# Crime and Justice

# Crime and Justice
## A Review of Research
### Edited by Michael Tonry

VOLUME 17

*The University of Chicago Press, Chicago and London*

This volume was prepared under Grant Number 90-IJ-CX-0015 awarded to the Castine Research Corporation by the National Institute of Justice, U.S. Department of Justice, under the Omnibus Crime Control and Safe Streets Act of 1968 as amended. Points of view or opinions expressed in this volume are those of the editors or authors and do not necessarily represent the official position or policies of the U.S. Department of Justice.

The University of Chicago Press, Chicago 60637
The University of Chicago Press, Ltd., London

96 95 94 93   4 3 2 1

ISSN: 0192-3234

ISBN: 0-226-80818-1

LCN: 80-642217

# Contents

# Preface

The correctional tail looks soon likely to be waving the criminal justice dog. Between 1980 and the end of 1992, American prison populations increased by 179 percent. The jail and probation increases were comparable. In recent years, the increases have resulted largely from strategic policy choices by the architects of the "War on Drugs." Because, however, the frontline combatants tend to work from within police departments and prosecutors' offices, federal funding increases have disproportionately supported those sectors of the criminal justice system. Funding for institutional and community correctional programs received lower priority. The results are well known—overcrowded institutions and programs, development of intermediate sanctions programs to divert offenders from incarceration, more than forty states under federal court orders related to crowding.

There are some signs that a change in official and public attitudes toward crime policy may be under way. The U.S. Sentencing Commission and the federal judiciary have outspokenly expressed their opposition to mandatory minimum penalties, and bills have been recently introduced into the U.S. Congress to reduce the number of mandatory minimum provisions. In the fiscally tight times facing state and local governments in the 1990s, the search for ways to avoid increasing prison and jail costs becomes ever more energetic.

This volume of *Crime and Justice* preponderantly attends to issues of corrections and sentencing. This was neither quite by coincidence nor entirely by design. A series that specializes in state-of-the-art review essays of research related to the criminal justice system necessarily tracks subjects receiving research attention, and this is necessarily influenced by the policy interests and funding priorities of federal research agencies. Separately, however, the variable gestations of individual essays caused the concentration. Six of the eight essays in this volume concern sentencing or corrections. Warren Young and Mark Brown present what is known about cross-national comparisons of the use of incarceration. Brian Gormally, Kieran McEvoy, and David Wall recount the evolution of interactions between political violence in Northern Ireland and the need to operate a corrections system that serves both political and ordinary offenders. Joan Petersilia and Susan Turner report on the largest experimental evaluation ever undertaken of intensive supervision programs in the United States. David Weisburd presents an overview of learning about experimental research designs on criminal justice, especially correctional, subjects. Barry Feld surveys knowledge concerning the evolution of the juvenile court, and I review experience with sentencing commissions and the guidelines they develop. Essays on research on bullying in North America and Western Europe by David Farrington and on victimization theories by Robert Meier and Terance Miethe round out the program.

This volume, like all of its predecessors, would not exist without support from the National Institute of Justice. I am, as always, grateful to Mary Graham, who oversees all things related to *Crime and Justice* for the National Institute of Justice; Paul Cascarano, the institute's assistant director, who initially proposed establishment of the series and has long given guidance to it; and James K. Stewart, director of the National Institute of Justice when support for this volume was awarded.

Michael Tonry

*Warren Young and Mark Brown*

# Cross-national Comparisons of Imprisonment

ABSTRACT

Cross-national comparisons of incarceration are often invoked, usually to make a critical comparison between the invoker's jurisdiction and others. Most such comparisons are limited to average numbers confined or census date populations and are inherently misleading. Some countries such as Sweden and the Netherlands, for example, have smaller average prison populations per capita than most countries but annual rates of prison admissions that are much higher. Better comparisons would take account of admissions and sentence lengths for both remand and sentenced populations and would take account of some or all of crime rates, prosecutions, convictions, and sentences. Various theories to explain incarceration trends have been offered and tend to have more explanatory significance within than between jurisdictions.

That per capita prison populations vary enormously in size, both over time and between one jurisdiction and another, is well known. Indeed, cross-national comparisons of prison rates are commonplace not only in the academic literature but also in political and popular debate on penal issues, particularly as a platform for lobbying on penal reform and the development of so-called alternatives to custody.

Yet there is still relatively little understanding of how these variations ought to be interpreted. Detailed analysis of trends in the use of imprisonment has generally been confined to individual jurisdictions.

Warren Young and Mark Brown are, respectively, professor of law and lecturer in the Institute of Criminology, Victoria University of Wellington, New Zealand. We are grateful to the U.K. Economic and Research Council for financial assistance with the study reported in this essay. We also acknowledge the substantial input of Ken Pease and Linda Harvey and the assistance of collaborators in each of the jurisdictions we studied, without whose help the study would not have been possible.

Comparative statistics have usually been employed in a crude and superficial way by politicians, penal administrators, and penal reformers, often for the purpose of making an unfavorable comparison between their own jurisdiction and another. There has been little systematic exploration of the meaning of these sorts of comparisons and what they tell us about both the nature and functions of punishment generally and the punishment practices of particular jurisdictions.

Yet much is to be gained by developing a greater understanding of the reasons for variations in prison populations. To begin with, the use of imprisonment provides one measure of a society's punitiveness. Admittedly, it is not the only measure; a true understanding of the nature of punishment practices would address the whole ensemble of sentencing options and the way in which they are used. However, imprisonment is the best measure of punitiveness that is readily accessible (Wilkins and Pease 1987, p. 20); it has become a central sanction in the penal systems of all western jurisdictions; and in most it is the major penalty of last resort for serious offenses. Thus trend analyses and cross-jurisdictional comparisons of prison populations have the potential to offer rich insights not only into how *forms* of punishment vary but also into the extent to which jurisdictions differ in the *severity* of punishment.

Second, although the recent thrust of actual or proposed sentencing reforms in countries such as the United States, Canada, and Australia has been the reduction or elimination of sentencing disparity, this is arguably not the most critical policy concern. The most intractable problems in many jurisdictions—such as prison overcrowding, riots, poor conditions, and inadequate work or other program opportunities for inmates—are caused in part by the sheer numbers in custody. These numbers are notoriously difficult to predict and routinely outstrip prison construction. American jurisdictions provide a telling illustration. In 1981, for example, New York State published a master plan for its prison system that projected a rise in the state prison population from 20,916 on April 1, 1980 to 24,057 on April 1, 1986. But by March 28, 1985, the population was already 34,754 (New York State Committee on Sentencing Guidelines 1985, p. 136). Similarly, the Correctional Population Projection Committee of the Pennsylvania Commission on Crime and Delinquency forecast an annual growth of 1,766 inmates for 1989, but the actual population grew by 2,561 (Pennsylvania Commission on Crime and Delinquency 1990, p. 14). Partly as a result of these sorts of inaccurate projections, correctional institutions or systems in the majority of American jurisdictions have been under federal court orders or consent decrees over the last several years because of overcrowding and other prison conditions held to be unconstitutional.

These problems of overcrowding and inaccurate projections of prison population growth arise not so much from sentencing inconsistencies as from the overall extent and intensity of prison use (Pease 1991). Unless we develop a better understanding of the influences on that use, therefore, official policies will not only continue to be preoccupied with ways of keeping prison populations within socially and economically manageable limits, but will also continue to have limited success in doing so. Furthermore, sentencing reforms introduced for other reasons will continue to be subverted by the overriding concern for prison numbers. It is significant, for example, that American sentencing reforms introduced for the purposes of reducing sentencing disparity have in fact been used increasingly as a means of ad hoc prison population control (Knapp 1989, p. 123).

This essay identifies major trends in the use of imprisonment, and identifies some of the factors associated with those trends. Although it draws on data from the Second and Third United Nations Crime Surveys (Centre for Social Development and Humanitarian Affairs 1991) and from Council of Europe publications, it uses as its primary data source a cross-national study of trends in the use of imprisonment in seven different jurisdictions—England and Wales, Scotland, France, West Germany, Sweden, the Netherlands, and New Zealand—over a twenty-year period from 1968 to 1987. Section I outlines both differences in prison rates *between* jurisdictions and changes in such rates within jurisdictions. Section II examines some of the difficulties in interpreting these rates. Of course, imprisonment occurs as a response to offending; Section III therefore considers the extent to which variations in its use can be attributed to differences in the nature and seriousness of offending. Finally, Section IV discusses the significance of cross-jurisdictional differences in prison rates, suggesting that prison rates are driven by punishment practices that are deeply culturally embedded and that are only marginally affected by specific political initiatives or by differences in short-term social and economic conditions.

## I. Prison Populations: Numbers and Trends

The most commonly employed indicator of the use of imprisonment is the number of persons imprisoned per 100,000 total population. This number is taken either from the total number incarcerated on a specific date (such as December 31 or June 30), or from the average daily population over the whole year. Since the numbers incarcerated can be subject to seasonal fluctuations, the average daily population is the most reliable indicator and is generally used where it is available. Even then, there are substantial variations in counting practice that reduce the comparability of the data (see below).

Table 1 shows the prison rate per 100,000, either at a particular time or as a daily average, for a number of selected jurisdictions. Four points arising from this table deserve further comment. First, it is worth repeating the obvious: even though the rates are not all taken from the same year, it is clear that there are dramatic differences in imprisonment practice when expressed in this way—from a low of forty-four in the Netherlands to a high of 398 in the United States. In other words, the proportion of the American population incarcerated is about ten times that of the Netherlands and four times that of the United Kingdom.

Second, to the extent that prison rates for eastern European countries are known, there seems to be a substantial difference between eastern and western European countries, with the eastern European rates, although still much lower than the American rate, generally being two or three times greater than western European rates. This pattern was also apparent in the Second UN Survey in 1980.

Third, even in jurisdictions with fairly similar political and economic systems, the differences in prison rates are startling, as the comparisons of New Zealand and Australia and of the United States and Canada in table 1 show. This is demonstrated even more clearly by differences between state or provincial jurisdictions within the same country. For example, in Canada in 1987 provincial prison rates (which relate to those serving sentences of less than two years) ranged from an average of thirty-nine in Quebec to 423 in Northwest Territories; in the United States state prison rates (excluding those in local jails on remand or serving sentences of less than twelve months) at the end of 1990 varied from sixty-seven in North Dakota and seventy-two in Minnesota to 447 in Nevada and 1,125 in the District of Columbia; and in Australia state prison rates, excluding the Australian Capital Territory, in February 1990 ranged from fifty in Tasmania to 245 in Northern Territory.

Finally, comparisons of the prison rate data of individual jurisdictions from different sources for the same time period almost invariably yield discrepancies. For instance, from our own study we calculated a

## TABLE 1

### Prison Populations per 100,000 for Selected Jurisdictions

| Country | Year | Source | Rate |
|---|---|---|---|
| United States (including local jails) | December 31, 1989 | Bureau of Justice Statistics (1990) | 398 |
| Poland | Average 1985 | Centre for Social Development . . . . (1991) | 265 |
| Hungary | Average 1985 | Centre for Social Development . . . . (1991) | 223 |
| Bulgaria | Average 1985 | Centre for Social Development . . . . (1991) | 178 |
| Canada | July 1986 | Collier and Tarling (1986) | 109 |
| New Zealand | Average 1989 | New Zealand Department of Justice (1992) | 106 |
| Scotland | February 1, 1990 | Council of Europe (1992) | 95 |
| England and Wales | February 1, 1990 | Council of Europe (1992) | 93 |
| France | September 1, 1990 | Council of Europe (1992) | 82 |
| West Germany | September 1, 1990 | Council of Europe (1992) | 78 |
| Australia | February 1990 | Australian Institute of Criminology (1990) | 75 |
| Sweden | September 1, 1990 | Council of Europe (1992) | 58 |
| Italy | September 1, 1990 | Council of Europe (1992) | 57 |
| Norway | September 1, 1990 | Council of Europe (1992) | 57 |
| Netherlands | September 1, 1990 | Council of Europe (1992) | 44 |

prison rate in 1985 of seventy-seven for France, and forty-three for
the Netherlands, which compared with eighty-two and thirty-eight,
respectively, in the Third UN Survey for the same year (Centre for
Social Development and Humanitarian Affairs 1991). Such discrepancies, which no doubt arise from counting differences or from inaccuracies in the collection or transmission of data, demonstrate that aggregate rates of this sort should be regarded as only rough approximations
of the real picture, and that it is generally inappropriate to make fine
distinctions between individual jurisdictions or to draw firm conclusions from individual data points.

When trends in prison rates within individual jurisdictions are examined, no consistent cross-national patterns emerge. In some, there has
been a dramatic growth in the size of the population over the last ten
to twenty years. For example, as figure 1 demonstrates, from 1968 to
1987 the per capita prison population increased by 45 percent in England and Wales, 34 percent in France, 16 percent in the Netherlands,
and 14 percent in New Zealand. These figures pale into insignificance
by comparison with the United States: between 1980 and 1990 there
was a 111 percent increase in the number of sentenced prisoners per
capita in state and federal prisons, and between the 1983 and 1988
censuses of local jails there was a corresponding 47 percent increase in
the numbers in local jails. In contrast, other countries have managed
to achieve a reduction in their prison rate over the same period: as
figure 1 again shows, the rate in Sweden declined by 26 percent, and
in the Federal Republic of Germany it declined by 4 percent during
the 1968–87 period.

Similar inconsistencies in trends occur between jurisdictions within
one federal system. For example, between 1968 and 1987 in Australia,
the prison rate dropped by 30 percent or more in Victoria, New South
Wales, and South Australia, while it increased by about 20 percent in
Queensland; and between 1980 and 1989 in America, the state prison
rate increased by only 15.5 percent in North Carolina and 22.2 percent
in West Virginia, compared with a massive 257.7 percent in New
Hampshire and 262.5 percent in California.

On the face of it, these recent rapid and unpredictable fluctuations
in prison rates in most jurisdictions render suspect explanations of
variations in prison rates that were generated during periods when they
showed greater stability. For example, the homeostatic or "stability of
punishment" model, developed by Blumstein and Cohen (1973) and
advanced further by Blumstein, Cohen, and Nagin (1976), was based

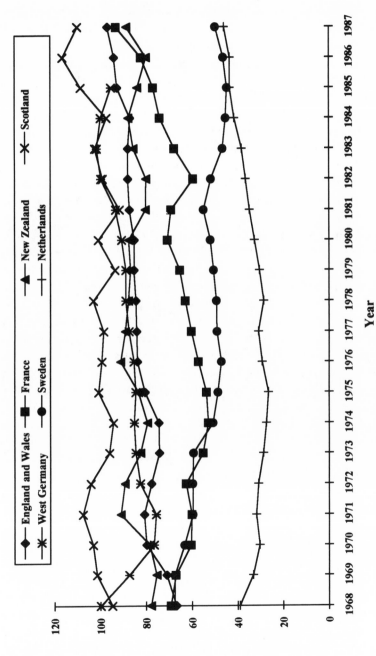

Fig. 1.—Average daily prison population per 100,000 population, 1968–87. Vertical axis represents number of prisoners

on the notion that the size of the custodial population in any particular society would remain fairly constant over time: that society needs a constant level of punishment to maintain social solidarity and that this is achieved through a continual readjustment of levels of punishment. Thus, as reception rates into prison rise or fall, the threshold of imprisonable behavior—or, to put it another way, the threshold of social tolerance—and the length of detention will be adjusted, officially or unofficially, to retain the prison population at a relatively constant level. This model appeared to fit the incarceration rates of a number of jurisdictions fairly well until the 1960s (see Blumstein and Moitra 1979; Tremblay 1986a), although it was called into question by others (see Cahalan 1979; Berk et al. 1981; Rauma 1981). It is much more difficult, however, to fit the model to the more recent trends identified above.

It should be noted that the stability-of-punishment model does not deny the possibility of revolutions in a society's penal climate; it claims only that such revolutions will be rare and that "the rate of punishment will be stable before and after these revolutions take place" (Tremblay 1986a, p. 177). It is possible that many jurisdictions have been undergoing such a revolution in recent years. If so, the stability-of-punishment theory does not explain such revolutions or predict their occurrence. Nor does it enable us to determine why the levels of punishment, whether stable or not, differ so much from one jurisdiction to another. Indeed, our data would suggest that there is much more stability in the differences *between* jurisdictions than in the trends *within* jurisdictions.

## II. Understanding and Interpreting Prison Rates

It should immediately be obvious—but seems not to be to most commentators, penal reformers, and academics—that rates of imprisonment per 100,000 total population are a potentially misleading way of both analyzing trends in the use of custody within particular jurisdictions and comparing the incarceration practices of different jurisdictions. At one level, they may simply be failing to measure the same thing because of changes (or differences) in counting rules. Much more significantly, they obscure the three most important dimensions in understanding imprisonment practices: the relative influence of the remand and sentenced populations, the relative influence of the number of custodial admissions and the average length of detention, and the effect of parole and remission.

## A. *Counting Rules*

Prison populations per 100,000 always provide only a partial count of the number of offenders effectively incarcerated at a particular time, since they exclude a number whose liberty is substantially restricted in one way or another. As far as we are aware, for example, all jurisdictions exclude offenders who are compulsorily or voluntarily committed to psychiatric institutions before trial or instead of conviction or sentence. This may be the reason for the fairly consistent finding of an inverse correlation between prison rates and the number of psychiatric hospitalization beds (see Penrose 1939; Biles and Mulligan 1973; Waller and Touchetta 1982; but, cf. Grabosky 1980): as the numbers subject to one form of confinement (psychiatric hospitalization) go up, the numbers subject to another form (penal custody) go down, and vice versa.

The extent to which other groups are excluded from the prison rate count, however, does differ to some extent between countries and over time, so that prison population rates are not necessarily measuring quite the same thing. For example, some jurisdictions (such as England and Wales and New Zealand) include all those who are physically in penal custody and those serving a full-time custodial sentence, regardless of age or type of institution; others (notably Canada) exclude persons who are under a specified age such as eighteen or who are serving their sentence in a youth custody institution. Some count only those who are actually in prison at the time; others count all prisoners who are within their jurisdiction, including those who have been transferred to hospitals or psychiatric institutions for treatment or are on work releases or home leave.

That in Canada offenders under the age of eighteen, not being the responsibility of adult correctional institutions, are not counted in prison rates means that the comparative Canadian rate in table 1 is substantially understated. Conversely, when American state prisons in 1977 changed from counting prisoners actually in custody to counting prisoners under their jurisdiction, there was an artifactual increase of nearly 3 percent in the average number of inmates (Bureau of Justice Statistics 1982), so that the comparative American figure is probably slightly inflated.

In other respects, however, the impact of differences in counting procedures is more difficult to quantify. For example, an examination of the proportion of prisoners reported by jurisdictions to be under the age of twenty-one would appear to suggest that a number of jurisdictions, as in Canada, largely exclude youth prisoners from their count: of the jurisdictions listed in table 1 for which information was available, the proportion ranged from 24 percent in the United Kingdom and in New Zealand to 12 percent in France, 7 percent in Norway, and 4 percent in Sweden. However, this variation is not simply a product of counting differences. As far as we have been able to determine, the Swedish and Norwegian custodial populations really do comprise a much lower proportion of young adults than elsewhere; in Sweden those under the age of eighteen are generally dealt with under the Social Welfare Act rather than being sentenced to a criminal sanction, while there is a presumption against the use of imprisonment for those aged under twenty-one. A few of these may be detained instead in juvenile "welfare" institutions of a custodial nature, but it seems unlikely that this can account for more than a small part of the differences in this respect.

In general, it can be concluded that only a few of the definitional or counting differences identified substantially affect the validity of the comparisons made in table 1. The Canadian figure is understated by the exclusion of those aged under eighteen, but in rough terms the other jurisdictions seem to be measuring much the same populations.

## B. The Relative Influence of Remand and Sentenced Populations

Prison population rates conflate two quite different groups—those on remand awaiting trial (pretrial detainees in the United States) or sentence and those in prison under sentence. The usual way of distinguishing these groups and identifying their respective contributions to the total population is to present the remand population as a percentage of the total prison population. An alternative is to calculate the remand population per 100,000 total population. Both of these figures are given in table 2, in all but three jurisdictions, as an average for the 1987 year.

It should be noted that definitions of "remand" and "sentenced" prisoners differ substantially from one jurisdiction to another. In countries like England and Wales and New Zealand, for example, a prisoner is classified as "sentenced" from the date at which he or she is received into prison following the imposition of a prison sentence. By contrast, in other jurisdictions—Italy and West Germany, for instance—prisoners are treated as remandees until the time for appeal has expired. Moreover, remand data do not usually distinguish between unconvicted prisoners awaiting trial and convicted prisoners awaiting sen-

## TABLE 2

### Remand Populations: Average 1987

| Country | Remand Population per 100,000 Total Population | Prison Population Comprising Remand Prisoners (%)* |
|---|---|---|
| France | 39.0 | 41.8 |
| Italy (September 1, 1988) | 29.8 | 49.3 |
| England and Wales | 21.1 | 21.8 |
| West Germany (September 1, 1988) | 19.0 | 22.4 |
| Scotland | 18.3 | 16.4 |
| Netherlands | 11.8 | 26.0 |
| Norway (September 1, 1988) | 11.1 | 23.0 |
| Australia | 9.6 | 15.5 |
| Sweden | 9.2 | 18.5 |
| New Zealand | 8.5 | 9.2 |

* Those awaiting trial or sentence.

tence. For these reasons, the Council of Europe (1990, p. 10) concluded that the available information "is still far from enabling us to calculate genuinely comparable rates of detention before trial." This suggests that at least some of the discrepancies between jurisdictions apparent from table 2 are an artifact of counting rules.

Nevertheless, even when that is taken into account, it seems clear that remand practice varies considerably and does not always mirror differences in overall imprisonment rates. For example, while the per capita prison population in the Netherlands in 1987 was a little over half that of Australia, the per capita remand population was slightly higher. Similarly, while the per capita prison population in New Zealand was about the same as England and Wales and Scotland, its per capita remand population (which as far as we can tell was calculated in the same way) was about half. The extent to which jurisdictions are willing to make use of custodial remands, it seems, is not directly related to the level of punitiveness they show in their use of sentences of imprisonment.

Important though this finding is, the significance of the distinction between sentenced and remand prisoners is even more clearly demonstrated by an analysis of the contribution of remand and sentenced prisoners to changes in imprisonment rates within individual jurisdictions over the last twenty years. Figure 2 shows changes in the propor-

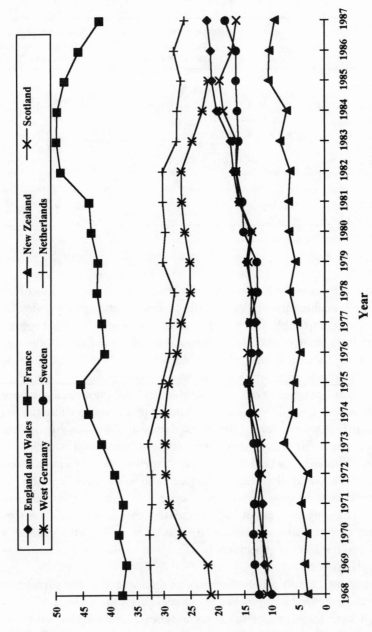

FIG. 2.—Proportion of average daily prison population comprising remand prisoners, 1968–87. Vertical axis represents percent

Year

- ◆ England and Wales
- ✳ West Germany
- ■ France
- ● Sweden
- ▲ New Zealand
- + Netherlands
- ✕ Scotland

tion of the average daily population comprising remand prisoners in the selected jurisdictions in our study from 1968 to 1987.

In this respect, jurisdictions roughly divide into three groups. In some, changes in the remand population largely paralleled changes in the sentenced population, so that the proportion of the total population on remand remained about the same. Although there were significant fluctuations in some years, France and West Germany generally fell into this category, with only small overall increases in the proportion on remand.

In other jurisdictions, the sentenced population moved in the opposite direction from changes in the remand population. In particular, while Sweden achieved a significant reduction in the number of sentenced prisoners, its per capita remand population actually increased by 11 percent, so that the proportion of the total population comprising remand prisoners has increased by over 50 percent.

In the third group of jurisdictions, while there was an increase in the number of both sentenced and remand prisoners, the growth of the latter significantly outstripped that of the former. For example, the per capita remand population increased in England and Wales by 221 percent, in France by 49 percent, and in New Zealand by 259 percent. By comparison, the per capita sentenced population increased by only 29 percent in England and Wales, 27 percent in France, and 15 percent in New Zealand. Similarly, in Australia between 1978 and 1989 the remand population increased by 88 percent, while the sentenced population increased by only 24 percent (Australian Institute of Criminology 1990).

The implications of this are plain: if efforts to reduce or manage prison populations are not to be misdirected, they require an understanding not only of the components of the prison population within a particular jurisdiction, but also of the way in which those components are changing. Of course, since sentenced prisoners comprise the bulk of the prison population, there is always a temptation to make sentencing practice the prime focus of penal reform. This analysis makes clear that that is not always appropriate. In England and Wales, for instance, while remandees still only make up around 20 percent of the total population, they were responsible for approximately half of the numerical increase in that population between 1968 and 1987, so that remand practice there assumes as much importance as sentencing practice in both the interpretation of prison population growth and the development of policy initiatives to limit or reverse that growth.

## C. Admissions and Length of Detention

Prison populations are self-evidently a function of the number of people sent to prison and the length of time they spend there. In other words, assuming a constant sentencing and remand practice, the prison population can be arrived at by multiplying the number of admissions with the average duration of detention. By the same token, the average duration can be obtained by dividing the prison population by the number of admissions.

These simple arithmetical equations demonstrate why prison population rates, even when divided into sentenced and remand categories, are a largely unhelpful way of measuring punishment practices in a society. Differences in population rates can result from differences in the number of admissions (the *breadth* of prison use) or in the average duration of actual detention (the *intensity* of prison use) or a combination of both. Different factors will affect each. Thus, for example, we might expect the number of persons charged or convicted to be a significant factor in driving admissions, but the average seriousness of offending to be a more important factor in determining length of detention.

Unfortunately, it is not possible to make a precise assessment of the extent to which cross-jurisdictional variations are attributable to differences in admissions or to differences in the length of detention. Few jurisdictions keep data on time served on remand or under sentence, and estimates, which assume stability in sentencing and remand practice, are often rendered dubious by volatility in prison population rates, especially in recent years. Moreover, comparisons of the number of admissions are affected by differences in counting rules: some jurisdictions, such as Germany, only regard as new admissions those persons entering "from liberty"; others, such as England and Wales and New Zealand, count as new admissions all those persons who were not in the particular prison the previous night, even if they were in custody (e.g., in another prison or in police cells) elsewhere. In the latter jurisdictions, this substantially inflates the number of admissions, especially of those received on remand.

In the light of these difficulties, the comparisons in table 3 are at best rough approximations that must be treated with a great deal of caution. Moreover, the number of admissions on remand in Sweden seems to include those who are arrested and held in police custody for even a few hours, so that the estimated average length of detention on remand is probably substantially understated. Nevertheless, in general

## TABLE 3

### Remand and Sentenced Prisoners: 1987

| Country | Sentenced Admissions per 100,000 | Estimated Effective Sentence Length (in Months) | Remand Admissions per 100,000 | Estimated Effective Remand Length (in Months) |
|---|---|---|---|---|
| England and Wales | 134.6 | 6.7 | 169.2 | 1.7 |
| West Germany (1986) | 84.4 | 10.6 | 78.0 | 3.0 |
| Scotland | 99.3 | 8.4 | 334.7 | .7 |
| France | 64.3 | 10.0 | 103.8 | 4.5 |
| Netherlands | 136.6 | 2.9 | N.A. | N.A. |
| Sweden | 178.0 | 2.7 | 405.2 | .3 |
| New Zealand | 190.1 | 5.3 | 203.0 | .5 |

NOTE.—N.A. = not available.

terms the figures do cast a different light on the prison population rates examined earlier. For example, as earlier commentators have noted (see Fitzmaurice and Pease 1982; Steenhuis, Tigges, and Esser 1983), the low prison rate in countries such as The Netherlands and Sweden is a function of very short average sentence length; the rate of admissions under sentence is comparable with or higher than many other European countries. By the same token, the comparatively high prison populations in England and Wales, Scotland, France, West Germany, and New Zealand generally have more to do with average length of detention than the numbers being sent to prison on remand or under sentence.

Differences in the average length of time on remand are probably primarily linked to both the workload and the efficiency of the criminal justice process.

Differences in average sentence length, by contrast, are likely to be the result not only of a more conscious set of policy choices but also, more importantly, of fundamental penal values (see below). Some jurisdictions, it seems, reserve full incarceration for a small minority of offenders, presumably the most serious or persistent ones; but when they resort to it, they deprive those offenders of their liberty for substantial periods of time. Others make more frequent use of imprisonment, but (perhaps for that reason) for shorter average duration.

It has been a matter of some debate whether these variations reflect differing overall levels of punitiveness. It has been argued, for example, that despite the fact that jurisdictions that use prison sentences sparingly but for longer times have higher prison rates, they may be no more punitive than those using prison sentences more often but for shorter periods. As Steenhuis, Tigges, and Esser (1983, p. 13) have put it, "After all, which climate is milder; one in which (imprisonment) is relatively rarely imposed but, when imposed, is of long duration, or one in which fairly frequent use is made of the sanction, but always using short or even extremely short sentences?"

However, the difficulty with the argument that higher prison rates do not necessarily indicate a greater level of punitiveness is that it takes no account of the relationship between imprisonment and other sanctions. As we shall see, those jurisdictions with high imprisonment rates also have comparatively large numbers of offenders subject to continuing community-based supervision or control, suggesting that even though they may not send proportionately more offenders to prison, the overall intrusiveness and severity of their punishment systems is greater.

It is equally instructive to examine the contribution of admissions and length of detention to prison population changes within particular jurisdictions. Our data enabled us to do such an analysis for six jurisdictions—Sweden, the Netherlands, England and Wales, France, New Zealand, and West Germany.

In two of the jurisdictions, the relative influence of admissions and length of detention was not clear-cut. In England and Wales, the prison population between 1968 and 1987 steadily increased through the equal contribution of an increase in sentenced admissions ($r = .88$, $p < .0001$) and an increase in remand length ($r = .90$, $p < .0001$). These two factors offset a decrease in sentence length ($r = -.77$, $p < .0001$). In West Germany, too, the sentenced prison population declined between 1968 and 1971 as a result of a decline in the sentenced admission rate (no data on the remand population being available until 1977), despite an increase in estimated average sentence length. After 1975, sentenced admissions fluctuated but showed a slight overall decline, while the population steadily rose until 1983 through a continuing increase in average sentence length and an increase in admissions on remand. As a result, there were moderate correlations between the prison population and both sentence length and admissions on remand ($r = .50$ and $.66$, respectively), although because of the small number of data points on remand prisoners only the former reached statistical significance.

In all other jurisdictions, it is clear that length of detention has played a much more significant role than admissions in prison population trends. In New Zealand there were significant moderate correlations between population changes from 1968 to 1987 and both sentence length ($r = .48$, $p < .02$) and remand length ($r = .59$, $p < .004$), but no significant correlation with admissions. In France, too, prison population changes were more strongly correlated with length of detention than with number of admissions, at least in relation to sentenced prisoners. In the remaining two jurisdictions—those with the lowest prison population rates—changes in those rates were by and large attributable to changes in length of detention. In Sweden the substantial decline in the prison rate from 1968 to 1987 was primarily due to a decrease in overall sentence length ($r = .80$, $p < .0001$), although there was also a significant but smaller correlation between prison population changes and a decline in the number of admissions on remand. Similarly, although the absence of remand data in the Netherlands makes it difficult to discern the overall pattern, it appears that the prison population there declined markedly from 1968 to 1975, primarily as a result of a decrease in sentence length, but then increased steadily after that in line with an increase in sentence length ($r = .90$, $p < .0001$).

Interpretation of these trends is by no means straightforward. An initial difficulty, of course, particularly in relation to sentenced prisoners, is that the two components are interdependent (see McMahon 1990). For example, if a policy of decarceration is successful, it is likely to be employed for those who would previously have received relatively short prison sentences. Unless there is also a consequential shortening of sentence length for the remainder of those who continue to receive imprisonment, average sentence length will necessarily increase as an artifact of the reduction in admissions. This seems to be the explanation for at least part of the trend from 1968 to 1971 in West Germany: reductions in sentenced admissions were, as expected, accompanied by increases in average sentence length.

However, at the risk of oversimplifying complex data, it is possible to draw some tentative conclusions from our small sample of jurisdictions. The first is that admissions and length of detention seem to be equally important contributors to *increases* in prison populations. In New Zealand and France, length of detention has been a more significant factor in population increases than admissions. The same was true in England and Wales from 1938 to 1968, where the number of sentenced admissions remained more or less constant while the population increased by 360 percent. As we have seen, however, since then sentenced admissions have been responsible for about half of the increase in the population. In the United States, too, the explosion in the prison population from 1973 through the mid-1980s seems to be attributable primarily to an increase in admissions: while both average nominal prison sentences and time served in prison did not lengthen, the chances of receiving a prison sentence after arrest grew as a ratio both of arrests and of nearly every type of recorded offense (Bureau of Justice Statistics 1990; Langan 1991).

In contrast, jurisdictions that have a comparatively low prison population or that have achieved a marked *reduction* in that population seem to be those that manage to regulate or effect changes to prison rates through length of detention, and especially sentence length, rather than through admissions. This is not uniformly the case. For example, Feest (1982) has claimed that the dramatic slump in the prison population in West Germany between 1968 and 1970 can be attributed to a variety of legislative reforms aimed at reducing admissions: many traffic offenses were made nonimprisonable; a number of nonviolent sex-related offenses were decriminalized; prison sentences of up to one year (instead of nine months) became suspendible; and, most important of all, fines were made a sentencing alternative for most crimes. Graham (1990) and Feest (1991) have also attributed the drop in the West German prison population between 1983 and 1988—a decline on average of 3.5 percent per annum—to a radical change in the practice of public prosecutors and judges that reduced the number of prosecutions and led to the growth of a number of projects designed to divert offenders from custody. Our own figures seem to support these claims; sentenced admissions dropped to less than one-half of their former level between 1968 and 1970 and then, after steadily rising again until 1983, experienced a marked decline after that. Average sentence length, in contrast, did not decline in either period. However, the West German experience is very much the exception and shows that significant reductions in the population are likely to be achieved only by enormous reductions in the number of admissions. Jurisdictions seem to be more successful in making substantial inroads into the prison population by tackling average length of detention, and particularly average sentence length.

This should come as no surprise, since prison populations are generally much more sensitive to changes in length of detention than to changes in admissions. The reasons for this are obvious. As has already been noted, reductions in the number of sentenced admissions will generally be achieved by the use of noncustodial sentences for those who would have received short custodial sentences. But since short sentence prisoners, while comprising a substantial proportion of *admissions*, make up a much smaller proportion of the *population*, the impact on the latter will be small. Bottomley and Pease (1986, p. 107), for example, have estimated that in England and Wales in 1983 sentences up to and including six months accounted for 51 percent of receptions but only 17 percent of the population, so that in order to reduce the prison population by a mere 17 percent, over half of the custodial decisions of the courts would have to be substituted with noncustodial decisions. A similar calculation in New Zealand shows that in 1988 prisoners serving sentences of less than twelve months accounted for over 57 percent of all admissions under sentence, but only about 25 percent of the actual population. Again, in order to achieve a 25 percent reduction in the prison population, we would have to replace 57 percent of prison sentences with noncustodial ones. In contrast, of course, a reduction in average sentence length will result in a proportionate reduction in the population.

A similar argument applies to remand prisoners. Any attempt to reduce the number of admissions on remand—for instance, by the more flexible use of bail, the development of bail hostels, etc.—will tend to be directed toward less serious offenders who spend comparatively short periods of time in custody. Those who spend long periods of time on remand and who contribute disproportionately to the remand population will be left unaffected. Clearly policies directed toward increasing the efficiency of the criminal justice system and reducing the average length of custodial remands across the board will deliver a greater return.

This points to the difficulty in expecting large-scale reductions in the prison population through the development of so-called alternatives to custody, or "intermediate punishments." It is undoubtedly true that those (e.g., Chan and Ericson 1981; Hylton 1981; Austin and Krisberg 1982; Cohen 1985) who have argued that intermediate punishments have a net-widening effect, by being used as enhanced community-based sentences rather than as alternatives to custody, have substantially overstated their case (see McMahon 1990). In most jurisdictions, an expansion in the use of community-based sanctions has been accompanied by a significant reduction in the *proportion* (although not necessarily the number) of offenders sent to prison. However, the point is that, to the extent that intermediate punishments are used as alternatives to custody, they are inevitably directed at those who would have served relatively short terms. There is no evidence that intermediate punishments in themselves are more likely than short prison terms to reduce the chances of reconviction or of imprisonment in the future. Hence, however desirable it might be to divert from custody offenders currently sentenced to or remanded in custody for short terms, this will not make substantial inroads into the prison population unless it is accompanied by a decrease in length of detention for the remainder. That is why, in New Zealand over the last twenty years, there has been a significant negative relationship between sentenced admissions and the use of community-based sanctions at the upper end of the tariff scale (periodic detention, community service, community care, and supervision), but no significant relationship at all between prison populations and the use of such sanctions. In other words, it seems that, although an expansion in the number of such community-based sanctions may have an effect on the number of people who are sent to prison, this may not have the expected impact on the prison population because it is not tackling the major factor driving that population. Accordingly, efforts to control prison population growth by developing and expanding alternatives to imprisonment may well be misplaced.

## D. *The Impact of Parole and Remission*

The population of sentenced prisoners is a reflection of both "front-end" and "back-end" decisions. At the front end, the legislature and the judiciary determine the offenses for which imprisonment should be available; the types of mandatory, maximum, and minimum sentences available; and the number and length of nominal sentences actually imposed. However, in almost all jurisdictions there is also a set of back-end executive decisions that directly shape the size of the sentenced population—decisions about both parole and remission.

Remission (known as "good time" in the United States) is generally more or less automatic—that is, in the absence of some sort of disciplinary infraction within prison that has resulted in some loss of remission, it is received by all prisoners as a matter of right. Moreover, although it may be accompanied by a formal period of supervision after release, it does not generally involve stringent conditions or close monitoring of released prisoners. Arguably, therefore, where remission exists it becomes an established part of the sentencing and punishment culture, and its existence is implicitly acknowledged in the nominal sentences imposed. In the short term, a change in the availability of remission may well have an impact on the prison population. However, there is some evidence that judges fairly quickly restore previous norms of effective sentence length by adjusting the nominal sentences imposed (e.g., Weatherburn 1985; South Australian Office of Crime Statistics 1989). Thus the longer-term effect of remission on the size of the prison population is likely to be relatively small. Arguments for the retention of remission to keep the lid on prison population growth are therefore short-term ones; the long-term benefits in this respect are much more debatable.

The impact of parole, however, is rather more complex and problematic. It is arguable that changes in parole eligibility or release policy can have a substantial limiting effect on the prison population. Since parole, for example, is generally a discretionary form of release offered to only some prisoners, it is less likely than remission to be absorbed into the sentencing culture and to be reflected in the nominal sentences imposed. Moreover, since parole boards have low public visibility, they are more likely to be responsive to administrative concerns about the effects of prison crowding than are legislators or judges. They are therefore likely to act as a mechanism to stabilize prison populations or check their growth.

We could not tell from our own data whether jurisdictions with more generous parole provisions tended to have lower prison populations. However, there is some evidence from elsewhere that parole can have such a "safety-valve" effect. For example, Bottomley and Pease (1986, p. 150) have shown that, without the existence of parole, fluctuations in the prison population of England and Wales during the twentieth century would have been much more marked than they were: parole thus produced some element of stability and predictability in the size of the prison population. Conversely, the dramatic increase in the American prison population from 1975 onward has been attributed in part to the abolition of parole or the curtailment in its use in many state jurisdictions over that period, which the adoption of alternative mechanisms like enhanced good time did little to counteract (Blumstein 1988; Bottomley 1990). In a cross-jurisdictional comparison, Steenhuis, Tigges, and Esser (1983, p. 10) have also suggested that the higher sentenced population in West Germany than in the Netherlands, which they attributed to longer sentence length, arose partly from West Germany's greater reluctance to use parole as a back-end method of reducing symbolically severe sentences.

While these examples suggest that parole does have the effect of containing prison populations, the picture is a more complex one. Parole tends to be accompanied by more stringent conditions than release on remission. In some jurisdictions those conditions have been more strictly enforced in recent years, resulting in higher rates of recall of parolees to prison to serve the remainder of their sentence. As a result, the effectiveness of parole as a safety valve for prison overcrowding has been diluted. For example, in California parole violators in 1981 accounted for 8 percent of admissions to prison, but by 1988 this had increased to 45 percent, so that parole violators accounted for about 16 percent of the Californian inmate population (California Blue Ribbon Commission 1989). Similar trends can be found in Texas, Pennsylvania, and a number of other American state jurisdictions. Thus parole violators have made a disproportionate contribution to increases in the prison population.

Moreover, it is commonplace in some jurisdictions to prosecute parole violators for the offense of breach of parole or for other offenses discovered in the course of enforcing parole conditions, as well as or instead of recall to prison on the original sentence. In this event, parole violators may well end up back in prison serving longer sentences than they would have without the existence of parole.

There is an added difficulty with the use of parole as a safety valve to keep prison populations at a manageable level. Parole is most needed to serve this function when prison populations are expanding through an increase in admissions or length of detention. Such an increase, however, is likely to occur at times of heightened concern about law and order, when public criticism of early release mechanisms is sharpest. As a result, an increase in admissions or length of detention may often be accompanied by political pressure to reduce the use of early release, so that the stabilizing potential of parole is largely lost. There is some evidence that this is precisely what occurs. Tremblay (1986*b*), for instance, has shown, by reference to historical incarceration trends in Montreal, that when the number of convictions per capita increased, there was no substantial corresponding increase in early release; and when the severity of punishment increased, there was actually a decrease in early release. More recently, attempts to use early release to overcome the effects of prison overcrowding in a number of American jurisdictions have met with both political and judicial resistance (see, e.g., Joyce 1992), and in New Zealand increases in nominal sentence length have been accompanied by the abolition of parole eligibility for a substantial proportion of longer-term inmates.

In summary, remission in the long term may not have any effect on the size of the prison population, although it is undoubtedly valuable in facilitating the smooth administration of prisons. But parole does have the potential to have a stabilizing effect on prison population growth. However, that effect is likely to be diluted by political pressure to reduce parole eligibility at times of maximum population growth, and it is also likely to be counteracted by any attempt at strict enforcement of parole conditions.

### III. The Impact on Prison Populations of Crime and Conviction Rates

People are not incarcerated at random: the use of custody, one hopes, is generally triggered by suspected or proven criminal behavior. Thus at least some of the variations that occur in the use of imprisonment, both over time and between one jurisdiction and another, are likely to be due to differences in the nature and seriousness of the offending coming before the courts. For example, if one country is processing a greater proportion of its citizens through the criminal justice system than another, one might expect the rate of admissions on remand and under sentence to be greater. Equally, if the average seriousness of offending in one country is greater than in another, one might expect this to be reflected in greater average length of detention.

Arguably the most appropriate means of assessing the extent to which differences or changes in prison population are attributable to the nature and extent of offending would be to express the total prison population as a rate of persons arrested and the population of sentenced prisoners as a rate of persons convicted. This is not without difficulty, since arrest and conviction rates do not take into account differences in clearance rates, rates of police cautioning, the use of other diversionary strategies, and so on. For example, if one country filters out more cases before arrest or conviction than another, the offenses for which sentences are imposed will on average be more serious, so that it will appear to have a harsher sentencing practice. As Steenhuis, Tigges, and Esser (1983) have shown, for instance, it is difficult to compare Germany with either the Netherlands or Sweden, because in the former prosecutions are brought in cases that in the Netherlands and Sweden would result in a waiver of prosecution on policy grounds. Even leaving aside this difficulty, few jurisdictions provide comparable arrest or conviction data. In our own study, for instance, we were able to obtain fairly comprehensive data on convictions from only three jurisdictions.

Most studies of the impact of the nature and seriousness of offending on prison populations have accordingly relied on an analysis of aggregate crime rates. For example, Nagel (1977) compared the crime rates of all American states in 1974 with their imprisonment rates in 1975, concluding that there was no clear relationship between the two. Biles (1979) refined Nagel's analysis and extended it to Canada and Australia. He found a positive relationship: states and provinces with a high crime rate also tended to have high prison populations. Bowker (1981) criticized the fact that these analyses were restricted to data at just one time. Instead, he examined crime and imprisonment rates between 1941 and 1978 in all American states, and found that although there were a few significant correlations on the basis of lagged time series analyses, the overall evidence was weak and contradictory and did not show any consistent relationship between levels of crime and the use of imprisonment. Zimring and Hawkins (1991) also compared imprisonment rates in the United States between 1949 and 1988 with reported FBI index crime rates and with rates in the four violent index felonies over the same period, and found no consistent relationship. They conceded that more sophisticated lagged statistical analysis might have disclosed some sort of complex relationship, but they maintained that their data demonstrated "the lack of a direct and simple relationship that would enable us to successfully explain most fluctuations in the rate of imprisonment by reference to changes in crime rates" (Zimring and Hawkins 1991, p. 124). Applying a similar time series analysis to data from Australian states, Biles (1982) discovered, in contrast with his earlier study, that there was a significant negative relationship between imprisonment rates and crime rates lagged for one, two, and three years. In other words, after crime rates had increased, imprisonment rates, contrary to expectation, decreased in the next one, two, and three years, with the drop being particularly marked in the third year. When he applied this analysis to England and Wales, however, he found the opposite picture: crime rates and imprisonment rates, both lagged and unlagged, showed a strong positive correlation between 1960 and 1979 (Biles 1983).

It is likely that at least part of the reason for these contradictory and confusing conclusions arises not only from the simplicity of the methodology employed but also from the reliance on aggregate crime figures in this way. Three particular problems arise in the use of such figures. First, there are often gross discrepancies in the crime data provided by individual jurisdictions that cannot be attributed to anything other than inaccuracies in its collation or transmission. For example, the second and third UN surveys both collected crime data from member countries on the 1980 year, and there were frequently very marked discrepancies between the two returns for the same year, even from countries with supposedly sophisticated recording systems. Second, and more importantly, some jurisdictions have much more comprehensive recording systems than others and thus record a much greater proportion of the trivial offenses coming to notice. As a result, such jurisdictions will seem much more restrained in their use of imprisonment. Even within a particular jurisdiction, reporting and recording practices may change markedly over time. Finally, aggregate crime rates take no account of differences or changes in the *seriousness* of offending; they simply measure the *volume* of offending.

In the light of these difficulties, the most practicable means of assess-

ing the influence of the nature and seriousness of offending on imprisonment rates is to consider those rates either in relation to a number
of very specific offense categories, or in relation to aggregate offenses
of a more serious kind. Admittedly, this does not overcome all counting
and definitional problems. Even definitions of serious offenses such as
homicide vary substantially from one jurisdiction to another: some
include attempted homicide within the figures, while others classify it
as serious assault; and some draw a distinction between intentional and
unintentional culpable homicide, while others do not. Moreover, the
counting of even fairly specific offenses within one jurisdiction can be
highly variable. Kalish (1988), for example, in a comparison of robbery
rates supplied by countries to Interpol and the United Nations for
1980, found that only one-quarter of countries reported the same or
nearly the same rates to both agencies.

Nevertheless, detailed small-scale comparisons by offense type do
at least offer the potential to take into account jurisdictional differences
in counting rules and arrest and charging practices and are probably
the most reliable basis for assessing the impact of the nature and seriousness of offending on the use of imprisonment. Studies of this sort
have tended to show that differences in the nature or seriousness of
offending do account for some of the variations in incarceration rates,
but by no means all. For instance, Waller and Touchetta (1982) found
that in a comparison between American states, between Canadian
provinces, and between Australian states, there was a statistically significant relationship between the incarceration rate and rates of homicide, robbery, rape, and serious assaults. Even so, however, these
correlations were of a fairly low order. More recently, Lynch (1988)
estimated the likelihood that a person arrested for robbery, burglary,
or theft in the United States, Canada, England, and West Germany
would eventually be sentenced to imprisonment. This study, which
was limited to the likelihood of admissions into prison rather than
length of imprisonment, found that most but not all of the differences
between the United States and the other three jurisdictions disappeared when arrest rates were taken into account. For example, of
those arrested for robbery, he estimated that 49 percent would be
incarcerated in the United States, 52 percent in Canada, 48 percent in
England and Wales, and between 23 and 58 percent in West Germany.
In contrast, he estimated that of those arrested for burglary, the rate
of incarceration was 35 percent in the United States, 30 percent in
England and Wales, and only 23 percent in Canada (no figures being

available for West Germany). This suggested that while the United States was a little more likely than other jurisdictions to imprison property offenders, much of the difference between American states and elsewhere arose from their substantially higher rate of violent offending.

In our own study, we collected data on all recorded offenses and on aggregate violent and sexual offenses and property offenses respectively. We then calculated prison populations per 10,000 offenses in each group. The results for 1987 are presented in table 4.

It will be seen that, as a proportion of both recorded violent and sexual offenses and recorded property offenses, New Zealand seems to have a comparatively low use of imprisonment. However, this is probably because, unlike most other jurisdictions, it has a national computerized system on which all incidents initially classified as offenses are recorded, no matter how trivial they are or what the subsequent outcome is, and because it has no "hierarchy rules" for multiple offenses brought against a single offender, so that one incident may produce several recorded offenses.

The ranking of other jurisdictions in terms of prison use is clearly affected by relative offense rates. For example, by comparison with England and Wales and West Germany, France's imprisonment rate increases; and, even though Sweden, like New Zealand, has no "hierarchy rules" for multiple offenses, it seems to make less use of imprisonment in relation to both recorded violent and sexual offenses and recorded property offenses than does the Netherlands. With these qualifications, however, the general patterns in cross-national prison use identified above still remain. In other words, it does appear, after taking into account the limited information we have on differences in counting rules and so on, that the volume of recorded crime seems to account for only a small part of the differences between one jurisdiction and another. This is demonstrated graphically by figures 3(a) to 3(c), which show that over a twenty-year period, while there is some fluctuation in the differences between one jurisdiction and another, the rankings generally show a remarkable degree of stability. In other words, while prison use might fluctuate markedly within jurisdictions from one period to another, its relationship to what is happening in other jurisdictions seems to remain more constant.

The influence of crime trends on prison population changes within individual jurisdictions is more problematic. Certainly the *impression* given by statistical data is that, at least in some jurisdictions, the influ-

## TABLE 4
## Prison Populations per 10,000 Recorded Crimes: 1987

| Country | Prison Populations per 100,000 Population | Prison Populations per 10,000 Recorded Crimes | Prison Populations per 10,000 Recorded Violent and Sexual Crimes | Prison Populations per 10,000 Recorded Property Crimes |
|---|---|---|---|---|
| England and Wales | 96.9 | 131.5 | 2,452.9 | 139.2 |
| West Germany | 95.4 | 130.0 | 2,048.2 | 141.7 |
| France | 93.1 | 166.2 | 3,967.7 | 178.9 |
| New Zealand | 88.5 | 79.3 | 1,164.9 | 98.5 |
| Netherlands | 45.2 | 64.9 | 1,492.2 | 68.8 |
| Sweden | 49.8 | N.A. | 559.1 | 49.2 |

NOTE.—N.A. = not available.

28

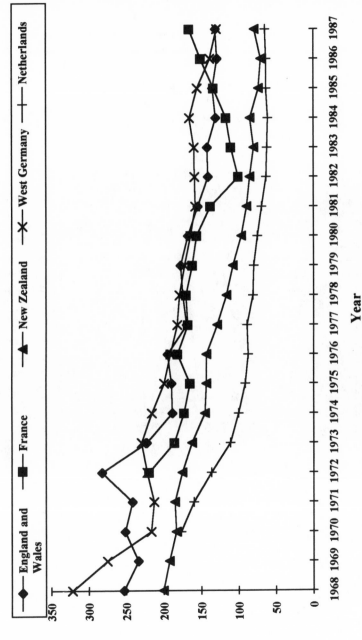

Fig. 3a.—Average daily prison population per 10,000 total recorded offenses, 1968–87. Vertical axis represents number of prisoners

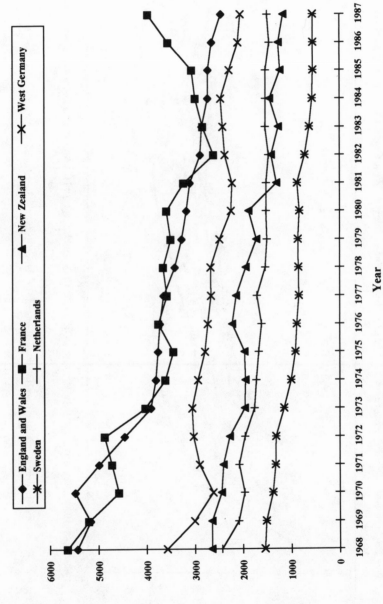

FIG. 3b.—Average daily prison population per 10,000 recorded violent offenses, 1968–87. Vertical axis represents number of prisoners

30

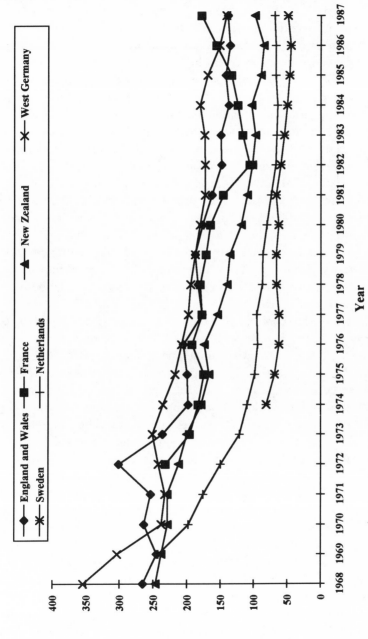

FIG. 3c. —Average daily prison population per 10,000 recorded property offenses, 1968–87. Vertical axis represents number of prisoners

31

ence, if it exists, is comparatively small. It is true that between 1960 and 1984 index crimes in the United States rose 278 percent and prison rates increased by 263 percent, so that there was a close parallel between the two trends. Between 1981 and 1986, however, prison rates continued to rise, while reported index crimes exhibited a steady decline, followed by an upturn in the latter half of the 1980s. In The Netherlands, too, while the number of recorded serious offenses has almost tripled since the Second World War, that country's prison population is now little more than half what it was in 1950.

However, an assessment of the relationship between trends in crime and incarceration rates really requires a more detailed and sophisticated assessment. The complexity, of course, arises because the influence is likely to be delayed, since there is a difference of up to seven years between the peak age of crime and the peak age of incarceration (Blumstein 1988, 1989): first offenders rarely receive imprisonment and most accumulate a number of convictions before their first prison sentence, so that several years may elapse between first offense and first period of imprisonment. Thus an increase in the crime rate or the conviction rate may produce an increase in the prison population some five to seven years later.

We attempted to explore this issue within each jurisdiction by correlating crime rates, both generally and within each offense category, with prison rates, and then by undertaking a similar lagged analysis, so that the crime rates were being correlated with prison rates occurring three to seven years later. In the event, this analysis was largely unhelpful in all jurisdictions. For example, in England and Wales the correlations of prison population rates and offense rates were highly significant when prison population rates remained unlagged ($r = .84$ to .93, all significant at $p < .0001$). However, the same pattern of highly significant correlations emerged when prison population rates were lagged for each of three to seven years. The problem appeared to be that both prison rates and offense rates were monotonically increasing over the period, so that when one was lagged it did not disturb the overall linear trend. Thus the strength of the overall upward trend in both sets of data was such that any perturbations in the time series on which a lagged effect might hinge were largely subsumed within that trend.

In order to overcome this difficulty, we calculated the first-order differences in the time series, that is, the difference or change between one year and the next. Thus the data were detrended in order to examine the lagged effects of offense rates on prison populations. The first-order offense rate differences were correlated with first-order differences lagged from zero to ten years. Using this method of analysis, only low to moderate correlations were found. Thus it must be concluded either that changes in crime rates were independent of changes in prison population rates and that increases in both were being driven by some third factor, or that any lagged or unlagged effects that were occurring were being masked by other more powerful influences on changes in the data.

Overall, therefore, our conclusion would be that only a small measure of the differences in prison populations between one jurisdiction and another or the changes in prison populations within particular jurisdictions seem to be related to crime rates. Moreover, to the extent that there is a relationship, we cannot be certain that it is a causal one; both official crime rates and prison rates may be affected by the level of punitiveness in a society—that is, attitudes toward crime and punishment may influence known criminality as well as sentencing practice.

## IV. Explaining Differences in Prison Use

If differences or changes in prison use cannot readily be explained by crime rates and conviction rates, to what can they be attributed? Three different approaches have traditionally dominated the literature in this area (for a review, see Young 1986). The first approach is based on the view that criminal justice practice somehow takes on a life of its own and reacts to justify the resources at its disposal regardless of the explicit policies governing its practice, and hence that the size of the prison population is at least partly driven by criminal justice expenditure, particularly prison capacity; the second argues that there is a direct relationship between prison rates and unemployment rates; and the third sees prison rates primarily as a function of policy choices and of attitudes within the criminal justice system itself.

### A. Traditional Approaches

The three different approaches, of course, are in reality interrelated; where prison capacity and unemployment rates are believed to affect the prison population, they are said to do so by influencing either judicial attitudes or public and political perceptions of appropriate punishment and consequent policy choices, or both. Even with this refinement, however, such traditional approaches are ultimately limited by their own narrow frame of reference; at most they point to one small ingredient in a complex web of political, economic, and cultural factors that drive punishment practices. However, it is useful to review them in some detail, because their assumptions and limitations do provide a contrast to the broader sociocultural explanation that will be developed in the subsequent section.

1. *Prison Capacity.* The view that prison capacity drives the size of the prison population is based on the notion that prison populations will be adjusted so that they do not unduly exceed the space available, and, more importantly, that prison populations will follow Parkinson's Law and expand to fill the available space, regardless of crime rates (see, e.g., Abt Associates 1980; Krisberg and Schwartz 1983).

It is, of course, easy to find a relationship between prison construction and population size, but as Blumstein (1988, p. 261) has said, it is a much more complex task to disentangle the "influence of population growth on the construction of capacity, and the influence of capacity limitations in encouraging or inhibiting the growth of prison populations." Such efforts as have been made to develop a statistical model for this purpose have not been successful (see, e.g., the criticism of Abt Associates [1980] by Blumstein, Cohen, and Gooding [1983], and Blumstein 1988).

As might be expected, there is anecdotal evidence to suggest that the prison population does tend to drive capacity, at least to a limited extent. For example, the dramatic increase in the U.S. prison population over the last decade or so has been accompanied by a vigorous prison construction program, although the growth in bed space has lagged significantly behind the growth in population. Similarly, New Zealand's 50 percent increase in the prison population between 1986 and 1991 necessitated a construction and refurbishment program producing a 47 percent increase in total cell capacity. That the number of prisoners does not drive capacity more directly can probably be attributed not only to inaccurate prison population projections and fiscal constraints, but also to the flexible nature of the notion of prison capacity (which in many jurisdictions allowed double or triple celling) and to the availability of various "back-end" methods to relieve overcrowding by executive fiat as an alternative to the construction of more prisons.

In contrast, anecdotal evidence in support of the proposition that capacity drives population is much more difficult to find. To the extent that there is such an effect, it seems likely to be simply a negative or limiting one. Overcrowded prisons may have a constraining effect on the number of people in prison, either because judges impose it more restrictively or because early release mechanisms are put in place to alleviate overcrowding problems. For example, to the extent that the introduction of determinate sentencing in the United States in the late 1970s and early 1980s increased the severity of sentences and produced overcrowding, this was to a limited extent counteracted by the use of "back-end" methods to regulate the prison population, such as more generous remission, emergency release, and administrative leave (Shane-Dubow, Brown, and Olsen 1985). Moreover, several sentencing commissions were mandated by their enabling legislation either to take account of prison capacity in formulating sentencing guidelines or to ensure that such guidelines were consistent with existing capacity. However, there is little reason to believe that a reverse Parkinsonian effect applies and that underused prisons produce more imprisonment than full but not overcrowded ones.

There is, of course, a policy dilemma here. If prison building programs substantially alleviate overcrowding and improve conditions within prisons, they may well lower the threshold at which imprisonment is used in the sentencing process. Conversely, a moratorium on prison construction or a reduction in prison capacity is likely to reduce the use of imprisonment only to the extent that it produces significant overcrowding, a result that penal reformers would no doubt eschew for other reasons.

That dilemma, however, is incidental to the main thrust of the argument here, which is that there is little reason to believe that in the long run prison capacity has a significant bearing on the size of the prison population within a particular jurisdiction and even less reason to believe that it can explain the differences between jurisdictions. In any case, even if prison capacity did have a significant bearing on the prison population, it would still not explain why capacity was fixed at a particular level or varied from one jurisdiction to another, and that is essentially the issue that the theory attempts to address.

2. *Unemployment Rates.* One of the most common explanations for differences in prison rates sees the rate of unemployment as affecting the rate and severity of imprisonment over and above changes in the volume or nature of reported crime or convicted offenders. The most sophisticated exposition of this explanation can be found in the Marxian analysis of Box and Hale (1982, 1986). They argue that the unemployed represent a "problem population" who can distance themselves

from the consent to be governed. As a consequence, they are likely to be perceived by those in positions of power and authority as potentially disruptive, thus constituting a threat to social discipline and law and order. For this reason, this problem population has to be tightly controlled, even by coercive means, in order to preserve ideological and social harmony (Box and Hale 1986, p. 79).

Not surprisingly, proponents of this view claim that the criminal justice system plays a major part in such a tightening of social control, which in turn affects the prison population. They argue that, whether or not unemployment does cause an increase in crime, judges are likely to share the prevailing political view that it does, and particularly in times of economic recession are likely to take the unemployment status of an offender into account in determining whether imprisonment is required and how long the sentence should be. Moreover, even if the unemployed are not singled out for more severe penal sanctions, the generally depressed economic climate that higher unemployment reflects may well provoke greater anxiety and social instability, which may in turn lead to a more punitive penal climate.

The evidence for such a link, however, is rather equivocal. There are certainly a number of studies that have shown a fairly strong and consistent relationship between increases in unemployment and increases in the prison population, irrespective of the volume of recorded criminal activity (e.g., Jankovic 1977; Wallace 1981; Box and Hale 1982). However, this is by no means invariably the case. There are a number of jurisdictions, such as Japan, the Netherlands, and Poland, where prison populations over particular periods of time have declined or remained stable against a background of rising unemployment (Greenberg 1980; Rutherford 1984).

One of the reasons for the inconsistencies in these findings may be that prison population rates may not always be sufficiently sensitive to discern the influence of unemployment rates on judicial practice. To the extent that there is such an influence, it may primarily affect the numbers remanded in custody and the numbers receiving short sentences of imprisonment: unemployed offenders might be regarded as having fewer community ties and therefore as presenting a higher risk of reoffending, thus increasing the likelihood that they will be remanded in custody; and likewise, they may be perceived as being unable to pay monetary penalties and as otherwise unsuitable for community-based punishments, thus rendering them eligible for short sentences of imprisonment. If this is so, it might be expected to have much more impact on prison admissions, particularly remand admissions, than on the prison population. There is some evidence that this is indeed the case; almost all studies that have explored the relationship between admissions and unemployment rates have found a relationship between the two. For example, Greenberg (1977) found that there was a close relationship between the rate of prison admissions and the official unemployment rate in Canada over the years 1945 to 1959; the correlation between the per capita prison population and the unemployment rate, although also positive, was considerably weaker. Sabol (1989) also found that in England and Wales, over the period 1946 to 1985, the changes in unemployment unambiguously affected growth in prison admissions. At a more detailed level, Crow et al. (1989) found in a sample of Magistrates' Courts in England and Wales that, while sentencers paid more attention to offending than to employment status, being unemployed nevertheless increased the risk of receiving an immediate custodial sentence.

Using our own data, we were able to examine the influence of unemployment rates on prison population differences between jurisdictions by comparing six jurisdictions (England and Wales, France, West Germany, Sweden, the Netherlands, and New Zealand) for four different years—1968, 1975, 1981, and 1987. In the latter three years, we lagged prison populations for one, two, and three years, hypothesizing that while anticipated unemployment may well have an immediate effect on judicial practice, that is likely to show up in prison population statistics only in subsequent years.

Although we did not have enough jurisdictions to test the statistical significance of the resulting correlations, there was little in our data to support the hypothesis of a positive relationship between cross-jurisdictional prison populations and unemployment rates; that is, there was little to suggest that jurisdictions with high unemployment rates tended to have higher prison populations than those with low unemployment rates. In 1968 and 1975 there was virtually no correlation at all when unlagged data were used, and when prison rates were lagged for one, two, and three years in 1975, the only correlations were negative ones. In 1981 and 1987 there were some positive correlations using both lagged and unlagged data, but they were weak, with only one extending beyond the .3 level.

In order to explore the hypothesis that unemployment rates might be more closely related to admissions than length of detention, we repeated the analysis for total admissions and for average length of detention in the same years. Although the small number of cases again precludes any firm conclusion, there was no evidence of the predicted relationship. Such correlations between admissions and unemployment rates as existed were negative.

When we explored the extent to which unemployment rates could account for trends within individual jurisdictions over time, a rather clearer and more consistent picture emerged. For the period 1968 to 1987, only Sweden did not show any sort of relationship. In England and Wales, West Germany, France, and the Netherlands, there were very high and significant correlations ($r$ = .68–.91), which generally grew stronger with lagging. As expected, in England and Wales and France, unemployment was more closely linked with changes in the remand population than changes in the sentenced population. In New Zealand, too, there was a highly significant positive correlation between unemployment rates and changes in the remand population, but not between unemployment rates and changes in the sentenced population. In contrast, however, in the Netherlands and West Germany, most or all of the influence of unemployment rates lay in their effect on the sentenced population. There was thus no consistent pattern for unemployment to affect remand practice more than sentencing practice.

In general, it seems clear that unemployment rates are more useful as a means of explaining trends in prison use within jurisdictions than of explaining differences between jurisdictions. In other words, fluctuations in unemployment may well alter the penal climate of a particular jurisdiction to some degree, but those fluctuations are within fairly narrow parameters and are unable to account for the more substantial differences in prison rates between one jurisdiction and another.

3. *Policy Choices.* In recent years, especially in the wake of actual or proposed sentencing reforms in many jurisdictions, a good deal of emphasis has been placed on the direct effect of policy choices in determining trends and differences in prison rates. For example, many have argued that the dramatic increase in the prison populations in many American states since the late 1970s has been the result of the development of determinate sentencing structures (including mandatory incarceration provisions), a declining faith in the effectiveness of rehabilitation programs, and the corresponding emergence of a "get tough" policy, which has at least implicitly been intended to result in an increase in the use and length of prison sentences for particular categories of offender (Blumstein 1988; Joyce 1992). Others have noted

that some jurisdictions seem to have been successful in maintaining comparatively low prison populations or reducing those populations by deliberate policy choices. West Germany's short-lived success in reducing the prison population between 1968 and 1970 by legislative change, and more durable success in reducing its population after 1983 by changes in prosecutorial and judicial decision making (Feest 1982, 1991; Graham 1990), provide perhaps the best illustration. Another example can be found in the sentencing guidelines of Minnesota and Washington, both of which have been designed to coordinate sentencing and correctional resources by requiring the sentencing commissions formulating the guidelines to ensure that they could be implemented without adverse fiscal consequences for the correctional system. They seem to have been largely successful in this regard; the rate of increase in their prison population has been significantly lower than in most other American jurisdictions, so that throughout much of the 1980s they were able to hold their prison populations within existing correctional capacity (Tonry 1991, pp. 311–13).

However, the view that prison populations are readily manipulated by legislative, judicial, or prosecutorial policy and that trends and variations in prison rates are often explicable in these terms is simplistic and largely unhelpful for two reasons. First, policies that are deliberately adopted to reduce the prison population frequently do not have their intended effect. Sometimes this is because the policies themselves are based on a misunderstanding of the factors driving the prison population and therefore do not have the effect anticipated. The consequences of the introduction of the suspended prison sentence in England and Wales in 1967 graphically demonstrate the point. More generally, the reliance on alternatives to custody or "intermediate punishments" as a means of achieving a significant reduction in the prison population is likely to fail in most jurisdictions for the reasons stated earlier. Sometimes, however, even if the stated policies themselves are appropriately targeted, they are thwarted by countervailing pressures within the criminal justice system itself or within the wider socioeconomic and political structure, such as conflicting policy directives or economic pressures, which drive the prison population in the opposite direction from that intended (Friedman 1981).

More significantly, the sharp distinction between socioeconomic and cultural variables and policy choices overlooks that, while individual policy initiatives may sometimes be in conflict with each other, the underlying policy parameters are driven or at least constrained by the socioeconomic and cultural framework within which they are being formulated. Choices about the nature and severity of penal sanctions are not simply dictated by rational decisions about the methods that will most efficiently control crime. They may be shaped by the economic structure and concerns of a particular society (Ignatieff 1978) and by the specific forms of power in a society and the way in which these are exercised through, and control imposed on, the powerless (Foucault 1977); in other words, they may be used to reinforce a particular conception of social order or shore up a particular set of political and economic interests and power relations. More importantly for the argument here, they are shaped by a variety of more intangible cultural factors. That is the reason, of course, why neither the formal structure of the criminal law nor the particular penal philosophies or principles supposedly underpinning it are able to explain divergent rates of imprisonment: even when the philosophies and structures of two jurisdictions seem to be uniform, their actual use of imprisonment is apt to vary considerably (Zimring and Hawkins 1991, p. xiii).

In summary, therefore, attempts to extend traditional explanations of prison rate variation to cross-jurisdictional differences have proved to be of limited value. Certainly, within jurisdictions there are some fluctuations that can, as traditionally predicted, be attributed to structural factors such as unemployment rates or to particular legislative, judicial, or executive changes in policy. However, to the extent that these fluctuations occur within fairly narrow bounds, the structural explanations advanced to account for them do not provide a satisfactory explanation of the more marked differences in the use of imprisonment between one jurisdiction and another. For that we must look to the underlying processes that shape the institution of punishment itself and, in particular, to the role of social and cultural forces.

## B. Cultural Attitudes and Penal Values

There has developed recently a body of literature that significantly advances our understanding of the processes framing attitudes toward the form and severity of punishment, exploring in detail the way in which behavioral norms and cultural conventions are related to the emergence and changing use of particular forms of punishment within particular societies (Spierenburg 1984; Garland 1990; Pratt 1992). It suggests that, while punishments may be *justified* by policymakers, judges, and penal administrators by reference to their instrumental goals (which tend to be similar across jurisdictions), their form and severity are in reality likely to be *chosen* on the basis of almost instinctive feelings about what the "right" punishment is—what Garland (1990, 1991) has called the public "sensibilities" that are deeply embedded in the cultural patterns of any society and that go to make up a society's penal values. Those feelings tend to be shared within a culture, leading to a surprisingly high degree of concordance between judicial sentencing practice and public opinion on sentencing (see Doob and Roberts 1988; Hough and Moxon 1988; Roberts 1992).

It follows that differences between jurisdictions in imprisonment practice are likely to mirror more general differences in judicial and public attitudes, not so much toward the rationale for punishment as toward the quantum of punishment. Some empirical support for that can be found in a recent international crime survey (Van Dijk, Mayhew, and Killias 1991), which found a fairly strong correlation between high per capita imprisonment rates and public support for imprisonment as the best sentencing option.

However, there has been little cross-cultural work describing the reasons why such penal values or public sensibilities differ between societies, even when they have superficially similar political and cultural traditions. It was beyond the scope of our study to collect data on this issue, but the recent work of Wilkins and Pease (Wilkins 1984, 1991; Wilkins and Pease 1987; Pease 1991) is illuminating and points to the direction that future investigations in this area should take.

Wilkins and Pease claim that one of the cultural determinants of a society's penal climate or its relative punitiveness is linked to its relative egalitarianism: the greater a society's tolerance of inequality, the more extreme the scale of punishment utilized. On this analysis, punishment is seen as a type of negative reward; just as positive rewards in the form of higher incomes and more social status are bestowed on those who succeed in business or professional careers, so negative rewards in the form of punishment are imposed on those who fail by breaking society's rules. Each is at an opposite end of the same continuum, so that differentials at one end of the continuum covary with differentials at the other. Thus the greater the differentials in the rewards provided for "success" at one end of the continuum, the greater the differentials in the scale of punishments (or, for that matter, in the scale of damages and other remedies under the civil law) at the other end of the continuum. Countries that have a highly individualistic and competitive ethos, premised on notions of meritocracy and equal opportunity, and have substantial gaps between rich and poor are likely to be comparatively severe in their penal outlook. Countries that have highly developed welfare systems and a less materialistic reward structure are likely to be comparatively mild.

In order to provide empirical support for this claim, Wilkins and Pease correlated World Bank measures of income inequality—the proportion of total income earned by the highest 5 percent of income earners and the proportion of total income earned by the lowest 20 percent of income earners—with both average receptions and average length of detention in seven European countries. While these are admittedly rather crude approximations of the extreme ends of the hypothesized reward/punishment continuum, they are probably the best data available for the purpose.

The results of this analysis were at least in some respects consistent with the hypothesis. There was a strong correlation of $+.81$ between the proportion of income earned by the highest 5 percent of income earners and the average length of detention, and a moderate to low correlation of $+.24$ between the proportion of income earned by the lowest 20 percent of income earners and the average length of detention, suggesting that "it may be relative extreme wealth rather than extreme poverty which holds the key to the relationships speculated upon" (Wilkins and Pease 1987, p. 28). However, the correlations with admissions were not consistent: while there was a positive correlation $(+.40)$ between the reception rate and the proportion of income earned by the lowest 20 percent, there was in fact a negative correlation $(-.50)$ between the reception rates and the proportion of income earned by the highest 5 percent.

At first sight, it is not easy to make sense of this; if differentials at the punishment end of the continuum mirror those at the reward end, it might be thought that those jurisdictions with greater income differentials would not only impose longer sentences on those who receive imprisonment, but also resort to it at an earlier point in the hierarchy of penalties.

In fact, the data produced by Wilkins and Pease are easier to reconcile with their hypothesis than appears at first sight. As we have seen, the jurisdictions characterized by high prison rates tend to be those with high average lengths of detention rather than high admission rates; in other words, they have higher prison populations not because they use imprisonment more often, but because they impose longer sentences. The reason for that can be found in a tendency toward a positive relationship between the availability and use of imprisonment and the use of the more severe and intrusive noncustodial sanctions. The Third UN Survey found that the availability of more noncustodial sanctions was related to some degree to higher prison population rates (Centre for Social Development and Humanitarian Affairs 1991). Similarly, a recent comparison of Australian states and New Zealand shows clearly that those jurisdictions with higher prison rates also have higher rates of the population subject to community-based sanctions with some element of ongoing supervision or control, such as community work or probation supervision (New Zealand Department of Justice 1992). Although this evidence is not conclusive, it does strongly suggest that jurisdictions with greater "differentials" in the scale of punishment have a more elaborate and more intrusive structure of noncustodial sentences, so that prison admission rates are not a reliable indicator of a society's penal climate. Hence the absence of a clear correlation between such rates and income differentials does not invalidate the Wilkins and Pease hypothesis.

That imprisonment and other punishment practices, and the policy choices underlying them, appear to be driven at least in part by deeply embedded sociocultural factors means that cross-jurisdictional differences in prison use are likely to remain fairly stable over time. Imprisonment rates *within* a particular jurisdiction are likely to fluctuate substantially on the basis of changes not only in the number of convicted offenders, but also in other conditions such as unemployment, the degree of political or social stability, or a shift in decision-making power within the criminal justice system from, say, parole boards or the judiciary to the legislature. But, as our earlier analysis showed, the gross differences that mark the comparisons *between* jurisdictions are likely to remain relatively unperturbed by these fluctuations.

That there is not a greater degree of comparative stability in prison trends historically can probably be accounted for on two grounds. The first is that sentencing practices do not always wholly reflect penal values in the public mind. In particular, there is often a clash between the perceived public demand for severe sentences and the resources that society wants or is able to expend on the penal system. Politicians and the public often want to get tough, or be seen to be getting tough, but do not want to pay for it. As a result, sentencing practice is often characterized by symbolically severe punishments that are later mitigated by "back-end" executive release mechanisms, such as parole, remission, and home leave. These mechanisms, of course, are in themselves influenced by the penal climate within which they operate, but only in an indirect way; and the availability of such mechanisms may well change from time to time within particular jurisdictions—depending on such factors as prison overcrowding and publicity over early releases gone wrong—without any significant shift in penal values themselves. The second factor affecting comparative stability in prison trends is that penal values are not impervious to sudden change. For instance, sudden and dramatic events within a culture, such as those experienced by some countries occupied during the Second World War, may alter the penal value of a unit of prison time over a very short period indeed.

## V. Summary

This essay has described and attempted some interpretation of variations in imprisonment rates both between jurisdictions and within individual jurisdictions over time. It has shown that increases in prison populations over time tend to be caused by changes in both admissions and length of detention, but that reductions in the prison population over time are more easily achieved through regulating the length of detention than the number of admissions. In cross-national comparisons, jurisdictions with high prison populations typically do not send proportionately more offenders to prison, but rather impose longer terms on those who do go to prison.

Traditional structural approaches to the explanation of these trends and differences in prison rates are ultimately limited and do not significantly advance our understanding of the processes which shape the use and form of punishment. In particular, offense or conviction rates account for only a small part of the variations in the use of imprisonment; prison capacity may affect the prison population only to the extent that overcrowding may constrain judicial sentencing practice or increase the use of early release mechanisms, but otherwise it has little bearing on the size of the population; and unemployment rates, although related to fluctuations in imprisonment rates *within* jurisdictions, seem largely unrelated to differences *between* jurisdictions.

Similarly, it is difficult to attribute variations in imprisonment practice simply to differences or changes in penal philosophies or in other policy choices within the criminal justice system. To begin with, penal policies frequently do not have their intended effect, either because they are inappropriately targeted or because other countervailing pressures within the criminal justice system or wider political and socioeconomic structure militate against their successful implementation. More importantly, penal policies are not simply based on rational decisions about the methods of punishment that will most efficiently control crime. Thus, although different jurisdictions may articulate the same set of concerns about crime and may espouse similar penal philosophies—whether it be retribution, deterrence, rehabilitation, or incapacitation—to deal with particular categories of offender, the expression given to those philosophies in the legislative structure and in sentencing practice is likely to vary substantially.

Such variations are driven by a range of more intangible cultural factors that are deeply rooted in a society's history, values, and socioeconomic structure. The form and severity of punishment, whatever the rationale provided, are shaped by public sensibilities about punishment, which go to make up a society's penal values. Those penal values seem to be related, among other things, to a society's relative egalitarianism: the greater the differentials in terms of income and other rewards and the greater the gaps between rich and poor in society, the more extreme the scale of punishment will be. While any sort of systematic cross-national investigation of this thesis has only recently been undertaken, the available evidence lends support to it.

This sort of analysis of imprisonment rates demonstrates the limitations of efforts at "rational" penal reform that attempt to alter penal practices by redefining penal philosophies or offering a greater choice in the smorgasbord of sanctions. Ultimately, effecting very substantial shifts in the use of imprisonment—for example, making English or New Zealand prison rates as low as those of the Netherlands—involves changing a range of sociocultural attitudes and values that go well beyond the technical penological agenda. To argue this is not to deny the possibility of change; it is rather to argue for a different level of social and political debate.

REFERENCES

Abt Associates. 1980. *American Prisons and Jails*, vol. 2. Washington, D.C.: U.S. Government Printing Office.

Austin, J., and B. Krisberg. 1982. "The Unmet Promise of Alternatives to Incarceration." *Crime and Delinquency* 28:374–409.

Australian Institute of Criminology. 1990. *Remand Imprisonment in Australia.* Trends and Issues in Crime and Criminal Justice, no. 27. Canberra: Australian Institute of Criminology.

Berk, R. A., D. Rauma, S. L. Messinger, and T. F. Cooley. 1981. "A Test of the Stability of Punishment Hypothesis: The Case of California, 1851–1970." *American Sociological Review* 46:805–29.

Biles, D. 1979. "Crime and the Use of Prisons." *Federal Probation* 43(2):39–43.

———. 1982. "Crime and Imprisonment: An Australian Time Series Analysis." *Australian and New Zealand Journal of Criminology* 15:133–53.

———. 1983. "Crime and Imprisonment: A Two-Decade Comparison between England and Wales and Australia." *British Journal of Criminology* 23:166–72.

Biles, D., and G. Mulligan. 1973. "Mad or Bad? The Enduring Dilemma." *British Journal of Criminology* 13:275–79.

Blumstein, A. 1988. "Prison Populations: A System Out of Control?" In *Crime and Justice: A Review of Research*, vol. 10, edited by Michael Tonry and Norval Morris. Chicago: University of Chicago Press.

———. 1989. "American Prisons in a Time of Crisis." In *The American Prison*, edited by Lynne Goodstein and Doris L. MacKenzie. New York: Plenum.

Blumstein, A., and J. Cohen. 1973. "A Theory of the Stability of Punishment." *Journal of Criminal Law and Criminology* 64:198–207.

Blumstein, A., J. Cohen, and W. Gooding. 1983. "The Influence of Capacity on Prison Population: A Critical Review of Some Recent Evidence." *Crime and Delinquency* 29:1–51.

Blumstein, A., J. Cohen, and D. Nagin. 1976. "The Dynamics of a Homeostatic Punishment Process." *Journal of Criminal Law and Criminology* 67:317–34.

Blumstein, A., and S. Moitra. 1979. "An Analysis of the Time Series of the Imprisonment Rate of the United States: A Further Test of the Stability of Punishment Hypothesis." *Journal of Criminal Law and Criminology* 70:376–90.

Bottomley, A. K. 1990. "Parole in Transition: A Comparative Study of Origins, Developments, and Prospects for the 1990s." In *Crime and Justice: A Review of Research*, vol. 12, edited by Michael Tonry and Norval Morris. Chicago: University of Chicago Press.

Bottomley, A. K., and K. Pease. 1986. *Crime and Punishment: Interpreting the Data*. Milton Keynes, England: Open University Press.

Bowker, L. H. 1981. "Crime and the Use of Prisons in the United States: A Time Series Analysis." *Crime and Delinquency* 27:206–12.

Box, S., and C. Hale. 1982. "Economic Crisis and the Rising Prisoner Population in England and Wales." *Crime and Social Justice* 17:20–35.

———. 1986. "Unemployment, Crime and Imprisonment, and the Enduring Problem of Prison Overcrowding." In *Confronting Crime*, edited by R. Matthews and J. Young. London: Sage.

Bureau of Justice Statistics. 1982. *Prisoners, 1925–81*. Washington, D.C.: U.S. Department of Justice.

———. 1990. *Prisoners in 1989*. Washington, D.C.: U.S. Department of Justice.

Cahalan, M. 1979. "Trends in Incarceration in the United States since 1880." *Crime and Delinquency* 25:9–41.

California Blue Ribbon Commission. 1989. *Final Draft Report: Blue Ribbon Commission on Inmate Population Management.* Sacramento: California Blue Ribbon Commission.

Centre for Social Development and Humanitarian Affairs. 1991. *Report to the General Assembly on the Second and Third United Nations Surveys.* Vienna: United Nations.

Chan, J., and R. Ericson. 1981. *Decarceration and the Economy of Penal Reform.* Toronto: University of Toronto, Centre of Criminology.

Cohen, S. 1985. *Visions of Social Control.* Cambridge: Polity Press.

Collier, P., and R. Tarling. 1986. "International Comparisons of Prison Populations." *Home Office Research Bulletin* 23:48–54.

Council of Europe. 1990. *Prison Information Bulletin No. 15.* Strasbourg: Council of Europe.

———. 1992. *Prison Information Bulletin No. 16.* Strasbourg: Council of Europe.

Crow, I., P. Richardson, C. Riddington, and F. Simon. 1989. *Unemployment, Crime and Offenders.* London: Routledge.

Doob, A. N., and J. Roberts. 1988. "Public Punitiveness and Public Knowledge of the Facts: Some Canadian Surveys." In *Public Attitudes to Sentencing: Surveys from Five Countries,* edited by N. Walker and M. Hough. Aldershot: Gower.

Feest, J. B. 1982. *Imprisonment and the Federal Republic of Germany.* Bremen: University of Bremen.

———. 1991. "Reducing the Prison Population: Lessons from the West German Experience?" In *Imprisonment: European Perspectives,* edited by John Muncie and Richard Sparks. New York: Harvester.

Fitzmaurice, C., and K. Pease. 1982. "Prison Sentences and Population: A Comparison of Some European Countries." *Justice of the Peace* 18:575–79.

Foucault, M. 1977. *Discipline and Punish: The Birth of the Prison.* Translated by Alan Sheridan. London: Penguin.

Friedman, L. M. 1981. "History, Social Policy and Criminal Justice." In *Social History and Social Policy,* edited by D. J. Rothman and S. Wheeler. New York: Academic Press.

Garland, D. 1990. *Punishment and Modern Society: A Study in Social Theory.* Oxford: Oxford University Press.

———. 1991. "Sociological Perspectives on Punishment." In *Crime and Justice: A Review of Research,* vol. 14, edited by Michael Tonry. Chicago: University of Chicago Press.

Grabosky, P. N. 1980. "Rates of Imprisonment and Psychiatric Hospitalisation in the United States." *Social Indicators Research* 7:63–70.

Graham, J. 1990. "Decarceration in the Federal Republic of Germany: How Practitioners Are Succeeding Where Policy-Makers Have Failed." *British Journal of Criminology* 30:150–70.

Greenberg, D. F. 1977. "The Dynamics of Oscillatory Punishment Processes." *Journal of Criminal Law and Criminology* 68:643–51.

———. 1980. "Penal Sanctions in Poland: A Test of Alternative Models." *Social Problems* 28:194–204.

Hough, M., and D. Moxon. 1988. "Dealing with Offenders: Popular Opinion and the Views of Victims in England and Wales." In *Public Attitudes to Sentencing: Surveys from Five Countries*, edited by N. Walker and M. Hough. Aldershot: Gower.

Hylton, J. H. 1981. "Community Corrections and Social Control: The Case of Saskatchewan, Canada." *Contemporary Crises* 5:193–215.

Ignatieff, M. 1978. *A Just Measure of Pain: The Penitentiary and the Industrial Revolution*. London: Macmillan.

Jankovic, I. 1977. "Labour Market and Imprisonment." *Crime and Social Justice* 8:17–31.

Joyce, N. M. 1992. "A View of the Future: The Effect of Policy on Prison Population Growth." *Crime and Delinquency* 38:357–68.

Kalish, C. B. 1988. *International Crime Rates*. Washington, D.C.: Department of Justice, Bureau of Justice Statistics.

Knapp, K. 1989. "Criminal Sentencing Reform: Legacy for the Correctional System." In *The American Prison*, edited by L. Goodstein and D. L. MacKenzie. New York: Plenum.

Krisberg, B., and I. Schwartz. 1983. "Rethinking Juvenile Justice." *Crime and Delinquency* 29:333–64.

Langan, P. 1991. "America's Soaring Prison Population." *Science* 251:1568–73.

Lynch, J. P. 1988. "A Comparison of Prison Use in England, Canada, West Germany and the United States: A Limited Test of the Punitive Hypothesis." *Journal of Criminal Law and Criminology* 79:180–217.

McMahon, M. 1990. "Net-Widening: Vagaries in the Use of a Concept." *British Journal of Criminology* 30:121–49.

Nagel, W. G. 1977. "On Behalf of a Moratorium on Prison Construction." *Crime and Delinquency* 23:154–72.

New York State Committee on Sentencing Guidelines. 1985. *Determinate Sentencing: Report and Recommendations*. Albany: New York State Committee on Sentencing Guidelines.

New Zealand Department of Justice. 1992. *Imprisonment as The Last Resort: The New Zealand Experience*. Wellington: Department of Justice.

Pease, K. 1991. "Punishment Demand and Punishment Numbers." In *Policy and Theory in Criminal Justice*, edited by D. M. Gottfredson and R. V. Clarke. Aldershot: Gower.

Pennsylvania Commission on Crime and Delinquency. 1990. *Containing Pennsylvania Offenders*. Harrisburg: Pennsylvania Commission on Crime and Delinquency

Penrose, L. S. 1939. "Mental Disease and Crime: Outline of a Comparative Study of European Statistics." *British Journal of Medical Psychology* 18:1–15.

Pratt, J. 1992. *Punishment in a Perfect Society*. Wellington: Victoria University Press.

Rauma, D. 1981. "Crime and Punishment Reconsidered: Some Comments on Blumstein's Stability of Punishment Hypothesis." *Journal of Criminal Law and Criminology* 72:1772–98.

Roberts, Julian. 1992. "Public Opinion, Crime, and Criminal Justice." In *Crime and Justice: A Review of Research*, vol. 16, edited by Michael Tonry. Chicago: University of Chicago Press.

Rutherford, A. 1984. *Prisons and the Process of Justice*. London: Heinemann.

Sabol, W. J. 1989. "The Dynamics of Unemployment and Imprisonment in England and Wales, 1946–1985." *Journal of Quantitative Criminology* 5(2):147–68.

Shane-Dubow, S., A. P. Brown, and E. Olsen. 1985. *Sentencing Reform in the United States: History, Content and Effect*. Washington, D.C.: U.S. Government Printing Office.

South Australian Office of Crime Statistics. 1989. *The Impact of Parole Legislation Change in South Australia*. Adelaide: Attorney General's Department.

Spierenburg, P. 1984. "The Sociogenesis of Confinement and Its Development in Early Modern Europe." In *The Emergence of Carceral Institutions*, edited by P. Spierenburg. Rotterdam: Erasmus University.

Steenhuis, D. W., L. C. M. Tigges, and J. J. A. Esser. 1983. "The Penal Climate in the Netherlands." *British Journal of Criminology* 23:1–16.

Tonry, M. 1991. "The Politics and Processes of Sentencing Commissions." *Crime and Delinquency* 37:307–29.

Tremblay, P. 1986a. "The Stability of Punishment: A Follow-up of Blumstein's Hypothesis." *Journal of Quantitative Criminology* 2(2):157–80.

———. 1986b. "The Evolution of Penitentiary Imprisonment, of Its Intensity, of Its Firmness and of Its Scope—the Case of Montreal, 1845–1913." *Canadian Journal of Criminology* 28:47–68.

Van Dijk, J., P. Mayhew, and M. Killias. 1991. *Experiences of Crime across the World: Key Findings from the 1989 International Crime Survey*. Boston: Kluwer Law and Taxation Publishers.

Wallace, D. 1981. "The Political Economy of Incarceration Trends in Late U.S. Capitalism: 1971–1977." *Insurgent Socialist* 10:59–66.

Waller, I., and L. Touchetta. 1982. *Canadian Crime and Justice in Comparative Perspective*. Ottawa: University of Ottawa, Department of Criminology.

Weatherburn, D. 1985. "Appellate Review, Judicial Discretion and the Determination of Minimum Periods." *Australian and New Zealand Journal of Criminology* 18:272–83.

Wilkins, L. T. 1984. *Consumerist Criminology*. London: Heinemann.

———. 1991. *Punishment, Crime and Market Forces*. Aldershot: Dartmouth.

Wilkins, L. T., and K. Pease. 1987. "Public Demand for Punishment." *International Journal of Sociology and Social Policy* 7(3):16–29.

Young, W. 1986. "Influences upon the Use of Imprisonment: A Review of the Literature." *Howard Journal* 25(2):125–36.

Zimring, F. E., and G. Hawkins. 1991. *The Scale of Imprisonment*. Chicago: University of Chicago Press.

*Brian Gormally, Kieran McEvoy, and David Wall*

# Criminal Justice in a Divided Society: Northern Ireland Prisons

ABSTRACT

Many societies are divided on political, ethnic, religious, national, or
linguistic lines; criminal justice systems require strategies to manage the
consequences of the resulting conflict and political violence. The prison
system in Northern Ireland provides a case study of three contrasting
methods of managing divided and politically motivated prisoners.
"Reactive containment" is a military-style response of suppression
combined with negotiation that treats inmates as prisoners of war.
"Criminalization" denies political legitimacy to the practitioners of
violence by imposing the symbols and regimes appropriate to ordinary
criminals. "Normalization" treats division and a certain level of violence
as commonplace, seeks to minimize conflict within the prisons, engages
constructively with politically motivated prisoners, and holds the greatest
promise for managing political violence without being an obstacle to
political progress.

Many nations and societies are chronically divided. The divisions may
be ethnic, religious, linguistic, or related to national identity, and can
lead to fundamental social and political discord. Quite often this discord gives rise to, or is associated with, political violence.[1] State and

Brian Gormally, Kieran McEvoy, and David Wall are deputy director, information
officer, and director, respectively, of the Northern Ireland Association for the Care and
Resettlement of Offenders (NIACRO), the major charity working with and campaigning
on behalf of prisoners and their families in Northern Ireland. The authors acknowledge
the importance and value of their working relationship with the Northern Ireland Office
Prison Service, prisoners, and prisoners' representatives, and also the help and encouragement of Tony Bottoms.
[1] In this essay we use the phrase "political violence" as defined in Section 31 of the
Emergency Provisions Acts (Northern Ireland), 1978 and 1987: "Terrorism means the
use of violence for political ends and includes any use of violence for the purpose of
putting the public or any section of the public in fear." After some deliberation we have
decided that we should use the word "terrorist" in quotation marks, since to do otherwise

51

particularly criminal justice system responses to such a continuing crisis are a matter of wide interest.

This essay examines the management of political violence in Northern Ireland since the late 1960s. It uses the prison system as a case study that illuminates three models of how a state can respond to political violence. These models serve as distinct theoretical constructs or Weberian "ideal types" (Weber 1949) that explain how a criminal justice system can operate in situations of extreme social discord.

We have chosen the prison system as a case study for a number of reasons. First, on a general level, as Ditchfield (1990, p. 8) has pointed out, "prisons are social institutions, located in particular societies at particular points in time. Like all social institutions, they reflect the norms and values of their societies and are inevitably affected by them." Prisons have much to tell us of how a particular society is directed, disciplined, and administered (Foucault 1977).

Second, on a more particular level, as practitioners in the criminal justice system, it is the area of work with which we are most closely involved. Third, the prisons in Northern Ireland have in many ways formed the key ideological terrain on which ongoing struggles, between those engaged in political violence and the authorities, have been waged.

We have termed the three models: "reactive containment" (1969–76), "criminalization" (1976–81), and "normalization" (1981 onward). By fixing dates on these models, however, we are not postulating "a Whig view of history" (Thompson 1975, 1980), where the system inexorably progresses from a cruder, less civilized past toward some more sophisticated, ultimately "liberal" preordained goal. While the strategies adopted by the Northern Ireland Prison Service are in part a product of and a response to the shortcomings of previous strategies, the changes within the Northern Ireland prison system also reflect and are influenced by broader societal and political changes. Depending on political perspective these changes can be seen as progressive or regressive. The models are neither evolutionary nor mutually exclusive. Their characteristics are not set in stone. They are constantly being challenged, prodded, and redefined in the ongoing struggle that is the essence of the management of political violence.

Each model has advantages and disadvantages. We do not aim to

would be to ignore the processes of criminalization and delegitimation of which we write. For a more detailed discussion of the difficulties of terminology, see Mani (1978) and Gearty (1991).

be prescriptive, though our preference among the models inevitably becomes clear. Nor do we intend to suggest that the "management" of political violence is, in itself, a good thing. Setting out to manage political violence may obscure the routes to the solution of the problems that cause it.

Our exposition starts with a definition of the three models in Section I. A brief overview of the Northern Ireland prison system is also included to identify institutions mentioned in the text. We continue with a brief account of basic interpretations of the Northern Ireland conflict in Section II. Our purpose is not to stress the uniqueness of that situation but to provide the basic information with which to make sense of the context in which the models of the management of political violence have been applied. The Irish context is rich in dramatic detail, which can have a fascination of its own. Our intention, however, in conjunction with dealing with the detail of that context, is to extract from it the patterns of operation and thus to construct ideal types, heuristic devices, for the management of political violence. These may then be more or less useful, in a wide variety of contexts, in illuminating the policies of state agencies or opening up directions for policy development.

We then discuss the first two models—reactive containment and criminalization—sketching in their basic characteristics through an essentially historical analysis in Sections III and IV, respectively. We examine the third model, "normalization," in considerable detail in Section V. There are several reasons for this concentration. First, this is the contemporary phase and so is more interesting. Second, it represents, in our view, a qualitatively new departure in British policy in Northern Ireland. Third, its principles might have a wider applicability beyond Northern Ireland than those of the other models. Concluding remarks are offered in Section VI.

I. Overview of the Prison System and the Three Models

Before discussing the three models it may be useful to familiarize readers with a broad outline of the current prison system in Northern Ireland, which we later discuss in greater detail.

A. *The Prison System in Northern Ireland*

There are five institutions, each with a fairly distinct and unique role. The system is designed to imprison politically motivated prisoners (over two-thirds of the daily average population), from different and implacably opposed paramilitary organizations, as well as "ordinary" criminals, or "ordinary decent criminals (odc's)" as they are colloquially called. Fifty-eight percent of the average population are serving long-term sentences (longer than five years), and 23 percent are serving life sentences.

1. *Crumlin Road.*   This, the oldest prison with the worst conditions, is the main male remand prison in Northern Ireland. It is a high-security prison housing both conforming political prisoners (i.e., those who by and large will conform to the prison regime, disavow their allegiance to their respective "terrorist" organization, and integrate with other political prisoners from oppositional paramilitary groups) and nonconforming political prisoners. It also contains "ordinary" re-manded prisoners, although these are kept on a different wing from the nonconforming politicals. The prison houses an assessment unit where recently sentenced prisoners are assessed to decide to which of the other prisons they should be sent. It has an optimum capacity of 433; in January 1993, there were 542 inmates.

2. *Maze Prison.*   This is the high-security male prison that houses mainly the sentenced, nonconforming political prisoners. Political pris-oners are segregated according to their paramilitary allegiances. They elect their own "officers commanding" (oc's), and other ranks of respon-sibility, for each prison subdivision and for the prison as a whole. There is a de facto recognition of the paramilitary command structures through which the authorities negotiate and manage the prison, and the prisoners have a large degree of autonomy on the wings. Formerly known as Long Kesh, it was the main prison under focus during the hunger strike era. The optimum capacity is 744 prisoners; there were 471 inmates in January 1993.

3. *Maghaberry Prison.*   Maghaberry is actually two separate prisons: one a medium-security, custom-built prison housing conforming sen-tenced male political prisoners and long-term "ordinaries" (opened No-vember 1987), and the other a female prison that houses all remand and sentenced female prisoners, conforming and nonconforming politi-cals as well as "ordinaries" (opened March 1986). Conditions in both prisons compare favorably with the vast majority of prisons in Britain. The male prison was built in order to give the authorities flexibility to offer an institution for those political prisoners who no longer wished to retain allegiance to their organization. The female prison was built to replace the old women's prison at Armagh, which, like Crumlin Road, was an old establishment in very poor condition. The men's

prison has an optimum capacity of 432; the number of inmates in January 1993 was 337. The women's facility has an optimum capacity of 56; the number of inmates was 42 in January 1993.

4. *Magilligan Prison.* Magilligan is a medium-security male prison that houses mainly "ordinary" sentenced prisoners who have either been given short-term sentences or are approaching the end of longer fixed sentences. Its optimum capacity is 288; the number of prisoners in January 1993 was 307.

5. *Young Offenders Centre.* The Young Offenders Centre is a male prison that houses mostly male "ordinary" remand and sentenced prisoners between the ages of 18 and 21, serving sentences of up to four years. The optimum capacity is 300. The number of prisoners in January 1993 was 155.

The prison population has stabilized over recent years at around 1,800–1,900 prisoners. This is a marked decrease in numbers from a high of over 3,000 in the mid-1970s. That decrease, which we discuss in greater detail when looking at the operation of the models, is due to factors such as the abandonment of internment (mass detention of suspected terrorists without trial), the sustained release of life (indeterminate) sentence prisoners, and the stabilization of levels of violence at a lower level.

Other features of the system are discussed below, particularly in Section V, including the increased use of prerelease parole, improvement in visiting provisions for families, and community support structures.

### B. The Three Models

The three models of how a state can deal with political violence are briefly introduced here. Experience with each is discussed in later sections.

1. *Reactive Containment.* This model can be seen as a relatively crude response to an actual, or potential, armed insurrection. It is fundamentally a military model though it can be implemented by police forces and other security bodies. Its mind-set is of a "war" against a distinct "enemy." It finds difficulty in engaging with the complexities of a divided society. It incorporates the military horror of a war on two fronts and, where there is more than one source of political violence, identifies one as the only, or main, enemy.

The essential characteristics of reactive containment are the suppression and containment of the insurrectionary enemy, a willingness to use conventional military force, the prorogation of aspects of civil liberties, and contemporaneous negotiation with the "enemy" and with other political forces in the search for a political settlement. The model implies an acceptance that the violence is political in origin, however "wrong," and therefore confers some kind of legitimacy on its perpetrators. In prison terms, it implies detention with the minimum of formality, yet with prisoners being given a relatively high status; their regime will approximate to that of "prisoners of war."

This approach was used time and again in the course of Britain's withdrawal from empire. It was familiar to soldiers, civil servants, and politicians, just as it was to several leaders of newly independent countries who ultimately made the journey from jail to the prime ministerial residence. Examples include Jomo Kenyatta in Kenya, Robert Mugabe in Zimbabwe, and, of course, Eamon de Valera in Ireland.

For the Northern Ireland prison system, this model meant internment without trial, "special category status" for those convicted through especially invented, no-jury courts, military guards on the prison camps, and, eventually, a huge, money-led recruitment drive for more prison officers.

2. *Criminalization.* This approach is fundamentally a redefinition of political violence as simple criminal activity. It is an attempt to remove any legitimacy from the "terrorists." Negotiations are more or less rejected, and the total defeat of violence is held out as a real possibility.

This is not simply a propaganda offensive against the perpetrators of violence; indeed, such campaigns are common in all models. It has practical consequences that are the result of clear judgments about the "enemy" and the institutions of the state. It means, first, an estimation that there is no existing insurrection that has any hope of even limited success. There is therefore little incentive to negotiate, and, indeed, in the context of this policy, dialogue is seen as counterproductive. Second, it expresses a confidence in the strength of the criminal justice system, even if it has had to be augmented with special powers and procedures. Third, it can recognize and deal with a variety of sources of political violence; they are perceived simply as varieties of criminals. Fourth, it expresses the belief that those convicted by the system can be coerced and cajoled into acceptance of their roles as criminals. Such an outcome would have a hugely delegitimizing effect on violence outside the prisons and cast fundamental doubt on the motivation of those involved.

This policy puts the prisons in the front line. Every symbol of "difference" between "terrorists" and ordinary criminals, any notion of the political character of some inmates, has to be removed from the system. So it involved the end of "special category status," the rigid enforcement of the wearing of prison uniforms and the doing of prison work, and a refusal to recognize the existence of paramilitary organizational structures.

3. *Normalization.*[2]  The third model represents a realization and acceptance that political violence and division are a "normality" of a given criminal justice system and society—part of a broader range of other "normalities" that should receive equal emphasis such as ordinary crime, ordinary policing, unemployment, and so forth—and an acceptance of the anomalies that this entails.

The main principles of normalization derive from a number of political decisions:

The first is an acceptance that the prison system, at any rate, is not a mechanism that can "defeat" political violence; rather it is a mechanism for managing some of its consequences, and an abandonment of the policy of criminalization, insofar as that is designed to coerce prisoners into a practical and symbolic acceptance of the status of common criminals.

The second is a recognition that political conflict and division are permanent (i.e., will exist for the foreseeable future) and hence must be seen as "normal."

The third is an acceptance of the "permanence" of "temporary" legislative and administrative structures that have been adapted to contain political violence and yet are seen as forming just one specialized part of the "normal" criminal justice system.

For the prisons normalization implies development of a number of strategic directions:

The recognition of groups of politically motivated prisoners who are

---

[2] We need to distinguish our use of the term "normalization" from that of the Republican movement in Ireland. In Republican parlance, "normalization" is used to describe a significant propaganda element in an aggressive anti-insurrectionary program. They see the British engaged in an attempt to deny the existence of the "war," to stress the appearances of ordinary life, to relegate the "liberation struggle" of the IRA to a minor nuisance that kills fewer people than road traffic incidents. In our terminology, however, normalization does not have the same aggressive, anti-insurrectionary connotations as its admittedly cognate use by Republicans. We see the strategy not so much as a method of defeating the IRA but as a way of incorporating their and other "terrorists' " existence in a stable but flexible system of administering and managing political violence as one of many structural problems within Northern Ireland.

distinct from "ordinary" prisoners and from each other is the first direction. This distinction includes elements of flexibility and negotiation; an attempt to limit, quarantine, and marginalize the paramilitary groupings; and through a carrot-and-stick approach, constructive engagement with their adherents.

The second is a policy of minimizing causes and occasions of conflict with prisoners and their families. This involves a culture of realism and a readiness to spend money to avoid trouble.

The third involves creating a culture of normality around the system by allowing much greater access for the media and the public to information and the institutions themselves and proactive and sophisticated media intervention.

These strategic directions can be perceived in the practice of the Northern Ireland Prison Service over the past few years. They are, however, forms of practice that are translatable to a wide variety of contexts where social division and political violence confront a criminal justice system.

## II. Interpretations of the Northern Ireland Conflict

For the purposes of this essay, we have felt it unnecessary to give a detailed account of the conflict in Ireland. However some brief, and thus by definition oversimplified, historical and theoretical context is required in order better to understand our three models for the management of political violence. We have included a chart of the main events, government reports, and prison episodes, covering the past quarter century, in the Appendix. Many of these are referred to in the text.

For those unfamiliar with the complexities of Irish history, it might be appropriate at this juncture to offer a very brief overview. Such a historical narrative might begin with the gradual conquest of the island of Ireland by English forces between 1169 and the Act of Union with Britain in 1801. Three years before, the first "Republican" uprising, designed to establish an independent Irish nation state, had been defeated. Similar armed or political uprisings occurred in every generation during the nineteenth century, culminating in the major political demand for "home rule," in the late nineteenth and early twentieth centuries. Meanwhile, in the North, the distinctly Protestant and pro-union-with-Britain character of the majority of the population was becoming clearer and politically organized.

An armed body, the Ulster Volunteer Force, was created to be the cutting edge of the Unionist campaign to resist home rule. They formed an alliance with the British Conservative party, which saw it as a political opportunity to hurt the Liberal government of the day. In the context of an unreliable British officer corps based in Ireland, and the outbreak of World War I, the political impetus for home rule in the British Parliament was dissipated.

In 1916 a Republican rebellion in Dublin was suppressed, and its leaders were executed. In the succeeding few years, insurrection became widespread in the South of the country, under the leadership of the Irish Republican Army (IRA). The result was the partition of the country into two states, with a civil war in the South and the establishment of an avowedly Protestant state in the North. The present political violence in Northern Ireland results from the clash of interpretations of this history and of the differing aspirations and allegiances to which it has given rise. These issues are dealt with in more detail in the exposition of varying historical interpretations given below.

Some of the best attempts at analyzing the nature of the conflict here, as elsewhere, have been marred by a quest for an illusory mono-causality (Ignatieff 1981). We have therefore chosen to adapt the typology developed by John Whyte (1991) in his seminal work, "Interpreting Northern Ireland," to analyze the potential sources of political violence from different perspectives. He argues that there are essentially four interpretations of the Northern Ireland conflict: traditional Nationalist; traditional Unionist; Marxist; and two-community, or internal, conflict (Whyte 1991, p. 114). In the following sections we show how each of the explanatory constructs can represent different perspectives on the origins of political violence in Northern Ireland.

## A. Traditional Nationalist

The principal perpetrator of politically motivated violence from this tradition has been the IRA (see also Section V on normalization). Their view is that when, in 1920, the British Parliament passed the Government of Ireland Act creating two devolved Irish Parliaments, they split the Irish nation against the wishes of the majority of its people. For them the establishment of the six-county state in the North of Ireland was done via a boundary commission and the arbitrary drawing of a border designed to ensure a Protestant majority in the North. As the North-Eastern Boundary Bureau (set up by the new Irish Free State government) put it in 1923: "The problem of the North-East Ulster is unique only in one respect—it is the only religious minority in the world which has, through the assistance of powerful outside influences, been able to frustrate the organic development of the nation for more than half a century, and then to insist on cutting off from the nation not only its own adherents, but a large minority whose traditional allegiance was to the nation as a whole" (1923, p. vi).

Both states were formed in the wake of what was, at least in military terms, the largely unsuccessful insurrection of 1916 (Cauldfield 1965; Kee 1972, 1982). This was followed by the more successful guerrilla campaign waged by the IRA against the British between 1919 and 1921 (Townsend 1975; Coogan 1990) and ultimately a meeting between the British and the IRA that led to the signing of the Anglo-Irish Treaty, the setting up of the boundary commission, and the establishment of the two states (Curran 1988).

The IRA, which had largely been the force behind the guerrilla war, split over the treaty—some wanting to hold out for the Republic they had sought, others arguing that the treaty gave "the freedom to win the freedom" and that the boundary commission established by the treaty would redraw the border in such a way as to make Northern Ireland economically unviable (Coogan 1990). A bitter civil war followed in 1922 and 1923, pitting the Free State army (largely made up of former members of the IRA) against their former comrades, before the "irregulars" accepted that they could not defeat the Free State army (Neeson 1967).

Most of those on the losing side in the civil war put aside their arms, formed the Fianna Fail party in 1926, and entered constitutional politics in the South under the leadership of Eamon De Valera. A few remained in Sinn Fein (the IRA's political wing) and gave their allegiance to what was left of the IRA, to the Proclamation of the Irish Republic (drawn up and signed by the leaders of the 1916 uprising), and to what they saw as the historically ordained mandate for a united Ireland (Coogan 1985). For them the establishment of the Irish Free State in the South in 1921, with its dominion status and the oath of allegiance to the Crown, was an illegal act, and all subsequent Dublin governments were, therefore, illegal. They claimed that the 1918 general election, the last to be held on an all-Ireland basis, where Sinn Fein had won a landslide victory, had given them and the IRA a mandate to seek a United Ireland by whatever means.

When De Valera assumed power in Dublin in 1932, he proscribed the IRA. De Valera was to a degree embracing a form of constitutional nationalism (as opposed to militant Republicanism), and this was formally expressed in the 1937 Irish Constitution, Article 2 of which declared, "The national territory consists of the whole island of Ireland, its islands and the territorial seas."

During the next thirty years the IRA made periodic attempts at mounting bombing campaigns in Britain and armed attacks on military and police installations in the North, its most sustained effort being the Border Campaign of 1956–62. The latter campaign was singularly unsuccessful as a result of a combination of lack of support, lack of funds, poor planning, and the effective use by the security forces on both sides of the border of the emergency powers available to them (Bowyer Bell 1979; Coogan 1985; Bishop and Mallie 1989).

In the current campaign the main perpetrator of Republican violence is the Provisional IRA, which split from the official IRA in 1969 (see the section below on Marxist interpretations). Tactics have included attacks on security force personnel in Northern Ireland, Britain and Europe, major political and judicial figures, workmen on military and police installations, and prominent Loyalists, as well as the bombing of commercial, military, and civilian targets. The legal political wing of the Provisional IRA is Sinn Fein, which operates as an open political party, though its spokespersons are denied full access to the broadcast media.[3] It receives approximately one-third of the Catholic vote in Northern Ireland.

The other 60–70 percent of the nationalist community in the North regularly vote for what could reasonably be described as constitutional nationalism, that is, a United Ireland by consent. Republicans point to the traditional discrimination in the North against Catholics in terms of employment opportunities and housing (cf. Teague 1987) as evidence of the unworkability of the Northern Ireland state. They see themselves engaged in a war of liberation against the British occupation, a war in which the British use a range of measures against them including military conflict, draconian Emergency powers, imprisonment, sponsoring loyalist violence, single-issue pressure groups, revisionist histories, and anything else that marginalizes or delegitimizes their struggle.

## B. *Traditionalist Unionist*

Even though they formed a permanent majority in the new Northern Ireland state, Protestants felt besieged. They felt under threat from within by the seditious Catholic minority and from without by the

---

[3] In October 1988, the government introduced a ban on hearing the spoken words of (principally) Sinn Fein spokespersons in the broadcast media. When such persons are interviewed, their words are spoken by an actor or given as subtitles.

hostile state to the South, which laid claim in its constitution to Northern Ireland as a part of its own national territory. Even the more charitable historical analysts have suggested that the most discreditable element to the state that was created was the concrete expression of that sense of fear and vulnerability (Stewart 1977).

The Unionist government established a special paramilitary police force, the "B-Specials" in 1920, in effect a Protestant militia to protect the state against the assaults of Republicans. They also introduced the Special Powers Act in 1922, which created wide powers including internment; powers to ban political parties, rallies, and marches; and powers to stop, search, and detain without warrants or reasonable suspicion. Section 1(i) read: "If any person does any act of such a nature as to be calculated to be prejudicial to the preservation of peace or the maintenance of order in Northern Ireland and not specifically provided for in the regulations, he shall be deemed guilty of an offense against the regulations."

In many ways, the special powers era represented a continuum of coercion. Thus there was sufficient force to achieve repression, the political will to pursue that policy, and the necessary legal means (Hogan and Walker 1989, p. 15).

Republicanism as the expression of extreme nationalism was seen as the real danger and threat. Loyalist violence was treated with greater ambivalence because it was commonly seen as reactive to republicanism rather than any real threat to the state (Boyd 1969). As Hogan and Walker (1989, p. 14) put it, "Most regulations appeared during campaigns of the IRA, whereas loyalist sectarianism rarely elicited any response."

The distrust of the Catholic minority was intense and institutionalized. Any compromise with Catholics with a political dimension to it was seen as undermining the Protestant hegemony. The result was widespread discrimination against Catholics, especially for jobs and housing (Smith 1990); a concentrated attempt to keep their numbers down by ensuring that the historic rates of emigration persisted; gerrymandering with the electoral process to ensure Protestant majorities (Purdey 1990); and a state where planning for infrastructure such as roads or the siting of major social institutions was determined along religious lines.

One of the most comprehensive expressions of Unionist ideology is expressed by M. W. Heslinga (1962) in his book, *The Irish Border as a Cultural Divide*. Heslinga (1962, pp. 14–16, 81, 93–94) argues that despite the division of Ireland in 1921, the British Isles remain in many ways one unit. He views Ulster Protestants as having a tradition of civil and religious freedom that is anathema to the quite clear Catholic ethos of the Republic and its constitution. He thus sees Northern Ireland Protestants as forming a separate nation (p. 62). While he does not stand over the details of the border (p. 49), he believes that it "represents, however arbitrarily, an important spiritual divide" (p. 78).

Unionists viewed the establishment of "a Protestant parliament for a Protestant people" as necessary to preserve their links with the rest of the United Kingdom and the Crown and to protect their religious independence. In particular it was felt necessary that Unionists dominated and ran the institutions of the state. In order to protect themselves against the seditious minority, who professed no loyalty to the Union, the Royal Ulster Constabulary (RUC), with its associated special militias, was structured and organized to operate on behalf of the Unionist majority. The RUC, despite recruitment drives at various stages of its history, has traditionally remained largely composed of Protestants. In 1991, Hugh Annsley, chief constable of the RUC, stated that Catholic membership was currently around 7 percent of full-timers and 3 percent of the part-time force (Mapstone 1992, p. 185). Originally the force was supported by part-time militia in the A-, B-, and C-Specials. The A- and C-Specials were disbanded in 1925, leaving only the B-Specials in support. They in turn were disbanded in 1969 on the recommendation of the Hunt Commission, which sought to restructure the RUC in the wake of the civil disturbances of that year (Hunt 1969; Brewer and Magee 1991).

Unionists have seen the threat to their position from three potential sources, the hostile government to the South (Kennedy 1988), the seditious minority of Catholics within the North (Stewart 1977), and a potentially treacherous British government that would sell them out for an end to political violence (Guelke 1988, p. 195). Unionists argue that economically the North is much better off as part of the United Kingdom. They believe that the economy of the Republic is structurally weak, and to become a part of it "would be to join economic hopelessness and a huge debt" (Paisley, Robinson, and Taylor 1982, pp. 50–52).

Whatever the merits of this economic analysis, the question of British identity is in any case much more important to Unionists. McCartney et al. (1981, p. 5) speak of the Unionist's ties with Britain as "psychologically bound to her with bonds of blood, history, and common adversity which cannot be bartered away in some logical package no matter how attractive that might seem." They object to the claim to the North in Article 2 of the Irish Constitution and "to the pseudo legality which it affords to the Provisional IRA's campaign of violence in the North" (McCartney et al. 1981, p. 2). Similarly the enshrinement of Catholic values in the Irish Constitution such as the prohibition on divorce and the difficulty of obtaining contraceptives are cited among the dangers of unification (McCartney et al. 1981, p. 5; Paisley, Robinson, and Taylor 1982, p. 5). It is, however, arguable whether changes to these elements would do much to assuage the Unionists' fears. As Whyte (1991, p. 151) put it, "Unionist attitudes are based more on perceptions of an atmosphere than on particular grievances."

Political violence from the Unionist camp comes from the two primary sources of the Ulster Defence Association (UDA) and the Ulster Volunteer Force (UVF) (see also Section V on normalization). They see attacks on the security forces by Republicans not merely as an attempt to force the Protestant community into a United Ireland with all that this entails but also as "a genocide against the Protestant people." They see the IRA as aided and abetted by the nationalist community and the authorities as lacking sufficient resolve properly to tackle the security threat posed by Republicans: "The IRA had stated publicly that without the help and support of the nationalist electorate its war machine could not function. Those who aid and abet the Republican war machine, either by the ballot box or by other means, are deemed as guilty as those who pull the trigger. . . . We will not stand idly by while the government allows the IRA to continue its genocide against our people and the wrecking of our cities" (New Ulster Defender 1992).[4]

Loyalist paramilitaries would thus claim that their violence is both defensive and reactive to that of the IRA. This means however that they have a much more ambivalent relationship with the state and its security infrastructure than Republicans. While they claim that they too are political prisoners, they have traditionally been more willing to accept the label of criminals and the due process of the system. "Their only crime is Loyalty" is the essence of Loyalist ideology.

## C. Marxist

Although Marxist analysis can be traced as far back as Marx and Engels themselves (Marx and Engels 1971), James Connolly, one of

[4] Statement released by the Ulster Freedom Fighters, a code name for the UDA, after the shooting of a Catholic taxi driver on February 2, 1992.

the participants executed by the British in the 1916 rising, was the first to apply it systematically to the Irish conflict (Ryan 1948). Connolly's proposition was that no victory for the worker over the bourgeois in Ireland could be achieved other than by national independence (Ryan 1948, p. 9). Connolly's major worry, ultimately realized, was that the country would be partitioned, keeping alive the national question at the expense of class politics. He believed that the result of partition would be to strengthen the most conservative forces in Ireland in both parts of Ireland, leading to "a carnival of reaction both North and South" (Ryan 1948, p. 111).

Connolly's writings have been substantially updated by works published just prior to and during the current spate of violence in the North (Devlin 1969; Farrell 1976; McCann 1980). The central thesis of all of these texts was that Connolly's carnival of reaction had in fact occurred and that Northern Ireland was governed by a capitalist class that kept the Catholic and Protestant working class repressed and divided. This was done by two techniques: beating the sectarian drum to the Protestant working class whenever the two classes showed signs of uniting by encouraging fears of Catholic take over, and marginally discriminating between Catholics and Protestants (exploiting Protestant workers but still giving them a narrow but visible margin over their Catholic workmates and neighbors) (Whyte 1991, p. 180).

The political violence that has originated from this perspective has largely come from left-wing Republican splinter groups. The IRA split in the early 1970s occurred because the provisional faction opposed the essentially Marxist direction the organization had taken during the 1960s, and because of the organization's decision to recognize Westminster and Leinster House (the Irish Parliament) (Bishop and Mallie 1989, p. 136). Although the "Provisionals" took up the mantle of traditional militant Republicanism, the "official IRA" has apparently continued to exist as the armed wing of the left-wing "Workers party." The Workers party, which was formed from the official faction of the IRA, and which had six members of parliament in the Republic, itself split in 1992 over the refusal of some of their members completely to abandon their links with a more militant past.

Other organizations such as the Irish National Liberation Army (INLA) and later the Irish Peoples Liberation Organisation (IPLO) were to emerge from this fusion of militant Republicanism and class politics (Dillon 1990, p. 280). Although this was the ideological basis for these groups, they have singularly failed to go beyond their Republican label to develop support from the Protestant working class. Indeed, they have been heavily criticized for being openly sectarian and involved in criminal activity. In 1992 the IRA launched a concerted series of armed attacks against members of the IPLO, accusing them of organized drug dealing. Under this onslaught, the organization declared itself dissolved.

### D. Two-Community/Internal Conflict

This perspective tends to lay more stress on the indigenous rather than the exogenous factors of the Northern Ireland conflict (O'Leary 1985). The Cameron Report, based on an investigation of the civil disturbances of 1969 (para. 229), suggested seven basic causes to the unrest; there was no mention of any cause outside Northern Ireland (Cameron 1969). O'Brien (1972), Darby (1976), and Boal and Douglas (1982) are just some of the better-known examples of this type of research. Similarly, Boyle and Hadden (1985), Watt (1981), and Rea (1982), while ascribing varying degrees of relevance to the British/Irish dimension, have all seen the "conflict in Northern Ireland as one between two different traditions, identities, and allegiances" (Rea 1982, p. 1).

The "internal conflict" thesis in official reports and academic research appears to be by far the most popular approach (Whyte 1991, p. 203). Political violence would therefore be seen largely as the product of the state of the relations between the two communities. The major difference between this and the other perspectives is that it negates the role of either the Irish or British states. Fox and Morison (1992, p. 10) describe this perspective as the creation and regulation of two officially sanctioned identities within Northern Ireland, that is, "the idea of making each mutually hostile faction equally valid—so long as they eschew the use of violence." It is for those who have the responsibility for managing political violence to decide whether taking their own neutrality for granted is a recipe for good and effective management.

### E. Conclusion

To a greater or lesser degree, the different organizations and institutions, both state based and community based, legal and illegal, operate on the basis of one or another of these models. This informs individual and collective behavior and has influenced the ways in which the state has managed political violence and the way in which paramilitary organizations have responded to the state. It is central to an understanding of Northern Ireland institutions in general and the Prison Service in particular, to recognize that the behavior and the conflict it generates is embedded in these alternative views of history.

### III. Reactive Containment, 1969–75

"Reactive containment" was a relatively crude military-led response to what was perceived in Britain as a quasi-colonial insurrection similar to those that had been faced in Kenya, Malaysia, Cyprus, Aden, and Oman. The essential similarity was seen to be that the government had to react because the locally based authorities had lost control. The army should be dispatched as a temporary measure to regain control. This should be allied with a fairly tough security policy; violence should be contained as a political solution is sought.

In the 1960s, influenced at least in part by similar agitations in America and other places in Europe, Catholic frustration and disenchantment at the way the Northern Irish state had functioned (Cameron 1969) began to express itself in a form other than the traditional Republican response of armed insurrection. That disenchantment was partially vindicated by the Cameron Commission, which was established by the Northern Ireland government in 1969 to look into the origins of the disturbances. It produced an explicit criticism of the way the Northern Ireland state had operated between 1921 and 1969. This commission, which consisted of a Northern Ireland Protestant, a Northern Ireland Catholic, and a Scottish judge as chairman concluded that there was widespread resentment among Catholics at inequities in housing allocation, discrimination in local government employment, gerrymandering of local government boundaries, and a partisan law enforcement system (Cameron 1969, para. 229).

The repeal of the special powers legislation, an end to discrimination in housing and jobs, and the cessation of gerrymandering formed the central demands of the Northern Ireland Civil Rights Association that was chiefly responsible for the mobilization of Catholic grievances (Purdey 1990). These took the form of civil rights marches. The demonstrations provoked in turn a hostile reaction from sections of the Protestant population. The Northern Ireland government reacted by clamping down severely on the marches, using the police and B-Specials to break them up by force. These measures, along with the failure to protect Catholic communities from sectarian attack, ensured that the usually precarious relationship between the Catholic population and the government, and in particular the RUC, was to deteriorate still further. As the violence and rioting escalated in both volume and frequency, the RUC, having lost the confidence of the Catholic community, found itself unable to cope and ultimately the British army was called in to play a peacekeeping role. Within months, that role had changed as the attitudes of Republicans and the colonial training of the British army combined to ensure that the army's role became seen as an exercise in counterinsurgency.

What is important to note at this stage of the conflict is that while the security measures introduced were quite harsh, including use of internment, severe interrogation techniques, and a temporary curfew on the predominantly Catholic Falls Road in Belfast, the political and ideological nature of the violence was implicitly accepted by the authorities.[5] Prisoners arrested and detained were given "special category" status. This meant that they were held separately from "ordinary" prisoners and allowed to wear their own clothes and to associate freely—essentially, in other words, to behave as prisoners of war.

In 1972, after a truce had been called, the British government met with the leaders of the IRA. Gerry Adams, now president of Sinn Fein, was released from prison to be part of the delegation. With the British army on the streets and the IRA the obvious enemy, the political aspect to the violence was simply not in question.

## A. Insurgency and Counterinsurgency: The Deployment of British Troops

The British army's leading expert on counterinsurgency, who arrived in Northern Ireland in September 1970, described the strategy governing troop deployment: "The British Army was struggling to adapt ideas gained in the colonies to the circumstances prevailing in part of the United Kingdom, i.e., Northern Ireland, and it was doing so in partnership with a number of London based politicians and civil servants who had thought very little about the problems of insurgency, and a number of Northern Ireland politicians and civil servants whose whole political system had been devised with this very problem in mind, but in a context that had become out of date from a political point of view. Progress was only made after an extended period of trial and error" (Kitson 1991, p. x).

---

[5] These interrogation techniques included hooding of prisoners, beatings, playing of constant humming noises, forcing prisoners to stand with arms outstretched, and other sensory deprivation techniques. In 1978 the European Court of Human Rights found these practices to be in breach of Article 3 of the European Convention of Human Rights, constituting "inhuman and degrading treatment." See Ireland v. UK (S310/71), Judgment (18.1.78) 23.I.

The British army was deployed by the Westminster government in Belfast and Derry in August 1969 initially to safeguard besieged Catholic enclaves. The army was welcomed at first by the Catholic communities, which saw it as offering protection from Protestant mobs that the RUC and B-Specials either could or would not. Elements within the IRA, however, which had been remobilized reluctantly to act as defenders of those communities, saw the symbolism of British troops on Irish soil as a means to regalvanize their ranks, until then depleted and disorganized because of the failure of the Border Campaign of a decade before. The organization had moved in a Marxist direction after that campaign, away from traditional Republicanism to a more socialist approach (Bowyer Bell 1979; Coogan 1985; Bishop and Mallie 1989). As noted earlier, in 1969 the traditionalists within the movement were to split and form the Provisional IRA, which took up the orthodox Republican mantle of attacking "Crown forces." It is largely this group that has continued that campaign for the past twenty-one years. The breakaway left-wing splinter groups of the Irish National Liberation Army and, to a much lesser degree, the Irish People's Liberation Organisation have also been a subsidiary source of this category of violence.

The British army was not under the authority of the local government at Stormont, so inevitably London gained considerable control over local security matters as a result. This created obvious strains and tensions in the relationship between London and Stormont and led ultimately to the establishment of direct rule when, in March 1972, the Unionist government at Stormont resigned over the transfer of security powers to Westminster. Apart from a brief period of devolved power—sharing government from June 1973 to May 1974, London has since then assumed direct control of the affairs of Northern Ireland.

The unsuitability of the army for the task they were given was demonstrated by a number of tragic events in the 1970s. In 1970, British soldiers shot dead four civilians and injured sixty in the Falls curfew incident as 3,000 troops, supported by armored vehicles and helicopters, fought skirmishes as they searched through an exclusively Catholic area of Belfast, "axing down doors, ripping up floor boards, disemboweling chairs, sofas, beds, and smashing the garish plaster statues of the Madonna, the Infant of Prague and the Saint Bernadette that adorned the tiny front parlours" (Bishop and Mallie 1989, p. 119).

Similarly, the events of "Bloody Sunday" on January 30, 1972, when members of the parachute regiment shot fourteen unarmed demonstrators dead in Derry, ensured that the relationship between the Catholic community and the soldiers was one of open hostility (McCann, Shields, and Hannigan 1992).

## B. Special Category Status

The most explicit recognition of the political nature of the violence was the "special category status" granted to prisoners convicted of "terrorist" crimes between 1972 and 1975. During this period there were three classes of prisoners in the Northern Ireland system. The first-class prisoners were the "ordinary criminals" convicted of "ordinary decent crimes." The second were internees who were held subject to administrative detention in segregated accommodation. The third were those convicted of offenses related to the troubles. Prior to the granting of special category status, these prisoners were held in Crumlin Road jail in nonsegregated accommodation, with no free association, and forced to wear prison uniforms.

In early 1972, Billy McKee, formerly head of the Belfast Brigade of the IRA, led forty Republican prisoners on a hunger strike for prisoner of war status. William Whitelaw, secretary of state for Northern Ireland, conceded special category status as McKee neared death. This was done partly because of fears of the inevitable reaction that would have followed McKee's death, but also it had been one of the IRA's preconditions for a ceasefire and talks held between the two sides in July 1972. Regardless of the reason for the government's capitulation, the apparent success of McKee's hunger strike was to have important ramifications within Republican folklore toward the end of that decade.

What special category status entailed was that prisoners had de facto prisoner of war status. They were held in segregated accommodation away from "ordinary" prisoners and prisoners of opposing paramilitary factions. Most sentenced prisoners were held in Nissen huts at Long Kesh with usually three huts within each compound or "cage." Prisoners were allowed freely to associate, wear their own clothes, drill and hold lectures, and essentially run their cages along military-style lines. Each cage had its own officer in command, and all negotiations with the prison authorities were done through him (Adams 1990).

As part of a review of the policies designed to deal with "terrorism," the government set up a committee headed by Lord Gardiner (Gardiner 1975). It recommended that, after March 1, 1976, no prisoner convicted of "terrorist" type offenses should be entitled to special category status. This became a key element of the government's new policy direction of "criminalization." It is important to note, however, that during this period what was going on within the prisons was a microcosm of what was happening outside the prison walls. In the same way as negotiations between the prison authorities and the prisoners were achieved through the paramilitary command structures, similarly, the government was involved in dialogue with their comrades on the outside.

The government had met with the leaders of the IRA in 1972, although these talks ultimately came to no conclusion, and hostilities were resumed within days. In 1975 an IRA Christmas truce, which had been set up after a group of Protestant churchmen had met the IRA, was extended from January 2 until February 10. Merlyn Rees, by then secretary of state for Northern Ireland, had established fairly intricate means of "monitoring" the truce by setting up "incident centers" manned by civil servants twenty-four hours per day with direct links to an operations room in Stormont Castle. IRA and Sinn Fein officials would bring allegations of abuses of the truce, and these were duly processed. A steadily growing number of incidents led to the centers being closed in November. The cease-fire was officially ended on January 23, 1976, with a raid by the British army on Sinn Fein offices.

This was in many ways indicative of a hard-line government security policy allied with a pragmatic approach to the necessity for dialogue with "the enemy." The government talked and acted tough, not in many ways out of a "principled abhorrence" with the methods of their adversaries, but, rather, in order to strengthen their hand at the negotiation table.

### C. Internment

Another example of the policy of reaction and containment of the era was the use of the power of internment or administrative detention without trial. This power had always existed in both jurisdictions since the formation of the two states. It had been introduced on three prior occasions in the North, in 1921–24, 1938–45, and 1956–61. It was reintroduced in Northern Ireland on August 9, 1971, by the Stormont government with the consent of Westminster and remained in force after the assumption of direct rule (Great Britain 1971). The introduction of internment was recognized as a political gamble, but it was felt to be worth the risk. The chief danger, ultimately realized, as perceived by both the army and the politicians was that if the operation was badly conceived, it would provoke yet more hostility among the Catholics, increase support for the IRA, and miss many of the people it was aimed at.

The legal mechanics for carrying out the procedure were fairly simple. Under the Detention of Terrorists Order 1972, Article 4 (a slightly modified version of the power under the old Special Powers Act), the secretary of state could order the "interim custody" of a "suspected terrorist" for up to twenty-eight days. That detention was then examined by a "commissioner," who was in theory at least "a person of legal experience." The defendant could be excluded from the hearing, evidence inadmissible in a criminal trial could be heard, and witnesses gave evidence from behind screens (Spujt 1986). If the commissioner was satisfied not only of concern in terrorism but also that "detention was necessary for the protection of the public," a detention order could be issued, to be reviewed in one year. The burden of proof was a very high degree of probability although, since there was no necessity for reasonableness, "bad faith" was the only effective grounds for challenge.

The means of getting people into the process were no more sophisticated. "Operation Demetrius," the army code name for internment, went into operation on August 9 at 4:00 A.M. Of the 342 men arrested around the North, 116 were released within forty-eight hours. Among those who were taken from their beds were many retired Republicans, trade unionists, middle-class civil rights campaigners, a drunk picked up at a bus stop, and several people held on mistaken identity. Several of the people on the army's list turned out to be dead (Bishop and Mallie 1989, p. 186). Between August 9, 1971, and February 14, 1972, 2,447 people were detained, with 934 of them later being released (Spujt 1986, pp. 7–8). It is now largely accepted by those who administered the internment system that many of those who were interned were either completely innocent or on the margins of political violence. As William Whitelaw, then secretary of state for Northern Ireland, put it: "Now if you say that I put some in who shouldn't have been in, yes I would think that is certainly right. . . . I have the greatest doubts looking back whether internment was ever right" (Spujt 1986, p. 729).

Internees were held at Crumlin Road prison in Belfast, in camps at Long Kesh and Magilligan, and for a time aboard the Maidstone prison ship moored in Belfast Lough, simply because the space was not available within the existing prison system. Once interned, individuals were interrogated using the variety of techniques described above.

Internment was activated almost exclusively against "suspected Republicans" and thus de facto against the Catholic community. In September 1971 the British home secretary stated quite candidly that the aim of the internment policy was "to hold in safety, where they can do no further harm, active members of the IRA and, secondly, to obtain more information about their activities, their conspiracy and their organisation to help the security forces in their job of protecting the public as a whole" (Spujt 1986, p. 731).

Detention of Loyalists barely reached seventy, and this was at the height of the Ulster Workers Council Strike in May 1974; otherwise it was around fifty.

The council strike was a general strike organized by the United Ulster Unionist Council in 1974 in protest at the Sunningdale agreement that had been signed that year giving the Republic's government a largely symbolic say in the affairs of Northern Ireland. Through industrial action and paramilitary intimidation (Dillon 1990, p. xxv), the strikers brought Northern Ireland to a virtual standstill, and the agreement collapsed.

The number of detained Republicans reached nearly 640 in December 1973 and remained above 550 until the government began a policy of phased release in July 1974 (Spujt 1986, p. 735). The explanation offered by the British government before both the European Commission and Court of Human Rights was that Loyalist paramilitaries were smaller and more amorphous and that Republicans were better organized and thus responsible for more death and destruction (*Ireland v. UK* [1978], para. 66). While statistics for these years are hard to compile, those published as an appendix to the New Ireland Forum Report suggest that between 1971 and 1975 Republicans killed 126, 255, 128, 98, and 102 people, respectively, for those years while Loyalists killed 21, 103, 80, 104, and 115 people (Dillon and Lehane 1984). Although body counts are a distasteful measure for levels of violence, the point is nonetheless important because the visible evenhanded distribution of justice becomes a key tenet of the later criminalization and normalization models of the management of political violence.

Apart from the political fallout, in purely military terms, internment was an unmitigated disaster. The degree and intensity of the violence in the aftermath of internment has not been matched either before or since. The principal justification for internment had been to take the principal "players" out of action and then make further inroads on their operations by gaining intelligence through interrogations. In the seven months prior to internment, eleven soldiers and seventeen civilians died; in the five months following internment, thirty-two British soldiers, five members of the Ulster Defence Regiment (UDR), and ninety-seven civilians were either shot dead or blown up (O'Malley 1990, p. 17). The intended objectives of internment had clearly not been achieved.

The policy was abandoned after the Gardiner Report of 1975 had criticized it as having brought the law into contempt, causing deep resentment, and increasing the terrorist legend as well as the proficiencies of detainees to perpetrate violence. It concluded, "Detention [which replaced internment as official nomenclature after 1972] cannot remain as a long term policy . . . the prolonged effects of its use are ultimately inimical to community life, fan a widespread sense of grievance and injustice, and obstruct those elements in Northern Ireland society which could lead to reconciliation" (Gardiner 1975, para. 148).

In many ways the conclusion of that report was to prove prophetic, as with the phasing out of special category status and internment the limitations of a reactive containment policy were increasingly obvious to policymakers.

## D. Diplock Courts

In 1972 Secretary of State Whitelaw announced that the government would look at "whether changes should be made in the administration of justice in order to deal more effectively with terrorism without using internment under the Special Powers Act" (Great Britain 1972). On October 18, 1972, Whitelaw announced that this matter would be investigated by a commission chaired by Lord Diplock. The report, which was published in December 1972, proposed a package of measures that were intended to overhaul the criminal justice system to enable the conviction of those suspected of involvement in paramilitary activities to be obtained more easily, thereby reducing reliance on internment.

Recommendations were made concerning, among other things, the extension of army and police powers to stop and question, search and seize, and arrest and detain; the relaxation of the law governing the admissibility of confessions in order to enable convictions on confession alone to be secured in a greater number of cases; and the suspension of jury trial for a list of offenses usually associated with the activities of paramilitary organizations. These were to be known as "scheduled offences" since they were listed in a schedule to the enabling legislation.[6] The commission concluded that jury trial was "not practicable in the case of terrorist crimes in Northern Ireland" because of the threat of intimidation of witnesses (Diplock 1972, para. 17) and the risk that Loyalist defendants would be perversely acquitted by predominately Protestant juries (Diplock 1972, paras. 35–37).

Although Diplock courts were established first in 1973, it is one thesis that they perhaps did not come properly into their own as a means of dealing with political violence until after 1976 and the period of criminalization. The notion of redefining the judicial process so that quasi-normal policing and court processing of defendants was the norm, was much more difficult during the period of military-led reactive containment. The disbandment of the B-Specials and a brief three-month period when the police were disarmed (Ryder 1989, pp. 117–19) were obvious attempts at making elements of the criminal justice system more evenhanded in carrying out their functions. This thesis would hold, however, that such a task of "normalization" was not really feasible with the military having such a high profile and the perception that an armed insurrection was going on evidenced by measures such as internment and special category status.

An alternative argument is that the Diplock courts have been a constant feature of all three models of the management of political violence. In the period of containment, their "special" nature allowed the granting of special category status to those convicted by them. In the criminalization phase, they were reinterpreted as standard criminal courts so that those sentenced by them were "common criminals." In the normalization phase they have become a permanent, specialized feature of the criminal justice system dealing with one among a variety of species of offenders.

---

[6] Scheduled offenses (those listed in a schedule, i.e., an appendix to the Emergency Provisions Act) included murder, manslaughter, serious offenses against the person, arson, malicious damage, riot, offenses under the Firearms Act (Northern Ireland) 1969 and the Explosive Substances Act 1883, robbery and aggravated burglary, intimidation, membership of proscribed organizations, and collecting information likely to be of use to terrorists. The act also empowered the attorney general to certify that particular cases of murder, manslaughter, and offenses against the person should not be treated as scheduled offenses and should, therefore, be tried by jury (i.e., treated as "ordinary crimes"). Since 1973 juries have continued to function in Northern Ireland in civil cases, in coroners' courts, and in courts trying nonscheduled indictable offenses.

*E. Emergency Legislation*

The bulk of the Diplock Commission's proposals were enacted by Parliament soon after in the Northern Ireland (Emergency Provisions) Act 1973 (EPA), section 2(1) of which provided: "A trial on indictment of scheduled offence shall be conducted by the court without a jury."

The EPA 1973 was intended to be a temporary measure, and as such it contained a provision requiring Parliament to reconsider every year whether it was still necessary.[7] In practice however these "renewal debates" in Parliament soon became a cosmetic exercise. The main British political parties, Conservative and Labour, supported the continuation of this legislation in an often uninterested and uncritical manner. Debates were poorly attended and the government of the day (at different times involving both major political parties) renewed the legislation without any serious consideration of its long-term use. It has been argued that in many ways the 1973 Act represented a retrograde step as far as the rights of the citizen are concerned. It put the authorities in the position where they could represent themselves as using the "normal" judicial procedures when, in fact, the procedures they were using consisted of special powers of arrest, nonjury "Diplock" courts, and special rules of evidence (Walsh 1983, p. 11).

It is doubtful if the British government envisaged these measures operating on a long-term basis. In 1973 it embarked on a political initiative aimed at tackling the roots of the problem in Northern Ireland. That initiative purported to recognize the dual national identities prevailing in Northern Ireland by proposing the establishment of a Council of Ireland giving the government of the Republic some token say in the affairs of the North. It also sought to give the Catholic minority a say in the government of the state for the first time by setting up a power-sharing assembly.

Although that initiative failed and the prospect of a cessation of violence receded, the government took the decision in the wake of the Gardiner Report (1975) that much of this emergency legislation could be retained and incorporated into a broader strategy of criminalization. In this we see the beginning of a realization that political violence is intricately linked to the structure and functioning of Northern Ireland.

---

[7] The Prevention of Terrorism Act, which was introduced in the wake of a series of IRA pub bombings in England in the 1970s and which applies throughout the United Kingdom, was recently made permanent (rather than subject to annual review). It could be argued that this too signals the permanence or "normality" of measures required to deal with "terrorism."

The violence could not be tackled in the short term by a military-led combination of a tough security policy and arbitrarily locking up the alleged combatants in extrajudicial proceedings in order to strengthen one's hand for the negotiations that would inevitably come.

## IV. Criminalization, 1975–81

"Criminalization" is a fusion of political and military thought into a strategy of continuing military conflict with the "terrorists" aligned with a concerted attempt to delegitimize and criminalize what had been hitherto accepted as explicit *political* violence. The phasing out of the use of special category status and internment as recommended by the Gardiner Report (1975) was in conjunction with security measures designed to reduce the role of the army and increase the role of the police and political and social measures designed to marginalize the "terrorists" from their own communities.[8] This policy under the direction of Roy Mason (who had replaced Merlyn Rees as secretary of state for Northern Ireland) became known as "Ulsterization." Mason's approach, which has been followed to a degree by successive Conservative administrations, included "relatively generous social policies on the one hand, and a strong military posture on the other" (Gaffikin and Morrissey 1990, p. 206).

The theoretical element to the strategy was quite simple but essential if the hitherto political offenders were to be criminalized. The obvious guerrilla undertones to the ongoing conflict between the IRA and the British army could to a degree be internalized if it was members of the RUC and locally based UDR who were on the front line. Rather than be seen as one side in the ongoing struggle, the British government felt that it could portray itself, at least to an international audience, as neutral, trying to keep the peace in the ongoing factional fighting between two communities divided on religious and historical grounds.

There was a big recruitment drive within the RUC and a commitment to reduce the number of British army regiments committed to Northern Ireland. In the spring of 1976, an Englishman, Kenneth

---

[8] Examples of this strand of government thinking include the introduction of the Fair Employment Act 1976 outlawing discrimination on the grounds of religion. (This act was given considerably greater legislative teeth in 1989, including the making of indirect discrimination lawful, the power to bring claims of religious discrimination directly before an industrial tribunal, and enlarged investigative powers for the commission.) Similarly, there has been for some time a concerted strategy of government-led investment in Northern Ireland, with investment under schemes like "Making Belfast Work" being aimed specifically at areas such as West Belfast, from where the IRA would be seen to derive their greatest level of support within the city.

Newman, was appointed as chief constable of the RUC with a brief to professionalize the force so that it could lose its historic tag of sectarianism among the Catholic community. In January 1977, for the first time since 1969, the policy of police primacy was formalized by an agreement between the army general officer commanding (GOC) troops in Northern Ireland and the RUC, putting the chief constable in charge of overall security (Ryder 1989, p. 159).

This trend was not, however, paralleled by a softening of the interrogation and security policies of the police. Between 1976 and 1979, 3,000 people were charged with "terrorist" offenses, most of them on evidence obtained by confessions (Bishop and Mallie 1989, p. 321). The RUC was under intense pressure to secure convictions, and it responded by resorting frequently to physical beatings, threats, verbal abuse, intimidation, and generally oppressive treatment in an effort to extract confessions in the holding centers (Taylor 1980; Walsh 1983, p. 94; Hogan and Walker 1989, p. 116). One individual, Brian Maguire, died as a result of injuries received during interrogation. The techniques used in police holding centers like Castlereagh in Belfast led Amnesty International (1978, p. 56) to conclude that "maltreatment of suspected terrorists by the RUC has taken place with sufficient frequency to warrant the establishment of a public inquiry to investigate it." The government refused to accede to Amnesty's demand for a wide-ranging enquiry and established a more narrowly focused committee under Lord Justice Bennett. Even this committee refused to accept that all of those injured while in police custody had injured themselves as the police had claimed (Bennett 1979, paras. 19, 63).

Although there was a simultaneous trend toward withdrawing most British army regiments, the British government admitted that the Special Air Services (SAS) Regiment, an elite highly trained group specializing in covert guerrilla activity, was being deployed on January 1, 1976. In fact there is much evidence to suggest that the SAS had been deployed since the early 1970s (Dillon 1990; Murray 1990), but it is nonetheless highly significant that the government chose this time to make their presence public. This controversial regiment has been involved in some of the most contentious shootings by the security forces in Northern Ireland (Urban 1992).

Criminalization thus included a fusion of processing "terrorists" through the amended "normal" criminal justice system of Diplock courts and emergency legislation, an attempt to marry more conventional professional policing methods with fairly harsh interrogation techniques, and passing the sharper edge of the military conflict to a specialist covert elite rather than the more open conflict of the earlier period.

While on ideological grounds from the government's perspective the notion of criminalization was more sophisticated in terms of the battle for legitimacy, it did bring with it certain pitfalls that were soon to manifest themselves. The first and most obvious of these is that by "normalizing" extensive emergency powers into part of the mainstream criminal justice system, serious deviations from internationally recognized standards of human rights evolve into exactly that, the "norm." The United Kingdom has been found guilty of breaches of the European Convention of Human Rights more often than any other signatory despite being the prime mover in establishing that forum in the first place. Some commentators have explained this perceived erosion of civil liberties in Britain as being linked, at least in part, to what has been happening in Northern Ireland (Hillyard 1990).

The second pitfall is that extensive police powers and the minimal protection for the accused in the courts will become the norm for dealing with not only the political violence but also ordinary crime (Boyle and Allen 1983; Rolston and Tomlinson 1986). Certainly the conduct of normal policing of ordinary crime has become considerably distorted when policing of political violence has taken precedence. There is evidence to suggest that policing of "ordinary crime" such as car theft is affected by the need for information on suspected terrorists. Young car thieves are regularly offered inducements of small amounts of money or charges being dropped in return for low-grade intelligence on suspected "players" (McEvoy 1991).

The third and perhaps most dangerous risk is that the tactic of publicly denying the offenders' political motivation distorts policymakers' understanding of the true political nature of the conflict. This leads to political decision making based on "principle," rather than pragmatic realism. During this period, what began as a strategy for the better management of political violence evolved, at least in the eyes of certain key politicians and managers, into a point of principle that, since it could only be enforced by the harshest and most repressive measures, ultimately became an obstacle to good management.

## A. The Prisons, 1976–81: Dirty Protests and Hunger Strikes

Any person convicted of a scheduled offense after March 1976 was treated as an ordinary criminal according to the new policy of criminalization. Men were sent to a newly constructed prison (quickly dubbed the "H-blocks" since they were built in the shape of the letter H) erected alongside the compounds in Long Kesh and women to the old prison at Armagh. The legs of each H comprised a wing of twenty-five centrally heated eight-by-twelve-foot cells; a toilet area; and dining, recreation, and handicraft rooms. The central bar of the H was used for medical and administration quarters. With the abolition of special category status Long Kesh thus became two prisons. The compounds, with their Nissen huts, continued to hold the declining number of special category prisoners, since anyone convicted of a political offense before March 1, 1976, continued to hold this status, while prisoners convicted of such offenses after that date were confined to cells in the H-blocks. In order to signify the new policy direction, Long Kesh was renamed the "Maze Prison" although most prisoners and relatives persist in referring to it as Long Kesh.

The British government claimed the new facilities were among the best in Europe. In a document released to counter Republican propaganda called "H Blocks: The Reality," it claimed that "the Cellular Maze Prison [is] one of the most modern in Western Europe. . . most comprehensive in the facilities it provides and administered in humanitarian fashion" (H Blocks 1980). This theme of the excellent facilities being misused and damaged by recalcitrant prisoners was to form one of the basic tenets of the government's public statements in the ensuing years of the dirty protest, and hunger strikes.

1. *Dirty Protests.* On September 14, 1976, Ciaran Nugent, an IRA prisoner, was the first prisoner sentenced under the new regime. When he was asked for his clothes size for a uniform, he reportedly replied, "They will have to nail a prison uniform on my back first" (Republican Fact File 1991). Nugent was placed in a cell without clothes, covering himself with the blanket for his bed. Several hundred Republican prisoners—at any given moment, between one-third and one-half of the men arriving at the Maze/Long Kesh—followed Nugent "on the blanket."

Since it was an offense under the prison rules to leave one's cell improperly dressed, prisoners were thus confined to their cells for twenty-four hours per day. They were refused access to television, books, and newspapers. The refusal to cooperate with the authorities was a breach of prison discipline and thus meant that they were not entitled to the 50 percent remission scheme operating in Northern Ireland at that time (remission rates in Northern Ireland are now 33 percent; this change came into effect in 1989 and is currently governed by Sections 14 and 70 of the Emergency Provisions Act 1991; it is discussed in more detail below). Cooperating prisoners are entitled to three "privileged visits" and one statutory visit per month, but their noncooperation meant the cancellation of the three privileged visits, and their refusal to wear the uniform to the visiting area cost prisoners the fourth visit. Their contact with the outside world was thus limited to one censored letter per week (Beresford 1987, p. 27). After some confrontations with prison officers in which furniture was smashed, prisoners had their beds and footlockers removed, leaving them with two men per cell, each with a mattress, three blankets, and a Bible.

After several months the prisoners compromised and wore the uniform for their statutory visit, and thus the pattern of confrontation and brinkmanship began to take shape.

In 1978 a dispute arose over the circumstances in which prisoners were allowed to wash and go to the toilet. The authorities permitted them to go down the corridors provided they had a towel lapped around them, but they were refused a second towel to dry themselves. The prisoners began to refuse to leave their cells and thus the "no wash" protest had begun. The no wash protest was mirrored by nonconforming Republican prisoners in Crumlin Road, Magilligan, and Armagh Women's prison. Similarly, after several brawls between prison officers and prisoners in the Maze over the emptying of their chamber pots, prisoners began to throw the contents out through the windows of their cells and the spy holes in the doors. Prison officers responded by throwing it back in the cells and the prisoners began to smear the excrement on the walls, floors, and ceilings of their cells.

O'Malley's (1990, p. 21) description of the spiraling deterioration in prison management is worth reproducing: "Every gesture of noncooperation on the part of the protesting prisoners brought a harsher response; further punishment and stricter enforcement of the prison regulations. . . when prisoners baited warders, refusing to comply with even the simplest of orders, warders beat prisoners; when prisoners tried to defend themselves against warders, or assault them, warders administered savage retaliation; when the IRA, which had added prison officers to their list of legitimate targets, shot prison officers (eighteen were shot during this period), warders took their revenge on the prisoners."

By September 1980, there were approximately 1,400 prisoners at the Maze/Long Kesh. Of these, 370, half of whom were Republican and half Loyalist, had special status. Of the others, about 700 were Republican and 300 Loyalist, and close to 450 were "on the blanket" (Northern Ireland Prison Service 1980a). Random cell searches, mirror searches where prisoners were forced to squat naked over a mirror before and after visits and during wing shifts, forcible bathing in scalding water, and delousing were carried out with force and often vengeful brutality (O'Malley 1990, p. 22).

Prisoners had attempted to use the European Convention to argue that their detention was in breach of several of the articles, but this was ultimately rejected by the commission in June 1980. The commission reported that "the protest campaign was designed and co-ordinated by the prisoners to create the maximum publicity and to enlist public sympathy and support for their political aims. That such a strategy involved self-inflicted debasement and humiliation to an almost sub-human degree must be taken into account" (European Commission 1980). Similarly, a report by Amnesty International (1980) condemned the IRA tactic of assassinating prison officers and concluded that Amnesty did not support a special status for any prisoner.

2. *Hunger Strikes.* "Hunger-striking, when taken to the death, has a sublime quality about it: in conjunction with terrorism it offers a consummation of murder and self sacrifice which in a sense can legitimize the violence which precedes and follows it" (Beresford 1987, p. 38).

Given the conditions in which the prisoners were living, and the apparent failure of the efforts outside prison to resolve their plight,[9] it was perhaps inevitable that the prisoners within the jail would seek redress in the tactic of hunger striking, by which Billy McKee and others had secured special category status in the first place. They had for some time been pressuring the leadership of the IRA outside the prison to give permission for a hunger strike to begin (Beresford 1987, p. 360).

Finally on October 10, 1980, the IRA Army Council having given their consent, Sinn Fein announced that a hunger strike would be called in ten days. On October 27 an initial seven prisoners at the Maze went on hunger strike, being joined thirty-five days later by

---

[9] Apart from the initiative of the European Commission, there was an attempt by the Irish Commission for Justice and Peace to act as a "clarifier" between the two sides, as well as the attempts to broaden support for the prisoners' demands beyond the IRA sympathizers by the establishment of campaign groups known as the National H Block Committees.

three Republican women prisoners at Armagh and on December 13, five days before the hunger strike ended, by thirty more Republican men in the Maze. This first hunger strike ended when Humphrey Atkins, then secretary of state, presented a thirty-four page document to a mediator that appeared to contain the basis of a settlement. The hunger strikers sought clarification on several points, but before he received this clarification, Brendan Hughes, officer in command at the Maze, called off the hunger strike (O'Malley 1990, p. 33). He had been encouraged by the fact that another line of communication had been opened up (to the traditionally more sympathetic Foreign Office). Despite serious reservations by some of the hunger strikers, with Sean McKenna, youngest of the original hunger strikers, near death, the IRA took a gamble (Beresford 1987, p. 43).

The official Republican history of this deal is that "all the phrases contained in the document about the situation not being static, work not being interpreted narrowly and the prison regime being progressive, humane, and flexible were soon shown to be empty platitudes. On January 9, Atkins reneged by reversing the order by which POWs received their own clothes" (Republican Fact File 1991).

It is often difficult in hindsight to ascertain exactly why the details of one deal are acceptable and those of another are not. Certainly it appears in retrospect that the IRA had badly overcalculated the degree of flexibility the government would permit in order to enable a peaceful settlement. The concessions given, such as the staged issue of "civilian-style" clothing simultaneous with prisoners being allowed their own clothes and the experimental movement of prisoners into clean cells with furniture, were subject to delays, demands, and brinkmanship by both sides. The prisoners felt that they had called off the hunger strike too early, without a firm enough commitment in either form or will from the authorities. As O'Malley has argued, the view of the authorities may well have been that "the prisoners had backed down when they saw McKenna's life was on the line" (O'Malley 1990, p. 32).

As a result of the breakdown in negotiations a second hunger strike began on March 1, the fifth anniversary of the end of political status. The strikers' cause crystallized into five demands: the rights to wear their own clothes; to refrain from prison work; to associate freely with one another; to organize recreational facilities and to obtain one letter, visit, and parcel a week; and to have lost remission time restored.

Bobby Sands, who was leader of this second hunger strike, issued the following statement as it began: "We are still able to declare that the criminalization policy which we have resisted and suffered, has failed. . . . If a British government experienced such a long and persistent resistance to a domestic policy in England, then that policy would almost certainly be changed. . . . We have asserted that we are political prisoners and everything about our country, our arrests, interrogations, trials and prison conditions, show that we are politically motivated" (*Iris* 1991, p. 17).

The principal event that focused world attention on this hunger strike was the death of Frank McManus, nationalist member of Parliament (MP) for Fermanagh South Tyrone, on March 5, and Sands's ultimate election as MP on April 9 (two further H-block candidates were elected to the Dail in the Republic). Margaret Thatcher announced that the result changed nothing, "A crime is a crime is a crime. . . . It is not political, it is a crime" (O'Malley 1990, p. 60). Four days later the Northern Ireland Office announced that Sands was in critical condition, and on April 17 his death produced a worldwide response.[10] Three other hunger strikers had joined Sands two weeks into his fast; as hunger strikers died (or were taken off the hunger strike by their families in the later stages), the process continued until ultimately ten hunger strikers were to starve themselves to death.

The hunger strike ended on Saturday, October 3, 217 days after it had begun. A few days earlier the new secretary of state, James Prior, had replied to a question as to whether he was seeking to defeat the prisoners. We believe that the tone of this statement is tacit recognition of the mistakes that had been made during this period: "I do not believe in talking in those terms, because I always believe that they do more harm than good. I am saying to the hunger strikers: Give up. When it is clear that you have given up, we can amplify the statements that have already been made about prison reform, and progress in prison. If there is any doubt about that Lord Gowrie [prison minister] will, of course, amplify that and set things straight" (*Belfast Telegraph* 1981).

---

[10] "*The Hong Kong Standard* said it was 'sad that successive British governments have failed to end the last of Europe's religious wars.' *The Hindustani Times* said Mrs. Thatcher had allowed a fellow member of Parliament to die of starvation, an incident which had never before occurred in a civilised country. Teheran announced it would be sending its ambassador in Sweden as a representative at the funeral. . . . In India, Opposition members of the Upper house stood for a minute's silence in tribute. Members of Indira Gandhi's ruling Congress party refused to join in. In Portugal members of the Opposition stood for him. . . . ABC said he was a political kamikaze who got his strategy wrong. . . . In Russia *Pravda* described it as 'another tragic page in the grim chronicle of oppression, discrimination, terror, and violence in Ireland' " (Beresford 1987, p. 132).

## B. Conclusion

After the end of the hunger strike the majority of the prisoners' demands were quickly implemented. Prior announced in a press conference a few days later that prisoners could wear their own clothes, something that surely would have prevented the hunger strike in the first place had Atkins offered it a year before. Remission was restored on condition of good behavior; the demands relating to mail and visits had already been met. Prison work was ultimately abandoned as constituting too great a security risk after thirty-eight Republican prisoners escaped from the Maze in 1983 (Hennessey 1983–84; Dunne 1989).[11]

The five demands of the prisoners were at the center of the ideological battle over legitimacy between the authorities and the prisoners. We believe that the authorities adhered too rigidly to the principles of criminalization rather than viewing it as a matter of pragmatic management of political violence. Rather than a strategy for the more effective management of political violence as was originally intended, it became almost a political principle that justified and indeed necessitated the introduction of violent and repressive measures that inevitably presented structural obstacles to prevent effective management. This was a lesson that the authorities were to use with a great deal more subtlety and sophistication during the period we refer to as "normalization."

## V. Normalization, 1981 Onward

The prison system, as it exists at the beginning of 1993, was described earlier. Within the constraints of limited size and number of institutions, the aim is to provide a flexible range of regimes that can cope with the diverse political character and offending history of the prison population. It has been the recent ambition of the Prison Service to expand its options with a new, "high-tech" prison, but budgetary considerations have prevented this. To recapitulate, in brief: there are three main options for sentenced prisoners—the Maze, where nonconforming politicals are segregated; Maghaberry, where conforming politicals and some ordinaries mix in good physical conditions and a relatively relaxed regime; and Magilligan, which contains mainly ordinary prisoners, including a high proportion of sex offenders. Remand prisoners are kept in the Crumlin Road in Belfast, which, in conditions of great tension, forces politicals of opposing factions to mix, but segre-

---

[11] Although most of these prisoners have been subsequently caught, killed "on active service," or extradited from other countries, several remain at large.

gates them from ordinaries. Young adults (eighteen to twenty-one years) serving less than four years are placed in the Young Offenders Centre. It is within this system that the policy we describe below is implemented.

The current stance of the Prison Service is characterized by a set of policies and practices that amount to a particular application of the principle of normalization. That does not necessarily mean, however, that the policy has been centrally determined, described, and promulgated. Our perception is that the decisions that have led to the application of the policy of normalization have been taken relatively autonomously by the managers of various elements of the state structure who have come to similar conclusions. The policy appears to be the result of pragmatic judgments by those close to the ground. Indeed it may be argued that certain elements within the armed security forces have yet to come to the conclusions involved in a policy of normalization.

The relative autonomy of the generation of the policy by the Prison Service seems particularly marked. Ministerial control over operational policy is a constitutional fiction rather than a reality. Ministers in charge of prisons in Northern Ireland tend to be subject not only to the whims of the electorate but also to the perception that Northern Ireland is often seen as the "outer Siberia" of British political appointments. Consequently, civil servants have been seen as a much less transient population. The generation of ideas seems to take place within formal and informal groupings of these civil servants. Their relative autonomy and their ability to take decisions breaking with past policy relies on acquiescence by politicians, at the least. They are, however, working in a gray area, and "outside" political intervention can always take place.

At least three dynamics affect the way the relatively autonomous layer of prison managers operates. There is direction, or "interference," from above, by their Westminster-based political masters. There is inertia and occasional outright opposition from below from the organized ranks of prison officers. There is also a tendency, in the managerial level itself, toward overconfidence in their own methods of operation that can involve erecting into an article of faith a principle that began as a pragmatic management tool (see, e.g., the discussion below on segregation).[12]

[12] The authors have deliberated for some time on the possibility of a fourth dynamic that may have an influence on managerial decisions, that of the professional interest taken in the prisons by the security and intelligence services. We are aware that one

The concept of "normalization" is an explanatory construct. As such it does not account for all aspects of current policy and practice, neither does it comprehend all the motives of people involved. We do believe, however, that it does explain the general direction or tendency of policy. There are, of course, exceptions to this direction. Two of these—the continuing confrontational policies at Crumlin Road and the mass strip search at the female prison in March 1992, both discussed below, are failures to implement normalization properly.

The principle of normalization appears to rest on three clearly political decisions. The first is an acceptance that the prison system, at any rate, is not a mechanism that can "defeat" political violence, rather, that it is a mechanism for managing some of its consequences. This is quite a radical view, given the standard political rhetoric about defeating terrorism and hunting its perpetrators without let or mercy. It is appropriate, however, for an agency dealing with the individuals, often for very many years, that the other parts of the criminal justice system deliver to it.

A clear consequence of this policy is the abandonment of the principle of criminalization, at least in a pure form. For a major element in that position was to coerce prisoners into a practical and symbolic acceptance of the status of common criminals. That has quite clearly been dropped; unregenerate, politically motivated prisoners are, by and large, recognized as such and are segregated from other inmates.

However, in a more general sense, criminalization underpins normalization. For politically motivated prisoners are regarded as legally the same as "ordinary" prisoners; they are held in the same prisons and subject to similar regimes. It is just that the authorities are now prepared to tolerate some diversity in location of groups of prisoners and regimes in order to avoid unnecessary conflict.

The second major political decision amounts to a recognition that political conflict and division will exist for the foreseeable future and must be seen as "normal." This is the quintessence of the change from attempting to solve a problem to trying to manage it. This does not simply refer to the violence. The phrase "an acceptable level of violence," first attributed to Merlyn (now Lord) Rees, secretary of state

---

reason for the posting of "high-flyers" in the British civil service to Northern Ireland is to give them experience in working with the "funnies," members of the secret services. Since this is, by definition, a highly secretive area of which we have only second-hand anecdotal accounts, we felt that to include it in the main text would have been overly speculative.

for Northern Ireland, 1974–76, has a long currency. Yet the idea of containing rather than crushing the violence always went hand in hand with the search for comprehensive and final political solutions. That quest can be said to have ended with the Anglo-Irish Agreement of 1985, which can be seen on one level as an interstate contract establishing good management practice in handling the affairs of a region in which both countries have an interest.[13]

The policy of normalization does not halt political activity; neither does it suppress the British government's desire for a political accommodation. Rather, it expresses a rebuttable presumption that some level of division and violence will continue, whatever the politicians do.

The underlying argument of this aspect of normalization is that most developed countries—to say nothing of the underdeveloped—have chronic problems of racial, ethnic, sectarian, or linguistic division. In Europe, Yugoslavia has violently disintegrated, Spain has Basque and Catalan nationalism to contend with, France faces several centrifugal regional pressures and increasing racism directed against Arab immigrants, Germany has difficulty with Turkish "guest workers" and now its underprivileged Easterners, Belgium is deeply divided by a language barrier, and so on. In North America, the United States has major ethnic divisions and conflicts, and Canada faces great partitionist pressures. Great Britain itself has racial problems, inner-city riots, a North-South divide, and powerful separatist movements in Scotland and Wales. Why should Northern Ireland be any different?

Those responsible for normalization believe that, if they can, they should manage the situation without too gross a derogation from international norms of civil liberties, develop and maintain a stable civil society, and support a reasonable—and in some respects, excellent— quality of life for the majority of people.

This is perhaps a fanciful and overcynical interpretation of the policy. Yet we believe it is demonstrable that political feelings such as those described underlie the policy of normalization. A tiny, but inter-

---

[13] This agreement, signed between the British and Irish governments, exchanged greater cooperation by the Republic in cross-border security for a mechanism to give Dublin influence over the administration of Northern Ireland. A system of regular intergovernmental meetings serviced by a permanent secretariat, with Irish civil servants based in Belfast, was set up. The agreement provoked major opposition by the Unionists and, in the resulting civil unrest, the Royal Ulster Constabulary received widespread praise for their determined stance against Loyalist provocation and intimidation.

esting, indicator is the new logo of the Prison Service. It is a diamond within a diamond, each vertically divided into two shades of blue. A senior official, perhaps tongue in cheek, interpreted it to us as the outer diamond representing a divided society and the inner diamond, representing the prisons, partitioned equally in a controlled and structured response. Of course, in Northern Ireland, the very replacement of the Crown by a new, "secular," logo is itself highly symbolic.

The third major political decision underpinning normalization is an acceptance of the "permanence" of "temporary" legislative and administrative structures that have been adapted to contain political violence.[14] This decision is the operational consequence of the acceptance of the normality of division and violence. It means that the "special" procedures for dealing with politically motivated offenders will be part of the criminal justice system for the foreseeable future.

This does not simply amount to the recognition of an unfortunate reality. For the essence of normalization is to reduce the structures erected to deal with political violence from something abnormal to just one specialized part of the "normal" criminal justice system. So, for example, the police have their specialized arms—traffic branch, drugs squad, community relations branch, and so on—among which the special branch and its associated support groups dealing with "terrorism" represent just one professional discipline.

Similarly, the Prison Service has its array of techniques for dealing with the needs and demands of prisoners and their security; politically motivated prisoners are just one special "client group" among others.

In one sense, this is very much the "technical" response to "terrorism," that denies it any political significance. However, what we might call "good practice" in normalization does recognize the reality of political motivation and that it is part of real currents in the community. Prisons can be managed effectively only by understanding, and to an extent engaging with, the politics of different groups of inmates. Indeed, it would be our contention that most of the failures of the normal-

[14] The two major pieces of legislation forming the legal response to terrorism are the Emergency Provisions Act (first passed in 1973) and the Prevention of Terrorism Act 1989. The former was subject to annual parliamentary enactment until 1989 when it was given a five-year lifespan. It is still reported on annually by a judge appointed for the purpose by the government. Both laws are subject to an annual parliamentary renewal debate but are, to all intents and purposes, permanent pieces of legislation. Of course, Northern Ireland, since its foundation, has always had laws that were perceived to infringe on civil liberties, but they were usually deemed "special," "temporary," or "emergency."

ization policy have been the result of political miscalculation or misunderstandings.

The political decisions listed above appear to have led to the development of a number of strategic directions for the Prison Service. We have identified three, and within each a number of policies and practices that result. These are changed relations with politically motivated prisoners, a policy of minimizing conflict, and creating through the media and other methods a culture of normality around the prison system.

## A. Relations with Politically Motivated Prisoners

This strategic direction involves the recognition of groups of politically motivated prisoners who are distinct from "ordinary" prisoners and from each other. This is not simply a passive or grudging acceptance of reality. It is an open-eyed, determined attempt to manage the consequences of incarcerating quantities of disciplined, politically motivated people, divided into two or more mutually hostile groups. It is proactive and designed to win the political objectives of normalization. The policy includes elements of flexibility and negotiation; an attempt to limit, quarantine, and marginalize the paramilitary groupings; and, through a carrot and stick approach, constructive engagement with their adherents.

Before considering in more detail the nature of the Prison Service's engagement with politically motivated prisoners, we should describe, in more detail than elsewhere, the characteristics of the main groupings involved and their current ideological stances toward the prison system.

Politically motivated prisoners can be regarded as falling into two groups, Loyalist and Republican. On the Loyalist side there are two main paramilitary groupings, the Ulster Defence Association and the Ulster Volunteer Force. These have clear separate identities and, mainly, separate command structures within the prisons. However, there is little or nothing to choose between their attitudes to the prison system, and they have by and large until recently acted in concert within the prisons.

Loyalist ideology with regard to prison is a reflection of their rather divided attitude toward the state in general. They proclaim their loyalty to the Crown and the United Kingdom, and yet they commit crimes against the state in pursuit of what they see as its best interests. As far as the prisons are concerned, then, Loyalists accept their legitimacy. They would even sometimes use the language of "ordinary" penology, as in "there is not enough done for the 'rehabilitation' of our men when they are released." They would perhaps go so far as to accept that their actions had been "crimes." However, they are very clear that their political motivation, their "loyalty," excuses those crimes. They would blame the British government and pusillanimous politicians for forcing them into illegality to defend their people, their culture, and their state. So, while they would wish to exact from the Prison Service a due recognition of their political motivation, they accept the right of the prisons to exist and the legitimacy of their role.

On the Republican side, by far and away the biggest organization is the Provisional IRA. A score or two of prisoners belong to one of the small "Republican socialist" splinter groups, but, apart from the odd flare up of tension, they effectively accept the leadership of the Provisionals.

In contrast to the Loyalists, Republicans refuse any legitimacy to the prison system. They regard it as part of the apparatus of repression of an occupying force—part of the "British war machine." They regard the activities that got them into prison as acts of war, no more criminal than the actions of a uniformed soldier on the field of battle. They regard themselves as prisoners of war with the consequent duty to continue the fight within the prisons and, in particular, to escape. The prisoners' welfare organization attached to Sinn Fein, the IRA's political wing, is called the "Prisoner of War Department." Every symbol of legitimate imprisonment, such as prison clothes or prison work, is anathema to Republicans. They are consistent in their attempts to win recognition of themselves as separate, political, and noncriminal— in a phrase, to win political status.

In daily practice, the pure ideology of the prisoner-of-war thesis is not adhered to rigidly in all particulars. There is, however, another element that holds significant potential for disruption and violence. That is the long history of seeing the prisons as a political battleground. This tradition goes back at least to the 1920s and was seen at its most extreme and tragic point in the hunger strikes of 1980–81.

However, that episode was traumatic all round and both the government and Republicans appear to have edged away from deliberate trials of strength. Republicans still see prison issues and support for their prisoners as major elements in their political stance, but not with first-rank mobilizing potential.

1. *Flexibility.*    The first element in the prison authorities' strategic

engagement with politically motivated prisoners consists of a practice of flexibility and negotiation. Flexibility is an essential part of any prison regime. Where large numbers of men are forcibly detained, the potential for disruption and violence is always there. Rigidity and strict legalism are likely to provoke dissent and, perhaps, violent outbursts. That is particularly the case when groups of inmates have a coherent ideology that will lead them to seize on grievances, injustices, and rigidities within the regime as points of mobilization for organized protest.

The fundamental issue at stake between prison authorities and both sets of politically motivated prisoners is their political status. Given that formal political status (i.e., recognition of noncriminality and acceptance that they were imprisoned only for political opposition) has never been on the practical agenda since the beginning of the troubles, arguments have revolved around symbols that can be seen to point in the direction of political recognition or, conversely, toward criminalization.

One of the most important of these has been "segregation." Simply, this means housing those of a similar political allegiance in one part of a prison. In conformity with the spirit of normalization, the prison authorities could simply shrug and say they are recognizing realities by segregating politicals from "ordinaries" and each other. To an extent, that is what they have done, but only reluctantly and with a lively appreciation of the practical consequences.

Segregation means the easy establishment of paramilitary command structures, the imposition of discipline on waverers, the possible intimidation or subornation of prison officers, and easier planning for escape.[15] So there has been a marked reluctance to accept segregation by the prison authorities and a consistent campaign to resist its extension and to increase the number of "integrated" areas of prisons (Colville 1992).[16]

[15] Such discipline on waverers is not just a question of sanctions against potential dissidents. It may also have a political purpose in, for example, subordinating the raising of individual grievances to an overall political campaign. There have also allegedly been occasions when individual prisoners have been prevented from using the lawyers of their choice in preference to those on an "approved list" and being instructed as to which plea will be acceptable to the movement.

[16] The Colville enquiry was set up to investigate the management of paramilitary prisoners in Crumlin Road after IRA prisoners planted a bomb in the prison canteen that killed two Loyalist inmates. The report supported the authorities' refusal to extend segregation. Its main conclusion recommended against formal segregation at Crumlin Road, but the report could be seen as a major text of normalization in Northern Ireland's prisons. It is based on wide consultation, including hundreds of prisoners, is open-eyed

The prison system now contains segregated and nonsegregated areas and a range of regimes with differing levels of security. To some observers, this range of provision may seem unexceptional. However, given the relatively small size of the system and its history, we believe the variety of regimes is quite impressive.

In principle, the system can process, in an appropriate way, everyone from a fine defaulter serving a few days in prison to a notorious "terrorist" sentenced to life. In January 1993, the various categories of sentenced prisoners recognized by the system (in practice rather than in theory) seem to be the following: young prisoners (seventeen to twenty-one years) serving up to four years, ordinary and political ($N$ = 120); ordinaries ($N$ = 300); "nonconforming" politicals, divided into Loyalist and Republican ($N$ = 470); long-term conforming politicals ($N$ = 375); short-term conforming politicals ($N$ = 90); a disparate category of prisoners who might be at risk from other prisoners—sex offenders, informers, ex-security force personnel, schismatics from paramilitary groups, and so on.[17] Prisoners in this last category are held together in the remand prison because of what the authorities deem their collective vulnerability ($N$ = 25).

2. *Negotiation.* Negotiation and consultation with prisoners might be seen as an indispensable part of prison management. After all, it is an axiom in prison management that prisons require the consent of prisoners to operate at all. Indeed, it is part of the policy of normalization that negotiation should take place. However, in relation to politically motivated prisoners, there are decisions on matters of principle to be taken.

Negotiation with politically motivated prisoners means negotiation with a paramilitary chain of command. That is obviously to give a level of recognition to the paramilitary organization and, it might be argued, to go some way down the road of recognizing them as prisoners of war.

Normalization rejects the symbolism of such negotiation. It is pragmatic; it chooses the most effective routes to the avoidance of conflict;

---

and severely realistic, and demonstrates a high degree of empathy with the self-image of politically motivated prisoners.

[17] These figures are rough estimates based on the official figures for January 1993. The prison population statistics are not centrally collated within these categories, so we have made our own approximations. A better term for short-term conforming politicals might be "ex-politicals," except that many of these prisoners maintain strong political beliefs. "Conforming" basically indicates that they have withdrawn from the formal paramilitary command structure; they may still remain strong Republicans or Loyalists.

it does not waste time and effort willfully ignoring the fact that paramilitary prisoners do elect spokesmen and that they are the only route
of communication with the authorities that the prisoners will use.[18]

The parameters of negotiation will always be an issue, of course.
From the authorities' point of view, the narrower the range, the more
discussions center on prosaic details of prison life, the more prisoners
are accepting the de facto legitimacy of the prison system. From the
paramilitaries' point of view, the fact of negotiations themselves gives
legitimacy to their own command structure. It seems a reasonable quid
pro quo.

Negotiation works in the Northern Ireland prison system. It provides a reliable channel of communication between inmates and author-
itiesthatcanreducetension,defusepotentialincidents,andavforthisefficacy
is the paramilitary discipline of the various groups involved. Paradoxi-
cally, good relations within the prison depend on the existence of a
factor that is officially abhorrent to the authorities and, indeed, may
continue to be abhorrent to many of theities and, indeed, may
continue to be abhorrent to many of the prison officers who actually
take part.

An interesting light is thrown on this subject by the experience at
Maghaberry Prison. In that regime there are conforming politicals and
long-term ordinaries, and so formal paramilitary structures do not exist. The authorities have found difficulties at times in running the
prison effectively "because they have no one to talk to." The idea of
elected spokesmen or even a prison council has been floated by officials
used to getting things done by striking deals with the oc's of paramilitary groupings.

Like any negotiations, the discussions between paramilitaries and
officials within Northern Ireland prisons are an extension of war by
other means. The fact of negotiation does not mean that a political
struggle has ceased to exist. "Dirty tricks" are used by both sides in
negotiation as well as in the continuing battle outside that forum. In
particular, there is an undeclared intelligence war that is subject to all
the distortions, delusions, and illusions of omniscience that characterize such conflicts outside.

[18] It seems the general rule that paramilitary prisoners elect their command structure
within the prisons. "The Green Book" (the IRA's constitution), as revised by Oglaidh
Na hEireann (IRA) General Headquarters General Army Orders 1987, rule 4 states,
"Any volunteer committed to prison forfeits all previous rank and shall report to the
Oglaidh Na hEireann structure for debriefing and further instruction" (Irish Republic
Army 1987). It is not clear, of course, what pressures might be put on this electoral
process by the organizations outside the prisons.

However, routine negotiation with politically defined groups of prisoners is a prime—and successful—characteristic of normalization. Normalization does not imply softness or even a climate of tolerance. It is not neutral in respect of terrorism; it simply tries to be realistic in its war aims and to pick with some care the ground it fights on.

3. *Segregation and Marginalization.* In relation to politically motivated prisoners, a key element of normalization's strategy is to attempt to limit, quarantine, and marginalize paramilitary groupings. It is clearly and explicitly understood and stated by the leadership of the Prison Service that they are engaged in a struggle with the paramilitaries. Their existence and reasons for existence are recognized, but they are regarded as opponents of the state and of democracy whose influence must be limited and challenged.

In an administration where the proponents of political violence were a small minority, the process of marginalization would be a matter of "putting them in their place." Their place being, of course, just one particularly idiosyncratic variety of inmate among many others. That is the way politically motivated Irish prisoners, almost all Republicans, are treated in British prisons. Their special status is recognized in that they are always given the highest security classification, but they are split up throughout the system into small groups and subject to intense supervision. Association is limited and paramilitary command structures are prevented from developing.

In the Northern Ireland system, however, politically motivated prisoners form around two thirds of the daily population. In dealing with this reality, normalization accepts a level of segregation of these factions of prisoners from each other and from "ordinary" prisoners. The attempt at marginalization, therefore, is more a question of squeezing their room for maneuver, of making them work hard for any recognition of their special status.

Thus the Prison Service strategic plan drew a line at the status quo in late 1991: "We shall create conditions which will offer all prisoners. . . the opportunity to serve their sentences free from the influence of paramilitary organisations: by continuing to resist further segregation which acts against the best interest of prisoners, the efficiency of the Service and the long term stability of the wider community" (Northern Ireland Prison Service 1991*d*, p. 12).[19]

The public line of the Prison Service is that segregation is an evil,

[19] This document, "Serving the Community," is probably the basic text of normalization in Northern Ireland's prisons, as will become clear in our numerous references below.

to be entertained reluctantly only when there is no other option. They claim that escapes are made easier, backing up the point with comments made by Sir James Hennessey in his report on the Maze breakout of 1983: "The segregation of the Provisional IRA prisoners in H7 made it easier for them to plan and execute the escape. Having seen segregated and integrated blocks and work and having talked to staff, we have little doubt that prisoners in segregated blocks are generally better able to plan and execute subversive activities of all kinds" (Hennessey 1983–84).

The Prison Service further argues that paramilitary prisoners in segregated conditions can deal with staff from a position of strength and that this adversely affects staff morale. It also says that segregation is costly because it limits the freedom to use the prison estate in the most economic fashion.

In spite of the passion with which these arguments are propounded, the reality is that segregation has existed within the system for many years and is accepted with a degree of equanimity by the Prison Service. However, these arguments have been deployed to justify the refusal to grant formal segregation at Crumlin Road prison in Belfast. This controversy is one that we shall examine below as an example of the contradictions within a system that, in general, is adopting the principles of normalization.

4. *Constructive Engagement.* Another major element that the policy of normalization suggests in terms of relations with politically motivated prisoners is a practice of what we might call "constructive engagement" with individual prisoners. Another description would be a "hearts and minds" campaign designed, as a primary objective, to wean prisoners away from their paramilitary allegiances. A secondary objective is to reduce the level of military-political activism among those who insist on maintaining their adherence to paramilitary organizations. This involves a carrot and stick approach, as, perhaps, do all such campaigns.

First, the stick—which, in the sense of purely coercive tactics, actually plays quite a small part in the process. The authorities claim that segregated conditions demand more security, and thus the regime is not as relaxed and open as it could be and access to facilities is restricted. In the Maze, the life of a prisoner revolves very much around the twenty-four cell wing of an H-block. In Maghaberry and Magilligan, there is greater access to work, education, and leisure facilities. However, it is debatable which is the best regime from the perspective of the prisoner. On segregated wings, prisoners have considerable freedom of movement. Prison officers infrequently enter the wings and prisoners associate freely from 8 A.M. to 8 P.M. As prisoners do no prison work, apart from the need to attend visits, there are relatively few occasions when prisoners need to, or can, leave the wing. Prisoners prepare their own food and organize their own entertainment. Education is conducted by tutors visiting individual prisoners within the area of the wing. Thus prisoners are very much self-regulated, but within the strict confines of the wing.

However, prisoners in Maghaberry are managed and controlled along more traditional lines by prison staff. There are better opportunities to use a range of facilities but fewer opportunities to be self-organized.

The other main coercive element refers only to life sentence prisoners (Rolston and Tomlinson 1986, 1988). The decision on release from this indeterminate sentence is made by the secretary of state for Northern Ireland, a member of the British cabinet. However, there is an elaborate advisory procedure that involves individual reports on prisoners from prison staff, probation officers, and others, and reference to a life sentence review board, a panel made up of civil servants and individual experts. We will look at the operation of this procedure and the home leave scheme in Northern Ireland since both offer interesting examples of normalization.

Section 14 of the Life Sentence Explanatory Memorandum, which was released in January 1985 to explain the system, describes the extent to which paramilitary allegiance is taken into account in deciding on release. It suggests that problems of assessing the risk of an individual committing further acts of violence if released are "specially difficult where the crime which led to the imposition of the life sentence was committed on behalf of a paramilitary organisation, where the organisation concerned is still perpetuating acts of violence, and where there is no convincing evidence that the prisoner has entirely given up his affiliation to it" (Northern Ireland Prison Service 1985b, para. 14).

This passage not only implies that those who renounce their paramilitary affiliation will be released earlier but also suggests that paramilitary prisoners are hostages for the behavior of their organizations outside. Certainly, some of the shortest "life" sentences have been served by those with affiliations to the official IRA, which has not committed major acts of political violence since the middle 1970s.

In fact, however, it appears that this "political" test of supposed risk is of little enough importance. It is impossible to prove statistically, but informed commentators guess that there might be, on average, about six months difference between the length of time reformed and unregenerate paramilitaries actually serve. Most life sentences for politically motivated crimes last about fifteen years in Northern Ireland.

So much for the stick; there is no evidence of any particular harshness in the attitude of prison officers to segregated prisoners. One measure, the number of prison offenses committed leading to adjudications, bears this out. In 1990–91, out of 1,249 such offenses, only sixteen were reported from the Maze (Colville 1992, p. 8). However, an alternative explanation of this low level of conflict between staff and inmates is that the regime of segregation, based on prisoner self-regulation, provides for far fewer potential contact points between staff and prisoners, which may lead to actions resulting in disciplinary charges.

More recently, the governor of Maze Prison was attacked when he visited one of the Loyalist wings. Two hooded prisoners attacked him and a prison officer, who were alone on the wing and at some physical distance from other prison staff. At the time of writing, the prisoners who carried out the attack have not been identified. That this attack was possible, and that no prisoner has been identified as responsible, indicates the considerable autonomy groups of prisoners have on segregated wings.

In this case, the carrot, or, at least, policies that have both a carrot and stick element, are more widely used. We have noted that "reformed" paramilitaries, serving indeterminate sentences, can expect to serve a little less time than their unreformed colleagues. In terms of regimes, the reverse of the somewhat stricter security imposed on segregated areas of the system is supposed to be a more relaxed and open lifestyle for conforming prisoners.

It is Maghaberry Prison, the new, purpose-built establishment, completed on a green field site some six years ago, that is the flagship of the system's engagement with ex-paramilitary prisoners. In good physical condition with enhanced access to education and work opportunities, conforming prisoners are encouraged to prepare for life outside (Northern Ireland Prison Service 1989–90a).

It would be wrong to overemphasize the benefits of the regime at Maghaberry, however. In educational terms, for example, inmates of the Maze seem to do as well as those in Maghaberry. Moreover, ex-

prisoners have complained of the rigidities of the regime in Maghaberry. Given the experience of many of these prisoners, who were
previously housed in the self-governing wings of the Maze, this is
hardly surprising. Also, without organization to back them up, inmates
feel vulnerable to the power of prison officers.

This is one side of the Prison Service's declared commitment to
individuality of treatment, that is, treating prisoners as individuals
regardless of religious or political beliefs. This is a policy that is presented as humane and flexible, but it is also specifically seen as anti-
paramilitary. It is declared that individual needs cannot be properly
met when a prisoner is shielded from view and contact with the authorities by a paramilitary command structure. In fact, however, none of
the paramilitary organizations have policies preventing their members
from taking advantage of welfare or other facilities. It is unclear, moreover, just what advantages will accrue to an inmate by individuality
of treatment. If there are any, it is probably more due to a slightly
more relaxed attitude toward security of conforming prisoners. It may
be, for example, that compassionate leave to visit a sick relative or
attend a family funeral will be more easily given to a conforming
prisoner.

It is perhaps surprising that the prison authorities have not taken
the opportunity to enhance the positive aspects of the individual approach at Maghaberry. Improved opportunities for earning wages,
linked to the possibility of purchasing luxury items with earnings,
could easily be introduced at Maghaberry, reflecting positively on the
regime without destabilizing the segregated regime at the Maze.

The downside of individualization of treatment is, however, being
a lone prisoner faced with the power and authority of the whole system. It is an example of the paternalism that runs through the Northern
Ireland Prison Service's concept of normalization that individuality of
treatment is assumed to be an unalloyed good. If the system were
totally benevolent, that might well be the case. Needless to say, individual prisoners sometimes find it hard to discern that benevolence
and, on the contrary, experience prison as a hostile institution.

5. *Life Sentence Prisoners and the Life Sentence Review Board.* The theory of individualization justifies an interesting feature of the Northern
Ireland system. That is the relatively "early" release of life sentence
prisoners. The average length of time served in a life sentence in
Northern Ireland for those convicted of "terrorist crimes" is twelve

to thirteen years, whereas individuals convicted of similar offenses in England serve a minimum of twenty years.

This is clearly a political decision and part of a policy designed to limit the activism of those released. However, it is implemented through the complex life sentence review procedure that we mentioned above. As noted, a board of "independent" experts reviews cases, at the latest after ten years have been served, on the basis of reports from prison sources and sometimes from the probation service and written representations from the prisoner, his or her family, and any other person or agency that has a view. The board consists of senior civil servants, the chief probation officer, a psychiatrist, and a medical officer.

The Prison Service claims that reports on nonconforming prisoners are less complete and reliable and that this is the justification for holding them slightly longer. In any event, the board can recommend release or a further review after a set period (maximum three years). If the recommendation is for release, the trial judge (if alive) and the lord chief justice are consulted. The secretary of state takes the final decision.

Since 1985, approximately 200 lifers and over fifty "at the secretary of state's pleasure" (SOSPs) have been released.[20] At the time of writing only a handful have had their licence revoked for further offending. Lifers and SOSPs are on license for the remainder of their lives and can be recalled to prison by the secretary of state for alleged reoffending or risky conduct without recourse to the courts. Possibly one reason for this is that they do not feel they have been held unreasonably for a long time beyond what would be seen as fair. On the whole, ex-lifers are not embittered, institutionalized rejects but early middle-aged men, often very mature, anxious to make something of the rest of their lives. A punitive refusal of reasonable release would change that very much for the worse.

There is some evidence that released lifers are not expected by their respective paramilitary organizations to become reinvolved in organized violence. Their military value is of limited use because the authorities know who they are. Also they are considered to have served

[20] This means that they were under eighteen years old when sentenced to an indeterminant sentence under section 73(i) of the Children and Young Persons Act (Northern Ireland) 1968. Effectively, they serve as long or longer as someone sentenced to a life sentence.

their time and "made their contribution to the struggle." Unlike ordinary offenders, within their own communities many released lifers are much respected. In Catholic West Belfast, for example, there is a club, with extensive facilities for members, called the "Felon's Club." Conditions of membership require that members have been convicted of, or interned for, offenses related to the achievement of Republican objectives.

Furthermore, the release process itself is a good example of constructive engagement with politically motivated prisoners. It is a sophisticated exercise in the management of a massive change in the life circumstances of a group of human beings. It is also an exercise in the control of potentially violent enemies of the state.

Unlike some other jurisdictions, in Northern Ireland life sentence prisoners are not required to sign any renunciation of unlawful activity or any undertaking to be of good behavior. Such a formal declaration would be anathema to Republicans, certainly, and would give the government the embarrassment of keeping them in prison indefinitely. They are required to sign their license form, but only as an indication that they have understood its conditions.

A life sentence prisoner in the United Kingdom jurisdictions is on "license" for the term of his or her natural life. The power of recall to prison is the coercive element that underlies the whole release process. That it has hardly been used emphasizes its effectiveness in controlling the behavior of ex-lifers.

Yet before license is finally granted, the prisoner is put through a process that exquisitely blends coercion and inducement. This is known as the "working out scheme." It is divided into three "phases." During the first phase, the secretary of state sets provisional dates for release, and, while still in custody, the prisoner is offered a series of seminars on issues such as housing, welfare rights, and reestablishing relationships. Help with obtaining employment is also offered by the probation board for Northern Ireland. The prisoner must find work, either voluntary or paid, before he moves to the second phase of the scheme.

For the next three months, the prisoner goes to work from the prison each day, returning again at night (Monday to Thursday). Weekends are spent at home. Help for men without weekend accommodation is available from the probation board.

The third and final stage of the scheme lasts approximately three months. During these months the prisoner "lives out" completely, only reporting to the prison at regular intervals. At the end of this phase, the prisoner should receive his or her life license and be released into the community with no further reporting requirement.

This program is a mixture of practical assistance in reintegrating into the outside community and a testing process that can impose severe psychological pressure. From the authorities' point of view, the working out and returning process is a test of risk. If, during this period, the prisoner behaves himself, he is safe to be released. In practice, however, the process is more a test of cooperation with the system. This process is not designed to deal with psychologically unstable people who might commit violent crime as soon as they are outside the prison gates. It is a process for disciplined "terrorists" or "ex-terrorists."

Thus in the early part of the process, the prisoner has to return voluntarily each night to the prison, submitting to a strip search on the way in at night and on the way out in the morning. He must live a normal working life during the day, though avoiding alcohol or subversive associates, and then resubmit to the constraints of prison life each evening. This cooperation must be seen to have a political significance.

However, it would be wrong to see this process as a humiliation that breaks the political will of participants. Rather, it is an example of the pragmatism that is the paramilitaries' dominant response to the positive features of a prison system operating a policy of normalization. Yet idealism can only survive so much pragmatism; it is part of the policy of normalization to extend the areas where paramilitaries are forced to choose between uncomfortable rejectionism and the practical benefits of cooperation.

6. *Home Leave.* An extraordinary example of this process is the system of home leave that operates in Northern Ireland. All prisoners, in the last few months of their sentence, are entitled to periods of home leave in order to get used to outside society. These are usually a couple of days every month or so. However, more interesting is the availability of Christmas and summer home leave. These are offered to almost all prisoners who have served more than twelve years. For about five days over the Christmas holiday and for two weeks in the summer, hundreds of committed paramilitary prisoners, approximately one-third of the prison population, are allowed out to stay with their families. So far not a single paramilitary prisoner has failed to return in

the years of the scheme's operation. This is a privilege also extended to ordinary prisoners, although a small number of them either fail to return or return late. Only the most notorious escapers have been refused this privilege.[21]

It is curious that paramilitary prisoners, many of whom define themselves as prisoners of war with the duty of escape, voluntarily walk out of their prison and walk back, twice a year. It is equally paradoxical that the authorities feel they can release "terrorists" for a summer holiday but maintain they are too dangerous to be released finally. It is hard to find logic in a practice like this. It is easy, however, to find good sense and a pragmatic collaboration between supposed enemies.

This scheme relies, of course, on the discipline of paramilitary prisoners. They will return, for a failure to do so would deny the privilege to their comrades. There is some anecdotal evidence that paramilitary organizations actually police the return of their own prisoners. It is recognized by the organizations that a breach by a paramilitary prisoner of release conditions could jeopardize the whole system. For the same reason, they are unlikely to engage in any obvious illegality. It is a scheme that offers obvious benefits to prisoners and their families and to the prison authorities in terms of happier prisoners and an important privilege unlikely to be put at risk by violent protest. Yet it is only a prison system convinced by the policy of normalization that would have the confidence to implement it.

The final example of constructive engagement with politically motivated prisoners is less startling. This is the support that government has given to the statutory and voluntary organizations that assist in the resettlement of ex-offenders. Of course, this is a general policy but, as the various organizations have shown an ability and willingness to work with paramilitary ex-prisoners, so has enthusiasm for their activity increased.

The main organizations involved are the probation board, a statutory body appointed by the secretary of state, the Northern Ireland Association for the Care and Resettlement of Offenders (NIACRO) (for which the authors work), and Extern, the last two being charitable associations. These groups offer a range of services, including employment, training, advice, and accommodation. At times, the Probation

---

[21] For example, Brendan McFarlane, one-time officer commanding the Provisionals in the Maze and recaptured leader of the successful 1983 breakout from the prison, has so far been refused home leave on the grounds that he is a "Red Book," or maximum security, prisoner.

Service and NIACRO are used as alternative channels of communication between politically motivated ex-prisoners and the government.

### B. Minimizing Conflict

One of the Prison Service's other main strategic directions arising from the principle of normalization is a policy of minimizing causes and occasions of conflict with prisoners and their families. This involves, like other aspects of normalization, a culture of realism and a readiness to spend money to avoid trouble. It also recognizes that an overt commitment by the Prison Service to the development of a humane prison system and, for example, the provision of good support services for prisoners' families reflects well on the Prison Service and counters the Republican view of the repressive British state.

The fundamental purpose here is not simply to avoid trouble for its own sake but also to avoid occasions and issues around which politically motivated prisoners and their supporters might mobilize. We have seen that prisons in Northern Ireland are, to some extent, a political battleground, yet one where the actual terrain of conflict is severely limited. Over large tracts, the supposed combatants actually coexist and collaborate. Only a few pieces of territory are actually contested. It is the Prison Service's policy to reduce the number and extent of areas of conflict.

To use a slightly different analogy—conflict in the prisons is far from total war. It is more akin to semiritual battles of the Middle Ages, where rules of chivalry and codes of war restricted actual fighting to a controlled and limited passage of arms. It is the policy of the Prison Service to extend the areas of agreement and remove, as far as possible and without compromising on principle, each and every casus belli.

Examples of the avoidance of occasions of conflict abound. Many have to do with not imposing the symbols of imprisonment on politically motivated prisoners. In the Northern Ireland system, prisoners can wear their own clothes (subject to a ban on paramilitary-style uniforms), receive food parcels from outside, buy a wide range of goods in "tuck shops," listen to personal radios, and play musical instruments.

More important, in the segregated wings of the Maze, men do no prison work, enjoy free association, and organize their own lives to a great degree. Censorship has been minimized, and while there are frequent individual cases of petty restriction or delay, these are usually due more to bureaucratic indecision than to a particularly strict policy.

So, most publications available outside, including those of the political wings of paramilitary organizations, are allowed into the prisons. Several prison officers have also been taught Irish so that publications in that language can be allowed in. There are strong indications that access to telephones will be allowed in the near future.

The removal of these symbols of criminalization, while maintaining the reality of incarceration, is very important politically. It is difficult to protest against the fact of imprisonment itself, especially when it is the consequence of a judicial process that contains recognizable elements of natural justice, however much "adjusted" to combat "terrorism."

Furthermore, if you loudly proclaim yourself a soldier in an insurgent army, it ill becomes the image to cry foul if the enemy locks you up when he catches you. It is necessary, rather, to find potent symbols of the "injustice" of labeling "prisoners of war" as "criminals."

As we noted earlier, it was around a number of these symbols that the five demands of the hunger strikes were organized. To recap briefly, the right to wear their own clothes; to refrain from prison work; to associate freely with one another; to organize recreational facilities; to obtain one letter, visit, and parcel a week; and to have lost remission time restored were their demands.

None of those five demands are now issues in the Northern Ireland prison system. The first four are standard for sentenced, segregated prisoners, and loss of remission is not now imposed as a punishment on nonconforming prisoners. Taken individually, none of these issues represent matters of principle for the Prison Service. Removed as symbols of "convict" life, they are removed as occasions of conflict.

All this illustrates what is, perhaps, the defining distinction between the policy of normalization and the previous policy of criminalization. As we noted in the section on criminalization, from March 1976 to the end of 1981, the prison authorities did everything they could to break the protest against the end of special category status.

Normalization avoids these pointless and tragic battles that claimed the lives of ten hunger strikers and eighteen assassinated prison officers. It is now accepted that politically motivated prisoners, especially Republicans brought up in a long tradition of prison protest, will not accept the symbols of criminality. Normalization drops those as unessential to the purpose of imprisonment. It maintains what is essential: political prisoners stay locked up and offer that level of cooperation that allows a prison to run. Why should the system demand any more?

1. *The Prison Officers.* In any prison, there is always a risk of conflict between prisoners and prison officers. It is a principle aim of normalization to reduce that risk. In that aim, the prison authorities face formidable barriers. First, a custodial variant of macho culture pervades the younger and lower-ranking elements of the uniformed prison service in particular. This is probably characteristic of most corps of custodial guardians, especially uniformed ones (Thomas 1972). It involves a continuing process of acting out dominance over prisoners and their visitors. It is expressed in bullying, rigidity over regulations, and sometimes curious sartorial displays. It can, of course, lead to physical brutality.

The Northern Ireland Prison Service uniform (worn by all those below governor grades) includes a black peaked cap. In the past, some officers would distort the cap so that the peak came down right over their eyes. This necessitates a tilting of the head backward so that the wearer can see. It was a conscious imitation of the parade-ground style of certain elite units of the British army; though perhaps unintended, it also evoked a reminiscence of the headgear of the Nazi SS. This practice was widely regarded as offensive and intimidating and has now been banned.

A second obstacle peculiar to Northern Ireland is the religious composition of the prison service, which is overwhelmingly Protestant; a certain sectarianism toward Catholic prisoners is to be expected (Helsinki Watch 1992). At times this has reached worrying intensity, and there has been evidence of extreme views among prison officers. There has not been serious evidence, however, of any widespread infiltration by or collaboration with Loyalist paramilitaries. Indeed, as might be expected, relations between imprisoned Loyalist paramilitaries and prison officers are often very sour.

The third obstacle lies in industrial relations. Uniformed prison officers belong to a trade union, the Prison Officer's Association. It has great industrial strength, which it uses to win high material rewards for its members, with the average wage of a Northern Ireland prison officer being over £30,000 per annum despite needing no formal entrance qualifications. There is also a perception that it stands against progress in terms of the development of the prison regime. The Prison Officers' Association (POA) refused to endorse the code of conduct (discussed below), and its endorsement of the Prison Service Strategic Plan was lukewarm, at best. However, the relations between the leadership of the prison service and the POA are complex and outside the scope of this study. Suffice it to say, that those who implement any policy are organized in a body that has its own agenda; however proper that may be, it does put a question mark over the extent to which the prison service management can implement its will in any given case.

The industrial strength of the prison officers, and the perception of a moral debt being owed to them as a guardian force under stress and threat from society's enemies, can lead to a lack of industrial discipline. The sickness and absenteeism rates of the prison service are very high and put a limit on developments that require increased staffing.

The leadership of the Prison Service has attempted to overcome these obstacles through a number of means. It nailed its colors to the mast of normalization with the publication of a code of conduct for the Prison Service. This emphasized good practice and a commitment to "treat all prisoners as individuals regardless of their religious beliefs or political opinions" (Northern Ireland Prison Service 1990c, p. 9).

It was, however, declaratory, general, and not directly binding in a disciplinary sense. Similarly, the Prison Service strategic plan makes a range of general commitments to good behavior by staff. These statements are important as a public declaration of direction, but more significant are concrete measures within the service itself. Training of prison officers, both on induction and in-service, has been extended and broadened. Some discussions have taken place about involving outside groups and interests, such as prisoners' families, in such training.

There has clearly been a tightening up of management over the past few years and a series of internal messages that "rotten apples" would not be tolerated. In particular, it has been made clear that organized but unauthorized brutality will not be tolerated in the future. This goes along with a private recognition that this has happened in the past, as well as the public recognition through the payment of compensation to abused prisoners in numerous cases.[22] We do not know, however, what the actual progress of this campaign for improved professional practice has been. Certain indicators are positive, and are discussed below, but there is clearly some resistance. The issue may not be so simple as a struggle between an enlightened management

[22] In 1989 the Irish Republic's Supreme Court refused to extradite Dermot Finucane, one of the Maze escapers, largely on the grounds that he would be liable to be beaten on his return to the Maze. The Northern Ireland Office's case that he would not be beaten was substantially weakened by the fact that they had already paid out compensation to several other returned Maze escapers and thus in effect admitted that such events occurred.

and a benighted rank and file, but that there is a struggle around the implementation of the principles of normalization, we have no doubt. It is, however, largely silent, internal, and unsusceptible to external analysis.

The major indicator of change comes from a less than objective source—the attitude of paramilitary prisoners. In the dialectic of conflict and cooperation, which is the leitmotif of relations between guards and guarded in all prisons, paramilitary prisoners have an extra edge: the potential for violent intimidation by their organizations on the outside. This has been extensively used in the Northern Ireland situation. Since 1969, twenty-eight prison officers have been assassinated, although this has not occurred now for several years.

An indication of this trend was demonstrated by the capture by the Provisional IRA of two prison officers and a policeman in 1990 as they returned from a fishing trip in the Republic. The policeman was executed, and the prison officers were released without harm. Indications are that this decision by a South Armagh unit of the IRA reflected a general view of Republican paramilitary organizations that prison officers are not now, in general, "legitimate targets." This is remarkable in the context of the extension, by the IRA, of the list of so-called legitimate targets to include ordinary building workers engaged in any construction for the security forces and firms who supply the police or the army with any kind of goods.

It would be quite wrong to analyze this development as a sign that the paramilitaries have succeeded in creating a docile and cowed prison service through intimidation. Indeed, conflicts still arise, threats are still occasionally made against prison officers (indeed both groups have made sporadic use of intimidatory attacks in the recent past), and this policy could be reversed as the result of any major incident in the prisons. It represents more the success of a policy and practice of distinguishing the prison service from the security forces, that is, the British army (including the Ulster Defence Regiment, now merged with the regular regiment, the Royal Irish Rangers) and the Royal Ulster Constabulary.

The concept being pressed strongly is that the prison service is a civilian service, doing its duty of humane incarceration, and taking no stand on how prisoners come to be in prison. Instances of sectarianism or lack of professionalism are not of course eradicated. The perception being pushed, however, is that a "normalized" prison service should see itself as a body of civilian professionals with management and interpersonal skills valued much more highly than the traditional job requirements of military-style discipline and knowledge of control and restraint techniques.

2. *Security.* The demands of security will always provide occasions for conflict with prisoners. There is no suggestion in the Northern Ireland system that standards of security will, in general, be lowered. However, the Prison Service strategic plan makes an interesting commitment to imposing "no higher degree of security than is necessary to discharge the warrant of the court." Again, this is merely a general statement, with no necessary implications for practice. In principle, however, it could be very important. Usually, the demands of security are regarded as paramount, and any derogation from them, for reasons of practicality or humanity, are regarded as problematic. The burden of proof is on those who wish to relax or compromise security for some particular reason. In theory, the above declaration should reverse that burden of proof; any given aspect of security would require to be positively justified. Time will tell if that will be the reality in practice.

3. *The Prison Rules.* Of more significance may be the promulgation of a revised set of prison rules.[23] At the time of writing, the Prison Service has commissioned one of its former senior employees to attempt a complete redraft of the present rules that, despite some amendments in the early 1980s, date back to 1953. The declared aim is to implement in the rules the recent changes in the Northern Ireland system and the relevant recommendations in the Woolf Report (1990). This report by Lord Justice Woolf is viewed by many as a watershed in British penal reform. Initiated in the wake of serious disturbances in several British prisons, it is based on wide consultation with prisoners, reform groups, and interested bodies. The ultimate recommendations, if implemented, would mean a complete overhaul of the British prison system. While the report did not extend to the Northern Ireland system, and indeed the system here is in many ways showing the way to the British system, it is of such major importance that the Northern Ireland Office evidently wished to ensure that it was in compliance with its principal recommendations.

---

[23] The prison rules are a statutory instrument—a series of regulations—made by the appropriate government minister under the authority of the Prison Act (Northern Ireland) 1953. They include regulations for the running of the prisons, certain minimum standards or rights for prisoners (such as access to chaplains and the right to one visit per month), and a list of disciplinary offenses. After the act itself, the rules form the basic legal and administrative foundation of the prison system. A plethora of confidential standing orders regulate the day-to-day life of the prisons.

This redraft will be most important evidence of the progress and depth of the policy of normalization. While it would be idle to speculate about the redraft's contents in any detail, certain predictions can be made. It is unlikely to make a major shift to a rights-based system from the paternalistic structure that grants privileges at the discretion of the authorities and that is the norm in the English system of administrative law. It is likely to remove some of the more objectionable disciplinary offenses (such as "making false and malicious allegations against an officer," rule 31[14], and "making repeated and groundless complaints," rule 31[16]) but not create a qualitatively new disciplinary structure.

It is no part of normalization's agenda to create sticks to beat the authorities' back. This would be the perception of a rights-based system that was open to straightforward legal challenge. As it is, a recent substantial growth in the use of judicial review in prison matters has been viewed with some concern by the Prison Service. If normalization has a crucial weakness, it is in its neglect of enforceable rights. NIACRO made this point in responding to the publication of the Prison Service Strategic Plan: "Our major criticism of this first section of the Prison Service Plan is its lack of any reference to justice. Whatever about the process that gets people to prison, the service administering custodial institutions should have an explicit commitment to operating them according to the principles of natural justice. Later in the Plan there are references to fairness; in our view these are inadequate, expressing a paternalistic concept which is dependent on the goodwill of the authorities" (Northern Ireland Association for the Care and Resettlement of Offenders 1992, p. 2).

4. *Family.* The quality of contact between prisoner and family can be a source of stability or of innumerable causes of conflict. When the dimension of politics is added to this relationship, it becomes a crucial factor in determining the character of the prison system.

The dynamics of the family-prisoner relationship in Northern Ireland are complex and not all strictly relevant to this study. Paramilitary organizations and their associated political parties give some assistance to relatives of their imprisoned members and help organize them in various ways around various issues. The extent of political involvement by relatives varies as does the extent to which they view their family member's problems in the context of some overall political struggle.

A number of nonprofit organizations offer practical services to prisoners' families and some take up issues on their behalf. The social security system gives some assistance to relatives on benefit or low incomes by financing one "assisted visit" to prison a month. The prison service itself controls the quality of the visiting experience within the prisons.

In the context of normalization, the main concern of the prison service is to reduce occasions of conflict with the families and to resolve any issues that might be seen as grievances by prisoners. It would be wise to point out, however, the perception that the service also has a further agenda: to use the families to undermine the will of the prisoners to fight the system. That is not a perception that we fully share. It is true that the Northern Ireland Office would like to weaken the relationship between relatives and paramilitary organizations. It would prefer to replace any services provided by the paramilitaries with ones provided by its own organization or government-funded voluntary organizations. It is also true that it would prevail on relatives to concentrate on the practical comfort and well-being of their family member rather than support any struggle against symbols of "oppression."

However, it can be argued that it is hard to discern anything contrary to the interests of prisoners or their relatives in better services, better regimes, and better conditions for visits. If the prison authorities provide these things in the pursuit of their own political objective of reducing conflict, so be it. In some ways, decent prison conditions sharpen up the debate about why people are in prison and about the political conditions that may have contributed to their actions and hence incarceration. Poor conditions should be a subject of legitimate protest in themselves, irrespective of how people come to suffer them. To mix the two issues can be of detriment to both, as is arguable in the example of the hunger strikes.

The quality of the visiting experience is a matter largely determined by the attitudes and policies of the prison authorities. In September 1989, the Northern Ireland Prison Service introduced its "interface" policy. This was designed to make major improvements in the visiting experience and, hence, reduce occasions of conflict between visitors and the prison as an institution. The purpose expressed was "to enhance the relationship between the public and the Prison Service, by improving the conditions and arrangements for visits to prisons" (Northern Ireland Office 1990a).

None of the proposals in this policy were in themselves particularly radical, but they were designed to add up to a qualitatively new experience for visitors and prisoners. Procedures at visitors' receptions were to be streamlined by removing the requirement for proof of identity (the undoubted security objections must have been overridden). Prisoners were to be allowed to send visiting permits directly to visitors and enclose correspondence. Waiting rooms and visiting areas were to be upgraded to include televisions or piped music, toys for children, pictures on walls, and easy access to toilets, where possible.

Special training for staff involved in visits was to be introduced, more information was to be offered to visitors, and governors would regularly monitor the treatment of visitors. Quite simply, staff was told to treat visitors as human beings rather than enemies. Visits could be extended beyond the standard thirty minutes, where practicable, and a new visitor's center would be built at Magilligan prison. Support would be given to voluntary organizations in providing transport to the prisons.

In February 1990, NIACRO and other nonprofit organizations carried out a survey of visitors to monitor the impact of these changes. Rather surprisingly, given the fact that most relatives surveyed would have an ideological bias against the prisons, an overall majority said the visiting experience had improved since the implementation of the new policy. Indeed 63 percent of visitors to the Maze, all relatives of paramilitary prisoners, noticed improvements. In contrast, 78 percent of those visiting the remand prison at Crumlin Road said there had been no improvements. While the physical constraints of a Victorian building make improvements difficult at Crumlin Road, there seems to be a consistent failure of management at the prison in implementing developments that have significant impact in other areas of the system.

A detailed report was drawn up, and working parties at each prison discussed the findings. The result has been further improvement, though Crumlin Road remains a problem. The visiting experience in the Northern Ireland system is probably now as good as anywhere in the United Kingdom. Visits take place at open tables, and limited physical contact is permitted. In Maghaberry and Magilligan there are staffed play areas within the visiting rooms so that children can play as well as interact with their parents. Every prison has a visitors' center, run by voluntary organizations, that offers a creche, canteen facilities, and advice and information. Visits are usually a good deal longer than the half-hour minimum.

There is a considerable level of support for prisoners' families in the community, mostly funded by government. The probation service and

NIACRO, in particular, cooperate to provide a network of self-help groups, child-care provision, advice, and counseling to prisoners' families. In this respect, Northern Ireland appears to be one of the most advanced and best organized regions in Europe (Northern Ireland Association for the Care and Resettlement of Offenders 1991).

5. *"Ordinary Decent Criminals."* One other interesting consequence of a prison system that has a majority of political prisoners is the dynamics that this creates between the politicals, the authorities, and the "ordinary decent criminals," as they are known in Northern Ireland. The political prisoners, especially Republicans, establish rules and codes of conduct that are designed to counter the authorities' attempts to criminalize the political nature of their offenses.

As we have already described, all prisoners, including ordinary prisoners, take advantage of the special home leave arrangements for long-term prisoners and for those nearing the end of their sentences. The failure by a small number of ordinary prisoners to return to prison at the end of the period of home leave is rarely the result of a serious attempt to avoid imprisonment. Often such failures are related to unresolved domestic difficulties, consumption of too much alcohol, and other relatively mundane personal contingencies.

Thus one of the consequences of developing a liberal home leave policy, which tacitly depends on the discipline of paramilitary organizations, is that a small number of ordinary prisoners will fail to honor parole arrangements. In informal discussion with senior prison staff the inevitability of such breaches is recognized; a concern is expressed, however, that bad publicity surrounding such escapes could jeopardize the home leave scheme as a whole. To date no prisoner who has breached parole conditions has generated adverse publicity.

It is difficult to assess the general impact of imprisonment on prisoners convicted of offenses not related to the political situation. Before the present period of civil conflict, Northern Ireland had only one prison (Crumlin Road) housing fewer than 600 prisoners. In 1966 the average daily prison population stood at 493. From 1960 to 1965 only six people were convicted of murder. Indeed the relatively small prison population seems to reflect a generally low level of crime. A much quoted 1988 International Victimisation Survey demonstrates that Northern Ireland apparently continues to have a comparatively low crime rate. Northern Ireland had the lowest victimization rate (15 percent of adults being victims one or more times during 1988) of the fifteen countries surveyed, which included the United States (29 percent), Australia (28 percent), and England and Wales (19 percent) (Northern Ireland Office 1990*b*).

There is no evidence that the very high level of paramilitary prisoners in the prison system has significantly altered the impact of imprisonment on ordinary offenders, with respect to reconviction rates or behavior while in prison. However, there are marked differences in the regime and conditions that ordinary prisoners enjoy largely because of the substantial number of paramilitary prisoners and their long-term impact on the prison system. All of the privileges extended to prisoners after the hunger strikes ended are enjoyed by ordinary prisoners. They can wear their own clothes, they have the opportunity for three extra visits per month as well as the one statutory visit, they have access to the same extended privileges as regards receipt of mail and parcels, and there is no compulsion to do prison work.

As in most prisons, some trusted prisoners are used by the prison authorities to carry out some prison work. It is not surprising that in Northern Ireland these trusted prisoners are drawn almost exclusively from the ranks of ordinary prisoners. At the Maze prison, which houses paramilitary prisoners in segregated conditions, a small number of ordinary prisoners are housed there quite specifically for the purpose of enabling them to do prison work as trusted prisoners. However, one unfortunate consequence for these ordinary prisoners is the failure of the prison service to develop a prison regime suitable for low-risk prisoners. Consequently all prisoners are held in prisons where security is the first and major consideration.

There have been relatively few publicly expressed concerns by ordinary prisoners about the nature of their confinement. Clearly, ordinary prisoners lack the cohesive organization that facilitates effective public relations. In early 1992, after a bombing in Crumlin Road prison, a group claiming to represent ordinary prisoners complained that they were suffering because of the ongoing conflict between paramilitary prisoners. They claimed that their voice was going unheard. However, suspicions have been voiced in some quarters that this group (which apparently produced only one press statement) was itself a fictitious product of political manipulation.

One particular group of ordinary prisoners, sexual offenders, has benefited from the influence of paramilitary prisoners. The Northern Ireland Prison Service states in its annual report that 9 percent of Northern Ireland's sentenced prisoners are people convicted of sexual offenses (1991*d*, p. 5). However, unlike in the rest of the United Kingdom and indeed many other European jurisdictions, these offenders are integrated with the rest of the prisoners. Again, unlike in so many other jurisdictions, physical attacks on such prisoners by other inmates are extremely rare. While Republican prisoners in particular express revulsion at sex offenders, this is usually not translated into physical violence since this would be seen as a traditional "criminal" prisoner response. Anecdotal evidence suggests that the political prisoner's ability to use the paramilitary command infrastructure as a support mechanism reduces the need for prisoners to fall into the usual informal prison hierarchies in which sex offenders are invariably at the bottom. Indeed in many ways there is a free-rider effect in which the concessions won primarily by Republican prisoners, such as the right to wear their own clothes, are extended to all prisoners.

Finally there are undoubtedly prisoners whose offenses were significantly motivated by the wish for personal advantage or gain who are considered to be paramilitary prisoners and who may therefore be contained in the segregated wings in the Maze prison. A period of civil conflict involving the development and maintenance of paramilitary organizations over a long period of time means that such organizations contain both individuals largely driven by ideological commitment and individuals more concerned with personal betterment. Particularly within Loyalist paramilitary groups there have been a number of internal conflicts, resulting in assassinations of individuals who were accused of using their positions in such organizations for personal financial gain. However, there is little evidence that the nature of paramilitary organizations and hence the prisoners who claim allegiance to them is other than ideologically driven.[24] Thus, in large part, there is a very clear distinction between ordinary prisoners and paramilitary prisoners, and unlike the period of attempts to criminalize paramilitary prisoners, the Prison Service now adopts a pragmatic approach to the management of all prisoners.

Efforts are beginning to develop a prison regime that is more directly designed to deal with the needs of ordinary prisoners. Magilligan prison, which holds more ordinary prisoners than any other (largely because prisoners are held there who have short-term sentences) is

[24] The RUC has set up a special unit to deal with the use of legitimate businesses by paramilitary organizations, and indeed special legislation has been introduced to assist the police in the control of this kind of income generation by paramilitary organizations (see Emergency Provisions Act [Northern Ireland] 1991, secs. 35–42, 47–64).

exploring options for prison work that would be unlikely to be successful with paramilitary prisoners. An innovative scheme in which prisoners make goods for sale, the proceeds of which go toward supporting charitable work with prisoners' families, is being explored.

It is perhaps surprising that the Prison Service has not seized more opportunities for improving the conditions and privileges of ordinary prisoners. Such developments would give them further opportunities to provide inducements for paramilitary prisoners to conform to the prison system. As the processes of normalization continue, this kind of inducement is likely increasingly to be developed as a further informal control mechanism.

### C. Prison Policies, the Media, and Outside Agencies

One key tenet of the policy of normalization is that the progress made in terms of prison management is assessed and presented in the most positive light possible for the managers. This is achieved by carefully targeting the general public and key agencies who have an interest in the operation of the prisons. Since 1981 the prison authorities have been quite successful in establishing the terms of reference, and the terms, in the debate on prisons.

1. *Prisons and the Media.*    The importance of the media in defining the limits of the conflict in Northern Ireland has never been far from the forefront of government strategy. The techniques employed by the government have ranged from informal censorship of television and press by pressuring journalists and their controllers (Chibnall 1977; Madden 1979; Curtis 1984), to black propaganda (Foot 1989), and to "psychological operations" (Hooper 1983), and since 1989 to the imposition of a television ban on spoken words of members of Sinn Fein and the Ulster Defence Association. The techniques employed by the Prison Service over the past eleven years, while encompassing at least some of the above elements, have arguably been somewhat more sophisticated.

We believe the dynamic for this change in the public relations direction came from the obvious failings of the hunger strike era. During that time the British government was widely perceived and portrayed, particularly by the international press, as being unsubtle, recalcitrant, and unfeeling (Beresford 1987; O'Malley 1990). Senior civil servants are privately quite candid that these were the darkest days for the service, where the IRA without doubt "won the propaganda war." Since that time the public relations branch to prison regimes has become among the best organized and most efficient in the Northern Irish government.

"Off the record" briefings, a policy of glasnost allowing BBC television cameras to make a detailed documentary inside the Maze in 1990, long-term strategic planning in public relations to preempt emotive prison-based anniversaries such as internment and the hunger strikes, a Royal visit by Princess Anne to Maghaberry in May 1992—these are all examples of a service that had learned the important lesson of an era where Republicans were by and large allowed to make most of the running during the hunger strikes. The central text of the public relations agenda of normalization is to demonstrate how "normal," "well run," and "forward looking" are our prisons.

A television documentary for which the producers were given virtually unlimited access to interview prisoners and use whatever footage they wished was particularly instructive. The decision was made to let the public see quite openly the operation of the paramilitary command structure within the prison. Although this undermined the old adages of criminalization to which lip service is still paid, it was obviously felt that any ideological inconsistency would be counterbalanced by the visible depiction of a peaceful prison. The principal bone of contention for Republican prisoners in the documentary, many of whom had been in the dirty protest and on hunger strikes, was the substandard size of the sausage rolls. In public relations terms the debate had come full circle.

2. *Prisons and Stakeholders.*    Aside from the paramilitary organizations and their respective political parties (by definition ostracized and marginalized by the media because of their espousal of the use of violence), the only real challenge that can be presented to the government's view of things comes from those who are de facto authoritative sources because of their "technical expertise" in prison policy or service provision.

Agencies such as NIACRO with a policy comment or service delivery brief to prisoners and their families are the obvious port of call for any journalist who wishes to look beyond the official line. In preparing their long-term strategic document, "Serving the Community," the Prison Service set up a series of "stakeholder" meetings where preordained stakeholders in the criminal justice system were allowed to present their views in an interchange with the government. There is a culture of amenability where major figures within the prison establishment are willing to leave themselves open to meetings and discussion.

Debates in public and private are often frankly and strongly argued, but are rarely acrimonious.

Even paramilitary organizations themselves have to a degree been included. While organizations like NIACRO would once have been dismissed by Republicans as at best "liberal do-gooders" and at worse as part of the "British war machine," there is an increasing awareness of the degree of professional cultures of independence and technical proficiency. We accept that this must by definition be within the limitations of the operation of the prison system, yet such a dialogue between the managers of a system and quasi-independent expert "outsiders" is central to the development of the normalization thesis. Questioning of official policy, which during the periods of reactive containment and criminalization would have been "giving succour to terrorism," has been transformed to "constructive criticism" by normalization.

### D. Exceptions to Normalization

We are not postulating, either among the models or indeed within them, that the prison system is evolving irrevocably toward some predetermined "liberal" goal of improved relations and minimal conflict. In this section we discuss two recent contrary episodes that highlight and reinforce this point. We feel they do not contradict our general thesis about the policy of normalization. Rather, they demonstrate that the policy is implemented only with halts and reversals and that it may not be applied uniformly at all levels of the prison service.

1. *Strip Searching.* On the morning of Monday, March 2, 1992, male prison officers entered the wings of Mourne House, the female section of Maghaberry Prison, allegedly singing, "Happy Days Are Here Again." All thirty-two inmates, Republican, Loyalist, and "ordinary," were informed that they were to be strip searched.[25] Twenty-two Republican prisoners refused to cooperate and all, except one who was recovering from a hysterectomy, were forcibly stripped and searched one by one in a process taking ten hours. Male warders were used to break down cell doors and were apparently on the wings when the searches were carried out by female prison officers. Several prisoners and prison officers received injuries, and five women were charged

[25] In a strip search, the prisoner is made to remove all his or her clothes, and the naked body is visually inspected. An open-sided sheet, with a hole for the head, is offered though most prisoners refuse it, holding that it simply prolongs the process and increases the indignity. No physical probing is supposed to be carried out, and internal examinations of the vagina or anus have not as far as we are aware been carried out on female prisoners in Northern Ireland.

with assaulting prison officers in the course of resisting the search. This was the first time ever that all inmates of the female prison had been strip searched in such a manner.

Strip searching of female prisoners in Northern Ireland has a highly charged history. From November 1, 1982 (when the practice was first introduced), to March 11, 1983, 772 strip searches of women, then housed in the since closed Armagh Prison, were carried out. This practice led to widespread protest, especially from women's groups and church people. Throughout the eighties, every International Women's Day saw large protests, involving many women from Britain, outside Armagh and then Maghaberry. Trade unions, civil liberties groups, voluntary organizations, and politicians spoke out against the practice. Yet the actual frequent and regular use of strip searches lasted less than six months.

From March 1983 on women were no longer routinely searched entering or leaving the prison, and searches became "random," according to the Northern Ireland Office. The number of searches dropped dramatically, though no figures are available, and the issue lost a great deal of its prominence. Women prisoners were transferred to Maghaberry Prison on March 18, 1986, and, while strip searching still occasionally took place, it appeared to be a dead issue politically. This makes the events of March 2, 1992, all the more extraordinary.

It is hard to discern the security reason for strip searching. A clothed rubdown accompanied by the use of mechanical or electronic detecting devices of various kinds can discover virtually everything a strip search can. In the entire history of such searches—since November 1982— nothing of serious security interest has ever been found. Only internal examinations—rightly regarded as unacceptable—could achieve a further level of security.

Not surprisingly, the suspicion is maintained in some quarters that strip searching is used as a method of domination and control. It is perhaps significant that this is clearly more effective with women than men. It is also the case that the prison system seems to find it more difficult to deal with politically motivated women than men. Some of the most dedicated paramilitary operatives have been women, and some formidable agitators have passed through the women's prison in Northern Ireland.[26] The comparisons and contrasts between the

[26] Mairead Farrell, e.g., served fourteen years in Armagh and Maghaberry prisons and was, for much of that time, officer commanding of the Provisionals. She uncompromisingly refused to cooperate with prison institutions. In 1989 she and two male companions (all of them unarmed), were shot dead in Gibraltar by British SAS operatives while apparently planning a bombing mission.

management of male and female paramilitary prisoners would require a separate study. However, the theory has been put forward that, at a time of change in the leadership of the Prison Service, lower-ranking elements wished to demonstrate publicly their domination over these prisoners. Some significance has also been attached to the fact that the search took place two days before the publication of the Colville Report (1992) (discussed below).

Whatever the reason for this event, the consequence was political embarrassment for the Prison Service and the government. It would be an exaggeration to say that the matter became a major issue, but there was considerable press coverage and several civil liberties, volunteer, and trade union organizations protested. The Provisionals were handed another issue for political mobilization. No benefit accrued to the authorities. The female prison, as a result, will be arguably harder to manage, and there is no evidence that any breach of security was averted.

Indeed, it appears that the Northern Ireland Office has recognized the negative repercussions of the event. Their press office has accused the Provisionals of deliberately provoking the search. This kind of response, which simultaneouly admits operational and political incompetence, shows that actions such as this mass search fall outside the carefully crafted contours of overall prison policy.

2. *The Demand for Segregation at Crumlin Road.* The issue of segregation in the remand prison has been a battleground between politically motivated prisoners, both Loyalist and Republican, and the authorities for many years. In 1990, however, the campaign intensified, and there were many incidents of violence between Loyalists and Republicans and attacks on prison staff. These culminated, in November 1991, in the placing of a bomb by Republicans in the canteen area that exploded when Loyalists were using it, killing two. This incident led to the appointment of Lord Colville to enquire into the management of paramilitary prisoners in Crumlin Road (Colville 1992).

It could well be argued that the official position taken by the prison authorities was an error, leading to unnecessary conflict. However, in effect, Lord Colville has accepted this drawing of a line under the present level of segregation. He and the authorities have decided to gamble that a display of firmness on the issue will discourage further violence or effective campaigns for segregation in Crumlin Road. Thus, a firm boundary will have been established, beyond which, it is argued, segregation will never be extended. The authorities will have established a quarantine fence around the most committed politically motivated prisoners; their future task will be to narrow its boundaries as far as may be practicable.

This particular passage in the history of Northern Ireland's prisons shows that a hard line is not incompatible with normalization. Furthermore, while we may criticize particular decisions from a standpoint of normalization, the Colville Report (1992) was written very clearly from within its culture. It supported the refusal to grant more formal segregation but also supported the continuance of the self-segregation system that already exists.

Paramilitary prisoners are effectively separated from the "ordinaries"—the mixed bag of nonpolitical remand prisoners, short-term sentenced prisoners, and fine defaulters in for a few days—which Crumlin Road also contains, though they are supposedly integrated. In a good example of the pragmatism of normalization, the prison staff on an "integrated" wing in Crumlin Road prison on alternate days unlock the cells of Republicans first, then Loyalists. On one day, one faction will take exercise in the morning, on the next day it will take it in the afternoon. One day one faction will eat in the canteen and get "evening association," the next day they will spend the time in their cells. Loyalists and Republicans—who are not, of course, "integrated" in the same cells—voluntarily undergo a limited regime in order to avoid contact with each other. This is known as the "good day, bad day" system and is actively facilitated by the authorities.

Colville (1992) has taken this further by proposing the segregation of visits, which has been implemented by the prison, so that the families of Republicans use one visiting area and those of Loyalists use another. So, in this supposedly integrated regime, Loyalists and Republicans will rarely, if ever, meet.

The reality of the events at Crumlin Road in the winter of 1991–92 was therefore that the authorities won on the principle of segregation and so were able to establish the boundaries of their quarantine fence around politically motivated prisoners. However, the practical regime within the prison conceded a great deal of the substance of the prisoners' demands: a fairly obvious example of the principles of normalization. It is unlikely that such concessions will prove sufficient to alleviate the situation, and the likelihood of violence persisting would seem strong.[27]

[27] In December 1992 Loyalist paramilitaries launched a rocket-propelled grenade (RPG-7) rocket from outside the prison at a dining room in which Republican prisoners were eating. In January 1993 the authorities discovered a small quantity of semtex explosives in a dining room in a routine search.

VI. Conclusion

Our purpose, in this essay, has been to isolate and identify those aspects of the development of the prison system in Northern Ireland that might have resonances for the wider world.

We have tried to use a different method of analysis from those usually employed to study the criminal justice system in Northern Ireland. There are three traditional ways: a narrow, technical examination of black letter law; law seen as a simple instrument for the defeat of terrorism; and the civil liberties critique of "emergency" laws by reference to international human rights norms. We offer a complementary approach that involves an analysis of the fluid set of structures, practices, and relationships that make up a functioning system.

This does not aim to be an abstracted sociological analysis. We have attempted to place this functioning system within its political context. This means that, first, a historical approach, which uses events to illuminate both the process and the content of decision making, has been employed. This historical perspective has allowed us to discern patterns in the policies that have governed the management of the prison system in Northern Ireland, that is, the three models that we have discussed at length. Second, we have located the analysis firmly within the realm of political studies by seeing the primary actor as the British state, engaged in its governance of Northern Ireland and interacting with a variety of political forces on that terrain.

Thus our analysis has examined the Northern Ireland prison system as a real, functioning system, from a historical perspective and as an element in a unique regional arm of the central state, constructed to govern this part of the United Kingdom. The result has allowed us to describe the three historical phases of the management of the prison system and also to abstract from them the basic principles of governance that underlie them. We have ended up with three models of the management of politically motivated prisoners, and we have suggested that these have wider relevance, as a case study, first, for the management of political violence and, second, for the direction of criminal justice systems that must deal with both politically motivated and ordinary offenders.

These models have relevance for countries, such as Italy, Spain, or Israel, which have past or current experience of explicitly political violence. They may also be of interest to those countries where societal division and resulting violence have taken a less overtly political form. Problems of race relations, national or cultural identity, or the integration of ethnic minorities, have affected countries such as the United States, Germany, Australia, and Canada; their criminal justice systems must reflect and take account of these divisions.

We have deliberately chosen not to draw on other typologies of prison management (e.g., Ditchfield 1990). Most have paid insufficient attention to the diversity of prison populations. While the Northern Ireland system has evolved particularly to deal with politically motivated offenders, the principle that a system should reflect the variety and interaction of the people it processes has obvious implications for all prison systems. Prisoners are not an amorphous mass to be managed as a whole. Prisons inevitably contain offenders of different races, ages, and cultural backgrounds who have committed a wide variety of offenses. Management models and the systems they influence need to recognize this reality.

Extracting the management principles underlying phases of policy has led to a concentration on the actions and motives of the managers of the prison system. It therefore fails to do justice to the continuing dialectic between them and other political forces. In particular, and with the exception of our description of the hunger strike period, we have underplayed the level of activity and influence of the prisoners and their organizations themselves. An analysis of the principles and tactics of opposition and accommodation to the policies of the prison authorities, used by prisoners over the past twenty years, would be a useful complementary study to ours. This task is important, not simply to elucidate the continuing interactions we have pointed to, but also because of the importance of political prisoners in any ultimate solution. History, in Ireland and elsewhere, would suggest that the fate of such persons is central to the cementing of a binding political agreement. A good example is the way in which the amnesty for political prisoners (explicitly including those convicted of offenses of violence) was a necessary prerequisite to the present negotiations in South Africa over a new system of government and society.

We might also note that taking the management perspective does not imply a position on the causes or origins of political violence. If we talk about a "response" to political violence, this is not, in itself, a critique of those who argue that the policies and practices of the state played a role in provoking the violence in the first place. Both Republicans and Loyalists would claim that the activities of the state (or rather the lack thereof in the case of the latter) are the key to understanding their resort to violence. Rather, we are simply concerned to trace the development of an institution and its policies in conditions of political violence; ongoing issues of provocation, accommodation, or conciliation are relevant to that, questions of original causality are not.

We have been unable to delve too deeply into the interaction between prison authorities and forces in wider society. Northern Ireland has lacked any form of democratic regional government, apart from a brief period, since 1972. Under "direct rule" from Westminster, the state in Northern Ireland is a detachment of the central state without any formal responsibility to the local electorate. This "democratic deficit," as it is sometimes called, creates political problems of legitimacy and accountability. It also creates managerial problems.

Any state needs strong roots in civil society if it is to function effectively. In a democratic society, elected parliaments or assemblies are fundamental links between the state structure and civil society, as are the wide variety of social groupings that include state personnel and "civilians." The state structure in Northern Ireland lacks many of these roots, partly because it has always been seen as a temporary formation, managing the region until local political forces agree on a form of government. Yet the necessity for feedback on policies and initiatives, as part of a managerial practice of monitoring and evaluation, remains. It is in this light that we might wish to see the Prison Service's development of the concept of "stakeholders" and its increasing use of the media and public dialogue in general. The varying forms of political influence that this situation creates and the decline in the role of the political party might have interesting parallels for other situations where a "democratic deficit" applies.

Our concentration in this essay has been on the principle of normalization. We regard it, in some measure, as a sophisticated and sensible model for the management of political violence. But, from another perspective, we could see it as "marginalization." In the earlier periods of reactive containment and criminalization, the prisons were in the forefront of the political crisis in Northern Ireland. Under normalization, with periodic exceptions, they are not. It is as if the policies of normalization can direct one element of the state structure into a backwater, away from the mainstream of political conflict.

Certainly the policies and practices of the police and army have more direct political impact than prisons in Northern Ireland today. This is an interesting commentary on the idea, promoted by Foucault (1977) and others, that the prison is a central element in society's systems of discipline and control. This is not to dismiss the idea that the penitentiary can be seen as a microcosm of society's disciplinary apparatus. It may be arguable, however, that the greater the social discord, the more political conflict approaches open warfare, the less significant is the system for processing captives and the more significant are the actions of the forces on the battlefield.

This argument begs the question as to whether the "front line" elements of the state can adopt a policy of normalization when confronted with political violence. As we have noted, it is our view that the policies and practices of neither police nor army in Northern Ireland amount to a full program of normalization. Yet there are signs that some elements are working toward that, while some actions and policies seem designed to provoke violent opposition rather than manage it. A study into this question might be particularly rewarding.

In this essay we have examined three different, but not mutually exclusive, models for the management of political violence. We believe that the development of the normalization model is one that governments have followed and will continue to follow as they attempt to come to terms with political violence. What normalization has done in Northern Ireland is to use parts of the criminal justice system and in particular the prisons as a managerial tool to contain what is seen essentially as a managerial problem. The danger in conceiving political violence in the same terms as the economy, the health service, or transport policy is, of course, that it either ignores, or designates insoluble, the political and structural reasons that create the problem that needs management.

If violence can be contained within certain areas or between certain groups, it evolves into "an acceptable level of violence" that becomes only slightly more irksome (in managerial terms) than other elements of the criminal justice system such as too many fine defaulters being admitted to prison or erratic sentencing practices. In other words the cost in human terms is subsumed in the language and actions of the ostensible moral neutrality of management. While the development of an abridged but essentially "normal" criminal justice system is useful to cope with the ongoing management of violent political conflict, it adds little impetus to the search for a solution to that violence.

Having said that, the actual practice of normalization does not present a concrete obstacle to political progress. Indeed, to some extent, the practices of normalization might point the way to at least limited progress. For, in one sense it can be seen as the policy of organized hypocrisy. As a senior IRA prisoner told one of the authors: "The history of the prison struggle here is that the authorities never cave in on the macro-ideological level, but we get what we want de facto a couple of years later or hedged around with conditions."[28] If it were possible to give the political forces competing over the terrain of Northern Ireland much of what they want without anyone having to admit it, that might be a recipe for solid political progress.

APPENDIX
Northern Ireland Conflict, 1968–92

*A. Reactive Containment, 1968–75*

1. *General Events*

| | |
|---|---|
| October 1968 | Civil rights march violently stopped by police in Derry |
| August 1969 | Sectarian fighting involving police in Belfast and Derry; British troops deployed between factions |
| January 1970 | IRA splits into "official" and "provisional" wings |
| April 1970 | "B-specials" disbanded; replaced by Ulster Defence Regiment |
| May 1970 | Conservative government elected at Westminster |
| July 1970 | Falls Road "curfew"—search and seize operation by British army in Catholic areas |
| August 1971 | Internment without trial introduced |
| January 1972 | "Bloody Sunday"—fourteen marchers shot dead by paratroopers; the *Cameron Report* (1969)—report into the civil disturbances; appointed by government of Northern Ireland; Northern Ireland Parliament prorogued—direct rule from Westminster |
| July 1972 | Negotiations between IRA and British government; "Bloody Friday"—IRA bombs kill nine people in Belfast; "Operation Motorman"—IRA "no-go" areas opened up by British army assault |
| June 1973 | Elections to "power-sharing" assembly |
| February 1974 | Labour party elected to govern at Westminster |
| May 1974 | Loyalist bombs kill twenty-two in Dublin; Ulster Worker's Council strike brings down "power-sharing" executive |

---

[28] Interview with author, May 1992.

| | |
|---|---|
| October/November 1974 | Guildford and Birmingham bombings kill nineteen and injure 200 in England |
| Christmas 1974 | IRA declare cease-fire |
| February 1975 | "Incident centers" set up to monitor IRA/British army truce |
| May 1975 | "Constitutional convention" established for local politicians to discuss future |
| November 1975 | Truce finally breaks down and incident centers closed |

### 2. Prison Events

| | |
|---|---|
| August 1971 | Internment—internees held in Crumlin Road, Maidstone prison ship and Magilligan and Long Kesh ex-army camps |
| November 1971 | Nine men escape from Crumlin Road |
| June 1972 | "Special category status" granted after McKee hunger strike; first sentenced "politicals" arrive at Long Kesh |
| January 1973 | Two hundred sentenced "politicals" move to Long Kesh from Crumlin Road |
| October 1974 | Republicans burn Long Kesh compounds |
| November 1974 | Hugh Coney, internee, shot dead while escaping |
| 1975 | Building of "H-blocks" at Long Kesh begins; prison renamed "the Maze" (the name of the local townland) |

### 3. Major Reports

| | |
|---|---|
| 1970 | *Hunt Report*—report on the police after events in 1969 |
| 1972 | *Widgery Report*—cleared British paratroopers after deaths of civilians on Bloody Sunday |
| 1972, 1973 | *Diplock Report*—report to amend criminal justice system to deal with terrorism; introduced Diplock courts |
| 1975 | *Gardiner Report*—recommended end to special category status |

## B. Criminalization, 1976–81

### 1. General Events

| | |
|---|---|
| March 1976 | Constitutional convention dissolved without agreement |
| August 1976 | "Peace People" established |
| January 1977 | "Ulsterization" policy—primacy of the police—announced |
| May 1977 | Second Loyalist strike fails |
| March 1979 | Airey Neave, chairman of Conservative party, killed by INLA bomb in London |

| | |
|---|---|
| May 1979 | Conservative party elected to government in Westminster |
| August 1979 | Lord Mountbatten, the Queen's cousin, killed by IRA; eighteen paratroopers killed in ambush by IRA |
| October 1979 | Ex-head of British Foreign Intelligence Service (MI6) appointed to coordinate security and intelligence |
| April 1981 | Bobby Sands elected as member of Westminster Parliament in by-election |

2. *Prison Events*

| | |
|---|---|
| February 1976 | Frank Stagg dies on hunger strike in England; in protest at refusal to transfer him to Ireland |
| March 1976 | Special category status abolished for those convicted after this date; automatic 50 percent remission introduced; opening of first H-blocks |
| September 1976 | Ciaran Nugent goes on "blanket protest" against refusal of special category status |
| December 1976 | Last internee released; power to intern no longer used though still on statute book |
| 1977 | H-block completed; start of building at Maghaberry; all compounds closed at Magilligan |
| March 1978 | "No wash" protest begins |
| November 1978 | Albert Miles, deputy governor of Maze, shot dead, bringing to eight the number of prison staff members shot in three years |
| 1979 | Nine prison officers, including one assistant governor, killed during year |
| October 1980 | First hunger strike—thirty-seven men and three women became involved; "five demands" elaborated to mark special status; strike called off on the basis of "Atkins" document when McKenna was near death; strike by prison officers in support of pay demand by colleagues in Britain causes opening of "Foyle Prison" staffed by army and RUC |
| January 1981 | Second hunger strike—claims that Britain reneged on Atkins document; Bobby Sands first striker; others joined on staggered basis |
| June 1981 | Eight remand prisoners, including Joe Doherty, escaped from Crumlin Road using guns |
| October 1981 | After ten deaths, hunger strikes are called off; gradual granting of five demands in practice |

3. *Major Report*

| | |
|---|---|
| 1979 | *Bennett Report*—report on police interrogation procedures; it found that not all injuries were self-inflicted |

## C. Normalization, 1981

### 1. General Events

| | |
|---|---|
| October 1982 | Elections for "rolling devolution"; mainly the Catholic Social Democratic and Labour party (SDLP) boycotted meetings |
| November/December 1982 | "Shoot to kill" policy alleged about RUC in ambushes against suspected Republicans |
| March 1983 | "New Ireland Forum" set up by Republic of Ireland |
| April 1983 | First "surpergrass" trial ended |
| June 1983 | Republican leader, Gerry Adams, wins election as Westminster MP for West Belfast |
| May 1984 | Stalker enquiry into "shoot to kill" allegations set up |
| October 1984 | IRA bomb in Brighton kills four, narrowly missing Prime Minister Thatcher |
| December 1984 | Private Iain Thain convicted of the murder of a civilian; served two and one-half years and returned to regiment |
| November 1985 | Anglo-Irish Agreement signed |
| January 1986 | Mass protests against agreement; police confront Loyalist crowds and are attacked in their homes in Loyalist areas |
| March 1986 | Opening of female prison at Maghaberry and closure of Armagh; male prison opened with small number of selected inmates |
| May 1986 | Stalker removed from enquiry three days before final report is due |
| June 1986 | "Rolling devolution" assembly finally dissolved |
| November 1987 | IRA Bomb Remembrance Day ceremony in Enniskillen, killing eleven |
| March 1988 | Three IRA operatives killed by British agents in Gibraltar; three killed at funerals by Loyalist; two soldiers killed by crowd at subsequent funerals |
| October 1988 | Voices of Sinn Fein members and other "supporters of violence" banned from being broadcast |
| October 1989 | "Guildford four" released after being found not guilty of 1974 bombing |
| 1990 | "Birmingham six" released after not guilty finding on appeal, sixteen years after conviction |
| 1991 | Secretary of state, Peter Brooke, starts talks process with local politicians during "break" in meetings under the Anglo-Irish Agreement |
| April 1992 | Conservatives elected to fourth term in government; political talks restart |

## 2. *Prison Events*

| | |
|---|---|
| November 1982 | Strip searching of all female prisoners entering and leaving prison instituted |
| March 1983 | After international protests, level of strip searching dramatically reduced; Life Sentence Review Board holds first meeting; fourteen lifers released on license |
| September 1983 | Thirty-eight IRA prisoners escape from Maze, killing a prison officer |
| August 1984 | Loyalists go on hunger strike in Magilligan, demanding segregation; called off after two months |
| January 1985 | Public launch of life sentence release procedure with release of "Explanatory Memorandum" about the system |
| February 1985 | Introduction of Christmas home leave scheme; 105 prisoners allowed home |
| June 1988 | Closure of last three special category compounds |
| 1989 | Publication of aims and objectives of Prison Service; campaign for segregation at Crumlin Road grows during year |
| August 1989 | Summer home leave introduced for lifers; 143 released for long weekends; 100 lifers released on license in year |
| October 1989 | Attempted major escape from Crumlin Road; "interface" policy on improved visits is introduced |
| Early 1990 | Two policemen shot when captured by IRA on border; prison officer released unharmed |
| 1990 | Strategic review within the Prison Service using outside consultants and involving "stakeholders" |
| June 1991 | Launch of Prison Service strategic plan, "Serving the Community" |
| November 1991 | Continuing campaign for segregation culminates in IRA bomb in Crumlin Road prison that kills two Loyalists; entire female prison strip searched for the first time; resisters forcibly stripped; Joe Doherty extradited from the United States |
| March 1992 | *Colville Report* refuses segregation, but physical changes in prison begin to be made, assisting process of self-segregation |

## 3. *Major Reports*

| | |
|---|---|
| 1983–84 | *Hennessey Report*—report into security at Maze following escape of thirty-eight Republican prisoners |

1990                                     *Woolf Report*—report after prison rioting in
                                         Strangeways and others; recommendations
                                         did not extend to Northern Ireland but seen
                                         as a watershed for penal reform
1992                                     *Colville Report*—report into holding of Loyalist
                                         and Republican prisoners at Crumlin Road
                                         refuses to allow official segregation of prison

REFERENCES

Adams, G. 1990. *Cage Eleven*. Dingle: Brandon.

Amnesty International. 1978. *Report of an Amnesty Mission to Northern Ireland*. London: Amnesty.

————. 1980. Amnesty Annual Report. London: Amnesty.

*Belfast Telegraph*. 1981. "Prior Urges Hungerstrikers to Give Up" (September 28), p. 1.

Bennett, H. 1979. *The Bennett Report: A Report of the Committee of Inquiry into Police Interrogation Procedures in Northern Ireland*. Cmnd. 7397. London: Her Majesty's Stationery Office.

Beresford, D. 1987. *Ten Men Dead*. London: Grafton.

Bishop, P., and E. Mallie. 1989. *The Provisional IRA*. London: Corgi.

Boal, F. W., and N. H. Douglas. 1982. *Integration and Division: Geographical Perspectives on the Northern Ireland Problem*. London: Academic Press.

Bowyer Bell, J. 1979. *The Secret Army*. Dublin: Academy Press.

Boyd, A. 1969. *Holy War in Belfast*. Tralee: Anvil Books.

Boyle, K., and M. Allen. 1983. *Sentencing Law and Practice*. London: Sweet & Maxwell.

Boyle, K., and T. Hadden. 1985. *Ireland: A Positive Proposal*. Harmondsworth: Penguin.

Brewer, J. D., and K. Magee. 1991. *Inside the RUC—Routine Policing in a Divided Society*. Oxford: Oxford University Press.

Cameron, Lord. 1969. *A Report into Disturbances in Northern Ireland: Report of the Commission Appointed by the Governor of Northern Ireland*. Cmnd. 532. Belfast: Her Majesty's Stationery Office.

Cauldfield, M. 1965. *The Easter Rebellion*. Dublin: Frederic Muller.

Chibnall, S. 1977. *Law and Order News*. London: Tavistock.

Colville, M. 1992. *The Colville Report: A Report on the Operational Policy in Belfast Prison for the Management of Paramilitary Prisoners from Opposing Factions*. Cmnd. 1860. London: Her Majesty's Stationery Office.

Coogan, T. P. 1985. *The IRA*. London: Fontana.

————. 1990. *Michael Collins: A Biography*. London: Hutchinson.

Curran, G. 1988. *The Birth of the Irish Free State (1921–23)*. Birmingham: Alabama University Press.

Curtis, L. 1984. *Ireland: The Propaganda War*. London: Pluto.

Darby, J. 1976. *Conflict in Ireland: The Development of a Polarised Community*. Dublin: Gill & Macmillan.

Devlin, B. 1969. *The Price of My Soul*. London: Pan.

Dillon, M. 1990. *The Dirty War*. London: Arrow.

Dillon, M., and P. Lehane. 1984. *New Ireland Forum: The Cost of Violence Arising from the NI Crisis since 1969*. Dublin: Republic of Ireland Stationery Office.

Diplock, Lord. 1972. *The Diplock Report: The Report of the Commission to Consider Legal Procedures to Deal with Terrorist Activities in Northern Ireland*. Cmnd. 5186. Belfast: Her Majesty's Stationery Office.

Ditchfield, G. 1990. *Control in Prisons: A Review of the Literature*. London: Her Majesty's Stationery Office.

Dunne, D. 1989. *Out of the Maze: The True Story of the Biggest Jail Escape since the War*. Dublin: Gill & Macmillan.

European Commission. 1980. *Decision of the European Commission on Human Rights*. European Commission Reports no. 3. Strasbourg: European Commission.

Farrell, M. 1976. *Northern Ireland: The Orange State*. London: Pluto.

Foot, P. 1989. *Who Framed Colin Wallace?* London: Macmillan.

Foucault, M. 1977. *Discipline and Punish: The Birth of the Prison*. New York: Pantheon.

Fox, M., and J. Morison. 1992. "Lawyers in a Divided Society: Legal Cultures and Legal Services in Northern Ireland." *Journal of Law and Society* ("Special Issue on Tomorrow's Lawyers") 19:124–45.

Gaffikin, F., and M. Morrissey. 1990. *Northern Ireland: The Thatcher Years*. London: Red Books.

Gardiner, Lord. 1975. *The Gardiner Report: The Report of a Committee to Consider in the Context of Civil Liberties and Human Rights, Measures to Deal with Terrorism in Northern Ireland*. Cmnd. 5847. Belfast: Her Majesty's Stationery Office.

Gearty, C. 1991. *Terror*. London: Faber & Faber.

Great Britain. Parliament. House of Commons. 1971. *House of Commons Debates*. Hansard Parliamentary Reports. Vol. 823 (September), cols. 8–212. London: Her Majesty's Stationery Office.

———. 1972. *House of Commons Debates*, p. 34. Hansard Parliamentary Reports. London: Her Majesty's Stationery Office.

Guelke, A. 1988. *Northern Ireland: The International Perspective*. Dublin: Gill & Macmillan.

H Blocks. 1980. *The Reality*. London: Her Majesty's Stationery Office.

Helsinki Watch. 1992. *Report on British Prisons*. New York: Helsinki Watch.

Hennessey, James. 1983–84. *The Hennessey Report: A Report of an Inquiry by H.M. Chief Inspector of Prisons into the Security Arrangement at H.M.P. Maze*. Cmnd. 203. London: Her Majesty's Stationery Office.

Heslinga, M. W. 1962. *The Irish Border as a Cultural Divide*. Aesin: Van Gorcum. (Originally published 1971.)

Hillyard, P. 1990. "From Belfast to Brixton." In *Lessons from Northern Ireland*, edited by G. Hayes and P. O'Higgins. Belfast: SLS Legal Publications.

Hogan, G., and C. Walker. 1989. *Political Violence and the Law in Ireland.* Manchester: Manchester University Press.

Hooper, A. 1983. *The Military and the Media.* Aldershot: Gower.

Hunt, Lord. 1969. *The Hunt Report. The Report of the Advisory Committee on Police in Northern Ireland.* Cmnd. 535. Belfast: Her Majesty's Stationery Office.

Ignatieff, M. 1981. "State, Civil Society, and Total Institutions: A Critique of Recent Social Histories Of Punishment." In *Crime and Justice: An Annual Review of Research,* vol. 3, edited by M. Tonry and N. Morris. Chicago: University of Chicago Press.

*Iris.* 1991. "The H. Block Hunger Strike," no. 16 (May), pp. 2–64.

Irish Republic Army. 1987. *The Green Book: The Constitution of Oglaidh na Heireann (the Provisional IRA)* (as amended). Dublin: Republican Press Centre.

Kee, R. 1972. *The Green Flag: A History of Irish Nationalism.* London: Weidenfield & Nicholson.

———. 1982. *Ourselves Alone.* London: Quartet.

Kennedy, D. 1988. *The Widening Gulf: Northern Attitudes to the Independent Irish State (1919–1949).* Belfast: Blackstaff.

Kitson, F. 1991. *Low Intensity Operations: Subversion, Insurgency and Peacekeeping.* 2d ed. London: Faber & Faber.

McCann, E. 1980. *War and an Irish Town.* 2d ed. Harmondsworth: Penguin; London: Pluto.

McCann, E., M. Shields, and B. Hannigan. 1992. *Bloody Sunday in Derry: What Really Happened?* Dingle: Brandon.

McCartney, R., H. L. McCracken, P. Smith, G. Smyth, and B. Somers. 1981. *The Unionist Case.* Typescript. Belfast.

McEvoy, K. 1991. "Joyriding in West Belfast." Master of Science thesis. University of Edinburgh, Centre for the Study of Criminology and the Philosophy of Law.

Madden, P. 1979. "Banned, Censored and Delayed." In "Campaign for Free Speech in Ireland. The British Media and Ireland: Truth the First Casualty." Pamphlet. London: Information on Ireland.

Mani, V. 1978. "International Terrorism: Is a Definition Possible?" *Indian Journal of International Law* 18:206–32.

Mapstone, R. 1992. "Police Attitudes in a Divided Society." *British Journal of Criminology* 32:183–192.

Marx, K., and F. Engels. 1971. *On Ireland.* London: Lawrence & Wisehart.

Murray, R. 1990. *The SAS in Ireland.* Dublin: Mercier.

Neeson, E. 1967. *The Civil War in Ireland.* Cork: Mercier.

*New Ulster Defender.* 1992. "The Pan-Nationalist Front." *New Ulster Defender* 1(i):1–31.

North-Eastern Boundary Bureau. 1923. *Handbook of the Ulster Question.* Dublin: State Stationery Office.

Northern Ireland Office. 1990a. "Interface: Initiatives for the Improvement of Visits and Contact with the Public in Northern Ireland Prisons." Unpublished memorandum. Belfast: Northern Ireland Association for the Care and Resettlement of Offenders.

————. 1990*b. A Review of Research.* No. 1. Belfast: Northern Ireland Office Statistics Branch.

Northern Ireland Prison Service. 1973–91*a. Annual Reports on the Administration of the Northern Ireland Prison Service.* Belfast: Her Majesty's Stationery Office.

————. 1985*b.* Life Sentence Prisoners in Northern Ireland. An explanatory memorandum. Belfast: Her Majesty's Stationery Office.

————. 1990*c. The Code of Conduct of the NI Prison Service 1990.* Belfast: Her Majesty's Stationery Office.

————. 1991*d. Serving the Community: The Northern Ireland Prison Service in the 1990's.* Belfast: Her Majesty's Stationery Office.

Northern Ireland Association for the Care and Resettlement of Offenders. 1991. *Silent Sentence: Working with Prisoners' Families. A Conference Report and Guide to Practice.* Belfast: Northern Ireland Association for the Care and Resettlement of Offenders.

————. 1992. *Justice, Safety and Openness: NIACRO Response to the Prison Service Strategic Plan.* Belfast: Northern Ireland Association for the Care and Resettlement of Offenders.

O'Brien, C. C. 1972. *States of Ireland.* London: Hutchinson.

O'Leary, B. 1985. "Explaining Northern Ireland: A Brief Study Guide." *Politics* 5(1):35–41.

O'Malley, P. 1990. *Biting at the Grave: The Irish Hungerstrikes and the Politics of Despair.* Belfast: Blackstaff.

Paisley, I. K., P. Robinson, and J. Taylor. 1982. *Ulster: The Facts.* Belfast: Crown.

Purdey, B. 1990. *Politics in the Street: The Origins of the Civil Rights Movement in Northern Ireland.* Belfast: Blackstaff.

Rea, D., ed. 1982. *Political Co-operation in Divided Societies. A Series of Papers Relevant to the Conflict in Northern Ireland.* Dublin: Gill & Macmillan.

Republican Fact File. 1991. "Republican Prisoners and the Prison Struggle in Ireland—Criminalisation: Defeated by Prison Resistance." Belfast: Sinn Fein Foreign Affairs Bureau.

Rolston, B., and M. Tomlinson. 1986. "Long Term Imprisonment in Northern Ireland. Psychological or Political Survival?" In *The Expansion of European Prison Systems.* Working Papers in European Criminology no. 7, edited by B. Rolston and M. Tomlinson. Stockholm: European Group for the Study of Deviance and Control.

————. 1988. "The Challenge within Prisons and Propaganda in Northern Ireland." In *Whose Law and Order?* edited by M. Tomlinson, T. Varley, and C. McCullagh. Belfast: Queen's University Bookshop.

Ryan, D., ed. 1948. *Socialism and Nationalism: A Selection from the Writings of James Connolly.* Dublin: Three Candles.

Ryder, C. 1989. *The RUC: A Force under Fire.* London: Methuen.

Smith, D. 1990. *Equality and Inequality in Northern Ireland.* 2d ed. London: London Policy Studies Institute.

Spujt, R. J. 1986. "Internment and Detention without Trial in Northern Ireland (1971–75)." *Modern Law Review* 49:712–39.

Stewart, A. T. Q. 1977. *The Narrow Ground: Aspects of Ulster, 1906–1969.* London: Faber & Faber.

Taylor, P. 1980. *Beating the Terrorists: Interrogation in Omagh, Gough and Castlereagh.* Harmondsworth: Penguin.

Teague, P. 1987. *Beyond the Rhetoric: Politics, the Economy and Social Policy in Northern Ireland.* London: Lawrence & Wisehart.

Thomas, J. E. 1972. *The English Prison Officer since 1850: A Study in Conflict.* London: Routledge & Kegan Paul.

Thompson, E. P. 1975. *Whigs and Hunters: The Origins of the Black Act.* London: Penguin.

————. 1980. *The Making of the English Working Class.* 3d ed. London: Penguin.

Townsend, C. 1975. *The Civil War in Ireland.* Dublin: Mercier.

Urban, M. 1992. *Big Boy's Rules: The Secret Struggle against the IRA.* London: Faber & Faber.

Walsh, D. 1983. *The Use and Abuse of Emergency Regulation in Northern Ireland.* Nottingham: Russell.

Watt, D., ed. 1981. *The Constitution of Northern Ireland: Problems and Prospects.* National Institute of Economics and Social Policy Research. Policy Studies Institute. Royal Institute of International Affairs. Joint Studies in Public Policy no 4. London: Heinemann.

Weber, M. 1949. "Objectivity in Social Science and Social Policy." In M. Weber, *The Methodology of the Social Sciences.* Translated by E. A. Schils and F. Finch. Glencoe, Ill.: Free Press.

Whyte, J. 1991. *Interpreting Northern Ireland.* Oxford: Oxford University Press.

Widgery, Lord. 1972. *The Widgery Report. A Report of the Tribunal Appointed to Inquire into the Events on Sunday 30th January 1972 which Led to Loss of Life in Connection with the Procession in Londonderry That Day.* Belfast: Her Majesty's Stationery Office.

Woolf, Lord Justice. 1990. *The Woolf Report: The Report of an Inquiry by L. J. Woolf and Judge Stephen Tumin.* London: Her Majesty's Stationery Office.

*Michael Tonry*

# Sentencing Commissions and Their Guidelines

ABSTRACT

Sentencing commissions, administrative agencies charged to develop and promulgate standards for sentencing, were first proposed early in the 1970s and first established in 1978. Of four recent major sentencing reform approaches—the others being parole guidelines, voluntary sentencing guidelines, and statutory determinate sentences—only sentencing commission systems continue to be created. Despite controversies associated with the highly unpopular federal guidelines, commissions and their guidelines have achieved their primary goals. Some commissions have achieved specialized technical competence, have adopted comprehensive policy approaches, and have to a degree insulated policy from short-term political pressures. Guidelines have reduced disparities and gender and sex differences in sentencing and by tying policies to available resources have enabled some jurisdictions to resist national trends toward greatly increased prison populations.

The sentencing commission is alive and well. Proposed by Judge Marvin Frankel more than twenty years ago as a device for reducing sentencing disparities and judicial "lawlessness," sentencing commissions were to be specialized administrative agencies charged to set standards for sentencing (Frankel 1972). Some commissions have operated much as Judge Frankel hoped they would; they have achieved and maintained specialized institutional competence, have to a degree insulated sentencing policy from short-term "crime of the week" political pressures, and have maintained a focus on comprehensive system-wide policy-making. Guidelines promulgated by commissions have altered sentenc-

Michael Tonry is Sonosky Professor of Law and Public Policy at the University of Minnesota Law School.

ing patterns and practices, have reduced sentencing disparities and gender and race effects, and have shown that sentencing policies can be linked to correctional and other resources, thereby enhancing governmental accountability and protecting the public purse.

Many readers may be surprised by the preceding summary of experience with sentencing commissions and their guidelines. The controversial story of the best-known commission, the U.S. Sentencing Commission, is well known. The U.S. commission's guidelines are easily the most disliked sentencing reform initiative in the United States in this century. They are commonly criticized on policy grounds (that they unduly limit judicial discretion and unduly shift discretion to prosecutors), on process grounds (that they foreseeably cause judges and prosecutors to devise hypocritical stratagems to circumvent them), on technocratic grounds (that they are too complex and are hard to apply accurately), on fairness grounds (that by taking only offense elements and prior criminal history into account, very different defendants receive the same sentence), and on normative grounds (that they greatly increased the proportion of offenders receiving prison sentences and are generally too harsh). How, a reader might reasonably ask, can the commission idea be a success if its most prominent example is so controversial?

The answer is that the experience of the U.S. commission is misleading in two ways. First, the federal commission is but one of twenty that have been established and of a dozen or more now in existence. In some states, notably including Delaware, Minnesota, Oregon, Pennsylvania, and Washington, the experience has been much happier. Second, and as important for assessment of the viability of Judge Frankel's proposal, the evidence documenting the policy failures and unpopularity of the U.S. guidelines at the same time demonstrates the institutional capacities of sentencing commissions. However misguided the U.S. Sentencing Commission's policies, and however ineffective its efforts to elicit acceptance from practitioners, it has become a specialized agency of technical competence and has managed through its guidelines radically to alter sentencing practices in the federal courts.[1]

The sentencing commission idea will survive the federal debacle. To be sure, the federal example raises skepticism in many states. In both North Carolina and Texas, for example, commissions at early meetings

---

[1] This point, that an increasingly effective organization is behind the deeply unpopular federal guidelines, is obvious enough once noted but has long gone unnoted. Doob (1993) pointed it out to me, and I have developed the idea elsewhere (Tonry 1993a).

adopted resolutions expressly repudiating the federal guidelines as a model for anything they might develop (Knapp 1993). The North Carolina commission euphemistically abjured use of the word "guidelines" in its legislative proposals (North Carolina Sentencing and Policy Advisory Commission 1993) so as not to conjure up images of the federal guidelines (Orland and Reitz 1993). At a meeting of state sentencing commissions in Boulder, Colorado, in February 1993, an Ohio representative reported that the Ohio commission early in its work resolved that "Ohio should not adopt the type of rigid sentencing guidelines exemplified by the federal guidelines" (Orland and Reitz 1993). State policymakers can and do distinguish the merits and promise of Judge Frankel's proposal from the demerits and policy failures of the U.S. federal experience.

Sentencing reform remains on the policy agendas of many common law jurisdictions in the United States and elsewhere. The Criminal Justice Act 1991, which took effect in October 1992, is a major reconstitution of sentencing laws and practices in England and Wales (Wasik and Taylor 1991; Ashworth 1992; Thomas 1993). In Australia, although the 1980 call of the Australian Law Reform Commission for abolition of parole fell on deaf ears, in 1989 New South Wales (Gorta 1992, 1993) enacted truth-in-sentencing laws not greatly different from those in some American states; in 1991 Victoria enacted the Sentencing Act of 1991, which made significant changes to that state's sentencing laws (Fox 1991; Freiberg 1993). Although the 1987 recommendation of a Canadian national commission that Canada establish a permanent sentencing commission was not adopted by the Canadian Parliament (Canadian Sentencing Commission 1987, chap. 14), major sentencing reform legislation has been repeatedly considered (see, e.g., Roberts and von Hirsch 1993).

In American states, the sentencing commission is the only institutional survivor of two decades' experimentation with comprehensive approaches to sentencing reform. During the 1970s, four differing reform approaches contended (Blumstein et al. 1983, chap. 3). Parole guidelines, the earliest dating initially from the late 1960s, were an effort to reduce disparities in prison sentences by structuring the discretion of parole boards in setting release dates. A number of states, notably including Oregon, Washington, and Minnesota, and the federal system, adopted parole guidelines (e.g., Gottfredson, Wilkins, and Hoffman 1978; Arthur D. Little, Inc. 1981; Bottomley 1990). Because parole boards, however, have no jurisdiction over jail sentences or nonincarcerative penalties, or over the decision whether to incarcerate in state prisons, parole guidelines were at best a partial solution to sentencing disparities and were repealed to be replaced by sentencing guidelines in the jurisdictions mentioned. Some states continue to develop and to use parole guidelines, but they are promoted as relevant to parole administration and not as a stand-alone sentencing reform.

Next in order, expressly building on experience with parole guidelines and dating initially from pilot projects in Denver and Vermont in the mid-1970s, were sentencing guidelines that were "voluntary" in the two senses that they were developed by judges without a statutory mandate and that judicial compliance with them was entirely discretionary with the individual judge (Wilkins et al. 1978; Kress 1980). By the early 1980s, voluntary guidelines had been developed in most states (Blumstein et al. 1983, pp. 138–39), sometimes at the state level (e.g., Maryland, Florida, Massachusetts, Michigan, New Jersey, and Wisconsin) and more often at county or judicial district levels (Shane-DuBow, Brown, and Olsen 1985). The voluntary guidelines were often created by judges in hopes that by putting their own houses in order they would forestall passage of mandatory or determinate sentencing laws (e.g., Carrow et al. 1985, pp. 126–27). Evaluations showed that voluntary guidelines typically had little or no demonstrable effect on sentences imposed (Rich et al. 1982; Blumstein et al. 1983, chap. 4; Carrow 1984; Carrow et al. 1985), and in most places they were abandoned. They continue in effect in a number of states, including Michigan and Wisconsin, but no evaluations have been published. The notable exception to the generally pessimistic story of voluntary guidelines is in Delaware, where they took effect in the mid-1980s and appear to have normative and collegial, albeit they do not have formal legal, authority (e.g., Quinn 1990, 1992; Gebelein 1991). In Delaware, also, no major independent or other evaluations have been published.

Third in sequence were statutory determinate sentencing schemes dating from the mid-to-late 1970s like those in California, Illinois, Indiana, and North Carolina. They were diversely specific, ranging from California where, initially, for example, robbery was specified to warrant a three-year prison term in the ordinary case, but two or four years if mitigating or aggravating circumstances were present, to Indiana where statutes prescribed ranges of ten to forty years for some offenses (Blumstein et al. 1983, chap. 3). Few of the statutory schemes were subjected to independent evaluations by outsiders. The exceptions are California, where many evaluations were conducted (for a complete list, see Cohen and Tonry 1983, table 7-15), and North Carolina, where Stevens Clarke and colleagues completed a number of evaluations (Clarke et al. 1983; Clarke 1984, 1987). In both states, statutory determinate sentencing laws reduced sentencing disparities and (remarkably, in retrospect) led to reductions in average sentence lengths. Nonetheless, no state known to me (and I have said this often in places where, if I am wrong, I should have been corrected) has adopted a statutory determinate sentencing system for more than ten years.

After nearly two decades of experimentation, the guideline-setting sentencing commission is the only reform strategy that commands widespread support and continues to be the subject of new legislation. Legislation to establish the first two commissions, in Minnesota and Pennsylvania, was enacted in 1978. In other places I have told the story of sentencing commissions through the mid-1980s (Tonry 1987, 1988). Suffice to say that by 1987, presumptive guidelines created by sentencing commissions were in place in Minnesota, Washington, and (after an initial legislative rejection) Pennsylvania. Voluntary guidelines in Maryland and Florida, which had been created with federal demonstration project money, were adopted statewide; Florida's were converted into (nominally) presumptive guidelines, and the judicial steering committee that oversaw the demonstration project evolved into a sentencing commission (Carrow et al. 1985). Entities called sentencing commissions had been created in South Carolina (von Hirsch, Knapp, and Tonry 1987, pp. 24–25, 117–24), New York (Griset 1991), Connecticut (Shane-DuBow, Brown, and Olsen 1985), and Maine (von Hirsch, Knapp, and Tonry 1987, pp. 20–21), but either decided not to develop guidelines (Maine and Connecticut) or tried to do so but were unable to persuade state legislatures to ratify the guidelines proposed (New York and South Carolina).

The pace of sentencing commission activity increased after the mid-1980s. The federal legislation was passed in 1984, commissioners were appointed in 1985, and the guidelines took effect in 1987. Oregon's guidelines took effect in 1989; with Washington and Minnesota, Oregon has the most sophisticated guidelines now in use. Guidelines created by sentencing commissions took effect in Tennessee, Louisiana and, after legislative rejection of initial proposed guidelines, in Kansas in 1993 (Gottlieb 1991). At the time of writing, sentencing commissions are at work in Ohio, North Carolina, and Alaska, and commissions with wider charges to consider sentencing and corrections policies and laws are working in Texas and Arkansas (Knapp 1993).

Supreme Court Justice Louis Brandeis once observed that "it is one of the happy incidents of the federal system that a single, courageous state may, if its citizens choose, serve as a laboratory and try social and economic experiments without risk to the rest of the country" (*New State Ice Co. v. Liebmann*, 285 U.S. 262, 311 [1932]). Amid discussion, development, promulgation, enactment, rejection, celebration, and denunciation of American's experiments with sentencing commissions, it seems a good time to take stock of what has happened to Judge Frankel's suggestion that sentencing policy be made the subject of administrative rule making.

Numerous entities of different sorts have been called sentencing commissions but my focus here is principally on those that fall within Judge Frankel's proposals for statutory creation of an administrative body charged with developing rules for sentencing that would be presumptively applicable, subject to a judge's authority to impose some other sentence if reasons were given, with that judgment being subject to review on appeal by a higher court (von Hirsch, Knapp, and Tonry 1987, chap. 1). At least ten commissions fit that definition (more or less in chronological order, Minnesota, Pennsylvania, Maine, Washington, South Carolina, the U.S. Sentencing Commission, Oregon, New Mexico, North Carolina, Kansas, and Ohio). Excluded are commissions with more general charges to consider sentencing or corrections issues, or both, and formulate recommendations. The most celebrated commission of this type was the Canadian Sentencing Commission (1987); notable American instances occurred in New York (Griset 1991), Texas (Reynolds 1993), and Arkansas (Knapp 1993).

This essay consists of three sections. The first examines experience with sentencing commissions in relation to the effects of their guidelines on sentencing patterns and correctional practices and in relation to their institutional properties (specialized competence, insulation from short-term emotionalism and political pressures, a systemic approach to policy-making). The second section canvasses the major policy issues that current commissions have addressed and that future commissions must resolve. The third provides a diagnosis of the state of health of Judge Frankel's proposal and its long-term prospects.

Before beginning, one final prefatory note concerning sources is necessary. The scholarly and evaluation literatures on sentencing commissions and their guidelines are slight. Besides Judge Frankel's book, only three others have discussed commissions (as opposed to their guidelines) in any detail (O'Donnell, Churgin, and Curtis 1977; von

Hirsch, Knapp, and Tonry 1987; Parent 1988) and only a handful of articles (Tonry 1979, 1991; Frankel and Orland 1984; Wright 1991). Private foundations and the federal research-sponsoring agencies have shown little interest in sentencing for many years and, as a result, little has been added to the literature since the last time I took stock of the sentencing commission experience (Tonry 1988). The only major exception concerns the U.S. Sentencing Commission on which a modest evaluation literature (e.g., Schulhofer and Nagel 1989; Heaney 1991; Karle and Sager 1991; U.S. Sentencing Commission 1991*a*, 1991*b*; Dunworth and Weisselberg 1992; Meierhoefer 1992; Nagel and Schulhofer 1992; U.S. General Accounting Office 1992) and a sizable policy literature (e.g., Wright 1991; Freed 1992; Doob 1993; Tonry 1993*b*) have accumulated. The bimonthly *Federal Sentencing Reporter* published by the University of California Press for the Vera Institute of Justice is a treasure trove of otherwise fugitive reports and analyses of the federal sentencing commission and its guidelines; the December 1992 issue is devoted entirely to evaluation issues. In addition, most sentencing commissions collect monitoring data in greater or lesser detail and publish annual or more frequent statistical reports. There are a handful of recent empirical writings by others, using commission data, in Minnesota (e.g., Frase 1991, 1993*a*) and Washington (Boerner 1993), and a small number of articles have described the policies and processes of state sentencing commissions (Kramer and Scirica 1985; Parent 1988; Bogan 1990, 1991; Griset 1991; Lieb 1991, 1993; Dailey 1992; Kramer 1992; Gottlieb 1993; Wright and Ellis 1993) and the federal sentencing commission (Breyer 1988, 1992; von Hirsch 1988; Stith and Koh 1993; Tonry 1991, 1993*b*). Finally, five law reviews have recently devoted symposium issues to sentencing.[2] This essay draws on these sources and also on personal contacts with state and federal policymakers and practitioners.

## I. Experience with Commissions

The crux of Judge Frankel's proposal concerned the institutional capacities of administrative agencies. Rule-making authority has been delegated by legislatures in the United States to countless state and federal agencies on the bases that, better than any legislature, they can achieve

---

[2] The *Yale Law Journal* (vol. 101, no. 8), the *University of Southern California Law Review* (vol. 66, no. 1), the *University of California Davis Law Review* (vol. 25, no. 3), the *Wake Forest Law Review* (vol. 28, no. 2), and the *University of Colorado Law Review* (vol. 64, no. 3).

and maintain specialized competence concerning complex subjects, they have some degree of insulation from short-term popular emotions and political pressures, and they can adopt comprehensive, long-term approaches to policy-making. Because the sentencing commission was proposed as a tool for establishing standards for sentencing and reducing disparities, any stocktaking must consider two questions. First, have commissions successfully developed and implemented sentencing guidelines that have changed sentencing practices and reduced disparities? Second, as administrative agencies, have sentencing commissions developed specialized competence, achieved some insulation from knee-jerk politics, and adopted comprehensive, long-term approaches to policymaking?

## A. Effects on Sentencing Practices

Guidelines developed by commissions have changed sentencing practices and patterns, reduced disparities, ameliorated racial and gender differences, and helped states control their prison populations. That statement camouflages deep disagreements about the wisdom of decisions made by commissions. In the federal system, for example, numerous observers charge that the new sentencing patterns are too severe and that the new practices are undesirable because lawyers and judges commonly, and foreseeably, manipulate the guidelines to avoid imposing sentences that they believe are too harsh (Federal Courts Study Committee 1990; Freed 1992; Nagel and Schulhofer 1992; Tonry 1993b). In the federal, Minnesota, and Oregon systems, critics argue that disparities have been reduced by violating the second half of the equality injunction ("and treat different cases differently"). Racial and gender differences have been reduced but, controlling for current offenses and criminal histories, women and whites continue more often to receive mitigated sentences than do men and blacks and, conversely, men and blacks more often receive aggravated sentences. Gender differences have been ameliorated but only by increasing the relative severity of women's punishments compared with preguidelines patterns in which women's sentences were markedly less severe than men's (e.g., Knapp 1984, pp. 67–68). Racial differences have diminished in some jurisdictions, but only by limiting standard sentencing criteria to current offense and criminal history information (which in any case has a systematically unfavorable disparate impact on black defendants) and by forbidding judges to adjust sentences on the basis of biographical information such as education, employment, and family status,[3] which lessens chances of favorable treatment of nondisadvantaged defendants but in many individual cases penalizes disadvantaged defendants who have to some degree overcome dismal life chances. Finally, although some jurisdictions have managed to regulate their prison populations, some never tried and the U.S. commission, despite a statutory directive, failed to do so.

Nonetheless, while reasonable people can disagree about the wisdom of policies commissions have adopted and regret that they have not been more successful at reducing unwarranted disparities and eliminating harsher treatment of minority defendants, no informed person can disagree that some commissions and their guidelines have altered sentencing practices and patterns in their jurisdictions.

1. *Conformity with Guidelines.* Data are available from four states and the federal system on judges' compliance with guidelines. It is clear that judges in a large majority of cases will conform the sentences they announce to applicable authorized sentencing ranges. That assertion requires two important caveats. First, guideline developers have often insisted that guidelines should be disregarded when a case's special features warrant different treatment (Gottfredson, Wilkins, and Hoffman 1978); they are after all guidelines, not mandatory penalties,[4] and judges' reasons for imposing some other sentence can be stated for the record and examined by higher courts. From this perspective, a guidelines system that elicited 100 percent compliance would be undesirable because judges would not be discriminating among cases as they should.

Second, if judges are willing to give plea bargaining free rein, compliance may be more apparent than real. Guidelines make sentencing predictable. Picture a guidelines grid as a dart board. Figure 1 as an example shows the initial 1989 Oregon grid. Each cell specifies a range of presumptively appropriate sentences; to fix the game counsel need only be sure that their dart hits the right cell. This they can do by means of charge dismissals. If counsel negotiate a fifteen-month prison sentence, and the applicable sentencing range for offense $X$ is fourteen to sixteen months, the defendant need only plead guilty to $X$ and the

---

[3] The federal guidelines, for example, in § 5H1.6 provide: "Family ties and responsibilities . . . are not ordinarily relevant in determining whether a sentence should be outside the guidelines" (U.S. Sentencing Commission 1992a). Comparable rules apply to education and employment.

[4] Although the U.S. Sentencing Commission has muddied the distinction by describing its own presumptive guidelines as "mandatory guidelines" (U.S. Sentencing Commission 1991a, p. i).

| Criminal History Scale | | | | | | | | |
|---|---|---|---|---|---|---|---|---|
| Multiple (3+) Felony Person Offender | Repeat (2) Felony Person Offender | Single (1) Felony Person/Non-Person Offender | Single (1) Felony Person Offender | Multiple (4+) Felony Non-Person Offender | Repeat (2-3) Felony Non-Person Offender | Significant Minor Criminal Record | Minor Criminal Record | Minor Misdemeanor or No Criminal Record |
| **A** | **B** | **C** | **D** | **E** | **F** | **G** | **H** | **I** |

| Crime Seriousness Scale | | A | B | C | D | E | F | G | H | I |
|---|---|---|---|---|---|---|---|---|---|---|
| Murder | 11 | 225-269 | 196-224 | 178-194 | 149-177 | 149-177 | 135-148 | 129-134 | 122-128 | 120-121 |
| Manslaughter I, Assault I, Rape I, Arson I | 10 | 121-130 | 116-120 | 111-115 | 91-110 | 81-90 | 71-80 | 66-70 | 61-65 | 58-60 |
| Rape I, Assault I, Kidnapping I, Arson I, Burglary I, Robbery I | 9 | 66-72 | 61-65 | 56-60 | 51-55 | 46-50 | 41-45 | 39-40 | 37-38 | 34-36 |
| Manslaughter II, Sexual Abuse I, Assault II, Rape II, Using Child in Display of Sexual Conduct, Drugs—Minors, Cult/Manuf., Del., Comp., Prostitution, Neg. Homicide | 8 | 41-45 | 35-40 | 29-34 | 27-28 | 25-26 | 23-24 | 21-22 | 19-20 | 16-18 |
| Extortion, Coercion, Supplying Contraband, Escape I | 7 | 31-36 | 25-30 | 21-24 | 19-20 | 16-18 | 180/90 | 180/90 | 180/90 | 180/90 |
| Robbery II, Assault III, Rape III, Bribe Receiving, Intimidation, Property Crimes (more than $50,000), Drug Possession | 6 | 25-30 | 19-24 | 15-18 | 13-14 | 10-12 | 180/90 | 180/90 | 180/90 | 180/90 |
| Robbery III, Theft by Receiving, Trafficking Stolen Vehicles, Property Crimes ($10,000 - $49,999) | 5 | 15-16 | 13-14 | 11-12 | 9-10 | 6-8 | 180/90 | 120/60 | 120/60 | 120/60 |
| Failure to Appear I, Custodial Interference II, Property Crimes ($5,000 - $9,999) Drugs—Cult/Manuf./Del. | 4 | 10-10 | 8-9 | 120/60 | 120/60 | 120/60 | 120/60 | 120/60 | 120/60 | 120/60 |
| Abandon Child, Abuse of Corpse, Criminal Nonsupport, Property Crimes ($1,000 - $4,999) | 3 | 120/60 | 120/60 | 120/60 | 120/60 | 120/60 | 120/60 | 90/30 | 90/30 | 90/30 |
| Dealing Child Pornography, Violation of Wildlife Laws, Welfare Fraud, Property Crimes (less than $1,000) | 2 | 90/30 | 90/30 | 90/30 | 90/30 | 90/30 | 90/30 | 90/30 | 90/30 | 90/30 |
| Altering Firearm ID, Habitual Offender Violation, Bigamy, Paramilitary Activity, Drugs—Possession | 1 | 90/30 | 90/30 | 90/30 | 90/30 | 90/30 | 90/30 | 90/30 | 90/30 | 90/30 |

* In white blocks, numbers are presumptive prison sentences expressed as a range of months.
* In gray blocks, upper number is the maximum number of custody units which may be imposed; lower number is the maximum number of jail days which may be imposed.

FIG. 1.—Oregon sentencing guidelines grid, 1989. Source: Ashford and Mosbaek (1991).

prosecutor to dismiss any other charges to assure the agreed sentence. Of course, different prosecutors may offer different deals to like-situated offenders, who may therefore plead guilty to offense $Y$ or offense $Z$. So long as the judge imposes the agreed sentence from within the applicable guideline range in every case, nominal compliance will be absolute, however disparate the sentences like-situated offenders receive.

There is considerable evidence that counsel do bargain around guidelines, which makes before-and-after-guidelines comparisons of sentencing difficult; the meaning of a plea to, say, second-degree aggravated assault may be different before and under guidelines. Comparisons of

## TABLE 1

Conviction Offenses by Seriousness Levels, 1982 and 1985 (%)

| Level | FY 1982 | January–June 1985 | Difference |
|---|---|---|---|
| XIV | .2 | .1 | − .1 |
| XIII | .5 | .3 | − .2 |
| XII | .3 | .2 | − .1 |
| XI | .1 | .2 | + .1 |
| X | .9 | .4 | − .5 |
| IX | 5.6 | 3.6 | − 2.0 |
| VIII | 1.4 | .6 | − .8 |
| VII | 3.4 | 2.0 | − 1.4 |
| VI | 4.7 | 5.7 | + 1.0 |
| V | .8 | .7 | − .1 |
| IV | 10.6 | 9.7 | − .9 |
| III | 8.3 | 10.1 | + 1.8 |
| II | 34.5 | 33.3 | − 1.2 |
| I | 28.7 | 31.1 | + 2.4 |
| Unranked | .0 | 1.9 | + 1.9 |
| Total | 100.0 | 99.9 | |

SOURCE.—Washington State Sentencing Guidelines Commission (1985), p. 3.
NOTE.—Level XIV is the most serious category (aggravated murder). Percentages do not equal 100 due to rounding. FY = fiscal year.

plea bargaining in Minnesota before and under guidelines showed a marked shift away from sentence bargaining and toward charge bargaining (Knapp 1984, chap. 6). Frase, in a quantitative analysis of Minnesota sentencing patterns through 1989, concluded, "It appears likely that whatever plea-trial disparities there were before the guidelines went into effect continued to exist in the early post-guidelines years, and still exist today; plea bargaining, and its accompanying charge and sentence disparities, is 'alive and well' in Minnesota" (1993a, p. 34).

In Washington State, as table 1 shows, there was a marked shift in offense-of-conviction patterns after the guidelines took effect. In general, convictions of offenses subject to presumptive state-prison sentences declined, and convictions of other offenses increased. Similarly, among the six lowest offense levels, in which the presumption generally is against state incarceration, there was a marked shift toward more convictions for the least serious crimes, for which the guidelines did not call for any incarceration.

In Pennsylvania, a more subtle pattern appeared which shows how guidelines can accommodate different patterns of plea bargaining. Table 2 shows patterns of guideline compliance in Pennsylvania in 1983 and 1986.[5] Pennsylvania has a unique set of guidelines that establish standard, aggravated, and mitigated ranges for every offense and, like most jurisdictions,[6] recognize various severity levels of some crimes (e.g., first-, second-, and third-degree robbery). Two patterns stand out from table 2. For most sets of offenses, fewer than half of those convicted of the most serious grade of the offense received sentences within the standard range; mitigated-range sentences were high, and downward departures were very high. Among those convicted of the lowest-grade offense in each set, from 62 to 96 percent received standard-range sentences; mitigated-range and downward-departure sentences were much less common. The most plausible explanation is that these patterns reveal the operation of diverse plea negotiation conventions within Pennsylvania. Where sentence bargaining is common, defendants plead guilty to the most serious offense charged with an understanding that the judge will impose a mitigated sentence or depart downward. Where charge bargaining is common, defendants plead to a charge which bears a presumptive penalty they will accept, and judges then impose a standard-range sentence.

In theory, plea bargains should not distort application of the federal guidelines because they are based on the defendant's "relevant conduct" as determined by a preponderance of the evidence at sentencing and not merely on the conviction offense. Nonetheless, there is substantial evidence from research sponsored by the U.S. commission (Schulhofer and Nagel 1989; U.S. Sentencing Commission 1991*b*, chap. 6; Nagel and Schulhofer 1992) and research by others (Heaney 1991) that counsel, often with tacit judicial approval, do bargain around the guidelines. Sometimes this is done by having the defendant plead guilty to an offense for which the maximum lawful sentence is less than the applicable guideline range. Sometimes it is done by counsel stipulating to facts that omit details like weapon use or victim injury or a larger quantity of drugs that require a stiffer sentence. Sometimes it is done by understandings that the judge will ignore the guidelines and that neither party will appeal. Sometimes it is done in even more

---

[5] Comparable patterns continued in 1991 although reclassification of some offenses makes exact comparisons impossible (Pennsylvania Commission on Sentencing 1993, table 4).

[6] The North Carolina Sentencing and Policy Advisory Commission (1993) has proposed that North Carolina adopt guidelines patterned on Pennsylvania's separate set of ranges for standard, mitigated, and aggravated sentences (see also Lubitz 1993).

## TABLE 2

### Statewide Conformity in Pennsylvania in 1983 and 1986, Selected Offenses (in Percent)

| Offense | Standard Range | | Aggravated Range | | Mitigated Range | | Departure Up | | Departure Down | |
|---|---|---|---|---|---|---|---|---|---|---|
| | 1983 | 1986 | 1983 | 1986 | 1983 | 1986 | 1983 | 1986 | 1983 | 1986 |
| Aggravated assault: | | | | | | | | | | |
| Felony2 | 36 | 47 | 4 | 5 | 12 | 12 | 2 | 3 | 46 | 33 |
| Felony3 | 100 | N.A. | 0 | N.A. | 0 | N.A. | 0 | N.A. | 0 | N.A. |
| Misdemeanor1 | 70 | 71 | 1 | 2 | 10 | 8 | 0 | 1 | 19 | 18 |
| Arson: | | | | | | | | | | |
| Felony1 | 13 | 33 | 0 | 4 | 10 | 16 | 0 | 3 | 77 | 44 |
| Felony2 | 62 | 48 | 0 | 8 | 11 | 10 | 5 | 1 | 22 | 33 |
| Burglary: | | | | | | | | | | |
| ogs 7 | 39 | 40 | 3 | 4 | 25 | 18 | 3 | 9 | 29 | 29 |
| ogs 6 | 49 | 56 | 3 | 4 | 14 | 13 | 4 | 5 | 31 | 22 |
| ogs 5 | 78 | 77 | 2 | 4 | 5 | 5 | 2 | 3 | 12 | 11 |
| Retail theft: | | | | | | | | | | |
| Felony3 | 62 | 65 | 2 | 2 | 9 | 12 | 1 | 0 | 25 | 20 |
| Misdemeanor1 | 91 | 96 | 0 | 0 | 4 | 1 | 0 | 0 | 5 | 2 |
| Robbery: | | | | | | | | | | |
| Felony1 | 48 | 59 | 6 | 7 | 10 | 10 | 15 | 11 | 25 | 12 |
| Felony2 | 67 | 73 | 4 | 4 | 6 | 7 | 6 | 4 | 20 | 12 |
| Felony3 | 85 | 87 | 1 | 3 | 4 | 3 | 2 | 2 | 17 | 5 |

SOURCES.—Pennsylvania Commission on Sentencing (1984), table 1; Pennsylvania Commission on Sentencing (1987), table 4.

NOTE.—ogs = offense gravity scale; N.A. = not available.

Byzantine ways.[7] Although no one has devised a credible estimate of how often the guidelines are deceptively evaded, commission-sponsored research acknowledges that bargaining distorts guideline application in at least 25 to 35 percent of cases (Nagel and Schulhofer 1992).

Keeping in mind therefore that compliance rates may mean less than appears, table 3 shows compliance and departure rates for selected recent years for Minnesota, Oregon, Pennsylvania, Washington, and the federal system. Departure rates are low in every jurisdiction, which shows that guidelines have moral force in each of them. Judges sworn to enforce the law are presumably more comfortable not "departing" from guidelines that the legislature has adopted or ratified. Not much else can be concluded from table 3. Because guideline ranges vary substantially from Minnesota's very narrow ones (e.g., for rape with no prior record: eighty-one to ninety-one months) to Pennsylvania's very broad combination of standard, aggravated, and mitigated ranges (e.g., for rape with no prior record: twenty-seven to seventy-five months), comparisons of departure rates across jurisdictions offer no comparative insights into sentencing consistency. Moreover, jurisdictions count departures in different ways. In the federal system, sentence reductions awarded defendants for "substantial assistance to the government" are not considered departures. Nor in Pennsylvania are sentences in the aggravated and mitigated ranges considered departures. Nor in Washington are sentence reductions under "First-Time Offender Waiver" and "Sex Offender Sentencing Option" provisions.

Once all the caveats are taken into account, and ignoring plea-bargaining complications, it would appear that the greatest levels of guidelines compliance occur in Oregon and Minnesota. Here too, unfortunately, things are not as simple as appears. As Frase has pointed out (1991; 1993a, p. 17 and figs. 4–6), gross compliance rates are misleading; a better inquiry would focus on departures from what to what. He shows, for example, that in Minnesota rates of mitigated dispositional departures (that is non-state-prison sentences when the guidelines specify state prison) annually represented 3–7 percent of all felony sentences between 1981 and 1989, but represented from 19 to 33 per-

---

[7] Rule 5.k.1., e.g., allows the judge to disregard the guidelines altogether if the prosecutor files a motion requesting a mitigated sentence because of the defendant's "substantial assistance to the government"; if the prosecutor's real motive is to avoid an unduly harsh sentence, observers can not know whether the claimed "substantial assistance" was provided or was useful.

TABLE 3

Departure Rates, American Guidelines Systems, Recent Years (in Percent)

| | Ad hoc Aggravated Departures | Approved Aggravated Sentences | Standard Sentences | Approved Mitigated Sentences | Ad hoc Mitigated Sentences |
|---|---|---|---|---|---|
| Federal (1991) | 1.7 | ... | 80.6 | 11.9 | 5.8 |
| Minnesota (1989)* | 6.4 | ... | 80.9 | ... | 12.7 |
| Minnesota (1989)† | 6.8 | ... | 75.3 | ... | 17.9 |
| Oregon (1991) | 3 | ... | 94 | ... | 3 |
| Pennsylvania (1991) | 2 | 2 | 74 | 8 | 13 |
| Washington (1991) | 1.6 | ... | 80.7 | 15.4 | 1.7 |

Sources.—Ashford and Mosbaek (1991), pp. 31, 37; Minnesota Sentencing Guidelines Commission (1991a), figs. 10, 13; Pennsylvania Commission on Sentencing (1993), table 4; U.S. Sentencing Commission (1992b), table 56; Washington State Sentencing Guidelines Commission (1992a).

\* Dispositional departures only (state incarceration or not).

† Durational departures (length of sentence).

cent of all presumptive prison sentences. This is because guidelines presume state imprisonment for only approximately 20 percent of convicted felons. If, therefore 7 percent of all cases are mitigated dispositional departures, they represent a third of those presumed bound for prison.

One last permutation on compliance-and-departure calculations is to disaggregate for types of offense. Pennsylvania's guidelines, for example, cover felonies and misdemeanors. Although 87 percent of Pennsylvania sentences in 1983 fell within the applicable guideline ranges, when the data are broken down, 97 percent of misdemeanor sentences were compliant but only 79 percent of felony sentences (Tonry 1988, table 8). Significantly lower compliance rates characterized escape (40 percent), arson (64 percent), involuntary deviate sexual intercourse (68 percent), and aggravated assault (70 percent) (Tonry 1988, table 9). Data for 1991 show an 85 percent overall compliance rate which breaks down much as the 1983 data did (Pennsylvania Commission on Sentencing 1993, table 9).

For all the qualifications, however, judges much more often than not impose sentences that comply with applicable guidelines.

2. *Disparity Reduction.*    Every sentencing commission claims that its guidelines have reduced sentencing disparities compared with sentencing patterns before guidelines took effect. Research on disparities, however, faces a number of formidable problems, some of which mirror the problems posed by data on compliance with guidelines. First, promulgation of guidelines may affect plea bargaining and before-and-after comparisons may be confounded if charging and bargaining practices change with the guidelines. If offenses labeled as second-degree aggravated assaults are systematically different before and under guidelines, analyses of disparities in sentencing for that offense may involve apples-and-oranges comparisons. If, for example, less serious second-degree assaults under guidelines more often result in pleas to less serious charges than before, cases resulting in convictions of second-degree assault may be more homogeneously serious and apparently reduced disparity a product of that greater homogeneity. Second, as was true during most of the last decade, if public and officials' attitudes toward offenders became more punitive over time, sentences are likely to have become harsher with or without guidelines and that rising tide complicates disparity analyses. Third, and most important, is a combined conceptual and methodological problem. Most disparity-reduction analyses use the offense severity and criminal history classifications

that are expressed in the relevant guidelines as the basis of comparisons, rather than comprehensive statistical models of sentencing before and under guidelines, and this inevitably exaggerates the extent to which disparities have been reduced. This last problem has greatest relevance to the federal guidelines; recent evaluations of the federal sentencing guidelines by the U.S. Sentencing Commission (1991*b*) and the U.S. General Accounting Office (1992) illustrate the problem, and it is discussed in some detail below.

Because the evidence is clearer in the states and because the federal guidelines present special problems for disparity analyses, I discuss them in separate subsections. First, however, some prefatory remarks about disparity studies are in order. Most of the analyses discussed are efforts to compare sentencing disparities in the first year, or few years, under a guidelines system with sentencing in some period before guidelines took effect. As time goes by, it becomes increasingly difficult, and soon impossible, to reach conclusions about disparities. After a few years, hypothetical comparisons must be made with sentencing patterns as they would have been had guidelines not been adopted. This is impossible to do. The public and political attitudes and sensibilities that led to creation of a sentencing commission would presumably have influenced sentencing patterns without guidelines. In addition, political and policy environments change over time, and these changes would also alter sentencing patterns with or without guidelines.

a. *Disparity Reduction in the States.*   There are plausible grounds for believing that the state guidelines in their early years reduced disparities. In Minnesota, where more evaluations have been conducted than in any other state, an evaluation of the first four years experience concluded, "disparity in sentencing decreased under the sentencing guidelines. This reduction in disparity is indicated by increased sentence uniformity and proportionality" (Knapp 1984, pp. v–vi). Outside evaluators agreed: Minnesota "was largely successful in reducing pre-guideline disparities in those decisions that fall within the scope of the guidelines" (Miethe and Moore 1985, p. 360). Frase, drawing on data for 1981 to 1989, concludes that "the Minnesota guidelines have achieved, and continue to achieve" most of their goals, including disparity reduction, and "have been modestly successful in achieving greater honesty and uniformity in sentencing" (Frase 1993*a*, p. 3).

No independent evaluations have been published concerning the Oregon, Pennsylvania, Washington, and Delaware guidelines, but each commission, relying on its regularly collected monitoring data, has concluded that disparities declined. The Washington commission, relying on 1985 data, concluded, "the Sentencing Reform Act has clearly increased consistency in the imprisonment decision" (Washington State Sentencing Guidelines Commission 1986, p. 7). Looking back over the first six years' experience with guidelines, the Washington commission reported, "the high degree of compliance with sentencing guidelines has reduced variability in sentencing among counties and among judges" (Washington State Sentencing Guidelines Commission 1992*b*, p. 12). On the early years of the Pennsylvania guidelines, its commission concluded for 1983, "it appears that Pennsylvania's guidelines are accomplishing their intended goal of reducing unwarranted sentencing disparity" (Pennsylvania Commission on Sentencing 1984, p. i), and for 1984, "sentences became more uniform throughout the state" (Pennsylvania Commission on Sentencing 1985, p. i). Kramer and Lubitz (1985) agreed. Finally, reporting on the first fifteen months' guidelines experience in Oregon, its commission concluded, "the guidelines have increased uniformity in sentencing considerably. Dispositional variability for offenders with identical crime seriousness and criminal history scores has been reduced by 45 percent over the variability under the pre-guidelines system" (Ashford and Mosbaek 1991, p. viii).

In Delaware, no evaluation has been published of the effects of its voluntary guidelines on disparities. However, a number of publications by the chairman (Gebelein 1991) and director (Quinn 1990, 1992) of Delaware's Sentencing Accountability Commission list "consistency and certainty" among the guidelines' goals and present data showing that the guidelines have succeeded in increasing use of incarceration for violent offenders and use of intermediate punishments for nonviolent offenders. This at least arguably supports an inference of greater consistency in Delaware sentencing.

Most likely, sentencing guidelines reduced disparities in all these jurisdictions compared with what they would have been without guidelines. Judge Frankel's complaints about lawlessness in sentencing presumably strike a responsive chord in most judges and lawyers. Because presumptive guidelines set authoritative standards for sentences where none existed, it would be astonishing if they had no effect on sentencing decisions. Even when plea bargaining, which is nearly ubiquitous in American courts, is taken into account, it is likely that the bargaining takes place in the shadow of the guidelines and that the bargained sentences are more consistent than otherwise they would have been.

Nonetheless, the evaluation research evidence on this question is less definitive than it appears or than its celebrants claim.

b. *Disparity-Reduction in the Federal System.* The evidence on federal sentencing disparities is mixed, and the best conclusion at present is that we do not know whether disparities have increased or decreased (Rhodes 1992; Weisburd 1992; Tonry 1993*b*). Although the U.S. commission, on the basis of an evaluation of the first four years experience with federal guidelines, claims "the data . . . show significant reductions in disparity" (U.S. Sentencing Commission 1991*b*, p. 419), there is reason to doubt that conclusion. Because both the U.S. commission and the U.S. General Accounting Office (GAO) devoted extensive efforts to measuring changes in sentencing disparities, I discuss the subject at some length.

For a discussion of the federal evaluation to be intelligible to readers not already familiar with the federal guidelines, some description of the system is necessary. Judges in setting sentences are supposed first to consult a schedule for the particular offense (table 4 shows the schedule for robbery) which specifies a "base offense level." Then, on the basis of various offense circumstances, such as whether the offender was armed and if so with what, whether the weapon was used and with what injurious result, and the value of any property taken, the offense level is adjusted upward or downward (almost always upward). Next the judge must determine the offender's criminal history score (mostly a measure of prior convictions). Finally the judge is to consult a two-dimensional grid (see table 5) to learn the presumptive sentence for the offender, given his adjusted offense level and his criminal history. Thus, a hypothetical offender who was convicted of robbery (base offense level in table 5: 20) of $15,000 (increase by one level) of a bank (increase by two levels), in which he possessed and discharged a firearm (increase by seven levels), causing a minor injury (increase by two levels), would, with no prior record, fall within level thirty-two and be presumed to receive a prison sentence between 121 and 151 months.

The federal guidelines, uniquely among American guideline systems, are based not on the offense to which the defendant pled guilty or of which he was convicted at trial, but on "actual offense behavior," which the commission calls "relevant conduct." The chairman and general counsel of the commission have explained that the relevant conduct approach was intended to offset efforts by prosecutors to manipulate the guidelines by dismissing charges to achieve a conviction

# TABLE 4

## Robbery, Extortion, and Blackmail

§2B3.1 Robbery

a) Base offense level: 20
b) Specific offense characteristics

1. If the property of a financial institution or post office was taken, or if the taking of such property was an object of the offense, increase by 2 levels.
2. (A) If a firearm was discharged, increase by 7 levels; (B) if a firearm was otherwise used, increase by 6 levels; (C) if a firearm was brandished, displayed, or possessed, increase by 5 levels; (D) if a dangerous weapon was otherwise used, increase by 4 levels; (E) if a dangerous weapon was brandished, displayed, or possessed, increase by 3 levels; or (F) if an express threat of death was made, increase by 2 levels.
3. If any victim sustained bodily injury, increase the offense level according to the seriousness of the injury:

   Degree of bodily injury and increase in level

   A) Bodily injury, add 2 levels
   B) Serious bodily injury, add 4 levels
   C) Permanent or life-threatening bodily injury, add 6 levels
   D) If the degree of injury is between that specified in subdivisions A and B, add 3 levels; or
   E) If the degree of injury is between that specified in subdivisions B and C, add 5 levels.

   Provided, however, that the cumulative adjustments from (2) and (3) shall not exceed 11 levels.

4. (A) If any person was abducted to facilitate commission of the offense or to facilitate escape, increase by 4 levels; or (B) if any person was physically restrained to facilitate commission of the offense or to facilitate escape, increase by 2 levels.
5. If a firearm, destructive device, or controlled substance was taken, or if the taking of such item was an object of the offense, increase by 1 level.
6. If the loss exceeded $10,000, increase the offense level as follows:

| Loss (Apply the Greatest) | Increase in Level |
| --- | --- |
| A) $10,000 or less | no increase |
| B) More than $10,000 | add 1 |
| C) More than $50,000 | add 2 |
| D) More than $250,000 | add 3 |
| E) More than $800,000 | add 4 |
| F) More than $1,500,000 | add 5 |
| G) More than $2,500,000 | add 6 |
| H) More than $5,000,000 | add 7 |

SOURCE.—U.S. Sentencing Commission (1992a).

offense that, under the guidelines, prescribed the preferred sentence (Wilkins and Steer 1990).

The complexity of the federal guidelines and their reliance on relevant conduct present nearly insuperable difficulties for a before-and-after disparity analysis. Information concerning drug quantity or purity or the presence of an unused firearm or the occurrence of uncharged crimes, all of which are "relevant conduct" and have incremental punitive significance, was often not material before the guidelines took effect. Consequently, there was no reason for probation officers to obtain or record such information, and for periods before November 1987 it is not systematically and reliably available. The GAO observed, "significant differences in much of the offender data available made it difficult to reliably match and compare groups of preguidelines and guidelines offenders. Preguideline offender data focused on personal information, such as socioeconomic status and family and community ties, that was supposed to be irrelevant under the guidelines in all or most cases. Conversely, most of the detailed data available on guidelines offenders, such as role in the offense, were not available for preguidelines cases" (1992, p. 10).

The commission and GAO approached disparities in two ways—by asking participants whether they believed disparities had been reduced and by conducting sophisticated quantitative analyses. All that can be learned from the interviews and surveys is that prosecutors and probation officers were likelier to believe that disparities had been reduced than were judges and defense lawyers. Table 6 shows answers to questions about reduced disparities from GAO interviews in four sites, commission interviews in twelve sites, and a commission mail survey.

Table 6 shows that most judges and defense counsel did not believe disparities to have been reduced (significant and slight majorities of prosecutors and probation officers disagreed). An earlier analysis of the guidelines by the Federal Courts Study Committee (1990) reported that many judges and the committee itself believed that disparities had increased.

The quantitative analyses were also inconclusive. The GAO's conclusion, based both on examination of the U.S. commission's statistical analyses and reanalysis of the commission's data is that "limitations and inconsistencies in the data available for preguidelines and guideline offenders made it impossible to determine how effective the sentencing guidelines have been in reducing overall sentencing disparity" (1992, p. 10).

## TABLE 5

## U.S. Sentencing Commission Sentencing Table (in Months of Imprisonment)

| Offense level | Criminal History Category (Criminal History Points) | | | | | |
|---|---|---|---|---|---|---|
| | I (0 or 1) | II (2 or 3) | III (4,5,6) | IV (7,8,9) | V (10,11,12) | VI (13 or more) |
| 1 | 0–6 | 0–6 | 0–6 | 0–6 | 0–6 | 0–6 |
| 2 | 0–6 | 0–6 | 0–6 | 0–6 | 0–6 | 1–7 |
| 3 | 0–6 | 0–6 | 0–6 | 0–6 | 2–8 | 3–9 |
| 4 | 0–6 | 0–6 | 0–6 | 2–8 | 4–10 | 6–12 |
| 5 | 0–6 | 0–6 | 1–7 | 4–10 | 6–12 | 9–15 |
| 6 | 0–6 | 1–7 | 2–8 | 6–12 | 9–15 | 12–18 |
| 7 | 1–7 | 2–8 | 4–10 | 8–14 | 12–18 | 15–21 |
| 8 | 2–8 | 4–10 | 6–12 | 10–16 | 15–21 | 18–24 |
| 9 | 4–10 | 6–12 | 8–14 | 12–18 | 18–24 | 21–27 |
| 10 | 6–12 | 8–14 | 10–16 | 15–21 | 21–27 | 24–30 |
| 11 | 8–14 | 10–16 | 12–18 | 18–24 | 24–30 | 27–33 |
| 12 | 10–16 | 12–18 | 15–21 | 21–27 | 27–33 | 30–37 |
| 13 | 12–18 | 15–21 | 18–24 | 24–30 | 30–37 | 33–41 |
| 14 | 15–21 | 18–24 | 21–27 | 27–33 | 33–41 | 37–46 |
| 15 | 18–24 | 21–27 | 24–30 | 30–37 | 37–46 | 41–51 |
| 16 | 21–27 | 24–30 | 27–33 | 33–41 | 41–51 | 46–57 |
| 17 | 24–30 | 27–33 | 30–37 | 37–46 | 46–57 | 51–63 |
| 18 | 27–33 | 30–37 | 33–41 | 41–51 | 51–63 | 57–71 |
| 19 | 30–37 | 33–41 | 37–46 | 46–57 | 57–71 | 63–78 |

| | | | | | | |
|---|---|---|---|---|---|---|
| 20 | 33–41 | 37–46 | 41–51 | 51–63 | 63–78 | 70–87 |
| 21 | 37–46 | 41–51 | 46–57 | 57–71 | 70–87 | 77–96 |
| 22 | 41–51 | 46–57 | 51–63 | 63–78 | 77–96 | 84–105 |
| 23 | 46–57 | 51–63 | 57–71 | 70–87 | 84–105 | 92–115 |
| 24 | 51–63 | 57–71 | 63–78 | 77–96 | 92–115 | 100–125 |
| 25 | 57–71 | 63–78 | 70–87 | 84–105 | 100–125 | 110–137 |
| 26 | 63–78 | 70–87 | 78–97 | 92–115 | 110–137 | 120–150 |
| 27 | 70–87 | 78–97 | 87–108 | 100–125 | 120–150 | 130–162 |
| 28 | 78–97 | 87–108 | 97–121 | 110–137 | 130–162 | 140–175 |
| 29 | 87–108 | 97–121 | 108–135 | 121–151 | 140–175 | 151–188 |
| 30 | 97–121 | 108–135 | 121–151 | 135–168 | 151–188 | 168–210 |
| 31 | 108–135 | 121–151 | 135–168 | 151–188 | 168–210 | 188–235 |
| 32 | 121–151 | 135–168 | 151–188 | 168–210 | 188–235 | 210–262 |
| 33 | 135–168 | 151–188 | 168–210 | 188–235 | 210–262 | 235–293 |
| 34 | 151–188 | 168–210 | 188–235 | 210–262 | 235–293 | 262–327 |
| 35 | 168–210 | 188–235 | 210–262 | 235–293 | 262–327 | 292–365 |
| 36 | 188–235 | 210–262 | 235–293 | 262–327 | 292–365 | 324–405 |
| 37 | 210–262 | 235–293 | 262–327 | 292–365 | 324–405 | 360–life |
| 38 | 235–293 | 262–327 | 292–365 | 324–405 | 360–life | 360–life |
| 39 | 262–327 | 292–365 | 324–405 | 360–life | 360–life | 360–life |
| 40 | 292–365 | 324–405 | 360–life | 360–life | 360–life | 360–life |
| 41 | 324–405 | 360–life | 360–life | 360–life | 360–life | 360–life |
| 42 | 360–life | 360–life | 360–life | 360–life | 360–life | 360–life |
| 43 | life | life | life | life | life | life |

SOURCE.—U.S. Sentencing Commission (1992a).

## TABLE 6

Percentage of Practitioners Who Believe Unwarranted Disparities Have Been Reduced

|  | Judges | Prosecutors | Federal Defenders | Private Attorneys | Probation Officers |
|---|---|---|---|---|---|
| USSC interviews | 50 | 76 | 41 | 32 | 59 |
| USSC mail survey | 32 | 51 | 11 | 19 | 52 |
| GAO interviews | 20 | 83 | (————37————) | | 50 |

SOURCES.—For USSC interviews, U.S. Sentencing Commission (1991*b*), table 27; for USSC mail survey, U.S. Sentencing Commission (1991*b*), table 28; for GAO interviews, U.S. General Accounting Office (1992), table 3.

NOTE.—USSC = U.S. Sentencing Commission; GAO = U.S. General Accounting Office.

The commission would put a different gloss on its and GAO's findings on disparity reduction. The GAO entitled its report "Sentencing Guidelines—Central Questions Remain Unanswered." Commission Chairman Wilkins urged instead, "Sentencing Guidelines: Disparity Reduced, but Some Questions Remain" (GAO 1992, p. 182).

The insurmountable problem that comparable pre- and postguidelines data are not available served as the basis for GAO's agnosticism, though it noted that commission analyses showed reduction in disparities for some selected offenses. The GAO's own analysis showed that "unwarranted disparity continued" in relation to offenders' race, gender, employment status, age, and marital status (1992, p. 12).

Because of data limitations, the commission confined its empirical analyses of disparity reduction to four categories of robbery (with no or moderate criminal history, with and without a weapon), two categories of embezzlement ($10,000–$20,000 loss, $20,000–$40,000 loss), heroin trafficking (100–400 grams), and cocaine trafficking (500–2000 grams). Sample sizes were tiny (preguidelines samples were 17, 13, 25, 18, 27, 36, 40, and 44 cases; postguidelines samples were 80, 38, 57, 24, 56, 71, 72, and 81 cases). Sentences from downward departures for "substantial assistance to the government" were excluded from the analysis. For each of the eight offenses examined, sentences "pre" and "post" guidelines (both sentences announced and sentences "expected to be served") were characterized in terms of means, medians, and the range in months within which the middle 80 percent of cases fell. The breadth of the ranges of the middle 80 percent of sentences declined for all eight offenses, though for five of those offenses the decline was not statistically significant. As commentators have stressed, the "not statistically significant" caveat means that the apparent reduction in disparity in five of the eight offenses studied may result from random chance and have nothing to do with the guidelines (Rhodes 1992; Weisburd 1992).

There are, unhappily, five reasons why even these modest findings are suspect. The first two are the inherent data limitations mentioned earlier and the tiny sample sizes. The third is that the commission's own process evaluation and several other studies (Schulhofer and Nagel 1989; Nagel and Schulhofer 1992) suggest that "substantial assistance" notions are commonly used to permit judges to impose sentences less severe than guideline sentences that the judge and the prosecutor consider too severe. In fiscal year 1991, of all disposed cases, 11.9 percent were downward departures for substantial assistance; 21 percent of drug offense dispositions were substantial assistance departures (U.S. Sentencing Commission 1992b, table 55). Since judges are completely free of the guidelines once a substantial assistance motion is filed, opportunity for disparity is great. Excluding those departures from the disparity analysis inevitably understates the degree of variation in sentences, especially for drug cases.

The fourth problem is that two of the offenses examined, heroin and cocaine trafficking, became subject to mandatory minimum five-year sentences after the cases in the preguidelines sample were decided. Thus any apparent reduction in disparity for those offenses is likelier to result from passage of the mandatory minimum legislation than from implementation of the guidelines.

The fifth, and most important problem, however, is conceptual. "Unwarranted disparity" is not defined in the Sentencing Reform Act of 1984, and the commission selected a self-serving definition that inevitably exaggerated disparity reduction. Much research on sentencing disparities uses multivariate analyses and mathematical models to describe sentencing patterns before and after a policy or law change (e.g., Blumstein et al. 1983, chap. 2). Observed changes, assuming they are statistically significant and theoretically plausible, are then attributed to the change. The commission, instead, defined unwarranted disparities solely in terms of its own guidelines offense and criminal history characteristics.

The commission's approach is misleading for two reasons. First, because federal law and guidelines now set very precise standards for sentences in relation to offenses and criminal history, and the previous law had only maximum authorized sanctions and a few mandatory minimums, it would be astonishing if the new guidelines had no effect on sentencing patterns. Previously there were no targets to shoot at but under guidelines there were. Unless judges completely ignored the guidelines, sentences should on average have become closer to the targets. Second, however, the commission's approach might completely miss increases in disparity in relation to variables other than current offense and criminal history characteristics.

Doob (1993), for example, hypothesizes a situation in which pre-guideline sentencing decisions were premised solely on rehabilitative considerations and, in light of the relevant criteria, perfectly consistent. By using its culpability-based offense and criminal history categories to measure disparities, and superimposing them on the preguidelines data, the commission's methodology would miss the prior perfect consistency (by reference to different criteria) and most likely and unsurprisingly conclude that sentences were less disparate by its criteria after guidelines than before.

Suppose, for another example, that before the guidelines took effect, employed offenders with dependent children typically received lighter sentences because of judges' concern for the effects of a prison sentence on spouses, children, and household stability (as Wheeler, Mann, and Sarat [1991] suggest). The federal guidelines, which forbid judges to take account of employment prospects or family status, may have made the effects of employment plus dependents less consistent than before the guidelines; some judges foreseeably will circumvent the guidelines to achieve sentences that appear to them just and that follow the previous conventions, while others will adhere to the guidelines. Thus, in relation to employment and family status, sentencing under the guidelines will be more, not less, disparate than under the old system. By defining and looking for "unwarranted disparities" as it did, the commission undertook an impoverished look at disparity that was likely to produce a finding that disparities declined.

These methodological, measurement, and conceptual problems increased the odds that the commission would find that unwarranted disparities have declined. That statistically significant findings of reduced disparities were achieved for only three of eight selected crimes suggests that disparities have not declined very much or at all, or, as GAO more cautiously concluded, that decline cannot be demonstrated.

Absence of evidence is not, of course, evidence of absence. My best guess is that the state commissions are right and that sentencing in their states became more consistent and that disparities declined. It is harder to be sure about the federal guidelines because their complexity, rigidity, and severity have fostered such wholesale circumvention that much case disposition has been forced below ground, and it is unclear how reliable federal data are on the characteristics of disposed cases.

3. *Sentencing Patterns.* Most commissions have adopted "prescriptive" guidelines that are intended to change existing sentencing patterns (rather than "descriptive" guidelines intended to reproduce, with greater consistency, past sentencing practices). Minnesota and Washington sought to increase use of imprisonment for violent offenses and to decrease it for property offenses and assert that their monitoring data show that those objectives were achieved in the guidelines' early years (Knapp [1984], p. 31; Washington State Sentencing Guidelines Commission [1986], fig. 1; these analyses are discussed in some detail in Tonry [1988], pp. 306–9). Oregon had the same goals and found that the proportion of offenders convicted of felonies against persons who received state prison sentences increased from 34 percent before guidelines to 48 percent under guidelines while the proportion of property felons sentenced to state prisons declined from 19 to 9 percent; imprisonment for sex abuse felonies tripled from 13 to 42 percent (Ashford and Mosbaek 1991, pp. viii, 11). Pennsylvania sought to increase sentencing severity and appears to have succeeded; for most serious crimes, the proportion of convicted offenders incarcerated and their average minimum sentences before parole eligibility increased after the guidelines took effect (Pennsylvania Commission on Sentencing 1987, table 19). In Delaware, published monitoring data are less detailed than elsewhere but, as figure 2 shows, after the guidelines took effect the proportion of violent offenders among Delaware prisoners increased and the proportion of nonviolent offenders decreased (Gebelein 1991, p. 12). The U.S. Sentencing Commission also attempted to increase sentencing severity by decreasing use of probation, increasing the proportion of offenders incarcerated, and greatly increasing sentence lengths; it succeeded on all counts (U.S. Sentencing Commission 1991*b*; Tonry 1993*b*).

The effects of changes in sentencing patterns appear to vary with the abruptness of the new policies' departure from past practices. Where that change is modest, as in the initial guidelines in Pennsylvania and Minnesota, practices appear likely to revert to their prior pat-

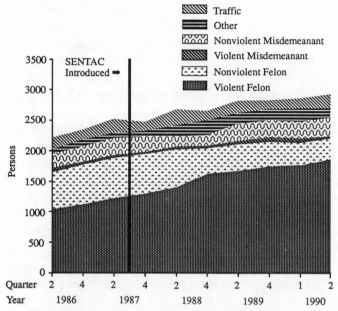

FIG. 2.—Composition of Delaware's incarcerated population before and after effective date of SENTAC guidelines. Source: Gebelein (1991).

terns once the system has settled down. Where the change is sharp and the new sentencing policies are much more severe than past practice, there has been less evidence of reversion.

Published analyses are available from three jurisdictions— Minnesota, Washington, and the federal system—that describe system acceptance or rejection of substantial changes to sentencing policies. In Minnesota, amidst the commission's general policy of emphasizing prison use for violent offenses and deemphasizing its use for property offenses, major controversies included decisions to reduce the use of imprisonment for property offenders and to prescribe lengthy prison terms for sex offenders, especially for intrafamilial sex offenders. Frase (1993a) tells both stories; in each, the commission's policy changes were resisted.

Prosecutors actively resisted the policy decision to preclude imprisonment for most property offenders. Under the initial guidelines, minor property offenders were prison bound only if they had accumulated many prior convictions. A common prosecutorial strategy, in response, was to build criminal histories. A shoplifter might, for example, contrary to an earlier practice of taking a plea to one offense with other charges being dismissed, be required to plead guilty to five offenses; the next time that offender was convicted of shoplifting, his five prior convictions would produce a presumptive prison sentence. The commission responded by changing the criminal history scoring rules so as to offset the bargaining pattern change (Parent 1988). This time prosecutors responded by insisting on guilty pleas to multiple charges and arguing that the sentence for the last contemporaneous plea must take account of the defendant's minutes-earlier prior convictions. In *State v. Hernandez*, 311 N.W. 2d 478 (1981), the Minnesota Supreme Court upheld that practice and the prosecutors won. By 1983, the proportion of property offenders imprisoned had risen to preguidelines levels and continued to rise through 1989 (Frase 1993*a*, p. 38).

The intrafamilial sex offense story is less tortured, but the moral is no less clear. Responding to heightened public concern, the commission prescribed prison sentences for most persons convicted of sexual offenses, regardless of the offender's prior record. Child sex abuse cases are especially complicated because of practitioners' recognition of many offenders' psychopathology, concern for maintaining households, and fear of making children feel guilty for having caused a parent's imprisonment and broken up the family. As a result, departure rates for child sex abuse cases have been high throughout the guidelines period and in 1987, despite the guidelines presumption of lengthy prison terms, the imprisonment rate for intrafamilial sex abuse cases was only 40 percent and the rate for nonfamilial statutory rape cases was only 58 percent (Frase 1993*a*). Frase's analysis does not demonstrate that sentences for sex offenders did not increase; they did, for those offenders for whom downward departures did not occur. Minnesota's sex-offender policies thus increased disparities among persons convicted of child sexual abuse offenses but, among those imprisoned, increased the severity of penalties.

Boerner has shown how changes in guideline severity adopted in Washington were quickly followed by increases in average sentence severity. Because criminal code changes that increase penalties must be made prospectively, for constitutional reasons, during transition periods grandfathered cases must be sentenced under the earlier, less harsh, standards and new cases under the new standards, allowing for examination of the effects of the new standards. Figure 3 shows sentencing patterns from 1988 to 1992 for second degree burglaries committed before and after the effective date of guideline amendments that divided second degree burglary into residential and nonresidential

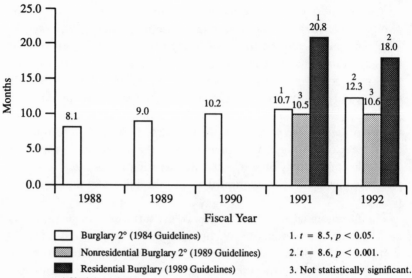

FIG. 3.—Average sentence length, burglary. Source: Boerner (1993, fig. 5)

types and increased penalties for each. Average sentences for residential burglary increased substantially, while sentences for grandfathered cases (both nonresidential and residential) increased only slightly. Figure 4 shows comparable data for sentencing in first degree statutory rape and first degree "rape of child" cases from 1987 to 1992, which offenses Boerner writes are comparable because code changes in 1988 that increased penalties also relabeled statutory rape as "rape of a child;

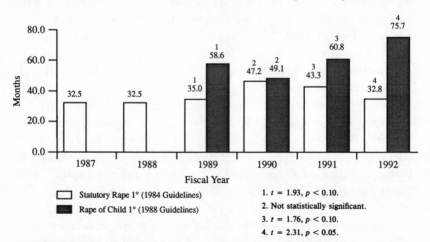

FIG. 4.—Average sentence length, statutory rape and rape of child. Source: Boerner (1993, fig. 7).

the behavior covered by each of the degrees is essentially the same" (Boerner 1993, p. 25). Sentences for grandfathered cases under the original 1984 guidelines fluctuated but remained essentially the same through 1992, while cases sentenced under the 1988 guideline revision were substantially higher.

Boerner gives many such examples, all of which tend to demonstrate that changes in guidelines sentence severity were quickly followed by increases in the severity of sentences for affected offenses. As always, the data tell less than an omniscient observer would want to know. Because Boerner's data are average sentences received by incarcerated offenders sentenced for the designated offenses, it is impossible to know whether and how often the harsher sentences were avoided by plea bargains in which the defendant was allowed to plead guilty to a less serious offense than would have happened before the guideline revisions took effect. It would, however, require an unrealistically cynical hypothesis thereby to explain away all or most of the apparent increases in sentencing severity, leaving the conclusion that Washington's guideline changes did indeed significantly increase sentencing severity.

If the Washington data leave any doubt that sentencing policy changes through guidelines can alter sentencing practices, the U.S. Sentencing Commission experience should remove that doubt. The commission chose greatly to increase the proportion of offenders sentenced to imprisonment and greatly to increase the average lengths of prison sentences. It succeeded in both objectives.

The commission's evaluation showed that overall the percentage of convicted federal offenders sentenced to probation declined from 52 percent in late 1984 to 35 percent in June 1990. The commission isolates only three offenses for separate study (drugs, robbery, and "economic offenses"); use of nonincarcerative sentences fell sharply for each.

Reduction in the use of probation as a sentence was even greater than the commission reports. The commission's evaluation overstates the use of probation, presumably by counting split sentences that include some period of incarceration as a condition of "probation." The commission's 1991 annual report (U.S. Sentencing Commission 1992b, table 23) shows that only 14.5 percent of offenders in 1991 received "probation only" sentences. Although the evaluation does not report probation-only sentences before the guidelines took effect, some insight can be gained by comparing 1985 probation-only rates for selected offenses with 1991 rates. The 1985 data were reported by the commission in 1987. The first number in each of the following pairs is the 1985 probation-only rate; the second is the 1991 rate: robbery—18 percent, 0.3 percent; fraud—59 percent, 22 percent; immigration—41 percent, 16.8 percent (U.S. Sentencing Commission 1987, p. 68; 1992*b*, table 3).

The severity of prison sentences likewise increased. The commission reports that the mean "expected to be served" sentence for all offenders increased from twenty-four months in July 1984 to forty-six months in June 1990 (1991*b*, p. 378). Prison sentences for drug offenses increased by 248 percent from 1984 to 1990 and from an average sixty months for robbery in 1984 to seventy-eight months in 1990. Although the commission's evaluation does not discuss other offenses, most offense categories would probably demonstrate stark increases.

The record, though not uncomplicated, seems to show that commissions through their policy choices can alter sentencing patterns substantially. That this can happen despite deep judicial dislike of the new policies is illustrated by the federal experience in which several judges have resigned rather than impose sentences they believe are unduly harsh, in which a California judge in tears imposed a lengthy sentence because the guidelines required it and then resigned, and in which one not unrepresentative appellate judge voted to uphold an aggregate 140 years imprisonment for four defendants, only to observe, "these sentences defy reason, but as I have already noted—such is our system" (Bright 1993).

4. *Racial and Gender Differences.*   Every sentencing commission has included reduction or elimination of racial and gender discrimination in sentencing among its goals (e.g., Minnesota Sentencing Guidelines Commission 1980), and most claim to a considerable extent to have succeeded. The Minnesota commission's three-year evaluation concluded that racial differences in sentencing declined under guidelines; nonetheless, minority defendants were likelier than whites to be imprisoned when the presumptive sentence prescribed non-state-imprisonment, minority defendants received longer sentences than similarly categorized whites, and men received longer prison sentences than similarly categorized women (Knapp 1984, p. 61). Miethe and Moore (1985, pp. 352–55), using the same data but more sophisticated statistical techniques, agreed that overall racial and gender differences declined under guidelines. Frase (1993*a*, pp. 23–31), using the commis-

sion's monitoring data through 1989, also agreed that racial and gender differences diminished compared with preguidelines practices but painted a more complex picture. Controlling for current offense and criminal history, women continued to receive gentler handling; they were less than half as likely to be subject to aggravated departures and more likely to benefit from mitigated departures. Black defendants had equal or higher aggravated departure rates compared with whites in each of five years studied and lower mitigated departure rates in all five years.

Washington's evaluation revealed similar patterns. The initial evaluation found an overall decline in racial differences in sentencing but that "substantial racial and gender disparity was found in the use of sentencing alternatives"; whites were almost twice as likely as blacks to benefit from special mitigating provisions for first-time and some sex offenders (Washington State Sentencing Guidelines Commission 1987, p. 59). In a ten-year review of Washington sentencing reforms, although concluding that racial and gender differences had diminished, the commission in 1992 acknowledged "significant gender and ethnic differences in the application of options" to incarceration (Washington State Sentencing Guidelines Commission 1992b, p. 12).

The Oregon racial data from the first fifteen months' guidelines experience are difficult to disentangle because most analyses compare whites and "minorities," a category that includes blacks, Hispanics, Asians, and Native Americans, groups whose patterns of criminality vary substantially. In addition, most of the data are presented in tabular form without controls or multivariate analyses to take account of systematic differences in the kinds of crimes and criminal histories that characterize various groups. Noting that the data are crude, the following can be observed. First, the overall probability of state incarceration for whites fell from 17 percent before guidelines to 12 percent under guidelines. For minorities, the rate fell slightly from 23.9 percent to 23 percent (with six-point decreases for blacks and Asians and three- and five-point increases for Native Americans and Hispanics; Ashford and Mosbaek [1991], p. 47). Whites were slightly less likely than minority defendants to receive upward dispositional departures, slightly more likely to receive downward dispositional departures, and much more likely to benefit from an "optional probation" alternatives program (Ashford and Mosbaek 1991, pp. 49–52). As whites are to minority defendants in Oregon sentencing, so women are to men: women were less likely to receive upward departures, more likely to receive downward departures, and more likely to be sentenced to optional probation.

Curiously, although the U.S. Sentencing Commission's self-evaluation and the GAO reanalyses of the commission's data involved much more sophisticated data-analytic methods than any of the state evaluations, the research design precluded any overall conclusions about racial and gender disparities. The commission's basic study, recall, was of disparity before and under guidelines using the commission's offense severity and criminal history schemes as the measure of consistency, but focusing on eight categories of cases involving small numbers in each category. As a result, the rote conclusion (U.S. Sentencing Commission 1991a, pp. 302, 324) was that "cell sizes were inadequate to test or no significant relationships were found with respect to . . . race, gender, age." Exclusion from the analysis of departures for "substantial assistance to the government" leaves open the possibility that those mitigated sentences are skewed in terms of race or gender. In addition, as with the general disparity analysis, there is no basis for generalizing from the specific offenses the commission analyzed to federal offenders generally (U.S. General Accounting Office 1992, p. 64).

Because of the small sample sizes, the numbers of mitigated departures were insignificant, and no meaningful analyses of race and gender effects in departures could be made. In relation to disparities within the guidelines (i.e., whether some racial or gender groups are likelier to receive sentences at the top or bottom of the guideline ranges), the commission found that "race was found to be statistically significant across all offense categories [but] . . . only slight variations between sentencing of black and white offenders were found." However, "women were statistically more likely to receive sentences at the bottom of the range" (U.S. Sentencing Commission 1991a, p. 324).

The GAO, in a more sophisticated analysis, concluded that "blacks were more likely than whites to receive sentences at the bottom or top of the guidelines range rather than in the middle" and that "females were twice as likely (i.e., 1.91 times as likely, to be exact) as males to receive sentences at the bottom rather than in the middle of the range" (U.S. General Accounting Office 1992, p. 92).

The commission somewhat formalistically disagreed with the GAO's depiction of sentencing differences within guidelines as disparity, arguing that Congress authorized guideline ranges in which the maximum sentence was 25 percent longer than the minimum and accordingly by definition there could be no "unwarranted disparities," on racial or any other grounds, among sentences within applicable ranges (U.S. General Accounting Office 1992). Probably the fairest summary of the federal evaluations is that they are inconclusive on the effect of guidelines on racial disparities and consistent with state evaluations in finding gender disparities in favor of women.

The available evidence thus shows that guidelines have ameliorated but not eliminated racial and gender disparities in sentencing and that whites more often than nonwhites, and women than men, benefit from alternatives to incarceration and mitigated departures from guidelines. The difficulties in all this are that racial sentencing comparisons are confounded by systematic socioeconomic differences between races and that both racial and gender comparisons are confounded by group differences in criminality. Because blacks for reasons both of racial discrimination and social disadvantage tend to be likelier than whites to participate in common law crimes and to accumulate criminal records, guidelines based primarily on the current crime and the past criminal record in the nature of things treat blacks more severely than whites (and a parallel pattern distinguishes men from women). These differences in crime participation and criminal history accumulation are well known and are illustrated in tables 7 and 8 from Oregon's fifteen-month evaluation. Classification of offenders by ethnicity and criminal history ("A" is highest, "I" is lowest) shows more blacks than whites, and more men than women, with extensive criminal histories.

In order to combat racial disparities in sentencing, most sentencing commissions have forbidden judges to give weight in sentencing to socioeconomic factors such as education, employment, and family stability which are known to be correlated with race, in order not systematically to disadvantage members of minority groups. Unfortunately, the "neutral" criteria of current offense and criminal history have the same effect. Since most guideline disparity analyses control for criminal history, they define away much of the differentially adverse sentencing experienced by members of minority groups as "not disparity."

5. *Prison Populations.* The Oregon, Washington, Minnesota, and federal commissions operated under enabling legislation which directed them to give substantial consideration to the impact of their guidelines on correctional resources, which was generally interpreted to refer to prison beds and capacity. The federal commission ignored that charge, despite unambiguous language in Section 994(g) of the Sentencing Re-

## TABLE 7
### Criminal History Classification by Race, Oregon (in Percent)

| Criminal History Category | Race | | | | | Total |
|---|---|---|---|---|---|---|
| | White | Hispanic | Black | Native American | Asian | |
| A | .5 | .4 | 3.9 | .8 | .0 | .7 |
| B | 1.8 | 1.3 | 4.9 | 1.7 | .0 | 1.9 |
| C | 5.6 | 3.2 | 12.7 | 9.9 | 6.9 | 5.9 |
| D | 3.1 | 2.0 | 6.0 | 11.6 | .0 | 3.3 |
| E | 8.7 | 3.6 | 8.3 | 7.4 | .0 | 7.9 |
| F | 13.4 | 9.4 | 13.0 | 22.3 | 10.3 | 12.9 |
| G | 21.0 | 17.4 | 15.3 | 18.2 | 20.7 | 20.0 |
| H | 14.9 | 9.1 | 11.7 | 17.4 | 3.4 | 13.8 |
| I | 30.9 | 53.6 | 24.4 | 10.7 | 58.6 | 33.5 |
| Total | 100.0 | 100.0 | 100.0 | 100.0 | 100.0 | 100.0 |
| Number | 4,300 | 834 | 386 | 121 | 29 | 5,670 |

SOURCE.—Ashford and Mosbaek (1991), p. 49.
NOTE.—Cases where criminal history is missing have been excluded; $p < .0001$.

## TABLE 8
### Criminal History Classification by Gender, Oregon (in Percent)

| Criminal History Category | Gender | | Total |
|---|---|---|---|
| | Male | Female | |
| A | .9 | .0 | .7 |
| B | 2.1 | .4 | 1.9 |
| C | 6.7 | 1.4 | 5.9 |
| D | 3.7 | 2.0 | 3.4 |
| E | 8.7 | 4.2 | 8.1 |
| F | 13.3 | 12.4 | 13.2 |
| G | 20.3 | 17.5 | 19.9 |
| H | 13.3 | 16.7 | 13.8 |
| I | 31.0 | 45.4 | 33.1 |
| Total | 100.0 | 100.0 | 100.0 |
| Number | 5,200 | 910 | 6,110 |

SOURCE.—Ashford and Mosbaek (1991), p. 56.
NOTE.—Cases where criminal history is missing have been excluded; $p < .0001$.

form Act of 1984: "The sentencing guidelines prescribed under this chapter shall be formulated to minimize the likelihood that the federal prison population will exceed the capacity of the federal prisons," and promulgated guidelines that were predicted to triple the federal prison population within a decade (U.S. Sentencing Commission 1987, chap. 7). The other states heeded their charges and, rarities among American states, as figure 5 shows, managed to restrain population growth and hold prison populations within capacity for extended periods (and Oregon to the present). In Minnesota and Washington, sensational crimes in each state in 1989 provoked anticrime hysteria, and the legislatures increased penalties for many crimes; both prison populations thereafter rose rapidly (Frase 1993*b*; Lieb 1993).

Nonetheless, the experience in Washington, Oregon, and Minnesota shows that sentencing commissions and their guidelines can adopt policy approaches that treat prison beds as scarce and expensive resources and that those policies can succeed in constraining prison population growth and associated public spending.

## B. *Effectiveness as Administrative Agencies*

Were there not a federal sentencing commission, no one would question that Judge Frankel's proposed new approach to formulation of sentencing policy has been markedly successful, both substantively and institutionally. In 1978, just a few years after the appearance of Judge Frankel's book, *Criminal Sentences: Law without Order*, and long before passage of the Federal Sentencing Reform Act of 1984, Minnesota and Pennsylvania enacted sentencing commission legislation and, in 1980 and 1982, respectively, guidelines took effect. Since then, guidelines developed by sentencing commissions have taken effect in Washington, Oregon, Louisiana, Tennessee, and Kansas. Commissions are at work in Ohio, North Carolina, and elsewhere.

Of guidelines now in effect, those in Minnesota, Pennsylvania, Washington, and Oregon have been in operation long enough that evidence concerning their operation is available. The preceding subsection showed that commissions have in significant degree achieved many of their substantive policy goals. State commissions have also achieved Judge Frankel's institutional purposes. They have established and sustained specialized technical competence. In all four states, the commissions have survived to serve as their state's principal forum for sentencing policy proposals. Each has developed a monitoring system and has from time to time considered or implemented guidelines changes to

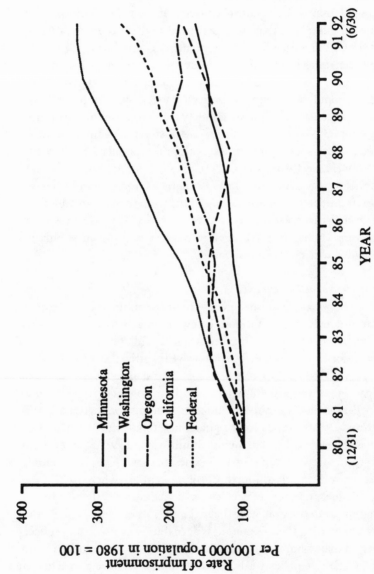

FIG. 5.—Rate of prison population growth for selected states and the federal system, 1980–92. The top solid line is the rate for California; the bottom solid line is the rate for Minnesota. Sources: Bureau of Justice Statistics (1992a, table 2; 1992b, table 1); Flanagan and Maguire (1992, table 6.72).

respond to implementation problems revealed by monitoring programs. Each conducts regular training sessions. Each publishes annual statistical reports. Minnesota's commission in 1984 prepared the most sophisticated evaluation of a state sentencing initiative ever published (Knapp 1984). All four are wrestling with current policy issues. Pennsylvania, in particular, is now considering a major overhaul of its guidelines and some of their underlying policy premises (Pennsylvania Commission on Sentencing 1993, pp. 3–7). Oregon and Washington are both working on guidelines for misdemeanants and for non-state-prison-bound felons (Bogan 1991; Washington State Sentencing Guidelines Commission 1992*b*). Minnesota has been working for years on nonincarceration guidelines, drug-offense policy, and day fines (e.g., Minnesota Sentencing Guidelines Commission 1991*b*, 1992).

The state commissions have served to some degree to insulate sentencing policy from short-term emotionalism and law-and-order sloganeering. Sentencing policies did eventually change in both Minnesota and Washington to reflect the law-and-order politics of the 1990s; perhaps it is no coincidence that penalties in both states increased substantially in 1989, only months after Willie Horton's voter-galvanizing appearance in the 1988 presidential campaign. In Minnesota, the anticrime reaction was so strong that the legislature amended the enabling legislation to make "public safety" the primary factor in setting sentencing standards and, while allowing some role for resource concerns, provided that resources should no longer warrant substantial consideration (Frase 1993*b*).

No legislative delegation of rule-making authority to administrative agencies can forever or completely insulate policy from partisan political influence, nor should it. Powerful and determined political forces can overrule an agency's policies directly through legislation or indirectly through informal political pressure or appointment of new commissioners committed to different policies. In the short term, however, especially in the face of less powerful or less determined opposition, administrative agencies can buffer policy from episodic emotions and sometimes can protect elected officials from constituent pressures. Especially in the past dozen years in the United States, criminal justice policies have been highly contentious. Political pressures and emotions tend to support increased penalties for currently topical crimes and to provide little support for comprehensive unemotional approaches to crime control policies. Where the political will exists to try to buffer sentencing policies from short-term emotions, the experience in the states shows that commissions can provide that buffer—so long as the supportive political will survives.

The state sentencing commissions also adopted comprehensive systems approaches to sentencing policy. Minnesota, Washington, and Oregon all fitted their sentencing policies to available (or foreseeable) prison resources, taking the theretofore unknown but unassailable position that responsible policy-making requires that states face up to the programmatic and financial implications of the sentencing policies they adopt. Policy can be tailored to fit resources, or resources can be expanded to meet projected needs; one way or the other a "resource constraint" policy requires conscious and responsible decision making, a practice conspicuously absent in the 1980s in most American states, where punishments were repeatedly raised without regard to resources and foreseeably resulted in unprecedented prison overcrowding and federal court intervention. As a result of the resource constraint policy, each of the commissions had consciously to reduce penalties for some crimes when pressures arose to increase penalties for others.

To this point, the experience of the federal and state commissions is institutionally similar. Where the experience differs is in the quality of the guidelines the state commissions produced, their successful efforts to win (at least grudging) support from judges and other practitioners, their success in achieving an institutional esprit among commission staff, and their abilities to insulate policy from politics at least for a time (e.g., Tonry 1991, 1993b). Three points of difference stand out.

First, unlike the federal guidelines, which remain deeply unpopular with judges and lawyers six years after their effective date, the guidelines in Washington, Delaware, Pennsylvania, Minnesota, and Oregon are generally supported by criminal court practitioners. In no state is there heated debate about the guidelines' desirability and legitimacy and in no state is there organized opposition to them.

Second, as noted earlier, until legislative changes in Washington and Minnesota led to toughened guidelines, those states successfully maintained prison populations within available capacity and maintained lower than average incarceration rate increases, thereby avoiding out-of-control corrections spending and federal court intervention. In Oregon, population control continues. By contrast, the U.S. commission ignored its statutory directive to link policy to resources and, as a result, the federal prison population grew by 60 percent between year-end 1987 and mid-1992, and the federal prisons in 1992 were operating at 158 percent of capacity (Bureau of Justice Statistics 1992*b*).

Third, unlike the state commissions, the U.S. Sentencing Commission suffered from internal dissension, high staff turnover, ineffective management, and political infighting. The state commissions have been remarkably stable. The Pennsylvania commission's director, appointed in 1978, remained in place early in 1993, and several of the senior staff remained with the commission for ten years or longer. The current director of the Minnesota commission was promoted from within and has worked with the commission for more than a decade. The Washington commission's director was its initial research director, and the initial director remains active in sentencing policy deliberations. The director of the Oregon Criminal Justice Council, under the auspices of which Oregon's guidelines were developed, has held that position since before that state's guidelines were developed.

The U.S. Sentencing Commission experience has been less stable and less harmonious. The U.S. General Accounting Office (1990), when asked by the Congress to assess the commission's management and operations, found "organizational disarray." In four years the commission had four staff directors and one interim director and was without a research director for one and one-half years. "According to former staff directors, it was difficult to manage in an environment where they could not maintain authority over staff because of commissioners' involvement," the GAO observed. Moreover, "part of the problem has been finding qualified candidates who would be willing to take the [research director's] position, given perceptions that the working environment is complicated by commissioner involvement and other matters" (p. 15). The May 1990 issue of the *Federal Sentencing Reporter* reprints critical statements about the commission's management from numerous agencies and spokesmen. Two members of the commission and one ex officio member have resigned on principle over the commission's failures (Robinson 1987; Block 1989).

To be sure, not all state sentencing commissions have succeeded. Some, like those in New York and South Carolina, developed guidelines but could not persuade legislatures to adopt them. In Pennsylvania and Kansas, legislatures rejected initial sets of proposed guidelines, and commissions came forth with less ambitious but salable successors. In some states—for example, Florida—the guidelines are not well respected and are of little influence (Florida Legislature 1991).

If the controversies associated with the U.S. Sentencing Commission, and the wisdom of its policies, are set aside, from a purely technical perspective even it can be seen as an institutional success. Successful administrative agencies achieve and maintain specialized competence concerning complex subjects (that is why they are created), they have some degree of insulation from short-term political emotions and pressures (that is why typically their members are appointed for fixed terms and can only be removed for cause), and they can adopt comprehensive and long-term approaches to policy-making (this also is why they are created and why public funds are spent to develop cadres of policy experts).

From that perspective, even the U.S. commission has been at least a partial success. No one can doubt that it has achieved specialized competence. Through its rule-making processes, it has proposed and promulgated hundreds of changes to its guidelines, policy statements, and supporting commentary in efforts to rein in what it sees as willfully noncompliant judges and to fine-tune its policies. Through its monitoring and evaluation staffs, it has assembled mountains of data and published numerous annual and evaluation reports, at least some of which, notably its report on mandatory penalties (1991a), demonstrate high levels of technical competence and policy sophistication.

The commission has taken a comprehensive systems approach to policy-making, as is evidenced by its efforts to devise guidelines for all federal offenses, to monitor the guidelines' implementation, to counterbalance the plea-bargaining strategies of prosecutors and defense counsel, and to train probation officers to serve as guardians of the guidelines.

The most powerful evidence that the U.S. commission has succeeded institutionally is that federal sentencing practices have been radically altered. No matter how misguided the guidelines and despite their inability to win support from the people who must implement them (which means they will fail in the long term), the guidelines have succeeded in recasting federal sentencing. Sentencing patterns changed as the commission intended: the proportion of cases sentenced to probation declined greatly, and average prison terms for many offenses became longer.

Where Judge Frankel's model failed in the federal system was in respect of political insulation. Most proponents of guidelines have seen its one-step-removed-from-politics character as a great strength (e.g., Frankel and Orland 1984). The U.S. commission, by contrast, made no effort to insulate its policies from law-and-order politics and short-term emotions. One sign of this is a repeated invocation by the commission of the "reduction of undue leniency" in sentencing as one of the guidelines' primary objectives (1991a, p. i),[8] even though the Sentencing Reform Act of 1984 includes no equivalent language among its enumerated statutory purposes (18 USCA § 3553[a][2]; 28 USCA, chap. 58, § 991[b]). The commission apparently decided that the U.S. Department of Justice and the most law-and-order members of the U.S. Congress were its primary constituency, and it established and attempted to enforce policies that pleased that constituency. This is presumably why the commission ignored a statutory directive that it should tie its policies to available correctional resources,[9] why it chose to ignore a statutory presumption against incarceration of first offenders not convicted of violent or other serious crimes,[10] and why it reacted to harsh mandatory minimum penalty provisions for many drug offenses by making the guidelines even harsher (e.g., Tonry 1992).

Thus the federal experience shows that, as an institution, a sentencing commission can operate much as do administrative agencies on other subjects. The state experience supports that conclusion but also shows that commissions can also develop successful sentencing policies that win the support of practitioners, that tie policy to resource allocation, and that achieve substantively sound sentencing policies.

## II. Issues Facing Commissions

For the foreseeable future, sentencing commissions are here to stay. Their guidelines have been completely successful nowhere, in part because there can be no consensus about the meaning of success. So long as people have discussed punishment there have been major differences in perspective between those who see the criminal law and sentencing primarily or exclusively as institutions concerned with alleged offenders' moral culpability and those who see the criminal law and

[8] See, e.g., U.S. Sentencing Commission (1991a, p. i): "The goals of the Sentencing Reform Act of 1984 were to reduce unwarranted disparity, increase certainty and severity, and correct past patterns of undue leniency."

[9] Section 994(g): "The Commission in promulgating guidelines . . . shall take into account the nature and capacity of the penal, correctional, and other services and facilities available. . . . The sentencing guidelines prescribed under this chapter shall be formulated to minimize the likelihood that the federal prison population will exceed the capacity of the federal prisons."

[10] Section 994(j): "The Commission shall insure that the guidelines reflect the general appropriateness of imposing a sentence other than imprisonment in cases in which a defendant is a first offender who has not been convicted of a crime of violence or an otherwise serious offense."

sentencing primarily as institutions concerned with prevention of crime and maximization of public safety. Even without fundamental differences in punishment philosophy, differences in officials' perspectives breed disagreements. Legislators and sentencing commissioners are concerned with policy in the aggregate. If disparity reduction is the goal, clear bright-line standards are the simplest to express and against which to measure progress. Judges, lawyers, and defendants are concerned with situationally just or appropriate penalties and often find clear and simple standards arbitrary and simplistic. Disagreements about punishment purposes and differences in perspective make it impossible to achieve perfect compliance with guidelines. Commissions have, however, managed to make sentencing more accountable, more consistent, and less disparate in its impact on minority group members, and those are not small achievements.

As the sentencing commission enters its third decade, two sets of policy issues must continue to be addressed. One set of issues poses fundamental policy-making challenges—plea bargaining, intermediate punishments, misdemeanor guidelines—that no commission has adequately resolved. Another, however, involves issues on which there has been slow but steady progress, on which commissions have gradually refined their approaches, and on which commissions have learned from one another. This section sketches the contours of those issues. Discussing them in detail would require another essay, and to my knowledge there is no published literature (except, perhaps, Parent [1988]). Interested readers, however, are invited to contact the commissions listed in the Appendix. All have wrestled with these issues and most have prepared, and are willing to share, staff or commission reports on the policy rationales and considerations behind detailed policy choices.

## A. Major Systemic Issues

Four major systemic issues affecting sentencing guidelines have faced sentencing commissions from the outset. On one, the desirability of tying sentencing policy and its projected operations to correctional resources, there is slow but steady movement toward choosing to do so. Other major systemic issues—controlling prosecutorial discretion under guidelines and developing guidelines for misdemeanors and for nonincarcerative penalties—have been discussed by every sentencing commission but nowhere have they as yet been adequately resolved

(unless doing nothing or virtually nothing is seen as adequate resolution).

1. *Guidelines for Noncustodial Sanctions and Misdemeanors.* Although
no commission in its initial years attempted to develop guidelines for
nonincarcerative sentences, in part because development of incarceration guidelines was challenge enough, in part because of the lack of
community-based punishments in most jurisdictions, and in part because no one knew how to do it, commissions today are at work in
many states on proposals to integrate intermediate and noncustodial
penalties into guidelines and to devise systems of interchangeability
between prison and nonprison sanctions.

There has been considerable conceptual progress, but little practical
policy-making, since the Minnesota commission declined a legislative
invitation (Laws of Minnesota for 1978, chap. 723, § 9[5][2]) to devise
nonincarceration guidelines: "The sentencing guidelines promulgated
by the commission may also establish appropriate sentences for prisoners for whom imprisonment is not proper. Any [such] guidelines . . .
shall make specific reference to noninstitutional sanctions including but
not limited to the following: payment of fines, day fines, restitution,
community work orders, work release programs in local facilities, community based residential and nonresidential programs, incarceration in
a local correctional facility, and probation and the conditions thereof."
In the event, the Minnesota commission's guidelines created presumptions as to who went to prison (roughly 20 percent of convicted felons)
and for how long, but set no presumptions for sentences for nonimpris-
onment or local jail sanctions for felons or for sentences of any kind
for misdemeanants.

Since then, each commission has considered misdemeanor and non-
imprisonment guidelines, and a few have taken small steps. Three
basic approaches have been considered. The first is to create "punishment units" in which all sanctions can be expressed. If guidelines, for
example, set "120 punishment units" as the presumptive sentence, a
judge could impose any combination of sanctions that represented 120
units. Oregon's guidelines specify presumptive sentences for many offenders in punishment units (Bogan 1990, 1991), but do not provide for
how the units are to be calculated. This has been the critical problem in
every jurisdiction that has considered the punishment unit approach.
Preoccupation with prison sentences as the standard punishment has
so far stymied development of the concept. Jurisdictions have typically

begun with prison time and then attempted to specify punitively equivalent nonprison sentences. In a number of jurisdictions, for example, one day's imprisonment has been made equivalent to one, or even three, days' community service. This limits substitution of noncustodial for custodial penalties to very short prison terms. The best-known American community service program (McDonald 1986) and the national policy in England and Wales (Pease 1985), respectively, set 70 and 240 hours as the maximum enforceable length of a community service sentence. At three days' community service to one day's incarceration, community service would be exchangeable for three to ten days' incarceration.

Besides the difficulty in reaching agreement about exchange rates between custodial and noncustodial penalties, two other problems have impeded policy development (Morris and Tonry 1990, chap. 8). Few American jurisdictions have large numbers of well-managed, credible, noncustodial penalties in operation, which makes it difficult to promulgate guidelines premised on their availability. In an era of constrained public resources, it has been difficult obtaining new money to create new programs (even though diversion of prison-bound offenders to community penalties should in the long run conserve public funds). The second, related, problem is that county governments in most American states pay for all or most noncustodial corrections programs. This means both that available programs differ substantially between counties within a state and that new programs must be paid for from county revenues (or from state funds, but in tight times, states are no more eager to appropriate new money than are counties).

The second approach is to create different presumptive bands within sentencing guideline grids—(strong presumptive "in"; weak presumptive "in"; weak presumptive "out"; strong presumptive "out")—and to allow judges to create individualized noncustodial punishments that take account of those presumptions. The D.C. Superior Court Sentencing Guidelines Commission (1987) first proposed such a system, and Pennsylvania more recently has adopted one. The problem with this approach is that it authorizes use of noncustodial penalties and contemplates some interchangeability between custodial and noncustodial penalties but sets no standards for their use when they are authorized (Morris and Tonry 1990, chap. 3).

The third approach is simply to specify equivalent custodial and noncustodial penalties and to authorize judges to impose them in the alternative. Washington's commission did this (Boerner 1985) and later proposed a more extensive system (Washington State Sentencing Guidelines Commission 1992*b*, pp. 19–23), which the legislature did not adopt. Like the punishment unit proposals, so far the equivalency approaches have been unable to overcome the psychological and political pressures to make "equivalent" punishments as subjectively burdensome as prison, which limits their use to the most minor offenses and offenders. Advice from academics (Wasik and von Hirsch 1988; Morris and Tonry 1990, chap. 4) has not proven enormously helpful.

2. *Tying Sentencing Policy to Corrections Resources.* The wisdom of the Minnesota-Washington-Oregon decision to tie sentencing policies to corrections resources has become ever clearer, and other states are beginning to follow suit. Pennsylvania's commission, for example, which initially chose not to take correctional resources into account in devising its guidelines, is reconsidering that decision (Kramer 1992). The North Carolina Sentencing and Policy Advisory Commission (1993) and the Texas Punishment Standards Commission (Reynolds 1993) have proposed that their states adopt policies of tying sentencing policy to correctional resources. The Kansas commission proposed, and the legislature accepted, an "early warning system" approach in which the commissioner of corrections would certify an impending resource problem and the sentencing commission would review current practices and make recommendations for changes to the legislature (Kansas Sentencing Commission 1991; Gottlieb 1993).

3. *Controlling Plea Bargaining.* No jurisdiction has as yet devised an adequate system for controlling plea bargaining under a sentencing guidelines system. Washington State came closest. Aware of criticisms that guidelines for sentencing shift discretion to prosecutors, the Washington legislature authorized its sentencing commission to promulgate statewide charging and plea-bargaining standards. Because of concern that strong standards would be unenforceable (or invite judicial scrutiny of prosecutorial discretion that prosecutors adamantly opposed) and opposition on the merits from prosecutors, the commission developed weak aspirational standards (Boerner 1985, app. 6).

Sentence bargains, if allowed, can undermine any system of guidelines (Alschuler 1978). Charge (or "fact") bargaining in systems based on conviction offenses like Minnesota's or Oregon's enable plea bargaining lawyers to pick the applicable guideline range and thereby greatly to limit the judge's options. A number of proposals have been made for regulating plea bargaining under guidelines (Schulhofer 1980; Tonry and Coffee 1987). One is to provide an explicit percentage or other mechanical sentence discount for defendants who plead guilty (Gottfredson, Wilkins, and Hoffman 1978). The U.S. Sentencing Commission in effect does this by allowing a two- or three-level sentence reduction for "acceptance of responsibility" evidenced by a guilty plea. The most radical proposal has been to adopt "real offense" sentencing in which penalties are based not on the defendants' conviction offense but on his "actual behavior." Only the U.S. Sentencing Commission has adopted a real-offense system. The U.S. commission adopted its "relevant conduct" approach to sentencing in order to offset plea bargaining's influence (Wilkins and Steer 1990); by requiring judges at sentencing to take account of uncharged behavior, and behavior alleged in dropped or acquitted charges, the commission's approach raises difficult issues of principle (Lear 1993; Reitz 1993). In addition, that approach has not managed to avoid increased prosecutorial influence. Many judges argue that the guidelines have shifted power to the prosecutor (Federal Courts Study Committee 1990; Heaney 1991).

### B. Evolutionary Issues

The earliest guidelines, it is easy to forget, represented a radical departure from the indeterminate sentencing systems that they displaced. Before guidelines, judges had almost complete discretion to impose any lawful sentence, and parole boards could set any release date between the minimum parole eligibility date and the maximum set by the judge (often three times the minimum). That some policy choices made by the early commissions were cautious and others in retrospect relatively crude should be no surprise. In this brief section, I identify a number of issues on which there has been gradual movement in some states toward more refined policy choices.

1. *Scaling Offenses.* In early guideline systems, commissions for the most part stayed very close to statutory definitions of offenses, however broadly defined. As time has passed, commissions have partitioned statutory offense definitions into subcategories of different severity. The Pennsylvania commission, for example, has recently reconsidered its offense severity rankings and its subdivisions of crimes. The extreme case is the U.S. Commission (see table 4) which has added numerous extrastatutory elements to its system of offense scaling.

2. *Criminal Histories.* The earliest guidelines systems used broad generic criminal history measures. In Minnesota, for example, every prior felony conviction was given one "point," every prison misdemeanor one-fourth point, and every prior gross misdemeanor one-half

point. More recent systems, including revisions to Minnesota's, are subtler. Some give greater weight to prior violent than to prior property convictions. Some cross tabulate so that a prior violent conviction weighs more heavily for a current violent conviction than for a current nonviolent conviction. Some weight prior convictions in relation to their severity under the guidelines system's offense severity scaling for current convictions. In similar fashion, guidelines commissions are becoming more subtle in their chronological weighing of past crimes, tending more often to build in express "decay" provisions in which convictions prior to some date (e.g., five or ten years before the current crime) are no longer taken into account.

There are numerous other issues, of course, on which policy thinking continues to evolve. These include such things as the handling of aggravating and mitigating circumstances, the number of offense levels in a guidelines grid, the relative location of particular crimes in offense severity rankings, and the development of special procedures and rules for regularly recurring policy issues presented by sex abuse cases, first offenders, and drug cases.

### III. The Future of the Sentencing Commission

The commissions that Judge Frankel proposed have shown that they can achieve much of what he had in mind. They can attain and sustain specialized in. ..tional competence of a variety of kinds. They can develop and implement comprehensive, jurisdiction-wide standards for sentences. Their guidelines can reduce sentencing disparities, diminish racial and gender differences, and help jurisdictions link their criminal justice policies to their criminal justice budgets. That is on the bright side.

Commissions have limits as policy tools. There is evidence that, after the enthusiasms and satisfactions of innovation have passed, institutional hardening of the arteries can set in and commissions can lose their influence and lapse into passivity (e.g., Knapp 1987, pp. 127–41). Commissions are premised in part on belief in norms of instrumental rationality and empirically informed policy-making. When the political environment is such that elected officials insist on treating criminal justice policy-making primarily as symbolic politics, as happened in New York (Griset 1991) and the federal system (von Hirsch 1988) and with Pennsylvania's first set of proposed guidelines (Martin 1984), there is little that commissions can do to resist in the long run. In the short run, as the success of Minnesota's, Oregon's, and Washington's commissions at defying the national trends toward increased use of imprisonment indicates, commissions can resist the politicization of criminal justice policy. In both Washington and Minnesota, perhaps because prison populations began to climb after get-tough guidelines amendments were enacted in the late eighties, legislators have begun to have second thoughts and to look for ways to regain the policy rationality their guidelines systems once had (Frase 1993*b;* Lieb 1993).

This overview of experience with sentencing commissions paints a partial picture and relies on literatures that more often support hypotheses than answer questions. In part, this is because so few evaluations have been carried out. With the exception of one series of outside evaluations of Minnesota's guidelines (e.g., Miethe and Moore 1985, 1987; Moore and Miethe 1986), which relied largely on the Minnesota commission's data, and the GAO's (1992) federal analysis, all of the evaluations to date have been internal efforts carried out by permanent staff. This has two obvious consequences. The commissions have a predictable institutional self-interest in establishing the success of their policies. The extreme instance is the U.S. commission's institutional defensiveness and distortion. Its self-evaluation defined disparity in a self-serving way that was foreordained to demonstrate success, evidence was presented in the most favorable possible light, and implementation problems were attributed not to the lack of wisdom in the commission's policies but to stubborn resistance of judges (e.g., U.S. Sentencing Commission 1991*b*, pp. 419–20). The second, and more common, problem is that ongoing commission budgets tend not to be adequate to support sophisticated evaluations. The only data available for analysis are routinely collected monitoring data which are limited in coverage and may not be comprehensive (in Oregon's fifteen-month evaluation, e.g., reporting forms had been filed for only 74 percent of cases sentenced under the guidelines; Ashford and Mosbaek [1991], p. x). Funds are not likely to be available to hire research consultants and supplementary staff to carry out the analysis. Minnesota's justly celebrated three-year evaluation was made possible only by grants from the National Institute of Corrections and the MacArthur Foundation, which supported supplementary data collection and paid for specialist research staff (Knapp 1984).

Thus, for a number of reasons, there are severe limitations inherent in having commissions evaluate their own handiwork. To date, however, with the exception of the Miethe and Moore and GAO studies, and recent reanalyses of commission data by Frase in Minnesota (1991,

1993*a*) and Boerner in Washington (1993), there have been no outside empirical assessments. With the exception of the federally funded self-evaluation by the U.S. Sentencing Commission (and the GAO follow-up), the federal government, including its research agencies, has not funded a single evaluation of sentencing commissions or their guidelines for nearly a decade, which seems a pity when so many states have tried, or are trying, to recast their sentencing policies and practices with the help of sentencing commissions.

Twenty years on, at least in an American context, sentencing commissions and their guidelines have proven themselves as the most effective prescription thus far offered for the ills of lawlessness, arbitrariness, disparity, and discrimination that were widely believed to characterize indeterminate sentencing.

Perhaps in time private and public funding agencies will realize that the states' experiments with sentencing reform are continuing and will provide the financial support that is needed to help states better understand where they have been and where they are going.

### APPENDIX

Most commissions are willing to share materials with interested observers and to answer questions. The names and mailing addresses of the major commissions at the time of writing were:

Delaware Sentencing Accountability Commission (SENTAC)
State Office Building
820 French Street
Wilmington, Del. 19801

Kansas Sentencing Commission
Jayhawk Tower
700 Jackson, Suite 501
Topeka, Kans. 66603

Louisiana Sentencing Commission
2121 Wooddale Blvd.
Baton Rouge, La. 70806

Minnesota Sentencing Guidelines Commission
The Meridian National Bank Building
205 Aurora Avenue
Suite 205
St. Paul, Minn. 55103

North Carolina Sentencing and Policy Advisory Commission
P.O. Box 2472
Raleigh, N.C. 27602

Oregon Criminal Justice Council
School of Urban and Public Affairs
632 SW Hall Street, Room 314
P.O. Box 751
Portland State University
Portland, Oreg. 97207

Pennsylvania Commission on Sentencing
Commonwealth of Pennsylvania
P.O. Box 1200
State College, Pa. 16801

United States Sentencing Commission
One Columbus Circle NE
Suite 2-500 South Lobby
Washington, D.C. 20002-8002

Washington Sentencing Guidelines Commission
421 So. Capitol Way, Suite 303
P.O. Box 40927
Olympia, Wash. 98504-0927

Wisconsin Sentencing Commission
Suite 701
2 East Mifflin Street
Madison, Wis. 53703

REFERENCES

Alschuler, Albert W. 1978. "Sentencing Reform and Prosecutorial Power." *University of Pennsylvania Law Review* 126:550–77.
Arthur D. Little, Inc. 1981. "An Evaluation of Parole Guidelines in Four Jurisdictions." Report prepared for the National Institute of Corrections, Washington, D.C., and Cambridge, Mass.: Authur D. Little, Inc.
Ashford, Kathyrn, and Craig Mosbaek. 1991. *First Year Report on Implementation of Sentencing Guidelines: November 1989 to January 1991*. Portland: Oregon Criminal Justice Council.
Ashworth, Andrew. 1992. "The Criminal Justice Act 1991." In *Sentencing,*

*Judicial Discretion, and Training*, edited by Colin Munro and Martin Wasik. London: Sweet & Maxwell.

Australia Law Reform Commission. 1980. *Sentencing of Federal Offenders*. Canberra: Australian Government Publishing Service.

Block, Michael K. 1989. "Emerging Problems in the Sentencing Commission's Approach to Guidelines Amendments." *Federal Sentencing Reporter* 1:451–55.

Blumstein, Alfred, Jacqueline Cohen, Susan E. Martin, and Michael Tonry, eds. 1983. *Research on Sentencing: The Search for Reform*. 2 vols. Washington, D.C.: National Academy Press.

Boerner, David. 1985. *Sentencing in Washington—a Legal Analysis of the Sentencing Reform Act of 1981*. Seattle: Butterworth.

———. 1993. "The Legislature's Role in Guidelines Sentencing in 'The Other Washington.'" *Wake Forest Law Review* 28:381–420.

Bogan, Kathleen M. 1990. "Constructing Felony Sentencing Guidelines in an Already Crowded State: Oregon Breaks New Ground." *Crime and Delinquency* 36:467–87.

———. 1991. "Sentencing Reform in Oregon." *Overcrowded Times* 2(2):5, 14–15.

Bottomley, A. Keith. 1990. "Parole in Transition: A Comparative Study of Origins, Developments, and Prospects for the 1990s." In *Crime and Justice: A Review of Research*, vol. 12, edited by Michael Tonry and Norval Morris. Chicago: University of Chicago Press.

Breyer, Stephen. 1988. "The Federal Sentencing Guidelines and the Key Compromises upon Which They Rest." *Hofstra Law Review* 17:1–50.

———. 1992. "The Key Compromises of the Federal Sentencing Guidelines." In *Sentencing, Judicial Discretion, and Training*, edited by Colin Munro and Martin Wasik. London: Sweet & Maxwell.

Bright, Myron. 1993. "These Sentences Defy Reason, but as I Have Already Noted—Such Is Our System." *Overcrowded Times* 4(3):20.

Bureau of Justice Statistics. 1992a. *Prisoners in 1991*. Washington, D.C.: U.S. Department of Justice, Bureau of Justice Statistics.

———. 1992b. "Four Percent More Prisoners in First Half of 1992." News release. Washington, D.C.: U.S. Department of Justice, Bureau of Justice Statistics.

Canadian Sentencing Commission. 1987. *Sentencing Reform: A Canadian Approach*. Ottawa: Canadian Government Publishing Centre.

Carrow, Deborah M. 1984. "Judicial Sentencing Guidelines: Hazards of the Middle Ground." *Judicature* 68:161–71.

Carrow, Deborah M., Judith Feins, Beverly N. W. Lee, and Lois Olinger. 1985. *Guidelines without Force: An Evaluation of the Multijurisdictional Sentencing Guidelines Field Test*. Report to the National Institute of Justice. Cambridge, Mass.: Abt.

Clarke, Stevens H. 1984. "North Carolina's Determinate Sentencing Legislation." *Judicature* 68:140–52.

———. 1987. *Felony Sentencing in North Carolina, 1976–1986: Effects of Presumptive Sentencing Legislation*. Chapel Hill: University of North Carolina at Chapel Hill, Institute of Government.

Clarke, Stevens H., Susan Turner Kurtz, Glenn F. Lang, Kenneth L. Parker, Elizabeth W. Rubinsky, and Donna J. Schleicher. 1983. *North Carolina's Determinate Sentencing Legislation: An Evaluation of the First Year's Experience.* Chapel Hill: University of North Carolina at Chapel Hill, Institute of Government.

Cohen, Jacqueline, and Michael Tonry. 1983. "Sentencing Reforms and Their Impacts." In *Research on Sentencing: The Search for Reform,* vol. 2, edited by Alfred Blumstein, Jacqueline Cohen, Susan E. Martin, and Michael Tonry. Washington, D.C.: National Academy Press.

D.C. Superior Court, Sentencing Guidelines Commission. 1987. *Initial Report of the Superior Court Sentencing Guidelines Commission—the Development of Felony Sentencing Guidelines.* Washington, D.C.: D.C. Superior Court, Sentencing Guidelines Commission.

Dailey, Debra L. 1992. "Minnesota's Sentencing Guidelines—Past and Future." *Overcrowded Times* 3(1):4, 12–13.

Doob, Anthony. 1993. "The United States Sentencing Commission's Guidelines: If You Don't Know Where You Are Going, You May Not Get There." Paper prepared for the Colston International Sentencing Symposium, Bristol, England, April.

Dunworth, Terence, and Charles D. Weisselberg. 1992. "Felony Cases and the Federal Courts: The Guidelines Experience." *Southern California Law Review* 66:99–153.

Federal Courts Study Committee. 1990. *Report.* Washington, D.C.: Administrative Office of the U.S. Courts.

Flanagan, Timothy J., and Kathleen Maguire. 1992. *Sourcebook of Criminal Justice Statistics—1991.* Washington, D.C.: Bureau of Justice Statistics, U.S. Department of Justice.

Florida Legislature. 1991. *An Alternative to Florida's Current Sentencing Guidelines—a Report to the Legislature and the Sentencing Guidelines Commission.* Tallahassee: Florida Legislature, Economic and Demographic Research Division, Joint Legislative Management Committee.

Fox, Richard. 1991. "Order Out of Chaos: Victoria's New Maximum Penalty Structure." *Monash University Law Review* 17:106–31.

Frankel, Marvin E. 1972. *Criminal Sentences: Law without Order.* New York: Hill & Wang.

Frankel, Marvin, and Leonard Orland. 1984. "Sentencing Commissions and Guidelines." *Georgetown Law Journal* 73:225–47.

Frase, Richard S. 1991. "Sentencing Reform in Minnesota, Ten Years After." *Minnesota Law Review* 75:727–54.

———. 1993a. "Implementing Commission-based Sentencing Guidelines: The Lessons of the First Ten Years in Minnesota." *Wake Forest Law Review* (forthcoming).

———. 1993b. "Prison Population Growing under Minnesota Guidelines." *Overcrowded Times* 4(1):1, 10–12.

Freed, Daniel J. 1992. "Federal Sentencing in the Wake of Guidelines: Unacceptable Limits on the Discretion of Sentences," *Yale Law Journal* 101:1681–1754.

Freiberg, Arie. 1993. "Sentencing Reform in Victoria: A Case Study." Paper prepared for the Colston International Sentencing Symposium, Bristol, England, April.

Gebelein, Richard S. 1991. "Sentencing Reform in Delaware." *Overcrowded Times* 2(2):5, 12–13.

Gorta, Angela. 1992. "Impact of the Sentencing Act of 1989 on the NSW Prison Population." *Current Issues in Criminal Justice* 3(3):308–17.

———. 1993. "Truth-in-Sentencing in New South Wales." *Overcrowded Times* 4(2):4, 11–12.

Gottfredson, Don M., Leslie T. Wilkins, and Peter B. Hoffman. 1978. *Guidelines for Parole and Sentencing.* Lexington, Mass.: Lexington Books.

Gottlieb, David J. 1991. "A Review and Analysis of the Kansas Sentencing Guidelines." *Kansas Law Review* 39:65–89.

———. 1993. "Kansas Sentencing Guidelines Take Effect." *Overcrowded Times* 4(3):1, 10–13.

Griset, Pamela L. 1991. *Determinate Sentencing—the Promise and the Reality of Retributive Justice.* Albany: State University of New York Press.

Heaney, Gerald W. 1991. "The Reality of Guidelines Sentencing: No End to Disparity." *American Criminal Law Review* 28:161–233.

Kansas Sentencing Commission. 1991. *Recommendations.* Topeka: Kansas Sentencing Commission.

Karle, Theresa Walker, and Thomas Sager. 1991. "Are the Federal Sentencing Guidelines Meeting Congressional Goals? An Empirical and Case Law Analysis." *Emory Law Review* 40:393–444.

Knapp, Kay A. 1984. *The Impact of the Minnesota Sentencing Guidelines—Three Year Evaluation.* St. Paul: Minnesota Sentencing Guidelines Commission.

———. 1987. "Implementation of the Minnesota Guidelines: Can the Innovative Spirit Be Preserved?" In *The Sentencing Commission and Its Guidelines,* by Andrew von Hirsch, Kay A. Knapp, and Michael Tonry. Boston: Northeastern University Press.

———. 1993. "Allocations of Discretion and Accountability within Sentencing Structures." *Colorado Law Review* 64:679–705.

Kramer, John. 1992. "The Evolution of Pennsylvania's Sentencing Guidelines." *Overcrowded Times* 3(4):6–9.

Kramer, John H., and Robin L. Lubitz. 1985. "Pennsylvania's Sentencing Reform: The Impact of Commission-established Guidelines." *Crime and Delinquency* 31:481–500.

Kramer, John H., and Anthony J. Scirica. 1985. "Complex Policy Choices: The Pennsylvania Commission on Sentencing." Paper presented at the annual meeting of the Academy of Criminal Justice Sciences, Las Vegas, April.

Kress, Jack M. 1980. *Prescription for Justice: The Theory and Practice of Sentencing Guidelines.* Cambridge, Mass.: Ballinger.

Lear, Elizabeth T. 1993. "Is Conviction Relevant?" *UCLA Law Review* (forthcoming).

Lieb, Roxanne. 1991. "Washington State: A Decade of Sentencing Reform." *Overcrowded Times* 2(4):1, 5–8.

————. 1993. "Washington Prison Population Growth Out of Control." *Overcrowded Times* 4(1):1, 13–14, 20.

Lubitz, Robin L. 1993. "North Carolina Legislature Considers Sentencing Change." *Overcrowded Times* 4(2):1, 9–10.

McDonald, Douglas. 1986. *Punishment without Walls: Community Service Sentences in New York City.* New Brunswick, N.J.: Rutgers University Press.

Martin, Susan. 1984. "Interests and Politics in Sentencing Reform: The Development of Sentencing Guidelines in Pennsylvania and Minnesota." *Villanova Law Review* 29:21–113.

Meierhoefer, Barbara. 1992. "The Role of Offense and Offender Characteristics in Federal Sentencing." *Southern California Law Review* 66:367–99.

Miethe, Terance D., and Charles A. Moore. 1985. "Socioeconomic Disparities under Determinate Sentencing Systems: A Comparison of Preguideline and Postguideline Practices in Minnesota." *Criminology* 23:337–63.

————. 1987. *Evaluation of Minnesota's Felony Sentencing Guidelines.* Report to the National Institute of Justice, Washington, D.C.

Minnesota Sentencing Guidelines Commission. 1980. *Report to the Legislature—1980.* St. Paul: Minnesota Sentencing Guidelines Commission.

————. 1991a. *Summary of 1989 Sentencing Practices for Convicted Felons.* St. Paul: Minnesota Sentencing Guidelines Commission.

————. 1991b. *Report to the Legislature on Intermediate Sanctions.* St. Paul: Minnesota Sentencing Guidelines Commission.

————. 1992. *Report to the Legislature on Controlled Substance Offenders.* St. Paul: Minnesota Sentencing Guidelines Commission.

Moore, Charles A., and Terance D. Miethe. 1986. "Regulated and Unregulated Sentencing Decisions: An Analysis of First-Year Practices under Minnesota's Felony Sentencing Guidelines." *Law and Society Review* 20:253–77.

Morris, Norval, and Michael Tonry. 1990. *Between Prison and Probation: Intermediate Punishments in a Rational Sentencing System.* New York: Oxford University Press.

Nagel, Ilene H., and Stephen Schulhofer. 1992. "A Tale of Three Cities: An Empirical Study of Charging and Bargaining Practices under the Federal Sentencing Guidelines." *Southern California Law Review* 66:501–66.

North Carolina Sentencing and Policy Advisory Commission. 1993. *Report to the 1993 Session of the General Assembly of North Carolina.* Raleigh: North Carolina Sentencing and Policy Advisory Commission.

O'Donnell, Pierce, Michael Churgin, and Dennis Curtis. 1977. *Toward a Just and Effective Sentencing System.* New York: Praeger.

Orland, Leonard, and Kevin R. Reitz. 1993. "Epilogue: A Gathering of State Sentencing Commissions." *Colorado Law Review* 64:837–45.

Parent, Dale. 1988. *Structuring Sentencing Discretion: The Evolution of Minnesota's Sentencing Guidelines.* Stoneham, Mass.: Butterworth.

Pease, Ken. 1985. "Community Service Orders." In *Crime and Justice: A Review of Research,* vol. 6, edited by Michael Tonry and Norval Morris. Chicago: University of Chicago Press.

Pennsylvania Commission on Sentencing. 1984. *1983 Report: Sentencing in Pennsylvania.* State College: Pennsylvania Commission on Sentencing.

————. 1985. *1984 Report: Sentencing in Pennsylvania*. State College: Pennsylvania Commission on Sentencing.

————. 1987. *1986–1987 Annual Report*. State College: Pennsylvania Commission on Sentencing.

————. 1993. *Sentencing in Pennsylvania—1991*. State College: Pennsylvania Commission on Sentencing.

Quinn, Thomas J. 1990. "Delaware Sentencing Guidelines Achieving Their Goals." *Overcrowded Times* 1(3):1–2.

————. 1992. "Voluntary Guidelines Effective in Delaware." *Overcrowded Times* 3(1):1, 9, 11.

Reitz, Kevin. 1993. "Sentencing Facts: Travesties of Real-Offense Sentencing." *Stanford Law Review* 45:523–73.

Reynolds, Carl. 1993. "Texas Commission Proposes Corrections Overhaul." *Overcrowded Times* 4(2):1, 16–17.

Rhodes, William. 1992. "Sentence Disparity, Use of Incarceration, and Plea Bargaining: The Post-guideline View from the Commission." *Federal Sentencing Reporter* 5:153–55.

Rich, William D., L. Paul Sutton, Todd D. Clear, and Michael J. Saks. 1982. *Sentencing by Mathematics: An Evaluation of the Early Attempts to Develop Sentencing Guidelines*. Williamsburg, Va.: National Center for State Courts.

Roberts, Julian, and Andrew von Hirsch. 1993. "Statutory Sentencing Reform: A Review of Bill C-90." Unpublished manuscript. Ottawa: University of Ottawa, Department of Criminology.

Robinson, Paul. 1987. *Dissenting View of Commissioner Paul H. Robinson on the Promulgation of Sentencing Guidelines by the United States Sentencing Commission*. Washington, D.C.: U.S. Government Printing Office.

Schulhofer, Stephen. 1980. "Sentencing Reform and Prosecutorial Power." *University of Pennsylvania Law Review* 126:550–77.

Schulhofer, Stephen J., and Ilene Nagel. 1989. "Negotiated Pleas under the Federal Sentencing Guidelines: The First Fifteen Months." *American Criminal Law Review* 27:231–88.

Shane-DuBow, Sandra, Alice P. Brown, and Erik Olsen. 1985. *Sentencing Reform in the United States: History, Content, and Effect*. Washington, D.C.: U.S. Government Printing Office.

Stith, Kate, and Steve Y. Koh. 1993. "The Politics of Sentencing Reform: The Legislative History of the Federal Sentencing Guidelines." *Wake Forest Law Review* 28:223–90.

Thomas, David A. 1993. "Sentencing Reform: England and Wales." Paper prepared for the Colston International Sentencing Symposium, Bristol, England, April.

Tonry, Michael. 1979. "The Sentencing Commission in Sentencing Reform." *Hofstra Law Review* 7:315–53.

————. 1987. *Sentencing Reform Impacts*. Washington, D.C.: U.S. Government Printing Office.

————. 1988. "Structuring Sentencing." In *Crime and Justice: A Review of Research*, vol. 10, edited by Michael Tonry and Norval Morris. Chicago: University of Chicago Press.

————. 1991. "The Politics and Processes of Sentencing Commissions." *Crime and Delinquency* 37:307–29.

————. 1992. "Salvaging the Sentencing Guidelines in Seven Easy Steps." *Federal Sentencing Reporter* 4:355–59.

————. 1993*a*. "The Success of Judge Frankel's Sentencing Commission." *Colorado Law Review* 64:713–22.

————. 1993*b*. "The Failure of the U.S. Sentencing Commission's Guidelines." *Crime and Delinquency* 39:131–49.

Tonry, Michael, and John C. Coffee, Jr. 1987. "Enforcing Sentencing Guidelines: Plea Bargaining and Review Mechanisms." In *The Sentencing Commission and Its Guidelines*, by Andrew von Hirsch, Kay A. Knapp, and Michael Tonry. Boston: Northeastern University Press.

U.S. General Accounting Office. 1990. *U.S. Sentencing Commission: Changes Needed to Improve Effectiveness*. Testimony of Lowell Dodge before the Subcommittee on Criminal Justice of the Committee on the Judiciary, United States House of Representatives, March. Washington, D.C.: U.S. General Accounting Office.

————. 1992. *Sentencing Guidelines—Central Questions Remain Unanswered*. Washington, D.C.: U.S. General Accounting Office.

U.S. Sentencing Commission. 1987. *Sentencing Guidelines and Policy Statements, April 13, 1987*. Washington, D.C.: U.S. Government Printing Office.

————. 1991*a*. *Mandatory Minimum Penalties in the Federal Criminal Justice System*. Washington, D.C.: U.S. Sentencing Commission.

————. 1991*b*. *The Federal Sentencing Guidelines: A Report on the Operation of the Guidelines System and Short-term Impacts on Disparity in Sentencing, Use of Incarceration, and Prosecutorial Discretion and Plea Bargaining*. Washington, D.C.: U.S. Sentencing Commission.

————. 1992*a*. *Sentencing Commission Guidelines Manual*. Washington, D.C.: U.S. Sentencing Commission.

————. 1992*b*. *Annual Report—1991*. Washington, D.C.: U.S. Sentencing Commission.

von Hirsch, Andrew. 1988. "Federal Sentencing Guidelines: The United States and Canadian Schemes Compared." Occasional Papers from the Center for Research in Crime and Justice, no. 4. New York: New York University Law School.

von Hirsch, Andrew, Kay Knapp, and Michael Tonry. 1987. *The Sentencing Commission and Its Guidelines*. Boston: Northeastern University Press.

Washington State Sentencing Guidelines Commission. 1985. *Sentencing Practices under the Sentencing Reform Act*. Olympia: Washington State Sentencing Guidelines Commission.

————. 1986. *Preliminary Evaluation of Washington State's Sentencing Reform Act*. Olympia: Washington State Sentencing Guidelines Commission.

————. 1987. *Preliminary Statistical Summary of 1986 Sentencing Data*. Olympia: Washington State Sentencing Guidelines Commission.

————. 1992*a*. *A Statistical Summary of Adult Felony Sentencing*. Olympia: Washington State Sentencing Commission.

————. 1992*b*. *A Decade of Sentencing Reform: Washington and Its Guidelines, 1981–1991.* Olympia: Washington State Sentencing Commission.

Wasik, Martin, and Richard D. Taylor. 1991. *Criminal Justice Act 1991.* London: Blackstone.

Wasik, Martin, and Andrew von Hirsch. 1988. "Noncustodial Sentences and the Principles of Desert." *Criminal Law Review* 1988:555–72.

Weisburd, David. 1992. "Sentencing Disparity and the Guidelines: Taking a Closer Look." *Federal Sentencing Reporter* 5:149–52.

Wheeler, Stanton, Kenneth Mann, and Austin Sarat. 1991. *Sitting in Judgment: The Sentencing of White-Collar Criminals.* New Haven, Conn.: Yale University Press.

Wilkins, Leslie T., Jack M. Kress, Don M. Gottfredson, Joseph C. Calpin, and Arthur M. Gelman. 1978. *Sentencing Guidelines: Structuring Judicial Discretion—Report on the Feasibility Study.* Washington, D.C.: U.S. Department of Justice.

Wilkins, William W., Jr., and John R. Steer. 1990. "Relevant Conduct: The Cornerstone of the Federal Sentencing Guidelines." *South Carolina Law Review* 41:495–531.

Wright, Ronald F. 1991. "Sentencers, Bureaucrats, and the Administrative Law Perspective on the Federal Sentencing Commission." *California Law Review* 79:1–90.

Wright, Ronald F., and Susan P. Ellis. 1993. "Progress Report on the North Carolina Sentencing and Policy Advisory Commission." *Wake Forest Law Review* 28:421–61.

*Barry C. Feld*

# Criminalizing the American Juvenile Court

ABSTRACT

Progressive reformers envisioned a therapeutic juvenile court that made individualized treatment decisions in the child's "best interests." The Supreme Court's *Gault* decision provided the impetus for transforming the juvenile court from an informal welfare agency into a scaled-down criminal court. Since *Gault*, the juvenile court procedures increasingly resemble those of adult courts, although in some respects, such as assistance of counsel, juveniles receive less adequate protections. Judicial and legislative changes have altered the juvenile court's jurisdiction over noncriminal status offenders and serious young offenders—as the former are diverted from the system, the latter are transferred to adult criminal courts. Juvenile courts increasingly punish youths for their offenses rather than treat them for their "real needs." These charges eliminate most differences between juvenile and criminal courts. The juvenile court must either develop a new rationale and mandate or face further erosion and redundancy.

The Supreme Court's decision *In re Gault*, 387 U.S. 1 (1967), began transforming the juvenile court into a very different institution than the Progressives contemplated. Progressives envisioned an informal court whose dispositions reflected the "best interests" of the child. In *Gault*, the Supreme Court engrafted formal procedures at trial onto the juvenile court's individualized treatment sentencing schema. Although the Court's decisions were not intended to alter the juvenile court's therapeutic mission, subsequent legislative, judicial, and administrative responses to *Gault* have modified the court's jurisdiction, purpose, and

Barry C. Feld is Centennial Professor of Law at the University of Minnesota Law School.

procedures (Feld 1984, 1987, 1988*b*). As a result, juvenile courts now converge procedurally and substantively with adult criminal courts.

Legislative recognition that juvenile courts often failed to realize their benevolent purposes has led to two jurisdictional changes. The first concerns status offenses—misconduct by juveniles such as truancy or incorrigibility that would not be a crime if committed by an adult. Recent reforms limit the dispositions that noncriminal offenders may receive or remove status offenses from juvenile court jurisdiction altogether. A second jurisdictional change is the criminalizing of serious juvenile offenders. Increasingly, some youths are transferred from juvenile courts to criminal courts for prosecution as adults.

As the juvenile court's jurisdiction contracts, its commitment to rehabilitating offenders is also changing. The sentences that delinquents charged with crimes receive increasingly are based on the idea of just deserts rather than their "real needs." Proportional and determinate sentences based on the current offense and prior record, rather than the "best interests" of the child, dictate the length, location, and intensity of intervention. An increased emphasis on formal procedural justice has accompanied the enhanced role of punishment in sentencing juvenile offenders. Although in principle juvenile courts' procedural safeguards closely resemble those of criminal courts, in practice, the procedural justice routinely afforded juveniles is far less than the minimum insisted on for adults.

Throughout its history, the juvenile court has been marked by a disjunction between its rehabilitative rhetoric and its punitive reality (Rothman 1980; Feld 1990*b*). As the Supreme Court noted in *Kent v. United States*, 383 U.S. 541, 555 (1966), "The child receives the worst of both worlds: he gets neither the protections accorded to adults nor the solicitous care and regenerative treatment postulated for children." Even as states increasingly punish young offenders, most juvenile codes provide neither special procedural safeguards to protect juveniles from their own immaturity nor the full panoply of adult criminal procedural safeguards to protect them from punitive state intervention. Rather, juvenile courts employ procedures that assure that youths continue to "receive the worst of both worlds," treating delinquents just like adult criminal defendants when formal equality redounds to their disadvantage while providing less adequate juvenile court safeguards when those deficient procedures redound to the advantage of the state (Feld 1984, 1990*b*). This is most evident, for example, in the continuing absence of counsel for many juveniles in many states (Feld 1988*a*, 1989, 1991; Kempf, Decker, and Bing 1990).

The substantive and procedural convergence between juvenile and criminal courts eliminates virtually all of the conceptual and operational differences in strategies of social control for youths and adults. Even with the juvenile court's transformation into a scaled-down criminal court, however, its modes of operation continue virtually unchanged from an era when its processes were informal by design and its purposes expressly rehabilitative. Despite juvenile courts' inability to prevent or reduce youth crime, they survive and even prosper. Despite statutory and judicial reforms, official discretion arguably has increased rather than decreased. This raises the question whether there is any longer any reason to maintain a punitive juvenile court separate from the adult criminal court whose only distinction is its persisting procedural deficiencies.

This essay draws on judicial opinions, legislative changes, empirical research, and theoretical writings to evaluate the contemporary juvenile court. Its purpose is to describe and analyze the transformation of the juvenile court from a benevolent, therapeutic institution into a scaled-down criminal court for young people and to assay the policy implications of these changes. Section I examines the assumptions underlying the original juvenile court and its subsequent constitutional domestication after *Gault*. Section II provides an overview of the sources of knowledge and data-analytic techniques used to examine juvenile courts. Section III examines the shift from informal to formal procedure᠎ ᠎᠎᠎᠎᠎᠎᠎᠎᠎᠎᠎᠎᠎᠎᠎᠎᠎᠎n following *Gault*. Section IV exami᠎᠎᠎᠎᠎᠎᠎᠎᠎᠎᠎᠎᠎᠎᠎᠎᠎e juvenile court's response to noncri᠎᠎᠎᠎᠎᠎᠎᠎᠎᠎᠎᠎᠎᠎᠎ analyzes changes in the response t᠎᠎᠎᠎᠎᠎᠎᠎᠎᠎᠎᠎᠎᠎n VI employs a variety of indicators᠎᠎᠎᠎᠎᠎᠎᠎᠎᠎᠎᠎᠎shift in sentencing policy from treat᠎᠎᠎᠎᠎᠎᠎᠎᠎᠎᠎shing them. Section VII considers ᠎᠎᠎᠎᠎᠎᠎᠎᠎᠎᠎urt and the policy issues they raise.

## I. The Transformation of the Juvenile Court

Ideological changes in cultural conceptions of children and in strategies of social control during the nineteenth century led to the creation of the juvenile court in Cook County, Illinois, in 1899 (Sutton 1988;

Ainsworth 1991). Progressive reformers applied new theories of social control to new ideas about childhood and created a social welfare alternative to criminal courts to treat criminal and noncriminal misconduct by youths (Fox 1970a; Empey 1979; Mennel 1983; Sutton 1988). Before the juvenile court, the only special protections accorded young offenders charged with crimes were those afforded by the common law's infancy mens rea defense (Fox 1970b; McCarthy 1977a; Weissman 1983; Walkover 1984). The criminal law presumed that rational actors made blameworthy choices and exempted from punishment categories of people who lacked the requisite moral and criminal responsibility (Kadish 1968). At common law, children less than seven years old were conclusively presumed to lack criminal capacity, while those fourteen years of age and older were treated as fully responsible. Between the ages of seven and fourteen years, there was a rebuttable presumption of criminal incapacity (Fox 1970b; McCarthy 1977a; Weissman 1983). If found to be criminally responsible, youths as young as twelve years of age could be and were executed (Streib 1987).

Historically, the criminal law presented the stark alternatives of a criminal conviction and punishment as an adult or an acquittal or dismissal that freed a youth from all supervision. Jury or judicial nullification to avoid punishment excluded many youths from control, particularly those charged with minor offenses (Fox 1970a; Platt 1977). To avoid these consequences, special institutions for youths proliferated. In the early to mid-nineteenth century, the first youth institutions, Houses of Refuge, made their appearance in the East Coast urban centers (Fox 1970a; Hawes 1971; Rothman 1971; Mennel 1973). By mid-century, reformatories and youth institutions spread to the rural and midwestern regions (Rothman 1980; Sutton 1988). By the end of the century, juvenile courts completed the process of differentiating the social control of youths from adults (Platt 1977; Ryerson 1978; Rothman 1980).

## A. The Progressive Juvenile Court

By the end of the nineteenth century, America had changed from a rural, agrarian society to an urban, industrial society (Wiebe 1967). Between 1870 and World War I, railroads fostered economic growth, changed the processes of manufacturing, and ushered in a period of rapid social and economic modernization (Hofstadter 1955; Hays 1957; Kolko 1963; Wiebe 1967). Traditional social patterns faced new challenges as immigrants, primarily from southern and eastern Europe, and rural Americans flooded into the burgeoning cities to take advantage of new economic opportunities. The "new" European immigrants differed in language, religion, political heritage, and culture from the dominant Anglo-Protestant Americans who had preceded them (Hofstadter 1955; Higham 1988). They predominantly were peasants; their cultural and linguistic differences from the dominant culture, coupled with their numbers, hindered their assimilation. Overburdened by numbers, cities proved unable to provide even basic needs (Trattner 1984). Crowded ethnic enclaves, urban ghettos, poverty, disorder, crime, and inadequate social services were untoward features of modern urban industrial life.

Changes in family structure and functions accompanied the economic transformation and included a reduction in the number and spacing of children, a shift of economic functions from the family to other work environments, and a modernizing and privatizing of the family that substantially modified the roles of women and children (Kett 1977; Lasch 1977; Demos and Boocock 1978; Degler 1980). The latter development was especially noticeable in the upper and middle classes, which had begun to view children as corruptible innocents whose upbringing required special attention, solicitude, and instruction (DeMause 1974; Kett 1977). The social construction of childhood as a recognizable developmental stage is a relatively recent phenomenon (Ainsworth 1991). While Aries (1962) contends that, prior to the past two or three centuries, young people were regarded as miniature adults, small versions of their parents, clearly by the end of the nineteenth century, a newer view of childhood and adolescence emerged (Kett 1977; Hawes and Hiner 1985; Ainsworth 1991). Children increasingly were seen as vulnerable, innocent, passive, and dependent beings who needed protection and extended preparation for life (Kett 1977; Platt 1977; Zimring 1982; Hawes and Hiner 1985).

The social and economic changes associated with modernization and industrialization sparked the Progressive Movement (Hofstadter 1955; Wiebe 1967). Progressivism encompassed a host of ideologies and addressed issues ranging from economic regulation to criminal justice and social and political reform. One unifying theme was that professionals and experts could develop rational and scientific solutions to social problems that would be administered by the state (Sutton 1988). Progressive reliance on the state reflected a fundamental belief that state action could be benevolent, that government could rectify social problems, and that Progressive values could be inculcated in others (Allen

1964, 1981). Progressives felt no reservations when they attempted to "Americanize" the immigrants and poor through a variety of agencies of assimilation and acculturation to become sober, virtuous, middle-class Americans (Platt 1977; Rothman 1978, 1980).

The Progressives' trust of state power coupled with the changing cultural conception of children and child rearing led them into the realm of "child saving" (Platt 1977). Child-centered Progressive reforms, such as the juvenile court system, child labor and welfare laws, and compulsory school attendance laws, both reflected and advanced the changing imagery of childhood (Cremin 1961; Trattner 1965; Wiebe 1967; Kett 1977; Tiffin 1982). Progressive programs attempted to structure child development, control and mold children, and protect them from exploitation. The goals and the methods of these programs, however, often reflected the Anglo-Americans' antipathy to the immigrant hordes and a desire to save the second generation from perpetuating the Old World ways (Platt 1977; Empey 1979).

Changes in ideological assumptions about human behavior and social deviance led Progressives to new views on criminal justice and social control policies (Rothman 1980; Allen 1981). Positivism—the effort to identify the various factors that cause crime and deviance—challenged the classic formulations of crime as the product of free will choices (Matza 1964; Allen 1981). Positive criminology, as distinguished from "free will," asserted a scientific determinism of deviance, sought to identify the causal variables producing crime and delinquency, and informed many Progressive criminal justice reforms (Allen 1964; Platt 1977; Rothman 1980). Assuming that criminal behavior was determined rather than chosen reduced actors' moral responsibility and led to a focus on reforming offenders rather than punishing them for their offenses (Allen 1964, 1981; Matza 1964; Rothman 1980). Applying medical analogies to the treatment of offenders, a growing class of social science professionals fostered the "rehabilitative ideal" (Platt 1977; Ryerson 1978; Allen 1981).

A flourishing "rehabilitative ideal" entails certain assumptions about means and ends. It requires a belief in the malleability of human behavior and a basic moral consensus about the appropriate directions of human change (Allen 1964, 1981). Progressives believed that the new behavioral sciences provided them with the tools for systematic reform and that it was proper to impose the virtues of a middle-class lifestyle on immigrants and the poor (Rothman 1980; Allen 1981). The "rehabilitative ideal," which permeated Progressive criminal justice reforms such as probation and parole, indeterminate sentences, and the juvenile court (Allen 1964, 1981; Rothman 1980), emphasized open-ended, informal, and highly flexible policies. Discretion was necessary because diagnosing the causes of and prescribing the cures for delinquency required an individualized, case-by-case strategy that precluded uniform treatment or standardized criteria (Rothman 1980). It is probably not coincidental that the increased flexibility, indeterminacy, and discretion in social control practices corresponded with the increasing volume and changing ethnic characteristics of offenders during this period (Fox 1970*a;* Sutton 1988).

Progressive "child savers" described juvenile courts as benign, nonpunitive, and therapeutic, although modern writers disagree as to whether their movement should be seen as a humanitarian attempt to save poor and immigrant children (Hagan and Leon 1977; Sutton 1988) or as an effort to expand state social control over them (Fox 1970*a;* Platt 1977). The legal doctrine of *parens patriae,* the state as parent, legitimated intervention (Cogan 1970; Rendleman 1971). The *parens patriae* doctrine drew no distinction between criminal and noncriminal conduct, a view that supported the Progressive position that juvenile court proceedings were civil rather than criminal in nature. The civil nature of the proceedings fulfilled the reformers' desire to remove children from the adult criminal system and allowed greater supervision of children and greater flexibility in treatment (Hawes 1971; Platt 1977; Rothman 1980). Because the reformers eschewed punishment, through the juvenile court's "status jurisdiction" they could respond to noncriminal behavior such as smoking, sexual activity, truancy, immorality, or living a wayward, idle, and dissolute life—activities that previously might have been ignored but that the Progressives wished to end because it betokened premature adulthood (Rosenberg and Rosenberg 1976; Schlossman and Wallach 1978; Garlock 1979). Status jurisdiction reflected the reformulated conception of childhood and adolescence that had emerged during the nineteenth century and authorized predelinquent intervention to forestall premature adulthood, enforce the dependent position of youth, and supervise children's moral upbringing (Platt 1977; Rothman 1980).

The "rehabilitative ideal," as implemented in the juvenile court, envisioned a specialized judge trained in social sciences and child development whose empathic qualities and insight would aid in making individualized dispositions. Specialized judges, assisted by social service personnel, clinicians, and probation officers, would act in the "best interests of the child" (Ryerson 1978; Rothman 1980). Progressives assumed that a rational, scientific analysis of facts would reveal the proper diagnosis and prescribe the cure, and the juvenile court's methodology encouraged collecting as much information as possible about the child. The resulting factual inquiry into the whole child accorded minor significance to the specific crime since the offense indicated little about a child's "real needs." Because the reformers' aims were benevolent, their solicitude individualized, and intervention guided by science, they saw no reason to circumscribe narrowly the power of the state. Rather, they maximized discretion to provide flexibility in diagnosis and treatment and focused on the child's character and lifestyle rather than on the crime.

By separating children from adults and providing a rehabilitative alternative to punishment, juvenile courts rejected both the criminal law's jurisprudence and its procedural safeguards such as juries and lawyers. Court personnel used informal procedures and a euphemistic vocabulary to eliminate any stigma and implication of an adult criminal proceeding (Mack 1909; President's Commission on Law Enforcement and Administration of Justice 1967b). Hearings were confidential and private, access to court records was limited, and youths were "adjudicated" to be "delinquent" rather than convicted and found to be guilty of an offense. Theoretically, a child's "best interests," background, and welfare guided dispositions (Mack 1909). Since a youth's offense was only a symptom of the "real" needs, sentences were indeterminate, nonproportional, and potentially continued for the duration of minority. The events that brought the child before the court affected neither the degree nor the duration of intervention because each child's needs differed and no limits could be defined in advance.

## B. The Constitutional Domestication of the Juvenile Court

By the 1960s, several forces combined to erode the rehabilitative premises of the Progressive juvenile court and undermine support for discretionary, coercive socialization in juvenile courts, criminal justice, and social welfare. A flourishing "rehabilitative ideal" entails assumptions about means and ends: faith in human malleability and the existence of an effective change technology, and a social consensus regarding what it means to be "rehabilitated"—that is, agreement about the nature of the "finished product" (Allen 1981). Progessives believed that the new social sciences and the medicalization of deviance provided them with the tools for reformation and that it was proper to socialize and acculturate the children of the poor and immigrants to become middle-class Americans (Rothman 1978, 1980; Ryerson 1978).

By the time of *Gault*, the Progessives' consensus about state benevolence, the legitimacy of imposing certain values on others, and what rehabilitation entailed and when it had occurred were all matters of intense dispute (Rothman 1978; Allen 1981). The decline in deference to the professionalism and benevolence of rehabilitative experts led to an increased emphasis on procedural formality, administrative regularity, and the rule of law.

Several forces unraveled support for the rehabilitative enterprise and led to the imposition of due process safeguards in juvenile and criminal justice: left-wing critiques of rehabilitation that characterized all governmental programs as coercive instruments of social control through which the state oppresses the poor and minorities (American Friends Service Committee 1971), liberal disenchantment with the unequal and disparate treatment of similarly situated offenders resulting from treatment officials' exercise of clinical discretion (Rothman 1978), and conservative advocates of a "war on crime" during the turbulent 1960s who favored repression over rehabilitation (Graham 1970).

The reevaluation of juvenile and criminal justice social control strategies in the 1960s was occasioned by the dramatic increase in youth crime and urban disorders as the children of the post–World War II "baby boom" came of age. The demographic bulge in the cohort of fourteen- to twenty-four-year-olds overwhelmed many traditional socializing institutions, led to fears of the young, an increase in social disorder associated with the young, and increased demands for their social control (Coleman et al. 1974). Black migration from the rural South to the urban North during and after World War II greatly increased minority concentrations in urban ghettos and gave impetus to the civil rights movement (Hodgson 1976). Urban riots in the 1960s exacerbated the crisis of "law and order," added fuel for the advocates of repression, and led to the elections of Richard Nixon as president and Ronald Reagan as governor of California.

The decline of support for rehabilitation accompanied the declining legitimacy of public authority (Allen 1981). Where Progressive claims of benevolence legitimated a program, by the 1960s, bureaucratic assertions of benevolence elicited skepticism and scrutiny (Rothman 1978). Empirical evaluations of treatment programs raised substantial doubts about the effectiveness of efforts to coerce change and concerns about the subjectivity inherent in therapeutic justice (Martinson 1974; Allen

1981). Questioning the scientific bases of rehabilitation also implicated the processes by which it was implemented as critics equated discretionary expertise with standardless subjectivity that lent itself to discriminatory applications (American Friends Service Committee 1971).

Although constitutional criminal procedural safeguards served to protect citizens against governmental power, the Progressives had redefined coercion as benevolent social services, rejected the antagonism of governmental power and citizens' liberty interests, and insulated many forms of intervention from formal legal limitations (Rothman 1978). As the relationship between state benevolence and coercion became more apparent and the expertise of the intervenors more suspect, the Supreme Court resorted to adversarial procedures and rule-oriented limitations to protect individual liberties.

In the 1960s, the issue of race in American society was the crucial factor linking distrust of governmental benevolence, concern about social service personnel's discretionary decision making, the crisis of "law and order," and the Supreme Court's due process jurisprudence (Graham 1970; Debele 1987). The Warren Court's "due process revolution," which reformed the criminal process and the administration of social services, reflected a judicial effort to expand civil rights, protect minorities from state officials, and infuse governmental services with greater equality through the imposition of the rule of law and procedural restraints on official discretion (Graham 1970; Rothman 1978). Beginning with the struggle for racial justice in school desegregation in *Brown v. Board of Education*, 347 U.S. 483 (1954), during the 1960s the Warren Court interpreted the Constitution to restrict the scope of governmental intervention in citizens' lives, extended equality to minorities and the disenfranchised, and regularized administrative decision making. In the context of criminal justice, the Supreme Court simultaneously applied many of the provisions of the Bill of Rights to the states, redefined and expanded the meanings of those rights to control the actions of local law enforcement officials, and extended constitutional safeguards to administrative officials previously immune from judicial scrutiny (Graham 1970).

The Supreme Court's juvenile court decisions in *Gault* and several later cases mandated procedural safeguards in delinquency proceedings and focused judicial attention initially on whether the child committed an offense as prerequisite to sentencing (Feld 1984, 1988b). In shifting the formal focus of juvenile courts from "real needs" to legal guilt, *Gault* identified two crucial gaps between juvenile justice rhetoric and reality: differences between the theory and the practice of rehabilitation and between procedural safeguards afforded adults and those available to juveniles. The *Gault* Court emphasized that juveniles charged with crimes who faced institutional confinement required elementary procedural safeguards including advance notice of charges, a fair and impartial hearing, assistance of counsel, an opportunity to confront and cross-examine witnesses, and the privilege against self-incrimination (Paulsen 1967; Rosenberg 1980; McCarthy 1981; Feld 1984). Thus began the procedural convergence of the juvenile justice system with the adult criminal process.

In *In re Winship*, 397 U.S. 358 (1970), the Court concluded that the risks of unwarranted convictions and the need to protect against government power required delinquency to be proved by the criminal law's standard of proof "beyond a reasonable doubt" rather than by lower civil standards of proof. In *Breed v. Jones*, 421 U.S. 519 (1975), the Court posited a functional equivalence between criminal trials and delinquency proceedings and applied the bar on double jeopardy to delinquency convictions.

In *McKeiver v. Pennsylvania*, 403 U.S. 528 (1971), however, the Court denied to juveniles the constitutional right to jury trials and halted the extension of full procedural parity with adult criminal prosecutions. In contrast to its analyses in earlier decisions, the *McKeiver* Court reasoned that "fundamental fairness" in delinquency proceedings required only "accurate factfinding," a requirement that can be satisfied as well by a judge as by a jury. Unlike *Gault* and *Winship*, which recognized that procedural safeguards protect against governmental oppression, the Court in *McKeiver* denied that such protection was required and invoked the stereotype of the sympathetic, paternalistic juvenile court judge (Feld 1984, 1988*b*). Although the *McKeiver* Court relied on the differences between juvenile courts' *treatment* rationale and criminal courts' *punitive* purposes to justify the procedural differences in the two settings, it did not analyze the differences between treatment as a juvenile and punishment as an adult that warranted those procedural differences (Feld 1987, 1988*b*).

Together, *Gault*, *Winship*, and *McKeiver* precipitated a procedural and substantive revolution in the juvenile court system that unintentionally but inevitably transformed it from its original Progressive conception. By emphasizing criminal procedural regularity in the determination of delinquency, the Supreme Court shifted the focus of juvenile courts from paternalistic assessments of a youth's "real needs" to proof of the commission of criminal acts. By formalizing the connection between criminal conduct and coercive intervention, the Court made explicit a relationship that previously was implicit and unacknowledged.

Since those decisions, a variety of legislative, judicial, and administrative actions have transformed the juvenile court. Four developments—increased procedural formality, removal of status offenders from juvenile court jurisdiction, waiver of serious offenders to the adult system, and an increased emphasis on punishment in sentencing delinquents—are manifestations of the criminalizing of the juvenile court. These reforms have not been implemented as intended, have not had their expected effects, and as a result, the juvenile court has been transformed but remains unreformed. While the remainder of this essay examines these changes and their implications for the juvenile court, it is first necessary to identify some of the sources of knowledge about juvenile courts and their administration.

## II. Sources of Knowledge about the Juvenile Court

Juvenile courts are a study in contradictions marked by disjunctions between theory and practice, between rehabilitative rhetoric and punitive reality, and between the law on the books and the law in action (Feld 1990*b*). Analyses are complicated further because juvenile courts are almost exclusively state statutory entities with only a secondary federal judicial role. Among the fifty separate state systems, juvenile courts differ substantially in both their legislative definitions and processing of young offenders. In different states, a juvenile court may be a division of the court of general jurisdiction, a separate court, or part of an inferior court system (Edwards 1992). In most states, juvenile court jurisdiction encompasses criminal and noncriminal misconduct by all persons under eighteen years of age. However, in twelve states, adult criminal court jurisdiction begins at sixteen or seventeen years of age, while in Wyoming, it may not begin until a youth is nineteen (Hamparian et al. 1982; Feld 1988*b*). In addition, even where general juvenile court jurisdiction extends until eighteen years of age, some states may automatically place younger youths charged with serious offenses in adult criminal court (Feld 1987). In a few states, juvenile and criminal courts exercise concurrent jurisdiction over young offenders, which means that the prosecutor's decision to charge a youth as a juvenile delinquent or as an adult criminal determines the forum in which the case will be heard (Feld 1978, 1987; Hamparian et al. 1982).

As a consequence of variations in legislative definitions, juvenile courts in different jurisdictions may confront widely divergent clientele. While it is possible to generalize about juvenile courts, analyses of juvenile justice administration necessarily must be qualified by specific references to each state's legislative nuances and judicial opinions.

## A. Sources of Knowledge

Analyzing states' juvenile court "law on the books" is the relatively straightforward task of legal scholarship and involves analyses of statutes, judicial opinions, and court rules. For example, juvenile courts' procedures are structured by an amalgam of United States Supreme Court constitutional decisions such as *Gault*, state statutes, judicial opinions, and court rules of procedure; juvenile court procedures are analyzed by comparing those used in different jurisdictions or in criminal courts (Rosenberg 1980; McCarthy 1981; Feld 1984). Legal scholars also analyze juvenile court substantive law, for example, by examining statutes and judicial opinions regulating juvenile court sentencing practices (Walkover 1984; Feld 1988*b*) or the bases for transferring some juveniles to criminal courts (Vereb and Hutzler 1981; Hamparian et al. 1982; Feld 1987).

Analyzing the "law in action" in juvenile courts is a more complicated matter. There have been relatively few intensive ethnographic studies of juvenile courts that provide detailed information about the operations of a single juvenile court (Cicourel 1968; Emerson 1969; Bortner 1982). Such studies typically involve participant observation of a court's operations over a period of months or years, extensive interviews with selected or random samples of court personnel, observations of court hearings and other decisions, identification and tracking of individual juveniles' cases through the process, or statistical analyses of cases processed during the observation period (Cicourel 1968; Emerson 1969; Bortner 1982). While these studies provide a richness of data and analyses, unfortunately they are somewhat dated and do not reflect the contemporary reality of juvenile justice administration. Moreover, in order to preserve the anonymity of the court sites being observed, the authors do not provide enough information about the courts' social structural contexts to permit generalization to other courts in other settings.

Many studies of juvenile justice administration rely on secondary analyses of official data collected by local or state agencies: police, probation, prosecution, juvenile courts, corrections, and the like (e.g.,

Henretta, Frazier, and Bishop 1986; Feld 1989, 1991; Bishop and Frazier 1992). Reliance on official police crime statistics is frequently criticized because of concerns about underreporting of crime by victims to the police as well as by police departments to the FBI and selection bias by police in detecting, recording, and reporting crime (Sampson 1986).

Official juvenile court statistics reflect further population selection biases. The typical juvenile delinquency or status offense case begins with a juvenile's referral by police, parents, probation officers, or school officials to either the county prosecuting attorney, a county's juvenile court, or the court's juvenile probation or intake department. These prosecutorial and intake "gatekeepers" may screen cases on a discretionary basis for legal sufficiency, social welfare needs, or both to determine whether formal juvenile court intervention is appropriate (Feld 1989). Many referrals are dismissed by prosecutors or closed by the social services staff at intake with some type of *informal* disposition —dismissal, counseling, warning, diversion or referral to another agency, or informal probation—that does not result in the filing of a petition. In the remaining cases, the juvenile process is *formally* initiated by the filing of a petition, typically by the prosecuting attorney. In many jurisdictions, referrals that do not result in formal charges may not generate systematic records that can be retrieved or analyzed. This is an important source of population selection bias in juvenile records since informal screening and formal charging practices vary considerably among states, as well as among counties within a state. Between 1957 and 1982, for example, approximately half of all delinquency referrals nationwide were handled by formal petition, ranging from a high of 54 percent in some years to a low of 41 percent in others (Nimick, Szymanski, and Snyder 1985, p. 12). In 1988, 48 percent of all delinquency referrals and 22 percent of all status referrals resulted in the filing of a formal petition (Snyder et al. 1990, pp. 14, 99). One study reported that in four states the proportion of juvenile court referrals that resulted in the filing of petitions ranged from 10.7 percent to 62.8 percent (Feld 1988a).

For those cases that become official juvenile court statistics, access to and secondary analyses of juvenile court data becomes somewhat easier in many jurisdictions. Following passage of the Juvenile Justice and Delinquency Prevention Act of 1974, the Office of Juvenile Justice and Delinquency Prevention within the U.S. Department of Justice has supported the National Juvenile Court Data Archive (NJCDA) at the National Center for Juvenile Justice (NCJJ). In the mid-1970s, state and local juvenile courts began to adopt automated record keeping and statistical reporting systems. Thirty states or metropolitan courts now contribute case-level data or court-level aggregate statistics to NJCDA (National Center for Juvenile Justice 1991). While the amount of data and types of variables contained in the respective states' data sets vary considerably, these official data have considerable validity because they were designed and collected by state and local juvenile courts to meet their own calendar, information, planning, and operational needs (Snyder et al. 1990).

Each year, data contributed to NJCDA are merged to create a national data set containing detailed descriptions of cases handled by the states' juvenile courts (Snyder et al. 1990).[1] Although the individual states collect, code, and report different types of information about a case, NJCDA has developed a standardized, national coding format that enables it to recode the raw data provided by the states into a more uniform format. The staff study codebooks and operation manuals, interview data suppliers, and analyze data files to maximize their understanding of each information system.

The diversity and quantity of data in NJCDA permit analyses that would not be possible within a more general and uniform national coding system such as the FBI's Uniform Crime Reports. In one study of 17,195 individual juveniles' cases in Minnesota in 1986, Feld (1989) analyzed the delivery of legal services and the impact of counsel in juvenile courts and reported considerable variation in juvenile justice administration in counties in which lawyers routinely, occasionally, and seldom appeared.[2] In a second analysis of that NJCDA data file,

---

[1] The NJCDA's unit of count is "cases disposed." Each "case" represents a youth whose case is disposed of by the juvenile court for a new delinquency or status referral. A case is "disposed" when some definite action is taken, whether dismissal, warning, informal counseling or probation, referral to a treatment program, adjudication as a delinquent with some disposition, or transfer to an adult criminal court (Nimick et al. 1985, p. 3). As a result of multiple referrals, one child may be involved in several "cases" during a calendar year. Moreover, each "case" referral may contain more than one offense or charge. The multiple referrals of an individual child may tend to overstate the numbers of youths handled annually. Multiple charges in one petition may appear to understate the volume of delinquency in a jurisdiction. Because the unit of count is "case disposed," one cannot generalize from the data either the number of individual youths who are processed by the court annually or the number of separate offenses with which juveniles are charged.

[2] While normally the NJCDA data unit is "case disposed," the NJCDA was able to convert its case-based data file into a youth-based data file, permitting Feld (1989, 1991) to analyze the cases of *individual juveniles* against whom *petitions* were filed in 1986. The annual data collected by the Minnesota Supreme Court's Judicial Information System

Feld (1991) reported that there was "justice by geography"; urban, suburban, and rural courts screened, detained, and sentenced similarly situated offenders differently. Because Feld's (1989, 1991) research was not experimental with random assignments, multivariate analyses controlling for the effects of the present offense, prior record, and other legal variables on variations in juveniles' sentences could not account for local differences in precharge screening practices and population selection biases that may account for some of the differences found in juvenile justice administration.

Some of the better studies analyzing juvenile court dispositional practices attempt to account for precharge screening by collecting data directly through the individual court itself and at several decision-making points (Dannefer and Schutt 1982; McCarthy and Smith 1986; Fagan, Slaughter, and Hartstone 1987). McCarthy and Smith (1986) analyzed racial discrimination in juvenile justice processing by collecting data at intake screening, detention, adjudication, and disposition. They used path analyses to examine the cases of an original sample of 649 youths referred to one southeastern, metropolitan juvenile court for delinquency; they also examined subsamples of 406 petitioned youths and 186 adjudicated youths to assess the effects of race and sample selection biases on juvenile justice processing. Their multivariate analyses of sequential screening processes concluded that cumulative decisions produced a legally more homogeneous population in which social class and race became "increasingly important as direct influences on final disposition as youths are selected into the system for further processing" (McCarthy and Smith 1986, p. 58).

Fagan et al. (1987) extended McCarthy and Smith's (1986) strategy and analyzed screening decision making by using a stratified, random sample of youths at six decision points in the juvenile justice process in a metropolitan area in a western state. They collected data on actions taken by the police, the prosecutor, the juvenile court, the probation department, and the state correction agency. The police records included demographic characteristics, prior contacts, and the instant offense. The prosecutor's records included charging information, and the court-processing data, collected directly from court files, contained summaries of findings and actions taken at each hearing, motions filed

included information on the data of referral, county and source of referral, referral offense(s), the offense(s) for which the youth was ultimately adjudicated, the youth's detention status, the nature of the juvenile's defense representation, the eventual disposition, the juvenile's birthdate, race, and sex.

by counsel, and predispositional and other reports and records relevant to the case. They used simple two- and three-way contingency tables to control for demographic, offense history, and specific violent offense characteristics in the apprehension, detention, charging, adjudication, and sentencing of 114 Anglo and 120 minority youths accused of violent, serious, and other offenses. They concluded, after controlling for a wide range of offense and offender characteristics, that minority youths consistently received harsher and more punitive dispositions than did Anglo youths. Like McCarthy and Smith, however, Fagan et al. were only able to control weakly for social class and social status, which correlate with race and which may provide an alternative, nondiscriminatory explanation for the juvenile courts' dispositions.

Clarke and Koch (1980) used court records to conduct a quasi experiment that examined the effects of legal representation and court-processing variables on juveniles' dispositions. They collected 1,435 court records from a period six months prior to the start of a juvenile legal representation project and for six months after it was implemented. They constructed matched sets of cases on the basis of seriousness of offense and prior records within which the disposition rates were homogeneous. Controlling for the offense variables, they examined the effects of certain risk factors—race, sex, age, home structure, parental presence at hearing, source of referral, legal representation, and detention—on dispositions. Because Clarke and Koch worked from "raw" court records, they were able to construct an offense-seriousness index based on more information than simply the type of offense charged. While the present offense and prior record accounted for most of the variance in sentencing, after controlling for their effects, juveniles against whom probation officers and parents were complainants, those held in pretrial detention, and those with legal representation received more severe sentences.

Hamparian et al.'s (1982) study of juveniles waived to criminal court and prosecuted as adults is one of the most ambitious juvenile court data collection projects undertaken. Hamparian conducted a complete nationwide census of every juvenile, defined as persons under eighteen years of age, waived from juvenile court or tried as an adult in 1978. Her project, which produced a summary volume and five volumes of individual state-by-state data, entailed preliminary telephone surveys of state and local agencies, followed by physical data retrieval in 3,100 counties. Data were gathered from state court administrative offices, juvenile courts, prosecutors, and adult criminal courts. State data sets were verified by contacting the local units of government. In each state, data on each youth's age, sex, race, offense, adult court judgment, sentence, and maximum sentence if confined were collected in the most populous 10 percent of the counties and in all counties in which five or more youths were waived. The types of "official" records available included "everything from very sophisticated data tapes to court records kept in penciled, handwritten notebooks" (Hamparian et al. 1982, p. 238).

Although juvenile court records increasingly are computerized, Hamparian et al.'s description of the range of quality of data in juvenile courts is apt. Like all official records, the validity, reliability, completeness, and accuracy of the information recorded and transmitted varies substantially. Moreover, different components of the juvenile justice system—police, intake, probation, prosecutors, courts, corrections—collect different types of information for different administrative purposes. There are virtually no consistent identifiers that enable researchers or policy planners to link individual case files in different agencies or to track offenders through various stages of "loosely coupled" systems or over time. While most states' automated juvenile court data systems include data on a youth's date of birth, county, offense, and disposition, very few juvenile court information systems routinely and consistently collect data on important legal and sociodemographic variables such as family status, income, school performance, use of weapons, injury to victims, representation by counsel, or the like (National Center for Juvenile Justice 1991). For example, only six states routinely code and collect data on whether juveniles had the assistance of counsel in juvenile court proceedings (Feld 1988a). While sociodemographic information is regularly collected and included in a juvenile's social services records, those social services records are less accessible to researchers or policy analysts and entail substantially greater costs in order to put them into an analytically useable format.

### B. Varieties of Juvenile Courts

The idealized portrayal of the traditional juvenile court is one of procedural informality in the quest of the goals of treatment and rehabilitation (Mack 1909). The historical focus on characteristics of the young offender fostered judicial discretion and organizational diversity rather than formality and consistency, such that "any attempt to analyze the workings of a given court demanded a lengthy evaluation of its judge" (Rothman 1980, p. 238). Evaluations of contemporary juvenile courts continue to emphasize the diversity of judges and the highly discretionary legal framework that allows for "very individualistic interpretation and clearly different application" of laws (Rubin 1985, p. 7).

With *Gault's* imposition of formal procedures and the emergence of punitive as well as therapeutic goals (Feld 1984, 1988*b*), a state's juvenile courts can no longer be assumed to conform to the traditional rehabilitative model or even to be similar to one another. One cannot generalize from intensive ethnographic studies of a single juvenile court to other courts in other locales. The few comparative studies of juvenile courts reveal some of the complexities of goals, philosophies, court structures, and procedures that characterize the juvenile court as an institution (Sarri and Hasenfeld 1976; Cohen and Kluegel 1978, 1979).

Recent research indicates that juvenile courts vary on a number of structural, philosophical, and procedural dimensions (Stapleton, Aday, and Ito 1982; Hasenfeld and Cheung 1985). Stapleton et al. (1982) at the National Center for State Courts developed a detailed questionnaire to elicit information on ninety-six theoretically relevant variables about juvenile courts' jurisdiction, administrative structure, procedures, and options at intake, detention, adjudication, and disposition. They interviewed two respondents, a judge and a court administrator, in a saturated sample of 150 metropolitan juvenile courts. They compared the two sets of responses from each court and called back or made site visits to resolve discrepancies. Through factor analyses, they identified clusters of factors—status offender orientation, centralization of authority, formalization of procedure, and intake screening discretion—around which courts varied and developed an empirical typology of metropolitan juvenile courts. Their typology confirmed "the existence of the two major types of juvenile courts ('traditional' and 'due process') suggested in the literature. More important, however, it reveals variations in court structure and procedure that are not captured adequately by existing simplistic typologies" (Stapleton et al. 1982, p. 559). For example, their factor analyses identified "transitional courts," which represent an intermediate point in the transformation from traditional, therapeutic courts to formal, due process courts.

Traditional courts intervene in a child's "best interests" on an informal, discretionary basis, while the legalistic courts emphasize more formal, rule-oriented decision making and recognition of a juvenile's legal rights. "Traditional" and "due process" courts may be arrayed across a continuum from informal to formal procedures with corresponding structural and substantive differences (Stapleton et al. 1982). Traditional, informal, cooperative courts and formal, adversarial courts differ considerably in the presence of counsel, which is one important indicator of procedural, substantive, and structural variations among juvenile courts (Handler 1965; Stapleton and Teitelbaum 1972; Cohen and Kluegel 1978; Feld 1984, 1989, 1991). Whether attorneys are present routinely, in turn, affects many other aspects of juvenile justice administration. Recent studies indicate that the presence of counsel, which is associated with a formal, due process orientation, is also related to differences in pretrial detention, sentencing, and case-processing practices (Cohen and Kluegel 1978; Carrington and Moyer 1988*a*, 1988*b;* Feld 1988*a*, 1989, 1991; Kempf et al. 1990).

While juvenile courts vary substantially among the states, they vary considerably within a single state as well. Although the same laws typically apply to all juvenile courts within a state, there is substantial structural and geographic administrative variation (Mahoney 1987; Kempf et al. 1990; Feld 1991). For example, whether youths live in metropolitan areas with full-time juvenile courts or in rural areas with part-time juvenile judges affects how their cases are screened, processed, and sanctioned (Kempf et al. 1990; Feld 1991). Differences in social structure are associated consistently with differences in juvenile crime rates and in juvenile justice administration (Kempf et al. 1990; Feld 1991). In Minnesota's urban counties, which are more heterogeneous and racially diverse, and less stable, than rural counties, juvenile court intervention is more formal and due process oriented. Feld's (1989, 1991) research demonstrates both a theoretical and an empirical relationship between variations in social structure and juvenile justice administration. Feld (1989) compared counties with high (95 percent), medium (46 percent), and low (19 percent) rates of representation and reported considerable variation in detaining, sentencing, and processing of juveniles. Feld (1991) reported that attorneys appeared in 62.6 percent of all cases in urban courts, where a more formal, due process model of justice occurs, whereas they appeared only in 25.1 percent of cases in rural juvenile courts, where a more traditional, informal model of justice occurs.

There also appears to be a relationship between social structure, procedural formality, and severity of sanctions. In the more formal, urban courts, 12.9 percent of all juveniles were held in pretrial detention as contrasted with 4.8 percent of suburban youths and 4.4 percent of rural juveniles (Feld 1991). Urban courts also sentenced similarly charged youths more severely than did judges in suburban or rural courts. For youths charged with felony offenses, for example, urban judges removed 42.3 percent from their homes as compared with 23.7 percent of suburban judges and 29.5 percent of rural judges (Feld 1991). Multiple regression analyses using an urban "dummy" variable indicate that being tried in an urban court aggravates the severity of a youth's sentence (Feld 1991).

Kempf et al. (1990) examined juvenile justice administration in Missouri and found similar variations:

> The results of this study show differential processing within two distinct court systems operating in Missouri juvenile justice. One court type is rural and the other is primarily urban. . . . Rural courts typically are guided by one judge who holds the position for several years where the majority of decisions are made by one chief juvenile officer. Rural courts rarely have separate detention facilities, and have less access to local treatment facilities. Decisions are made individually, that is, on a case by case basis. . . . In urban courts the judges rotate to other types of courts frequently. Different staff are responsible at different stages in the process. Decisionmaking is guided more often by written standards, but policies still enable discretionary choices. Urban courts operate their own facilities, and have greater access to both home and residential placement services. These two types of courts function by different standards as well. Rural courts seem to adhere to traditional, pre*Gault*, juvenile court *parens patriae* criteria in their handling of youths. Urban courts appear more legalistic in orientation and process cases more according to offense criteria. [Kempf, Decker, and Bing 1990, p. 118]

There is also some macrolevel evidence from which to infer a relationship between process formality and sentencing severity. An interstate analysis of appointment of counsel reported that rates of representation in more urban, industrial states—California (84.9 percent), Pennsylvania (86.4 percent), and New York (95.9 percent)—were about double the rates in more rural, Midwestern states—Minnesota (47.7 percent), North Dakota (37.5 percent), and Nebraska (52.7 percent) (Feld 1988a). Perhaps related to its greater procedural formality, California is also one of the leaders in "cracking down" on youth crime (Private Sector Task Force on Juvenile Justice 1987; Forst and Blomquist 1991). And New York's "designated felony" legislation has been characterized as "one of the harshest juvenile justice [sentencing] systems in the country" (Woods 1980, p. 2).

The intrastate and interstate variations raise the question whether there is a relationship between procedural formality and severity of sanctions. Does greater urban crime engender more punitive responses, which then require more formal procedural safeguards as a prerequisite? Or, does urban bureaucratization lead to more formal procedural safeguards, which then enable judges to exact a greater toll than they otherwise might? Perceived increases in urban crime may foster a "war-on-crime" mentality that places immense pressures on the juvenile justice system to "get tough" and furthers the convergence between juvenile and criminal courts. In short, structural features associated with juvenile crime and its repression may also be associated with process formality and sentencing severity.

These recurring findings of extensive interstate and intrastate variations in procedural formality, representation by attorneys, and detention and sentencing practices raise important issues for understanding juvenile courts. Finding "justice by geography" and substantial judicial diversity in ostensibly similar counties and under identical legal regimes vastly complicates the tasks of criminologists. There is both a theoretical and empirical relationship between variations in social structure and in juvenile justice administration. If a state's juvenile courts are not a single, uniform justice system, then research must identify and account for these systemic and structural differences. Studies that analyze and interpret aggregated statewide data without accounting for procedural, contextual, and structural characteristics or intrastate variations may systematically mislead and obscure, rather than clarify. Studies reporting differences in juvenile courts' decision making actually may reflect sampling errors, population biases, or system differences. Subject to these caveats, the next sections of this essay examine the juvenile court as an institution in transition.

### III. Procedural Justice in Juvenile Courts

Procedure and substance are inextricably intertwined in juvenile courts. The increased procedural formality since *Gault* has been associated with a corresponding shift in emphasis, both in legal theory and in administrative practice, away from therapeutic, individualized dispositions toward more punitive, offense-based sentences (Gardner 1987; Feld 1988*b*; Forst and Blomquist 1991). In 1970, when the Supreme Court decided *McKeiver*, juvenile court judges' discretion was not constrained by determinate or mandatory minimum sentencing statutes or administrative guidelines. In the mid- to late 1970s, several states adopted "designated felony" and serious offender sentencing legislation and determinate sentencing guidelines (Feld 1988*b;* Ainsworth 1991). Since 1980, eleven more states have adopted mandatory minimums, determinate sentences, or administrative release guidelines. Legislative revisions of juvenile courts' purpose clauses eliminate even rhetorical support for rehabilitation, and court decisions endorsing punishment contradict the therapeutic premise of juvenile dispositions (Walkover 1984; Feld 1988*b*). As a result, about one-third of the states use at least some explicitly punitive sentencing strategies (Feld 1988*b*). A similar pattern occurred in the use of offense criteria to structure the waiver decision that places some juvenile offenders in adult criminal courts (Feld 1987).

These changes repudiate many of the original juvenile courts' basic assumptions that juveniles should be treated differently than adults, that juvenile courts operate in a youth's "best interest," and that rehabilitation is an indeterminate process that cannot be limited by fixed-time punishment (Coates, Forst, and Fisher 1985). These changes also contradict *McKeiver's* premise that therapeutic juvenile dispositions require fewer procedural safeguards than do adult criminal prosecutions and raise questions about the quality of juvenile justice that the Court avoided.

The formal procedures of juvenile and criminal courts have converged under *Gault's* impetus (Feld 1984, 1988*b*). There remains, however, a substantial gulf between theory and reality, between the law on the books and law in action. Theoretically, delinquents are entitled to formal trials and the assistance of counsel. In actuality, the quality of procedural justice is far different. Despite the criminalizing of juvenile courts, most states provide neither special procedures to protect juveniles from their own immaturity nor the full panoply of adult procedural safeguards.[3] Based on depictions of courtroom dramas and publicized criminal trials, young people have a cultural expectation of what a "real" trial should be. The contrast between the ideal-typical jury trial with vigorous defense representation and the "actualized caricature" of a juvenile bench trial fosters a sense of injustice that may delegitimatize the legal process (Ainsworth 1991, p. 1119).

## A. *Jury Trials*

The right to a jury trial is a critical procedural safeguard when sentences are punitive rather than therapeutic. Only thirteen states'

[3] Feld (1984) elaborated the thesis that states treat juveniles like adult criminal defendants when equality redounds to their disadvantage and use less adequate juvenile court safeguards when those deficient procedures provide an advantage to the state by comparing juvenile and adult criminal procedural safeguards.

case law or statutes grant juveniles the right to jury trials (Feld 1988*b;* Ainsworth 1991), while the majority of states follow the Supreme Court's lead in *McKeiver v. Pennsylvania* and deny access to juries. Without citing any empirical evidence, the *McKeiver* Court posited virtual parity between the factual accuracy of juvenile and adult adjudications to rationalize denying juveniles a jury trial. But juries provide special protections to assure factual accuracy, use a higher evidentiary threshold when they apply *Winship's* "proof beyond a reasonable doubt" standard, and acquit more readily than do judges (Kalven and Zeisel 1966). Greenwood, Lipson, Abrahamse, and Zimring (1983) analyzed arrest disposition rates for similar types of cases in juvenile and adult courts in California and concluded that "it is easier to win a conviction in the juvenile court than in the criminal court, with comparable types of cases" (Greenwood, Lipson, Abrahamse, and Zimring 1983, pp. 30–31).

Ainsworth (1991) offers a variety of reasons why juvenile court judges convict more readily than juries. Fact finding by judges and juries is intrinsically different since the former try hundreds of cases every year while the latter hear only one or two. As a result of hearing many cases routinely, judges may become less meticulous in considering evidence, may evaluate facts more casually, and may apply less stringently the concepts of reasonable doubt and presumption of innocence than do jurors (Ainsworth 1991). The personal characteristics of judges differ from those of jurors, and it is more difficult for a defendant to determine how those personal characteristics will affect the decision in a case. Through voir dire, litigants may examine jurors about their attitudes, beliefs, and experiences as they may bear on the way they will decide the case; there is no comparable opportunity to explore a judge's background to determine the presence of judicial biases. In addition to the novelty of deciding cases, juries and judges evaluate testimony differently. Juvenile court judges hear testimony from the same police and probation officers on a recurring basis and develop a settled opinion about their credibility. Similarly, as a result of hearing earlier charges against a juvenile, or presiding over a detention hearing or pretrial motion to suppress evidence, a judge already may have a predetermined view of a youth's credibility and character (Feld 1984; Ainsworth 1991). Fact finding by a judge differs from that by a jury because an individual fact finder does not have to discuss either the law or the evidence with a group before reaching a conclusion. Although a jury must be instructed explicitly about the law to be applied to a case, the judge in a bench trial is not required to articulate the law, and it is more difficult to determine whether the judge correctly understood and applied it (Ainsworth 1991).

Moreover, *McKeiver* ignored that constitutional procedures also prevent governmental oppression (Feld 1981*a*, 1984, 1988*b*). In *Duncan v. Louisiana*, 391 U.S. 145 (1968), the Court held that adult criminal proceedings required a jury to assure both factual accuracy *and* protection against governmental oppression. *Duncan* emphasized that juries protect against a weak or biased judge, inject the community's values into law, and increase the visibility and accountability of justice administration. These protective functions are even more crucial in juvenile courts, which labor behind closed doors immune from public scrutiny. Appellate courts acknowledge that juvenile cases exhibit far more procedural errors than do adult criminal cases and suggest that secrecy may foster a judicial casualness toward the law that visibility might constrain (*R.L.R. v. State*, 487 P.2d 27 [Alaska 1971]; *In re Dino*, 359 So.2d 586 [Louisiana 1978]).

Few of the states that sentence juveniles punitively provide jury trials; several have rejected constitutional challenges (e.g., *State v. Schaaf*, 743 P.2d 240 [Washington 1987]; Feld 1988*b*). Juries have symbolic significance for the juvenile court out of all proportion to their practical impact since even in states where they are available, they are seldom used (Feld 1988*b*). A survey of jury trials in those few jurisdictions that give juveniles access to a jury reported that the rates ranged between .36 percent and 3.2 percent (Shaughnessy 1979). There are no data available on the rates of juvenile jury trials compared with adult jury trials for comparable offenses. As a symbol, however, the jury requires candor and honesty about punishment that is imposed in the name of treatment and the need to protect against even benevolent governmental coercion.

## B. The Right to Counsel

Procedural justice hinges on access to and the assistance of counsel. When *Gault* was decided, an attorney's appearance in delinquency proceedings was a rare event, occurring in perhaps 5 percent of cases (*Harvard Law Review* 1966; President's Commission on Law Enforcement and Administration of Justice 1967*b*). Despite *Gault's* formal legal changes, however, the actual delivery of legal services lagged behind. In the immediate aftermath of *Gault*, observers in two metropolitan juvenile courts systematically monitored institutional compliance with the decision and reported that juveniles were neither adequately advised of their right to counsel nor had counsel appointed for them (Lefstein, Stapleton, and Teitelbaum 1969). Ferster and Courtless's (1972) analysis of court records in 1968 showed that 27 percent of juveniles were represented, and observations of sixty-four hearings in 1969 included only 37.5 percent in which juveniles had counsel at the adjudicatory stage; in 66.7 percent of those cases in which lawyers were present, they did not participate in any way.

In the two decades since *Gault*, the promise of legal representation remains unrealized; in many states half or less of all juveniles receive the assistance of counsel to which they are constitutionally entitled. In the only study that reports statewide data or makes interstate comparisons of the delivery of legal services, Feld (1988*a*) reported that in three of the six states surveyed, only 37.5 percent, 47.7 percent, and 52.7 percent of juveniles charged with delinquent and status offenses were represented. Clarke and Koch's (1980) evaluations of legal representation in North Carolina in 1978 found that the juvenile defender project represented only 22.3 percent of juveniles in Winston-Salem, North Carolina, and only 45.8 percent in Charlotte, North Carolina. Aday (1986) found rates of representation of 26.2 percent and 38.7 percent in the southeastern jurisdictions he studied. Walter and Ostrander (1982) observed that only 32 percent of the juveniles in a large north central city were represented by counsel. A study of a large, midwestern county's juvenile court found that only 41.8 percent of juveniles were represented by an attorney (Bortner 1982). In Minnesota, a majority of all juveniles are unrepresented: in 1984, 53.2 percent of juveniles appeared without counsel (Feld 1984, 1988*a*); in 1986, 54.7 percent were unrepresented (Feld 1989, 1991); in 1988, 58.9 percent had no attorney (Minnesota Supreme Court 1990). Feld (1989) reported enormous county-by-county variations in rates of representation within Minnesota, ranging from a high of 100 percent in one county to a low of less than 5 percent in several others. A substantial minority of youths removed from their homes (30.7 percent) or confined in state juvenile correctional institutions (26.5 percent) lacked representation at the time of their adjudication and disposition (Feld 1989).

Juveniles charged with more serious offenses are more likely to be represented. In Minnesota, where only 45.3 percent of youths overall had counsel, 66.1 percent of those charged with a felony offense, 46.4 percent of those charged with misdemeanors, and only 28.9 percent of those charged with status offenses had lawyers (Feld 1991). Emphasizing the variability of juvenile justice, however, for youths in Minnesota's seventy-seven rural counties, even a majority of those charged with felony offenses (50.4 percent) appeared without counsel (Feld 1991). While youths charged with serious offenses are more likely to be represented, they constitute a small part of juvenile court dockets in most states (Feld 1988a, 1989). In Minnesota in 1986, for example, only 18.4 percent of youths were charged with a felony, and most of those were felony offenses against property, such as burglary. In 1984, in California, 35.9 percent of youths were charged with felony offenses; in New York, 23.1 percent; and in Nebraska, 12.1 percent (Feld 1988a), with property felony crimes predominating in all jurisdictions. The largest group of unrepresented youths and those most likely to be incarcerated without representation are charged with minor property offenses like shoplifting (Feld 1988a, 1989).

There are a variety of possible explanations for why so many youths appear unrepresented in juvenile courts: parental reluctance to retain an attorney, inadequate public defender legal services in nonurban areas, a judicial encouragement of and readiness to find waivers of the right to counsel in order to ease administrative burdens on the courts, cursory and misleading judicial advisories of rights that inadequately convey the importance of the right to counsel and suggest that the waiver litany is simply a technicality, a continuing judicial hostility to an advocacy role in a traditional treatment-oriented court, or a judicial predetermination of dispositions with nonappointment of counsel where probation is the anticipated outcome (Feld 1984, 1989; Bortner 1982; Lefstein et al. 1969; Stapleton and Teitelbaum 1972). In many instances, juveniles may plead guilty and have their case disposed at the same hearing without benefit of counsel. Whatever the reason, many juveniles facing potentially coercive state action never see a lawyer and waive their right to counsel without consulting with an attorney or appreciating the legal consequences of relinquishing counsel.

The most common explanation for why so many juveniles are unrepresented is that they waive their right to counsel (Lefstein et al. 1969; Stapleton and Teitelbaum 1972; Bortner 1982; Feld 1984, 1989). Most state courts use the adult legal standard—"knowing, intelligent, and voluntary" under the "totality of the circumstances"—to assess the validity of juveniles' waivers of constitutional rights (*Fare v. Michael C.*, 442 U.S. 707 [1979]; Feld 1984, 1989). The crucial issue, as for adults, is whether a waiver of counsel can be "knowing, intelligent, and voluntary" if it is made by a child alone without consulting with an attorney. The problem is exacerbated when, in closed confidential proceedings, judges who expect waivers immediately create an impression that waiver is a meaningless technicality and have responsibility for interpreting the juvenile's response (Feld 1989).

The "totality" approach to juveniles' waivers of rights has been criticized extensively as an example of treating juveniles just like adults when formal equality puts them at a disadvantage (Grisso 1980; Rosenberg 1980; Feld 1984; Melton 1989). Juveniles simply are not as capable as adults to waive their constitutional rights in a knowing and intelligent manner (Grisso 1980, 1981). Grisso (1980, 1981) evaluated juveniles' understanding of their *Miranda* rights by administering multiple tests to determine whether they could paraphrase the words in the warning, whether they could define six critical words in the *Miranda* warning such as "attorney," "consult," and "appoint," and whether they could give correct true-false answers to twelve rewordings of the *Miranda* warnings. The structured interviews, designed by a panel of psychologists and lawyers, were administered to three samples of juvenile subjects, 431 in all, who varied by age, race, social class, and juvenile court experience, and to two samples of adult subjects, 203 parolees residing in a halfway house, and fifty-seven volunteers from university and hospital custodial services. The adult samples were used to compare the juveniles' performances with adult norms. The findings indicated that most juveniles who receive legal advisories do not understand them well enough to waive their constitutional rights in a "knowing and intelligent" manner. Only 20.9 percent of the juveniles, as compared with 42.3 percent of the adults, demonstrated adequate understanding of the four components of a *Miranda* warning, while 55.3 percent of juveniles as contrasted with 23.1 percent of the adults exhibited no comprehension of at least one of the four warnings (Grisso 1980, pp. 1153–54). The most frequently misunderstood *Miranda* advisory was that the suspect had the right to consult with an attorney and have one present during interrogation. Problems of understanding and waiving rights are particularly acute for younger juveniles. "As a class, juveniles younger than fifteen years of age failed to meet both the absolute and relative (adult norm) standards for comprehension. . . . The vast majority of these juveniles misunderstood at least one of the four standard *Miranda* statements, and compared with adults, demonstrated significantly poorer comprehension of the nature and significance of the *Miranda* rights" (Grisso 1980, p. 1160). The recognition that children have different competencies than adults is reflected in the host of legal disabilities imposed on children for their own protection that limit their ability, for example, to enter into contracts, convey property, marry, drink, drive, or even donate blood. While several states recognize this developmental fact with respect to waivers of counsel, most states allow juveniles to waive constitutional rights such as *Miranda* and the right to counsel without restriction and confront the power of the state alone and unaided (e.g., Iowa Code Ann. § 232.11 [West 1985]; Wis. Stat. Ann. § 48.23 [West 1983]; American Bar Association—Institute of Judicial Administration 1980*a;* Feld 1984).

The questionable validity of juvenile waivers of counsel rights raises several collateral legal issues. Absent a valid waiver, appointment of counsel is a constitutional prerequisite to any sentence restricting an adult defendant's liberty (*Scott v. Illinois,* 440 U.S. 367 [1979]). It is also a constitutional violation to use prior convictions obtained without counsel to enhance later sentences (*United States v. Tucker,* 404 U.S. 443 [1972]; *Burgett v. Texas,* 389 U.S. 109 [1967]; *Baldasar v. Illinois,* 446 U.S. 222 [1980]). Every time a juvenile court judge incarcerates a youth without representation, or uses prior uncounseled convictions to sentence a juvenile, to impose a mandatory minimum or enhanced sentence, to waive a juvenile to criminal court, or to "bootstrap" a status offender into a delinquent through the contempt power, he or she compounds the problems associated with the original denial of counsel (Feld 1989).

Even when juveniles are represented, attorneys may not represent their clients effectively. Organizational pressures to cooperate, judicial hostility toward adversarial litigants, role ambiguity created by the dual goals of rehabilitation and punishment, reluctance to help juveniles "beat a case," or an internalization of a court's treatment philosophy may compromise the role of counsel in juvenile court (Fox 1970*a;* Clarke and Koch 1980; Feld 1989). Institutional pressures to maintain stable, cooperative working relations with other personnel in the system may be inconsistent with effective adversarial advocacy (Lefstein et al. 1969; Stapleton and Teitelbaum 1972; Bortner 1982).

Several studies indicate that juveniles with lawyers in juvenile courts may be at a disadvantage when compared with similarly situated unrepresented youths; that is, procedural formality may constitute an aggravating factor in sentencing. While the relationships between the factors producing more severe dispositions and the factors influencing the appointment of counsel are complex, the presence of counsel appears to aggravate the sentences that juveniles receive (Feld 1989). Stapleton and Teitelbaum (1972), Clarke and Koch (1980), Bortner (1982), and Feld (1988a, 1989) all reported that juveniles with lawyers are more likely to be incarcerated than juveniles without counsel. For example, Feld (1989) reported that 28.1 percent of all juvenile offenders with lawyers were removed from their homes as contrasted with 10.3 percent of those appearing without counsel. Multiple regression analyses that controlled for a host of legal variables indicate that the presence of an attorney accounts for about 1.5 percent of the variance in home removal dispositions and about .6 percent of the variance in secure confinement sentences (Feld 1989, p. 1308). In a methodologically more sophisticated study, Clarke and Koch (1980) applied a variable-selection procedure to the association between dispositions and all variables potentially related to it, except for court administrative variables such as detention status or representation by counsel, to construct matched sets of cases. Using court files, they constructed a more sensitive offense seriousness index. Comparing the disposition rates for juveniles in different risk categories, they concluded that "there was a significant and consistent difference in the commitment rates of un-counseled and counseled cases: *children without counsel were less likely to be committed*, especially if they were in the intermediate risk groups" (Clarke and Koch 1980, p. 301). Research on legal representation in Canadian juvenile courts also reports a negative impact of counsel on juveniles' sentences in some settings (Carrington and Moyer 1988a, 1988b, 1990). An evaluation of the impact of counsel in six states' delinquency proceedings reported that, "in virtually every jurisdiction, representation by counsel is an aggravating factor in a juvenile's disposition. . . . While the legal variables [of seriousness of present offense, prior record, and pretrial detention status] enhance the probabilities of representation, the fact of representation appears to exert an independent effect on the severity of dispositions" (Feld 1988a, p. 393).

There are several possible explanations for the apparent relationship between procedural formality, as evidenced by the presence of counsel, and more severe sentences. One is that the lawyers who appear in juvenile court are incompetent and prejudice their clients' cases (Knitzer and Sobie 1984). While systematic qualitative evaluations of the actual performance of counsel in juvenile courts are lacking, the available evidence suggests that even in jurisdictions where counsel routinely are appointed, there are grounds for concern about their effectiveness (Knitzer and Sobie 1984; Feld 1989). Or it may be that, early in a proceeding, a juvenile court judge's familiarity with a case alerts him or her to the eventual disposition that will be imposed on conviction, and counsel may be appointed in anticipation of more severe consequences (Aday 1986; Feld 1989). In most jurisdictions, the same judge who presides at a youth's arraignment and detention hearing will later decide the case on the merits and then pronounce a sentence. Perhaps the initial decision to appoint counsel is based on evidence obtained in the preliminary stages that also influences later dispositions. If so, the court's extensive familiarity with a case prior to the fact-finding hearing raises basic questions about the fairness and objectivity of the adjudicative process (Ainsworth 1991).

Another possible explanation for the aggravating effect of lawyers on sentences is that juvenile court judges may treat more formally and severely juveniles who appear with counsel than those without. Within statutory limits, judges may feel less constrained when sentencing a youth who is represented since adherence to the form of due process may insulate sentences from appellate reversal. In short, there may be a price for the use of formal procedures similar to that experienced by adult criminal defendants who insist on a jury trial rather than pleading guilty. While not explicitly punishing juveniles who are represented because they appear with counsel, judges may be more lenient toward those youths who appear unaided and contritely "throw themselves on the mercy of the court." At the very least further research is needed on the delivery of legal services, the role and effect of counsel, and the relationship between procedural formality and sentencing severity in juvenile court.

### IV. Jurisdiction over Noncriminal Status Offenders

While the notion of helping troubled children is inherently attractive, the definition and administration of status jurisdiction has been criticized extensively in the post-*Gault* decades (Teitelbaum and Gough 1977; Allinson 1983). Beginning with the President's Commission on Law Enforcement and Administration of Justice (1967*a*, 1967*b*), which recommended narrowing the range of conduct for which court intervention is authorized, many professional organizations have advocated reform or elimination of the juvenile court's status jurisdiction (National Council on Crime and Delinquency 1975; American Bar Association—Institute of Judicial Administration 1982). Critics focus on its adverse impact on children, its disabling effects on families, schools, and other agencies that refer status offenders, and the legal and administrative issues status offenses present (Andrews and Cohn 1974; Katz and Teitelbaum 1978; Rosenberg 1983).

Status offenses traditionally were treated as a form of delinquency; status delinquents were detained and incarcerated in the same institutions as criminal delinquents even though they had committed no crimes (Handler and Zatz 1982). Parental referrals overloaded juvenile courts with intractable family disputes, diverted scarce judicial resources from other tasks, and exacerbated rather than ameliorated family conflict (Andrews and Cohn 1974). Social agencies and schools used the court as a "dumping ground" to impose solutions rather than to address sources of conflict. Status jurisdiction raised legal issues of "void for vagueness," equal protection, and procedural justice (Katz and Teitelbaum 1978; Rubin 1985). Judges were granted broad discretion to prevent unruliness or immorality from ripening into criminality, and intervention often reflected individual judges' values and prejudices. The exercise of standardless discretion to regulate noncriminal misconduct had a disproportionate impact on poor, minority, and female juveniles (Chesney-Lind 1977, 1988; Sussman 1977; Teilmann and Landry 1981).

Three post-*Gault* trends—diversion, deinstitutionalization, and decriminalization—reflect judicial and legislative disillusionment with the court's treatment of noncriminal youths and efforts to respond to these criticisms (Empey 1973). The Federal Juvenile Justice and Delinquency Prevention Act of 1974, 42 U.S.C. §§ 5601 *et seq.* (1983), required states to begin a process of removing noncriminal offenders from secure detention and correctional facilities. Federal and state restrictions on commingling status and delinquent offenders in secure institutions provided the impetus to divert some status offenders from juvenile courts and decarcerate those who remained in the system (Klein 1979; Handler and Zatz 1982).

## A. Diversion

Since *Gault*, one juvenile justice reform strategy focuses on providing services on an informal basis through diversion programs (Klein 1979). Just as the original juvenile court diverted youths from adult criminal courts, diversion programs shift away eligible youths from juvenile court who otherwise would enter that system. Klein (1979) and Polk (1984) question whether diversion programs have been implemented coherently or been effective when attempted. The ideology of juvenile justice—early identification and treatment—is inherently expansive and lends itself to overreaching. Klein (1979), for example, contends that diversion programs have not restricted themselves to youths who would otherwise have entered the juvenile justice system but have also encompassed "young people who are normally counseled and released by the police, if indeed they have any dealings with the police" (Klein 1979, p. 165). Moreover, many diversion programs are operated either by police or juvenile court personnel, who thereby retain effective control over juvenile offenders (Klein 1979). As a result, diversion, which theoretically was intended to reduce the court's client population, has had the opposite effect of "widening the net of social control" (Klein 1979; Polk 1984). The number of juveniles referred to court remains relatively constant despite a declining youth population, while juveniles who previously would have been released are subjected to other forms of intervention. For example, Decker (1985) analyzed juvenile court referrals for a four-year period prior to and after the adoption of a status offender diversion program in St. Louis. Although the number of status offenders referred to juvenile court declined somewhat following the introduction of diversion, the overall percentage of youth population at risk and the number of youths referred to juvenile court actually increased from an annual average of 5,276 prior to the introduction of the program to 6,615 in the four years following its implementation (Decker 1985). Moreover, diversion provides a rationale for shifting discretion from the juvenile court itself, where it is subject to some procedural formality as a result of *Gault*, to police or intake "gatekeepers" who continue to operate on an informal pre-*Gault* basis with no accountability. In his comprehensive study of the history of regulating "stubborn children," Sutton (1988, p. 215) concludes that diversion "sanctified and encouraged a strategy for circumventing due process, assured that programs would stay in the discretionary hands of local officials, and encouraged the privatization of long-term social control." Similarly, Decker's "net-widening" analysis concludes that, "because of the vagueness of the statutes defining status-offense conduct, the low visibility of police decisions in such situations, and the low probability of judicial review of these decisions, these programs present an even greater opportunity for abuse" (Decker 1985, p. 215).

## B. Deinstitutionalization

Federal and state bans on secure confinement provided an impetus to deinstitutionalize noncriminal youths. Although the numbers of status offenders in secure detention facilities and institutions declined by the mid-1980s (Handler and Zatz 1982; Krisberg and Schwartz 1983; Schneider 1984), only a small proportion of status offenders ever were sent to secure institutions; most remain eligible for commitment to "forestry camps" and other medium-security facilities (Sutton 1988). Amendments to the Federal Juvenile Justice Act in 1980 weakened even the restrictions on secure confinement; status offenders who run away from nonsecure placements or violated court orders may be charged with contempt of court, a delinquent act, and incarcerated (42 U.S.C. § 5633(a)(12)(A) [1983]; Costello and Worthington 1981; Schwartz 1989a). Bishop and Frazier (1992) report that using contempt power to "bootstrap" status offenders into delinquents is an important continuing source of gender bias in juvenile justice administration. "The typical female offender not in contempt has a 1.8 percent probability of incarceration, which increased markedly to 63.2 percent if she is held in contempt. In short, females referred to juvenile court for contempt following an earlier adjudication for a status offense receive harsher judicial dispositions than their male counterparts" (Bishop and Frazier 1992, p. 1183). Even though subsequent probation violations may result in incarceration, juveniles initially charged with status offenses enjoy fewer procedural rights than do youths charged with delinquency. For example, states use the prohibition on secure confinement as a rationale to deny youths charged with noncriminal misconduct the privilege against self-incrimination (*In re Spalding*, 273 Md. 690 [1975]), the right to counsel (*In re Walker*, 282 N.C.28 [1972]; Feld 1988a, 1989), or to proof beyond a reasonable doubt (*In re Henderson*, 199 N.W.2d 111 [Iowa 1972]).

## C. Decriminalization

Until recent reforms, status offenses were classified as a form of delinquency. Beginning with jurisdictional redefinitions in California in 1961 and in New York in 1962, almost every state has decriminalized conduct which is illegal only for children—incorrigibility, runaway, truancy—by relabeling it into new nondelinquency classifications such as Persons or Children in Need of Supervision (PINS) (Rubin 1985). The most recent legislative strategy is to relabel "juvenile nuisances" as dependent, neglected, or in need of protection and services (Rosenberg 1983; Bishop and Frazier 1992). Such label changes simply shift youths from one jurisdictional category to another without significantly limiting courts' dispositional authority, other than secure confinement. By manipulating labels, former status offenders may be relabeled downward as "dependent" or "neglected" youths, upward as "delin-quent offenders," or laterally into the private sector (Klein 1979; Handler and Zatz 1982; Schneider 1984). Based on courtroom observations, Mahoney and Fenster (1982) report that, following the decriminaliza-tion of status offenses in 1979, many girls were charged with criminal-type offenses—for example, loitering—for behavior that previously would have been charged as status offenses—for example, running away.

Many youths who formerly would have been status offenders, espe-cially those who are middle-class and female, now are shifted into the private mental health or chemical dependency treatment systems by diversion, court referral, or voluntary parental commitment (Schwartz 1989*b*). The Supreme Court in *Parham v. J.R.*, 442 U.S. 609 (1979), ruled that the only process juveniles are due when their parents "volun-tarily" commit them to secure treatment facilities is a physician's deter-mination that it is medically appropriate (Weithorn 1988). Most states' civil commitment laws do not provide juveniles with the same proce-dural safeguards as they do adults. Clearly, some children's psychologi-cal dysfunctions or substance abuse require medical attention. How-ever, many commitments result from status-like social or behavioral conflicts, self-serving parental motives, and medical entrepreneurs cop-ing with underutilized hospitals (Ellis 1974). Weithorn (1988, p. 799) observes that, "whereas in prior years, the juvenile justice system insti-tutionalized troublemaking youth as status offenders, recent legal re-forms have closed the doors of juvenile justice institutions to a sizable population of difficult children. Families and community agencies seek-ing intensive intervention have turned increasingly to mental hospitals: the only institutional alternative that is available, provides easy access, and is adequately funded by third-party payment." Coinciding with the deinstitutionalization of status offenders, Schwartz, Jackson-Beeck, and Anderson (1984, p. 375) report that the rate of juvenile psychiatric commitments in Minneapolis-St. Paul Hospitals doubled between 1976 and 1983 from ninety-one youths per 100,000 to 184. Jackson-Beeck (1985) reports that between 1978 and 1984 in Minnesota, juvenile psy-chiatric inpatients as a proportion of total inpatients increased from 16 percent to 26 percent, and juvenile chemical dependency inpatients in hospitals and treatment centers increased from 17 percent to 22 percent.

The combination of psychiatric hospitals seeking profits, insurance and Medicaid coverage for inpatient mental health care, and the malleability of diagnostic categories permits deviance to be "medicalized" and troublesome children to be incarcerated without meaningful judicial supervision, thereby providing an attractive alternative response for "youthful nuisances" (Schwartz et al. 1984; Weithorn 1988; Schwartz 1989b). Compared with adults, juveniles admitted for inpatient mental health treatment suffer from less serious disorders but stay longer once hospitalized (Schwartz et al. 1984; Jackson-Beeck, Schwartz, and Rutherford 1987).

Historically, the child welfare, juvenile justice, and mental health systems have dealt with relatively interchangeable youth populations that shift from one system to another depending on social attitudes, available funds, and imprecise legal definitions. The numbers of juveniles entering the "hidden system" of private psychiatric and chemical dependency treatment facilities has increased as the confinement of status offenders has declined (Schwartz et al. 1984; Jackson-Beeck et al. 1987). Weithorn (1988) reports that adolescent admissions to private hopitals' psychiatric units between 1980 and 1984 increased more than fourfold from 10,764 to 48,375. Lerman (1980) describes the private sector of the mental health industry as the juvenile justice system's institutional successor for the care and control of problematic youths and contends that deinstitutionalization has resulted in transinstitutionalization, with the transfer of some noncriminal juveniles from publicly funded facilities to private institutions (Lerman 1982, 1984).

Whether incarceration is for the juvenile's "best interests," for "adjustment reactions" symptomatic of adolescence, or for "chemical dependency," these trends revive the imagery of diagnosis and treatment on a discretionary basis without regard to formal due process considerations. The appropriate social and legal response to minor, nuisance, and noncriminal youngsters goes to the heart of the juvenile court's mission and the normative concept of childhood on which it is based. The debate polarizes advocates of authority and control of youth (Arthur 1977) and those who view intervention too often as discriminatory and a denial of rights (Murray 1983; Rubin 1985). While a few states—for example, Washington and Maine—have eliminated status jurisdiction entirely and allow noncriminal intervention only in cases of dependency or neglect, juvenile court judges strongly resist removal of status jurisdiction since any contraction of their authority over children leads to further convergence with criminal courts (Klein 1979; Handler and Zatz 1982). Sutton's (1988) seminal historical analysis of status offenders concludes that much of the policy debate is symbolic, that many of the adaptations are cosmetic, and that the differentiation of status offenders from delinquents perpetuates the traditional juvenile court by reserving the former for informal treatment while consigning the latter to formal punishment.

## V. Waiver of Jurisdiction over Serious Juvenile Offenders

The post-*Gault* era has witnessed a fundamental change in the jurisprudence of juvenile sentencing, as considerations of the offense, rather than the offender, increasingly dominate the decision. A shift in sentencing philosophy from rehabilitation to retribution is evident both in the response to serious juvenile offenders and in the routine sentencing of delinquent offenders (Feld 1987, 1988*b*).

Whether persistent or violent young offenders should be sentenced as juveniles or adults poses difficult theoretical and practical problems. The decision implicates both juvenile court sentencing practices and the relationship between juvenile and adult court sentencing practices. Virtually every state has a mechanism for prosecuting some juveniles as adults (Feld 1978, 1987). While few in number, these youths challenge juvenile courts' rehabilitative assumptions about nonpunitive, short-term social control (Feld 1990*a*).

Two types of statutes—judicial waiver and legislative offense exclusion—which focus repectively on characteristics of the offender or on the seriousness of the offense, highlight the differences between juvenile and criminal courts' sentencing philosophies (Thomas and Bilchik 1985; Feld 1987; Bishop and Frazier 1991).[4] Since juvenile courts traditionally emphasize individualized treatment of offenders, with judicial waiver a judge may transfer jurisdiction on a discretionary basis after a hearing to determine whether a youth is amenable to treatment or a threat to public safety. With legislative offense exclusion, by statutory definition youths charged with certain offenses, typically capital crimes or the most serious felonies—such as murder, rape, or armed robbery—simply are not within juvenile court jurisdiction (Feld 1987).

Judicial waiver's focus on the offender and legislative exclusion's focus on the offense illustrate the jurisprudential choices respectively

---

[4] A third mechanism for removing juvenile offenders from the juvenile system is prosecutorial waiver, or concurrent jurisdiction between juvenile and criminal courts over certain offenses (Feld 1978, 1987; Hamparian et al. 1982; Thomas and Bilchik 1985; Bishop and Frazier 1991). Since this analysis focuses primarily on the differences between the juvenile and adult justice systems and their respective emphases on offenders and offenses in sentencing, prosecutorial waiver is not discussed.

posed by emphasizing treatment and punishment. Punishment is retrospective and imposes unpleasant consequences for past offenses, while treatment is prospective and seeks to improve offenders' future welfare. Punitive sentences based on the offense typically are determinate and proportional, while individualized sentences based on the offender are indeterminate and nonproportional (Morris 1974; von Hirsch 1976, 1986). When youths are transferred to criminal court, legislative exclusion uses the seriousness of the offense, sometimes in combination with chronicity, to control the decision to prosecute a youth as an adult, whereas judicial waiver looks to individualized clinical assessments of the offender's amenability to treatment or dangerousness (Feld 1978, 1987).

## A. Judicial Waiver

Judicial waiver embodies the juvenile court's approach to individualized sentencing with its focus on characteristics of the offender to decide whether a youth should be treated as a juvenile or punished as an adult (Zimring 1991). In *Kent v. United States*, 383 U.S. 541 (1966), the Supreme Court mandated that formal procedural due process must be observed in judicial waiver determinations. Subsequently, in *Breed v. Jones*, 421 U.S. 519 (1975), the Court applied the double jeopardy provisions of the Constitution to the adjudication of juvenile offenses and thereby required states to make the dispositional determination before proceeding against a youth on the merits of the charge.

Although *Kent* and *Breed* provide the formal procedural framework within which the judicial waiver decision occurs, the substantive bases of the waiver decision pose the principal difficulties. Most jurisdictions provide for discretionary waiver based on a juvenile court judge's assessment of a youth's amenability to treatment or dangerousness, as indicated by age, the treatment prognosis, and the juvenile's dangerousness, as reflected in the seriousness of the present offense and prior record (Feld 1983). While many jurisdictions limit judicial waiver to felony offenses and establish some minimum age for adult prosecution, typically fourteen or fifteen, some states provide neither offense nor minimum age restrictions (Feld 1987).

1. *Waiver Disparities.* As sentencing criteria, "amenability to treatment" and "dangerousness" implicate some of the most fundamental and difficult issues of penal policy and juvenile jurisprudence. The underlying legislative assumptions that there are effective treatment programs for serious or persistent juvenile offenders, classification sys-

tems that differentiate the treatment potential or dangerousness of various youths, and validated and reliable diagnostic tools that enable a clinician or juvenile court judge to determine the proper disposition for a particular youth are all highly problematic and controversial. Similarly, asking a judge to decide whether a youth poses a threat to public safety requires judges to predict future dangerousness even though clinicians lack the technical capacity reliably to predict low base-rate serious criminal behavior (Monahan 1981; Morris and Miller 1985).

Judicial waiver statutes give judges broad, standardless discretion. While some legislation includes lists of amorphous and contradictory factors such as those appended to the *Kent* decision, those lists do not guide discretion but rather reinforce it by allowing judges selectively to emphasize one factor or another to justify any decision (*Kent v. United States*, 383 U.S. at 566 [1966]; Twentieth Century Fund Task Force on Sentencing Policy Toward Young Offenders 1978; Zimring 1981*a*). Because judges interpret and apply the same law inconsistently, discretionary statutes are not administered on an evenhanded basis (Hamparian et al. 1982; Feld 1978, 1987). Rural youths are more likely to be waived than are similarly situated urban offenders (Hamparian et al. 1982; Feld 1990*a*). Feld (1990*a*) found that, in Minnesota, 88.6 percent of waived urban juveniles were charged with a felony, as contrasted with 53.6 percent of rural juveniles. In addition, 48.6 percent of waived urban youths previously had been removed from their homes, as compared with 28.6 percent of waived rural juveniles. Hamparian et al.'s (1982) nationwide evaluation of judicial waiver in 1978 demonstrates that waiver is often inconsistent. Highlighting the interstate variability of juvenile justice administration, under similar statutory regimes among the states that rely on judicial waiver to transfer youths to criminal court, the rates of waiver vary from a high of 13.5 per 10,000 youths at risk to a low of .07.

Fagan and Deschenes (1990) analyzed waiver petitions filed against a sample of 201 violent youths in Boston, Detroit, Newark, and Phoenix in 1981–84. The violent offender population was defined as persons currently charged with a crime of violence and having at least one prior felony adjudication. Data on offense and offender characteristics were collected from police reports, court records, and social histories. Fagan and Deschenes analyzed the governing statutes, compared the rates of waiver—Boston (21 percent transferred), Detroit (31 percent), Newark (41 percent), and Phoenix (71 percent)—and concluded that no uniform or consistent criteria guided the transfer decision in any jurisdiction: "Neither did we find a strong relationship between transfer and more offense-related variables, including the nature of the offense, number of coparticipants or number of victims. What we found was a rash of inconsistent judicial waiver decisions, both within and across sites" (Fagan and Deschenes 1990, p. 347).

A youth's race may also affect waiver decisions (Fagan, Forst, and Vivona 1987). Eigen (1981a, 1981b) reported an interracial effect in transfers in Philadelphia; black youths with white victims were significantly more at risk for waiver. In their study of transfer of violent youths, Fagan, Forst, and Vivona (1987) also found disparities in the rates of transfer of minority and white offenders. Although there was no direct evidence of sentencing discrimination, "it appears that the effects of race are indirect, but visible nonetheless" (Fagan, Forst, and Vivona 1987, p. 276).

2. *Waived Juveniles' Criminal Court Dispositions.*   Because young people are not irresponsible children one day and responsible adults the next, except as a matter of law, juvenile and adult courts may pursue inconsistent sentencing goals when juveniles make the transition to criminal courts. Despite public concern with youth violence, most juveniles who are judicially waived are charged with felony property crimes like burglary, rather than with serious offenses against the person (Hamparian et al. 1982; Feld 1987, 1990a). When they appear in criminal courts as adult first offenders, typically they are not imprisoned (Greenwood, Petersilia, and Zimring 1980; Hamparian et al. 1982; Greenwood 1986).

Hamparian et al.'s (1982) nationwide study of waiver reported that, of the 7,318 juveniles judicially transferred in 1978, less than one-third (32 percent) of the youths were charged with offenses against the person; the largest proportion (45 percent) were charged with property crimes (Hamparian et al. 1982). Nimick et al. (1986), at the NJCDA, analyzed 127,163 petitioned delinquency cases disposed in 1982 and found waiver petitions were filed in about 2,335 cases, or less than 2 percent of all filings. They report that "waiver was not reserved for youth charged with a violent offense; in this sample only a third [34.3 percent] of all youth waived to criminal court were charged with an index violent offense. A greater percentage of waived cases were charged with an index property offense [40.3 percent], and nearly one-quarter [25.4 percent] of all waived cases involved what are commonly considered the less serious nonindex offenses" (Nimick et al. 1986, p. 2).

When Hamparian et al. (1982) traced the subsequent sentences of judicially waived youths in criminal court, they found that the majority were fined or placed on probation. Even among those confined, 40 percent had maximum sentences of one year or less. In part, these relatively lenient dispositions reflect the fact that most waived youths were not violent offenders. In analyzing the relationships between the offense for which jurisdiction was waived and the eventual adult sentence, Hamparian concluded that "there seems to be a direct correlation between low percentage of personal offenses waived and high proportion of community dispositions (as opposed to incarceration)" (Hamparian et al. 1982, p. 112). Heuser's (1985) evaluation in Oregon of the adult sentences received by waived juvenile felony defendants showed that the vast majority were property offenders rather than violent offenders and that, as a consequence, only 55 percent of the youths convicted of felonies were incarcerated, with the rest receiving probation. Moreover, even of those youths incarcerated as adults, nearly two-thirds received jail terms of one year or less and served an average of about eight months, approximately the same terms that juveniles with prior records who were convicted within juvenile court would receive (Heuser 1985). Gillespie and Norman's (1984) study of youths waived in Utah between 1967 and 1980 revealed that the majority of juveniles who were transferred were not charged with violent offenses, and the majority of juveniles convicted as adults were not imprisoned. Bortner's (1986) study of 214 waived juveniles in a western metropolitan county reported that less than one-third (30.8 percent) of the juveniles convicted in adult proceedings were sentenced to prison.

Greenwood, Abrahamse, and Zimring (1984) examined dispositions of youths tried as adults in several jurisdictions and found substantial variation in sentencing practices. In New York City and in Franklin County (Columbus), Ohio, they found that, controlling for offense seriousness, youthful offenders faced a substantially lower chance of being incarcerated than did older offenders; that youthful violent offenders got lighter sentences than did older violent offenders; and that, for approximately two years after becoming adults, youths were the beneficiaries of informal lenient sentencing policies in adult courts. Another study reported that, although the seriousness of a juvenile's offense is the primary determinant of the severity of the adult sentence imposed in Washington, D.C., "youth, at least through the first two years of criminal court jurisdiction, is a perceptible mitigating factor" (Twentieth Century Fund Task Force on Sentencing Policy Toward Young Offenders 1978, p. 63).

The lack of congruence between juvenile courts' maximum sanction, waiver, and adult criminal courts' sentencing practices occurs because the typical youth who is waived is an older juvenile charged with burglary rather than violence, because of qualitative differences in the nature of juveniles' offenses relative to adults', because of differences in sentencing philosophies between the two systems when youths make the transition from the one to the other, and because of the failure to integrate juvenile and adult criminal records for sentencing purposes. Even within the more serious categories of crimes, for example, there are age-related patterns of seriousness that may affect eventual sentences: younger offenders are less likely than adults to be armed with guns, inflict as much injury, or steal as much property (Greenwood, Petersilia, and Zimring 1980; McDermott and Hindelang 1981). Adult criminal courts tend to rely primarily on the seriousness of the present offense and the prior adult criminal history in making sentencing decisions. Their failure to include fully the juvenile component of the offender's criminal history stems from the confidential nature of juvenile court records, the functional and physical separation of the respective court services staffs, and the difficulty of compiling and maintaining criminal histories through several different bureaucracies (Greenwood, Petersilia, and Zimring 1980; Petersilia 1981; Greenwood 1986). As more states' criminal courts consider juvenile convictions as part of adult criminal history scores, however, juvenile records may become more fully integrated into and play a larger role in adult sentencing regimes (Feld 1981a).

Ultimately, waiver involves the choice of appropriate disposition of offenders who chronologically happen to be juveniles. The distinction between treatment as a juvenile and punishment as an adult is based on an arbitrarily chosen age that has no criminological significance other than its legal consequences. There is a strong relationship between age and crime; crime rates for many offenses peak in mid to late adolescence (Greenberg 1979; Hirschi and Gottfredson 1983; Farrington 1986; Greenwood 1986). Rational sentencing policy requires coordinated responses to young offenders on both sides of the juvenile/ adult line using a standardized means to identify and sanction serious and chronic young criminals (Twentieth Century Fund Task Force on

Sentencing Policy Toward Young Offenders 1978; Greenwood 1986; Feld 1987, 1990*a*).

Although juvenile and adult courts' sentencing practices may work at cross-purposes when youths make the transition to criminal court, Bortner (1986) contends that juvenile courts' organizational and political considerations explain more about waiver decisions than does the seriousness or intractability of a youth. By relinquishing a small fraction of its clientele and portraying these juveniles as the most intractable and dangerous in the system, juvenile courts create the appearance of protecting the public, preserve their jurisdiction over the vast bulk of juveniles, and deflect more comprehensive criticisms (Bortner 1986; Feld 1978, 1987).

## B. Legislative Exclusion of Offenses

Legislative offense exclusion defines juvenile court jurisdiction as not encompassing certain offenses (Feld 1978, 1987). Some jurisdictions exclude only capital crimes or murder while others may place youths charged with rape, armed robbery, and other offenses automatically in adult criminal court (Hamparian et al. 1982; Feld 1987). While most prescribe some minimum age for "automatic adulthood," typically sixteen years of age, youths as young as thirteen charged with murder in New York are prosecuted as adults (Feld 1987). Since juvenile courts are statutory entities, legislatures may modify their jurisdiction as they please, although it is often not apparent which of several alternative sentencing policies are being pursued when they redefine jurisdiction to exclude offenses.

Legislatively defining adulthood entails both empirical judgments and value choices. One normative judgment sometimes made is that certain crimes are so serious or so controversial that those who commit them deserve to be tried as adults and subjected to adult sanctions (Feld 1978, 1987). An empirical judgment involves an effort to identify persistent or serious offenders by selecting offense and recidivism criteria that differentiate between the relatively few serious or chronic young offenders who would be prosecuted as adults and the vast majority of juveniles who would remain within the jurisdiction of the juvenile court.[5] The policy choice is between having judges make these

---

[5] If the legislative goal in redefining juvenile court jurisdiction is to incapacitate chronic offenders selectively, for example, then excluding offenders solely on the basis of the seriousness of their present offense may not be the most effective strategy. Offenders who are both persistent and violent are legislatively distinguishable from their less criminally active peers on the basis of chronic criminal activity but not on the basis of

empirical and normative decisions on an ad hoc clinical basis or developing standard legislative criteria that integrate juvenile and adult sentencing practices and enable criminal courts to sentence violent or chronic juveniles more consistently (Feld 1983, 1990a).

Zimring (1981a, 1991) and Feld (1978, 1990a) contend that waiver should occur only when the minimum period of appropriate confinement for an offense substantially exceeds the maximum sentence available to a juvenile court. This criterion would identify "principal offenders accused of criminal homicide, and a few repetitively violent offenders accused of life-threatening crimes" (Zimring 1991, p. 276). One empirical impetus to waiver is a judge's perception that a juvenile requires a longer sentence than is available in the juvenile court (Feld 1990a). Fagan and Deschenes (1990) report that the length of time from age at offense to the maximum age jurisdictional limit, rather than prior record, predicts judicial transfer decisions.

## C. Offense Criteria and Waiver Decisions

Judicial waiver and legislative offense exclusion statutes present many of the same sentencing policy issues as the choice between indeterminate or determinate sentencing for adults. In the adult context, determinate sentences based on just deserts provide an alternative sentencing rationale to indeterminate sentences (American Friends Service Committee 1971; von Hirsch 1976; Petersilia and Turner 1987). Just deserts sentencing emphasizes concern for proportionality and equality, defines similar cases as similar based primarily on the seriousness of the offense and prior record, and limits consideration of individual status or circumstances. By contrast, individualized decisions envisioned by indeterminate sentencing can take account of all personal characteristics as relevant and rely heavily on professional discretion to weigh every factor (Matza 1964). Proponents of just deserts approaches reject individualization because treatment programs are seen as ineffective (Martinson 1974; Greenberg 1977; Sechrest, White, and Brown 1979; Lab and Whitehead 1988), individualization vests broad discretion in experts who often cannot justify treating similarly situated offenders differently, and clinical subjectivity often produces unequal

---

the seriousness of any given act. The research on criminal careers indicates that young offenders do not "specialize" in particular types of crime, that violence occurs within an essentially random pattern of delinquent behavior, and that a small number of chronic delinquents are responsible for many offenses and most of the violent offenses committed by juveniles (Blumstein et al. 1986).

and unjust results (von Hirsch 1976, 1986; Feld 1988b, 1990a). The just deserts sentencing philosophy has influenced several states' juvenile waiver and sentencing statutes (Feld 1987, 1988b).

Within the past two decades, concern for offense seriousness rather than reliance on judges' clinical assessments has come to dominate the waiver decision (Feld 1987, 1990a). Legislatures use offense criteria either as dispositional guidelines to limit judicial discretion or automatically to exclude certain youths (Feld 1987). More than twenty states have amended their judicial waiver statutes to reduce their inconsistency and to improve the fit between juvenile waiver and adult sentencing practices (Feld 1987). Legislatures use offense criteria to structure judicial discretion by specifying that judges may waive only certain serious offenses, identifying certain categories of serious current offenses or combinations of offenses and prior record for special procedural handling, or by prescribing the dispositional consequences that follow from proof of serious offenses or prior records (Feld 1987). Such legislative strategies restrict judicial waiver to serious offenses such as murder, rape, or robbery, use offense criteria to make transfer hearings mandatory, or shift to the juvenile the burden of affirmatively proving amenability to treatment rather than requiring the state to prove non-amenability (Feld 1987).

Evaluations of California's statutory waiver changes in 1976, adopting offense criteria and shifting the burden of proof to the juvenile, indicate that there was a dramatic increase in the numbers of youths who were tried as adults after being charged with one of the enumerated offenses (Teilmann and Klein n.d.). After accounting for possible fluctuations in juvenile crime rates, evaluators reported that "Los Angeles County experienced a 318 percent increase in certification hearings and a 234 percent increase in certifications" between 1976 and 1977 (Teilmann and Klein n.d., p. 30). Juveniles who were waived and tried as adults were almost as likely to be convicted as youths tried in juvenile court; following their convictions, they were more likely to be incarcerated than were their juvenile courtparts. Similarly, although Greenwood, Petersilia, and Zimring (1980) reported substantial variation in sentencing practices in several jurisdictions, they found that juveniles tried as adults in Los Angeles were not sentenced more leniently than other offenders; that for more serious crimes the seriousness or violence of the crime, not the age or record of the offender, determined the sentence; and that in sentencing marginal crimes like burglary the prior juvenile record appeared to influence the severity of the first adult sentence. Thus, restricting waiver to serious offenses and specifying special procedures may limit judicial discretion and increase the likelihood that significant adult sanctions will occur if waiver is ordered.

Nearly half of the states have excluded some offenses and offenders from juvenile court jurisdiction. While some states exclude only youths charged with capital crimes, murder, or offenses punishable by life imprisonment, others exclude longer lists of offenses or youths charged with repeat offenses (Feld 1987). The Illinois legislature, for example, redefined juvenile court jurisdiction in 1982 to exclude any youth aged fifteen or older who was charged with murder, armed robbery, or rape. In the seven years prior to the offense exclusion legislation, Cook County averaged forty-seven judicially waived youths per year. In the first two years following the enactment of the offense exclusion legislation, adult criminal prosecutions of juveniles more than tripled to 170, of which 151 resulted from the automatic transfer provision (Knoohuizen 1986). New York, which has no judicial waiver provisions and where juvenile court jurisdiction ends at age sixteen, adopted legislation in 1978 that excluded juveniles thirteen years or older charged with murder and fourteen years or older charged with kidnapping, arson, or rape (Singer and McDowall 1988).

Legislative amendments of judicial waiver statutes or exluded offense laws that target serious offenses or that couple serious offenses with prior records also increase the likelihood of significant adult sentences for serious young offenders. One way to examine the effects of such laws is to compare the sentences of juveniles tried as adults in jurisdictions in which they are targeted as serious offenders with the sentences received in more discretionary jurisdictions. Hamparian et al.'s national waiver survey showed that most judicially waived juveniles were property offenders, not violent offenders, and were not sentenced to prison (Hamparian et al. 1982; Nimick et al. 1986). By contrast, Thomas and Bilchik's (1985) study of waived youths' dispositions in Florida, where prosecutors can charge juveniles directly in adult court, reports that the majority of youths tried as adults were older males with prior delinquency adjudications and multiple present felony charges and that approximately two-thirds of these youths were sentenced to substantial terms of imprisonment. Rudman et al. (1986) evaluated the processing and dispositions of youths charged with a violent offense who had a prior felony conviction who were waived in four urban sites and reported that over 90 percent were incarcerated, and their sentences were five times longer than youths with similar characteristics who were retained in juvenile court. Even among this sample of violent offenders, however, Fagan and Deschenes (1990) were unable to identify factors that distinguished between those who were waived and those who were not. Heuser (1985) reported that, while violent and repetitive juvenile offenders were a small subset of the juveniles waived in Oregon, 75 percent of the juveniles convicted of violent offenses were incarcerated and received prison sentences in excess of six years. Hamparian et al. (1982) examined the adult sentences received by youths in excluded offense jurisdictions. They found that 97.8 percent of such youths were excluded for offenses against the person. They were only able to retrieve adult sentence data in Pennsylvania, where 62 percent of convicted youths were sent to adult correctional facilities.

Legislative strategies that use offense criteria as sentencing guidelines to structure judicial waiver discretion or to exclude certain offenses from juvenile court jurisdiction provide one indicator of a policy shift from an offender-oriented treatment sentencing philosophy to a more retributive one. Legislation structuring or elimination of judicial discretion repudiates rehabilitation at least with respect to "hard-core" offenders, narrows juvenile court jurisdiction, marginally reduces its clientele, and denies juvenile courts the opportunity to treat certain youths without even inquiring into their personal characteristics. Indeed, the increased emphasis on punishing serious young offenders as adults exposes at least some youths to the possibility of capital punishment for the crimes they committed as juveniles (Streib 1987).[6]

## VI. Sentencing Delinquent Offenders

For the Supreme Court in *McKeiver*, the basic justification for denying jury trials in delinquency proceedings and for maintaining a juvenile justice system separate from the adult one was based on the differences between juvenile treatment and criminal punishment (Gardner 1982; Feld 1988b). Despite the fundamental importance of the rehabilitation-retribution distinction, however, the Court did not analyze the differences between the two. There are several factors that the *McKeiver*

---

[6] In *Thompson v. Oklahoma*, 108 S.Ct. 2687 (1988), a plurality of the Supreme Court ruled that executing an offender for a crime committed at fifteen years of age violated the Eighth Amendment constitutional prohibition on "cruel and unusual punishment." However, in *Stanford v. Kentucky*, 109 S.Ct. 1969 (1989), a majority of the Court concluded that imposing capital punishment on an offender for a crime committed at sixteen or seventeen years of age did not violate the Constitution.

Court might have considered to decide whether a juvenile court is punishing a youth for his past offenses or treating him for his future welfare. This section examines legislative purpose clauses and court opinions, juvenile court sentencing statutes and sentencing practices, and conditions of institutional confinement and evaluations of their effectiveness to determine whether a juvenile is being treated or punished (Feld 1988*b*). All of these indicators consistently reveal that, despite persisting rehabilitative rhetoric, treating juveniles closely resembles punishing adult criminals.

Punishment involves state imposition of burdens on an individual who has violated legal prohibitions for purposes of retribution or deterrence. Punishment assumes that responsible, freewill moral actors make blameworthy choices and deserve to suffer the prescribed consequences for their acts because of *past offenses* (Hart 1968; von Hirsch 1976). Treatment, by contrast, focuses on the mental health, status, and *future* welfare of the individual rather than on the commission of prohibited acts (Allen 1964, 1981). Most forms of rehabilitative treatment assume that there is a degree of determinism, that antecedent factors caused the undesirable behavior, and that intervention strategies can be applied that will improve the offender's *future well-being*.

Whether juvenile court sentencing decisions are based on the past offense or the offender's future welfare provides an indicator of the governing sentencing philosophy. Just deserts sentencing, with its strong retributive foundation, punishes offenders according to their past behavior rather than on the basis of who they are or may become, and sentences are typically determinate and proportional. Similarly situated offenders are defined and sanctioned on the basis of relatively objective and legally relevant factors such as seriousness of offense, culpability, or criminal history (von Hirsch 1976, 1986). By contrast, sentences based on characteristics of the offender are typically open-ended, nonproportional, and indeterminate. Individualized justice deems all personal and social characteristics as relevant and does not assign controlling significance to any one factor.

The influence of just deserts principles for sentencing adults has spilled over into the routine sentencing of juveniles as well as to the waiver decision (Feld 1987, 1988*b*; Gardner 1987). But punishing juveniles has constitutional consequences since the *McKeiver* Court justified the procedural differences of juvenile court by positing a therapeutic, rather than punitive, purpose. Moreover, juveniles currently may serve longer sentences than their adult counterparts convicted of the same offense because they purportedly receive treatment rather than punishment.[7]

## A. The Purpose of Juvenile Courts

Among the factors which the Supreme Court considers to determine whether seemingly punitive and coercive governmental intervention constitutes punishment or an "alternative purpose" of treatment is the stated legislative purpose (*Allen v. Illinois*, 478 U.S. 364 [1986]; Gardner 1982). Most states' juvenile court statutes contain a purposes clause that declares the underlying legislative rationale as an aid to courts in interpreting the statute. These preambles provide one indicator of the goals of juvenile court intervention (Feld 1988*b*).

Forty-two states' juvenile codes contain a legislative purpose clause (Feld 1988*b*). In the decades since *Gault* and *McKeiver*, about one-quarter of the states have redefined their juvenile codes' statements of legislative purpose (Feld 1988*b*, p. 842, n. 84). These amendments deemphasize rehabilitation and intervention in the child's "best interest" and assert the importance of "provid[ing] for the protection and safety of the public" (Cal. Welf. & Inst. Code § 202 [West Supp. 1988]), "protect[ing] society . . . [while] recognizing that the application of sanctions which are consistent with the seriousness of the offense is appropriate in all cases" (Fla. Stat. Ann. § 39.001(2)(a)[West Supp. 1988]), "render[ing] appropriate punishment to offenders" (Haw.Rev.Stat. § 571-1 [1985]), "protect[ing] the public by enforcing the legal obligations children have to society" (Ind. Code Ann. § 31-6-1-1 [Burns 1980]), and the like (Feld 1981*a*, 1988*b*; Walkover 1984).

Many courts recognize that these changes signal a basic philosophical reorientation in juvenile justice (*State ex rel. D.D.H. v. Dostert*, 269 S.E.2d 401 [West Virginia 1980]). The Washington Supreme Court reasoned that "sometimes punishment is treatment" and upheld the legislature's conclusion that "accountability for criminal behavior, the

---

[7] The California Supreme Court in *People v. Olivas*, 17 Cal. 3d 236, 551 P.2d 375, 131 Cal. Rptr. 55 (1976), limited the maximum sentence that could be imposed on an adult misdemeanant committed to the California Youth Authority to the maximum length that could be imposed on an adult sentenced for the same offense. By contrast, in *People v. Eric J.*, 25 Cal. 3d 522, 601 P.2d 549, 159 Cal. Rptr. 317 (1979), the Court refused to apply the *Olivas* adult sentence limitations to juveniles committed to the Youth Authority and upheld a longer term imposed on a juvenile than could be imposed on an adult sentenced for the same offense. In rejecting *Eric J.*'s equal protection claim, the Court emphasized that, unlike "punitive" sentences for adults, "there has been no like revolution in society's attitude toward juvenile offenders. It is still true that 'Juvenile commitment proceedings are designed for the purposes of rehabilitation and treatment, not punishment.'" Id. at 554.

prior criminal activity and punishment commensurate with age, crime and criminal history does as much to rehabilitate, correct and direct an errant youth as does the prior philosophy of focusing on the particular characteristics of the individual juveniles" (*State v. Lawley*, 91 Wash.2d 654, 656, 591 P.2d 772, 773 [1979]). The Nevada Supreme Court endorsed punishment and held that "by formally recognizing the legitimacy of punitive and deterrent sanctions for criminal offenses juvenile courts will be properly and somewhat belatedly expressing society's firm disapproval of juvenile crime and will be clearly issuing a threat of punishment for criminal acts to the juvenile population" (*In re Seven Minors*, 99 Nev. 427, 423, 664 P.2d 947, 950 [1983]).

### B. Sentencing Legislation and Practices

Sentencing statutes and practices provide another indicator of whether a juvenile court is punishing or treating delinquents. Originally, juvenile court sentences were indeterminate and nonproportional to achieve the child's "best interests" (Mack 1909; Rothman 1980). Recently, however, many states' juvenile court sentencing legislation has shifted toward a greater emphasis on punishment (Feld 1988*b*).

1. *Determinate Sentences in Juvenile Court.* Despite the court's history of indeterminate sentencing, about one-third of the states now use the present offense, the prior record, or both, to regulate at least some juvenile court sentencing decisions through determinate or mandatory minimum sentencing statutes or correctional administrative guidelines (Feld 1988*b*). The clearest departure from traditional juvenile court sentencing practices occurred in 1977 when Washington state enacted just deserts legislation that based presumptive juvenile sentences on a youth's age, present offense, and prior record (Schneider and Schram 1983; Fisher, Fraser, and Forst 1985). The Washington code creates three categories of offenders—serious, middle, and minor—with presumptive sentences and standard ranges for each. A sentencing guidelines commission developed dispositional ("in/out") and presumptive length-of-stay guidelines in the form of standard ranges that are proportionate to the seriousness of the present offense, age, and prior record (Feld 1988*b*). Evaluations concluded that sentences became more uniform, consistent, and proportionate to the seriousness of the offense than under the prior rehabilitative sentencing regime (Schneider and Schram 1983; Fisher et al. 1985; Forst and Blomquist 1991).

In New Jersey, juvenile court judges consider offense, criminal history, and statutory "aggravating and mitigating" factors when sentencing juveniles determinately (N.J. Stat.Ann. §§ 2A:4A-43(a), 44(a), (d)[West 1987]). In 1987, Texas adopted determinate sentencing legislation for juvenile offenders charged with serious offenses if the prosecutor submits the petition to a grand jury (Tex. Fam. Code Ann. §§ 53.045, 54.04(d)(3)[Vernon Supp. 1988]; Dawson 1988; 1990*b*). Although the Texas legislation was intended to increase juvenile courts' sentencing powers over young offenders and to provide an alternative to judicial waiver, Dawson (1990*b*) contends that one unintended consequence of the law was to increase prosecutors' plea-bargaining leverage.

2. *Mandatory Minimum Terms.* A number of states—for example, Georgia, New York, and Ohio—impose mandatory minimum sentences for certain "designated felonies" (Feld 1988*b*). While some mandatory minimum sentencing statutes allow judges discretion whether to impose the mandated sanctions, other jurisdictions—for example, Delaware—require the court to commit youths for the mandatory minimum (Feld 1988*b*). These "therapeutic" mandatory sentencing laws are addressed to "violent and repeat offenders," "aggravated juvenile offenders," "serious juvenile offenders," or "designated felons" (Feld 1988*b*). Terms of mandatory confinement range from twelve to eighteen months, to age twenty-one, or to the adult limit for the same offense (Feld 1988*b*). Basing mandatory minimum sentences on the offense precludes any individualized consideration of the offender's "real needs."

3. *Administrative Sentencing and Parole Release Guidelines.* Several states' departments of corrections—for example, in Arizona, Georgia, and Minnesota—have adopted administrative guidelines that use offense criteria to specify proportional mandatory minimum terms, and these provide another form of just deserts sentencing (Forst, Friedman, and Coates 1985; Georgia Division of Youth Services 1985; Arizona Department of Corrections 1986; Feld 1988*b*). Minnesota's Department of Corrections adopted determinate "length-of-stay" guidelines based on the current offense and other "risk" factors (Minnesota Department of Corrections 1980). The juvenile risk factors—prior record, probation or parole status—are the same as those used in Minnesota's adult-sentencing guidelines, which are designed to achieve just deserts. In California, juveniles committed to the Youth Authority are released by the Youthful Offender Parole Board (Forst and Blomquist 1991). The board uses offense categories to establish parole eligibility based on its assessment of the "seriousness of the specific [offense] and the

degree of danger those committed to the Youth Authority pose to the public" (Cal. Admin. Code tit. 15, § 4945 [1987]; Private Sector Task Force on Juvenile Justice 1987).

4. *Empirical Evaluations of Juvenile Court Sentencing Practices.* Juvenile court judges decide what to do with a child, in part by reference to statutory mandates. Practical bureaucratic considerations and paternalistic assumptions about children influence their discretionary decisions as well (Matza 1964; Cicourel 1968; Emerson 1969; Bortner 1982).

The exercise of broad discretion associated with individualized justice raises concerns about its discriminatory impact (Dannefer and Schutt 1982; McCarthy and Smith 1986; Fagan, Slaughter, and Hartstone 1987; Krisberg et al. 1987; Pope and Feyerherm 1990a, 1990b). Poor and minority youths are disproportionately overrepresented in juvenile correctional institutions relative to white youths (Krisberg et al. 1987; Pope and Feyerherm 1990a, 1990b). Do discretionary sentences based on social characteristics result in more severe sentencing of minority youths (McCarthy and Smith 1986; Fagan, Slaughter, and Hartstone 1987; Krisberg et al. 1987)? Or, despite a theoretical commitment to individualized justice, are sentences based on offenses, and does the racial disproportionality result from real differences in rates of offending by race (Wolfgang, Figlio, and Sellin 1972; Hindelang 1978; Huizinga and Elliott 1987)? Or, does the structure of justice decision making—for example, racial differences in rates of pretrial detention or representation by counsel—act to the detriment of minority juveniles (Pope and Feyerherm 1990a, 1990b)? In short, to what extent do legal offense factors, social variables, or system-processing variables influence juvenile court judges' sentencing decisions and explain racial disparities?

While evaluations of juvenile court sentencing practices are somewhat contradictory, two general findings emerge (McCarthy and Smith 1986; Fagan, Slaughter, and Hartstone 1987). First, the present offense and prior record account for most of the variance in juvenile court sentencing that can be explained (Barton 1976; Clarke and Koch 1980; Horowitz and Wasserman 1980; Phillips and Dinitz 1982; McCarthy and Smith 1986; Feld 1989). In multivariate studies (Clarke and Koch 1980; McCarthy and Smith 1986; Fagan, Slaughter, and Hartstone 1987; Feld 1989), offense variables typically explain about 25–30 percent of the variance in sentencing. Practical bureaucratic considerations provide an impetus to base sentences on the offense. Avoiding scandals and unfavorable political and media attention constrain juvenile court judges to impose more formal and restrictive sentences on more serious delinquents (Cicourel 1968; Emerson 1969; Bortner 1982). Moreover, complex organizations that pursue multiple goals develop bureaucratic strategies to simplify individualized assessments (Matza 1964; Marshall and Thomas 1983). Since juvenile courts routinely collect information about present offenses and prior records, these legal factors provide bases for decisions. Despite juvenile courts' claims to individualize sentences, their practices are similar to adult courts' in their emphases on present offense and prior record. A survey of juvenile sentencing practices in California concluded that "juvenile and criminal courts in California are much more alike than statutory language would suggest in the degree to which they focus on aggravating circumstances of the charged offense and the defendant's prior record in determining the degree of confinement that will be imposed" (Greenwood et al. 1983, p. 51).

A second finding is that, after controlling for offense variables, the individualized justice of juvenile courts is often associated with racial disparities in sentencing juveniles (McCarthy and Smith 1986; Krisberg et al. 1987; Fagan, Slaughter, and Hartstone 1987; Pope and Feyerherm 1990a, 1990b). McCarthy and Smith (1986) and Fagan, Slaughter, and Hartstone (1987) report that, while initial screening decisions were not overtly discriminatory, racial effects were amplified as minority youths were processed through the system. Bishop and Frazier (1988) also report that race, as well as legal factors, influenced sequential processing decisions and that, as they proceeded further into the system, black youths were at a disadvantage relative to white youths. Bishop and Frazier analyzed all 54,266 referrals to juvenile court in Florida between January 1, 1979, and December 31, 1981. While black youths made up 28.4 percent of the initial referrals, court intake recommended formal processing of 59.1 percent of the cases involving black youths, compared with 45.6 percent of the white youths. Youths formally petitioned to juvenile court included 47.3 percent of black youths, compared with 37.8 percent of the whites, thereby increasing the minority composition of the cohort from 28.4 percent black to 32.4 percent black (Bishop and Frazier 1988). Of the youths adjudicated delinquent, 29.6 percent of black youths were incarcerated, compared to 19.5 percent of white youths. "The probability of an initial referral resulting in movement through the system of a disposition of incarceration/transfer is nearly twice as great for blacks (10.2 percent) as for whites (5.4 percent)" (Bishop and Frazier 1988,

p. 251). After multivariate controls and measures of interaction effects, Bishop and Frazier (1988) concluded that "race is a far more pervasive influence in processing than much previous research has indicated. Blacks are more likely to be recommended for formal processing, referred to court, adjudicated delinquent, and given harsher dispositions than comparable white offenders" (p. 258). Reports by McCarthy and Smith (1986), Fagan, Slaughter, and Hartstone (1987), and Bishop and Frazier (1988) emphasize the importance of analyzing juvenile justice decision making as a multistage process rather than focusing solely on the final dispositional decision. For example, Bortner and Reed (1985), Frazier and Cochran (1986), and Feld (1989) report that black youths are more likely to be detained than white youths and that detained youths are more likely to receive severe sentences.

While legal variables exhibit a stronger relationship with dispositions than do social variables, most of the variation in sentencing juveniles remains unexplained (Thomas and Fitch 1975; Clarke and Koch 1980; Horowitz and Wasserman 1980). The recent legislative changes in juvenile sentencing statutes reflect disquiet with the underlying premises of individualized justice, the idiosyncratic exercises of discretion, and the inequalities that result (Feld 1987, 1988b). If there are racial differences in patterns of offending, then coupling the legislative emphases on offense seriousness with the cumulative impact of race on multistage screening and processing decisions amplifies the disproportionate over-representation of minority youths in correctional institutions (Krisberg et al. 1987).

## C. Conditions of Confinement

The correctional facilities to which young offenders are sentenced provide another indicator of whether juvenile courts are punishing or treating them. The Court in *Gault* belatedly recognized the longstanding contradictions between rehabilitative rhetoric and punitive reality; conditions of confinement motivated the Court to insist on minimal procedural safeguards for juveniles. Rothman's (1980) study of the early Progressive training schools provides a dismal account of institutions which failed to rehabilitate and were scarcely distinguishable from adult penal facilities. Schlossman (1977) offers an equally negative account of Progressive juvenile correctional programs. Historical studies of the juvenile court's institutional precursor, the House of Refuge, provide similar descriptions of custodial, rather than rehabilitative, facilities (Hawes 1971; Rothman 1971; Mennel 1973; Sutton 1988).

Contemporary evaluations of juvenile institutions reveal a continuing gap between rehabilitative rhetoric and punitive reality (Bartollas, Miller, and Dinitz 1976; Feld 1977, 1981*b;* Lerner 1986). Research in Massachusetts described violent and punitive institutions in which staff physically abused inmates and were frequently powerless to prevent inmate violence and predation (Feld 1977, 1981*b*). A study in Ohio described a similarly violent and oppressive institutional environment for the "rehabilitation" of young delinquents (Bartollas et al. 1976). Studies in other jurisdictions report staff and inmate violence, physical abuse, and degrading make-work (Guggenheim 1978; Lerner 1986). The daily reality for juveniles confined in many "treatment" facilities is one of violence, predatory behavior, and punitive incarceration.

Coinciding with these post-*Gault* evaluation studies, lawsuits challenged conditions of confinement, alleged that they violated inmates' "right to treatment," inflicted "cruel and unusual punishment," and provided another outside view of juvenile corrections (Feld 1978, 1984).[8] During the 1970s, courts attempted to define the juvenile "treatment" that justified fewer procedural safeguards, although they decided most cases either on procedural grounds or by prohibiting clearly punitive institutional practices such as excessive use of solitary confinement and physical beatings.[9] Juvenile conditions-of-

[8] The right to treatment follows from the state's invocation of its *parens patriae* power to intervene for the benefit of the individual. In a variety of settings other than juvenile corrections, such as institutions for the mentally ill and mentally retarded, states confine individuals without affording them the procedural safeguards associated with criminal incarceration for punishment. In all of these settings, it is the promise of benefit that justifies the less stringent procedural safeguards. The constitutional rationale of the civil commitment cases has been invoked to secure treatment for juveniles incarcerated in state training schools. The right to treatment has been relied on in juvenile institutions in cases in which rehabilitative services were not forthcoming and custodial warehousing or barbaric practices were shown.

[9] In *Nelson v. Heyne*, 355 F. Supp. 451 (N.D. Ind. 1972), *aff'd*, 491 F.2d 352 (7th Cir. 1974), the Court found that inmates were beaten with a "fraternity paddle," injected with psychotropic drugs for social control purposes, and deprived of minimally adequate care and individualized treatment. In *Inmates of Boys' Training School v. Affleck*, 346 F. Supp. 1354 (D.R.I. 1972), the Court found inmates confined in dark and cold dungeonlike cells in their underwear, routinely locked in solitary confinement, and subjected to a variety of antirehabilitative practices. In *Morales v. Turman*, 383 F. Supp. 53 (E.D. Tex. 1974), *rev'd on other grounds*, 535 F.2d 864 (5th Cir. 1976), the Court found numerous instances of physical brutality and abuse, including hazing by staff and inmates, staff-administered beatings and teargassings, homosexual assaults, extensive use of solitary confinement, repetitive and degrading make-work, and minimal clinical services. In *Morgan v. Sproat*, 432 F. Supp. 1130 (S.D. Miss. 1977), the Court found youths confined in padded cells with no windows or furnishings and only flush holes for toilets and denied access to all services or programs except a Bible. In *State v. Werner*, 242 S.E.2d 907 (West Virginia 1978), the Court found inmates locked in solitary confinement, beaten, slapped, kicked, and sprayed with mace by staff, required to scrub floors with a

confinement litigation in the 1980s focused on juvenile pretrial detention facilities as well as institutions and attempted to define
constitutionally adequate minimum living conditions without prescribing any affirmative obligations associated with "treatment."[10]

Although the courts' analytic strategies vary and outcomes of cases
differ, judicial descriptions of custodial institutions emphasize that rehabilitative euphemisms such as "providing a structured environment"
cannot disguise the punitive reality of juvenile confinement. The institutional experiences of confined juveniles are not as unmitigatedly bad
as those of adult prison inmates (Forst, Fagan, and Vivona 1989). Based
on interviews with fifty-nine chronic juvenile offenders in state training
schools and eighty-one comparable youths in adult correctional facilities, Forst et al. (1989) report that juveniles in training schools rated
their treatment and training programs, services, and institutional personnel more positively than did the youths in prison. Despite their
relative superiority, however, juvenile correctional facilities certainly
are not so benign and therapeutic as to justify depriving those who
face commitment to them of adequate procedural safeguards.

Evaluations of juvenile institutions conclude that violent inmate subcultures are a function of security arrangements; the more staff impose
authoritarian controls to facilitate security, the higher the levels of
covert inmate violence within the subculture (Bartollas et al. 1976;
Feld 1977, 1981b). Juveniles sentenced to long terms under "get-tough"
legislation are the most serious and chronic offenders, yet facilities
designed to handle them often suffer from limited physical mobility,
inadequate program resources and staff, and intense interaction among
the most difficult and troubled youths in the system. The result is a
situation that can easily produce a juvenile correctional "warehouse"
with all of the worst characteristics of adult penal incarceration. The
recent changes in juvenile court sentencing legislation exacerbate the
deleterious side effects associated with institutional overcrowding
(Krisberg et al. 1986).

The "medical model" underlying the rehabilitative juvenile court
assumes that social or psychological factors cause delinquent behavior,

---

toothbrush, and subjected to punitive practices such as standing and sitting for prolonged
periods without changing position.

[10] In *D.B. v. Tewksbury*, 545 F.Supp 896 (D.C. Ore. 1982), the Court found that the
conditions of juvenile pretrial detainees who were incarcerated in an adult jail were
punitive and worse than those experienced by adult convicts. Other courts have found
similar conditions violate either juveniles' Fourteenth Amendment due process rights or
the Eighth Amendment's prohibition against cruel and unusual punishment.

that sentences should be individualized based on assessments of treatment needs, that release should occur based on when the juvenile improves, and that successful treatment will reduce recidivism (Kassebaum and Ward 1991). Evaluations of the effectiveness of juvenile rehabilitation programs on recidivism rates provide scant support for the conclusion that juveniles confined in institutions are being treated rather than punished (Lab and Whitehead 1988; Whitehead and Lab 1989). Martinson's (1974, p. 25) general observation that "with few and isolated exceptions, the rehabilitative efforts that have been reported so far have had no appreciable affect on recidivism" challenged the fundamental premise of therapeutic dispositions and the juvenile court. More recent evaluations of the impact of correctional programs on recidivism counsel skepticism about the availability of programs that consistently or systematically rehabilitate adult or serious juvenile offenders (Greenberg 1977; Sechrest et al. 1979; Whitehead and Lab 1989). The National Academy of Science's Panel on Research on Rehabilitation Techniques concluded that "the current research literature provides no basis for positive recommendations about techniques to rehabilitate criminal offenders. The literature does afford occasional hints of intervention that may have promise, but to recommend widespread implementation of those measures would be irresponsible. Many of them would probably be wasteful, and some would do more harm than good in the long run" (Sechrest et al. 1979, p. 102). A meta-analysis of juvenile correctional treatment evaluations appearing in the professional literature between 1975 and 1984 and meeting certain methodological criteria concluded that "the results are far from encouraging for rehabilitation proponents" (Lab and Whitehead 1988, p. 77).

While the general conclusion that "nothing works" in juvenile or adult corrections has not been persuasively refuted, it has been strenuously resisted (Melton 1989). Gendreau and Ross (1979, 1987), Garrett (1985), Greenwood and Zimring (1985), Izzo and Ross (1990), Palmer (1991), and Roberts and Camasso (1991), for example, offer literature reviews, meta-analyses, or program descriptions that stress that some types of intervention may have positive effects on selected clients under certain conditions. However, even Palmer's (1991, p. 340) optimistic assessment of the rehabilitation of "rehabilitation" concludes only that "several methods seem promising, but none have been shown to usually produce major reductions [in recidivism] when applied broadly to typical composite samples of offenders." The issue for the juvenile court is not whether some programs work for some offenders under some conditions, but whether the possibility of an effective rehabilitation program should be used to justify confining young offenders "for their own good" and with fewer procedural safeguards than are provided to adults.

## VII. Conclusion

For more than two decades since *Gault*, juvenile courts have deflected, co-opted, ignored, or accommodated constitutional and legislative reforms with minimal institutional change. Despite its transformation from a welfare agency into a criminal court, the juvenile court remains essentially unreformed. Public and political concerns about drugs and youth crime encourage the repression rather than the rehabilitation of young offenders. With fiscal constraints, budget deficits, and competition from other interest groups, there is little likelihood that treatment services for delinquents will expand. Coupling the emergence of punitive policies with a societal unwillingness to provide for the welfare of children in general (National Commission on Children 1991), much less for those who commit crimes, there is scant reason to believe that the juvenile court, as originally conceived, can be revived.

The recent changes in procedures, jurisdiction, and sentencing policies reflect ambivalence about the role and purpose of juvenile courts and the social control of children. As juvenile courts converge procedurally and substantively with criminal courts, is there any reason to maintain a separate court whose only remaining distinctions are procedures under which no adult would agree to be tried (McCarthy 1977b; Wizner and Keller 1977; Guggenheim 1978; Wolfgang 1982; Dawson 1990a; Federle 1990; Ainsworth 1991)? While most commentators acknowledge the emergence of a punitive juvenile court, they recoil at the prospect of its outright abolition, emphasizing that children are different and that distinctions between "delinquents" and "criminals" should be maintained (Rubin 1979; Gardner 1987; Melton 1989; Dawson 1990a; Springer 1991). Most conclude, however, that the juvenile court sorely needs a new rationale, perhaps one that melds punishment with reduced culpability and procedural justice (Rubin 1979; American Bar Association—Institute of Judicial Administration 1980b; Walkover 1984; Gardner 1989; Melton 1989; Springer 1991).

There are three plausible responses to a juvenile court that punishes in the name of treatment and simultaneously denies young offenders elementary procedural justice: restructure juvenile courts to fit their original therapeutic purpose, embrace punishment as an acceptable and appropriate part of delinquency proceedings but coupled with criminal procedural safeguards (American Bar Association—Institute of Judicial Administration 1980*b;* Melton 1989; Forst and Blomquist 1991), or abolish juvenile court jurisdiction over criminal conduct and try young offenders in criminal courts with certain modifications of substantive and procedural criminal law (Feld 1984, 1988*b;* Ainsworth 1991).

## A. Return to an Informal, "Rehabilitative" Juvenile Court

Some proponents of an informal, therapeutic juvenile court contend that the "experiment" cannot be declared a failure since it has never been implemented effectively (Ferdinand 1991). From their inception, juvenile courts and correctional facilities have had more in common with penal facilities than with welfare agencies, hospitals, or clinics (Schlossman 1977; Rothman 1980). By the 1960s and the *Gault* decision, the failures of implementation were readily apparent (President's Commission on Law Enforcement and Administration of Justice 1967*a*, 1967*b*). Any proposal to reinvigorate the juvenile court as an informal, therapeutic welfare agency must first explain why the resources and personnel that have not been made available previously will now become available (Edwards 1992).

Even if a coterie of clinicians suddenly descended on a juvenile court, it would be a dubious policy to recreate the juvenile court as originally conceived. The central critique of individualized justice is that juvenile courts are substantively and procedurally lawless. Despite the existence of statutes and procedural rules, juvenile courts operate effectively unconstrained by the rule of law. To the extent that judges make dispositions based on individualized assessments of an offender's "best interests" or "real needs," judicial discretion is formally unrestricted. If there are neither practical scientific nor clinical bases by which judges can classify for treatment (Sechrest 1987), then the exercise of "sound discretion" is simply a euphemism for idiosyncratic judicial subjectivity. If intervention were consistently benign and effective, perhaps differential processing would be tolerable. But juveniles committed to institutions or whose liberty is restrained regard the experience as a sanction rather than as beneficial (Wizner and Keller 1977). At the least, similarly situated offenders will be handled differently based on extraneous personal characteristics for which they are not responsible. At the worst, if juvenile courts effectively punish, then discretionary sentences based on individualized assessments introduce unequal and discriminatory sanctions on invidious bases.

The critique of the juvenile court does not rest on the premise that "nothing works" or ever can work. Indeed, some demonstration model programs may produce positive changes in some offenders under some conditions. And some treatment programs may be more effective than the evaluation studies indicate. However, after a century of unfulfilled promises, a continuing societal unwillingness to commit scarce resources to rehabilitative efforts, and intervention strategies of dubious or marginal efficacy, the possibility of an effective treatment program is too fragile a reed on which to construct an entire separate adjudicative apparatus. We should exercise caution in delegating coercive powers to penal therapists to use on a subjective, nonscientific basis.

Procedural informality is the concomitant of substantive discretion. The traditional juvenile courts' procedures are predicated on the assumption of benevolence. If clinical decision making is not constrained substantively, then it cannot be limited procedurally, either, since every case is unique. A primary role of lawyers is to manipulate legal rules for their clients' advantage; a discretionary court without objective laws or formal procedures is unfavorable terrain. The limited presence and role of counsel in many juvenile courts may reflect judicial adherence to a treatment model that no longer exists, if it ever did. But the absence of lawyers reduces the ability of the legal process to invoke existing laws to make courts conform to their legal mandates. The closed, informal, and confidential nature of delinquency proceedings reduces visibility and accountability and precludes external checks on coercive intervention.

The fundamental shortcoming of the traditional juvenile court is not a failure of implementation but a failure of conception. The original juvenile court was conceived of as a social service agency in a judicial setting, a fusion of welfare and coercion (Springer 1991). But providing for child welfare is ultimately a societal responsibility rather than a judicial one. It is unrealistic to expect juvenile courts, or any other legal institutions, to resolve all of the social ills afflicting young people or to have a significant impact on youth crime. Despite claims of being a child-centered nation, we care less about other people's children than we do our own, especially when they are children of other colors or cultures (Edelman 1987; National Commission on Children 1991). Without a societal commitment to a social welfare system that adequately meets the minimum family, health, housing, nutrition, and educational needs of all young people on a voluntary basis, the juvenile court provides a mechanism for involuntary control, however ineffective it may be in delivering services or rehabilitating offenders. Historical analyses of juvenile justice suggest that when social services and social control are combined in one setting, social welfare considerations quickly are subordinated to custodial ones (Platt 1977; Rothman 1980; Sutton 1988; Ferdinand 1989, 1991).

In part, the juvenile court's subordination of individual welfare to custody and control stems from its fundamentally penal focus. Rather than identifying the characteristics of children for which they are not responsible and that could improve their life circumstances—their lack of decent education, their lack of adequate housing, their unmet health needs, their deteriorated family and social circumstances (National Commission on Children 1991)—juvenile court law focuses on a violation of criminal law that is their fault and for which they are responsible (Fox 1970*b*). As long as juvenile courts emphasize the characteristics of children least likely to elicit sympathy and ignores the social conditions most likely to engender a desire to nurture and help, the law reinforces retributive rather than rehabilitative impulses. So long as juvenile courts operate in a societal context that does not provide adequate social services for children in general, intervention in the lives of those who commit crimes inevitably will be for purposes of social control rather than social welfare.

## B. Due Process and Punishment in Juvenile Court

Articulating the purposes of juvenile courts requires more than invoking treatment versus punishment formulae since in operation there are no practical or operational differences between the two. Acknowledging that juvenile courts punish imposes an obligation to provide all criminal procedural safeguards since "the condition of being a boy does not justify a kangaroo court," *In re Gault*, 387 U.S. at 28 (1967). While procedural parity with adults may realize the *McKeiver* Court's fear of ending the juvenile court experiment, to fail to do so perpetuates injustice. Treating similarly situated juveniles dissimilarly, punishing them in the name of treatment, and denying them basic safeguards fosters a sense of injustice that thwarts any reform efforts (Melton 1989).

Articulating alternative rationales for handling young offenders requires reconciling the two contradictory impulses provoked by recognizing that the child is a criminal and the criminal is a child. If the traditional juvenile court provides neither therapy nor justice and cannot be rehabilitated, then the policy alternatives for responding to young offenders are either to make juvenile courts more like criminal courts or to make criminal courts more like juvenile courts. In reconsidering basic premises, issues of substance and procedure must be addressed whether young offenders ultimately are tried in a separate juvenile court or in a criminal court (Feld 1988b). Issues of substantive justice include developing and implementing a doctrinal rationale—diminished responsibility or reduced capacity—for sentencing young offenders differently, and more leniently, than older defendants (Twentieth Century Fund Task Force on Sentencing Policy Toward Young Offenders 1978; Feld 1988b; Gardner 1989; Melton 1989). Issues of procedural justice include providing youths with *all* of the procedural safeguards adults receive *and* additional protections that recognize their immaturity (Rosenberg 1980; Feld 1984; Melton 1989).

Many recent commentators conclude that "the assumptions underlying the juvenile court shows it to be a bankrupt legal institution" (Melton 1989, p. 166) and that it is increasingly penal in character. Rather than proposing to abolish the juvenile court, they propose to transform the juvenile court into an explicitly penal one, albeit one that limits punishment based on reduced culpability and provides enhanced procedural justice (Rubin 1979; American Bar Association—Institute of Judicial Administration 1980b; Walkover 1984; Gardner 1989; Melton 1989; Forst and Blomquist 1991). Springer (1991, p. 398), for example, argues that "no longer will the juvenile court be seen as a quasi-judicial court-clinic but, rather, as a real court, administering real justice in its traditional retributive and distributive meanings. . . . Juveniles should have to pay for their crimes; but . . . society has a duty to its young delinquents to help them to gain moral and civic equilibrium."

The paradigm of the new juvenile court is that propounded by the American Bar Association—Institute of Judicial Administration's Juvenile Justice Standards Project. The twenty-six volumes of Juvenile Justice Standards recommend the repeal of jurisdiction over status offenders, the use of proportional and determinate sentences to sanction delinquent offenders, the use of restrictive offense criteria to regularize pretrial detention and judicial transfer decisions, and the provision of all criminal procedural safeguards, including nonwaivable counsel and jury trials (McCarthy 1977a; Wizner and Keller 1977; Flicker 1983). Under the Juvenile Justice Standards, "the rehabilitative model of juvenile justice is rejected and the principles of criminal law and procedure become the cornerstones of a new relationship between the child and the state" (McCarthy 1977*a*, p. 1094).

While proponents of the "criminal juvenile court" advocate fusing reduced culpability sentencing with greater procedural justice (Gardner 1989; Melton 1989; Springer 1991), they often fail to explain why these principles must be implemented within a separate juvenile court rather than in a criminal court. The Juvenile Justice Standards assert that "removal of the treatment rationale does not destroy the rationale for a separate system or for utilization of an ameliorative approach; it does, however, require a different rationale" (American Bar Association—Institute of Judicial Administration 1980*b*, p. 9, n. 5). Unfortunately, even though the standards propose a virtual replication of adult criminal procedure, they do not provide any rationale for doing so in a separate juvenile system.

Other commentators have suggested some possible rationales. Rubin (1979), for example, speculates that, since some specialized juvenile procedures and dispositional facilities would be needed, it is more practical and less risky to retain specialized juvenile divisions of general trial courts rather than to abolish juvenile courts entirely. Given institutional and bureaucratic inertia, however, it may be that only a clean break with the personnel and practices of the past could permit the implementation of the procedures and policies he endorses.

Proponents of a criminal juvenile court point to the deficiencies of criminal courts—overcriminalization, ineffective defense representation and excessive caseloads, poor administration, insufficient sentencing alternatives—to justify retaining a separate juvenile court (Rubin 1979). Unfortunately, these are characteristics of juvenile courts as well (Dawson 1990*a*). While certain elements of the criminal justice system, such as bail, might pose additional problems if applied without modification to juveniles (Dawson 1990*a*), those are not compelling justifications for retaining a complete and separate judicial system. Rather, such arguments suggest a comparison of the relative quality of juvenile and criminal justice in each state to determine in which system young people are more likely to be treated justly and fairly.

The only real substantive difference between the "criminal juvenile court" and adult courts is that the Juvenile Justice Standards call for shorter sentences than criminal courts would impose (Wizner and Keller 1977). Particularly for serious young offenders, the quality and quantity of punishment imposed in juvenile court is less than that in criminal courts. Maintaining a separate court may be the only way to achieve uniformly shorter sentences and insulate youths from criminal courts' "get tough" sentencing policies (Gardner 1989).

If there is a relationship between procedural formality and substantive severity, could a "criminal juvenile court" continue to afford leniency? As juvenile courts move in the direction of greater formality— lawyers insisting on adherence to the rule of law; openness, visibility, and accountability; proportional and determinate sentencing guidelines—will not the convergence between juvenile and criminal courts increase their repressiveness and further erode sentencing differences? Can juvenile courts only be lenient because their substantive and procedural discretion is exercised behind closed doors? Would the imposition of the rule of law prevent them from affording leniency to most youths? These issues are not even recognized, much less answered, by the Juvenile Justice Standards.

## C. Young Offenders in Criminal Court

If the child is a criminal and the primary purpose of formal intervention is social control, then young offenders could be tried in criminal courts alongside their adult counterparts. Before returning young offenders to criminal courts, however, there are preliminary issues of substance and procedure that a legislature should address. Issues of substantive justice include developing a rationale for sentencing young offenders differently, and more leniently, than older defendants. Issues of procedural justice include affording youths alternative safeguards *in addition* to full procedural parity with adult defendants. Taken in combination, legislation can avoid the worst of both worlds, provide more than the protections accorded to adults, and do justice in sentencing.

1. *Substantive Justice—Juveniles' Criminal Responsibility.* The primary virtue of the contemporary juvenile court is that serious young offenders typically receive shorter sentences than do adult offenders for comparable crimes. As a policy goal, young offenders should survive the mistakes of adolescence with their life chances intact (Twentieth Century Fund Task Force on Sentencing Policy Toward Young Offenders 1978; Zimring 1982). This goal is threatened if youths sentenced in criminal courts received the same severe sentences frequently inflicted on eighteen-year-old "adults." And, of course, the contemporary juvenile court's seeming virtue of shorter sentences for serious offenders is offset by the far more numerous minor offenders who receive longer "rehabilitative" sentences as juveniles than they would if they were simply punished as adults.

Shorter sentences for young people do not require that they be tried in separate juvenile courts. Both juvenile and adult courts are supposed to separate the adjudication of guilt or innocence from sentencing, with discretion confined largely to the sentencing phase (Dawson 1990a). Adult courts are capable of dispensing lenient sentences to youthful offenders when appropriate (Wizner and Keller 1977), although explicit and formal recognition of youthfulness as a mitigating factor is desirable (Zimring 1981a, 1991).

There are a variety of doctrinal and policy justifications for sentencing young people less severely than their adult counterparts. The original juvenile court assumed that children were immature and irresponsible (Ainsworth 1991). These assumptions about young people's lack of criminal capacity built on the common law's infancy mens rea defense, which presumed that children less than seven years old lacked criminal capacity, those between seven and fourteen years rebuttably lacked criminal capacity, while those fourteen years of age and older were fully responsible (Fox 1970b; McCarthy 1977b; Weissman 1983; Walkover 1984). Juvenile court legislation simply extended upward by a few years the general presumption of youthful criminal incapacity.

Common-law infancy and other diminished responsibility doctrines reflect developmental differences that render youths less culpable or criminally responsible and provide a conceptual basis for shorter sentences for juveniles than for their adult counterparts. When sentencing within a framework of deserved punishment, it would be fundamentally unjust to impose the same penalty on a juvenile as on an adult. Deserved punishment emphasizes censure, condemnation, and blame (von Hirsch 1976, 1986). Penalties proportionate to the seriousness of the crime reflect the connection between the nature of the conduct and its blameworthiness.

Because commensurate punishment proportions sanctions to the seriousness of the offense, it shifts the analytical focus to the meaning of seriousness. The seriousness of an offense is the product of two components—harm and culpability (von Hirsch 1976, p. 79). Evaluations of harm focus on the degree of injury inflicted, risk created, or value taken. The perpetrator's age is of little consequence when assessing the harmfulness of a criminal act. Assessments of seriousness also include the quality of the actor's choice to engage in the conduct that produced the harm. It is with respect to the culpability of choices—the blameworthiness of acting in a particular harm-producing way—that the issue of youthfulness becomes especially troublesome.

Psychological research indicates that young people move through

developmental stages of cognitive functioning with respect to legal reasoning, internalization of social and legal expectations, and ethical decision making (Piaget 1960; Kohlberg 1969; Tapp and Levine 1974; Tapp
and Kohlberg 1977). The developmental sequence and changes in cognitive processes are strikingly parallel to the imputations of responsibility associated with the common-law infancy defense and suggest that
by midadolesence individuals acquire most of the legal and moral values and reasoning capacity that will guide their behavior through later
life (Kohlberg 1964; Tapp 1976).

Even a youth fourteen years of age or older who knows "right from
wrong" and abstractly possesses the requisite criminal mens rea is still
not as blameworthy and deserving of comparable punishment as an
adult offender. Relative to adults, youths are less able to form moral
judgments, less capable of controlling their impulses, and less aware
of the consequences of their acts: "Adolescents, particularly in the
early and middle teen years, are more vulnerable, more impulsive, and
less self-disciplined than adults. Crimes committed by youths may be
just as harmful to victims as those committed by older persons, but
they deserve less punishment because adolescents have less capacity to
control their conduct and to think in long-range terms than adults"
(Twentieth Century Fund Task Force on Sentencing Policy Toward
Young Offenders 1978, p. 7). Because juveniles' criminal choices are
less blameworthy than adults and their responsibility is diminished,
they "deserve" less punishment than an adult for the same criminal
harm.

The crimes of children are seldom their fault alone. The family,
school, and community are responsible for socializing young people,
and society shares at least some of the blame for their offenses. Moreover, to the extent that the ability to make responsible choices is
learned behavior, the dependent status of youth systematically de-
prives them of opportunities to learn to be responsible (Zimring 1982).
Finally, children live their lives, as they commit their crime, in groups.
Young people are more susceptible to peer group influences than their
older counterparts, which lessens, but does not excuse, their criminal
liability (Zimring 1981b).

The Supreme Court in *Thompson v. Oklahoma*, 487 U.S. 815 (1988),
analyzed the criminal responsibility of young offenders and provided
additional support for shorter sentences for reduced culpability even
for youths older than the common-law infancy threshold of age fourteen. In vacating Thompson's capital sentence, the plurality concluded

that "a young person is not capable of acting with the degree of culpability that can justify the ultimate penalty" (*Thompson v. Oklahoma*, 108 S.Ct. at 2692 [1988]). A plurality of the Supreme Court subsequently upheld the death penalty for youths who were sixteen or seventeen at the time of their offenses (*Stanford v. Kentucky*, 109 S.Ct. 2969 [1989]). While recognizing that juveniles as a class may be less culpable than adults, the Court in *Stanford* decided on the narrow grounds that there was no clear national consensus that such executions violated "evolving standards of decency" encompassed in the Eighth Amendment's prohibition against "cruel and unusual" punishment.

The Court in *Thompson* reaffirmed earlier decisions holding that youthfulness was a mitigating factor at sentencing and concluded that juveniles are less blameworthy for their crimes than are their adult counterparts. Since deserved punishment must reflect individual culpability and "there is also broad agreement on the proposition that adolescents as a class are less mature and responsible than adults" (*Thompson v. Oklahoma*, 108 S.Ct. at 2698 [1988]), even though Thompson was responsible for his crime, simply because of his age he could not be punished as severely as an adult:

> Our history is replete with laws and judicial recognition that minors, especially in their earlier years, generally are less mature and responsible than adults. Particularly "during the formative years of childhood and adolescence, minors often lack the experience, perspective, and judgment" expected of adults. . . . The Court has already endorsed the proposition that less culpability should attach to a crime committed by a juvenile than to a comparable crime committed by an adult. . . . Inexperience, less education, and less intelligence make the teenager less able to evaluate the consequences of his or her conduct while at the same time he or she is much more apt to be motivated by mere emotion or peer pressure than is an adult. The reasons why juveniles are not trusted with the privileges and responsibilities of an adult also explain why their irresponsible conduct is not as morally reprehensible as that of an adult. [*Thompson v. Oklahoma*, 108 S.Ct. at 2698-99 (1988)]

The Court cited other instances—serving on a jury, voting, marrying, driving, and drinking—in which states act paternalistically and impose disabilities on youths because of their presumptive incapacity, lack of experience, and judgment. The Court emphasized that it would be both inconsistent and a cruel irony suddenly to find juveniles as culpable as adult defendants for purposes of capital punishment.

Quite apart from differences in culpability, there are other reasons why juveniles deserve less severe punishment than adults for comparable crimes. Penalties—whether adult punishment or juvenile "treatment"—are measured in units of time—days, months, or years. However, the ways that youths and adults subjectively and objectively conceive of and experience similar lengths of time differ (Piaget 1969; Cottle 1976; Friedman 1982). The developmental progression in thinking about and experiencing time—future time perspective and present duration—follows a sequence similar to the development of criminal responsibility. Without a mature appreciation of future time, juveniles are less able to understand the consequences of their acts. Because a juvenile's "objective" sense of time duration is not comparable to an adult's, objectively equivalent sentences are experienced subjectively as unequal. While a three-month sentence may be lenient for an adult offender, it is the equivalent of an entire summer vacation for a youth, a very long period of time. Because juveniles are more dependent on their parents, removal from home is a more severe punishment than it would be for adults. Thus, sentencing adults and juveniles to similar terms for similar offenses would be unjust.

Shorter sentences for reduced responsibility is a more modest rationale for treating young people differently than the rehabilitative justifications advanced by the Progressive child savers. Adult courts could impose shorter sentences for reduced culpability on a discretionary basis, although it would be preferable for a legislature explicitly to provide youths with categorical fractional reductions of adult sentences. This could take the form of a formal "youth discount" at sentencing. For example, a fourteen-year-old might receive 33 percent of the adult penalty, a sixteen-year-old 66 percent, and an eighteen-year-old the full penalty. A proposal for explicit fractional reductions in youth sentences can only be made against the backdrop of realistic, humane, and determinate adult sentencing practices in which "real-time" sentences can be determined. Several of the "serious juvenile offender" or "designated felony" sentencing statutes provide terms for serious young offenders that are considerably shorter than sentences for their adult counterparts. For youths below the age of fourteen, the common-law infancy mens rea defense would acquire new vitality for proportionally shorter sentences or even noncriminal dispositions.

A graduated age/culpability sentencing scheme could avoid some of the inconsistency and injustice associated with the binary either/or juvenile versus adult sentencing played out in judicial waiver proceedings. Depending on whether transfer is ordered, the sentences that youths receive can differ by orders of magnitude (Fagan and Deschenes 1990). Because of the differences in consequences, transfer hearings consume a disproportionate amount of juvenile court time and energy (Dawson 1990a). Abolishing juvenile courts would eliminate the need for transfer hearings, save considerable resources which are ultimately expended to no purpose, eliminate the punishment gap that occurs when youths make the transition between systems, and assure similar consequences to similar offenders.

Trying young people in criminal courts with full procedural safeguards would not especially diminish judges' expertise about appropriate dispositions for young people. The Progressives envisioned a specialized juvenile court judge who possessed the wisdom of a *kadi* (Matza 1964). Increasingly, however, district court judges handle juvenile matters as part of their general docket or rotate through juvenile court on short-term assignments without acquiring any particular juvenile dispositional expertise (Edwards 1992). Even in specialized juvenile courts, the information necessary for appropriate dispositions resides with the court services personnel who advise the judge on sentences, rather than with the court itself. Even if criminally convicted, court services personnel advise the judge as to the appropriate sentence, and, within the time limits defined by the offense, young offenders could be transferred to a family court or social services agency if a welfare disposition is appropriate.

Even a punitive sentence does not require incarcerating juveniles in adult jails and prisons. The existing detention facilities, training schools, and institutions provide the option of age-segregated dispositional facilities. Moreover, insisting explicitly on humane conditions of confinement could do at least as much to improve the lives of incarcerated youths as has the "right to treatment" or the "rehabilitative ideal" (Feld 1977, 1981b). A recognition that most young offenders will return to society imposes an obligation to provide the resources for self-improvement on a voluntary basis.

2. *Procedural Justice.*   Since *Gault*, many of the formal procedural attributes of criminal courts are routine aspects of juvenile justice administration as well. The same laws apply to arresting adults and taking juveniles into custody, to searches, and to pretrial identification procedures (Dawson 1990a). Juveniles charged with felony offenses

now are routinely subjected to similar fingerprinting and booking procedures. The greater procedural formality and adversary nature of the juvenile court reflects the merger of the court's therapeutic mission and its social control functions. The many instances in which states choose to treat juvenile offenders procedurally like adult criminal defendants, even when formal equality redounds to their disadvantage, is one aspect of this process (Feld 1984).

Differentials in age and competency suggest that youths should receive more protections than adults, rather than less. The rationales to sentence juveniles differently than adults also justify providing them with *all* of the procedural safeguards adults receive *and* additional protections that recognize their immaturity (McCarthy 1977*b*; Rosenberg 1980; Feld 1984; Melton 1989). This dual-maximal strategy would provide enhanced protection for children explicitly because of their vulnerability and immaturity.

One example where this dual-maximal procedural strategy would produce different results is waivers of Fifth and Sixth Amendment constitutional rights. Although the Supreme Court in *Gault* noted that the appointment of counsel is the prerequisite to procedural justice, *Gault's* promise of counsel remains unrealized because many judges find that youths waived their rights in a "knowing, intelligent, and voluntary" manner under the "totality of the circumstances." A system of justice that recognizes the disabilities of youths would prohibit waivers of the right to counsel or the privilege against self-incrimination without prior consultation with counsel (American Bar Association— Institute of Judicial Administration 1980*b*). The right to counsel would attach as soon as a juvenile is taken into custody and would be self-invoking; it would not require a juvenile affirmatively to request counsel as is the case for adults (*Moran v. Burbine*, 475 U.S. 412 [1986]). The presence and availability of counsel throughout the process would assure that juveniles' rights are respected and implemented. This is the policy that the Juvenile Justice Standards propose, albeit in a juvenile court setting.

Full procedural parity in criminal courts, coupled with alternative legislative safeguards for children, can provide the same or greater protections than does the current juvenile court. Expunging criminal records and eliminating collateral civil disabilities following the successful completion of a sentence could afford equivalent relief for an isolated youthful folly as does the juvenile court's confidentiality.

Abolishing the juvenile court would force a long overdue and critical reassessment of the entire social construct of "childhood" (Ainsworth 1991). As long as young people are regarded as fundamentally different from adults, it becomes too easy to rationalize and justify a procedurally inferior justice system. The gap between the quality of justice afforded juveniles and adults can be conveniently rationalized on the grounds that "after all, they are only children," and children are entitled only to custody, not liberty (*Schall v. Martin*, 467 U.S. 253 [1984]). So long as the view prevails that juvenile court intervention is "benign" coercion and that in any event children should not expect more, youths will continue to receive "the worst of both worlds."

But issues of procedure and substance, while important, focus too narrowly on the legal domain. The ideology of therapeutic justice and its discretionary apparatus persist because the social control is directed at children. Despite humanitarian claims of being a child-centered nation, our cultural and legal conceptions of children support institutional arrangements that deny the personhood of young people. A new purpose for the juvenile court cannot be formulated successfully without critically reassessing the meaning of "childhood" and creating social institutions to assure the welfare of the next generation.

### REFERENCES

Aday, David P., Jr. 1986. "Court Structure, Defense Attorney Use, and Juvenile Court Decisions." *Sociological Quarterly* 27:107–19.

Ainsworth, Janet E. 1991. "Re-imagining Childhood and Reconstructing the Legal Order: The Case for Abolishing the Juvenile Court." *North Carolina Law Review* 69:1083–1133.

Allen, Francis A. 1964. "Legal Values and the Rehabilitative Ideal." In *The Borderland of Criminal Justice: Essays in Law and Criminology*. Chicago: University of Chicago Press.

——. 1981. *The Decline of the Rehabilitative Ideal: Penal Policy and Social Purpose*. New Haven, Conn.: Yale University Press.

Allison, Richard, ed. 1983. *Status Offenders and the Juvenile Justice System*. Hackensack, N.J.: National Council on Crime and Delinquency.

American Bar Association—Institute of Judicial Administration. 1980a. *Juvenile Justice Standards Relating to Pretrial Court Proceedings*. Cambridge, Mass.: Ballinger.

——. 1980b. *Juvenile Justice Standards Relating to Juvenile Delinquency and Sanctions*. Cambridge, Mass.: Ballinger.

———. 1982. *Juvenile Justice Standards Relating to Noncriminal Misbehavior.* Cambridge, Mass.: Ballinger.

American Friends Service Committee. 1971. *Struggle for Justice.* New York: Hill & Wang.

Andrews, R. Hale, and Andrew H. Cohn. 1974. "Ungovernability: The Unjustifiable Jurisdiction." *Yale Law Journal* 83:1383–1409.

Aries, Philippe. 1962. *Centuries of Childhood: A Social History of Family Life.* New York: Vintage Books.

Arizona Department of Corrections. 1986. *Length of Confinement Guidelines for Juveniles.* Tucson: Arizona Department of Corrections.

Arthur, Lindsay G. 1977. "Status Offenders Need a Court of Last Resort." *Boston University Law Review* 57:631–44.

Bartollas, Clemens, Stuart J. Miller, and Simon Dinitz. 1976. *Juvenile Victimization.* New York: Wiley.

Barton, William. 1976. "Discretionary Decision-making in Juvenile Justice." *Crime and Delinquency* 22:470–80.

Bishop, Donna M., and Charles S. Frazier. 1988. "The Influence of Race in Juvenile Justice Processing." *Journal of Research in Crime and Delinquency* 25:242–63.

———. 1991. "Transfer of Juveniles to Criminal Court: A Case Study and Analysis of Prosecutorial Waiver." *Notre Dame Journal of Law, Ethics and Public Policy* 5:281–302.

———. 1992. "Gender Bias in Juvenile Justice Processing: Implications of the JJDP Act." *Journal of Criminal Law and Criminology* 82:1162–86.

Blumstein, Alfred, Jacqueline Cohen, Jeffrey A. Roth, and Christy A. Visher, eds. 1986. *Criminal Careers and "Career Criminals."* Washington, D.C.: National Academy Press.

Bortner, M. A. 1982. *Inside a Juvenile Court.* New York: New York University Press.

———. 1986. "Traditional Rhetoric, Organizational Realities: Remand of Juveniles to Adult Court." *Crime and Delinquency* 32:53–73.

Bortner, M. A., and W. L. Reed. 1985. "The Preeminence of Process: An Example of Refocused Justice Research." *Social Science Quarterly* 66:413–25.

Carrington, Peter J., and Sharon Moyer. 1988a. "Legal Representation and Workload in Canadian Juvenile Courts." Ottawa: Department of Justice, Canada.

———. 1988b. "Legal Representation and Dispositions in Canadian Juvenile Courts." Ottawa: Department of Justice, Canada.

———. 1990. "The Effect of Defence Counsel on Plea and Outcome in Juvenile Court." *Canadian Journal of Criminology* 32:621–37.

Chesney-Lind, Meda. 1977. "Judicial Paternalism and the Female Status Offender: Training Women to Know Their Place." *Crime and Delinquency* 23:121–30.

———. 1988. "Girls and Status Offenses: Is Juvenile Justice Still Sexist?" *Criminal Justice Abstracts* 20:144–65.

Cicourel, Aaron V. 1968. *The Social Organization of Juvenile Justice.* New York: Wiley.

Clarke, Stevens H., and Gary G. Koch. 1980. "Juvenile Court: Therapy or Crime Control, and Do Lawyers Make a Difference?" *Law and Society Review* 14:263–308.

Coates, Robert, Martin Forst, and Bruce Fisher. 1985. *Institutional Commitment and Release Decision-making for Juvenile Delinquents: An Assessment of Determinate and Indeterminate Approaches—a Cross-State Analysis.* San Francisco: URSA Institute.

Cogan, Neil H. 1970. "Juvenile Law, Before and After the Entrance of *'Parens Patriae.'*" *South Carolina Law Review* 22:147–81.

Cohen, Lawrence E., and James R. Kluegel. 1978. "Determinants of Juvenile Court Dispositions: Ascriptive and Achieved Factors in Two Metropolitan Courts." *American Sociological Review* 27:162–76.

———. 1979. "The Detention Decision: A Study of the Impact of Social Characteristics and Legal Factors in Two Metropolitan Juvenile Courts." *Social Forces* 58:146–61.

Coleman, James S., Robert H. Bremner, Burton R. Clark, John B. David, Dorothy H. Eichorn, Zvi Griliches, Joseph F. Kett, Norman B. Ryder, Zahava Blum Doering, and John M. Mays. 1974. *Youth: Transition to Adulthood.* Chicago: University of Chicago Press.

Costello, Jan C., and Worthington, Nancy L. 1981. "Incarcerating Status Offenders: Attempts to Circumvent the Juvenile Justice and Delinquency Prevention Act." *Harvard Civil Rights–Civil Liberties Law Review* 16:41–81.

Cottle, Thomas. 1976. *Perceiving Time: A Psychological Investigation with Men and Women.* New York: Wiley.

Cremin, Lawrence. 1961. *The Transformation of the School: Progressivism in American Education, 1876–1957.* New York: Vintage Books.

Dannefer, Dale, and Russell Schutt. 1982. "Race and Juvenile Justice Processing in Court and Police Agencies." *American Journal of Sociology* 87:1113–32.

Dawson, Robert O. 1988. "The Third Justice System: The New Juvenile Criminal System of Determinate Sentencing for the Youthful Violent Offender in Texas." *St. Mary's Law Journal* 19:943–1016.

———. 1990a. "The Future of Juvenile Justice: Is It Time to Abolish the System?" *Journal of Criminal Law and Criminology* 81:136–55.

———. 1990b. "The Violent Juvenile Offender: An Empirical Study of Juvenile Determinate Sentencing Proceedings as an Alternative to Criminal Prosecution." *Texas Tech Law Review* 21:1897–1939.

Debele, Gary A. 1987. "The Due Process Revolution and the Juvenile Court: The Matter of Race in the Historical Evolution of a Doctrine." *Journal of Law and Inequality* 5:513–48.

Decker, Scott H. 1985. "A Systematic Analysis of Diversion: Net Widening and Beyond." *Journal of Criminal Justice* 13:206–16.

Degler, Carl. 1980. *At Odds: Women and the Family in America from the Revolution to the Present.* New York: Oxford University Press.

DeMause, Lloyd. 1974. "The Evolution of Childhood." In *The History of Childhood,* edited by Lloyd DeMause. New York: Psychohistory Press.

Demos, John, and Sarane Spence Boocock. 1978. *Turning Points: Historical and Sociological Essays on the Family.* Chicago: University of Chicago Press.

Edelman, Marian Wright. 1987. *Families in Peril: An Agenda for Social Change.* Cambridge, Mass.: Harvard University Press.

Edwards, Leonard P. 1992. "The Juvenile Court and the Role of the Juvenile Court Judge." *Juvenile and Family Court Journal* 43:1–45.

Eigen, Joel. 1981a. "The Determinants and Impact of Jurisdictional Transfer in Philadelphia." In *Readings in Public Policy,* edited by John Hall, Donna Hamparian, John Pettibone, and Joe White. Columbus, Ohio: Academy for Contemporary Problems.

———. 1981b. "Punishing Youth Homicide Offenders in Philadelphia." *Journal of Criminal Law and Criminology* 72:1072–93.

Ellis, James W. 1974. "Volunteeering Children: Parental Commitment of Minors to Mental Institutions." *California Law Review* 62:840–916.

Emerson, Robert M. 1969. *Judging Delinquents: Context and Process in Juvenile Court.* Chicago: Aldine.

Empey, LaMar T. 1973. "Juvenile Justice Reform: Diversion, Due Process, and Deinstitutionalization." In *Prisoners in America,* edited by Lloyd E. Ohlin. Englewood Cliffs, N.J.: Prentice-Hall.

———. 1979. "The Social Construction of Childhood and Juvenile Justice." In *The Future of Childhood and Juvenile Justice,* edited by LaMar T. Empey. Charlottesville: University Press of Virginia.

Fagan, Jeffrey, and Elizabeth Piper Deschenes. 1990. "Determinates of Judicial Waiver Decisions for Violent Juvenile Offenders." *Journal of Criminal Law and Criminology* 81:314–47.

Fagan, Jeffrey, Martin Forst, and Scott Vivona. 1987. "Racial Determinants of the Judicial Transfer Decision: Prosecuting Violent Youth in Criminal Court." *Crime and Delinquency* 33:259–86.

Fagan, Jeffrey, Ellen Slaughter, and Eliot Hartstone. 1987. "Blind Justice? The Impact of Race on the Juvenile Justice Process." *Crime and Delinquency* 33:224–58.

Farrington, David P. 1986. "Age and Crime." In *Crime and Justice: An Annual Review of Research,* vol. 7, edited by Michael Tonry and Norval Morris. Chicago: University of Chicago Press.

Federle, Katherine H. 1990. "The Abolition of the Juvenile Court: A Proposal for the Preservation of Children's Legal Rights." *Journal of Contemporary Law* 16:23–51.

Feld, Barry C. 1977. *Neutralizing Inmate Violence: Juvenile Offenders in Institutions.* Cambridge, Mass.: Ballinger.

———. 1978. "Reference of Juvenile Offenders for Adult Prosecution: The Legislative Alternative to Asking Unanswerable Questions." *Minnesota Law Review* 62:515–618.

———. 1981a. "Juvenile Court Legislative Reform and the Serious Young Offender: Dismantling the 'Rehabilitative Ideal.'" *Minnesota Law Review* 69:141–242.

———. 1981b. "A Comparative Analysis of Organizational Structure and Inmate Subcultures in Institutions for Juvenile Offenders." *Crime and Delinquency* 27:336–63.

————. 1983. "Delinquent Careers and Criminal Policy: Just Deserts and the Waiver Decision." *Criminology* 21:195–212.

————. 1984. "Criminalizing Juvenile Justice: Rules of Procedure for Juvenile Court." *Minnesota Law Review* 69:141–276.

————. 1987. "Juvenile Court Meets the Principle of Offense: Legislative Changes in Juvenile Waiver Statutes." *Journal of Criminal Law and Criminology* 78:471–533.

————. 1988a. *"In re Gault* Revisited: A Cross-State Comparison of the Right to Counsel in Juvenile Court." *Crime and Delinquency* 34:393–424.

————. 1988b. "Juvenile Court Meets the Principle of Offense: Punishment, Treatment, and the Difference it Makes." *Boston University Law Review* 68:821–915.

————. 1989. "The Right to Counsel in Juvenile Court: An Empirical Study of When Lawyers Appear and the Difference They Make." *Journal of Criminal Law and Criminology* 79:1185–1346.

————. 1990a. "Bad Law Makes Hard Cases: Reflections on Teen-aged Axe-Murderers, Judicial Activism, and Legislative Default." *Journal of Law and Inequality* 8:1–101.

————. 1990b. "The Punitive Juvenile Court and the Quality of Procedural Justice: Disjunctions between Rhetoric and Reality." *Crime and Delinquency* 36:443–66.

————. 1991. "Justice by Geography: Urban, Suburban, and Rural Variations in Juvenile Justice Administration." *Journal of Criminal Law and Criminology* 82:156–210.

Ferdinand, Theodore N. 1989. "Juvenile Delinquency or Juvenile Justice: Which Came First?" *Criminology* 27:79–106.

————. 1991. "History Overtakes the Juvenile Justice System." *Crime and Delinquency* 37:204–24.

Ferster, Elyce Zenoff, and Thomas F. Courtless. 1972. "Pre-dispositional Data, Role of Counsel and Decisions in a Juvenile Court." *Law and Society Review* 7:195–222.

Fisher, Bruce, Mark Fraser, and Martin Forst. 1985. *Institutional Commitment and Release Decision-making for Juvenile Delinquents: An Assessment of Determinate and Indeterminate Approaches, Washington State—a Case Study.* San Francisco: URSA Institute.

Flicker, Barbara. 1983. *Standards for Juvenile Justice: A Summary and Analysis.* 2d ed. Cambridge, Mass.: Ballinger.

Forst, Martin, and Martha-Elin Blomquist. 1991. "Cracking Down on Juveniles: The Changing Ideology of Youth Corrections." *Notre Dame Journal of Law, Ethics and Public Policy* 5:323–75.

Forst, Martin, Jeffrey Fagan, and T. Scott Vivona. 1989. "Youth in Prisons and Training Schools: Perceptions and Consequences of the Treatment-Custody Dichotomy." *Juvenile and Family Court Journal* 40:1–14.

Forst, Martin, Elizabeth Friedman, and Robert Coates. 1985. *Institutional Commitment and Release Decision-making for Juvenile Delinquents: An Assessment of Determinate and Indeterminate Approaches, Georgia—a Case Study.* San Francisco: URSA Institute.

Fox, Sanford J. 1970*a*. "Juvenile Justice Reform: An Historical Perspective." *Stanford Law Review* 22:1187–1239.

———. 1970*b*. "Responsibility in the Juvenile Court." *William and Mary Law Review* 11:659–84.

Frazier, C. E., and J. K. Cochran. 1986. "Detention of Juveniles: Its Effects on Subsequent Juvenile Court Processing Decisions." *Youth and Society* 17:286–305.

Friedman, W. 1982. *The Developmental Psychology of Time.* New York: Academic Press.

Gardner, Martin. 1982. "Punishment and Juvenile Justice: A Conceptual Framework for Assessing Constitutional Rights of Youthful Offenders." *Vanderbilt Law Review* 35:791–847.

———. 1987. "Punitive Juvenile Justice: Some Observations on a Recent Trend." *International Journal of Law and Psychiatry* 10:129–51.

———. 1989. "The Right of Juvenile Offenders to Be Punished: Some Implications of Treating Kids as Persons." *Nebraska Law Review* 68:182–215.

Garlock, Peter D. 1979. " 'Wayward' Children and the Law, 1820–1900: The Genesis of the Status Offense Jurisdiction of the Juvenile Court." *Georgia Law Review* 13:341–447.

Garrett, Carol J. 1985. "Effects of Residential Treatment on Adjudicated Delinquents: A Meta-analysis." *Journal of Research in Crime and Delinquency* 22:287–308.

Gendreau, Paul, and Bob Ross. 1979. "Effective Correctional Treatment: Bibliotherapy for Cynics." *Crime and Delinquency* 25:463–89.

———. 1987. "Revivification of Rehabilitation: Evidence from the 1980s." *Justice Quarterly* 4:349–407.

Georgia Division of Youth Services. 1985. *Policy and Procedure Manual.* Atlanta: Georgia Department of Human Resources.

Gillespie, L. Kay, and Michael D. Norman. 1984. "Does Certification Mean Prison? Some Preliminary Findings from Utah." *Juvenile and Family Court Journal* 35:23–34.

Graham, Fred. 1970. *The Self-inflicted Wound.* New York: Free Press.

Greenberg, David F., ed. 1977. *Corrections and Punishment.* Beverly Hills, Calif.: Sage.

———. 1979. "Delinquency and the Age Structure of Society." In *Criminology Review Yearbook,* edited by Sheldon Messinger and Egon Bittner. Beverly Hills, Calif.: Sage.

Greenwood, Peter. 1986. "Differences in Criminal Behavior and Court Responses among Juvenile and Young Adult Defendants." In *Crime and Justice: An Annual Review of Research,* vol. 7, edited by Michael Tonry and Norval Morris. Chicago: University of Chicago Press.

Greenwood, Peter, Allan Abrahamse, and Franklin Zimring. 1984. *Factors Affecting Sentence Severity for Young Adult Offenders.* Santa Monica, Calif.: RAND.

Greenwood, P., A. Lipson, A. Abrahamse, and F. Zimring. 1983. *Youth Crime and Juvenile Justice in California.* Santa Monica, Calif.: RAND.

Greenwood, Peter, Joan Petersilia, and Franklin Zimring. 1980. *Age, Crime, and Sanctions: The Transition from Juvenile to Adult Court.* Santa Monica, Calif.: RAND.

Greenwood, Peter, and Franklin Zimring. 1985. *One More Chance: The Pursuit of Promising Intervention Strategies for Chronic Juvenile Offenders*. Santa Monica, Calif.: RAND.

Grisso, Thomas. 1980. "Juveniles' Capacities to Waive Miranda Rights: An Empirical Analysis." *California Law Review* 68:1134–66.

———. 1981. *Juveniles' Waiver of Rights*. New York: Plenum Press.

Guggenheim, Martin. 1978. "A Call to Abolish the Juvenile Justice System." *Children's Rights Reporter* 2:7–19.

Hagan, John, and Jeffrey Leon. 1977. "Rediscovering Delinquency: Social History, Political Ideology and the Sociology of Law." *American Sociological Review* 42:587–98.

Hamparian, Donna, Linda Estep, Susan Muntean, Ramon Priestino, Robert Swisher, Paul Wallace, and Joseph White. 1982. *Youth in Adult Courts: Between Two Worlds*. Washington, D.C.: Office of Juvenile Justice and Delinquency Prevention.

Handler, Joel F. 1965. "The Juvenile Court and the Adversary System: Problems of Function and Form." *Wisconsin Law Review* 1965:7–51.

Handler, Joel F., and Julie Zatz, eds. 1982. *Neither Angels nor Thieves: Studies in Deinstitutionalization of Status Offenders*. Washington, D.C.: National Academy Press.

Hart, H. L. A. 1968. *Punishment and Responsibility*. New York: Oxford University Press.

*Harvard Law Review*. 1966. "Juvenile Delinquents, the Police, State Courts, and Individualized Justice." 79:775–810.

Hasenfeld, Yeheskel, and Paul P. Cheung. 1985. "The Juvenile Court as a People-processing Organization: A Political Economy Perspective." *American Journal of Sociology* 90:801–24.

Hawes, Joseph. 1971. *Children in Urban Society: Juvenile Delinquency in Nineteenth-Century America*. New York: Oxford University Press.

Hawes, Joseph, and N. Hiner, eds. 1985. *American Childhood: A Research Guide and Historical Handbook*. Westport, Conn.: Greenwood Press.

Hays, Samuel P. 1957. *The Response to Industrialism, 1885–1914*. Chicago: University of Chicago Press.

Henretta, John C., Charles E. Frazier, and Donna M. Bishop. 1986. "The Effects of Prior Case Outcomes on Juvenile Justice Decision-making." *Social Forces* 65:554–62.

Heuser, James Paul. 1985. *Juveniles Arrested for Serious Felony Crimes in Oregon and "Remanded" to Adult Criminal Courts: A Statistical Study*. Salem: Oregon Department of Justice Crime Analysis Center.

Higham, John. 1988. *Strangers in the Land: Patterns of American Nativism, 1860–1925*. 2d ed. New Brunswick, N.J.: Rutgers University Press.

Hindelang, Michael. 1978. "Race and Involvement in Common Law Personal Crimes." *American Sociological Review* 43:93–109.

Hirschi, Travis, and Michael Gottfredson. 1983. "Age and the Explanation of Crime." *American Journal of Sociology* 89:552–84.

Hodgson, Godfrey. 1976. *America in Our Time: From World War II to Nixon*. New York: Vintage Books.

Hofstadter, Richard. 1955. *The Age of Reform: From Bryan to F.D.R.* New York: Knopf.

Horowitz, Allan, and Michael Wasserman. 1980. "Some Misleading Conceptions in Sentencing Research: An Example and Reformulation in the Juvenile Court." *Criminology* 18:411–24.

Huizinga, David, and Delbert S. Elliott. 1987. "Juvenile Offenders: Prevalence, Offender Incidence, and Arrest Rates by Race." *Crime and Delinquency* 33:206–23.

Izzo, Rhena L., and Robert R. Ross. 1990. "Meta-analysis of Rehabilitation Programs for Juvenile Delinquents." *Criminal Justice and Behavior* 17:134–42.

Jackson-Beeck, Marilyn. 1985. "Institutionalizing Juveniles for Psychiatric and Chemical Dependency Treatment in Minnesota: Ten Years' Experience." Minneapolis: Minnesota Coalition on Health Care Costs.

Jackson-Beeck, Marilyn, Ira M. Schwartz, and Andrew Rutherford. 1987. "Trends and Issues in Juvenile Confinement for Psychiatric and Chemical Dependency Treatment." *International Journal of Law and Psychiatry* 10: 153–65.

Kadish, Sanford H. 1968. "The Decline of Innocence." *Cambridge Law Journal* 26:273–90.

Kalven, Harry, and Hans Zeisel. 1966. *The American Jury*. Chicago: University of Chicago Press.

Kassebaum, Gene G., and David A. Ward. 1991. "Analysis, Reanalysis and Meta-analysis of Correctional Treatment Effectiveness: Is the Question What Works or Who Works?" *Sociological Practice Review* 2:159–68.

Katz, Al, and Lee Teitelbaum. 1978. "PINS Jurisdiction, the Vagueness Doctrine and the Rule of Law." *Indiana Law Journal* 53:1–34.

Kempf, Kimberly, Scott H. Decker, and Robert L. Bing. 1990. *An Analysis of Apparent Disparities in the Handling of Black Youth within Missouri's Juvenile Justice System*. St. Louis: University of Missouri, Department of Administration of Justice.

Kett, Joseph F. 1977. *Rites of Passage: Adolescence in America, 1790 to the Present*. New York: Basic Books.

Klein, Malcolm W. 1979. "Deinstitutionalization and Diversion of Juvenile Offenders: A Litany of Impediments." In *Crime and Justice: An Annual Review of Research*, vol. 1, edited by Norval Morris and Michael Tonry. Chicago: University of Chicago Press.

Knitzer, Jane, and Merril Sobie. 1984. *Law Guardians in New York State: A Study of the Legal Representation of Children*. Albany: New York State Bar Association.Knoohuizen, Ralph. 1986. *Juveniles Tried as Adults: Cook County, 1975–1984*. Evanston, Ill.: Chicago Law Enforcement Study Group.

Knoohuizen, Ralph. 1986. *Juveniles Tried as Adults: Cook County, 1975–1984*. Evanston, Ill.: Chicago Law Enforcement Study Group.

Kohlberg, Lawrence. 1964. "Development of Moral Character and Moral Ideology." In *Review of Child Development Research*, vol. 1, edited by Martin Hoffman and Lois Hoffman. New York: Russell Sage Foundation.

———. 1969. "Stage and Sequence: The Cognitive-Developmental Approach to Socialization." In *Handbook of Socialization Theory and Research*, edited by David Goslin. Chicago: Rand McNally.

Kolko, Gabriel. 1963. *The Triumph of Conservatism: A Reinterpretation of American History, 1900–1916*. New York: Free Press of Glencoe.

Krisberg, Barry, and Ira Schwartz. 1983. "Rethinking Juvenile Justice." *Crime and Delinquency* 29:333–64.

Krisberg, Barry, Ira Schwartz, Gideon Fishman, Zvi Eisikovits, Edna Guttman, and Karen Joe. 1987. "The Incarceration of Minority Youth." *Crime and Delinquency* 33:173–205.

Krisberg, Barry, Ira Schwartz, Paul Lisky, and James Austin. 1986. "The Watershed of Juvenile Justice Reform." *Crime and Delinquency* 32:5–38.

Lab, Steven P., and John T. Whitehead. 1988. "An Analysis of Juvenile Correctional Treatment." *Crime and Delinquency* 34:60–83.

Lasch, Christopher. 1977. *Haven in a Heartless World: The Family Besieged*. New York: Basic Books.

Lefstein, Norman, Vaughan Stapleton, and Lee Teitelbaum. 1969. "In Search of Juvenile Justice: *Gault* and Its Implementation." *Law and Society Review* 3:491–562.

Lerman, Paul. 1980. "Trends and Issues in the Deinstitutionalization of Youths in Trouble." *Crime and Delinquency* 26:281–98.

———. 1982. *Deinstitutionalization and the Welfare State*. New Brunswick, N.J.: Rutgers University Press.

———. 1984. "Child Welfare, the Private Sector, and Community-based Corrections." *Crime and Delinquency* 30:5–38.

Lerner, Steven. 1986. *Bodily Harm*. Bolinas, Calif.: Common Knowledge Press.

McCarthy, Belinda, and Brent L. Smith. 1986. "The Conceptualization of Discrimination in the Juvenile Justice Process: The Impact of Administrative Factors and Screening Decisions on Juvenile Court Dispositions." *Criminology* 24:41–64.

McCarthy, Francis Barry. 1977*a*. "The Role of the Concept of Responsibility in Juvenile Delinquency Proceedings." *University of Michigan Journal of Law Reform* 10:181–219.

———. 1977*b*. "Should Juvenile Delinquency Be Abolished?" *Crime and Delinquency* 23:196–203.

———. 1981. "Pre-adjudicatory Rights in Juvenile Court: An Historical and Constitutional Analysis." *University of Pittsburgh Law Review* 42:457–514.

McDermott, M. J., and Michael J. Hindelang. 1981. *Juvenile Criminal Behavior in the United States: Its Trends and Patterns*. Washington, D.C.: U.S. Government Printing Office.

Mack, Julian W. 1909. "The Juvenile Court." *Harvard Law Review* 23:104–22.

Mahoney, Anne Rankin. 1987. *Juvenile Justice in Context*. Boston: Northeastern University Press.

Mahoney, Anne Rankin, and Carol Fenster. 1982. "Female Delinquents in a Suburban Court." In *Judge, Lawyer, Victim, Thief: Women, Gender Roles and Criminal Justice*, edited by Nicole Hahn Rafter and Elizabeth Anne Stanko. Boston: Northeastern University Press.

Marshall, Ineke H., and Charles W. Thomas. 1983. "Discretionary Decision-making and the Juvenile Court." *Juvenile and Family Court Journal* 34(3): 47–59.

Martinson, Robert. 1974. "What Works? Questions and Answers about Prison Reform." *Public Interest* 35:22–54.

Matza, David. 1964. *Delinquency and Drift*. New York: Wiley.

Melton, Gary B. 1989. "Taking *Gault* Seriously: Toward a New Juvenile Court." *Nebraska Law Review* 68:146–81.

Mennel, Robert M. 1973. *Thorns and Thistles: Juvenile Delinquents in the United States, 1825–1940*. Hanover, N.H.: University Press of New England.

———. 1983. "Attitudes and Policies toward Juvenile Delinquency in the United States: A Historiographical Review." In *Crime and Justice: An Annual Review of Research*, vol. 4, edited by Michael Tonry and Norval Morris. Chicago: University of Chicago Press.

Minnesota Department of Corrections. 1980. *Juvenile Release Guidelines*. St. Paul: Minnesota Department of Corrections.

Minnesota Supreme Court. 1990. *Report of the Juvenile Representation Study Committee*. St. Paul: West.

Monahan, John. 1981. *The Clinical Prediction of Violent Behavior*. Rockville, Md.: U.S. Department of Health and Human Services.

Morris, Norval. 1974. *The Future of Imprisonment*. Chicago: University of Chicago Press.

Morris, Norval, and Marc Miller. 1985. "Predictions of Dangerousness." In *Crime and Justice: An Annual Review of Research*, vol. 6, edited by Michael Tonry and Norval Morris. Chicago: University of Chicago Press.

Murray, John P. 1983. *Status Offenders: A Sourcebook*. Boys Town, Nebr.: Boys Town Center.

National Center for Juvenile Justice. 1991. *Guide to the Data Sets in the National Juvenile Court Data Archive*. Pittsburgh: National Center for Juvenile Justice.

National Commission on Children. 1991. *Beyond Rhetoric: A New American Agenda for Children and Families*. Washington, D.C.: U.S. Government Printing Office.

National Council on Crime and Delinquency. 1975. "Jurisdiction over Status Offenses Should Be Removed from the Juvenile Court: A Policy Statement." *Crime and Delinquency* 21:97–99.

Nimick, Ellen H., Howard N. Snyder, Dennis P. Sullivan, and Nancy J. Tierney. 1985. *Juvenile Court Statistics, 1983*. Washington, D.C.: Office of Juvenile Justice and Delinquency Prevention.

Nimick, Ellen, Linda Szymanski, and Howard Snyder. 1986. *Juvenile Court Waiver: A Study of Juvenile Court Cases Transferred to Criminal Court*. Pittsburgh: National Center for Juvenile Justice.

Palmer, Ted. 1991. "The Effectiveness of Intervention: Recent Trends and Current Issues." *Crime and Delinquency* 37:330–46.

Paulsen, Monrad. 1967. "The Constitutional Domestication of the Juvenile Court." *Supreme Court Review* 1967:233–66.

Petersilia, Joan. 1981. "Juvenile Record Use in Adult Court Proceedings: A Survey of Prosecutors." *Journal of Criminal Law and Criminology* 72:1746–71.

Petersilia, Joan, and Susan Turner. 1987. "Guideline-based Justice: Prediction and Racial Minorities." In *Prediction and Classification: Criminal Justice Decision Making*, edited by Don M. Gottfredson and Michael Tonry. Vol. 9 of *Crime and Justice: A Review of Research*, edited by Michael Tonry and Norval Morris. Chicago: University of Chicago Press.

Phillips, Charles D., and Simon Dinitz. 1982. "Labelling and Juvenile Court Dispositions: Official Responses to a Cohort of Violent Juveniles." *Sociological Quarterly* 23:267–78.

Piaget, Jean. 1960. *The Moral Judgement of the Child.* Glencoe, Ill.: Free Press. (Originally published 1932.)

———. 1969. *The Child's Conception of Time*, translated by A. J. Pomerans. London: Routledge & Kegan Paul.

Platt, Anthony. 1977. *The Child Savers.* 2d ed. Chicago: University of Chicago Press.

Polk, Kenneth. 1984. "Juvenile Diversion: A Look at the Record." *Crime and Delinquency* 30:648–59.

Pope, Carl E., and William H. Feyerherm. 1990*a*. "Minority Status and Juvenile Justice Processing: An Assessment of the Research Literature (Part I)." *Criminal Justice Abstracts* 22:327–35.

———. 1990*b*. "Minority Status and Juvenile Justice Processing: An Assessment of the Research Literature (Part II)." *Criminal Justice Abstracts* 22:527–42.

President's Commission on Law Enforcement and Administration of Justice. 1967*a*. *The Challenge of Crime in a Free Society.* Washington, D.C.: U.S. Government Printing Office.

———. 1967*b*. *Task Force Report: Juvenile Delinquency and Youth Crime.* Washington, D.C.: U.S. Government Printing Office.

Private Sector Task Force on Juvenile Justice. 1987. *Final Report.* San Francisco: National Council on Crime and Delinquency.

Rendleman, Douglas R. 1971. *"Parens Patriae:* From Chancery to the Juvenile Court." *South Carolina Law Review* 23:205–59.

Roberts, Albert R., and Michael J. Camasso. 1991. "The Effects of Juvenile Offender Treatment Programs on Recidivism: A Meta-analysis of 46 Studies." *Notre Dame Journal of Law, Ethics and Public Policy* 5:421–41.

Rosenberg, Irene M. 1980. "The Constitutional Rights of Children Charged with Crime: Proposal for a Return to the Not So Distant Past." *University of California Los Angeles Law Review* 27:656–721.

———. 1983. "Juvenile Status Offender Statutes—New Perspectives on an Old Problem." *University of California Davis Law Review* 16:283–323.

Rosenberg, Irene M., and Yale L. Rosenberg. 1976. "The Legacy of the Stubborn and Rebellious Son." *Michigan Law Review* 74:1097–1165.

Rothman, David J. 1971. *The Discovery of the Asylum.* Boston: Little, Brown.

———. 1978. "The State as Parent: Social Policy in the Progressive Era." In *Doing Good: The Limits of Benevolence*, edited by William Gaylin, Ira Glasser, Steven Marcus, and David Rothman. New York: Pantheon.

———. 1980. *Conscience and Convenience.* Boston: Little, Brown.

Rubin, H. Ted. 1979. "Retain the Juvenile Court? Legislative Developments, Reform Directions and the Call for Abolition." *Crime and Delinquency* 25:281–98.

———. 1985. *Juvenile Justice: Policy, Practice, and Law.* 2d. ed. New York: Random House.

Rudman, Cary, Eliot Hartstone, Jeffrey Fagan, and Melinda Moore. 1986.

"Violent Youth in Adult Court: Process and Punishment." *Crime and Delinquency* 32:75–96.

Ryerson, Ellen. 1978. *The Best-laid Plans: America's Juvenile Court Experiment.* New York: Hill & Wang.

Sampson, Robert J. 1986. "Crime in Cities: The Effects of Formal and Informal Social Control." In *Communities and Crime*, edited by Albert J. Reiss, Jr., and Michael Tonry. Vol. 8 of *Crime and Justice: A Review of Research*, edited by Michael Tonry and Norval Morris. Chicago: University of Chicago Press.

Sarri, Rosemary, and Yeheskel Hasenfeld. 1976. *Brought to Justice? Juveniles, the Courts and the Law.* Ann Arbor: University of Michigan, National Assessment of Juvenile Corrections.

Schlossman, Steven. 1977. *Love and the American Delinquent.* Chicago: University of Chicago Press.

Schlossman, Steven, and Stephanie Wallach. 1978. "The Crime of Precocious Sexuality: Female Juvenile Delinquency in the Progressive Era." *Harvard Educational Review* 48:65–94.

Schneider, Anne L. 1984. "Deinstitutionalization of Status Offenders: The Impact on Recidivism and Secure Confinement." *Criminal Justice Abstracts* 16:410–32.

Schneider, Anne L., and Donna Schram. 1983. *A Justice Philosophy for the Juvenile Court.* Seattle: Urban Policy Research.

Schwartz, Ira M. 1989a. In *Justice for Juveniles: Rethinking the Best Interests of the Child.* Lexington, Mass.: Lexington Books.

———. 1989b. "Hospitalization of Adolescents for Psychiatric and Substance Abuse Treatment." *Journal of Adolescent Health Care* 10:1–6.

Schwartz, Ira M., Marilyn Jackson-Beeck, and Roger Anderson. 1984. "The Hidden System of Juvenile Control." *Crime and Delinquency* 30:371–85.

Sechrest, Lee B. 1987. "Classification for Treatment." In *Prediction and Classification: Criminal Justice Decision Making*, edited by Don M. Gottfredson and Michael Tonry. Vol. 9 of *Crime and Justice: A Review of Research*, edited by Michael Tonry and Norval Morris. Chicago: University of Chicago Press.

Sechrest, Lee B., Susan O. White, and Elizabeth D. Brown, eds. 1979. *The Rehabilitation of Criminal Offenders.* Washington, D.C.: National Academy of Sciences.

Shaughnessy, Patricia L. 1979. "The Right to a Jury under the Juvenile Justice Act of 1977." *Gonzaga Law Review* 14:401–21.

Singer, Simon I., and David McDowall. 1988. "Criminalizing Delinquency: The Deterrent Effects of the New York Juvenile Offender Law." *Law and Society Review* 22:521–35.

Snyder, Howard N., Terrence A. Finnegan, Ellen H. Nimick, Mellissa H. Sickmund, Dennis P. Sullivan, and Nancy J. Tierney. 1990. *Juvenile Court Statistics, 1988.* Pittsburgh: National Center for Juvenile Justice.

Springer, Charles E. 1991. "Rehabilitating the Juvenile Court." *Notre Dame Journal of Law, Ethics and Public Policy* 5:397–420.

Stapleton, W. Vaughan, David P. Aday, Jr., and Jeanne A. Ito. 1982. "An Empirical Typology of American Metropolitan Juvenile Courts." *American Journal of Sociology* 88:549–64.

Stapleton, W. Vaughan, and Lee E. Teitelbaum. 1972. *In Defense of Youth: A Study of the Role of Counsel in American Juvenile Courts.* New York: Russell Sage.

Streib, Victor L. 1987. *Death Penalty for Juveniles.* Bloomington: Indiana University Press.

Sussman, Alan. 1977. "Sex-based Discrimination and the PINS Jurisdiction." In *Beyond Control*, edited by Lee H. Teitelbaum and Aidan R. Gough. Cambridge, Mass.: Ballinger.

Sutton, John R. 1988. *Stubborn Children: Controlling Delinquency in the United States.* Berkeley and Los Angeles: University of California Press.

Tapp, June L. 1976. "Psychology and the Law: An Overture." *Annual Review of Psychology* 27:359–74.

Tapp, June L., and Lawrence Kohlberg. 1977. "Developing Senses of Law and Legal Justice." In *Law, Justice, and the Individual in Society*, edited by June L. Tapp and Felice Levine. New York: Holt, Rinehart & Winston.

Tapp, June L., and Felice Levine. 1974. "Legal Socialization: Strategies for an Ethical Legality." *Stanford Law Review* 27:1–54.

Teilmann, Katherine S., and Malcolm Klein. n.d. *Summary of Interim Findings of the Assessment of the Impact of California's 1977 Juvenile Justice Legislation.* Los Angeles: University of Southern California, Social Science Research Institute.

Teilmann, Katherine S., and Pierre H. Landry, Jr. 1981. "Gender Bias in Juvenile Justice." *Journal of Research in Crime and Delinquency* 18:47–80.

Teitelbaum, Lee E., and Aidan R. Gough. 1977. *Beyond Control: Status Offenders in the Juvenile Court.* Cambridge, Mass.: Ballinger.

Thomas, Charles W., and Shay Bilchik. 1985. "Prosecuting Juveniles in Criminal Courts: A Legal and Empirical Analysis." *Journal of Criminal Law and Criminology* 76:439–79.

Thomas, Charles W., and W. Anthony Fitch. 1975. "An Inquiry into the Association between Respondents' Personal Characteristics and Juvenile Court Dispositions." *William and Mary Law Review* 17:61–83.

Tiffin, S. 1982. *In Whose Best Interest? Child Welfare Reform in the Progressive Era.* Westport, Conn.: Greenwood Press.

Trattner, Walter I. 1965. *Crusade for the Children: A History of the National Child Labor Committee and Child Labor Reform in New York State.* Chicago: Quadrangle Books.

———. 1984. *From Poor Law to Welfare State: A History of Social Welfare in America.* 3d ed. Westport, Conn.: Greenwood Press.

Twentieth Century Fund Task Force on Sentencing Policy Toward Young Offenders. 1978. *Confronting Youth Crime.* New York: Holmes & Meier.

Vereb, Thomas S., and John L. Hutzler. 1981. *Juveniles as Criminals: 1981 Statutes Analysis.* Pittsburgh: National Center for Juvenile Justice.

von Hirsch, Andrew. 1976. *Doing Justice.* New York: Hill & Wang.

———. 1986. *Past or Future Crimes.* New Brunswick, N.J.: Rutgers University Press.

Walkover, Andrew. 1984. "The Infancy Defense in the New Juvenile Court." *University of California Los Angeles Law Review* 31:503–62.

Walter, James D., and Susan A. Ostrander. 1982. "An Observational Study of a Juvenile Court." *Juvenile and Family Court Journal* 33:53–69.

Weissman, James C. 1983. "Toward an Integrated Theory of Delinquency Responsibility." *Denver Law Journal* 60:485–518.

Weithorn, Lois A. 1988. "Mental Hospitalization of Troublesome Youth: An Analysis of Skyrocketing Admission Rates." *Stanford Law Review* 40: 773–838.

Whitehead, John T., and Steven P. Lab. 1989. "A Meta-analysis of Juvenile Correctional Treatment." *Journal of Research in Crime and Delinquency* 26:276–95.

Wiebe, Robert H. 1967. *The Search for Order, 1877–1920*. New York: Hill & Wang.

Wizner, Steven, and Mary F. Keller. 1977. "The Penal Model of Juvenile Justice: Is Juvenile Court Delinquency Jurisdiction Obsolete?" *New York University Law Review* 52:1120–35.

Wolfgang, Marvin. 1982. "Abolish the Juvenile Court System." *California Lawyer* 2(10):12–13.

Wolfgang, Marvin, Robert Figlio, and Thorsten Sellin. 1972. *Delinquency in a Birth Cohort*. Chicago: University of Chicago Press.

Woods, John P. 1980. "New York's Juvenile Offender Law: An Overview and Analysis." *Fordham Urban Law Journal* 9:1–50.

Zimring, Frank. 1981a. "Notes toward a Jurisprudence of Waiver." In *Readings in Public Policy*, edited by John C. Hall, Donna Martin Hamparian, John M. Pettibone, and Joseph L. White. Columbus, Ohio: Academy for Contemporary Problems.

———. 1981b. "Kids, Groups and Crime: Some Implications of a Well-known Secret." *Journal of Criminal Law and Criminology* 72:867–902.

———. 1982. *The Changing Legal World of Adolescence*. New York: Free Press.

———. 1991. "The Treatment of Hard Cases in American Juvenile Justice: In Defense of Discretionary Waiver." *Notre Dame Journal of Law, Ethics and Public Policy* 5:267–80.

*Joan Petersilia and Susan Turner*

# Intensive Probation
# and Parole

ABSTRACT

Intensive supervision programs (ISP) have proliferated in the past d
They generally emphasize reduced caseload
testing, treatment, and employment. The R
randomized field experiment, evaluated a na
project in fourteen jurisdictions in nine state
implemented well, particularly with respect t
officers' contacts and drug testing but were le
treatment participation. Intensive supervision
the frequency or seriousness of new arrests b
of technical violations and jail terms. Stepped-
frequent drug tests increased incarceration rate                 p program
and court costs compared with routine supervision. Development of an
array of sentencing options to create a graduated sentencing system
should justify continued development and testing of ISP programs.

Intensive supervision probation and parole programs are community-based criminal sanctions that emphasize close monitoring. These programs are variously called intensive supervision, alternative sanctions, intermediate sanctions, and intermediate punishments. Some intensive supervision programs (ISP) are "prison-diversion" programs intended to divert offenders from prison, either at sentencing or by early release from prison. Some are "enhancement" programs intended to increase the intensity of routine probation or parole.

In this essay, we use ISP as a generic term. However, there is no generic ISP. The only common characteristic of ongoing ISP programs

Joan Petersilia is director of the Criminal Justice Program, RAND, and associate professor in the School of Social Ecology, University of California, Irvine. Susan Turner is a senior researcher in RAND's Criminal Justice Program.

is that they are more "intense" than routine supervision in a particular jurisdiction. Most programs call for some combination of multiple weekly contacts with a supervising officer, unscheduled drug testing, strict enforcement of probation or parole conditions, and requirements to attend treatment, to work, and to perform community service. Caseloads typically consist of thirty to fifty offenders per officer.

In the last ten years, ISP has been hailed by many as the most promising criminal justice innovation in decades and has been adopted, in some form, in virtually every state. Why have ISP programs been touted so highly and proliferated so rapidly?

There are two kinds of arguments for ISP. One is practical. Serious crime is on the rise, prisons are overcrowded, and resources are constrained. Some advocates believe that ISP can alleviate prison crowding at less cost than expanding prison capacity and without jeopardizing public safety more than traditional probation and parole do.

The other is an argument from principle. The United States has few intermediate punishments. Offenders are typically either incarcerated or given routine probation, which in some people's minds is equated with "letting them go." In many jurisdictions, the choice of criminal sanctions is between prison or nothing at all.

Because seriousness of crime does not fall into two neat compartments, sentencing often errs in one direction or another. It is either too harsh, putting people behind bars whose crimes and criminality do not warrant it, or too lenient, giving people probation whose crimes and criminality deserve stronger punishment. According to this argument, ISP provides for more punishment choices, making the punishment likelier to be scaled to the severity of the crime.

The practical argument has been the most often used to support ISP. In the early 1980s, the Georgia Department of Corrections published an internal evaluation of the state's ISP program (Erwin 1986). The evaluation claimed that ISP had produced a number of important benefits—participants had extremely low recidivism rates, and most offenders were able to maintain employment, make restitution, and pay a monthly supervision fee. Furthermore, probationer fees made the ISP program totally self-supporting. David Evans, Georgia's director of corrections, subsequently noted, "The ISP programs basically saved the cost of building at least two new prisons" (Erwin 1986, p. 24).

These results generated a great deal of media and professional interest. An August 16, 1985, a *Washington Post* article called Georgia's ISP "the future of American corrections" (Sawyer 1985). In commenting on solutions to prison crowding, the *New York Times* concluded, "The state that has led the way is Georgia, and the most common new program spreading across the South and the nation is modeled on the Georgia program of intensive probation supervision" (*New York Times* 1985, p. 12).

Other states moved quickly to adopt the "Georgia model," and by 1990 jurisdictions in every state had instituted ISP programs for adult offenders (U.S. General Accounting Office 1990).[1] Some of the newer ISP programs were subsequently evaluated, and the results were more ambiguous than those reported by Georgia. Some of the evaluations reported cost savings (e.g., Illinois and New Jersey), while others did not (e.g., Massachusetts, Wisconsin); some reported recidivism reduction (e.g., Iowa), while others did not (e.g., Ohio, Wisconsin).[2] Unfortunately, when these and other ISP evaluations were examined more closely, it became clear that the effects of ISP remained unknown, due to weak research designs and evaluations.

The most serious deficiency in previous ISP evaluations has been the inability to identify a truly matched comparison group. The selection procedures used to identify appropriate clients for ISP often ensure that no comparable cases can be found in the regular system, particularly if the ISP program is designed to accept all suitable offenders. This is true whether the ISP program targets high-risk probationers, leaving less serious probationers "untreated" (as in Massachusetts), or low-risk prisoners who are distinctly different from the higher-risk prisoners left behind (as in New Jersey), or whether the assignment procedures allow for such broad judicial discretion that the ISP participants resemble neither the routine probationers nor the prisoners (as in Georgia and Illinois).

Researchers urged that experiments be conducted in which eligible offenders were randomly assigned to ISP or to the relevant alternative

[1] Similar trends have also occurred in juvenile justice (Armstrong 1991). Intensive supervision programs are not entirely new. In the late 1970s Banks et al. (1977) identified forty-six operational or recently completed intensive supervision projects. Early ISP projects were primarily probation-management tools designed to determine the ideal caseload size for achieving rehabilitation. Newer ISP programs do not give priority to the offender's need for services but rather focus on the community's need for protection, sanction credibility, and cost savings (see Petersilia and Turner [1990b] and Harland and Rosen [1987] for fuller discussions).
[2] Previous ISP evaluation results are contained in McCarthy (1987), Byrne et al. (1989), U.S. General Accounting Office (1990), Pearson and Harper (1990), Petersilia and Turner (1990b), and Armstrong (1991).

sanction (prison or routine probation or parole). Random assignment helps ensure that the outcomes result from the manipulated variables (here, the sentence imposed) rather than from systematically biasing factors (e.g., less serious offenders being assigned to ISP).

In 1986, the Bureau of Justice Assistance (BJA) of the U.S. Department of Justice provided funding for an ISP demonstration involving random assignment. The primary intent was to determine how participation in ISP programs affected the subsequent behavior of adult offenders. Fourteen sites in nine states were chosen to participate in the demonstration that ran from 1986 through 1991. The authors of this essay were responsible for design and conduct of the external evaluation. In general, the evaluation findings show the ISP programs did not alleviate prison crowding and may have increased it in some states; they cost considerably more than most advocates have realized, particularly if agencies incarcerate offenders for technical violations and rule infractions; they were no more effective than routine probation and parole in reducing in-program recidivism (as measured by arrests and convictions); they did provide the means by which offenders were held more accountable for their crimes and community behavior; and they may have increased public safety.

To some degree, these results occurred because the ISP programs were more punitive than routine probation and parole. Intensive supervision programs achieved their punitive objective of providing midlevel punishments between prison and probation. Thus, under present conditions, the practical and principled rationales for ISP may directly conflict. The more stringently ISPs impose and enforce their "punitive conditions," the more likely they are to exacerbate prison crowding and to reduce or eliminate cost savings relative to imprisonment.

This essay synthesizes research on ISP and provides an overview of the RAND evaluation findings. Many details are omitted; readers who want more information on research methodology, conditions for successful program implementation, the nature of individual demonstration projects, and the effects of ISP on drug offenders should consult the various articles and reports describing those elements of the demonstration in detail.[3] Section I describes what ISPs have been expected

[3] Various reports and articles discuss the RAND evaluation: implementing the research design (Petersilia 1989); conditions that affect successful ISP implementation (Petersilia 1990); how offenders perceived ISP (Petersilia 1990); the effects of ISP on drug offenders (Petersilia, Turner, and Deschenes 1992; Turner, Petersilia, and Deschenes 1992a, 1992b); the results of the Oregon prison-diversion ISP (Petersilia and Turner 1990c); the results of the Texas parole ISP (Turner and Petersilia 1992); and the

to accomplish and the controversy that has resulted. Section II provides the rationale for a randomized field experiment and describes the ISP demonstration sites, their programs, and RAND's evaluation methodology. Section III presents the results. Research and policy implications are discussed in Section IV.

## I. ISP: The Expectations and the Controversy

The probation population increased dramatically during the late 1980s, increasing 5–7 percent each year in the later years. At the end of 1990, a record-breaking 2.6 million people, two-thirds of all people under correctional supervision, were on probation (Bureau of Justice Statistics 1991a). Not only has the size of the probation population increased, but a higher proportion of them appear to be serious offenders. More of the current probation population has been convicted of felonies as opposed to misdemeanors than in earlier periods, and a greater proportion are drug-dependent (Guynes 1988; Cunniff and Shilton 1991).

Probation was neither intended nor structured to handle large numbers of serious felons, and its effectiveness has been hampered by budget cuts. A survey recently conducted by the American Probation and Parole Association reports that all large probation agencies, and most smaller ones, are experiencing serious financial difficulties and having to reduce staff and special program initiatives as a result (Matthews 1991). Reduced staffing has made caseloads of 150–200 common, and "supervision" sometimes amounts to no more than probationers mailing a card to the probation officer once a month.

Unfortunately, felons are not good risks for routine probation. RAND published a study in 1985 showing that 65 percent of felons on probation in two California counties were rearrested during their sentences, many of them for burglary, assault, and robbery (Petersilia et al. 1985). Twenty-five percent of those offenders granted probation were indistinguishable from offenders sentenced to prison in terms of current crime or criminal records. A more recent Bureau of Justice Statistics report shows that, within three years, while still on state probation, 43 percent of felons were rearrested for another felony (Langan and Cunniff 1992). Something must be done about the public safety risks posed by felons on traditional probation, but what?

Prison does not seem to be a viable option. Nationwide, prison

California probation ISP results (Petersilia and Turner 1990a, 1990b, 1991; Petersilia and Turner 1991).

populations have tripled since 1975, and in the early 1990s, forty states were operating all or part of their correctional systems under court orders or consent decrees to reduce prison crowding (Maguire and Flanagan 1991, table 1.93). Given the high costs of incarceration and the increasing numbers of offenders being incarcerated, states cannot build themselves out of the prison-crowding problem. For example, as part of a $3.2 billion corrections budget, California is in the process of adding 37,000 jail and prison beds. But projections indicate that in 1994, after new construction, its prisons will be operating at 150 percent of design capacity (California Commission on Inmate Population Management 1990). Further, despite enormous public investment in prison expansion, the level of violent crime reported by the FBI is substantially higher than it was as recently as 1985 (Maguire and Flanagan 1991, table 3.1).[4] The specter of imprisonment has apparently not had the deterrent effect on crime that the investment in prisons was designed to achieve.

Historically, there have been few criminal punishments other than routine probation and prison, and this has provoked interest in ISP. Policymakers in a growing number of jurisdictions have come to believe that ISP, by providing increased supervision of serious offenders in the community, can relieve prison crowding, lessen public safety risks, and save money.

*A. Assumptions about ISP's Effects*

The interest in ISP is based on a number of assumptions about how prison crowding, costs, and crime control would be affected if these programs were expanded.

One assumption is that a significant percentage of people now sent to prison are serious enough offenders that they should not be put on routine probation but not so serious that they could not be handled in the community under more stringent conditions than routine supervision.[5]

---

[4] The Federal Bureau of Investigation's Uniform Crime Reports (UCR), which provide national data on police-recorded crimes, report increases in violent crime. However, the National Crime Survey (a nationwide household interview survey that asks household members about the crimes they have suffered) reports a gradual decline in violent crime (Langan 1991).

[5] Petersilia and Turner (1989) concluded that, if commonly used ISP criteria were applied to offenders sentenced to U.S. prisons in 1986, about 33 percent of incoming inmates would qualify for ISP. Even under more stringent ISP eligibility criteria (e.g., excluding those convicted of drug offenses and those with alcohol abuse), about 20 percent of inmates still qualify.

A second assumption is that both prison-diversion and probation-enhancement ISP are cost-effective, in either the short or long term. Some prison-diversion ISPs directly reduce corrections costs by diverting offenders to ISP from imprisonment, and it presumably costs much less to maintain an offender in ISP than in prison. Probation and parole enhancement programs are said to prevent crimes through close surveillance and thereby to reduce need for future imprisonment. Probation-enhancement programs could also affect overall sentencing practices—assuming judges would be more willing to sentence felons to probation instead of prison if they believed the probationers would be subjected to closer scrutiny.

The arguments about crime control involve several implicit comparisons between sanctions, as well as assumptions about deterrence and incapacitation. Prison is assumed to provide the strongest crime prevention. It stops offenders from committing crimes against the public, and by its punitiveness may provide a deterrent to crime. Routine community supervision offers the weakest crime control. It often does not incapacitate, deter, or constrain people from committing crimes, and it imposes relatively few punitive conditions.

A third assumption is that ISP provides stronger crime control than routine supervision but less than prison. Theoretically, offenders should be deterred from committing new crimes because surveillance increases the chances of getting caught and being sent to prison. Offenders also should be constrained from committing crimes because the conditions of ISP limit their opportunities. Closer surveillance is likely to uncover more technical violations or rule infractions than routine probation (e.g., failure to attend drug treatment or to abstain from alcohol and drugs).

Some ISP supporters also assume that keeping offenders in the community has socialization and rehabilitation effects. It avoids possible criminogenic effects of imprisonment, keeps families and social networks together, and allows offenders to keep on working. With smaller caseloads, probation and parole officers can also more effectively act as brokers of community treatment programs and services for offenders who need them.

## B. Reservations about ISP Effects

Most of these assumptions seemed borne out by the early reports from programs like those in Georgia and New Jersey. Many ISP programs claimed to save at least $10,000 per year for each offender who would otherwise have been sentenced to prison (Byrne, Lurigio, and Baird 1989). Early reports also claimed low arrest rates, most of which were related to technical violations, and fewer than 5 percent of participants had been convicted of new offenses (Erwin and Bennett 1987; Petersilia 1987; Pearson and Harper 1990).

Yet despite these results, a number of major reservations have been voiced about the assumptions and what the outcomes really mean. Many of these reservations have come from independent agencies (e.g., U.S. General Accounting Office 1990). Some have been raised by scholars, such as Morris and Tonry (1990), who are proponents of intermediate punishment but believe many arguments for ISP are unsound. Finally, even supporters of the ISP concept have cautioned against premature judgment of the programs' effects (Petersilia 1987; Petersilia and Turner 1990b). In discussing the reservations about ISP, three questions are most often raised.

1. *Can ISP Materially Affect Prison Crowding?* Arguments against the assumptions about prison crowding are based on historical sentencing practices: who is likely to be placed on ISP, the size of ISP programs, and the mediating effects of other factors. Morris and Tonry (1990, p. 4) point out that "most felonies never were and are not now punished by imprisonment." Consequently, they argue that reducing prison crowding is a "false promise" for ISPs. They claim that "intermediate punishments tend at present to draw more from those who otherwise would be placed on unenforced probation or on suspended sentence than from those who otherwise would go to prison or jail." The U.S. General Accounting Office (GAO) report noted,

It is clear that existing programs have had little effect and are unlikely to have a sizable one on prison populations. This is because most programs have served a relatively small population of offenders. Programs that include *hundreds* of offenders cannot significantly affect prison populations that run into *tens of thousands*. In addition, the size of the intermediate sanction programs has not been the only factor limiting their utility for addressing the problem. . . . Even in the few states with large programs, other factors have worked to cancel out program effects. Florida, for example, operates a house arrest program that serves approximately 6,500 offenders, but it has not been able to offset an upward trend in inmate populations caused by an expanding offender population and harsher sentencing practices. As a result, *prison crowding in Florida is worse today than when the intermediate sanction program began.* [U.S. General Accounting Office 1990, p. 2, emphasis added]

Even if states would and could mount very extensive prison-diversion programs, how much actual diversion could they really expect to achieve? Fears about public reaction and public safety might well make judges reluctant to keep many of the people they now send to prison in the community. This reluctance could operate even though prison crowding may in practice cause all but the worst and most violent offenders to be returned to the streets before serving their complete sentences.

All of these arguments offer grounds for skepticism that ISP will significantly reduce prison crowding.

2. *Does ISP Provide a Cost-saving Alternative to Incarceration?* Most of the arguments about ISP's cost-saving potential have been based on per-offender costs. Virtually no one would question the claim that it costs more to keep an offender in prison than on probation. However, many observers have pointed out that per-offender costs are misleading and may vastly overstate the prospective cost savings from ISP. We broached this problem in the RAND report on felony probation: "Although ISPs would cost much less than new prisons, they would cost much more than traditional probation programs, so that if a substantial proportion of the felons who are now put on probation were put into ISPs, the total costs to the criminal justice system would rise precipitously" (Petersilia et al. 1985, p. xii).

Morris and Tonry also attack the issue of per-offender costs from another angle—how long offenders would actually be under each sanction: "If . . . the average cost per year per imprisoned offender is $12,000, and the average cost per year per intensively supervised offender is $4,000, comparison of those average annual costs is inherently misleading. If the average intensively supervised client serves 12 months ($4,000) but would otherwise have served 3 months in prison ($3,000), the intensive supervision program is more, not less, expensive" (1990, pp. 233–34).

The GAO report addresses the issue of marginal costs. Comparing per-offender costs for prison and ISP ignores the large proportion of prison costs (e.g., capital outlays and personnel) that are fixed costs: a new prison cell is not built or a new corrections officer hired for each new inmate, and diverting an offender from prison does not reduce the number or costs of cells and guards. Moreover, ISPs are highly labor intensive: "Maximum caseloads in intensive supervision, for example, are typically 25 offenders per supervisor or team of supervisors; thus, an increase of only 100 program participants would require the hiring and training of four to eight new employees. This not only increases direct outlays in the form of salaries and expanded overhead expenses but also produces longer-term financial commitments in the form of employment benefits and pensions. As these examples suggest, a more appropriate cost analysis would be based on comparison of marginal costs" (U.S. General Accounting Office 1990, p. 27).

Finally, the GAO report implicitly raises an issue that has been largely ignored—the costs incurred by offenders who fail on ISP: "Most intermediate sanction programs have a relatively high rearrest rate. The rate for Georgia's program, one of the most emulated, is 40 percent. If all were revoked, the state and local jurisdictions would have paid not only for the initial cost of processing offenders and supervisory costs while in the program but also the processing costs for revocation and the cost of imprisonment for 40 percent of the offenders. . . . Only when we begin to attain longitudinal data on relative program costs will we be able to provide relative estimates of the true costs of intermediate sanction programs" (U.S. General Accounting Office 1990, p. 28).

These arguments identify the empirical issues that need to be resolved before basing too much support for ISP on its potential for saving corrections costs.

3. *Can ISP Effectively Control Criminal Behavior?* The question of ISP's crime-control promise has been controversial since the beginning. Advocates of ISP have asserted that restrictive conditions and closer supervision will achieve greater crime control than routine supervision. Even some who criticize the arguments about effects on prison crowding and costs second that belief: "Intensive probation is a mechanism by which reality can be brought to all intermediate punishments. Allied to house arrest, treatment orders, residential conditions up to house arrest, buttressed by electronic monitoring where appropriate, and paid for by fees for service by the offender where that is realistic, intensive supervision has the capacity both to control offenders in the community and to facilitate their growth to crime-free lives" (Morris and Tonry 1990, p. 11).

Early reports suggested that ISP is an effective crime-control device, based on differences in recidivism rates (variously measured) between people on ISP and those on routine supervision. However, the groups

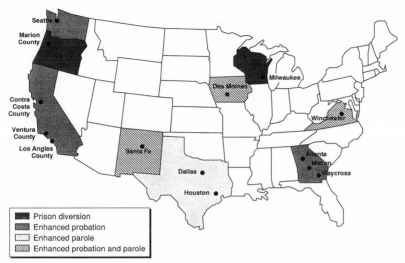

FIG. 1.—Sites and types of intensive supervision programs (ISPs) in the Bureau of Justice Assistance demonstration.

being compared in early studies may not have been comparable, so that the differences in outcomes resulted from the differences in the kinds of people in each sanction and not from program effects. The best way to overcome this difficulty is through experiments in which eligible offenders are randomly assigned to ISP or to the relevant alternative sanction (e.g., prison or routine probation or parole).

## II. The ISP Demonstration and Evaluation

In 1986, the Bureau of Justice Assistance issued a call for jurisdictions interested in participating in an experimental evaluation of ISP. Fourteen sites in nine states across the nation became part of that experiment.[6] Figure 1 shows the locations of the sites and the nature of the programs.

The fourteen sites tested ISP of three kinds: prison diversion, enhanced probation, and enhanced parole. Some diversion programs are commonly referred to as "front-door" programs because their goal is to keep offenders from entering the prison's front door. They generally identify lower-risk persons who have been sentenced to prison, or would have been, and divert them to the community to participate in

[6] The BJA funded the ISP demonstration programs (except Texas sites, which were funded by the Texas legislature), and the BJA and the National Institute of Justice funded the RAND evaluation at all sites.

an ISP program as a substitute for a prison term. "Back-door" diversion programs, like New Jersey's, release offenders from prison early into ISP programs. The enhancement programs select already-sentenced probationers and parolees for closer community supervision. People placed on enhancement ISPs are generally deemed too serious to be supervised on routine caseloads.

## A. ISP Programs in the Demonstration

The ISP demonstration programs constitute the largest randomized experiment in corrections undertaken in the United States. The sites were representative of ISP programs across the country. They included different types of ISP and varied by level of offender risk, by context (political, financial, social), and by agency organization (state, county). Nearly 2,000 offenders were involved.

1. *Requirements for Site Participation.* In the request for proposals to participate in the project, BJA stipulated that the sites agree to five conditions. First, they must design and implement an ISP program, following the general model developed in Georgia. In the Georgia ISP program, two officers supervised twenty-five offenders and enforced weekly contacts, unscheduled drug testing, strict probation conditions, and community service.[7] Second, the program must accept only adults. Third, the program must exclude offenders currently convicted of homicide, robbery, or sex crimes. Fourth, program managers must participate in training conferences and technical assistance activities provided by outside consultants.[8] Fifth, the program must participate in an independent evaluation conducted by RAND, which would require them to maintain core data elements and to cooperate in random assignment of cases.

Each of the chosen sites was funded for eighteen to twenty-four months at $100,000–$150,000 per site. The sites used these funds almost entirely for ISP staff salaries, as opposed to the provision of services (e.g., treatment, urinalysis).

2. *Nature of the Programs.* An innovation's chances of success are greatly enhanced if they are adapted to the local context (Ellickson et

---

[7] For complete descriptions of Georgia's ISP program, see Erwin (1986), Petersilia (1987), and Byrne et al. (1989). The ISP demonstration is not truly a test of the "Georgia model" since only general principles based on the Georgia program, not actual procedures, were incorporated in each site's locally designed ISP program.

[8] Training was directed by Carol Shapiro and Todd Clear of Rutgers University; technical assistance was provided by Douglas Holien and Audrey Bakke, formerly of the National Council on Crime and Delinquency.

al. 1983). The ISP demonstration took this into account. Except for the general guidelines noted above, BJA encouraged individual agencies to tailor program characteristics to their local clientele's needs and risks, the agencies' financial resources, and internal and external policy contexts. Each funded site began by making a number of policy and operational choices that shaped their programs: Which offenders would constitute the target group? Would the ISP target high-risk probationers or parolees, people currently in jail, or prison-bound offenders? Who would be excluded from participation (e.g., based on type of crime, prior record, drug or alcohol use, location of residence)? What aspects of the general ISP model would be incorporated in the local program (e.g., random urine testing, curfews, electronic monitoring, community service, probation supervision fees, victim restitution, and number of contacts)? What emphasis would be placed on treatment and rehabilitation services? How long would the various phases of ISP supervision last, and how would people be added to and removed from the ISP caseload? How would various types of infractions be handled, and at what point would offenders be revoked and an offender sentenced to incarceration?

No two programs were identical. As shown in table 1, both the programs and their clientele varied considerably.

Marion County and Milwaukee chose to implement strict prison-diversion programs; all other sites implemented enhancement programs, focusing on high-risk probationers or parolees. The distinction between probation/parole-enhancement and prison-diversion ISPs is important: enhancement ISPs complement routine supervision by providing stricter supervision for high-risk clients; prison-diversion ISPs apply a community sanction to offenders who would otherwise go to prison.

The Georgia sites, Des Moines, Contra Costa, Santa Fe, Seattle, and Winchester designed their ISP programs for drug offenders. Some programs used electronic monitoring equipment to monitor curfew restrictions (e.g., Macon, Los Angeles, and Des Moines). Others used random on-site drug testing (e.g., Atlanta). Others focused more on treatment participation (e.g., Santa Fe, Winchester).

Differences were also evident in the basic demographics and prior record characteristics of participants. The vast majority of study participants in all sites were males in their late twenties and early thirties. Most offenders had lengthy criminal records: the average number of prior arrests ranged from three in Atlanta to fifteen in Marion County.

# TABLE 1

## ISP Program and Offender Characteristics

| | Contra Costa, California | Los Angeles, California | Seattle, Washington |
|---|---|---|---|
| Study sample size | 170 | 152 | 173 |
| ISP characteristics: | | | |
| Target group | Probationers convicted of felony or misdemeanor drug offenses | High-risk probationers | Probationers convicted of drug-related offenses and drug dependent |
| ISP caseload size | 40:1 | 33:1 | 20:1 |
| Monthly ISP contact levels: | | | |
| Face-to-face | 4 | 16 | 12 |
| Phone/collateral | 8 | 8 | * |
| Drug tests | 4 | * | 8 |
| ISP emphasis | Drug testing | Active electronic monitoring | Surveillance, treatment referrals |
| Offender characteristics (in percentage of total sample): | | | |
| Sex, male | 81 | 87 | 73 |
| Race: | | | |
| White | 18 | 3 | 29 |
| Black | 79 | 86 | 64 |
| Hispanic | 3 | 11 | 5 |
| Average age | 28 | 29 | 31 |
| Current conviction crime: | | | |
| Violent[†] | 8 | 15 | 7 |
| Burglary/theft | 22 | 20 | 26 |
| Drug sale/possession | 69 | 59 | 66 |
| Other[‡] | 2 | 5 | 1 |
| Average no. of prior arrests | 6 | 7 | 9 |
| 1+ prior prison terms | 5 | 24 | 21 |
| Drug-dependent[§] | 42 | 41 | 99 |
| High/intensive risk score[‖] | 64 | 77 | 60 |

* No contact standard set.

[†] Homicide, rape, kidnap, assault, robbery.

[‡] Includes probation or parole revocations.

[§] Drug dependency not available for Contra Costa, Ventura, Los Angeles, Marion, and Milwaukee; for these sites we present the precent of ISP offenders with "high" drug treatment needs.

[‖] Risk score was constructed from the following variables: drug treatment needs, age at first or current conviction, prior probation terms, prior probation and parole revocations, prior felony convictions, and type of curent offense.

| Ventura, California | Atlanta, Georgia | Macon, Georgia | Waycross, Georgia |
|---|---|---|---|
| 166 | 50 | 50 | 50 |
| High-risk proba-tioners | High-need/low-risk felons with history of drugs | High-need/low-risk felons with history of drugs | High-need/low-risk felons with history of drugs |
| 19:1 | 25:2 | 25:2 | 25:2 |
| 16 | 12 | 12 | 12 |
| 8 | 8 | 8 | 8 |
| 4 | 8 | 8 | 8 |
| Police coordination, job training | Passive electronic monitoring | Active electronic mon-itoring | Treatment referrrals |
| 85 | 82 | 84 | 90 |
| 50 | 24 | 40 | 66 |
| 15 | 76 | 60 | 34 |
| 35 | 0 | 0 | 0 |
| 30 | 28 | 27 | 26 |
| 28 | 10 | 24 | 0 |
| 31 | 8 | 40 | 26 |
| 37 | 48 | 32 | 16 |
| 4 | 34 | 4 | 58 |
| 7 | 3 | 5 | 6 |
| 18 | 22 | 16 | 6 |
| 53 | 36 | 56 | 100 |
| 83 | 58 | 73 | 83 |

## TABLE 1 (*Continued*)

| | Santa Fe, New Mexico | Des Moines, Iowa | Winchester, Virginia |
|---|---|---|---|
| Study sample size | 58 | 115 | 53 |
| ISP characteristics: | | | |
| Target group | Probationers and parolees with high-risk/needs and drug dependent | Probationers and parolees convicted of drug offenses or drug-involved burglars | Probationers and parolees with drug-related conviction and/ or drug abuse history |
| ISP caseload size | 35:2 | 35:3 | 24:1 |
| Monthly ISP contact levels: | | | |
| Face-to-face | 12 | 16 | 12 |
| Phone/collateral | 8 | 4 | 4 |
| Drug tests | 4 | 8 | * |
| ISP emphasis | Counseling, employment | Active electronic monitoring | Substance abuse evaluation and outpatient treatment |
| Offender characteristics (in percentage of total sample): | | | |
| Sex, male | 88 | 75 | 81 |
| Race: | | | |
| White | 12 | 63 | 66 |
| Black | 0 | 34 | 34 |
| Hispanic | 88 | 1 | 0 |
| Average age | 30 | 30 | 27 |
| Current conviction crime: | | | |
| Violent[†] | 12 | 6 | 4 |
| Burglary/theft | 31 | 74 | 28 |
| Drug sale/possession | 17 | 15 | 40 |
| Other[‡] | 40 | 5 | 28 |
| Average no. of prior arrests | 8 | 7 | 9 |
| 1 + prior prison terms | 33 | 47 | 25 |
| Drug-dependent[§] | 96 | 97 | 96 |
| High/intensive risk score[‖] | 82 | 82 | 47 |

* No contact standard set.

† Homicide, rape, kidnap, assault, robbery.

‡ Includes probation or parole revocations.

§ Drug dependency not available for Contra Costa, Ventura, Los Angeles, Marion, and Milwaukee; for these sites we present the precent of ISP offenders with "high" drug treatment needs.

‖ Risk score was constructed from the following variables: drug treatment needs, age at first or current conviction, prior probation terms, prior probation and parole revocations, prior felony convictions, and type of curent offense.

| Dallas, Texas | Houston, Texas | Marion, Oregon | Milwaukee, Wisconsin |
| --- | --- | --- | --- |
| 221 | 458 | 24 | 72 |
| High-risk adult parolees with poor performance | High-risk adult parolees with poor performance | Adult felons sentenced to prison | Adult felons recommended to prison on presentence investigation report |
| 25:1 | 25:1 | 30:2 | 40:2 |
| 6 | 6 | 20 | 12 |
| 4 | 4 | * | * |
| * | * | * | 2 |
| Employment, case management/graduated sanctions | Employment, case management/graduated sanctions | Strict monitoring of law violations | Passive electronic monitoring |
| 92 | 93 | 79 | 90 |
| 29 | 29 | 67 | 24 |
| 65 | 55 | 12 | 68 |
| 6 | 16 | 17 | 8 |
| 28 | 29 | 27 | 28 |
| 23 | 19 | 8 | 3 |
| 67 | 58 | 50 | 46 |
| 5 | 17 | 4 | 18 |
| 5 | 6 | 38 | 33 |
| 9 | 8 | 15 | 10 |
| 86 | 83 | 67 | 50 |
| 19 | 28 | 71 | 51 |
| 98 | 97 | 96 | 94 |

Offenders in some sites had more serious prior records than in others. For example, 86 percent of the offenders in Dallas had served a prior prison term, contrasted with 5 percent of offenders in Contra Costa. The nature of the conviction offenses also varied considerably among sites, as did the racial composition of the study samples. In five sites, more than 96 percent of the offenders were judged to be drug-dependent.[9]

In general, the ISP programs were implemented well. Treatment was the one area where most programs fell short. For a variety of reasons, the agencies were not able to get many offenders into drug, alcohol, and other kinds of treatment programs. This was true even when treatment was a condition of participation in ISP. To many people, probation and parole by definition provide treatment services and support to their clients. These people are likely to assume that an ISP evaluation focuses on whether providing an intensive version of these treatment services to offenders affects their behavior. That was not the case in this demonstration. The ISPs studied here were not primarily "service and treatment programs"; they were oriented more toward "surveillance and supervision." This caveat should be kept in mind in considering the results and implications.

## B. Nature of the Evaluation

The demonstrations were intended to test the relative effectiveness of ISP and traditional sanctions. Specifically, data collection and analysis of the results were aimed at answering the following questions: Did ISP offenders receive more surveillance and services than offenders on routine supervision? How did participating in the ISP program affect offenders' future criminality? Did ISP affect the offenders' employment, treatment participation, community service, and victim restitution? How much does ISP supervision cost, relative to other sanctions? For whom was ISP most effective?

In designing the evaluation, RAND faced a reality of current experimental research and made a hard but considered choice. Experimental studies of this kind require multiple sites and large samples if the findings are to be generalizable. Unfortunately, government agencies provide limited funds to support criminal justice studies. Some of

[9] The drug-dependency item in the data collection form was worded, "At the time of the offender's arrest, indicate evidence of dependency on the following substances." Response choices were none, marijuana/hashish, LSD, PCP, uppers, downers, Quaaludes, cocaine, heroin, and other. Coders circled all that applied.

RAND's evaluation design choices reflect modest funding ($25,000 per site) rather than our best judgment about how to design and manage field experiments.

Nevertheless, this trade-off was acceptable because the project permitted a test of one of the most apparently promising criminal justice innovations in recent history. The disadvantage of modest funding was that some of the procedures employed make some results less than definitive.

1. *Characteristics of the RAND Evaluation.* The RAND evaluation was designed to operate similarly for all sites. Each site was required to follow identical procedures regarding random assignment and to collect identical data to support the evaluation. The evaluation had two unique features. First, all cases were assigned randomly to the ISP experimental or the control program (routine probation or parole or prison). Second, the sites themselves collected the data.

To randomize assignments, RAND used the pool of offenders that the sites deemed eligible for ISP programs. Each site had different eligibility criteria; once an offender met those criteria and thus was eligible for inclusion, random assignment between ISP and the control program was implemented by RAND project staff. Site officials provided lists of eligible offenders. Their names (and other information about them) were recorded on a master list for each site. RAND staff assigned offenders to either the ISP or the control program. The sites implemented the random assignment, putting the experimental cases in ISP, the controls in their respective programs.[10]

Three data collection forms were completed for each experimental and control offender. A background assessment was completed shortly after the offender was assigned to the study. This form recorded demographics, prior criminal record, current offense information, drug dependence, and treatment history. Six- and twelve-month review forms recorded the nature and type of probation and parole services received, participation in treatment and work programs, and recidivism (as measured by technical violations and arrests) during the one-year follow-up period. Specifically related to drug testing, the forms also recorded for each month of the follow-up the number of tests ordered and taken,

---

[10] Site personnel were told that deviations from the random assignment were allowed only in emergencies (e.g., an influential judge demanded that an offender get ISP). These "direct judicial commits" were discouraged, but, when they occurred, sites were asked to provide the names of the offenders. Across all fourteen sites, fewer than a dozen cases were directly committed to ISP caseloads; these cases were deleted from the final sample.

the types of drugs for which the offender tested positive, and the sanction imposed for a positive drug test. Data for all three forms were extracted from official record files. The sites also provided data on the organizational and political environment. For estimates of relative costs, the sites provided data on the daily costs of community sanctions and incarceration.

To record time-at-risk information, a status calendar was completed at the end of six months and at the end of one year. The calendar included dates when the offender was placed on and removed from ISP, electronic monitoring, or routine probation and dates of entry into and release from jail or prison. The calendars were filled out by the site coders, using information from the offenders' probation or parole files. These data were used to calculate contact rates and sanction costs.

Due to resource constraints, BJA staff decided at the outset that the sites would have to collect the data themselves. From a research standpoint, this was not ideal. Because the people collecting the data were also agency personnel, they could have competing priorities or biases that might compromise the research. RAND staff conducted validity checks at most of the sites, and believe the information was coded consistently and correctly.

RAND staff cleaned and edited all data, created analysis files for each site, and computed frequencies on the data. Sites were asked to review the preliminary data to see how closely they represented actual program operations and to flag any data items that seemed out of line with practice. In nearly every instance, the sites felt the data were being coded correctly (e.g., the number of contacts being made, the seriousness of the offenders they supervised).

2. *Analytic Methods.* The various reports and articles present a more detailed discussion of the evaluation methods.[11] Here, we summarize the methods used to address major questions in the analysis.

*a. Characterizing participants.* RAND collected a number of background characteristics for each offender, including sex, race, age at assignment, prior criminal record, drug use and treatment history, type of current offense, sentence characteristics, and conditions imposed. For each site, RAND summarized the characteristics of all experimental and control offenders in terms of means (for continuous variables) and proportions (for categorical variables).

---

[11] See n. 3 above.

To determine whether the comparison groups were comparable, the background characteristics of ISP and control offenders within each site were compared. With few exceptions, within a site experimental and control offenders were similar in terms of demographics, prior record, current offense, and risk of recidivism.[12] Random assignment ensures that, in the long run, experimental and control groups will be identical on background characteristics. We know, however, that random assignment does not guarantee this with any particular sample.

b. *Measuring intensity and treatment.* To measure program implementation, RAND calculated intensity of supervision and services delivered (e.g., the number of face-to-face and other contacts, counseling sessions, monitoring checks per month) as rates per month of street time. The rates were calculated by dividing the frequency of contacts by the offender's street time (days on probation but not incarcerated or on abscond status). These delivered rates were then compared with the rates specified in the program design. T-tests were used to compare for differences between the experimental and control groups within each site.[13]

c. *Measuring the effect of ISP on recidivism.* To be as comprehensive as possible, the ISP evaluations reported multiple indicators of recidivism, including both static and dynamic measures. Static measures represent simple counts of events, without taking into account the timing of the events. Dynamic measures take into account the timing of events, for example, the time to first arrest. The static measures included the proportion who were arrested, convicted, and incarcerated during the twelve months after program assignment, overall and by type of offense;[14] the proportion who experienced a technical violation during the twelve months after program assignment, overall and

[12] The exceptions: in Contra Costa, a higher percentage of ISP offenders had "high" drug treatment needs; in Los Angeles, ISP, electronically supervised probation, and routine probationers differed in age at current conviction; in Wisconsin, a higher percentage of experimental offenders had "high" alcohol treatment needs; in Oregon, control offenders had more prior probation and prior jail sentences; in Seattle, experimental offenders had more misdemeanor convictions; in Winchester, more control offenders were convicted of drug crimes; in Des Moines, a greater percentage of control offenders had "high" drug treatment needs. Given the large number of comparisons made within each site, this number of differences would be expected by chance alone. Risk-of-recidivism was predicted on the basis of employment history, attitude, mobility, drug and alcohol use, and prior incarcerations and convictions.

[13] To be precise, t-tests were performed on the log of the rates because of the skewed distribution.

[14] For control offenders who were imprisoned, recidivism is recorded for the time period following prison release if it occurred within the one-year follow-up period (e.g., six months in prison, followed by six months on parole).

by type of technical violation; and the most serious outcome each offender incurred over the entire twelve-month follow-up period.

Differences between offenders in ISP and routine supervision on each static measure were tested with $\chi^2$ tests. In addition, the analysis reported the rate of arrests, which refers to the number of arrests per year, per individual during the follow-up period. This measure takes into account follow-up period variation (i.e., street time). An individual's arrest rate was calculated as the number of arrests, divided by the offender's street time.

The final recidivism analysis used survival analysis, a technique that measures the pace of recidivism among offenders. The strength of this analysis, over fixed-period observations, is that it specifies the proportion of offenders who survive (and who fail) across specified intervals within the follow-up period, making it possible to describe these proportions within every month of the follow-up period. Survival analysis was used to analyze average time to first technical violation, time to first arrest, and time to first violation or arrest (whichever came first).

*d. Measuring the effect of ISP on social adjustment.* To measure program participation effects, RAND calculated the proportion of offenders who attended counseling programs or educational or vocational training; were employed; paid restitution, fees, or fines; or performed community service. These proportions were then compared for the experimental and control groups using $\chi^2$ tests on each measure of interest. The total period (days, hours) that each offender participated in each treatment or service program was recorded.

*e. Testing for correlations between background and outcome.* Logistic regression analyses were used to determine the interaction effect between assigned condition (ISP or routine supervision) and background characteristics on the various outcomes. The form of the logistic regression models was

$$\text{outcome} = \text{condition} + \text{background characteristic}$$
$$+ \text{condition} \times \text{background characteristic}.$$

*f. Estimating sanction costs.* One goal was to estimate the total criminal-justice dollars spent on each offender during the one-year follow-up period, including both corrections and court costs.[15] Proce-

---

[15] Zedlewski (1987) argues that crimes committed by offenders also entail social costs, such as victims' losses from missed work and hospital bills, as well as increased fear, which can be expressed in the purchase of more private security. No adequate method

dures were designed to take account of the marginal costs of different sanctions, how long offenders actually served under different sanctions, costs incurred for offenders subject to more than one sanction, and system costs for processing violations and new arrests. The cost calculations involved three steps. First, the costs of each type of local sanction or service used by the study sample were estimated, as were the costs of processing an arrest or technical violation.[16] Second, using information from the status calendar and the six- and twelve-month reviews, RAND determined where the offender was (in prison, on ISP, under routine supervision) on each day in the follow-up period and "billed" each offender for each service used. Third, RAND averaged across offenders within the experimental and control programs to estimate annual costs of both.

## III. Results of the Evaluation

The primary goal of the BJA demonstration project was to determine how ISP participation affected offenders' subsequent criminal behavior. The evaluation also examined cost-effectiveness and offender participation in counseling, work, and training programs. The participating sites had their own objectives and interests. Many hoped ISP would provide a means for reducing prison crowding. Most were interested in learning whether ISP served as an intermediate sanction, in which probation and parole conditions were monitored and enforced more credibly than has been customary in traditional probation programs with large caseloads.

### A. Effects on Prison Crowding

We cannot say whether prison-diversion ISP might reduce prison crowding. The two sites that attempted such programs—Marion County, Oregon, and Milwaukee, Wisconsin—had implementation difficulties that made the results equivocal. However, those problems, and the willingness of only two sites to try prison diversion, suggest that their potential in this regard is limited. To the contrary, evidence from other sites indicates that strict monitoring and enforcement of ISP conditions can result in a higher proportion of probationers and parolees being returned to prison and jail.

now exists for quantifying such social costs, so they are not included here; they are likely to be substantial.

[16] Information on the daily costs of supervision and incarceration was collected from each site. The average costs of processing an arrest, estimated as $1,500, were adapted from Haynes and Larsen (1984).

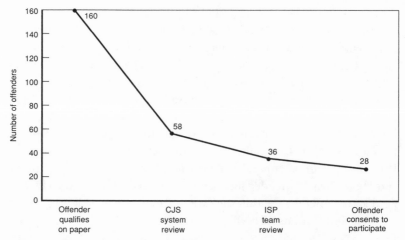

FIG. 2.—Stages of prison-diversion ISP screening: Marion County, Oregon

Experience in Milwaukee and Marion County indicates how difficult it would be to reduce prison crowding through ISP. As figure 2 shows, in Marion County the eligibility requirements were so stringent that few offenders qualified for the experiment. In Milwaukee, judges and probation officers often overrode the random assignment.

In Marion County, the primary criteria for eligibility were that the offender was convicted of a nonviolent felony and had no prior record of violence. The first criterion effectively limited ISP eligibility to property offenders. Since in some states such offenders comprise the majority of prisoners, an ISP program could take considerable pressure off the prisons, even with that restriction. However, in Oregon, property offenders who have no history of violence are not likely candidates for prison. Thus, the second criterion limited the pool of prison-bound eligibles considerably. During the eighteen-month period, 160 offenders were judged eligible for ISP based on these initial screening criteria.[17]

A special data collection effort was undertaken to understand why many apparently eligible offenders were rejected in Marion County. Individual case folders were examined, and practitioners were interviewed. We found no differences between the accepted and rejected cases in terms of race, prior criminal record, or status at the time of arrest. We did find, however, that 50 percent of those rejected had current burglary convictions—more than double the percentage among

[17] Complete Oregon results can be found in Petersilia and Turner (1990c).

cases accepted for ISP. This rejection of burglars points to a serious problem for prison-diversion ISP programs. Burglary is generally considered a nonviolent felony, and people serving sentences following burglary convictions comprise approximately 15 percent of the prison population on any given day (Maguire and Flanagan 1991). Yet, at least in Marion County, there seems to be strong resistance, whatever the eligibilty criteria, to use of ISP for burglars.

It is easy to understand why Marion County had so few participants. In most jurisdictions, a prison-diversion program that excludes violent offenders, convicted burglars, and people with any history of violence would have very few candidates left to divert. Some jurisdictions shrink the potential pool even further by excluding people with drug histories. Since about 75 percent of prisoners have either drug sale or use in their backgrounds (Bureau of Justice Statistics 1991b), in many states this restriction would put a prison-diversion ISP program out of business before it opened its doors.

The local judge in Marion County created another impediment to a random evaluation. He established an informed consent requirement, allowing diversion from prison only for those offenders who were willing. Eight (25 percent) of the remaining offenders refused, evidently preferring the certainty of prison to the uncertainties of ISP. The resulting sample size was too small to yield statistically reliable results.

The Milwaukee ISP experiment included two eligible offender pools: front-end cases (high-risk offenders newly convicted of nonviolent felonies) and back-end cases (probation or parole violators facing revocation for new nonviolent felonies or technical violations). These offenders were screened by ISP officers, and the names of those deemed eligible were called into RAND for random assignment to ISP or prison. The random-assignment recommendation was then made to the judge (for the front-end cases) or the supervisory agent (for the back-end cases).

Unfortunately, regardless of the random experimental designation, most front-end cases were sentenced to prison. Judges were evidently unwilling to divert half of these serious offenders to a community alternative. The back-end experimental cases were placed on ISP as recommended, but fewer than half of the control cases were sent to prison; the rest were sent to routine probation or parole. This selective sentencing for both groups effectively foiled the purpose of random assignment. We could no longer assume that the outcomes reflected program effects rather than the selection process. Comparison of the

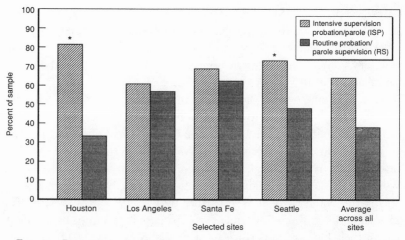

Fig. 3.—Percentage of offenders with any technical violation during one-year follow-up. Note.—Asterisk indicates that the ISP is significantly different from routine supervision, $p < .05$.

prisoners with those given ISP revealed that the prisoners had more serious conviction offenses.

## B. Increased Prison and Jail Commitments

Evidence from the RAND evaluation suggests that enhancement-type ISP might increase commitments to prison and jail, an effect that is directly contrary to proponents' hope to reduce prison populations. In general, ISP supervision was associated with more technical violations and more commitments to prison and jail. Figures 3 and 4 illustrate these two findings using results from four sample sites and the average for all participating sites. Figure 3 shows percentages of ISP and control offenders with any technical violation during the one-year follow-up. Figure 4 shows the percentage returned to prison during the one-year follow-up.[18] The results are consistent across all sites: more ISP than control offenders had technical violations, and a higher percentage were incarcerated during the one-year follow-up period. Twenty-seven percent of ISP offenders were placed in jail or prison during the follow-up, compared with 19 percent of the controls.

The higher rate of commitments from the experimental programs to jail and prison results mostly from higher rates of technical violations. Intensive supervision programs attempt to increase the credibility of

[18] Milwaukee and Marion County, the prison diversion sites, are deleted from the averages in figures 3–10.

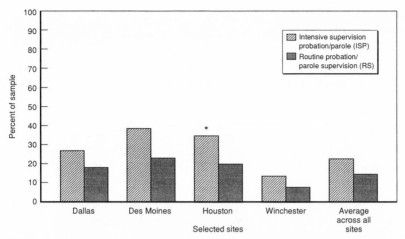

Fig. 4.—Percentage of offenders returned to prison during one-year follow-up. Note.—Asterisk indicates that the ISP is significantly different from routine supervision, $p < .05$.

community-based sanctions by making certain that conditions ordered by the court—including those considered "technical" in nature—are monitored and enforced and violations punished. Depending on how severely ISP staff (and their respective courts) choose to treat ISP infractions, commitments to prison and jails may rise significantly.

Figure 5 illustrates this phenomenon with data from Houston. The Houston program was a parole-enhancement ISP intended to reduce

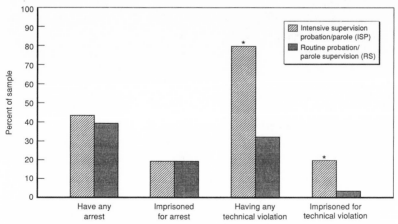

Fig. 5.—Houston response to arrest and technical violations during one-year follow-up. Note.—Asterisk indicates that the ISP is significantly different from routine supervision, $p < .05$.

recommitments to the Texas Department of Corrections.[19] The Houston program targeted parolees under supervision who had the highest probability of returning to prison if left on current caseloads (based on their risk-of-recidivism score and their current parole performance). Houston successfully implemented their ISP program protocol, which included increased face-to-face and home visits and more frequent drug testing.

There were no significant differences in new arrests between offenders in the ISP and control groups, but there were significant differences in technical violations and imprisonment. Eighty-one percent of the ISP offenders had technical violations, compared with 33 percent of those in the control group (routine parole). Five times as many ISP offenders were returned to prison for technical violations as were those on routine supervision (21 percent vs. 4 percent).

When both arrests and technical violations are considered, at the end of one year about 30 percent of the Houston ISP participants were in prison, compared with about 18 percent of the controls. Despite the program's intent to reduce prison use, putting people on ISP added more offenders to the prison population than did routine parole. Given random assignment, this can be interpreted as an ISP program effect, not the result of any difference in populations. Of course, these higher incarceration rates and costs must be weighed against the potential public safety gains.

## C. The Relative Costs of ISP

Much of the enthusiasm for ISP comes from its presumed cost-effectiveness. Dollars might be saved if enough prison-bound offenders are diverted to ISP. The costs per day per offender for imprisonment are much higher than costs per day for ISP. In most policy discussions, the annual operating costs of prisons (usually cited to be $14,000–$26,000 per year, per offender) are compared to the annual costs of ISP ($5,000–$8,000 per year, per offender). These comparisons fuel the popular notion that ISP is far cheaper than prison.

RAND's analyses show that ISP is more expensive than most people have understood. Much more needs to be considered than comparative

---

[19] To our knowledge, this is the only experimental evaluation of intensive parole supervision that has been completed. This type of ISP is receiving increased attention because parole revocation cases constitute an increasingly large share of prison admissions each year. Complete results for the Texas ISP evaluation are contained in Turner and Petersilia (1992).

per capita costs. Sizable increases in the number of people diverted to ISP from routine supervision could cause a considerable rise in total system costs.

In no site did ISP result in cost savings during the one-year follow-up period, even when, as in Texas, the program was designed specifically for that purpose. At all sites, ISP resulted in more technical violations, court appearances, revocations, and incarcerations, resulting in costs up to twice as high as the costs for routine probation and parole supervision. Variation in program costs is related to how ISP programs respond to violations. If violations were ignored, program costs were lower (because new court and incarceration costs were avoided). If violations led to increased revocations as a result of new arrests and technical violations, costs were higher.

1. *Cost of Imprisonment versus ISP.* In Oregon, RAND found that per capita ISP costs were about 75 percent of costs of imprisonment ($11,551 per offender per year vs. $15,526). These costs reflect a crossover effect. For the one-year study period, ISP offenders (the experimentals) and those sent originally to prison (the controls) spent about equal amounts of time incarcerated (local incarceration plus prison) during the one-year follow-up. The results graphically portray "revolving door" justice in Oregon, with many ISP and prison participants moving every couple of months between prison and the community.

Prison-bound offenders considered appropriate for an ISP-diversion program will likely be drawn from the lower-risk offenders being sentenced to prison. These people would probably serve shorter sentences anyway. When those offenders are sentenced to ISP, with restrictive rules and conditions and strict revocation policies, they may end up serving roughly the same amount of time in prison as if they were originally sentenced to prison. This cancels out the presumed cost savings states had hoped to realize.

2. *Cost of ISP versus Routine Probation and Parole.* High violation and incarceration rates for ISP offenders drove up estimated costs in the twelve probation/parole enhancement programs. ISP costs about 50 percent more per offender than routine probation or parole supervision. Annual ISP program costs averaged $7,200 per offender compared with about $4,700 per year for the control groups. These figures include judicial system costs and so are higher than those commonly reported for probation or parole supervision.

Tables 2 and 3 illustrate the various corrections programs that offenders in the two Texas parole-enhancement programs experienced

## TABLE 2

Texas ISP and Routine Supervision during One-Year Follow-Up

|  | Daily Costs for Dallas and Houston (in Dollars) | Average Days by Program | | | |
|---|---|---|---|---|---|
|  |  | Dallas | | Houston | |
|  |  | Routine Parole | ISP | Routine Parole | ISP |
| Supervision: |  |  |  |  |  |
| ISP | 5.39 | 0 | 260 | 0 | 166 |
| With electronic monitoring | 12.39 | 0 | .8 | 0 | 3 |
| Regular parole | 1.78 | 294 | 9 | 251 | 22 |
| With electronic monitoring | 8.78 | 2 | 0 | .6 | 0 |
| Residential | 26.91 | 0 | .4 | .3 | 14 |
| Custody: |  |  |  |  |  |
| Other confined (hospital) | 53.25 | 0 | .2 | 3 | 3 |
| Jail | 35.00 | 14 | 27 | 39 | 43 |
| Prison | 37.49 | 32 | 43 | 26 | 48 |
| Other: |  |  |  |  |  |
| Abscond/failure to appear/ escape | .50 | 20 | 18 | 33 | 58 |
| Other (transfer, dead) | .00 | 2 | 6 | 13 | 6 |

|  | Estimated Costs per Action (in Dollars) | Average Number of Court Actions | | | |
|---|---|---|---|---|---|
|  |  | Dallas | | Houston | |
|  |  | Routine Parole | ISP | Routine Parole | ISP |
| Court reprocessing: |  |  |  |  |  |
| Average number of arrests | 1,500.00 | .3 | .4 | .5 | .5 |
| Average number of technical violations | 500.00 | .1 | .2 | .4 | 2.2 |

during their one-year follow-up period, and the cost of each. Nearly two-thirds of the total costs of both ISP and routine supervision are due to the costs of incarcerating offenders in jail or prison.

Intensive supervision programs do not have the immediate cost-savings potential that their proponents imagined. If new community sanctions emphasize public safety and offender accountability, increases in program costs, not decreases, are likely to occur.

### D. Recidivism Rates

At no site did ISP participants experience arrest less often, have a longer time to failure, or experience arrests for less serious offenses

TABLE 3

Annual Costs for Texas ISP and Routine Parole,
per Offender (1988 Dollars)

| | Dallas | | Houston | |
| --- | --- | --- | --- | --- |
| Cost Components | Routine Parole | ISP | Routine Parole | ISP |
| Initial imposed sanctions | 524 | 1,420 | 446 | 932 |
| Court reprocessing costs | 526 | 736 | 995 | 1,930 |
| Intermediate sanctions | 18 | 33 | 170 | 577 |
| Other (abscond, escape) | 10 | 10 | 17 | 31 |
| Subsequent correctional custody: | | | | |
| Jail | 497 | 945 | 1,374 | 1,493 |
| Prison | 1,214 | 1,596 | 958 | 1,815 |
| Total annual program costs | 2,789 | 4,740 | 3,960 | 6,778 |

than did offenders under routine supervision.[20] This is a strong finding, given the wide range of programs, geographical variation, and clientele represented in demonstration projects. Figure 6 shows the percentage of offenders having at least one arrest during the one-year follow-up for selected sites and averaged across the participating sites. In only one instance was the proportion of ISP offenders arrested less than that for offenders on routine supervision. In all but three sites, arrest rates were higher for ISP than for the control groups, but not significantly so.[21] At the end of the one-year follow-up, about 37 percent of ISP and 33 percent of control offenders had been officially arrested.

If technical violations are used as a recidivism measure, the record for ISP looks somewhat grimmer (see figure 3); an average of 65 percent of the ISP clients experience a technical violation compared with 38 percent of the controls. However, technical violations may largely be program effects rather than evidence of criminal activity. Intensive supervision program clients are subject to much closer surveillance than others under supervision, and more of their violations may come

[20] The major outcome measure was officially recorded recidivism. Recidivism is however a product of the offender's conduct and the system's ability to detect and act on criminality. Offenders on ISP may be committing fewer crimes than comparable offenders, but heightened surveillance may increase the probability of detection. Without offender self-reports, it is impossible to disentangle offender behavior from enforcement activities.

[21] The sites with lower arrest rates for ISP were Des Moines, Macon, and Ventura County. In Ventura, a lower percentage of ISP than control offenses were arrested during the follow-up.

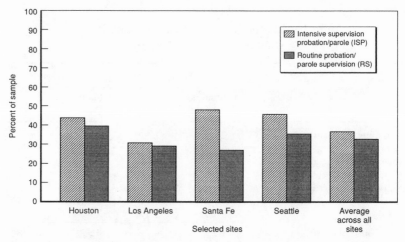

Fig. 6.—Percentage of offenders with any arrest during one-year follow-up

to official attention. This heightened scrutiny may make crime-control sense. Arrest rates correlate with criminal activity—the more crime an individual commits, the likelier he is to be arrested (Blumstein et al. 1986). Technical violations may also be proxies for commission of crimes. Noncompliance with technical conditions may signal that the offender is "going bad." Offenders who disregard court-imposed conditions may also be committing new crimes; either inference is often valid. Enforcement of conditions, however technical, should increase public safety.

To address this question, RAND examined the relationship in the California and Texas ISP programs between technical violations and arrests, correlating arrests and technical violations for all offenders combined and for each study group separately. There were no significant negative correlations between the number of arrests and the number of technical violations for any group. The analysis thus showed no support for the argument that violating offenders on technical conditions suppressed new criminal arrests.

When conviction rates are used as a recidivism measure, there were no differences between experimentals and controls. Conviction rates were much lower than arrest and technical violation rates for both groups. There were no significant differences across sites, and they tend to be quite similar within sites. For the ISP groups averaging across all sites, 21 percent of the ISP participants were convicted during the one-year follow-up, compared with 21 percent of the controls. These results lend little support to claims that ISP deters or constrains officially recorded criminal behavior more than routine supervision, at least during a one-year follow-up period.

## E. For Which Offenders Was ISP Most Effective?

Although ISP was not shown to be more effective than routine probation and parole in reducing recidivism overall, was it more effective for some subgroups?[22] If so, future ISP could be tailored to those subgroups. Resource constraints prevented investigation of this question except in California and Texas.

In this analysis, RAND used background characteristics that prior research has identified with recidivism: sex, race, age, risk-of-recidivism, prior record, living arrangement, drug-treatment needs, and employment (Petersilia et al. 1985; Petersilia, Turner, and Peterson 1986; Vito 1987). Interactions were examined between background characteristics and program type (ISP or control) in relation to three recidivism measures (technical violations, arrests, technical violations or arrests). In neither state did the analysis show consistent differences in recidivism for any subgroup of offenders (details are in Petersilia and Turner [1990*b*] and Turner and Petersilia [1992]).

Our ability to identify separate subgroups was hampered by the homogeneity of the sample. Within a site, the study samples were fairly homogeneous in terms of prior record, age, and drug use. When all offenders are fairly similar, it is difficult to find offender-program interactions.

## F. Treatment and Other Program Features

The ISP programs were, by design, oriented more toward surveillance than treatment. Bureau of Justice Assistance funds were used mostly to pay probation and parole staff salaries, not to purchase treatment services. Sites had to rely on existing treatment programs, which were minimal in some communities. Still, a higher percentage of ISP than control probationers and parolees participated in counseling and were employed. Figure 7 shows the percentages of ISP and control offenders who participated in any counseling (regardless of type and intensity) or were employed (regardless of length) during the one-year follow-up.

Across all sites, just under half of ISP offenders participated in some

[22] Erwin and Bennett (1987) speculate that ISP works best for drug offenders. Byrne and Kelly (1989) suggest that employed ISP offenders have lower recidivism rates and that higher levels of both treatment and surveillance are associated with success.

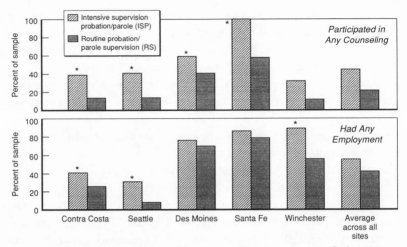

Fig. 7.—Percentage of offenders with any counseling or employment during one-year follow-up. Note.—Asterisk indicates that the ISP and routine supervision groups are significantly different, $p < .05$.

counseling during the follow-up period, compared with 22 percent of the controls. This difference is large, but given the serious records of these offenders, the overall counseling participation rate is notably low. The ISP programs generally had higher percentages of people in drug and alcohol counseling, but the differences were statistically significant only in Contra Costa, Houston, Los Angeles, Santa Fe, Des Moines, and Seattle. In Ventura and Waycross, ISP offenders experienced some of the highest rates of counseling, but routine supervision offenders also participated frequently in counseling in those sites, resulting in nonsignificant differences between ISP and routine supervision.

Findings were mixed for employment. Slightly more than one-half of ISP offenders in ISP programs were employed, compared with 43 percent of offenders on routine supervision. In Contra Costa, Los Angeles, Seattle, and Winchester, ISP offenders were more likely to be employed than their counterparts on routine supervision.

Participation in community service varied greatly across sites. The highest rates (greater than two-thirds of ISP offenders) were reported in the Georgia ISP programs, where community service has historically been a major component. In many sites community service was virtually nonexistent. In no site did ISP offenders participate significantly more often in community service than did routine supervision offenders. Restitution was paid by only a small minority of offenders. Across all sites, 12 percent of ISP offenders paid some restitution, compared with 3 percent of offenders on routine supervision. Only in Los Angeles and Des Moines were ISP offenders significantly more likely to pay restitution.

While treatment and program participation were generally low, supplementary analyses for California and Texas sites revealed a relationship between participation and recidivism. For this analysis, a summary score was created for each offender, with one point assigned for participation in each of the following: any employment during the follow-up year, any counseling sessions attended, any community service performed, and any restitution paid. Scores ranged from zero to four, with zero indicating no program participation and four indicating participation in all four activities. Cross tabulation between the summary participation scores and recidivism revealed that higher levels of program participation were associated with a 10–20 percent reduction in recidivism.

This analysis, however, does not incorporate the random assignment aspect of the study since offenders were not randomly assigned to different levels of program involvement. Thus, selection processes may be operating: "better" offenders not only may have lower recidivism rates but also may participate more often in programs. Measures of program participation and better outcomes may simply be correlated.[23] Future research should experimentally test the effects of enhanced treatment plus surveillance, compared with surveillance alone in order more reliably to determine the impact of treatment on offender recidivism.

## G. *Implementation*

The ISP programs were designed to be much more stringent than routine supervision, and, in general, they were. In Oregon and Wisconsin, the only sites that attempted true prison-diversion ISP, implementation problems make the results less than definitive. At the other sites, program protocols were implemented much as planned. There were significant differences between the ISP and control programs on dimensions that make the former more "intensive"—more contacts,

---

[23] This issue was investigated by incorporating the offender's risk-of-recidivism in the analyses. To determine whether the observed relationship between program participation and recidivism disappeared when the offender's risk level was statistically controlled, we used logistic regression to model recidivism as a function of offender risk and program participation. The relationship between participation and recidivism was nonsignificant for Ventura.

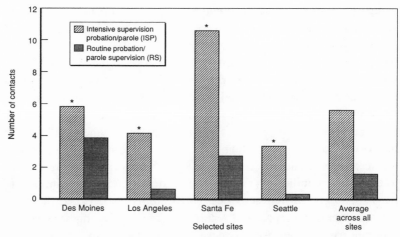

FIG. 8.—Number of monthly face-to-face contacts during one-year follow-up. Note.—Asterisk indicates that the ISP is significantly different from routine supervision, $p < .05$.

monitoring, and drug testing. Figure 8 shows the average number of face-to-face contacts for ISP and control programs. Figure 9 shows similar figures for drug testing.

Each site tailored its program to accomodate local needs and risks, the agencies' financial resources, and internal and external political contexts. Figures 8 and 9 reveal the varied ISP programs that resulted. In some programs, face-to-face contacts ranged upward from three per

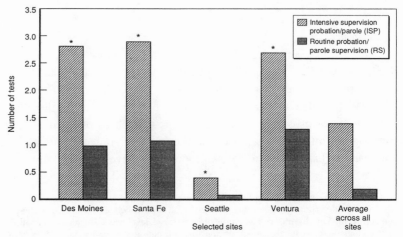

FIG. 9.—Number of monthly drug tests during one-year follow-up. Note.—Asterisk indicates that the ISP is significantly different from routine supervision, $p < .05$.

month; in others, offenders were contacted almost daily. Such wide variation is not peculiar to this study; others have noted similarly wide variations in ISP program intensity (Byrne et al. 1989).

No straightforward relationship was found between contact levels and recidivism. Within sites, ISP programs were more intensive than the control programs; however, no significant reductions in recidivism were observed as measured by new arrests. Contact rates also do not appear to be related to recidivism. For example, the average ISP face-to-face contacts in Seattle averaged 3.4 per month; average monthly ISP contacts in Macon were 16.1. Yet the percent of ISP offenders arrested in both sites was approximately forty.

RAND's conclusions concerning the relationship between intensity of contacts and recidivism is necessarily limited by the nature of the available data. The ISP programs were "packages" of contacts and services. It is difficult to isolate the independent effect of contact levels apart from other program emphases such as community service, electronic monitoring, or job placement services. In addition, RAND's data do not provide a test of widely disparate contact levels within a single jurisdiction—for example, the differential effects of an intensive program such as in Waycross with over twenty-two face-to-face contacts a month compared with a routine supervision program with only once-a-month contact.

Some people would not equate more frequent contacts and drug testing with punishment; after all, the offender has avoided the "real" punishment of incarceration. That attitude reflects the law-abiding citizen's perspective on crime and punishment, not necessarily the criminal's. Morris and Tonry observe, "Convicted criminals should not be spared punitive responses to their crimes; there is no point in imposing needless suffering, but effective sentencing will normally involve the curtailment of freedom either behind walls or in the community, large measures of coercion, and enforced diminutions of freedom; this is entirely properly regarded as punishment" (1990, p. 5).

By that standard, compared with the control programs, the ISP programs were punitive. Most of the ISP programs had significantly higher levels of various features that curtail freedom: face-to-face contacts, telephone and collateral contacts, law-enforcement checks, employment monitoring, and drug and alcohol testing. Both coercion and "enforced diminution of freedom" were higher, whether measured in terms of technical violations or responses to those violations.

Responses to technical violations, unlike arrests, are under the control of probation and parole staff.[24] Arrests are a police responsibility, although ISP officers did cooperate with the police at some of the sites. The degree of coercion and enforced diminution of freedom the ISPs can impose will come from detecting and responding strongly to technical violations.

## IV. Conclusions and Implications

Whether ISP can be said to "work" and whether jurisdictions should continue to invest in it will depend on local priorities, resources, and other considerations. In making decisions about ISP, jurisdictions need to consider several issues: what they hope to accomplish, how ISP should be structured, what protocol and political constraints will affect ISP, and how program effectiveness will be assessed.

### A. What Can ISP Be Expected to Accomplish?

The evidence to date suggests that ISP's proponents should be modest in their aspirations. Prison-diversion programs have encountered serious implementation impediments, and ISP in general has not been shown effective at reducing recidivism or relieving prison crowding.

1. *Is Prison Diversion a Viable Objective?*  Prison-diversion ISP programs are difficult to implement and are unlikely to be viable means of significantly reducing prison crowding in the immediate future unless educational campaigns can elicit more public and judicial support. The general public and criminal justice officials do not seem particularly receptive to prison-diversion ISP but appear more receptive to ISP programs that toughen the penalties of serious offenders who would otherwise receive ordinary community supervision. Several aspects of the demonstration project support this skeptical view. First, only two of the sites were willing to try prison diversion. Second, in Marion County, the review board imposed eligibility criteria so stringent that few offenders could qualify. Third, in Milwaukee, judges were unwill-

---

[24] Barry Nidorf, chief probation officer in Los Angeles County, believes that ISP staff worked closely with local police, thus possibly increasing their arrest probability. He writes, "The names of Los Angeles County ISP offenders and their conditions of probation were routinely given to the police. Any technical violations discovered by the police were reported to the probation officer. This increased the violation rate among ISP offenders. Further, when a crime was committed, police might have been more aware of the whereabouts of the ISP offenders, and therefore may have had a greater chance of connecting one of them to a crime, hence, raising his or her arrest probability. Intensive supervision program officers sometimes aided the police by facilitating searches of defendants' homes to find evidence of violations" (Nidorf 1991, p. 12).

ing to divert many prison-bound candidates to ISP and frequently overrode the random assignment.

Another consideration for prison diversion is how offenders in the demonstration fared on ISP. Except for Oregon and Wisconsin, all sites experimented with intensive probation or parole enhancement. Offenders were bound for or already under routine community supervision. Their high recidivism rates suggest that diverting more serious prison-bound offenders to ISP programs similar to those studied here would threaten recidivism rates at least as high. Offenders on ISP may in many of the sites have presented as serious risks as those being sentenced to prison; nonetheless, from a public safety perspective, ISP's failure to achieve more effective crime control than routine supervision does not augur well for ISP's potential as an alternative to imprisonment.[25]

2. *Can ISP Successfully Control Offenders?*   ISP's relative success at crime control raises complex questions. If ISP is intended to serve as an alternative to imprisonment, inevitably it is a less effective crime-prevention strategy than imprisonment during the time offenders would otherwise have been imprisoned. The U.S. General Accounting Office notes, "Offenders placed in prison pose no threat to public safety, at least for the period of their imprisonment. Judged by a standard of zero risk, all ISP programs fail to protect public safety" (1990, p. 45). However, prison-diversion programs are rare, and are likely to remain so, and the GAO observation does not undermine enhancement-ISP programs.

Most ISP programs have attempted to provide more stringent punishment for serious offenders who now experience nominal supervision. The GAO observed, "The premise of ISP programs is that they provide an intermediate sanction that, among other things, does not increase threats to public safety. This premise requires us to compare the recidivism rates of ISP programs to those of other community-based programs" (U.S. General Accounting Office 1990, p. 45).

Judged by that criterion, virtually all sites succeeded. Although they had higher technical violations, that was a function of more stringent conditions and closer supervision. More stringent conditions and monitoring provide opportunities for violations and for being found out.

Frequent drug testing, alone, is likely to generate high rates of technical violations. Few sites had a high proportion of low-risk offenders,

---

[25] Others offer more optimistic assessments about ISP as effective prison diversions (see Baird and Wagner 1990; Pearson and Harper 1990).

and the higher the risk rating, the likelier offenders are to be involved with drugs. Putting drug-dependent offenders in a program that forbids drug use, provides frequent drug testing, and provides no assured access to drug treatment virtually guarantees high violation rates. Few of the demonstration projects could obtain treatment for many offenders. Drug-related technical violations accounted for the highest proportion of total technical violations at most sites.

Technical violations aside, the RAND evaluation showed no worse recidivism for ISP clients than for offenders in the control groups. However, it seems odd to judge ISP successful if it merely "does not increase" threats to public safety. If these are not prison-diversion programs, they should be expected to impose more crime control than the less stringent programs for which they are alternatives. Otherwise, why should jurisdictions invest in them, except for reasons of principle?

It is quite possible that ISP may reduce ISP clients' criminal activity but that closer surveillance may increase the probability that they are caught for those crimes they do commit. The only way to investigate that possibility would be through offender interviews that obtain self-reports of criminal behavior.[26] Lacking those, the RAND evaluation provides no evidence that these types of ISP control crime more effectively than routine supervision.

## B. How Should ISP Be Structured?

Jurisdictions may want to reconstitute the elements of ISP differently from these programs in the BJA demonstration projects, depending on what they expect ISP to accomplish.

1. *Do Tougher Programs Achieve Better Crime Control?* Figure 8 showed that most ISP programs could be much tougher. In few of the sites were face-to-face contacts more frequent than eight per month. If an average face-to-face contact takes twenty minutes, ISP contacts of all kinds amounted to less than two hours a month. Figure 9 revealed a like story for drug testing. The cross-site average was just over two tests per month.

These findings suggest that ISP could be made significantly tougher,

[26] RAND conducted personal interviews with random samples of ISP and control offenders in Contra Costa, California. Offenders on ISP believed they were likely to get caught if they violated their probation conditions, particularly if the violation related to drugs. For most types of violations, ISP offenders believed they would be treated more harshly than would their counterparts on routine supervision. Complete offender interview results are contained in Buck (1989).

and tougher conditions might result in less recidivism. However, at least two questions remain: how much more constraining must conditions be, and could a jurisdiction afford it? RAND's results indicate that the more stringent the conditions, the more costly the program, and the more likely it is to drive up prison populations. Overall, ISP programs were more stringent than the control programs, but there was no evident payoff in deterrence or incapacitation (as measured by officially recorded recidivism).

2. *Would More Treatment Reduce Recidivism?*  Would strengthening the treatment component of ISP lower recidivism? The results on treatment may offer some hope. At all three California sites, offenders who received counseling, held jobs, paid restitution, and did community service were arrested 10–20 percent less often than were other offenders. Whether they were truly "rehabilitated" remains to be seen, and a longer follow-up would be needed to test that. Even these results must be viewed as tentative. Offenders were not randomly assigned to treatment within the experimental and control conditions, and lower recidivism rates could have been either treatment *or* selection effects. The positive outcomes may be a function of the kinds of offenders who got into the treatment programs and chose to be employed.

Outcomes might have been better if a greater proportion of the sample had participated in treatment. Participation in drug treatment, particularly, might have a high payoff.[27] Across all sites, about half the offenders were judged "drug-dependent" by their probation or parole officers. Many of the rest probably had some drug involvement. Yet ISP staff often reported difficulties obtaining drug treatment for these people. Although more ISP than control offenders participated in counseling, in some sites a large percentage of all studied offenders in need of drug treatment went untreated. It is not surprising, therefore, that about one-third of all new arrests were drug-related. A high priority for future research is to evaluate ISP programs that have high "doses" of both treatment and surveillance.

3. *Could Restructured ISP Achieve More Incapacitation?*  Incapacitation remains the strongest argument for imprisonment, but the system loses efficiency for handling many serious criminals because so many revocations from routine probation and parole must be accommodated. On any given day, about 20 percent of new admissions to American prisons are parole or probation violators (Petersilia and Turner 1989). Rates

[27] Some research literature gives credibility to this notion (Anglin and Hser 1990; Gendreau and Andrews 1990).

are higher in some states. In California, for example, technical revocations account for nearly half of all new prison admissions (California Commission on Inmate Population Management 1990). The crowding caused by this flood of revocation admissions means that—in some states—many offenders must be released after serving only small percentages of their sentences in order to keep crowding under control.

Given this effect, could jurisdictions more effectively incapacitate serious offenders by devising methods short of incarceration for responding to technical violations? Could offenders who have only violated supervision rules be kept on ISP but be subjected to additional conditions or constraints?

One contrary argument is that probationers and parolees who fail to obey conditions constitute a direct challenge to the authority of the court and the law. Disregard for conditions may demonstrate a more general rejection of social norms. Probation and parole professionals argue that technical revocation is often used as a less costly and more effective substitute for criminal prosecution. Many probationers and parolees whose noncustodial sentence is revoked for "rule violations," they argue, are actually being removed from supervision due to the commission of new crimes. For offenders not known to have committed new crimes, there is a "smoke-means-fire" argument: offenders who feel free to violate the court's rules are likely also to feel free to violate the law, and revoking their probation or parole will prevent crime.

There is some evidence against the assumption that technical violations signal new crimes and for the hypothesis that penalizing condition violations with sanctions short of incarceration could reduce prison crowding without higher risks to public safety. Consider events in the state of Washington.[28] In 1984, Washington officials began reconsidering sentencing and corrections policies regarding court-imposed conditions for probationers (routine, not ISP). Judges typically imposed a "standard" list of eight to ten conditions on probationers. As in other states with a large percentage of high-risk probationers, the result was that a great many probationers revolved in and out of prison because of technical violations.

This practice raised some provocative questions. Were the conditions imposed because they were relevant to the offenders' conviction crimes and past problem behavior? Did the specter of a Willie Horton-type situation prompt judges to make the record show that they always

---

[28] What we describe is not related to the Seattle ISP program in the BJA demonstration.

imposed as many constraints as possible? Is justice served by imposing conditions that are not strictly relevant to a case? Finally, how much was this practice contributing to prison crowding?

After considering these questions, the Washington State legislature developed new rules regarding conditions and the handling of violations (Washington State Sentencing Guidelines Commission 1983). Washington courts can now impose only conditions that are directly relevant to an offender's conviction crime and his past criminal behavior. This typically results in no more than two or three conditions. Further, prison cannot be used as a sanction for technical violations. Revocation on that ground carries a penalty of not more than sixty days in a local jail.

Preliminary results from Washington support the argument for deemphasizing technical conditions. They also suggest that technical violations often are not a proxy for criminal behavior. Although no empirical evaluations have been conducted, Washington officials believe that revocations for technical violations have decreased, while arrest rates for new crimes have remained roughly the same (Greene 1988). Decreasing the number of conditions imposed is likely to lower revocation rates somewhat. For example, if drug testing is not a condition, use of drugs will less often come to supervising officers' attention. If the assumption about the relation of technical violations to new crimes were true, arrest rates in theory should have risen. Since the rates have not risen, technical condition violations may not be strongly related to recidivism or public safety.

4. *Would De-emphasizing Technical Conditions Undercut the Punitive Intentions of ISP?* ISP is by design more punitive than ordinary probation or parole, largely because offenders are subject to tougher conditions. If jurisdictions followed Washington's lead on technical violations, would ISP retain its more punitive character? Could it still serve the sentencing objective of providing a mid-level punishment between prison and probation and scaled to the seriousness of the offender's crime?

Those questions can be approached from principle and from practical evidence. On principle, one might ask whether the common practice of imposing a standard set of conditions on all offenders under supervision appropriately proportions punishment to offense severity. It might be more just to impose only conditions that are relevant to an individual's case than to set standard conditions for all offenders. Moreover, imposing only relevant "special" conditions does not mean that offenders would be watched less closely. Instead, monitoring could concentrate on the limited conditions imposed and the offenders' general behavior. The intensity of supervision could continue to distinguish ISP from ordinary probation or parole, even if conditions were imposed in more discriminating ways.

There is strong, though limited, evidence that the conditions that make ISP intense are so onerous that some offenders prefer prison. Twenty-five percent of the Oregon offenders who were eligible for prison-diversion ISP chose not to participate. Conditions included contact with the probation officer at least five times a week, living only in approved locations, and submitting to unannounced drug and alcohol tests. There was also a one-year minimum time requirement for the ISP program. Evidently, those who opted out preferred the comparative certainty of prison to the chance of being assigned to ISP. Oregon's overcrowded prisons made it unlikely that ISP-eligible prisoners would serve a year in prison, and as it turned out, most men leaving the control group were released from prison after six months.

This pattern of calculated refusal to risk ISP conditions and remain in prison instead has been reported in Arizona and Texas. An Arizona parolee reported that he deliberately snorted cocaine prior to being tested for drugs. He wanted to be returned to prison where he could serve his full sentence ("max out") and be free of parole constraints (which were not even ISP constraints): "They sent me back to prison where I served the remaining three months of my maximum sentence and I got out. Now I'm free. No parole officer, no nothing . . . I knew exactly what I was doing and I still think it was the right decision."

Many people find it almost incomprehensible that anyone would prefer being in prison to being outside, no matter how restrictive the conditions. That serious criminals sometimes find the "more punitive" sanction preferable raises interesting questions about how societies develop penal codes and systems. Some criminals do not look at crime and punishment as the rest of society does. As prisons become more crowded and the lengths of sentence served decrease, ISP may come to seem increasingly punitive to offenders. If probation and parole administrators impose long lists of conditions and enforce them with vigor, ISP may gain so stern a reputation that many offenders request prison instead, and those who participate in ISP experience higher chances of revocation than had they received traditional supervision.

5. *Can Jurisdictions Afford the Kinds of ISP Programs They Want?*   Cor-

rectional cost calculations are complex. Per-offender costs for ISP are higher than is generally recognized. So are costs for routine supervision. If a jurisdiction wants to make ISP more constraining or more service-and-treatment-oriented than the BJA demonstration projects were, costs will be even higher.

Ventura County and Houston provide good examples of the effects of more constraining programs. Both imposed very stringent conditions and responded rigorously to technical violations. In Houston, the resulting per-offender costs of ISP were almost twice as high as for routine parole. Ventura had the highest costs among the ISP programs in California. The insufficiency of treatment slots even in Ventura suggests how expensive it would be for ISP programs to provide more treatment and service.

Whether jurisdictions want to make ISP tougher or more treatment-oriented, they must also consider what kind of return on investment they can expect. No one knows how much more intensive a program would have to be to reduce recidivism. Results in California suggest, but do not empirically demonstrate, the rehabilitative potential of providing more service and treatment. The GAO pointed out, "[W]e know that the per capita costs of these programs exceed those of traditional probation and parole but tend to be less than those of prison. However, current evaluations do not provide us with reliable evidence of how these per capita cost differentials affect overall correctional expenditures" (U.S. General Accounting Office 1990, p. 29).

One problem with making these calculations is that correction costs in most states are spread among many agencies and different levels of government. Local jurisdictions typically pay for jails and community sanctions, while the state pays for prisons. This distribution of costs creates political problems for ISP. If offenders who would normally be serving time in prison are diverted to or kept in an ISP program, who should bear the cost? Sheriffs and probation chiefs in many jurisdictions are resentful that their jails and agencies have had to absorb state-prison overflows, with no state funds to compensate for increases in their county-controlled budgets.

In states with centralized probation, parole, and prison administration (where authority for all corrections activity rests with a single administrative body), reallocation of a portion of the overall corrections budget from one program to another is straightforward (though not always easy to accomplish). But in states that are highly decentralized (where local corrections is administered by cities or counties), the issue arises of whether the state should reimburse the counties to offset some of the additional costs incurred by ISP.

## C. How Should ISP Outcomes Be Judged?

The criteria for judging an ISP program's success should be straight-forward—did it achieve what it was intended to accomplish? However, there are often diverse, sometimes conflicting, perceptions about ISP's character and objectives. This has been demonstrated in the responses of agency administrators to the reported ISP evaluation results. Jurisdictions need at the outset to specify their objectives, what mechanisms are supposed to accomplish those objectives, and how program effectiveness will be judged.

A primary stated goal of many agencies that participated in the BJA demonstration projects was to reduce recidivism in order to increase public safety. Intensive supervision, not treatment, was to be the means of achieving this goal; that goal was manifested in the structure of the programs. Most of the ISP programs emphasized stringent conditions and monitoring rather than treatment. The evaluation results show that official measures of recidivism (arrests and convictions) were about the same for the ISP and control programs. Measured for technical violations and revocations, recidivism was generally higher for the ISP programs.

If crime control rather than rehabilitation is the primary goal, that should be made explicit at the outset. If a jurisdiction is primarily interested in delivery of an intermediate punishment, even if it does not reduce recidivism rates, that also should be made clear. Otherwise, the public will see the observed changes in recidivism rates as an indication of "failure." Finally, if the aim is to reduce recidivism through a combination of intensive supervision and improved rehabilitation programs, that also needs to be made explicit, and the program should be structured to reflect it by devoting appropriate emphases and resources to treatment and surveillance.

## D. Recommendations for Future Research

Besides providing an experimental evaluation of ISP programs, the BJA demonstration projects showed that randomized experiments in criminal justice are feasible—contrary to what many had believed—and on a wide scale (see Weisburd, in this volume). It also demonstrated the economies of scale possible when funding agencies cooperate in undertaking large-scale projects: BJA supported the programs, training, and technical assistance, and the National Institute of Justice supported the analysis. Finally, the results suggest directions for future research.

Unlike medical research, criminal justice has not had an iterative tradition of experimentation, refining, and retesting, and criminal justice policy has suffered from that lack. Innovative criminal justice programs often have been designed, highly touted, and implemented, often without extensive—much less experimental—testing. When new programs have failed to meet expectations, they have been scrapped, and the feeling that "nothing works" has intensified. In the case of ISP, the RAND evaluation left many significant questions unasked and unanswered.

1. *Further Evaluation of Prison-Diversion ISP Programs.* The potential of ISPs as a prison diversion option remains to be tested. RAND's results were inconclusive but instructive. That only two sites were willing to attempt prison diversion may signal a general resistance (particularly among prosecutors and judges) to such programs. That signal was suggested by what happened in Milwaukee: judges simply overrode the random assignment mechanism and insisted on their own judgments of who should get prison or probation. In Marion County, eligibility requirements were so stringent that there were too few offenders to permit meaningful evaluation of program effects.

These results raise questions that merit further investigation.

*a. How large is the potential pool for prison diversion?* If states want to ease prison crowding through ISP, they need to look at the kinds and proportions of offenders currently in their prisons. Sentencing practices vary considerably from state to state, and as a result, the character of prison populations also varies. Research needs to document the most commonly utilized criteria for ISP eligibility, and estimate, for different states, the numbers of prisoners who would qualify given different eligibility criteria.

*b. Could system resistance be decreased by different mechanisms for prison diversion?* For example, there might be less resistance to prison diversion if offenders have already been sentenced to prison and prison officials, rather than judges and prosecutors, decide who is eligible. New Jersey has such a program. Offenders who have served at least one month of their prison sentence can apply for release to an ISP program. Those released remain within Department of Corrections' control and can thus be returned to prison at the first sign of misbehavior.

The New Jersey ISP program has been operating successfully since 1985, and nearly 3,000 inmates have been released to it. Its apparent success suggests several research questions: Is the system less resistant to this method of prison diversion because prison officials will take any blame if offenders go wrong? Does the possibility of prompt return to prison make officials and the community feel less at risk? Does this program "work" primarily because of "creaming"—because less serious applicants self-select into the program and prison officials further winnow out bad risks?

RAND is now evaluating a prison-diversion program in Minnesota using random assignment that is addressing some of those questions. This program is running into fewer implementation problems than arose in Marion County and Milwaukee. Nearly 100 offenders were screened by prison officials during the first few months of their sentences and released to either an ISP or a control program. This suggests that there may be a large enough pool of candidates to merit continued interest in prison diversion. So far, program effects on costs and community safety have not been analyzed, but recidivism (as measured by arrests) has been low.

From the standpoint of experimentation, findings in Minnesota corroborate the Marion County experience. Getting sufficient numbers for statistical analysis has been difficult because many offenders refuse to participate. They know they will be released to routine parole in a few months anyway. From the standpoint of corrections theory, it is worth investigating why some offenders prefer any time in prison to being in the community, regardless of the stringency or the duration of community supervision.

These preliminary findings raise other questions for research on prison diversion: What kinds of education programs will be required for judges? What kinds of procedures should be in place for quick revocation? What offender characteristics (e.g., prior record, current offense) are related to willingness to participate in ISP and to success in ISP? How did such programs affect prison crowding and associated costs, especially if there are high revocation rates?

2. *The Effects of Different ISP Models.*    A basic question is whether the RAND evaluation's results represent a failure of theory or a failure of implementation. The ISP programs RAND evaluated emphasized

surveillance, not treatment. Although most programs had surveillance levels that were significantly higher than in the control programs, virtually all of the ISPs had a low absolute level of contacts. They imposed much more drug testing than drug treatment, even though more than 50 percent of the samples were identified as drug abusers and some of the programs focused on drug offenders. Little wonder, then, that the ISP programs had significantly higher levels of technical violations, mostly as a result of positive drug tests.

The major research issue is whether ISP is a sound theoretical concept—if it were implemented differently. In California, RAND found that offenders who participated in drug counseling and other treatment programs had slightly lower recidivism rates than did offenders who did not participate in treatment programs. In Ventura County, which had the highest levels of surveillance, ISP offenders were less likely to be arrested. Evidence from Washington State suggests that imposing only probation and parole conditions that are related to the offender's crime and past record has resulted in lower revocation rates, without any obvious rise in arrest rates. These findings suggest that we need to give ISP more chances by revising and testing the model. These are some of the relevant research questions: Would recidivism rates be lower if programs had adequate drug treatment resources? Would more intense surveillance lower recidivism, and how intense must it be to make a difference? Would more selective ISP conditions result in lower revocation rates and with what, if any, effects on criminal behavior? What combination of conditions, surveillance, and treatment would get the best results?

Answering these questions will require a number of tests of different kinds, most of which should have an experimental design. Different models also need to be tested on different types of offenders. RAND is currently conducting such a test in Phoenix. Low-risk probationers are being assigned randomly to ISP with the following program differences: drug testing alone, drug testing plus officer contacts, and a strong treatment program. While this will provide information relevant to the questions posed, its usefulness may be limited because the population is relatively low risk. Different models should be tested on different risk populations.

3. *The Effects of ISP on Different Offender Populations.* Another explanation for why ISP didn't "work" in the RAND evaluation is that the ISP model was tested on the "wrong" population. The offenders were basically of the same type—serious and drug-involved. Many people

believe that ISP would work—but for a different, less serious group. The ISP model emphasizes specific deterrence. Deterrence-based programs attempt to change the offenders' perceptions of the costs associated with crime. The problem is that offenders have to share that perception and want to avoid the consequences.

Studies have shown that the more experienced offenders are, the lower they rate the risks of being caught and confined (Paternoster 1987). RAND's findings in Marion County and in Minnesota indicate that some of the serious, drug-involved offenders in those sites did not perceive prison as more punitive than ISP. Given these attitudes, it is worth investigating whether ISP would have different effects for less serious offenders who are not already confirmed in a criminal lifestyle and substance abuse.

4. *The Effects of Different ISP Components.*    RAND was not able to separate out the effects of different ISP components. Random assignment allows a test of the effect of the entire ISP package but does not allow us isolation of the effect of any particular program component.

By extension, RAND did not address questions about the effects of manipulations of program components. For example, RAND could not assess whether more contacts and surveillance would have an effect on recidivism. Unfortunately, neither can any other research. Although ISP proponents have assumed that at some threshold more contacts will lower recidivism, no empirical evidence is available that reveals what level (three, five, ten, twenty) contacts per week will achieve the effect. Although average contacts were higher in the ISP than in the control programs, the absolute levels were only about two contacts per week. RAND was similarly unable to draw any conclusions about the separate effects of drug testing, electronic monitoring, different curfew arrangements, or payment of fines. Future research could be designed to test the incremental effects of various ISP conditions on offender behavior.

5. *Effectiveness of ISP over Time.*    RAND's evaluation was based on a one-year follow-up. Recent research indicates that this is not long enough. Anglin and his colleagues found that offenders assigned to a program analogous to ISP in the 1970s did change gradually; however, it took three to eight years for the differences to emerge and ten years for them to reach statistical significance (Anglin and McGlothlin 1984). If the offenders in our study were followed up for a longer time, their behavior might ultimately differ from the controls' behavior. Future research should investigate ISP effects over longer follow-up periods.

6. *The Relationship between Technical Violations and Criminal Behavior.*
Technical violations are often seen as evidence that offenders under
supervision are "going bad." RAND's study showed that monitoring
for and responding to technical violations accounted for most of the
ISP officers' time and resulted in many commitments to prison and
jail. Handling technical violators also absorbs a great deal of court and
corrections time. Despite the policy significance of technical violations,
no serious research has focused on this issue. Future research should
focus on such issues as empirical evidence that technical violations are
related to criminal behavior; what technical conditions are currently
imposed, which conditions are monitored and enforced, and how
courts sanction various violations; the relationship between technical
conditions (imposition, enforcement, sanctioning) and the offender's
characteristics, agency and officer policy, and local and state resources;
how community corrections programs use technical conditions to manage offenders, encourage rehabilitation, promote agency credibility,
and protect the community; trends in the growth of the technical-
violator population and the effects of those trends on jails and prisons;
and innovative programs, administrative policies, and legal statutes
that have emerged specifically to deal with technical violators.

7. *Appropriate Outcome Measures.*   An important area for future corrections research is on outcome measures per se. Recidivism is the
outcome measure used in evaluating all sorts of interventions from
early childhood prevention programs to in-prison drug treatment. It is
almost the only measure used for corrections since rehabilitation has
been all but abandoned as a viable objective. The inability to reduce
recidivism frustrates researchers, policymakers, and program administrators and attracts media and public attention.

Given the centrality of recidivism to research and practice, its appropriateness as the sole or primary measure for particular interventions
should be reconsidered. It is not that recidivism is inappropriate for
evaluating program effects, but it should be only one of many measures. For some programs, it should, perhaps, not be the primary
measure.

For example, the American Probation and Parole Association
(APPA) has reaffirmed its commitment to ISP and its focus on rehabilitation. The APPA has issued a position paper asserting that behavioral
change, not recidivism, is the appropriate outcome measure. Such
changes would include negotiation skills, managing emotions, enhanced values, and attitude improvement. The APPA argues that these

aspects of human behavior should be the focus of ISP evaluations: "By measuring changes in an offender's cognitive development, we could ultimately pass judgment on a program's effectiveness."

If ISP programs are intended to control rather than to rehabilitate, it is still essential to rethink the use of recidivism as a measure of program effectiveness. One position is that higher recidivism rates should be seen as indicating a program's success. Barry Nidorf, chief probation officer for Los Angeles County, argues, "For years, probation has been measured only by recidivism rates. In today's environment, with over 70 percent of the caseload consisting of felony offenders, is it still realistic to use only this one criterion? Why isn't revocation and sentencing of a probation violator considered a 'success'? I believe it should be" (Nidorf 1991).

Nidorf is not arguing that reduced recidivism is never a measure of "success." Rather, he is arguing that detecting and sanctioning technical violations is a measure of a program's effectiveness, implicitly because these violations signal criminal behavior. If they do, then revocation means preventing crime. As for arrests and sentencing, Nidorf's assumption seems to be that the closer surveillance of probation helps make arrests possible and sentences stick.

These assumptions and the other issues raised above should be addressed in studies that ask probation and parole administrators to define a comprehensive set of appropriate measures for the goals of corrections that can be used by the field's practitioners and researchers.

These are not the only issues for future correctional research agendas, but they are currently the most pressing for research on the future of ISP.

### REFERENCES

Anglin, M. Douglas, and Yih-Ing Hser. 1990. "Treatment of Drug Abuse." In *Drugs and Crime*, edited by Michael Tonry and James Q. Wilson. Vol. 13 of *Crime and Justice: A Review of Research*, edited by Michael Tonry and Norval Morris. Chicago: University of Chicago Press.

Anglin, M. D., and W. H. McGlothlin. 1984. "Outcome of Narcotic Addict Treatment in California." In *Drug Abuse Treatment Evaluation: Strategies, Progress, and Prospect*, edited by F. M. Tims and J. P. Ludford. National Institute on Drug Abuse Research Monograph no. 51. Rockville, Md.: U.S.

Department of Health and Human Services, National Institute on Drug Abuse.

Armstrong, Troy L., ed. 1991. *Intensive Interventions with High-Risk Youths: Promising Approaches in Juvenile Probation and Parole.* Monsey, N.Y.: Criminal Justice Press.

Baird, S. Christopher, and Dennis Wagner. 1990. "Measuring Diversion: The Florida Community Control Program." *Crime and Delinquency* 36:112–25.

Banks, J., A. L. Porter, R. L. Rardin, T. R. Silver, and V. E. Unger. 1977. *Summary Phase I Evaluation of Intensive Special Probation Project.* Washington, D.C.: National Institute of Law Enforcement and Criminal Justice.

Blumstein, Alfred, Jacqueline Cohen, Jeffrey A. Roth, and Christy Visher. 1986. *Criminal Careers and "Career Criminals."* Washington, D.C.: National Academy Press.

Buck, Gerald. 1989. "Effectiveness of the New Intensive Supervision Programs." *Research in Corrections* 2(2):64–75.

Bureau of Justice Statistics. 1991*a*. *Probation and Parole.* Washington, D.C.: U.S. Department of Justice, Bureau of Justice Statistics.

———. 1991*b*. *Drugs and Crime Facts, 1991.* Washington, D.C.: U.S. Department of Justice, Bureau of Justice Statistics.

Byrne, James M., and Linda Kelly. 1989. "An Evaluation of the Implementation and Impact of the Massachusetts Intensive Probation Supervision Program." Unpublished report prepared for the National Institute of Justice, U.S. Department of Justice, Washington, D.C.

Byrne, James M., Arthur J. Lurigio, and Christopher Baird. 1989. "The Effectiveness of the New Intensive Supervision Programs." *Research in Corrections* 2(2):1–56.

California Commission on Inmate Population Management. 1990. *Final Report.* Sacramento: California State Legislature.

Cunniff, Mark A., and Mary K. Shilton. 1991. *Variations on Felony Probation: Persons under Supervision in 32 Urban and Suburban Counties.* Washington, D.C.: U.S. Department of Justice, Bureau of Justice Statistics.

Ellickson, Phyllis, Joan Petersilia, Michael Caggiago, and Sandra Polin. 1983. *Implementing New Ideas in Criminal Justice.* R-2929-NIJ. Santa Monica, Calif.: RAND.

Erwin, Billie S. 1986. "Turning Up the Heat on Probationers in Georgia." *Federal Probation* 50(2):17–24.

Erwin, Billie S., and Lawrence Bennett. 1987. "New Dimensions in Probation: Georgia's Experience with Intensive Probation Supervision (IPS)." *Research in Brief.* Washington, D.C.: U.S. Department of Justice, National Institute of Justice.

Gendreau, Paul, and D. A. Andrews. 1990. "Tertiary Prevention: What the Meta-analyses of the Offender Treatment Literature Tell Us about 'What Works.'" *Canadian Journal of Criminology* 32:173–84.

Greene, Richard. 1988. "Who's Punishing Whom?" *Forbes* 121(6):132–33.

Guynes, R. 1988. "Difficult Clients, Large Caseloads Plague Probation, Parole Agencies." *Research in Action.* Washington, D.C.: U.S. Department of Justice, National Institute of Justice.

Harland, Alan T., and Cathryn J. Rosen. 1987. "Sentencing Theory and Intensive Supervision Probation." *Federal Probation* 51(4):33–42.

Haynes, Peter, and C. Larsen. 1984. "Financial Consequences of Incarceration and Alternatives." *Crime and Delinquency* 30:529–50.

Langan, Patrick A. 1991. "America's Soaring Prison Population." *Science* 251:1568–73.

Langan, Patrick A., and Mark A. Cunniff. 1992. "Recidivism of Felons on Probation, 1986–89." *Special Report.* Washington, D.C.: U.S. Department of Justice, Bureau of Justice Statistics.

McCarthy, Belinda R., ed. 1987. *Intermediate Punishments: Intensive Supervision, Home Confinement and Electronic Surveillance.* Monsey, N.Y.: Willow Tree.

Maguire, Kathleen, and Timothy J. Flanagan, eds. 1991. *Sourcebook of Criminal Justice Statistics—1990.* Washington, D.C.: U.S. Department of Justice, Bureau of Justice Statistics.

Matthews, Timothy. 1991. *Survey of Probation Cost Considerations.* Lexington, Ky.: American Probation and Parole Association.

Morris, Norval, and Michael Tonry. 1990. *Between Prison and Probation: Intermediate Punishments in a Rational Sentencing System.* New York: Oxford University Press.

*New York Times.* 1985. "Crowded Prisons in South Lead to Tests of Other Punishments" (December 18), p. 12.

Nidorf, Barry. 1991. "Nothing Works Revisited." *Perspectives* 1991(Summer):12–13.

Paternoster, R. 1987. "The Deterrent Effect of the Perceived Certainty and Severity of Punishment: A Review of the Evidence and Issues." *Justice Quarterly* 4(2):173–217.

Pearson, Frank, and Alice G. Harper. 1990. "Contingent Intermediate Sentences: New Jersey's Intensive Supervision Program." *Crime and Delinquency* 36:75–86.

Petersilia, Joan. 1987. *Expanding Options for Criminal Sentencing.* R-3544-EMC. Santa Monica, Calif.: RAND.

———. 1989. "Implementing Randomized Experiments: Lessons from BJA's Intensive Supervision Project." *Evaluation Review* 13:438–58.

———. 1990. "Conditions That Permit Intensive Supervision Programs to Survive." *Crime and Delinquency* 36:126–45.

Petersilia, Joan, and Susan Turner. 1989. "Reducing Prison Admissions: The Potential of Intermediate Sanctions." *Journal of State Government* 62(2):65–69.

———. 1990a. "Comparing Intensive and Regular Supervision for High-Risk Probationers: Early Results from an Experiment in California." *Crime and Delinquency* 36:87–111.

———. 1990b. *Intensive Supervision Probation for High-Risk Offenders: Findings from Three California Experiments.* R-3936-NIJ/BJA. Santa Monica, Calif.: RAND.

———. 1990c. *Diverting Prisoners to Intensive Probation: Results of an Experiment in Oregon.* N-3186-NIJ. Santa Monica, Calif.: RAND.

———. 1991. "An Evaluation of Intensive Probation in California." *Journal of Criminal Law and Criminology* 82:610–58.

Petersilia, Joan, Susan Turner, and Elizabeth Piper Deschenes. 1992. "Intensive Supervision Programs for Drug Offenders." In *Smart Sentencing: The Emergence of Intermediate Sanctions*, edited by James Byrne, Arthur Lurigio, and Joan Petersilia. Newbury Park, Calif.: Sage.

Petersilia, Joan, Susan Turner, James Kahan, and Joyce Peterson. 1985. *Granting Felons Probation: Public Risks and Alternatives*. R-3186-NIJ. Santa Monica, Calif.: RAND.

Petersilia, Joan, and Susan Turner, with Joyce Peterson. 1986. *Prison versus Probation in California: Implications for Crime and Offender Recidivism*. R-3323-NIJ. Santa Monica, Calif.: RAND.

Sawyer, Kathy. 1985. "Tougher Probation May Help Georgia Clear Crowded Prisons." *Washington Post* (August 16), p. A1.

Turner, Susan, and Joan Petersilia. 1992. "Focusing on High-Risk Parolees: An Experiment to Reduce Commitments to the Texas Department of Corrections." *Journal of Research in Crime and Delinquency* 29:34–61.

Turner, Susan, Joan Petersilia, and Elizabeth Piper Deschenes. 1992a. "Evaluating Intensive Probation/Parole (ISP) for Drug Offenders." *Crime and Delinquency* 38:539–56.

———. 1992b. "The Implementation and Effectiveness of Drug Testing in Community Supervision: Results of an Experimental Evaluation." In *Drugs and the Criminal Justice System: Evaluating Public Policy Initiatives*, edited by D. MacKenzie and C. Uchida. Newbury Park, Calif.: Sage.

U.S. General Accounting Office. 1990. *Intermediate Sanctions: Their Impacts on Prison Crowding, Costs, and Recidivism Are Still Unclear*. Washington, D.C.: U.S. General Accounting Office.

Vito, Gennaro F. 1987. "Felony Probation and Recidivism: Replication and Response." *Federal Probation* 50(4):17–25.

Washington State Sentencing Guidelines Commission. 1983. *Preliminary Evaluation of Washington State's Sentencing Reform Act*. Olympia: Washington State Guidelines Commission.

Weisburd, David, with Anthony Petrosino and Gail Mason. In this volume. "Design Sensitivity in Criminal Justice Experiments."

Zedlewski, Edwin W. 1987. *Making Confinement Decisions*. Washington, D.C.: U.S. Department of Justice, National Institute of Justice.

*David Weisburd*
*with Anthony Petrosino and Gail Mason*

# Design Sensitivity in Criminal Justice Experiments

ABSTRACT

Interest in randomized experiments with criminal justice subjects has grown, in recognition that experiments are much better suited for identifying and isolating program effects than are quasi-experimental or nonexperimental research designs. Relatively little attention, however, has been paid to methodological issues. Using the statistical concept of power—the likelihood that a test will lead to the rejection of a hypothesis of no effect, a survey examines the design sensitivity of experiments on sanctions. Contrary to conventional wisdom advocating large sample designs, little relationship is found in practice between sample size and statistical power. Difficulty in maintaining the integrity of treatments and the homogeneity of samples or treatments employed offsets the design advantages of larger investigations.

Only experimental designs allow researchers to make an unambiguous link between effects and their causes. Random assignment of subjects into treatment and "control" groups—the defining feature of experimental research—provides a statistical basis for making the assumption that the outcomes observed in an experiment result from the interven-

David Weisburd is associate professor of criminal justice at Rutgers—The State University. Anthony Petrosino is research specialist, New Jersey Division of Criminal Justice. Gail Mason is a tutor in the Department of Legal Studies, La Trobe University. Research for this essay was supported by the National Institute of Justice (grant 88IJCX-0007) and by the School of Criminal Justice, Rutgers—The State University. We wish to thank Christopher Maxwell, Ana Lopes, and Martha J. Smith for their assistance. Helpful comments were provided by Ronald Clarke, Joseph Naus, Albert J. Reiss, Jr., Lawrence Sherman, Michael Tonry, Joel Garner, Lorraine Green, and Simcha Landau.

tions that are studied.[1] In contrast, correlational or quasi-experimental designs are always plagued by the possibility that some important confounding factor has not been taken into account by researchers. Randomized experiments thus have a distinct design advantage over nonexperimental studies. Nonetheless, the ethical and bureaucratic problems associated with random allocation of subjects in real-life criminal justice settings have generally led criminologists to other less controversial and more easily developed research methods.

Support for experimental methods in crime and justice has been growing over the last decade (e.g., see Farrington, Ohlin, and Wilson 1986) as has the number of important experimental studies (Garner and Visher 1988). Interest in experimentation, however, has been accompanied by a concern with the adequacy of experimental methods in criminal justice. Petersilia, for example, argues that little attention has been paid to the special difficulties of designing and managing field experiments in the justice system, or the potential strategies that might be used to overcome such problems (Petersilia 1989; see also Dennis 1988; Weisburd and Garner 1992). That most experimental studies in criminal justice have not led to statistically significant research findings adds support to such concerns (e.g., see Farrington 1983; Weisburd, Sherman, and Petrosino 1990), though the link between experimental design and study outcomes has not been explicitly tested. In this essay we examine this question in the context of a review of experimental studies in criminal justice sanctions conducted by Weisburd, Sherman, and Petrosino (1990). Focusing on the problem of statistical power, we challenge traditional assumptions about the relationship between research design and experimental results.

Statistical power provides the most direct measure of whether a study has been designed to allow a fair test of its research hypothesis. When a study is underpowered it is unlikely to yield a statistically significant result even when a relatively large program or intervention effect is found. For example, in the Kansas City Preventive Patrol Experiment (Kelling et al. 1974) inadequate statistical power biased the study toward the null hypothesis of no difference between the experimental and control conditions (see Feinberg, Larntz, and Reiss 1976). Had a more powerful study design been used, the study's major finding—that preventive patrol does not affect crime—might have

---

[1] In criminal justice experiments there is seldom a group that receives no treatment. More commonly, as is illustrated later, offenders are given different types of treatments—for example, intensive versus traditional probation.

been reversed for specific offenses (Sherman and Weisburd 1992). In the Kansas City experiment, as in much empirical study in the social sciences (see Chase and Chase 1976; Orme and Tolman 1986), research designs employed by investigators often make it very difficult for a study to obtain statistical support for the research hypothesis. In lay terms, such studies may be seen as "designed for failure," not because of inadequacies in the theories or programs evaluated, but because of the methods employed by investigators.

It is commonly assumed that increasing the size of a sample provides the most straightforward method for increasing the statistical power of a research design and thus avoiding the possibility that an investigation is biased toward a finding of no difference or no effect (e.g., see Kraemer and Thiemann 1987; Kolata 1990). Larger studies, all else being equal, are more powerful than smaller ones, which naturally leads researchers to the conclusion that bigger is better when it comes to experimental research. Our review of criminal justice experiments in sanctions suggests a much more cautious conclusion for researchers that takes into account the special difficulties that larger investigations present to those who have to manage, implement, and evaluate them.

The design benefits of larger studies are often offset by the implementation and management difficulties they present. Using sample estimates as a guide, the very largest investigations are no more powerful than the very smallest. Indeed, we find little relationship in practice between sample size and statistical power. While this conclusion is very much at odds with common assumptions in experimental research, it is consistent with our knowledge of the challenges that experimenters face in developing large-scale projects. In studies with larger samples it is often much more difficult to ensure that treatments are delivered consistently or effectively. Such studies are also more likely to include a wider diversity of subjects than are smaller investigations. Accordingly, all else is not equal in larger and smaller studies. Problems of implementation and the heterogeneity of larger studies make such investigations less likely to yield strong and consistent effects. Together they serve to constrain the design benefits that should derive from larger samples.

We begin our discussion of design sensitivity in randomized criminal justice studies with a general introduction to statistical power in Section I. Section II presents a brief description of the experimental studies examined, and Section III looks at general methodological characteristics of those experiments. In Section IV we examine the relationship between sample size and the actual outcomes of experiments. Our finding in that section, that larger studies should lead to more powerful research designs but do not, is discussed in Section V in terms of various components of the design and management of field experiments. In Section VI we suggest ways of overcoming the weaknesses of large sample designs and present some concluding comments on the implications of our findings for future experimental research.

## I. Statistical Power

There are two types of errors that can be made when deciding whether to reject or accept the null hypothesis (the hypothesis that an intervention will have no effect, or "null effect") in an empirical study. The most commonly discussed is type I error, which assesses the likelihood of falsely rejecting the null hypothesis based on findings in a sample when there is no difference between the groups under study in the population. This error is what is referred to when reporting the statistical significance of a study. Type II error, which is the central feature of statistical power, takes account of precisely the opposite type of risk. Its concern is with the possibility of falsely accepting the null hypothesis when there is a difference in the population characteristics of the groups examined.

In contrast to statistical significance—which identifies for the researcher the risk of stating that factors are related when they are not— statistical power provides an estimate of how often one would fail to identify a relationship that in fact existed. In statistical terms, power is defined as "1 − type II error," or one minus the probability of accepting the null hypothesis when it is false. Type II error occurs in an experiment when the researcher finds no difference in outcomes between treatment and control groups studied, but such differences do exist in the population from which they are drawn. Its relationship to the proposition that many experiments are designed for failure is straightforward. If examined at the outset, statistical power can identify when a research enterprise is likely to fail to provide support for the existence of an effect that is present in the population.

The importance of statistical power is often not fully understood by researchers, who are generally much more concerned with the concept of statistical significance. While little, if any, attention is paid to statistical power in the design of criminal justice studies (Brown 1989), researchers carefully set significance levels at the outset of an experiment in order to avoid accusations of bias later on. It has become virtually impossible to present research findings without attention to the statistical significance of research results, and norms concerning significance criteria are strongly established. Generally, a .05 level of significance is set. In other words, it is assumed that taking a risk of rejecting the null hypothesis five in 100 times, when it is in reality correct, is acceptable. Such clear standards for significance thresholds have allowed researchers to guard against the problem of biasing results to the research hypothesis.[2]

The notion that researchers may be biasing results against the research hypothesis (or for a finding of "no effect") has appeared less troubling to criminal justice scholars. Especially in experimental studies, which are often developed to test the effectiveness of expensive government interventions, the possibility that a study would be designed in a way that made it difficult to identify program success has appeared unlikely. Nonetheless, evidence from primarily nonexperimental criminological research (Brown 1989) suggests that criminal justice studies are often severely underpowered. This means that research is often designed in such a way that even if the effect the researcher posits is present in the population it is unlikely to be detected in the sample under study.

At this point it may be useful if we discuss a concrete example. Suppose a researcher wanted to examine the effects of methadone treatment on the six-month recidivism rate of drug addicts. Following the experimental method, addicts would be randomly allocated into control and treatment groups. The statistical power of this experiment is the probability that the statistical test employed would lead to a significant finding. Clearly, the researcher would not want to design a study that would make it highly unlikely to establish a relationship between methadone treatment and reduced recidivism if one existed. But, importantly, if a test is not statistically powerful, then the risk of such an error (a type II error) is very high. How then can one design a powerful study? More simply, what are the components that make up statistical power?

In understanding the factors that contribute to the power of an experimental study, four matters warrant consideration and are discussed

---

[2] When significance thresholds that make it easier to reject the null hypothesis (e.g., $p < .10$) are used, the researcher is generally expected to carefully explain his or her departure from established convention.

below.[3] First is the significance criterion employed in a statistical test. This is the threshold for rejection of the null hypothesis that an investigator sets at the outset of an experiment. Second is directionality, or the choice between employing a "one-tailed" or "two-tailed" test of significance. The third component of statistical power is what statisticians define as "effect size." Finally, and most commonly associated with the power of an experimental study, is the size of the sample examined by an investigator.

Clearly, the simplest way to decrease the likelihood of failing to reject the null hypothesis is to adjust the test statistic used as a threshold for statistical significance. One way to do this is to change the risk of type I error (the likelihood of rejecting the null hypothesis when it is in fact true) employed in an experiment. Because statistical power and statistical significance are directly related, when a less stringent level of significance is chosen (e.g., .10 as opposed to .05) it makes it easier to reject the null hypothesis and achieve statistical significance, and thus the experiment becomes more powerful. While this method for increasing statistical power is direct, it is usually not a practical suggestion since, as already discussed, norms concerning levels of significance are fairly well established.

A more practical method for changing the value of the test statistic needed to reject the null hypothesis is to limit the direction of the research hypothesis. A "one-tailed test" provides greater power than a "two-tailed test" for the same reason that a less stringent level of significance provides more power than a more stringent one. By choosing a one-tailed test of significance the researcher reduces the value of the test statistic needed to reject the null hypothesis. This occurs because the critical region (the part of a sampling distribution that defines the area of rejection of the null hypothesis) is shifted to test only one of the two potential outcomes in an experiment. For example, in the methadone experiment discussed above, the researcher could rule out the possibility at the outset that treatment might backfire and increase drug use. While there are many cases in which a directional research hypothesis is appropriate, once a one-directional test is posited, a sur-

---

[3] Though not discussed at length in the following paragraphs, the type of statistical test (e.g., chi-square or analysis of variance) used in an experiment can also affect its statistical power. Some tests are more appropriate in particular situations and provide more powerful tests of research hypotheses. Nonetheless, the differences between the power of different tests (equally appropriate to the problem at hand) is usually relatively small.

prising finding in the opposite direction cannot be touted as a major result.[4]

"Effect size" measures the influence of the intervention that is being assessed by taking the ratio of the magnitude of the differences between treatment and control groups to the standard deviation of those differences (see Cohen 1988).[5] Effect, as it is discussed here, is thus dependent on the size of the impact of a treatment, taking into account how much individuals in the sample vary in the outcomes measured. Statistinians do not simply examine the observed differences between the groups because they want to standardize the effects found in an experiment. Such standardization brings into perspective the differences between the groups and allows comparison of the size of an effect between studies that use different types of measures.

The relationship between statistical power and effect size is a straightforward one. When an effect in a population is larger it is harder to miss in any particular sample. Since statistical power asks what the likelihood is of detecting a particular effect (i.e., achieving statistical significance) in a given sample, when effect size is larger the experiment is more powerful. Where effects are hypothesized to be relatively small, other aspects of design must be maximized in order to achieve an acceptable level of statistical power.

Effect size is generally seen as the characteristic of statistical power that is most difficult to manipulate. A test is ordinarily conducted in order to determine the influence of an intervention on subjects. In experimental field research the intervention itself is usually arrived at through a complex series of negotiations between researchers and practitioners. Though, as we discuss later, effect size can be manipulated in ways that do not adversely affect the theoretical or practical goals of an experiment, there has been relatively little consideration of effect size in efforts to increase the power of experimental designs.[6]

The final component of statistical power, and the one most often used to manipulate power in social science research, is sample size (Kraemer and Thiemann 1987). Larger samples, all else being equal, provide more stable and reliable results than do smaller samples. The

[4] This is a case where you cannot have your cake and eat it too. If the advantage of a one-tailed test is sought, the researcher must sacrifice any finding in a direction opposite to that originally predicted. To do otherwise brings into question the integrity of the researcher's statistical design.

[5] We say more about the computation of effect size coefficients in Section IV below.

[6] For an important exception, see Lipsey (1990).

statistical logic is not complex. Larger samples are more "trustworthy" than smaller ones. For example, one would not be surprised to get two or three heads in a row from tosses of an honest coin. However, if the coin produced only heads in a sample of twenty-five tosses, we would be much more suspicious. Getting 100 heads in 100 coin tosses would lead even the most trusting person to doubt the fairness of the coin. In this same sense, larger samples are more powerful since they are more likely to be able to identify an effect, if it exists in a population, than are smaller studies. Conversely, as Kraemer and Thiemann note, "the smaller the sample size the smaller the power" (1987, p. 27). Because sample size provides a method for increasing statistical power that is straightforward and does not involve manipulations in either the significance levels employed or the treatments administered, it has played a central role in power analyses in the social sciences.

Returning to the methadone example, the researcher would, as David Farrington has suggested, "assess the size of effect (e.g., percentage difference) that would have practical significance and then calculate the sample size that would be needed to obtain statistical significance with this size of effect" (1983, p. 286). Put differently, the researcher's central problem is to identify the sample size needed to provide a powerful experiment based on the significance criteria and the effect size hypothesized. At a minimum, it is generally recommended that a statistical test have a power level greater than .50—indicating that the test is more likely to show a significant result than not (e.g., see Gelber and Zelen 1985, p. 413). But it is generally accepted that the most powerful experiments seek a power level of .80 or above (e.g., see Cohen 1973; Gelber and Zelen 1985). Such experiments are, given the researcher's assumptions about significance and effect size, highly likely to evidence a significant finding. The problem for our methadone researcher, simply stated, is to collect enough cases to achieve this threshold of power.

This is the process generally followed in developing powerful research designs. It is on its face a way of ensuring that a particular study is not designed for failure. While it makes assumptions about significance and effect size, it is primarily reliant on sample size to achieve a desired level of statistical power. It is based on the assumption that all else being equal, larger samples provide for a more powerful research design. But as we discuss below, the simple assumption that effect size is fixed, staying basically constant across samples of different sizes, is a flawed assumption.

## II. The Sample: Experiments in Sanctions

Our analysis of experimental design is drawn from a review carried out by Weisburd, Sherman, and Petrosino (1990). They attempted to identify all randomized studies reported in English that were conducted in criminal justice settings and used coercive "treatment" or "control" conditions. Five specific criteria were used for inclusion of studies: (1) that individuals were used as the primary unit of analysis, (2) that those individuals were randomly allocated into multiple treatment groups or treatment and control groups,[7] (3) that at least one outcome variable (whether self-report or drawn from a criminal justice agency) measured crime-related activities, (4) that the intervention or treatment (or the control condition) be coercively applied by a criminal justice agency in response to or in anticipation of a criminal act, and (5) that there be a minimum of fifteen cases included in at least two of the groups examined.[8] Weisburd, Sherman, and Petrosino identified seventy-six experiments that fit their criteria after a search of both computerized and noncomputerized criminal justice and general social science bibliographic indexes (see the Appendix).[9] Once identified,

[7] In seven cases, studies were included that randomized according to alternative allocation schedules. For example, in the Denver Drunk Driving Experiment (Ross and Blumenthal 1974, 1975) investigators allocated subjects based on alternative months. In the Hamilton Juvenile Services Project Experiment (Byles and Maurice 1979) and the California Juvenile Behavior Modification and Transactional Analysis Experiment (Jesness et al. 1972; Jesness 1975), the investigators used an odd/even system for placing offenders in treatment and control groups. In the Police Foundation Shoplifting Arrest Experiment, investigators noted that offenders were "alternatively assigned to an arrest or release category" (Williams, Forst, and Hamilton 1987). Such allocation procedures are random in the sense that there were not systematic biases in the choice of subjects who would be placed in each of the allocation sequences. However, because such studies might be seen as violating components of a classical experimental design, we replicated our basic analyses without them. The results do not differ substantially from those reported here.

[8] Farrington, Ohlin, and Wilson (1986, p. 66) argue that a "randomized experiment can control for all extraneous variables . . . only if a reasonably large number of people (at least fifty) are assigned to each condition." We could find no statistical reason for using this particular threshold, and Farrington, Ohlin, and Wilson do not detail their thinking on this question. The relatively low threshold used by Weisburd, Sherman, and Petrosino (1990) reflects their desire to include as broad a sample as possible.

[9] The search for studies began with a review of Farrington (1983) and Farrington, Ohlin, and Wilson (1986). From the references and studies included there, additional references and studies were reviewed, including bibliographies, qualitative works on the topic of randomized field experiments, and elaborations of studies already included in the sample. A search of the *Criminal Justice Abstracts* data base was also conducted. At the same time, additional narrative review articles on experimentation, deterrence, rehabilitation, sentencing, and corrections were examined. A search of the National Criminal Justice Reference System was completed in June 1989 for 1973–88 using the following key words: (a) randomization, (b) controlled study, (c) random assignment, (d) randomly assigned, (e) random allocation, (f) field experiment, (g) randomized experi-

each experiment was described in a registry and included in a computerized data base that detailed specifics of subjects, sanctions, methods, and outcomes.

Some mention should be made at the outset of the limitations created by identifying a sample of experiments through published studies and reports. A sample of what is reported is not the same as the universe of all studies. We might expect, for example, that studies that show a significant effect for criminal justice interventions would be more likely to be disseminated and published than studies showing no effect. Accordingly, there may be a bias to "successes" in this review as in others (see Coleman 1989). Studies conducted in criminal justice settings by agency researchers, as compared with studies supervised by university researchers, are also more likely to escape inclusion in a review of published materials. No doubt there are other biases that relate to the dissemination of research findings. Nevertheless, we do not want to over-emphasize such limitations. Most of the studies found did not report any statistically significant results, and many were conducted without any substantial university (or research institute) involvement.[10]

The criteria employed by Weisburd, Sherman, and Petrosino cast a fairly wide net for the identification of experimental criminal justice studies. There is, for example, tremendous diversity in the sanctions evaluated by researchers. While such penalties as probation, parole, and imprisonment occur most often in the studies examined, there are also studies evaluating police interventions, such as arrests (e.g., Sherman and Berk 1984a; Williams, Forst, and Hamilton 1987); prison tours, like the Scared Straight experiment in New Jersey (Finckenauer 1982); and restitution (e.g., Schneider and Schneider 1983; Schneider 1986).

Most often the experiments tested the influence of alternative criminal justice sanctions or the application of differing dosages of a particular sanction. For example, Ross and Blumenthal (1974, 1975) randomly assigned drunk drivers to three groups: a group that received a fine, one that received regular probation, or one that received therapeutic probation. In the Sacramento 601 Diversion Project (Baron, Feeney, and Thornton 1972, 1973), one of thirteen diversion studies in the review, juvenile delinquents were randomly assigned to an experimen-

---

ment, and (b) controlled trial. Almost 70 percent of the experiments were reported in scholarly journals or books. Twenty-eight percent were discussed in government publications, and 3 percent were identified only in nongovernmental research reports.

[10] In seven out of ten studies no significant differences were found between groups included in the experiment. Thirty-seven of the experiments were conducted without major support from a university or research institute.

tal group receiving family and individual counseling or to a control condition that went before the juvenile court. A number of parole studies varied the intensity of caseloads or supervision services. This was the case, for example, in the California Special Intensive Parole Experiment (Reimer and Warren 1957) conducted in the early 1950s. In one unusual probation study, Illinois parolees were randomly assigned to regular probation supervision or probation supervision carried out by volunteer lawyers (Berman 1975, 1978).

There are relatively few experiments where the experimental or control group was able to avoid criminal justice intervention altogether, though some of these are particularly well known.[11] For example, in the Minneapolis Domestic Violence Experiment (Sherman and Berk 1984*a*, 1984*b;* Berk and Sherman 1985, 1988) suspects were randomly allocated either to an arrest group, or to a group that received discretionary mediation, or to one in which suspects were ordered to stay away from home for eight hours. In the Police Foundation Shoplifting Arrest Experiment (Glick, Hamilton, and Forst 1986; Sherman and Gartin 1986; Williams, Forst, and Hamilton 1987) those in the experimental group were arrested after being identified as shoplifters. Members of the control group were released. While a few prison experiments contrasted continued incarceration with some type of work release or halfway house supervision (e.g., Lamb and Goertzel 1974*a*, 1974*b*), only one contrasted imprisonment with release. In the California Reduced Prison Sentence Experiment (Berecochea, Jaman, and Jones 1973; Berecochea and Jaman 1981), inmates were randomly assigned to six-month early release or a group that finished out their full sentences.

Eight of the studies tested the effects of group assignment to different institutional "wards," "regimes," or "communities." For example, in the Fricot Ranch Experiment (Jesness 1965, 1971*a*), male delinquents were randomly assigned to an experimental twenty-bed dormitory or to a more traditional fifty-bed unit. In the English Borstal Allocation Experiment (Williams 1970, 1975) youths were assigned to three types of borstal institutions: one that emphasized therapeutic treatment, one that included group counseling, or one that emphasized hard work and paternalistic control.

More than a quarter of the experiments involved treatments that are added onto traditional criminal justice sanctions, often in the context

---

[11] It could be argued that the diversion experiments did this as well. But when offenders were diverted from traditional criminal justice processing they usually received a fairly intrusive regimen of counseling or supervision.

of a prison or jail stay. Many of these studies would not have been seen by the original investigators as sanctioning experiments but rather as attempts at arriving at effective rehabilitative treatments. For example, in the Copenhagen Short Term Offender Experiment (Berntsen and Christiansen 1965), adult male prisoners were randomly assigned to an experimental group receiving psychological examination, interviews with social workers, or some form of individualized treatment geared toward resocialization. Members of the control group received services available through routine custody. In the California Juvenile Probation and Group Counseling Experiment (Adams 1965), juvenile male probationers were randomly assigned to an experimental group that received counseling sessions each week over six months or a control group that received normal probation services. Such experiments were included by Weisburd, Sherman, and Petrosino when inmates were coerced into participating. In cases where participation in the experiment was voluntary, the study was excluded (e.g., see Annis 1979).

The experiments reviewed included a substantial degree of diversity in the types of offenders examined. Nonetheless, most of the studies had predominantly male samples, and a majority of the subjects in most of the experiments were white. Half of the studies reviewed were conducted only with juveniles and most included offenders prosecuted for relatively minor offenses. Indeed, a number of the experiments specifically excluded high-risk offenders. Though, as already discussed, there are difficulties in making inferences from a sample of published materials, we suspect that the controversy surrounding random allocation of criminal justice interventions makes it more difficult to include offenders convicted of serious crimes and perhaps easier to conduct studies with juveniles. Still, half the experiments included some adult offenders and a few randomly allocated persons convicted of more serious crimes.[12]

The sample includes experiments from eighteen states as well as the District of Columbia. Fifteen studies were conducted outside the United States, with eleven carried out in England. Perhaps it is not surprising, given the tradition of support for empirical research in California, that more than 40 percent of the studies came from that state. Overall, most of the studies were carried out across institutions within a state or local jurisdiction. Nonetheless, two studies were car-

---

[12] For example, see the North Carolina Butner Correctional Facility Experiment (Love, Allgood, and Samples 1986) and the English Prison Intensive Social Work Experiment (Shaw 1974).

ried out across institutions in the federal justice system. Nineteen of the experiments were carried out in only one institution.

Weisburd, Sherman, and Petrosino thus identify a broad spectrum of experimental studies. Nonetheless, their inclusion criteria led them to exclude a number of better-known experiments in criminal justice. For example, the Kansas City Preventive Patrol Experiment (Kelling et al. 1974), which claimed to allocate varying amounts of police patrol randomly, was excluded because it involved random allocation of geographic areas (beats) rather than people.[13] Similarly, Tornudd's (1968) study of the effects of differential prosecutions on drunkenness randomly allocated towns rather than offenders.

The sanctioning criteria employed by Weisburd, Sherman, and Petrosino also led to the exclusion of a number of well-known studies. For example, the Living Insurance for Ex-Prisoners (LIFE) and the Transitional Aid Research Project (Tarp) experiments, both often thought of as criminal justice studies, were excluded from the sample (see Berk, Lenihan, and Rossi 1980; Rossi, Berk, and Lenihan 1980). These experiments randomly assigned subjects released from prison to groups that received weekly stipends or to a control group that did not. The study did not meet the requirements for inclusion in the sample because payments were not administered by criminal justice agents. The classic Cambridge-Somerville Youth Study (Powers and Witmer 1951) was excluded for similar reasons. It involved a social work response that could be refused by the subjects or their families.

The criterion that the experiment include crime-related outcome measures meant that studies like the Manhattan Bail Project (Ares, Rankin, and Sturz 1963), an often-cited experiment, also do not appear in this sample. There it was the success of pretrial recommendations for release or bail rather than the influence of sanctions on recidivism that was assessed. Similarly, Taylor's (1967) study of the effects of psychotherapy on Borstal girls was excluded because only psychological outcome measures were examined.

### III. Experiments in Sanctions: Methodological Characteristics

Comparatively few experimental studies in criminal justice provide very much detail about the methods employed in designing and carrying out research (Lipsey 1990). This is due, in part, to the norms of

[13] Had the Kansas City study met this criterion it might have been excluded as a result of questions raised concerning the randomization procedures used by investigators (see Feinberg, Larntz, and Reiss 1976; Farrington 1983).

report writing. There is just not the same demand for discussion of methodological details of research as there is for elaboration about outcomes or theoretical perspectives. Nonetheless, it is possible to examine in a general way a number of characteristics of the experimental research reviewed by Weisburd, Sherman, and Petrosino (1990). Before turning specifically to the relationship between effect size and sample size, we examine below a series of other design issues that are related to the power of experimental studies.

As described earlier, the size of a sample is directly related to the statistical power of an experiment. All else being equal, larger experiments are more powerful, and for this reason sample size has become the primary design characteristic manipulated by experimental researchers in order to increase the power of their research. Interestingly, while focusing on larger samples, few researchers have taken advantage of the fact that studies in which the sizes of the groups examined are relatively similar are more powerful than those in which the sizes of the groups are markedly different. While the benefit here is usually small, it can be large when the number of cases included in different groups examined in a study differ widely. And this is the case for a number of the experimental studies examined by Weisburd, Sherman, and Petrosino (1990).

The problem is illustrated by a formula for standardizing sample size in experimentation used by Cohen (1988, p. 42) in developing statistical power computations:

$$\frac{2(N_1)(N_2)}{N_1 + N_2}. \tag{1}$$

For example, if there is a total of 500 subjects in a study, but 400 in one group and 100 in another, the weighted or standardized sample size ($N$) per group used in power (and significance) calculations is only 160, while the $N$ for a two-group study equally divided between experimental and control groups is 250. Though the overall size of both studies is the same, the design of the latter is more powerful.

Often it is impossible to identify why the sizes of experimental and control groups are unequal.[14] We suspect that the reason is usually linked to randomization itself. Many studies randomly allocated subjects in ways that limited their control over the number of individuals

[14] It should be noted that four in ten of the studies reviewed did not describe how randomization was carried out.

TABLE 1

Statistical Power under Assumptions of Small, Moderate,
and Large Effect Size

| Standardized Sample Size | $N^*$ | Assumed Effect Size | | |
|---|---|---|---|---|
| | | Small | Moderate | Large |
| 15–50 | 12 | .12 | .49 | .82 |
| 51–100 | 25 | .26 | .87 | .99 |
| 101–200 | 21 | .37 | .98 | .99 |
| 201–400 | 5 | .60 | .99 | .99 |
| Over 400 | 11 | .91 | .99 | .99 |

*See note 25.

that fell in each group. For example, in the Sacramento Juvenile 601 Diversion Experiment (Baron, Feeney, and Thornton 1972, 1973), offenders were allocated to treatment and control groups based on randomly chosen days. Five of the experiments used a toss of a coin or a die to randomly allocate subjects. In eighteen of the forty-four experiments that described randomization procedures, researchers reported the use of random numbers tables. Though one might expect relatively equal groups using this technique, this was not always true.

Table 1 illustrates the direct relationship between statistical power and sample size. The experiments are divided into five categories based on the standardized number of cases per group in each study: "15–50," "51–100," "101–200," "201–400," and "over 400." Across the table are the average power coefficients for the experiments in each group given assumptions of "small," "moderate," and "large" effects (see Cohen 1988).[15]

Looking at table 1 it is clear that there is substantial diversity in the number of cases found in the samples examined by Weisburd, Sherman, and Petrosino (1990). For example, twelve of the studies include fifty or fewer standardized cases per group, and eleven include more than 400 standardized cases per group. As is to be expected, as the average sample size gets larger, the power levels associated with each

[15] Cohen's estimates are commonly used, but like other conventions are fairly arbitrary. As he notes in his widely cited text on statistical power: "Although arbitrary, the proposed conventions will be found to be reasonable by reasonable people. An effort was made in selecting these operational criteria to use levels of ES (effect size) that accord with a subjective average of effect sizes such as are encountered in behavioral science" (1988, p. 13).

TABLE 2

Statistical Power in Various Fields (under Assumptions of Small,
Moderate, and Large Effect Size)

| | Effect Size | | |
|---|---|---|---|
| Field | Small | Moderate | Large |
| Criminal justice experiments in sanctions (Weisburd, Sherman, and Petrosino 1990) | .39 | .86 | .96 |
| Gerontology (Levernson 1980) | .37 | .88 | .96 |
| Social work (Orme and Combs-Orme 1986) | .35 | .76 | .91 |
| Applied psychology research (Chase and Chase 1976) | .25 | .67 | .86 |
| Abnormal and social psychology (Sedlmeier and Gigerenzer 1989) | .21 | .50 | .84 |
| Education, general (Brewer and Owen 1973) | .28 | .79 | .91 |
| Speech pathology (Kroll and Chase 1975) | .16 | .44 | .73 |

hypothesized effect size also increase. For the smallest experiments, a very large effect would be needed for the researcher to be confident of identifying a statistically significant outcome. For the very largest experiments, however, even a small effect in the population would be very likely (power > .90) to lead to a statistically significant finding.

The experiments overall do not support the notion that randomized criminal justice studies are designed for failure, at least in terms of the number of cases examined by investigators. On average, experiments we examine allow a very high likelihood of detecting a moderate effect and are almost certain to detect a large effect (see table 2). While the power level achieved for a small effect is less than .40, here criminal justice experiments in sanctions are not very much different from research in other social sciences. When we compare experiments in sanctions with other reviews of statistical power in other disciplines, we find that criminal justice experiments are, on average, using these standardized criteria, fairly powerful (see table 2). In most areas where power has been assessed, studies have not been designed for detection of small effects, and in this regard criminal justice experiments in sanctions are more powerful than research in areas such as social work, applied and abnormal psychology, education, and speech pathology.

When experimenters are unable to ensure the integrity of the randomization process, the power of experimental research is also affected. Breakdowns in randomization bring into question the computed significance levels reported by investigators. Such levels are dependent on certain assumptions, fair randomization being one of them. While slight violations of this assumption, like others, are unlikely to bias study results seriously, in a number of cases randomization breakdowns were serious. For example, in the Denver Drunk Driving Sentencing Experiment (Ross and Blumenthal 1974, 1975), judges circumvented the randomization process in more than half the cases, mostly in response to defense attorney pleas to have their clients receive fines rather than the probation conditions. In sixteen of the studies reviewed by Weisburd, Sherman, and Petrosino (1990), randomization failures were reported by investigators.[16]

"Randomization overrides," where investigators allow practitioners to disregard randomization criteria because of institutional or public safety considerations, present similar problems, though when they are planned investigators can more carefully measure their influence on experimental results. For example, in the Minneapolis Domestic Violence Experiment (Sherman and Berk 1984a, 1984b, 1985; Berk and Sherman 1985, 1988), overrides were allowed if the offender attempted to assault the police, the victim demanded an arrest, a restraining order was violated, or offenders would not leave the premises when ordered to do so by the police. Though such overrides occurred in 18 percent of the cases, the investigators had carefully documented overrides and were able to analyze their occurrence and their influence on the experimental results. In eleven of the experiments, researchers reported that practitioners were allowed to override the randomization process.[17]

Treatment breakdowns have a direct impact on the statistical outcomes of experiments. When the investigator cannot ensure that a "treatment" or "control" condition has been administered, or that it has been administered in the dosage planned, the statistical power of a study is usually reduced.[18] This happens because the "effect" of an

[16] We suspect that such failures are underreported in published studies.

[17] A somewhat similar problem is evidenced in eight studies in which offenders were allowed to opt out of the less punitive sanction condition. For example, in the Ellsworth House Study (Lamb and Goertzel 1974a, 1974b), offenders could choose to remain in prison rather than be assigned to a halfway house. Breakdowns in assignment, like those reported in the Ellsworth House Experiment, were generally small because offenders were likely to want to take advantage of the more lenient randomized condition.

[18] Treatment integrity is usually discussed only in terms of the experimental condition. However, as noted earlier, most criminal justice studies compare alternative types of sanctions, and thus "control" groups may be better described as "comparison" groups. In such cases, there is also a "treatment" (often traditional criminal justice processing) that must be monitored and maintained. In the case of experiments with a more traditional "control" group, it is still the case that the experimenter must maintain the integrity of the "no sanction" condition.

experiment is directly related to the differences in treatment found between the experimental and control conditions. For example, in the California Special Intensive Parole Experiment (Reimer and Warren 1957), parole officers in the control group increased their contacts with parolees and thus simulated the treatments found in the experimental condition. Reimer and Warren (1957) offer this as one potential explanation for the small and insignificant differences found between the treatment and control groups studied in the second year of their study. Similarly, in the California Parole Research Project Experiment (Johnson 1962a, 1962b) control subjects often received more contact with their officers than did those in the experimental group, a factor that Johnson argues led to a finding of no difference between the experimental and control groups. In this case a nonexperimental reanalysis of the study showed that when supervision was classified by actual intensity (rather than experimental allocation), a strong relationship existed between parole success and increased contact (Johnson 1962b).

## IV. Statistical Power and Sample Size: A Reevaluation of Common Assumptions

Sample size is generally viewed as the most straightforward method for affecting the power of experiments.[19] All else being equal, the power of a study grows with each increment in the number of cases included. This fact was illustrated in table 1, where we estimated the expected power of the Weisburd, Sherman, and Petrosino (1990) experiments under assumptions of small, moderate, and large "effects." If we assumed a small effect, the average power of the studies grew from .12 for those with fifty or fewer standardized cases per group to over .90 for those with over four hundred cases. While the expected design benefits of larger samples decrease as assumed effect size grows (see Lipsey 1990), we still found an average difference of .50 in estimated power for the largest and smallest experiments under assumptions of moderate effects and a .17 difference if large effects were assumed.

These results help explain why researchers concerned with statistical power try to gather as many cases for inclusion in their samples as possible. In criminological research, which often tackles very serious public policy problems that are very difficult to affect, the benefits of

---

[19] Though Lipsey argues that affecting change in "effect size" is more cost-effective (1990, p. 169).

larger samples are particularly attractive. For example, it might not be expected that a particular prison program would have a very large influence on subsequent violence by offenders. Nonetheless, even if a relatively small group were deterred from committing future murders or rapes, the benefits for the community would be great. It is precisely in such studies, where researchers seek to design a test sensitive to even relatively small changes, that sample size has its largest influence on statistical power.

But the benefits associated with larger samples are based on the assumption that there is little relationship between the number of cases in a study and the effect of treatments on the subjects examined.[20] If, for example, we assumed that the effect of a study declined the larger it became, the gain in statistical power associated with larger samples would be offset by the smaller effect coefficients found in such studies. Given the reliance on sample size as a means of increasing statistical power, we set out to examine this relationship directly.[21]

[20] It also assumes that there is little relationship between sample size and significance criteria on the type of statistical tests employed. But in the case of these characteristics of power, an assumption of no relationship is not troublesome. The size of a study does not alter the substance of significance criteria, nor does it influence the basic characteristics of a statistical test—except to the extent that it affects the choices made by researchers.

[21] This can be illustrated by turning to measures of statistical significance and their relationship to the standardized effect coefficients and sample size estimates used in statistical power. Generally, significance tests in experimental research are derived by taking the ratio of the size of the differences between an experimental and control group to the standard error associated with those differences:

$$\frac{\text{size of difference}}{\text{standard error}}. \tag{2}$$

The size of the difference between the two samples is simply the magnitude of the difference in the dependent measures employed (usually means or percentages). The standard error associated with these estimates, the denominator of the equation, is a function of the pooled standard deviation of the outcomes observed and the number of cases included in the study. Taking a commonly used test, the $t$-test, we can see why larger studies are more powerful than smaller ones:

$$t = \frac{\overline{X}_1 - \overline{X}_2}{\hat{\sigma}\sqrt{\dfrac{N_1 + N_2}{N_1 N_2}}}. \tag{3}$$

As the number of cases grows, the standard error (the denominator of the $t$-test) will get smaller. This leads to a larger test statistic and thus a higher likelihood of rejecting the null hypothesis and achieving a statistically significant finding. The $t$-test also illustrates why tests with larger "effects" are, all else being equal, more powerful. In power analysis, effect size is generally computed by taking the ratio of the difference between sample estimates to the standard deviation of those estimates (see Cohen 1988; Lipsey 1990). In eq. (3), effect size would be expressed as $d$ (Cohen 1988, p. 20), which includes the ratio of the difference of means to the pooled within-group standard deviation of

Our primary empirical problem was to develop estimates of effect size for each of the experiments examined. We were aided in this process by the fact that many of the experiments included only one outcome measure, usually assessed at only one time period. Nonetheless, about six in ten of the studies reviewed included either multiple outcome measures or multiple follow-up periods or both. Our problem was to decide which of these estimates, or which combination of them, to use for identifying the "observed" effect size for each particular study.

One solution used by others who have reviewed effect size across studies (e.g., Chase and Chase 1976; Levernson 1980) is to take the mean of all of the outcome measures included by investigators. This solution has the benefit of not focusing on a "deviant" effect in a study. Because we wanted some degree of consistency across the experiments reviewed, we developed an "average effect size" (AES) measure by taking the mean of all the effect coefficients at the follow-up period closest to one year.[22] While "average effect size" provides one overall view of the influence of the studies on their subjects, it does not take into account that investigators often thought of their studies as tests of a series of research hypotheses, often linked to different outcome measures. In order to allow some sensitivity to this problem we developed an additional measure—maximum effect size (MES)—that provides an upper range of effect for the experiments.[23] "Maximum effect size" identifies the largest effect evidenced in each study for the twelve-month (or closest) follow-up period.[24]

Assessing effect size from these measures, our first conclusion relates not to the relationship between sample size and effect size but to the magnitude of the effects found in criminal justice experiments con-

---

those means (i.e., $\overline{X}_1 - \overline{X}_2/\hat{\sigma}$). As $d$ grows in size—either through a growth in the absolute difference in the means $(\overline{X}_1 - \overline{X}_2)$ or a decline in the amount of variability of the estimates $(\hat{\sigma})$—the $t$-statistic gets larger, and rejection of the null hypothesis is more likely. Returning to our earlier concern, if effect size were to get smaller as the number of cases in a study increased, then the benefits of a larger sample might be offset.

[22] Thirty-six of the studies used a one-year follow-up period; most of the others had a follow-up period somewhere between six and eighteen months. For experiments with more than one outcome measure, we took the mean of the effect size for each outcome measure. In experiments where the subjects were divided into more than two groups, the effect size was calculated by taking the difference between each of the groups and then calculating the mean of those differences.

[23] To calculate "maximum effect size" we also took the follow-up period closest to twelve months for each experiment. For experiments with more than one outcome measure, we took the measure with the largest effect size. If an experiment had only one outcome measure, the effect size for that measure was used.

[24] We also developed another measure that examines the largest standardized effect size for any outcome measure at any follow-up period. The results using this measure were similar to those reported in tables 3 and 4.

## TABLE 3

### Effect Size and Sample Size

| Average | | | | Maximum | | | |
|---|---|---|---|---|---|---|---|
| Effect Size | N | Percent | Mean Standard N | Effect Size | N | Percent | Mean Standard N |
| .00–.20 | 45 | 61 | 235 | .00–0.20 | 37 | 50 | 253 |
| .21–.40 | 20 | 27 | 118 | .21–.40 | 22 | 30 | 136 |
| .41–.60 | 3 | 4 | 37 | .41–.60 | 5 | 7 | 56 |
| .61–.80 | 5 | 7 | 51 | .61–.80 | 9 | 12 | 66 |
| .81–1.00 | 1 | 1 | 32 | .81–1.00 | 1 | 1 | 32 |

cerned with sanctions (see table 3). Of the seventy-four studies in which effect size estimates could be computed, less than four in ten have standardized effects above .20 using our average effect size measure.[25] Even using the less conservative maximum effect size estimates, only half of the studies have effects of this magnitude. This means that most of the studies did not achieve what is generally defined as the threshold for a small effect (see Cohen 1988). Only one experiment evidences what Cohen describes as a large effect (a standardized effect coefficient above .80) using either measure of effect size.

Following these results, we might conclude that adjustments in sample size are likely to have a large yield in criminal justice studies. As we noted earlier, it is precisely in the case where the investigator desires to detect small effects that the influence of the number of cases on statistical power is greatest. But this conclusion does not seem to hold when we turn to the relationship between sample size and effect size. If we look at the standardized number of cases (per group) for studies that fall in each of the effect size categories reviewed in table 3, we can see that there is a generally inverse relationship between sample size and effect size.[26] Indeed, the mean number of cases per group for the studies with the largest effects (.61–1.00) is between one-quarter and one-fifth of that for the studies with the smallest effects (0–.20), whether we use the maximum or average effect size measures. Only in the case of the comparison between studies with effects of .41–.60 and .61–.80 does the number of standardized cases increase, and here the change is relatively small.

[25] In two of the seventy-six cases insufficient information was provided by investigators to develop effect size coefficients. These cases are also excluded from analyses presented in tables 1 and 2.

[26] In experiments with more than one outcome measure, the standardized N was calculated by taking the mean of the standardized N's for each outcome measure.

## TABLE 4

### Average Effect Size and Statistical Power (by Sample Size)

| Standardized Sample Size | N | Mean Effect | Mean Power* |
|---|---|---|---|
| 15–50 | 12 | .42 | .46 |
| 51–100 | 25 | .23 | .29 |
| 101–200 | 21 | .17 | .33 |
| 201–400 | 5 | .18 | .45 |
| Over 400 | 11 | .08 | .35 |

\* Power estimates are derived by taking the mean power of all outcome measures examined.

What this means substantively is that estimates of statistical power arrived at by manipulating sample size, while assuming a constant effect size, are misleading. Although there is clearly a gain to be had from increasing the size of a sample, the negative relationship between sample size and effect size offsets, at least in part, the design benefits of increasing the number of cases studied.[27] How much of a loss is illustrated in table 4. Here we calculate the statistical power of the experiments based on average effect size coefficients evidenced in the samples studied.[28]

Quite surprisingly, given the general trend of using sample size as

[27] One anonymous reviewer suggested that this finding might result from investigators who "stop when they are winning." In other words, if a large and significant effect is achieved with a small number of subjects the investigator would stop the experiment and publish the results. If he or she gets a weak effect the experiment would be continued until the effect either is found to be significant or is viewed as unlikely to ever reach that threshold. Our own reading of the cases indicates that investigators usually define the randomization process at the outset of experiment and seldom analyze results early enough to substantively alter the basic design of a study. A second alternative explanation for these findings is that smaller studies are much less likely to be published if they do not achieve a significant result. While we cannot assess this speculation directly, we suspect that the rarity of experimental research in criminal justice leads to more unsuccessful studies being reported than is the case with nonexperimental designs. Among the larger studies this is particularly likely, and our basic finding holds for the largest sample size groupings. It is important to note that in some studies a finding of no difference (e.g., between prison and early release) would be taken by investigators as a program "success" since it indicates that a less expensive and less intrusive criminal justice intervention is as effective as the more punitive and costly sanction condition.

[28] While statistical power relates to the population characteristics of a study, we use these measures as a "best guess" of the true parameters under the assumptions made by investigators.

a method to increase statistical power, we do not find that larger studies have a power advantage. Indeed, the largest studies (those with more than 400 standardized cases per group) are less powerful under these assumptions than the smallest ones. They are also less powerful than studies with between 201 and 400 standardized cases and only marginally more powerful than those with 51–200 standardized cases per group. There is a slight increase in power between the second (51–100) and third (101–200) sample size categories and an increase in average power of .12 between the third and fourth (201–400) sample size groupings. However, the group that on average provides the most powerful investigations includes the smallest studies examined.

In the face of a result so at odds with conventional assumptions about statistical power, we were concerned that specific characteristics of our sample, rather than a more general process inherent to experimentation in criminal justice sanctions, might be responsible for our results. If, for example, a particular type of experimental research was more likely to include fewer subjects and such experiments were also more effective, this would explain in part our basic finding. Our efforts to examine this problem were hampered by the fact that the experiments varied so greatly. But we were able to look at the basic relationship between sample size and a series of specific characteristics that cut broadly across the studies. In the case of type of outcome measure (e.g., percent arrested or percent violating parole), type of investigator (practitioner vs. university researcher), type of sanction (e.g., parole or probation), and gender of subjects, we found little evidence that would lead us to challenge our conclusion that larger studies, regardless of their type, yielded generally smaller effects. However, we did find that the smallest studies were more likely to include only juvenile offenders or to involve treatments added onto conventional sanctions.[29]

Those experiments that were conducted primarily with juveniles are much more likely than others to fall into the smallest sample size categories (see table 5). Indeed, the larger the study, the less likely it is to involve primarily juvenile offenders. Nine of twelve of the studies including less than fifty standardized cases per group concentrated on

---

[29] We also found that studies with a six-month follow-up period or shorter were more likely to include fewer cases. We do not include this question in our discussion because the number of studies involved here is small (only eleven overall, with five in the fifteen to fifty sample size category) and makes a substantive analysis suspect. However, when we do examine the AES (average effect size) estimates across sample size categories for these eleven experiments, we find a similar pattern to that evidenced in our overall analysis.

## TABLE 5
### Average Effect Size for Experiments Including Only Juveniles

| Standardized Sample Size | N | Mean Effect |
|---|---|---|
| 15–50 | 9 | .52 |
| 51–100 | 16 | .22 |
| 101–200 | 7 | .21 |
| 201–400 | 2 | .28 |
| Over 400 | 3 | .09 |

these younger subjects. This was true for only three of the eleven studies in the largest sample-size grouping. Nonetheless, when we examine the relationship between sample size and effect size within the experiments including only juveniles, our results are generally consistent with the earlier findings (see table 5).

Experiments that involve treatments added onto conventional sanctions (e.g., coercive group counseling programs in a prison) accounted for less than one in three of the studies reviewed by Weisburd, Sherman, and Petrosino (1990). But they make up half of the experiments in the smallest sample grouping and none in the two largest categories. Accordingly, it might be argued that our basic finding reflects the relationship between sample size and experiment type. While it is the case that treatment experiments overall have larger effects than other experiments we reviewed, the relationship of sample size and effect size for treatment experiments follows the general pattern of our results (see table 6). There is a very large drop in effect size between the smallest studies and those with 51–200 standardized cases.

## V. Why Larger Studies Are Not More Powerful
The simple assumption that statistical power can be increased merely by adding cases to a study is not supported by our data. The largest studies are not necessarily more powerful than smaller ones; indeed, using sample estimates as a guide, the very largest investigations are no more likely to lead to rejection of the null hypothesis than are the very smallest. This challenges conventional wisdom in experimental research (e.g., see Kolata 1990). Nonetheless, we believe this result is consistent with the experiences of those who have approached the very

TABLE 6

Average Effect Size for "Treatment"
Experiments

| Standardized Sample Size | N | Mean Effect |
|---|---|---|
| 15–50 | 6 | .59 |
| 51–100 | 11 | .19 |
| 101–200 | 4 | .18 |
| 201–400 | . . . | . . . |
| Over 400 | . . . | . . . |

difficult task of designing and implementing randomized experiments in the real world of criminal justice.

It is generally easier to keep track of 100 or 200 subjects than 800 or 1,000. Similarly, three or four administrators are easier to monitor than twenty-five or fifty. As the scale of experimental research grows, so do the difficulties of implementation and management. But, even when criminal justice researchers set out with an awareness of the potential problems that large field studies entail, they are often surprised by the special difficulties they encounter. For example, Joan Petersilia, in describing her experience as an evaluator of a large Bureau of Justice Assistance probation study, provides a good example of how even experienced researchers are likely to underestimate the complexities of large-scale experimental research:

The author anticipated that monitoring a field experiment of these dimensions would require tremendous effort. However, the extra burdens imposed by high turnover and loss of motivation among the projects' staff and administrators was not anticipated. Nor did we realize how difficult it would be to get adequate data from the sites, which were responsible for collecting and forwarding the data to RAND. [Petersilia 1989, p. 452]

That larger studies are more difficult to monitor and control than smaller ones has two important implications for the statistical power of experimental research in sanctions. First, the management and monitoring problems associated with larger studies often lead to treatments being administered less effectively or less consistently than contemplated. Second, the need to gather large numbers of cases for study often leads to a great deal of heterogeneity in the nature of the samples studied. Because these characteristics of larger studies influence the magnitude of differences between groups in an experiment (the numerator of the effect size coefficient) and the variability of those differences (the denominator of effect size), they also influence the statistical power of experimental studies.

Problems in administering treatments in larger studies are illustrated in a number of the experiments we examined. In some cases, treatment failures result from the difficulty of keeping track of a very large number of subjects. For example, in the California Reduced Prison Experiment (Berecochea, Jaman, and Jones 1973; Berecochea and Jaman 1981), which included more than one thousand inmates, the experimental subjects, who were supposed to serve longer prison terms, sometimes served less prison time than the control group. But the difficulties in managing large numbers of criminal justice practitioners also led to treatments not being administered in the dosages proposed by experimenters. In the Vera Institute Pretrial Adult Felony Offender Diversion Experiment (Baker and Sadd 1979, 1981; Baker and Rodriguez 1979), for example, almost 40 percent of the diversion group ($N = 410$) never received the experimental treatment.[30]

These cases illustrate how an inability to ensure the implementation of treatments can have an impact on the outcomes of experiments by minimizing the differences between the experiences of treatment and control group members. But breakdowns in treatment integrity may also affect the variability of outcome measures. In the Memphis Juvenile Diversion Experiment, for example, the principal investigators note that the 785 youths in the experimental group received somewhere between 11 percent and 140 percent of their projected treatments

[30] We believe that treatment failures are more likely to occur in larger studies, and, when they do occur, are likely to be more serious. Nonetheless, using evidence of any treatment breakdowns as described by investigators, we do not find a clear linear relationship between sample size and treatment failure. There is comparatively little difference between the smallest studies and the sample groupings ranging up to 400 standardized cases per group. Among studies that fall into these categories, treatment failures noted by investigators average between 15 and 20 percent. The largest studies have a somewhat higher rate of failure, about a third, though the absolute difference here in the number of cases that have treatment failures (as contrasted with the smallest studies) is not large. These results reflect not only difficulties in administering treatment but also the attention paid by investigators to reporting such failures. We suspect it is likely that the greater attention given to detail in the smaller studies also led to more careful identification and reporting of problems encountered.

(Whitaker and Severy 1984). Because different offenders received different treatments, we would expect that the overall effects of the study would vary tremendously from subject to subject. While heterogeneity in the administration of treatment is common in both large and small experiments, our readings of the cases suggest that such variability is likely to be much greater in larger studies.

Variability is also increased by the heterogeneity of subjects studied in larger experiments. In planning such investigations it is often necessary to establish very broad eligibility requirements in order to gain the number of cases that investigators desire. For example, in the California Special Intensive Parole Experiment (Reimer and Warren 1957) described earlier, some 80 percent of the prison population qualified for inclusion in the study.[31]

Many times investigators in larger studies are forced to relax eligibility requirements once the project is ongoing. In the English Intensive Probation Experiments (Folkard et al. 1974; Folkard, Smith, and Smith 1976), for example, the original design, which called for high-risk male probationers, was changed when researchers saw that they were unable to fulfill project quotas. In the RAND study described by Petersilia, overestimation of the number of eligible offenders also led the sites involved to relax eligibility requirements in the midst of the experiment. Indeed, Petersilia argues that it eventually became "unclear who was participating" (1989, p. 450).

The effects of this heterogeneity in the subjects examined on the statistical power of experiments is illustrated in two studies that analyzed subgroups of offenders separately after the original project design had failed to yield significant results. The Police Foundation Shoplifting Arrest Experiment (Williams, Forst, and Hamilton 1987) examined shoplifters six years of age and older. Looking at the entire sample, no significant deterrent effects of arrest were noted. But when subjects were categorized into those under seventeen years of age, and those seventeen years of age and older, significant results were found for the juvenile group. In the Memphis Juvenile Diversion Experiment (Severy and Whitaker 1982, 1984; Whitaker and Severy 1984; Whitaker, Severy, and Morton 1984), investigators also found no significant differences when the entire sample was examined. But within

---

[31] Interestingly, even though the eligibility requirements were so broad, in the second phase of this project it was necessary to include subjects who were not eligible in the first phase.

the experimental group those youths needing social adjustment or education assistance were more likely to have a successful experience when compared to those needing family or individual counseling.

Though in both these cases the statistical design of the experiments was violated by a post facto division of the experimental and control groups, they follow a developing consensus among criminologists that different types of offenders will respond differently to different types of sanctions (see Farrington, Ohlin, and Wilson 1986). Where an experiment includes a heterogeneous population, effects of sanctions on one subgroup of offenders may be hidden by a different effect on another, as appears to be the case, for example, in the Police Foundation Shoplifting Arrest Experiment. Where there is less systematic variation in the study, but still great diversity in the types of subjects included, the variability of the estimates gained will grow, again leading to a smaller effect coefficient and thus a less powerful study.

Our observations on the relationship between sample size and problems of implementing and monitoring experimental research are based on a relatively small group of studies. Nonetheless, they are consistent with findings that develop out of a very large review of correctional treatment programs conducted by Lipton, Martinson, and Wilks (1975). Although they did not look specifically at the relationship between sample size and the quality of the 231 studies they examined, they did rate the studies in terms of the strength of the overall research design and the success of investigators in carrying out the studies.[32] In a reanalysis of these data, Palmer found "a strong inverse relationship between both quality and strength [of the studies], on the one hand, and sample size, on the other" (1978, p. 160). Among the better designed and implemented studies ("A" studies), the average sample size was 459. Among lower-quality studies ("B" studies), the average sam-

[32] Studies were selected for inclusion in the survey on the basis of the following criteria: the study must represent an evaluation of a treatment method applied to criminal offenders; it must have been completed after January 1, 1945; it must include empirical data resulting from comparison of treatment and control groups; and these data must be measures of improvement in performance on some relevant dependent variables. Studies specifically excluded were after-only studies without comparison groups, prediction studies, studies that only describe and subjectively evaluate treatment programs, and clinical speculations about feasible treatment methods. Following assessment by a professional researcher, each study was reviewed by a committee and allocated to one of three categories: "A" studies, acceptable for the survey with no more than minimal research shortcomings; "B" studies, acceptable for the survey with research shortcomings that place reservations on interpretation of the findings; and "Other Studies." Under "Other Studies" were reports and articles excluded because two or more of a possible eleven conditions existed. See Lipton, Martinson, and Wilks (1975, pp. 6–7) for a list of these conditions.

ple size was 900. While Palmer relegated these findings to an appendix, they suggest to us that our observations concerning the difficulties of developing and managing larger studies are not limited to our sample of criminal justice experiments in sanctions.

## VI. Implications and Conclusions

Our examination of the statistical power of experiments in sanctions leads to an ironic conclusion about the relationship between experimental design and study outcomes. Had more attention been paid to statistical power in developing sanctioning studies in criminal justice, the power of the studies themselves would probably not have increased significantly. The naive assumption behind much power analysis, that sample size is unrelated to effect size, is not consistent with our findings. Investigators of larger studies are likely to encounter more serious problems in implementing treatments than smaller studies. They are often forced as well to draw more heterogeneous samples. Both these factors influence the outcomes of experiments, and thus the power advantages of larger samples are often offset.

Our results suggest that larger studies are not to be preferred over smaller investigations. Nonetheless, there are significant difficulties in generalizing from small and restricted samples, and the design advantages they seem to offer do not offset the power disadvantages inherent to studies of such a small size. Using sample estimates as a guide, we found that the very smallest studies examined were more powerful than the very largest. Yet such studies did not offer even an equal chance of finding a statistically significant difference between treatment and control groups. Just as the small effects of large investigations offset the advantages of increasing the number of cases examined, the small samples in smaller investigations offset the advantages gained from larger effects. The task accordingly is to focus not on smaller studies but rather on strategies that will allow researchers to increase sample size while maintaining the integrity of treatments and minimizing variability.

Petersilia (1989) provides one lesson in this regard from the RAND Intensive Supervision Demonstration Project. Experimenters cannot allow practitioners to control the implementation of important aspects of study design, even though this is often one way of conserving much-needed research funds. As is the case for many other large-scale investigations, economic and practical constraints forced RAND to rely on practitioners to carry out many research tasks that would have been more directly controlled by researchers had the investigation been smaller. For RAND these decisions did not turn out to be cost-effective in the long run. They created both greater variability in treatments and in the pool of offenders examined than had been proposed in the original project design (Petersilia and Turner 1990; Turner 1991). More generally, the RAND experience illustrates the importance of maintaining researcher control over each stage of an experiment's design and implementation.

One example of a method for monitoring the implementation of treatments when they are controlled by practitioners is provided by the Minneapolis Hot Spots Patrol Experiment (Sherman and Weisburd 1992). Sherman and Weisburd randomly allocated increased police patrol to fifty-five of 110 high-crime locations, called "hot spots." While the number of cases in that study was relatively small, the number of practitioners involved was very large. Indeed, the entire patrol force in Minneapolis was used in increasing the patrol dosage in the experimental locations. In trying to avoid a problem encountered in the earlier Kansas City Preventive Patrol Experiment (Kelling et al. 1974), in which there was some doubt as to whether the treatments were successfully administered, Sherman and Weisburd conducted 6,500 hours of random observations of the experimental and control sites. While the observations were intended primarily as a means of documenting dosage, they also were seen by investigators as a method for keeping practitioners "honest."

Variability in the larger studies we examined often developed from overestimation of the number of cases that fit the original eligibility requirements of investigators. This problem has become widely recognized in recent experimental research (see Petersilia 1989) and has led a number of investigators to conduct what have been termed "case flow" studies. In the National Institute of Justice's Domestic Violence Replication Program, for example, researchers in each of the five sites involved in the program conducted a careful analysis before the study began of the potential universe of cases available for randomization (Uchida 1991). This process allowed investigators to avoid midstream changes in eligibility requirements. More generally, case flow studies provide an effective method for preventing the "watering down" of the experimental pool in order to achieve quotas set in the original research design.

Even when following the original project design, investigators often include a great deal of diversity in the types of subjects examined. As we observed earlier, larger studies are likely to be more variable than smaller ones, which explains in part the reduction in effect size that is found in the largest investigations. Statisticians offer one solution to this problem—randomization within blocks (e.g., see Lipsey 1990)—that has generally been ignored by criminal justice researchers. Block designs, which randomly allocate subjects within groups, minimize the effects of variability in an experiment by making sure that like subjects will be compared one to another. A commonly used method randomly allocates subjects within pairs, for example by random allocation of twins in psychological studies. While randomization of matched pairs is unlikely to be practical in criminological field experiments, blocking within larger groups does provide an effective method for minimizing the effects of variability in a study. Sherman and Weisburd (1989), for example, randomly allocated police patrol within five independent blocks based on prior crime activity. While blocking demands more complex statistical analyses than traditional experimental designs, it provides a relatively inexpensive method for dealing with the diversity of subjects found in most large studies.

These examples provide some evidence of recent attempts to manage the design difficulties that are likely to be encountered in large experiments. But such efforts have not been joined systematically, nor linked directly to the issues we have raised. The nature of the problems criminal justice researchers examine demand that they design for relatively large studies. Our findings suggest that there will be few gains from increasing sample size until the design difficulties that larger samples pose are directly addressed. For the future, this demands much greater attention to problems of method and design in experimentation than has been evident to date. For the present, it suggests that commonly used approximations of statistical power that do not take into account the relationship between sample size and effect size provide a very misleading view of the design advantages of larger studies.

APPENDIX

Studies Selected by Weisburd, Sherman, and Petrosino (1990)

| Name of Experiment | Source of Experiment |
|---|---|
| California Crofton House Experiment | Kirby 1969 |
| California Early Parole Discharge Experiment | Jackson 1978, 1983 |

| | |
|---|---|
| California Ellsworth House Experiment | Lamb and Goertzel 1974*a*, 1974*b* |
| California Fremont Program Experiment | Seckel 1967 |
| California Group Counseling Prison Experiment | Kassebaum, Ward, and Wilner 1971 |
| California Juvenile Behavior Modification and Transactional Analysis Experiment | Jesness, DeRisi, McCormick, and Wedge 1972; Jesness 1975 |
| California Juvenile CTP Phase I Experiment—Sacramento/Stockton | Stark 1963; Warren 1967; Palmer 1971, 1974 |
| California Juvenile CTP Phase I Experiment—San Francisco | Stark 1963; Warren 1967; Palmer 1971, 1974 |
| California Juvenile Probation and Group Counseling Experiment | Adams 1965 |
| California Parole Research Project Experiment | Johnson 1962*a*, 1962*b* |
| California Parole Work Unit Experiment | Burkhart 1969 |
| California Paso Robles Experiment | Seckel 1965 |
| California Pico Experiment | Adams 1970 |
| California Preston School Typology Experiment | Jesness 1971*b* |
| California Reduced Prison Sentence Experiment | Berecochea, Jaman, and Jones 1973; Berecochea and Jaman 1981 |
| California Short-Term Psychiatric Treatment Experiment—Preston | Guttman 1963 |
| California Short-Term Psychiatric Treatment Experiment—Nelles | Guttman 1963 |
| California Special Intensive Parole Experiment: Phase I | Reimer and Warren 1957 |
| California Special Intensive Parole Experiment: Phase II | Reimer and Warren 1958 |
| California Summary Parole Experiment | Star 1978 |
| California Unofficial Probation Experiment | Venezia 1972 |
| California Youth Training Center Experiment | Seckel 1965 |
| Canadian I-Level Maturity Probation Experiment | Barkwell 1976 |
| Clark County (Washington) Status Offender Deinstitutionalization Experiment | Schneider 1980 |

Copenhagen Short-Term Offender
Experiment
Denver Drunk Driving Sentencing
Experiment
English Borstal Allocation Exper-
iment
English Intensive Probation Experi-
ment—Sheffield


English Intensive Probation Experiment—Dorset


English Intensive Probation Experiment—London


English Intensive Probation Experiment—Staffordshire


English Intensive Welfare Experiment
English Juvenile Therapeutic Community Experiment

English Police Cautioning Exper-
iment
English Prison Intensive Social
Work Experiment
English Psychopathic Delinquent Ex-
periment

Fairfield School for Boys Exper-
iment
Florida Inmate Work Release Exper-
iment
Florida Project Crest Experiment
Fricot Ranch Delinquent Dormitory
Experiment
Hamilton (Canada) Juvenile Services
Project Experiment
Illinois Juvenile Tours Experiment


Illinois Volunteer Lawyer Parole Supervision Experiment

Berntsen and Christiansen 1965


Ross and Blumenthal 1974, 1975


Williams 1970, 1975


Folkard, Fowles, McWilliams,
Smith, Smith, and Walmsley 1974;
Folkard, Smith, and Smith 1976


Folkard, Fowles, McWilliams,
Smith, Smith, and Walmsley 1974;
Folkard, Smith, and Smith 1976


Folkard, Fowles, McWilliams,
Smith, Smith, and Walmsley 1974;
Folkard, Smith, and Smith 1976


Folkard, Fowles, McWilliams,
Smith, Smith, and Walmsley 1974;
Folkard, Smith, and Smith 1976


Fowles 1978


Clarke and Cornish 1972; Cornish
and Clarke 1975; Cornish 1987


Rose and Hamilton 1970


Shaw 1974


Craft, Stephenson, and Granger
1964


Persons 1966, 1967


Waldo and Chiricos 1977
Lee and Haynes 1978, 1980


Jesness 1965, 1971a


Byles and Maurice 1979
Greater Egypt Regional Planning
and Development Commission 1979


Berman 1975, 1978

Juvenile Diversion and Labeling Paradigm Experiment    Klein 1986; Lincoln, Klein, Teilmann, and Labin (n.d.)

Kentucky Village Psychotherapy Experiment    Truax, Wargo, and Silber 1966

Leeds (United Kingdom) Truancy Experiment    Berg, Consterdine, Hullin, McGuire, and Tyrer 1978; Berg, Hullin, McGuire, and Tyrer 1978; Berg, Hullin, and McGuire 1979

Los Angeles Community Delinquency Control Project Experiment    Pond 1970

Los Angeles Silverlake Experiment    Empey and Lubeck 1971

Memphis Drunk Driving Sanctioning Experiments—Social Drinkers    Holden, Stewart, Rice, and Manker 1981; Holden 1982, 1983

Memphis Drunk Driving Sanctioning Experiments—Problem Drinkers    Holden, Stewart, Rice, and Manker 1981; Holden 1982, 1983

Memphis Juvenile Diversion Experiment    Severy and Whitaker 1982, 1984; Whitaker and Severy 1984; Whitaker, Severy, and Morton 1984

Michigan Juvenile Offenders Learn Truth (JOLT) Experiment    Yarborough 1979

Minneapolis Domestic Violence Experiment    Sherman and Berk 1984a, 1984b, 1985; Berk and Sherman 1985, 1988

Minneapolis Informal Parole Experiment    Hudson 1973; Hudson and Hollister 1976

National Restitution Experiment—Boise    Schneider and Schneider 1983; Schneider 1986

National Restitution Experiment—Washington, D.C.    Schneider and Schneider 1983; Schneider 1986

National Restitution Experiment—Clayton County, Georgia    Schneider and Schneider 1983; Schneider 1986

National Restitution Experiment—Oklahoma County, Oklahoma    Schneider and Schneider 1983; Schneider 1986

New Jersey Juvenile Awareness Program (Scared Straight) Experiment    Finckenauer 1982

North Carolina Butner Correctional Facility Experiment    Love, Allgood, and Samples 1986

Ohio Juvenile Probationer Behavior Modification Experiment    Ostrom, Steele, Rosenblood, and Mirels 1971

Ontario (Canada) Social Interaction Training Experiment    Shivrattan 1988

Pinellas County (Florida) Juvenile Services Program Experiment    Quay and Love 1977

Police Foundation Shoplifting Arrest Experiment    Glick, Hamilton, and Forst 1986; Sherman and Gartin 1986; Williams, Forst, and Hamilton 1987

Ramsey County (Minnesota) Community Assistance Program Experiment    Owen and Mattessich 1987

Sacramento (California) Juvenile 601 Diversion Experiment    Baron, Feeney, and Thornton 1972, 1973

Sacramento (California) Juvenile 602 Diversion Experiment    Baron and Feeney 1976

San Diego (California) Chronic Drunk Offender Experiment    Ditman, Crawford, Forgy, Moskowitz, and Macandrew 1967

San Fernando (California) Juvenile Crisis Intervention Experiment    Stratton 1975

San Pablo (California) Adult Diversion Experiment    Austin 1980

San Quentin (California) Squires Program Experiment    Lewis 1979, 1981, 1983

Tacoma Juvenile Inmate Modeling and Group Discussion Experiment    Sarason and Ganzer 1973; Sarason 1978

Utah Provo Experiment    Empey and Rabow 1961; Empey and Erickson 1972

Vera Institute (New York) Pretrial Adult Felony Offender Diversion Experiment    Baker and Rodriguez 1979; Baker and Sadd 1979, 1981

Washington, D.C., Pretrial Supervision Experiment    Welsh 1978

Wayne County (Michigan) Project Start Experiment    Lichtman and Smock 1981

372     David Weisburd

REFERENCES

Adams, S. 1965. "An Experimental Assessment of Group Counseling with Juvenile Probationers." *Journal of the California Probation, Parole and Correctional Association* 2:19–25.

———. 1970. "The Pico Project." In *The Sociology of Punishment and Correction*, edited by N. B. Johnston, L. Savitz, and M. E. Wolfgang. New York: Wiley.

Annis, H. M. 1979. "Group Treatment of Incarcerated Offenders with Alcohol and Drug Problems: A Controlled Evaluation." *Canadian Journal of Criminology* 21:3–15.

Ares, C. E., A. Rankin, and H. Sturz. 1963. "The Manhattan Bail Project: An Interim Report on the Use of Pre-trial Parole." *New York University Law Review* 38:67–93.

Austin, J. F. 1980. "Instead of Justice: Diversion." Doctoral dissertation, University of California, Department of Sociology. Ann Arbor, Mich.: University Microfilms International.

Baker, S. H., and O. Rodriguez. 1979. "Random Time Quota Selection: An Alternative to Random Selection in Experimental Evaluation." In *Evaluation Studies Review Annual*, vol. 4, edited by L. Sechrest. Beverly Hills, Calif.: Sage.

Baker, S. H., and S. Sadd. 1979. *Court Employment Project: Evaluation.* Final report. New York: Vera Institute of Justice.

———. 1981. *Diversion of Felony Arrests; An Experiment in Pretrial Intervention: Evaluation of the Court Employment Project.* Summary report. Washington, D.C.: National Institute of Justice.

Barkwell, L. J. 1976. "Differential Treatment of Juveniles on Probation: An Evaluative Study." *Canadian Journal of Criminology and Corrections* 18:363–78.

Baron, R., and F. Feeney. 1976. *Juvenile Diversion through Family Counseling: A Program for the Diversion of Status Offenders in Sacramento County, California.* Washington, D.C.: National Institute of Law Enforcement and Criminal Justice.

Baron, R., F. Feeney, and W. E. Thornton. 1972. *Preventing Delinquency through Diversion: The Sacramento County Probation Department 601 Diversion Project, A First Year Report.* Sacramento, Calif.: Sacramento County Probation Department.

———. 1973. "Preventing Delinquency through Diversion." *Federal Probation* 37:13–18.

Berecochea, J. E., and D. R. Jaman. 1981. *Time Served in Prison and Parole Outcome: An Experimental Study.* Report no. 2. Sacramento: California Department of Corrections Research Division.

Berecochea, J. E., D. R. Jaman, and W. A. Jones. 1973. *Time Served in Prison and Parole Outcome: An Experimental Study.* Report no. 1. Sacramento: California Department of Corrections Research Division.

Berg, I., M. Consterdine, R. Hullin, R. McGuire, and S. Tyrer. 1978. "The Effect of Two Randomly Allocated Court Procedures on Truancy." *British Journal of Criminology* 18:232–44.

Berg, I., R. Hullin, and R. McGuire. 1979. "A Randomly Controlled Trial of Two Court Procedures in Truancy." In *Psychology, Law and Legal Processes*, edited by D. P. Farrington, K. Hawkins, and S. M. Lloyd-Bostock. Atlantic Highlands, N.J.: Humanities Press.

Berg, I., R. Hullin, R. McGuire, and S. Tyrer. 1978. "Truancy and the Courts: Research Note." *Journal of Child Psychiatry and Psychology* 18:359–65.

Berk, R. A., K. J. Lenihan, and P. H. Rossi. 1980. "Crime and Poverty: Some Experimental Evidence from Ex-offenders." *American Sociological Review* 45:766–86.

Berk, R. A., and L. W. Sherman. 1985. "Data Collection Strategies in the Minneapolis Domestic Assault Experiment." In *Collecting Evaluation Data: Problems and Solutions*, edited by L. Burstein, H. E. Freeman, and P. H. Rossi. Beverly Hills, Calif.: Sage.

———. 1988. "Police Responses to Family Violence Incidents: An Analysis of an Experimental Design with Incomplete Randomization." *Journal of the American Statistical Association* 83:70–76.

Berman, J. J. 1975. "The Volunteer in Parole Program." *Criminology* 13:111–13.

———. 1978. "An Experiment in Parole Supervision." *Evaluation Quarterly* 2:71–90.

Berntsen, K., and K. O. Christiansen. 1965. "A Resocialization Experiment with Short-Term Offenders." In *Scandinavian Studies in Criminology*, vol. 1, edited by K. O. Christiansen. London: Tavistock.

Brewer, J. K., and P. W. Owen. 1973. "A Note on the Power of Statistical Tests." *Journal of Educational Measurement* 10:71–74.

Brown, S. E. 1989. "Statistical Power and Criminal Justice Research." *Journal of Criminal Justice* 17:115–22.

Burkhart, W. 1969. "The Parole Work Unit Programme: An Evaluation." *British Journal of Criminology* 9:125–47.

Byles, J. A., and A. Maurice. 1979. "The Juvenile Services Project: An Experiment in Delinquency Control." *Canadian Journal of Criminology* 21:155–65.

Chase, L. J., and R. B. Chase. 1976. "A Statistical Power Analysis of Applied Psychological Research." *Journal of Applied Psychology* 61:234–37.

Clarke, R. V. G., and D. B. Cornish. 1972. *The Controlled Trial in Institutional Research—Paradigm or Pitfall for Penal Evaluators?* London: H.M. Stationery Office.

Cohen, J. 1973. "Statistical Power Analysis and Research Results." *American Educational Research Journal* 10:225–30.

———. 1988. *Statistical Power Analysis for the Behavioral Sciences*, 2d ed. Hillsdale, N.J.: Erlbaum.

Coleman, D. 1989. "Charge Dropped on Bogus Work." *New York Times* (April 4).

Cornish, D. B. 1987. "Evaluating Residential Treatments for Delinquents: A Cautionary Tale." In *Social Intervention: Potential and Constraints*, edited by K. Hurrelmann, F. Kaufmann, and F. Losel. Berlin: de Gruyter.

Cornish, D. B., and R. V. G. Clarke. 1975. *Residential Treatment and Its Effects on Delinquency*. London: H.M. Stationery Office.

Craft, M., G. Stephenson, and C. Granger. 1964. "A Controlled Trial of Authoritarian and Self-governing Regimes with Adolescent Psychopaths." *American Journal of Orthopsychiatry* 34:543–54.

Dennis, M. L. 1988. "Implementing Randomized Field Experiments: An Analysis of Criminal and Civil Justice Research." Doctoral dissertation, Northwestern University, Department of Psychology.

Ditman, K. S., G. G. Crawford, E. W. Forgy, H. Moskowitz, and C. Macandrew. 1967. "A Controlled Experiment on the Use of Court Probation for Drunk Arrests." *American Journal of Orthopsychiatry* 124:160–63.

Empey, L. T., and M. L. Erickson. 1972. *The Provo Experiment*. Lexington, Mass.: Heath.

Empey, L. T., and S. G. Lubeck. 1971. *The Silverlake Experiment*. Chicago: Aldine.

Empey, L. T., and J. Rabow. 1961. "The Provo Experiment in Delinquency Rehabilitation." *American Sociological Review* 26:679–96.

Farrington, D. P. 1983. "Randomized Experiments on Crime and Justice." In *Crime and Justice: An Annual Review of Research*, vol. 4, edited by M. Tonry and N. Morris. Chicago: University of Chicago Press.

Farrington, D. P., L. E. Ohlin, and J. Q. Wilson. 1986. *Understanding and Controlling Crime*. New York: Springer-Verlag.

Feinberg, S., K. Larntz, and A. J. Reiss, Jr. 1976. "Redesigning the Kansas City Preventive Patrol Experiment." *Evaluation* 3:124–31.

Finckenauer, J. O. 1982. *Scared Straight*. Englewood Cliffs, N.J.: Prentice-Hall.

Folkard, M. S., A. J. Fowles, B. C. McWilliams, D. D. Smith, D. E. Smith, and G. R. Walmsley. 1974. *IMPACT: Intensive Matched Probation and After-Care Treatment*. Vol. 1, *The Design of the Probation Experiment and an Interim Evaluation*. London: H.M. Stationery Office.

Folkard, M. S., D. E. Smith, and D. D. Smith. 1976. *IMPACT: Intensive Matched Probation and After-Care Treatment*. Vol. 2, *The Results of the Experiment*. London: H.M. Stationery Office.

Fowles, A. J. 1978. *Prison Welfare*. London: H.M. Stationery Office.

Garner, J., and C. A. Visher. 1988. "Experiments Help Shape New Policies." *NIJ Reports*, no. 211 (September/October).

Gelber, R. D., and M. Zelen. 1985. "Planning and Reporting Clinical Trials." In *Basic Principles and Clinical Management of Cancer*, edited by P. Calabrese, P. S. Schein, and S. A. Rosenberg. New York: Macmillan.

Glick, B., E. Hamilton, and B. Forst. 1986. "Shoplifting: An Experiment in Lesser Crimes and Punishments." Draft final report. Washington, D.C.: Police Foundation.

Greater Egypt Regional Planning and Development Commission. 1979. *Menard Correctional Center Juvenile Tours Impact Study*. Carbondale, Ill.: Greater Egypt Regional Planning and Development Commission.

Guttman, E. 1963. "Effects of Short-Term Psychiatric Treatment on Boys in Two California Youth Authority Institutions." Research Report no. 36. Sacramento: California Youth Authority.

Hays, W. L. 1981. *Statistics*. 3d ed. New York: Holt, Rinehart & Winston.

Holden, R. T. 1982. "Legal Reactions to Drunk Driving." Doctoral Dissertation, Vanderbilt University, Department of Sociology. Ann Arbor, Mich.: University Microfilms International.

———. 1983. "Rehabilitative Sanctions for Drunk Driving: An Experimental Evaluation." *Journal of Research in Crime and Delinquency* 20:55–72.

Holden, R. T., L. T. Stewart, J. N. Rice, and E. Manker. 1981. *Tennessee DUI Probation Follow-up Demonstration Project*. Final report. Springfield, Va.: Department of Transportation.

Hudson, C. H. 1973. *An Experimental Study of the Differential Effects of Parole Supervision for a Group of Adolescent Boys and Girls*. Summary report. Minneapolis: Minnesota Department of Corrections.

Hudson, J., and C. D. Hollister. 1976. "An Experimental Study of Parole Supervision of Juveniles and Social Service Utilization." *Iowa Journal of Social Work* 4:80–89.

Jackson, P. C. 1978. *The Bay Area Parole Study*. Sacramento: California Youth Authority.

———. 1983. "Some Effects of Parole Supervision on Recidivism." *British Journal of Criminology* 23:17–34.

Jesness, C. F. 1965. *The Fricot Ranch Study*. Sacramento: California Youth Authority.

———. 1971a. "Comparative Effectiveness of Two Institutional Treatment Programs for Delinquents." *Child Care Quarterly* 1:119–30.

———. 1971b. "The Preston Typology Study." *Journal of Research in Crime and Delinquency* 8:38–52.

———. 1975. "Comparative Effectiveness of Behavior Modification Transactional Analysis Programs for Delinquents." *Journal of Consulting and Clinical Psychology* 43:758–79.

Jesness, C. F., W. J. DeRisi, P. M. McCormick, and R. F. Wedge. 1972. *The Youth Center Research Project*. Sacramento: California Youth Authority.

Johnson, B. M. 1962a. *Parole Performance of the First Year's Releases: Parole Research Project: Evaluation of Reduced Caseloads*. Research Report no. 27. Sacramento: California Youth Authority.

———. 1962b. *An Analysis of Predictions of Parole Performance and of Judgments of Supervision in the Parole Research Project*. Research Report no. 32. Sacramento: California Youth Authority.

Kassebaum, G., D. Ward, and D. Wilner. 1971. *Prison Treatment and Parole Survival*. New York: Wiley.

Kelling, G. L., T. Pate, D. Dieckman, and C. E. Brown. 1974. *The Kansas City Patrol Experiment: A Technical Report*. Washington, D.C.: Police Foundation.

Kirby, B. C. 1969. "Crofton House: An Experiment with a County Halfway House." *Federal Probation* 33:53–58.

Klein, M. W. 1986. "Labeling Theory and Delinquency Policy: An Experimental Test." *Criminal Justice and Behavior* 13:47–79.

Kolata, G. 1990. "In Clinical Trials, Some Contend, Big is Beautiful." *New York Times* (April 15).

Kraemer, H. C., and S. Thiemann. 1987. *How Many Subjects? Statistical Power Analysis in Research*. Newbury Park, Calif.: Sage.

Kroll, R. M., and L. J. Chase. 1975. "Community Disorders: A Power Analytic Assessment of Recent Research." *Journal of Communication Disorders* 8:237–47.

Lamb, H. R., and V. Goertzel. 1974a. "Ellsworth House: A Community Alternative to Jail." *American Journal of Psychiatry* 131:64–68.

———. 1974b. "A Community Alternative to County Jail: The Hopes and the Realities." *Federal Probation* 38:33–39.

Lee, R., and N. M. Haynes. 1978. "Counseling Juvenile Offenders: An Experimental Evaluation of Project Crest." *Community Mental Health Journal* 14:267–71.

———. 1980. "Project Crest and the Dual-Treatment Approach to Delinquency: Methods and Research Summarized." In *Effective Correctional Treatment*, edited by R. R. Ross and P. Gendreau. Toronto: Butterworths.

Levernson, R. L., Jr. 1980. "Statistical Power Analysis: Implications for Researchers, Planners and Practitioners in Gerontology." *Gerontologist* 20: 494–98.

Lewis, R. V. 1979. *The Squires of San Quentin: Preliminary Findings on an Experimental Study of Juvenile Visitation at San Quentin Prison.* Sacramento: California Youth Authority, Division of Research.

———. 1981. *The Squires of San Quentin: An Evaluation of a Juvenile Awareness Program.* Sacramento: California Youth Authority, Division of Research.

———. 1983. "Scared Straight—California Style." *Criminal Justice and Behavior* 10:209–26.

Lichtman, G. M., and S. M. Smock. 1981. "The Effects of Social Services on Probational Recidivism." *Journal of Research in Crime and Delinquency* 18:81–100.

Lincoln, C. M., M. W. Klein, K. S. Teilmann, and S. Labin. N.d. "Control Organizations and Labeling Theory: Official versus Self-reported Delinquency." Unpublished manuscript. Los Angeles: University of Southern California.

Lipsey, M. W. 1990. *Design Sensitivity: Statistical Power for Experimental Research.* Newbury, Calif.: Sage.

Lipton, D., R. Martinson, and J. Wilks. 1975. *The Effectiveness of Correctional Treatment.* New York: Praeger.

Love, C. T., J. G. Allgood, and F. P. S. Samples. 1986. "The Butner Research Projects." *Federal Probation* 50:32–39.

Orme, J. G., and T. D. Combs-Orme. 1986. "Statistical Power and Type II Errors in Social Work." *Social Research and Abstracts* 22:3–10.

Orme, J. G., and R. M. Tolman. 1986. "The Statistical Power of a Decade of Social Work Education Research." *Social Service Review* 60:619–32.

Ostrom, T. M., C. M. Steele, L. K. Rosenblood, and H. L. Mirels. 1971. "Modification of Delinquent Behavior." *Journal of Applied Social Psychology* 1:118–36.

Owen, G., and P. W. Mattessich. 1987. *Community Assistance Program: Results of a Control Study of the Effects of Non-residential Corrections on Adult Offenders in Ramsey County.* St. Paul, Minn.: Wilder Foundation.

Palmer, T. B. 1971. "California's Community Treatment Program for Delinquent Adolescents." *Journal of Research in Crime and Delinquency* 8:74–92.

————. 1974. "The Youth Authority's Community Treatment Project." *Federal Probation* 38:3–14.

————. 1978. *Correctional Intervention and Research*. Toronto: Lexington Books.

Persons, R. W. 1966. "Psychological and Behavioral Change in Delinquents Following Psychotherapy." *Journal of Clinical Psychology* 22:337–40.

————. 1967. "Relationship between Psychotherapy with Institutionalized Boys and Subsequent Community Adjustment." *Journal of Consulting Psychology* 31:137–41.

Petersilia, J. 1989. "Implementing Randomized Experiments: Lessons from BJA's Intensive Supervision Project." *Evaluation Review* 13:435–58.

Petersilia, J., and S. Turner. 1990. *Intensive Supervision for High-Risk Probationers: Findings from Three California Experiments*. Santa Monica, Calif.: RAND.

Pond, E. M. 1970. *The Los Angeles Community Delinquency Control Project: An Experiment in the Rehabilitation of Delinquents in an Urban Community*. Sacramento: California Youth Authority.

Powers, E., and H. Witmer. 1951. *An Experiment in the Prevention of Delinquency: The Cambridge-Somerville Youth Study*. New York: Columbia University Press.

Quay, H. C., and C. T. Love. 1977. "The Effects of a Juvenile Diversion Program on Rearrests." *Criminal Justice and Behavior* 4:377–96.

Reimer, E., and M. Warren. 1957. "Special Intensive Parole Unit: Relationship between Violation Rate and Initially Small Caseload." *National Probation and Parole Association Journal* 3:222–29.

————. 1958. *Special Intensive Parole Unit, Phase II: Thirty-Man Caseload Study*. Sacramento: California Department of Corrections.

Rose, G., and R. A. Hamilton. 1970. "Effects of a Juvenile Liaison Scheme." *British Journal of Criminology* 10:2–20.

Ross, H. L., and M. Blumenthal. 1974. "Sanctions for the Drinking Driver: An Experimental Study." *Journal of Legal Studies* 3:53–61.

————. 1975. "Some Problems in Experimentation in a Legal Setting." *American Sociologist* 10:150–55.

Rossi, P. H., R. A. Berk, and K. J. Lenihan. 1980. *Money, Work and Crime*. New York: Academic Press.

Sarason, I. G. 1978. "A Cognitive Social Learning Approach to Juvenile Delinquency." In *Psychopathic Behavior: Approaches to Research*, edited by R. D. Hare and D. Schalling. Chichester: Wiley.

Sarason, I. G., and V. J. Ganzer. 1973. "Modeling and Group Discussion in the Rehabilitation of Juvenile Delinquents." *Journal of Counseling Psychology* 20:442–49.

Schneider, A. L. 1980. "Effects of Status Offender Deinstitutionalization: A Case Study." In *Evaluation and Criminal Justice Policy*, edited by R. Roesch and R. R. Corrado. Beverly Hills, Calif.: Sage.

————. 1986. "Restitution and Recidivism Rates of Juvenile Offenders: Results from Four Experimental Studies." *Criminology* 24:533–52.

Schneider, P. R., and A. L. Schneider. 1983. *An Analysis of Recidivism Rates in Six Federally-funded Restitution Projects in Juvenile Courts: A Statistical Summary*. Washington, D.C.: National Institute of Justice.

Seckel, J. P. 1965. *Experiments in Group Counseling at Youth Authority Institutions.* Sacramento: California Youth Authority, Division of Research.

―――. 1967. *The Fremont Experiment: Assessment of Residential Treatment at a Youth Authority Reception Center.* Sacramento: California Youth Authority, Division of Research.

Sedlmeier, P., and G. Gigerenzer. 1989. "Do Studies of Statistical Power Have an Effect on the Power of Studies?" *Psychological Bulletin* 105:309–16.

Severy, L. J., and J. M. Whitaker. 1982. "Juvenile Diversion: An Experimental Analysis of Effectiveness." *Evaluation Review* 6:753–74.

―――. 1984. "Memphis-Metro Youth Diversion Project: Final Report." *Child Welfare* 63:269–77.

Shaw, M. 1974. *Social Work in Prison.* London: H.M. Stationery Office.

Sherman, L. W., and R. A. Berk. 1984a. "The Deterrent Effects of Arrest for Domestic Assault." *American Sociological Review* 49:261–72.

―――. 1984b. *The Minneapolis Domestic Violence Experiment.* Washington, D.C.: Police Foundation.

―――. 1985. "The Randomization of Arrest." In *Randomization and Field Experimentation: New Directions for Program Evaluation, Number 28,* edited by R. F. Boruch and W. Wothke. San Francisco: Jossey-Bass.

Sherman, L. W., and P. R. Gartin. 1986. "Differential Recidivism: A Field Experiment of the Specific Sanction Effects of Arrest for Shoplifting." Paper presented at the American Society of Criminology annual meeting, Atlanta, November.

Sherman, L. W., and D. Weisburd. 1989. *Policing the Hotspots of Crime: A Redesign of the Kansas City Preventive Patrol Experiment.* Washington, D.C.: Crime Control Institute.

―――. 1992. "Does Patrol Prevent Crime: The Minneapolis Hot Spots Experiment." Paper presented at the Forty-seventh International Society of Criminology Course on Urban Crime Prevention, Tokyo, April.

Shivrattan, J. L. 1988. "Social Interactional Training and Incarcerated Juvenile Delinquents." *Canadian Journal of Criminology* 30:145–63.

Star, D. 1978. *Summary Parole: A Six and Twelve Month Follow-up.* Research Report no. 60. Sacramento: California Department of Corrections.

Stark, H. G. 1963. "A Substitute for Institutionalization of Serious Delinquents: A California Youth Study Experiment." *Crime and Delinquency* 9:242–48.

Stratton, J. G. 1975. "Effects of Crisis Intervention Counseling on Predelinquent and Misdemeanor Juvenile Offenders." *Juvenile Justice* 26:7–18.

Taylor, A. J. W. 1967. "An Evaluation of Group Psychotherapy in a Girl's Borstal." *International Journal of Group Psychotherapy* 17:168–77.

Tornudd, P. 1968. "The Preventive Effect of Fines for Drunkenness: A Controlled Experiment." *Scandinavian Studies in Criminology* 2:109–24.

Truax, C. B., D. G. Wargo, and L. D. Silber. 1966. "Effects of Group Psychotherapy with High Accurate Empathy and Non-possessive Warmth upon Female Institutionalized Delinquents." *Journal of Abnormal Psychology* 71:267–74.

Turner, Susan. 1991. Personal communication with author, February.

Uchida, Craig. 1991. Personal communication with author, February.

Venezia, P. S. 1972. "Unofficial Probation: An Evaluation of Its Effectiveness." *Journal of Research in Crime and Delinquency* 9:149–70.

Waldo, G. P., and T. G. Chiricos. 1977. "Work Release and Recidivism: An Empirical Evaluation of a Social Policy." *Evaluation Quarterly* 1:87–108.

Warren, M. Q. 1967. "The Community Treatment Project: History and Prospects." In *Law Enforcement Science and Technology*, edited by S. A. Yefsky. Washington, D.C.: Thompson.

Weisburd, D., and J. Garner. 1992. "Experimentation in Criminal Justice: Editor's Introduction." *Journal of Research in Crime and Delinquency* 29(1):3–6.

Weisburd, D., L. W. Sherman, and A. J. Petrosino. 1990. *Registry of Randomized Criminal Justice Experiments in Sanctions*. Sponsored by Rutgers—The State University and Crime Control Institute. Los Altos, Calif.: Sociometric Corporation, Data Resources Program of the National Institute of Justice.

Welsh, J. D. 1978. "Is Pretrial Performance Affected by Supervision?" In *Pretrial Services Annual Journal: 1978*, edited by D. A. Henry. Washington, D.C.: Pretrial Services Resource Center.

Whitaker, J. M., and L. J. Severy. 1984. "Service Accountability and Recidivism for Diverted Youth."*Criminal Justice and Behavior* 11:47–73.

Whitaker, J. M., L. J. Severy, and D. S. Morton. 1984. "A Comprehensive Community-based Youth Diversion Program." *Child Welfare* 63:175–81.

Williams, H., B. Forst, and E. E. Hamilton. 1987. "Stop! Should You Arrest That Person?" *Security Management* 31:52–58.

Williams, M. 1970. *A Study of Some Aspects of Borstal Allocation*. London: Home Office Prison Department, Office of the Chief Psychologist.

———. 1975. "Aspects of the Psychology of Imprisonment." In *The Use of Imprisonment: Essays in the Changing State of English Penal Policy*, edited by S. McConville. London: Routledge.

Yarborough, J. C. 1979. *Evaluation of JOLT as a Deterrence Program*. Lansing: Michigan Department of Corrections.

*David P. Farrington*

# Understanding and Preventing Bullying

ABSTRACT

Bullying is repeated oppression, psychological or physical, of a less powerful person by a more powerful one. The prevalence of bullying by and of school children is quite high; in some studies, about half of children were bullies, and over half were victims. Boys bully more than girls, but boys and girls are victimized about equally. Generally, bullies are aggressive, tough, strong, confident, and impulsive. Victims are unpopular, lonely, rejected, anxious, depressed, unwilling to retaliate, and lacking in self-esteem. Bullying occurs especially at places and times when adult supervision and surveillance is minimal. There is some continuity over time between bullying and violent crime. Prevention methods aim to improve the social and friendship skills of the victim and the empathy of the bully and to improve adult supervision and "whole-school" environments. In Norway, a nationwide campaign against bullying seemed to be successful.

Modern research on bullying in the English-speaking world began with the publication of *Aggression in the Schools* by Olweus (1978) describing studies of bullies and victims of bullying carried out in schools in Stockholm in the early 1970s (Olweus 1973).

Scandinavian research on bullying continued in the late 1970s and early 1980s (see Munthe 1989). Three well-publicized suicides of Nor-

David P. Farrington is professor of psychological criminology, Institute of Criminology, Cambridge University. Earlier versions of parts of this essay appeared in "Understanding and Preventing Bullying," an unpublished report prepared in February 1992 by the author under contract to the Crime Prevention Unit of the British Home Office. I am particularly grateful to David Hawkins, Dan Olweus, Peter Smith, Delwyn Tattum, and Richard Tremblay for helpful discussions and materials, and I would also like to acknowledge material kindly supplied by Valerie Besag, Graham Beck, John Coie, Michele Elliott, Diana Lamplugh, Barry McGurk, and Alison Skinner.

381

wegian boys, attributed to bullying, precipitated a nationwide campaign against bullying in Norwegian comprehensive schools by the Ministry of Education in October 1983 (Olweus 1990). Three years later, a large-scale follow-up study was carried out by Roland (1989). These Scandinavian developments, together with a Council of Europe seminar in Norway in 1987 (O'Moore 1988), stimulated research on bullying in a number of different countries in the late 1980s, including Spain and Portugal (Vieira da Fonseca, Fernandez Garcia, and Quevedo Perez 1989), Holland (Junger 1990), Scotland (Mellor 1990), Ireland (O'Moore and Hillery 1989), Canada (Ziegler and Rosenstein-Manner 1991), Australia (Rigby and Slee 1991), and the United States (Greenbaum, Turner, and Stephens 1989). Bullying has also been studied in many other countries, including Japan (Kikkawa 1987), France (Duyme 1990), and Malta (Borg and Falzon 1989). The most extensive bibliography of bullying research is by Skinner (1992).

In England in the 1970s, pioneering research on the correlates of bullying and victimization was carried out by Lowenstein (1978a, 1978b), independently of the Scandinavian tradition. A pioneering project on the prevention of bullying was carried out in 1979 to 1981 in a residential institution for young offenders by McGurk and McDougall (1991). However, English research did not really take off until the late 1980s and early 1990s, with the publication of four books on bullying in schools (Besag 1989a; Tattum and Lane 1989; Elliott 1991a; Smith and Thompson 1991a). The most extensive English research has been conducted in Sheffield by Whitney and Smith (1991). There has not been a great deal of research in the United States, but Perry, Willard, and Perry (1990) are trying to replicate some of Olweus's work.

This essay aims to summarize the current state of knowledge about bullying and victimization of children in schools and other institutions. Much of the research on victimization in institutions for offenders is not specifically concerned with bullying (but see Shields and Simourd 1991). There has been less research on other types of bullying, for example, between siblings, spouses, or cohabitees and in the armed forces.

Bullying is important in its own right. It is surprisingly common; there is evidence that over half of children have been victimized and over half have been bullies. It causes immediate harm and distress to the victim and has negative long-term consequences for the victim's mental health. It also has negative consequences for the bully since bullying may be reinforced by enjoyment and status, and hence the bully may become more likely to engage in other aggressive behavior.

Bullying is also important because of its relation to crime, criminal violence, and other types of aggressive antisocial behavior. Like offending, bullying arises from interactions between potential offenders and potential victims in environments that provide opportunities. However, bullying is more likely to be detected than offending because it occurs repeatedly between two people who typically know each other. Hence, bullying is potentially more controllable than offending. Certainly, it is easier to implement and evaluate bullying prevention programs in schools than more general crime prevention programs in the community. School bullying is to some extent a microcosm of offending in the community, and knowledge about causes and prevention gained more easily in the controlled setting of the school might be applicable to the less controlled setting of the community.

Just as criminological researchers might learn from findings on bullying, bullying researchers would gain by taking account of criminological findings. The explosion of recent research on bullying has led to quick advances in knowledge but has been carried out ahistorically, failing to benefit from research in related fields such as criminology. For example, bullying researchers could learn a great deal about measurement, reliability, and validity by taking account of more than thirty years of research on self-reports of offending. The application of the criminal careers perspective might enhance understanding of why bullying begins, why it continues, and why it ends and the relation between bullying careers and victimization careers. Bullying researchers could also learn from work on the prevention of aggression and delinquency.

Bullies tend to be aggressive in different settings and over many years. Adolescent bullies tend to become adult bullies and then tend to have children who are bullies. Like offenders, bullies tend to be drawn disproportionately from lower socioeconomic-status families with poor child-rearing techniques, tend to be impulsive, and tend to be unsuccessful in school. Victims of bullying tend to be unpopular and rejected by their peers, and tend to have low school attainment, low self-esteem, and poor social skills. There is evidence that social isolation and victimization tend to persist from childhood to adulthood, and that victimized people tend to have children who are victimized. Generally, bullying incidents occur when adult supervision or surveillance is low, as for example on playgrounds during recess.

Future research on bullying needs to isolate and disentangle the different kinds of bullying (e.g., teasing, intimidation, physical aggression) more carefully, to develop improved measurement techniques, and to relate self-reports to other measures such as playground observation, school records, and teacher reports. A key issue is the extent to which bullies are also victims, either at the same time or sequentially (e.g., children victimized at young ages becoming bullies as they grow older). An important problem for criminological researchers is to investigate how, when, and under what circumstances bullying escalates into criminal violence and to identify promising opportunities for intervention. Bullying prevention programs have been targeted on bullies, victims, or environments, but they need to be evaluated more rigorously.

Here is how this essay is organized. Section I reviews the epidemiology of bullying, including definitions, issues of measurement, reliability and validity, the prevalence and frequency of bullying and victimization, the overlap between bullies and victims, and bullying and victimization careers. Section II considers characteristics of bullies, characteristics of victims, environmental influences, and the consequences of bullying and victimization. Section III and the Appendix report new research results that show intragenerational continuity and intergenerational transmission of bullying and victimization. Sections IV and V examine prevention methods focusing on bullies, victims, and the environment and offer recommendations for future research.

## I. The Epidemiology of Bullying

There is no universally accepted operational definition of bullying. However, there is widespread agreement (e.g., Besag 1989a; Lane 1989; Pearce 1991; Smith and Thompson 1991b) that bullying includes several key elements: physical, verbal, or psychological attack or intimidation that is intended to cause fear, distress, or harm to the victim; an imbalance of power, with the more powerful child oppressing the less powerful one; absence of provocation by the victim; and repeated incidents between the same children over a prolonged period. Although a minority of researchers disagree over one or more of these elements (e.g., Stephenson and Smith 1989), the majority of researchers are quite concordant in their definitions.

Jones (1991, pp. 16–17) has provided some useful clarifications of the concept of bullying:

The bully is someone who is responsible for premeditated, continuous, malicious, and belittling tyranny. The victim is on the receiving end, repeatedly, defenselessly and typically without a champion. . . . None of us like children who make fun, and giggle, pointing fingers at others for their idiosyncrasies, but they are not career bullies; they are children growing up and doing what children do, rather cruelly, but predictably. . . . Nobody likes children who steal money or sweets from others, but beware of giving them the notoriety of being called bullies. They are thieves . . . . Bullies tend to extort money from a weak victim, or victims, systematically and repeatedly . . . . Teachers get remarkably fed up with children who fight or scrap with one another. But they are not bullies because they fight, and the one who wins is most certainly not a bully because he wins. The mindless and degrading violence of strong against weak may be bullying, but fighting, by definition, is not.

A major definitional problem is to decide where teasing ends and bullying begins. As Pearce (1991, p. 70) points out, "The overlap between bullying and teasing is an important one to recognise because teasing is usually considered to be quite acceptable. But if the teasing involves intimidation and results in distress, it clearly falls within the definition of bullying." Unfortunately for researchers, many different types of oppressive behavior are included under the heading of bullying: physical violence, mental cruelty, intimidation, extortion, stealing valued possessions, willful destruction of property, rubbishing other children's work, menacing stares, name calling (e.g., Cohn 1987), and "mother-cussing" (making derogatory remarks about mothers, e.g., implying prostitution or obesity; see Frost 1991, p. 30). It is important to establish the extent to which all these different types of behavior are interrelated. Perry, Kusel, and Perry (1988) in American research showed that peer ratings of beating up, hitting and pushing, picking on children, calling names, making fun of children, and trying to hurt their feelings were all interrelated.

Many researchers have distinguished between physical and psychological bullying and have argued that physical bullying is more characteristic of boys, while psychological bullying is more characteristic of girls (e.g., Stephenson and Smith 1989; Besag 1991; Smith and Thompson 1991b). Differences between boys and girls are graphically illustrated by Herbert (1989, p. 73):

Some years ago, a particular group of lower ability pupils began to exhibit unpleasant bullying tendencies. The boys were mostly aggressive and physically threatening. They would intimidate weaker or less confident pupils into providing them with treats such as sweets or cigarettes or sometimes money. The victim's school equipment would be hidden or scattered around playing fields, perhaps his homework destroyed. Sometimes the victim would be followed around school, so denied a hiding place. If the victim retaliated in any way, he was ridiculed and physically threatened. Only rarely was the victim hit. The bullies relied on the victim's fear of being hit, and the knowledge that he was incapable of defending himself. The girls were less physically threatening, although the same "treats" were expected. A victim would be isolated by a group of erstwhile friends and acquaintances. The girls would have a pact not to speak to one of their number, or sit next to her in lessons, as though she were unclean or smelled. The bullies would ridicule just the things of which young girls are acutely conscious: their developing figures, their clothes, their general appearance, their attempts at makeup. On one occasion a girl's sexual behavior was ridiculed; she was accused of being "common," a "slag," of having a venereal disease. Graffiti appeared on the toilet walls condemning her and her supposed boyfriends. The poor girl was made a social pariah. In such cases the problem is not the fear of physical violence but the constant condemnation, isolation and loneliness.

Few researchers have obtained children's own definitions of bullying. However, Arora and Thompson (1987) in Sheffield found that boys and girls, twelve to fourteen years old, and their teachers generally agreed on the actions most often perceived as bullying: "he or she tried to hurt me, tried to break something that belonged to me, tried to hit me, and tried to kick me." They also reported that children thought that bullying involved repeated incidents over a period of time with the same children involved, victims weaker than bullies, aggression for no reason, and several children "ganging up" on a single child. Unfortunately, they did not report actions that children thought did not constitute bullying. In Toronto, Ziegler and Rosenstein-Manner (1991) found that primary school children understood the concept of bullying and applied it to physical aggression, verbal taunting, threatening, and excluding children.

The most common definitions in use were adopted by Roland (1989) and Olweus (1991a) in their Norwegian research in the 1980s. Roland defined bullying as long-standing violence, physical or psychological, perpetrated by an individual or group and directed against an individual who cannot defend himself or herself. Olweus's definition is more carefully specified and hence possibly more restrictive. Olweus defined bullying as repeated, negative actions over time, including hitting, kicking, threatening, locking inside a room, saying nasty and unpleasant things, and teasing. There had to be an imbalance in physical or psychological strength between the bully and the victim since fights or quarrels between two people of approximately the same strength were not counted as bullying.

A. *Measurement, Reliability, and Validity*

Bullying has been measured using a variety of different techniques. In the earliest studies, Olweus (1978) and Lowenstein (1978b) primarily relied on teacher ratings and peer nominations, and later Scandinavian studies (e.g., Bjorkvist, Ekman, and Lagerspetz 1982) also used peer nominations. Staff ratings have been used in institutions for offenders (Mathai and Taylor 1985). Roland (1989) and Olweus (1990) mainly used anonymous self-report questionnaires, seeking information from both bullies and victims, and this method is now the most popular.

Table 1 summarizes characteristics of the six most important self-report studies of bullying (in six different countries). Three used Olweus's definition, and three Roland's. The sample size shown in table 1 is that on which prevalence estimates of victimization are based. For example, Olweus (1991a) reported that he obtained data from approximately 130,000 children in 715 schools, but his prevalence estimates of victimization are based on 83,330 children in 404 schools.

Individual interviews with children have also been used to obtain information about bullying and victimization in schools (e.g., Smith 1991). However, other useful methods, such as systematic observation (e.g., in playgrounds; see Tattum and Tattum [1992], pp. 140–44) and use of school records, have been neglected. Systematic observation has been used to study childhood aggression, for example, in nursery schools (e.g., Manning, Heron, and Marshall 1978). School records in Northern Ireland show that bullying is the offense for which corporal punishment is most frequently applied (Tattum 1989).

In the United States, there is a considerable literature on school violence and victimization (e.g., Toby 1983; Gottfredson and Gottfredson 1985; Parker et al. 1991). Detailed information about violence in schools was collected in the National Crime Victimization Survey

## TABLE 1

### Characteristics of Key Self-Report Studies of Bullying

| Principal Investigator | Location | Date | N | Age | No. Schools | No. Classes | Bullying Definition | Administrator |
|---|---|---|---|---|---|---|---|---|
| D. Olweus | Norway | Autumn 1983 | 83,330 | 8–16 | 404 | 4,100 | Olweus | teacher |
| M. O'Moore | Dublin | Easter 1988 | 783 | 7–13 | 4 | 30 | Roland | own teacher |
| A. Mellor | Scotland | Spring 1989 | 942 | 12–16 | 10 | ? | Roland | researcher |
| I. Fernandez Garcia | Madrid | 1989? | 1,200 | 8–12 | 10 | ? | Roland | teacher or researcher |
| S. Ziegler | Toronto | 1990 | 211 | 9–15 | ? | 14 | Olweus | teacher? |
| P. Smith | Sheffield | Autumn 1990 | 6,758 | 8–16 | 24 | 322 | Olweus | other teacher |

Sources.—Vieira de Fonseca et al. (1989); Mellor (1990); Olweus (1991a); O'Moore and Hillery (1989); Whitney and Smith (1991); Ziegler and Rosenstein-Manner (1991).

in 1989 (Bastian and Taylor 1991). A nationally representative sample of 10,449 young people aged twelve to nineteen who had attended a school in the previous six months completed the school crime supplement. This showed that 2.5 percent were victims of violence (mostly simple assaults) in or around school in the previous year, corresponding to a national estimate of 430,000 victims of school violence aged twelve to nineteen. About one in five (19 percent) feared an attack while traveling to or from school (especially on public transport or walking). The most common places avoided because of fear of crime were school washrooms and corridors. About 3 percent of boys and 1 percent of girls had taken a weapon to school for protection in the previous year.

In research on bullying, there has been insufficient concern with psychometric issues such as reliability and validity, despite hints about problems in the literature. For example, Roland (1989) speculated that girls were less likely than boys to answer questions truthfully about their own bullying. Researchers on bullying rarely provide information about the target population, about attrition, and about reasons for attrition, despite evidence that bullies and victims are disproportionately truants and hence disproportionately likely to be missing from school samples (e.g., Reid 1989). Precise figures about many topics in research reports on bullying are often missing, forcing the reader to engage in detective work (sometimes unsuccessfully).

There is some information relevant to the reliability and validity of bullying measures. Ahmad and Smith (1990) compared anonymous questionnaires with individual interviews one week later and with teacher and peer nominations for ninety-three Sheffield children. Agreement between questionnaires and interviews was about 90 percent for bullying and 95 percent for victimization (both scored dichotomously). However, only half of those who admitted bullying in the questionnaire admitted it in the interview, although 85 percent of those admitting victimization in the questionnaire admitted it in the interview. Ahmad and Smith concluded that the anonymous questionnaire was more valid, presumably because it yielded higher prevalence and because they implicitly assumed that denial was the main source of invalidity. They also reported that peer information agreed better with the questionnaire than did teacher information.

It has often been argued that most bullying is hidden from teachers and, hence, that teachers' reports are likely to underestimate its prevalence. In their Dublin study, O'Moore and Hillery (1991) found that teachers identified only 24 percent of self-reported bullies. However,

Olweus (1987), in a study of about ninety teachers and 2,000 children in Bergen, concluded that there was striking agreement between the percentages of bullies and victims identified by teachers and children's self-reports. Different data sources may agree in prevalence but disagree considerably in their identification of individual children. For example, in Pittsburgh, Loeber et al. (1989) systematically compared child, teacher, and parent reports of delinquent and antisocial behavior of 2,573 boys aged seven, ten, and thirteen. The percentage of seven-year-old boys who had shoplifted was almost identical according to children (7.9 percent) and parents (7.7 percent), suggesting considerable agreement between these sources. However, only seventeen boys were identified by both sources, while forty-eight were identified by parents but not boys, and fifty were identified by boys but not parents, suggesting considerable disagreement.

Stephenson and Smith (1989) in Cleveland (England) reported that teacher and peer nominations of which children were involved in bullying (as bullies or victims) in one school were highly correlated (.8). Olweus (1991a) reported high correlations (.4–.6) between self-reports and peer ratings of bullying and victimization. The most extensive reliability and validity research on bullying victimization was carried out in Florida by Perry et al. (1988). They found that peer-rated victimization scores correlated .62 with teacher-rated victimization scores and .42 with self-reported victimization scores.

More detailed comparisons between different measurement methods are needed. Given the current preference for self-report questionnaires, it would be helpful for investigators to build on the thirty years of research on the reliability and validity of measures of self-reported offending and antisocial behavior since similar issues arise in these different areas. (For reviews of self-reported offending, see Hindelang, Hirschi, and Weis [1981]; and Huizinga and Elliott [1986].) For example, Kulik, Stein, and Sarbin (1968) in California systematically compared anonymous and nonanonymous self-reported delinquency questionnaires and found that the total scores in the two conditions correlated .98, although they were about 10 percent higher when reported anonymously. Similarly, Hindelang et al. (1981) randomly assigned Seattle school children to an anonymous questionnaire, an anonymous interview, a nonanonymous questionnaire, or a nonanonymous interview and found that no method was consistently better or worse than any other on various criteria of reliability and validity.

Generally, delinquency researchers have validated self-report questionnaires concurrently and prospectively by comparing them with official records. Researchers on bullying in school could attempt to validate their self-report questionnaires against school records or teachers' reports. The key question is what proportion of teacher- or school-reported bullies, victims, and incidents are self-reported.

## B. Prevalence and Frequency

The prevalence of bullies and victims and the frequency of bullying and victimization of course depend on definitions and time periods. Unfortunately, key items of information such as these are often unclear in research reports on bullying. It is often unclear whether the prevalence of bullying at school includes incidents of social exclusion and whether it includes incidents on the way to and from school. The time period is rarely specified exactly. Most self-report questionnaires enquire about bullying "this term," but this can and does cover a period from one month to three months. Comparisons of reported prevalence rates will remain uncertain until bullying researchers begin to use standard time periods.

On the basis of teacher reports on 731 boys aged twelve to sixteen in eleven Stockholm schools, Olweus (1978) classified 5.4 percent as pronounced victims, 6.1 percent as less pronounced victims, 5.0 percent as pronounced bullies, and 5.3 percent as less pronounced bullies. Lowenstein (1978b) set a much stricter criterion for bullying, requiring identification by victims, by two or more teachers, and by two or more other children. Of 5,774 junior and secondary children in fifteen Hampshire schools, he identified only 1.4 percent as bullies. These must have been the most extreme cases. Stephenson and Smith (1989, 1991) in their study of 1,078 children aged ten to eleven in twenty-six Cleveland schools, relied on teacher reports and identified 16 percent as bullies and 13 percent as victims (including those who were both bullies and victims in these figures).

Chazan (1989) reported that 7.8 percent of boys and 4.9 percent of girls bullied other children in an Isle of Wight study of 435 five-year-olds. The corresponding percentages reported by teachers were 9.5 percent of boys and 7.6 percent of girls. In a national sample of 13,135 children born in one week of April 1970, the mothers reported that 15.4 percent bullied other children. Victimization figures from parents are even higher. Newson and Newson (1984) in their longitudinal study of 700 Nottingham children reported that the mothers said that 26 percent were bullied at school and 22 percent were bullied in the

## TABLE 2

### Prevalence of Bullying and Victimization

| Criterion and Site | Percent Bullies | | Percent Victims | |
|---|---|---|---|---|
| | Male | Female | Male | Female |
| Ever: | | | | |
| Dublin | 58 | 38 | 71.6 | 58.2 |
| Scotland | | 44 | 50 | |
| This term: | | | | |
| Dublin | 38.5 | 23.6 | 48.4 | 38.4 |
| Madrid | 18 | 15.5 | 16 | 19.6 |
| Toronto | 46.7 | 31.2 | 49.6 | 48.1 |
| Sometimes or more often: | | | | |
| Norway (primary) | 10.7 | 4.0 | 12.5 | 10.6 |
| Norway (secondary) | 11.3 | 2.5 | 7.4 | 3.3 |
| Scotland | | 4 | 6 | |
| Toronto | 25 | 9 | 18 | 19 |
| Sheffield (primary) | 15.7 | 7.4 | 27.6 | 26.7 |
| Sheffield (secondary) | 8.1 | 4.1 | 12.0 | 8.5 |
| Once a week or more often: | | | | |
| Norway | | 2 | 3 | |
| Dublin | 4 | 1 | 10.5 | 6.1 |
| Scotland | | 2 | 3 | |
| Toronto | | 2 | 11 | 6 |
| Sheffield (primary) | 5.8 | 1.4 | 9.8 | 9.8 |
| Sheffield (secondary) | 1.6 | .7 | 4.9 | 3.6 |

SOURCES.—See table 1.

street at age eleven. It seems likely that information about bullying by very young children will have to be obtained from parents and teachers, especially in light of evidence (Ziegler and Rosenstein-Manner 1991) that children under age six have difficulty understanding the concept of bullying.

Results from the most important studies of bullying, using self-report questionnaires, are summarized in table 2. A substantial proportion of children report that they have "ever" been victimized: 72 percent of boys and 58 percent of girls in Dublin (O'Moore and Hillery 1989, 1991) and 50 percent of children in Scotland (Mellor 1990, 1991). Substantial proportions also admit that they have "ever" bullied other children.

The proportions are less, of course, when the bullying is restricted to "this term." However, in Dublin, 48 percent of boys and 38 percent of girls said that they had been victimized this term, as did 49 percent of Toronto children (Ziegler and Rosenstein-Manner 1991). Somewhat fewer children admitted bullying, but the proportion was still substantial: for example, 39 percent in Toronto. The Madrid figures are lower than in Dublin and Toronto, at about 15–20 percent who were bullies and victims (Vieira da Fonseca et al. 1989). However, there is reason to believe that the Madrid figures for "physical and verbal bullying" exclude types of bullying included in other countries (mocking other children, stealing possessions, and social isolation), especially as there is apparently no Spanish word exactly equivalent to bullying (O'Moore 1988).

The questionnaires typically ask children to report whether bullying has occurred this term, not at all, once or twice, sometimes (now and then), about once a week, or more often. Since bullying is, by definition, repeated behavior, it is arguable whether aggression that occurs only once or twice should really be termed bullying. Table 2 shows the percentages of children who report being bullies and victims when bullying is restricted to sometimes or more often this term. Generally, the percentages of bullies and victims are higher in Sheffield and Toronto than in Scotland and Norway, possibly because of the urban nature of the Sheffield and Toronto samples, although in the Norwegian research bullying was not more prevalent in the big cities. Olweus (1990, 1991a) has translated the Norwegian percentages into 41,000 bullies and 53,000 victims in the whole country.

When the frequency for bullying is set even higher at once a week or more often, the prevalence of victims decreases to 10 percent or less, and the prevalence of bullies decreases to 5 percent or less (table 2). Dublin, Toronto, and Sheffield had higher rates of bullying than Scotland and Norway.

Bullies and victims are generally less prevalent in secondary schools (age eleven to sixteen in England) than in primary schools (age seven to eleven); detailed graphs published by Olweus (1990, 1991a) show that the prevalence of victims declined steadily with age for both males and females and that the prevalence of female bullies declined steadily with age, but the prevalence of male bullies stayed roughly constant between ages eight and sixteen. Bullies and victims are more prevalent in classes and schools for children with behavioral, emotional, or learning difficulties (e.g., O'Moore and Hillery 1989; Stephenson and Smith

1989; Ziegler and Rosenstein-Manner 1991). It would be interesting to investigate whether they are also more prevalent in institutions for offenders.

Table 3 summarizes the prevalence of the different types of acts included in the category of bullying. For example, 42 percent of Dublin children were victimized in school "this term"; about two-thirds of them suffered teasing, two-thirds were picked on, and two-thirds were hit or kicked (O'Moore and Hillery 1989). Nearly 46 percent of the Dublin sample were rejected or excluded, and 49.7 percent were victimized on their way to and from school, showing that neither of these categories was included in the victimization figures. The prevalence of different types of acts was lower in Sheffield (Smith 1992), lower in Madrid (Vieira da Fonseca et al. 1989), and lower still in Scotland (Mellor 1990). The Toronto figures for types of acts were only for acts committed sometimes or more often (Ziegler and Rosenstein-Manner 1991).

## C. The Overlap between Bullies and Victims

The most contentious issue in the bullying literature is the extent to which bullies are also victims, and vice versa. Olweus (1978) argued that there was little overlap between bullies and victims. His categories at each age were mutually exclusive, so that children could not simultaneously be bullies and victims. However, he showed that only 6 percent of the bullies at age thirteen became victims at age fourteen (in comparison with the chance expectation of prevalence of 12 percent), and that only 4 percent of the victims at age thirteen became bullies at age fourteen (in comparison with the chance expectation of prevalence of 12 percent). In his national study, Olweus (1991a) found that only one in ten bullies were also victims and only one in eighteen victims were also bullies.

The percentage of bullies who are victims, or vice versa, necessarily depends on the prevalences of bullies and victims and, hence, on the definitions of bullies and victims. Roland (1989) concluded that about 20 percent of victims were also bullies and that their bullying was nearly always directed against children who did not bully them. Stephenson and Smith (1989), on the basis of teacher reports, found that 10 percent of children were bullies, 7 percent were victims, and 6 percent were both bullies and victims. Assuming that these three groups did not overlap (since they also say that 23 percent of children were involved in bullying), it can be estimated that about 38 percent

# TABLE 3

## Prevalence of Types of Victimization

| Location and Type | Prevalence (in Percent) |
|---|---|
| Dublin: | |
|   Teased | 28.9 |
|   Picked on | 27.2 |
|   Hit/kicked | 28.0 |
|   Rejected/excluded | 45.6 |
| Scotland: | |
|   Picked on/called names | 15.4 |
|   Hit/kicked | 7.5 |
|   Rejected | 5.2 |
|   Extortion | 1.6 |
| Toronto (sometimes +): | |
|   Teased | 9.8 |
|   Hit/kicked | 10.6 |
|   Threatened/intimidated | 8.4 |

| | Prevalence (in Percent) | |
|---|---|---|
| | Male | Female |
| Madrid: | | |
|   Physical aggression | 14.4 | 9.2 |
|   Laughed at/mocked | 19 | 19.9 |
|   Hidden material/theft | 14.9 | 12 |
|   Rejected/isolated | 7.1 | 7.3 |

| | Prevalence (in Percent) | |
|---|---|---|
| | Primary | Secondary |
| Sheffield: | | |
|   Racial name calling | 8.5 | 2.9 |
|   Other name calling | 28.4 | 19.6 |
|   Hit/kicked | 20.7 | 8.3 |
|   Threatened | 17.1 | 8.1 |
|   Rejected | 10.1 | 2.3 |
|   Rumors spread | 14.7 | 7.7 |
|   Belongings taken | 8.6 | 3.0 |

SOURCES.—See table 1.

of all bullies were also victims, and that about 46 percent of all victims were also bullies—an overlap far in excess of chance expectation.

Mellor (1990) in Scotland, relying on self-reports, showed that about 15 percent were only victims, 7 percent were only bullies, and 3 percent were both bullies and victims (sometimes or more often during their school career). Yates and Smith (1989) in two Sheffield schools found that 20 percent of bullies were also victims, while 34 percent of victims were also bullies. O'Moore and Hillery (1989) in Dublin reported that 66 percent of bullies were also victims (higher than the prevalence of victims "this term" of 42 percent), and that 46 percent of victims were also bullies (higher than the prevalence of bullies "this term" of 29 percent).

The strength of the relationship between bullies and victims may decrease as the criteria for bullies and victims become more stringent. Bullies may also overreport their own victimization in order to provide some justification for their own behavior (Olweus 1991*b*). However, more research is needed to establish the concurrent overlap between bullies and victims according to different definitions, the extent to which victims at one age become bullies at a later age and vice versa, and the causal effect (if any) of victimization on later bullying. Widom (1989) showed that children who were physically abused were significantly likely to become violent offenders later on in life, and there may also be a tendency for victims later to become bullies.

## D. Bullying and Victimization Careers

Generally, boys bully more than girls, but boys and girls are equally victimized. Boys are overwhelmingly bullied by boys, while girls are equally bullied by boys and girls. Many victims are bullied by only one child at any given time. For example, Whitney and Smith (1991) in Sheffield reported that, of male primary school victims, 55.4 percent were bullied by one boy, 29.3 percent by several boys, 12.1 percent by both boys and girls, 1.3 percent by one girl, and 2.0 percent by several girls. Of female primary school victims, 27.4 percent were bullied by one boy, 12.7 percent by several boys, 22.1 percent by both boys and girls, 22.7 percent by one girl, and 15.2 percent by several girls. Most of the bullies were in the same class or the same year, while about 30 percent were older and fewer than 10 percent younger. These results are similar to those obtained in Norway, although a somewhat higher percentage of female victims were bullied by boys in Norway (Olweus 1990, 1991*a*).

These results do not reveal the extent to which a victim is always bullied by the same bully or bullies; a victim is bullied by children together in groups as opposed to several children consecutively; bullies are leaders, recruiters, or followers; children in groups are victimized; and one child bullies several different victims consecutively. Stephenson and Smith (1989) in Cleveland reported that 67 percent of bullies picked on more than one victim at any given time, and 78 percent of bullies had picked on different victims at different times. Similarly, the majority of victims were bullied by more than one child at any given time and had been bullied by different children at different times. Three-quarters of bullies had phases when they bullied interspersed with nonbullying phases, while 77 percent of victims had phases when they were victimized interspersed with nonvictim phases. Nearly half of the bullies (41 percent) encouraged other children to join them in bullying.

Perhaps because they were originally devised in ethnically homogeneous Scandinavian countries, the questionnaires typically ask the victims to report the age and sex of their bullies but solicit no information about ethnicity. It would be valuable to investigate whether certain ethnic groups differentially tend to bully other ethnic groups and how the prevalence of bullies and victims varies with ethnicity. The ethnicity of criminal offenders and crime victims is investigated in victim surveys such as the British Crime Survey (Mayhew, Elliott, and Dowds 1989) and the American National Crime Victimization Survey (Bureau of Justice Statistics 1991). However, the survey by Junger (1990) of Dutch, Moroccan, Turkish, and Surinamese boys in the Netherlands seems to be one of the few bullying projects focusing on ethnic differences. She found no ethnic differences in bullying victimization but that ethnic minority victims attributed their victimization to their ethnicity (unlike native Dutch victims). In Toronto, one in eight children over all, and one in three of those in inner-city schools, said that racial bullying often occurred in their schools (Ziegler and Rosenstein-Manner 1991).

Bullying tends to persist over time. For example, Yates and Smith (1989) in Sheffield reported that nearly two-thirds of bullies "this term" were also bullies last term. Similarly, Olweus (1978) in Stockholm found that two-thirds of bullies in one year were still bullies in the next year, while about two-thirds of victims in one year were still victims in the next year. Bjorkvist et al. (1982) in Finland reported 95 percent agreement between peer ratings of bullies or victims in one year and peer ratings in the next year. Stephenson and Smith (1989) discovered that 89 percent of the bullies had started bullying at least a year earlier, and 72 percent of the victims had been bullied for at least a year. Lane (1989) concluded that many victims had been victimized for two or three years.

It might be helpful to apply the concepts of criminal career research (see, e.g., Farrington 1992) to the investigation of bullying and victimization careers. A criminal career is defined as a longitudinal sequence of offenses. It has a beginning (onset), an end (desistance), and a career length in between (duration). Only a certain proportion of the population (prevalence) has a criminal career and commits offenses. During their careers, offenders commit offenses at a certain rate (frequency), and they may accelerate, decelerate, and have periods in remission. By investigating factors that influence onset, escalation, desistance, and so on, it should be possible to make recommendations about how to prevent criminal careers starting, how to prevent escalation after onset, and how to foster desistance. The factors influencing the onset of offending seem to be different from those influencing desistance; for example, parenting and peer factors influence onset, whereas employment and marriage foster desistance.

It would be interesting to investigate the cumulative prevalence of bullying and victimization at different ages, when and why bullying and victimization careers began, how long they persist, and when and why they end. For example, if the lifetime prevalences of bullying and victimization were very high, this might suggest that these behaviors were part of normal development. Information about why bullying ends should be helpful in knowing how to reduce bullying. It would also be interesting to study the frequency of bullying incidents during these careers. Another useful focus would be the onset, duration, and desistance of bully-victim pairs and of bullying groups and, more generally, the intertwining of bullying and victimization careers.

The career approach would encourage the developmental study of bullying and victimization, instead of the "snapshot" approach of cross-sectional surveys, which may not be very helpful in developing long-term prevention strategies. It would also facilitate better understanding of the relations between bullies and victims and particularly how often and why victims at one age become bullies at a different age. The same person may have both a bullying career and a victimization career, and it would be interesting to study the relationship between these two careers. Another interesting question concerns the effect on the observer of seeing someone victimized, which may be affected by the degree to which the observer feels empathy with the victim.

Longitudinal research on bullying and victimization would be needed to study the development of bullying and victimization careers, the effects of life events on these careers, and particularly developmental sequences linking bullying, victimization, and other behaviors. This should not be exclusively focused on schools since bullying and victimization also occur in other settings.

## II. Correlates, Predictors, and Consequences

Despite the methodological, measurement, and other limitations of the bullying literature, much can be learned from it about correlates, predictors, and consequences of bullying.

### A. Characteristics of Bullies

In his Stockholm research, Olweus (1978) concluded that male bullies had an aggressive personality, weak inhibitions against aggression, a strong need to dominate, and a favorable attitude toward aggression and that they obtained pleasure from bullying and recruited other boys to do it. They were relatively tough, strong, confident, somewhat below average in popularity, and had high testosterone levels and low adrenaline (reflecting underarousal). With the exception of a very small number of nervous bullies, they were not anxious or insecure. They had low empathy with victims and low guilt about bullying (Olweus 1984). They were slightly below average in school attainment and had negative attitudes toward school work and teachers. They were not close to their parents, reporting that their parents did not care for them, and negative to their fathers, who generally did not participate with them in leisure activities.

These results have generally been replicated in other studies. In Hampshire, Lowenstein (1978b) found that bullies were disruptive, hyperactive, slightly below average in intelligence and reading ability, and high in neuroticism on the Maudsley Personality Inventory. They had parents with marital difficulties who used poor child-rearing methods, and their parents tended to be high on authoritarian attitudes. In Finland, Bjorkvist et al. (1982) concluded that bullies were dominant and impulsive, while Lagerspetz et al. (1982) reported that they were strong, aggressive, and somewhat unpopular. In Scotland, Mellor (1990) reported that bullies tended to come from lower-class families, to have three or more siblings, and to live apart from their natural parents. In France, bullying was more common in lower-class families even for children who were adopted (Duyme 1990). In Dublin, O'Moore and Hillery (1991) showed that bullies tended to be unpopular, unhappy, with low self-esteem and low intellectual status. Half of them hated school, and a third (32 percent) met the criteria for conduct disorder on the Rutter (1967) questionnaire.

Perhaps the most extensive English information about bullying is provided by Stephenson and Smith (1989) in Cleveland. They discovered that bullies tended to be physically strong, active and assertive, easily provoked, enjoyed aggression, very confident, and of average popularity. In addition, they had poor concentration, poor school attainment, poor hygiene, and (unspecified) problems at home. About 18 percent were anxious bullies, with low popularity and low confidence, and those who were both bullies and victims also tended to have low popularity. In Toronto, Ziegler and Rosenstein-Manner (1991) asked the bullies why they bullied, and found that the most popular answers were to feel powerful and to be "cool."

The main issue in dispute is whether bullies are typically popular or unpopular. A key question is whether it is necessary or desirable to identify a minority of anxious bullies who are qualitatively different from the remainder. This is reminiscent of the long-standing debate about whether it is necessary to distinguish between "primary" or nonanxious psychopaths and "secondary" psychopaths who show anxiety (e.g., Blackburn 1988). In addition, it would be helpful to study differences between male and female bullies in detail.

## B. Characteristics of Victims

Olweus (1978, p. 123) found that male victims tended to be very unpopular, rejected by peers, anxious, weak, nonassertive, sensitive, and to have low self-esteem. They tended to be slightly low in school attainment. Their parents tended to be overanxious, "wrapping their boys in cotton wool." A small minority of victims were irritating, restless, or provocative. Olweus systematically investigated the prevalence of numerous external deviations, namely wearing glasses, physical handicaps, hearing problems, speech or language differences, obesity, small stature, physical weakness, appearance, skin color, personal hygiene, facial expression (e.g., grimacing), posture, and dress. Overall, he concluded that there was a weak tendency for victims to have negative physical deviations. However, the generally low prevalence of these deviations may have masked their importance as features of victims. For example, 27 percent of victims had three or more of these deviations, compared with 15 percent of bullies and 9 percent of controls. Large samples of victims are needed to establish the true importance of infrequently occurring physical deviations.

Olweus's conclusions about victims have largely been replicated by other researchers. In Hampshire, Lowenstein (1978*a*) concluded that victims tended to be less physically robust, less physically attractive, with odd mannerisms or physical handicaps, unwilling to retaliate, less sensitive to the feelings of others, and less likely to join in with others in work. In Finland, Bjorkvist et al. (1982) showed that victims were less attractive, less intelligent, and more depressed, while Lagerspetz et al. (1982) reported that they were unpopular, weak, with physical deviations and low self-esteem. In Scotland, Mellor (1990) found that victims tended to come from lower-class families and to be living apart from their natural parents. In Dublin, O'Moore and Hillery (1991) discovered that victims tended to be less popular, more anxious, and less happy than others, and had very low self-esteem. Perhaps because of the overlap between bullies and victims in Dublin, over one-quarter (28 percent) of victims met the criteria for conduct disorder on the Rutter (1967) questionnaire.

Stephenson and Smith (1989) in Cleveland reported that victims tended to be unpopular, passive, physically weak, and lacking in confidence. In addition, they were rated as thin and appearing different from other children in dress or speech (18 percent of victims as opposed to only 3 percent of bullies and other children). Like bullies, they tended to have poor concentration, poor school attainment, and poor hygiene. A minority of victims (17 percent) were classified as provocative, and the children who were both bullies and victims also tended to be provocative. In Sheffield, Yates and Smith (1989) found that victims tended to be alone at break times and to feel lonely and less well liked than other children. In a London primary school, Frost (1991) concluded that victims tended to be misfits because of appearance, lack of friends, low self-esteem, or being irritating or unusually compliant. Finally, Besag (1989*a*, 1991) highlighted the likelihood of clumsy children with problems of motor coordination becoming victims.

A key issue for future research is whether it is necessary or desirable to identify a minority of provocative victims who are qualitatively different from the remainder. In addition, it would be helpful to study differences between male and female victims in detail.

## C. Environmental Influences

As Frost (1991) pointed out, bullying flourishes at playtime (recess), when supervision is minimal. However, it also occurs in classrooms. Questionnaire studies show that the most common school location for bullying is in the playground. For example, Whitney and Smith (1991) found that in primary schools 76 percent of victims were bullied in the playground, 30 percent in the classroom, and 13 percent in the corridors. In secondary schools, 45 percent of victims were bullied in the playground, 39 percent in the classroom, and 30 percent in the corridors. Similarly, in Scotland, Mellor (1990) showed that 44 percent of victims said that bullying usually took place in the playground, 28 percent in the classroom, 15 percent outside school, 9 percent in corridors or washrooms, and 4 percent on the way to or from school. He considered that children were not supervised effectively on the playground in any of his ten schools, and that the design of the school influenced bullying (e.g., in schools with many long corridors, bullying occurred in the corridors).

Similar results were obtained in other countries. For example, in Toronto, Ziegler and Rosenstein-Manner (1991) found that children said that bullying occurred in the playground (57 percent), hallways (43 percent), classrooms (35 percent), lunchrooms (25 percent), on the way from school (24 percent), on the way to school (18 percent), and in washrooms (15 percent). In Madrid, Vieira da Fonseca et al. (1989) discovered that 42 percent of children said that bullying occurred during recess, and 20 percent that it occurred during class. Olweus (1991a) showed that two or three times as many children were bullied at school as on the way to or from school but that there was a marked tendency for children bullied on the way to or from school also to be bullied at school.

It might be expected that the rate of victimization of different age groups would be affected by the age range of the school. For example, ten- to eleven-year-olds in English primary schools, where they are the oldest age group, might have a lower rate of victimization than eleven- to twelve-year-olds in English secondary schools, where they are the youngest age group. The review by Tattum (1989) shows that victimization is one of the most common worries of children transferring from primary to secondary schools. For example, in a study of 173 first-form children in a London secondary school, Brown and Armstrong (1982) found that the most common worries (of twenty-two) were tests, detentions, being late, horrible pupils, doing wrong, and being bullied.

Many researchers have found that the prevalences of bullies and victims varied considerably between schools and have sought to discover school characteristics that distinguish between high-rate and low-rate schools. Generally, schools with a high prevalence of bullying at one time tend also to have a high prevalence some years later (Munthe 1989). In Scotland, Mellor (1991) reported that the proportion victimized sometimes or more often varied between 2 percent and 15 percent over ten schools. In Sheffield, Whitney and Smith (1991) showed that the proportion victimized sometimes or more often varied between 18 percent and 49 percent over seventeen primary schools and between 8 percent and 13 percent over seven secondary schools. The proportion bullying sometimes or more often varied between 7 percent and 28 percent over seventeen primary schools and between 3 percent and 9 percent over seven secondary schools.

In Olweus's earliest (1978) and later (1991a) research, the prevalence of bullying was not related to school size or class size, and Whitney and Smith (1991) came to the same conclusion in Sheffield. Stephenson and Smith (1989) in Cleveland reported that bullying was more prevalent in larger schools and in schools with larger classes but that the differences were not statistically significant over their twenty-six primary schools. Dale (1991) showed that bullying was more prevalent in single sex than in mixed-sex schools. Olweus (1991a) concluded that bullies and victims were not more prevalent in big city schools, but Ziegler and Rosenstein-Manner (1991) in Toronto found that more bullying was reported in inner-city schools. Also, Stephenson and Smith (1991) and Whitney and Smith (1991) showed that bullying was more prevalent in schools in socially disadvantaged areas. Bullying rates of Sheffield schools were not related to the proportion of non-white children (Whitney and Smith 1991).

Future research should attempt to investigate school factors that are correlated with the prevalence of bullies and victims. For example, Stephenson and Smith (1991) compared six high-bullying and six low-bullying schools and reported that head teachers in the low-bullying schools tended to express articulate, considered views on bullying and attached importance to controlling and preventing its occurrence. The key question is whether features of the school are related to bullying after allowing for features of the children at intake. This kind of question has been addressed in studies of delinquency rates in schools, which also vary dramatically from one school to another. For example, Farrington (1972) in London found that the delinquency rates of different secondary schools had little influence on the delinquency of boys after controlling for the secondary schools' differential intakes of troublesome boys from primary schools. Also in London, Rutter et al. (1979) showed that differences between secondary schools in delinquency rates could not be entirely explained by differences in the social class and verbal reasoning scores of their children at intake. Similar methodologies need to be used in studying the extent to which features of the schools might have some influence on bullying. If important school features are discovered, they could have momentous implications for the prevention of bullying.

While it is plausible to assume that bullying incidents arise from the interaction between potential bullies and potential victims in environments that provide opportunities for bullying, and while a great deal is known about characteristics of bullies, victims, and environments, no comprehensive theory of bullying that connects the disparate results has yet been developed. Researchers should attempt to develop such an all-embracing theory to guide future research and prevention efforts.

## D. The Aftermath of Bullying and Victimization

Not all bullying incidents come to the notice of teachers, of course, and many researchers have commented on children's inhibitions against "telling tales." In Scotland, Mellor (1990) reported that half of the victims had told nobody and that, of the remainder, 47 percent had told a parent and only 31 percent had told a teacher. In Sheffield, Whitney and Smith (1991) showed that between 43 percent and 63 percent of primary school victims had told a teacher (increasing with the frequency of victimization), and between 56 percent and 84 percent had told someone at home. The figures were lower in secondary schools. Between 22 percent and 40 percent of secondary school children had told a teacher and between 38 percent and 51 percent had told someone at home. In Toronto, 47 percent of victims had told a teacher, and 63 percent had told a parent (Ziegler and Rosenstein-Manner 1991).

Answers to hypothetical questions yield lower percentages who say that they would not tell. In Dublin, O'Moore and Hillery (1991) found that only 34 percent of children said that they would not tell a teacher and 15 percent would not tell a parent if they were bullied at school, while 55 percent would not tell if they saw someone else being bullied. Nearly half of the children (46 percent) thought that it was wrong to tell tales, and 54 percent were afraid that the bully might pick on them. Ziegler and Rosenstein-Manner (1991) asked bullies what victims should do, and ascertained that 51 percent said tell teachers, 50 percent said tell parents, 46 percent said fight back, 31 percent said tell friends, and 21 percent said talk to the bully. It would be useful to explore in more detail the reasons why victims do not tell teachers, just as the reasons for not reporting crimes to the police have been explored in detail in crime victimization surveys (e.g., Hough and Mayhew 1983). It might be expected that the probability of reporting would increase with the seriousness of the bullying behavior.

Teachers and other children do not always intervene to prevent bullying. In Sheffield, only 54 percent of primary school children and 48 percent of secondary school children reported that teachers sometimes or almost always intervened (Whitney and Smith 1991). In Toronto, only 39 percent of children thought that teachers nearly always or often intervened, 31 percent thought that teachers occasionally intervened, and 30 percent thought that teachers hardly ever intervened. However, 85 percent of teachers thought that they nearly always or often intervened, with only 8 percent considering that they occasionally intervened and 8 percent saying that they hardly ever intervened (Ziegler and Rosenstein-Manner 1991). It would be interesting to know why the perceptions of children and teachers about the frequency of intervention are so different.

In Sheffield, when children were asked what they usually did when they saw someone being bullied, 54 percent of primary and 34 percent of secondary children said that they tried to help; 27 percent of primary and 47 percent of secondary children said that they did nothing but thought that they ought to help; and 19 percent of both groups said that they did nothing and thought it was none of their business. More worryingly, only 65 percent of primary and 51 percent of secondary children thought that they could not join in bullying (Whitney and Smith 1991).

In a study of teasing among 175 inner-London primary school children, Mooney, Creeser, and Blatchford (1991) asked children how they had reacted to teasing. Just over half (52.7 percent) said that they had retaliated, while 43.8 percent had taken no notice and 26.8 percent had told a teacher. Afro-Caribbean boys were especially likely to retaliate rather than take no notice. Mooney et al. (1991) also asked victims why they thought they had been teased. The most common reasons were because of provocation (20.5 percent), enjoyment for the teaser (13.6 percent), envy of the teased child by the teaser (10.2 percent), the prestige of the teaser (10.2 percent), the teasing was accurate (9.1 percent), and the teaser disliked the teased child (8.0 percent).

Bullying and victimization have immediate and longer-term consequences. The victims may feel psychological or physical distress or pain, may find it difficult to concentrate on their schoolwork (Mellor 1991), and may be afraid to go to school because of their fear of being victimized. Reid (1989) found that victimization was the initial reason given by 15 percent of persistent absentees for first staying away from school, and 19 percent said it was one of the major reasons for their continued absence. Olweus (1992b) showed that victims tended to have low self-esteem and high depression seven to ten years later. The behavior of the bullies may escalate to more serious criminal acts, possibly because the pleasure of bullying reinforces their aggressive tendencies; for example, Olweus (1991a) reported that 60 percent of bullies in his Norwegian study were convicted of criminal offenses up to age twenty-four and that their prevalence of recidivist criminality was four times that of nonbullies.

### E. Bullying and Externalizing Problems

Up to this point, bullying has largely been discussed as though it were an isolated behavior. It is not. Bullying is only one element of aggression, just as aggression is only one element of a larger syndrome of antisocial behavior. In the psychiatric literature, this larger syndrome is usually termed "disruptive behavior disorders," comprising conduct disorder, attention deficit-hyperactivity disorder, and oppositional defiant disorder, and is distinguished from the anxiety disorders (American Psychiatric Association 1987). A similar distinction is drawn in British child and adolescent psychiatry (e.g., Graham and Rutter 1985).

The literature on child psychopathology is more relevant to this essay because of the widespread use of checklists of symptoms completed by teachers, parents, and children (e.g., Achenbach and Edelbrock 1984). In child psychopathology, this larger "broadband" antisocial syndrome is usually termed "externalizing problems" because the behaviors describe conflicts with other people, external to the child. The other broadband syndrome of "internalizing problems," involving internal conflicts and distress, is discussed in the next section. Generally, there is a great deal of concordance between behavior checklist syndromes and psychiatric diagnoses (e.g., Edelbrock and Costello 1988). The most widely used checklist is the Child Behavior Checklist of Achenbach and Edelbrock (1983). This has cross-cultural validity in identifying (through factor analysis) six behavioral syndromes in boys and girls aged six to eleven and twelve to sixteen: aggression, delinquency, attention problems (externalizing), anxious/depressed, shy/withdrawn, somatic complaints (internalizing: see Achenbach et al. 1989).

The aggression syndrome includes such items as bullying, teasing, starting fights, arguing, boasting, impulsivity, disobedience, sulking, swearing, showing off, stubbornness, screaming, demanding attention, and not feeling guilty. (For a factor analysis showing the links between bullying and these other items, see Tremblay et al. [1991].) Similar correlates of bullying have been noted in the education literature (e.g., Beck 1985). The Child Behavior Checklist does not contain an item specifically on bullying but includes items specifying "cruelty, bullying, or meanness to others," "teases a lot," and "threatens people." Researchers on bullying might be interested to see the prevalence figures for these items published in the literature. For example, Achenbach and Edelbrock (1981) reported a study of a random sample of 1,442 parents of boys and girls aged four to sixteen in the Washington, D.C., metropolitan area. The percentage reporting cruelty or bullying by their child in the previous six months decreased markedly with age for girls (from about 20 percent at four to about 2 percent at sixteen), but less so for boys (from 21 percent at four to about 14 percent at sixteen).

The childhood psychopathology literature also yields information about the stability of behaviors over time. For example, in the Netherlands, Verhulst and Althaus (1988) collected Child Behavior Checklists from 1,412 parents of boys and girls aged four to fourteen in 1983 and again at ages six to sixteen in 1985. Most of the items showed significant stability over this two-year interval, including the three mentioned above. Aggression scores had stability coefficients (correlations) averaging .66 over all age-sex groups, and broadband externalizing scores had stability coefficients averaging .62 over all age-sex groups. However, while there was relative stability, the absolute scores declined over the two years for both sexes. In other words, boys and girls became less aggressive with age, but the more aggressive children at the first time were still relatively more aggressive two years later. Teacher reports of aggressive and externalizing behaviors were also significantly stable over four years (Verhulst and Van der Ende 1991).

Many researchers have shown that there tends to be relative stability in measures of aggression over time for both males (e.g., Olweus 1979) and females (e.g., Olweus 1981). For example, the average stability coefficient in sixteen surveys of male aggression covering time intervals of up to twenty-one years was .68. Olweus (1984) reports that his interest in the stability of aggression arose because of his observation of the stability of bullying. He also considered how much this stability reflected the individual as opposed to the environment. Conceding that family and situational factors were important influences on aggression, he concluded that stable individual reaction tendencies were more important.

Several other studies show continuity between aggression in childhood and adolescence and later delinquency and crime, especially violent crime. Stattin and Magnusson (1989) followed 1,027 children from Orebro, Sweden, and found that teachers' ratings of aggression at ages ten and thirteen predicted officially recorded offending (and especially violent offending) up to age twenty-six. The teachers' ratings covered aggressiveness toward teachers and children, disturbing and quarreling with children, impertinence, and obstructiveness (Magnusson 1988). Similarly, Pulkkinen (1987) in Finland followed 369 children from ages eight to twenty and showed that offensive aggression at age fourteen (attacking and teasing without reason) predicted officially recorded violent offenses up to age twenty.

Eron et al. (1987) followed 518 children from New York State and found that peer-rated aggression at age eight significantly predicted criminal convictions up to age thirty (as well as aggression against spouses and the severity of physical punishment of children). The Eron study is often cited in the bullying literature as a study of the link between childhood bullying and later offending; actually, none of the peer nomination items at age eight specifically mentioned bullying; the closest items are saying mean things, taking other children's things, pushing or shoving children, doing things that bother others, and starting a fight over nothing (e.g., Lefkowitz et al. 1977). Other longitudinal studies of aggression (see, e.g., Pepler and Rubin 1991) and, indeed, of externalizing problems (e.g., White et al. 1990) are probably just as relevant to bullying. Studies of the childhood antecedents and later adult sequelae of adolescent aggression (e.g., Farrington 1991*b*) are also relevant to bullying.

## F. Victimization and Internalizing Problems

Victimization, like bullying, should not be studied in isolation. Victimization is probably one element of a larger syndrome of anxiety disorders or internalizing problems. However, as Perry et al. (1988, p. 807) pointed out, "despite the fact that all acts of interpersonal aggression involve two participants, a bully and a victim, almost all research devoted to understanding aggressive behavior has focused on the aggressor."

The Child Behavior Checklist does not include a specific question about being a victim of bullying. However, "feels others are out to get him or her," "fears going to school," and "complaining of loneliness" are all items included in the anxious/depressed syndrome, along with other fears, nervousness, self-consciousness, worrying, and unhappiness (Achenbach et al. 1989). Researchers on bullying might be interested in the prevalence figures for these items (according to parents) in the Washington, D.C., research of Achenbach and Edelbrock (1981). For example, loneliness generally decreased between ages four to five and age sixteen, but feeling persecuted increased up to ages eight to nine and then decreased. Another item related to victimization, "gets teased a lot," increased up to age ten to eleven and then decreased.

The Dutch research of Verhulst and Althaus (1988) provides information about the stability of these behaviors over a two-year period. For example, loneliness, feeling persecuted, and getting teased a lot were all significantly stable over time, but fearing school was not. Anxiety/depression scores had stability coefficients averaging .57 over all age-sex groups, compared with .59 for shyness/withdrawal (another likely correlate of victimization), and .54 for broadband internalizing scores. However, while there was relative stability, the absolute scores generally declined over the two years. In other words, the children tended to become less anxious, depressed, shy, or withdrawn over time, although the relatively more anxious children at one time were still relatively more anxious at the later time.

There is a long history of sociometric research on peer status among children, focusing on popularity or being rejected by peers (e.g., Croft and Grygier 1956). However, research on peer rejection has intensified in the last decade, largely because of the work of Coie and Dodge (1983). Generally, there are two main reasons for peer rejection: aggression and shyness/withdrawal (Coie 1990). The aggressive children tend to be actively rejected and disliked, whereas the shy or withdrawn children tend to be neglected, with few friends, and few children who nominate them as either most liked or most disliked.

Parker and Asher (1987) completed an extensive review of research on "low-accepted" children who are either rejected or neglected because of aggression or shyness. Their conclusions that children rejected by peers because of aggression tended to have later school problems (dropping out early) and to be involved in delinquency and crime were not surprising and were concordant with numerous other studies of the continuity of aggression mentioned earlier. However, they also reviewed several studies showing that children neglected by peers because of shyness did not tend to have later behavior problems such as delinquency but did tend to have later mental health problems such as schizophrenia and neuroses. Hence, researchers are likely to find that victims of bullying have later mental health problems even if there is no causal effect of the victimization.

Shyness seems to be apparent quite early in life. Kagan, Reznick, and Snidman (1988) showed that shy children at age two still tended to be significantly shy at age seven. They speculated that these inhibited children were born with a lower threshold for limbic-hypothalamic arousal to unexpected changes in the environment and that inherited variations in the threshold for arousal contributed not only to shyness in childhood but also to extreme degrees of social avoidance in adults.

Most recently, peer status research has focused explicitly on bullying. In North Carolina, Dodge et al. (1990) and Coie, Dodge, et al. (1991) systematically observed interactions between black boys aged seven (in first grade) and nine (in third grade) in experimentally designated play groups. They initially obtained peer nominations of boys who were aggressive or not and rejected or not and placed the different categories of boys together in play groups. Bullying was coded when an unprovoked boy taunted, dominated, coerced, made fun of, or abused a peer. The raters agreed in identifying a bullying incident 72 percent of the time. Most of the time, the victim submitted to the bullying, rather than trying to defend himself. Their results differed according to age. At age seven, surprisingly, popular boys tended to bully and aggressive boys tended to be victimized. At age nine, as expected, rejected boys tended to be bullies, and nonaggressive boys tended to be victimized. Coie, Dodge, et al. (1991) speculated that what they had labeled as bullying might be acceptable and adaptive behavior to establish dominance in the peer group at school entry (first grade) but less acceptable later on.

There is some suggestion in the literature of an interaction between shyness and aggression. In Chicago, Kellam (1990) reported that black boys who were both shy and aggressive in first grade committed more assaults as teenagers than boys who were only aggressive or only shy. Similarly, Kellam et al. (1983) found that the shy and aggressive boys were heavier substance users as teenagers, especially of cigarettes, beer, and wine. Whether shy and aggressive children are disproportionately bullies or victims (or both) is not clear, and research on this topic would be informative. In one of the few relevant studies, Lyons, Serbin, and Marchessault (1988) discovered that shy and aggressive children were disproportionately victimized and speculated that this was because they were provocative. It may be that shy and aggressive children tend to be both bullies and victims.

### III. Intragenerational and Intergenerational Continuity in Bullying

Little is known about continuities in male bullying from adolescence to adulthood, and whether males who bully tend to have children who bully. Similarly, little is known about the likelihood that males who are victims of bullying in adolescence will tend to have children who are victims of bullying, and the predictors and correlates of bullying and victimization. The Appendix reports analyses of data from a twenty-four-year follow-up of London boys on these questions. No other research project has followed up boys who are bullies in adolescence to investigate whether they tend to have children who are also bullies.

The results of the analyses show that there is intragenerational continuity in bullying. The bullies at age fourteen tended also to be bullies at age eighteen and at age thirty-two. There was specific continuity in bullying over and above the general continuity of aggressiveness. The most important predictors of bullying were low attainment at age eleven, convicted parents at age ten, physical neglect at age eight, and the father not joining in the boy's leisure activities at age twelve. Bullies did not tend to "have few or no friends" or to attend church at age eight.

The analyses also show that there is intergenerational continuity in bullying. The bullies at age fourteen tended at age thirty-two to have children who were bullies. There was specific transmission of bullying over and above any general tendency for antisocial men to have antisocial children. In addition to bullying at age fourteen, being unpopular at ages twelve to fourteen, having poor reading skills, and gambling heavily at age eighteen predicted having a child bully at age thirty-two. Boys who were unpopular at ages eight to ten, who had few friends at age eight, who suffered poor child rearing at age eight, and who were nervous and regular smokers at age fourteen tended at age thirty-two to have children who were victims of bullying. The fact that nervous and unpopular boys tended to have victimized children suggests that there is also intergenerational transmission of victimization.

## IV. Prevention of Bullying

Methods of preventing bullying can be classified into those focusing primarily on bullies, those focusing primarily on victims, and those focusing primarily on the environment (here, the school). Ideally, prevention methods should be based on well-developed theories, but in practice many are based on somewhat disconnected hypotheses.

### A. Prevention Focusing on Bullies

Many strategies proposed to reduce bullying can be classified under the familiar criminal justice headings of deterrence, retribution, reformation, incapacitation, denunciation, and reparation (see, e.g., Farrington 1978). For example, bullying was the most frequent offense leading to corporal punishment in Northern Ireland (Tattum 1989). In Cleveland, use of physical punishment to deter the bully was considered to be sometimes helpful by about half the teachers and about a third of the staff of the Psychological Service (Stephenson and Smith 1989). Also, the majority of children advocated the use of punishment. The techniques most favored by the teachers were using verbal reprimands to deter the bully and attempting to change the bully's behavior by reasoning. Stephenson and Smith (1991) advocated that teachers should aim to praise good behavior rather than use sanctions and that they should be careful not to bully themselves since the teachers would tend to serve as models for the children.

Frost (1991) and Jones (1991) provided practical suggestions for dealing with bullying, based on their experiences in inner-city primary and secondary schools, respectively. For example, Frost advocated "talking it through" with the bully and the victim and gave a useful example of a letter sent home to parents. This included statements such as, "I view this as such a serious problem that I intend in future to suspend children who have borne grudges and taken revenge days later, or ganged up with others to pick on one child, or indulged in violent, unprovoked behavior. I do hope that you will do all you can to support us in stamping out this undesirable trend towards violence. It is in everyone's interest that such antisocial behavior should be dealt with most severely" (Frost 1991, p. 33). She thought that the most effective sanction was peer group pressure and that children should be encouraged to be responsible for each other's safety. Jones pointed out the importance of helping children to tell teachers about bullying and also advocated bringing together bullies, victims, and their parents. He proposed that incidents should be recorded, bullies should be punished (e.g., by exclusion from school), and punishments should be recorded.

Several writers have focused on reparation and on promoting reformation by increasing empathy, rather than on deterrence, retribution, and incapacitation (exclusion). For example, Tattum (1989) emphasized the need for bullies to see things from the viewpoint of the victim. Pearce (1991) urged that the most effective measure was to insist that the bully should make amends to the victim for the distress caused. Any contract between the bully and the victim should be with the victim's agreement and closely supervised to make sure that it was successfully completed. Parents should be encouraged to teach caring and empathetic relationships, making the bully realize how the victim felt.

Foster and Thompson (1991) also recommended bringing bullies and victims together and working out some type of atonement that the bully could make to the victim. Also, they considered that children should be encouraged to report bullying. They proposed that teachers should meet with bullies and their parents, and with victims and their parents, to discuss the positive things that might happen at home to help their children not to get into these situations again. Foster and Thompson suggested that teachers needed training in counseling skills for these encounters. Goddard and Cross (1987) described a social skills training course for disruptive children which included sessions on teasing and bullying.

Several other workers have recommended a variety of strategies focusing on bullies. Lowenstein (1991) proposed making the bully aware of the victim's feelings, punishing the bully, providing opportunities for the bully to behave positively, and rewarding desirable behavior by the bully (e.g., using tokens that could be exchanged for extrinsic rewards such as sweets or privileges). Besag (1989b) advocated conflict resolution to achieve reconciliation between bullies and victims, counseling to help bullies and victims understand each other's point of view, class discussions so that the bullies could see that group opinion was against them, and behavioral programs for bullying focusing especially on rewarding desirable behavior. Priest (1989) also provided a useful summary of strategies targeted on the bully, including vigorous disapproval by adults, encouraging disapproval by peers, providing feedback on the extent of the distress caused, insisting on restitution, and rewarding desirable behavior.

Unfortunately, none of these strategies targeted on bullies has been systematically evaluated in controlled experiments. However, many programs designed to reduce aggression by children and adolescents have been systematically evaluated, especially in North America, and it might be expected that techniques that reduce aggression would also tend to reduce bullying.

One of the most relevant projects has been carried out in Seattle by Hawkins, Von Cleve, and Catalano (1991). This was designed to decrease aggressive behavior, delinquency, and drug abuse and to increase prosocial behavior by promoting social bonding. In eight Seattle schools, 458 first-grade children (ages six to seven) were randomly assigned to be in experimental or control classes and were followed up. The children in the experimental classes received special treatment at home and school that was designed to increase their attachment to their parents and their bonding to the school. Their parents were trained to notice and reinforce socially desirable behavior in a program called "Catch 'em being good." Their teachers were trained in classroom management, for example, to provide clear instructions and expectations to children, to reward children for participation in desired behavior, and to teach children prosocial methods of solving problems.

In an evaluation of this program eighteen months later, when the children were in different classes, Hawkins et al. (1991) found that the boys who received the experimental program were significantly less aggressive than the control boys, according to teacher ratings on the Child Behavior Checklist. They also scored less on broadband externalizing symptoms. These differences were obtained for white boys rather than black boys. The experimental white girls were not significantly less aggressive, but they were less self-destructive, nervous, and depressed.

Another highly relevant project was carried out in Montreal by Tremblay et al. (1991). This began with a kindergarten assessment at age six that identified 249 disruptive boys for the experiment. These boys were then randomly assigned to treatment or control groups. The treated boys received parent training and social skills training between ages seven and nine and were then followed up every year. The parent training was based on the work of Patterson (1982). Parents were trained to monitor children's behavior and to give positive reinforcement for prosocial behavior and negative reinforcement for antisocial behavior. The social skills training was carried out with small groups and included sessions on such themes as "what to do when I am angry" and "how to react to teasing."

Tremblay (1991) kindly supplied specific outcome data on teacher-rated bullying. This showed that the treated and control groups were not significantly different before treatment (age six) but that the treated group were significantly lower on bullying after the treatment (at age nine). Indeed, 62 percent of the controls, but only 42 percent of the treated boys, were rated as bullies at age nine. (These figures are high because all of the boys had been rated as disruptive at age six.) Unfortunately, the difference between treated and control boys decreased considerably at ages ten, eleven, and twelve. However, the published figures (Tremblay et al. 1991, 1992) show that the treated boys were significantly lower on self-reported fighting at age eleven and on teacher-rated fighting at age twelve. The differences at all ages were in the right direction, suggesting that the program had succeeded in reducing aggression.

Several extensive literature reviews (e.g., Kazdin 1987; Dumas 1989) show that parent training with preadolescents is often effective in reducing disruptive child behavior. Similarly, there are indications that cognitive-behavioral social skills training, both in schools (e.g., Coie, Underwood, and Lochman 1991) and in residential institutions (e.g., Pepler, King, and Byrd 1991), can be effective in reducing aggression. Both of these approaches might be used in research focusing on the prevention of bullying.

## B. Prevention Focusing on Victims

As with prevention focusing on bullies, there is no shortage of proposals for prevention focusing on victims, many based on practical experience. For example, Jones (1991) suggested that teachers should warn children about the possibility of being bullied when they arrived at the secondary school, or even before they arrived, on the induction day. He also recommended using drama to show children how to rebuff a bully or how to tell teachers about bullying. Besag (1989b) advocated holding workshops for parents to alert them to warning signs and to provide advice about what to do if they suspected that their child was bullying or being victimized. She also suggested that older children could be asked to "shadow" victims to observe the bullying problem and report it to teachers. Victims should develop strategies to avoid being victimized, such as staying with a group, not being last in the changing rooms, leaving valuable possessions at home, and not showing anger or distress when being bullied, as this encouraged the bullies to continue (Besag 1989a). Also, victims should be helped to develop confidence, self-esteem, and friendship skills.

Many other researchers have advocated attempts to improve the social and friendship skills of victims so that they are less likely to be isolated and rejected by other children. For example, Lowenstein (1978a) proposed that victims should be encouraged to develop a wider interest in what others were doing, should seek to praise or consider others, and should see situations from other children's viewpoints. Herbert (1989) described a social skills program with a group of eight victims, including brainstorming to identify concerns and role playing to model alternative ways of dealing with bullying. Victims were taught social skills such as listening, holding conversations, asking for help, dealing with feelings, negotiating, and responding to teasing. The sessions were held after school and led by a teacher and a social worker. Arora (1991) also described the use of victim support groups including eight victims and two adults, with one-hour sessions once a week, focusing on the enhancement of social skills through role playing. Tattum (1989) and Stephenson and Smith (1991) also advocated a focus on increasing friendship skills and self-esteem of victims.

Mellor (1991) reported remedies for bullying suggested by the children themselves. Boys argued that victims should stand up for themselves and fight back, while girls thought that victims should tell teachers and enlist support from other children so that they did not feel alone. Hoover and Hazler (1991) advocated peer tutoring and counseling for bullies and victims. Townsend-Wise and Harrison (1991) described a special free bullying telephone line set up for three months in 1990 to enable children to talk to counselors about bullying. More than 7,600 calls were received about bullying during this operation. The line was set up to find out more about bullying and about how to combat bullying, and the calls have been analyzed by La Fontaine (1991).

Unfortunately, the success in preventing victimization of any of these approaches focusing on victims does not seem to have been evaluated in any kind of empirical research, much less in controlled experiments. However, research on cognitive-behavioral interpersonal social skills training with delinquents has yielded hopeful results (e.g., Michelson 1987; Ross and Ross 1988).

## C. Prevention Focusing on the Environment

Most prevention efforts focusing on the school environment have centered on improving supervision (especially in the playground), on "bully courts," or on a "whole-school" approach to bullying. For example, Besag (1989b, 1991) pointed out the need to have well-supervised playgrounds, corridors, washrooms, and changing rooms. Unfortunately, lunchtime supervisors were often poorly paid, untrained, and of poor quality. She also recommended that it was desirable to have a greater variety of interesting activities available to children at lunchtimes, but this might require voluntary help from local parents. Jones (1991) proposed that teachers should be prominently around doing their proper duties and preventing the development of any "no-go" areas. Mellor (1991) suggested that playground supervision should be carried out by an adult trained to spot signs of bullying and to provide appropriate support for victims. Thompson and Smith (1991) also advocated improved supervision in the playground, possibly by extending a prefect system. Foster and Thompson (1991) argued that bullying might be decreased by segregating the children according to age and, in particular, grouping all first-year classes in the same area of a secondary school. Lunchtimes, playtimes, and lesson times could be staggered to minimize contact between different age groups.

The pioneering work on "bully courts" was completed by Laslett (1980, 1982) in a small day school for maladjusted children. The "justices" of this court were children elected by their peers, who heard complaints of bullying brought by other children and who set punishments, such as apologizing to the victim, doing pages of sums, keeping off the play area, washing the stairs, and doing something nice for the victim. Laslett reported that the bully court was in operation for ten years while he was the head teacher and for more than twenty years in total. He thought that it helped to decrease bullying, helped children to understand bullies and victims, and helped children to learn about making reparation and restitution. The children who bullied were influenced by criticism from other children.

Brier and Ahmad (1991) and Elliott (1991b) also described the operation of bully courts in schools. Brier and Ahmad's "bench" consisted of two teachers and five elected children. At first, the children wanted severe punishments for bullying, but later they became more moderate and chose punishments such as clearing rubbish from the playground for one week. The court helped the children understand the need for codes, laws, and sanctions. Brier and Ahmad presented figures showing that the prevalence of bullies and victims (according to self-reports) decreased in classes that had bully courts compared with other classes. However, the methodological problem was that the prevalence of victims in particular was much higher in the experimental classes before the intervention, so that the decrease might have been caused by regression to the mean.

Elliott (1991c) reported that the Kidscape organization had set up bully courts in thirty schools and monitored them in eight schools. In these eight schools, 70 percent of the children said that they had ever been victimized (presumably before the courts were introduced). At the end of the three-month "trial" (sic) period, 6 percent of the children said that they had been victimized (presumably in the three months). Elliott (1991c, p. 46) concluded that there had been "a dramatic drop in reported cases" and that "it would appear that the courts had been a major factor in reducing bullying, so why not introduce them everywhere?" However, of course, it is not clear that a 70 percent prevalence ever is greater than a 6 percent prevalence in three months. This evaluation falls far short of conventional methodological standards.

Improved supervision and bully courts, and indeed measures targeted on bullies and victims, are sometimes included in a "whole-school" approach to bullying. However, the key elements of the whole-school approach are the school taking responsibility for bullying and giving it a high priority, increasing awareness of bullying by teachers, children, and parents, publicizing explicit school policies designed to reduce bullying, and discussing bullying as part of the curriculum (see, e.g., Priest 1989; Tattum 1989; Foster, Arora, and Thompson 1990; Elliott 1991a; Stephenson and Smith 1991; Smith and Thompson 1991b). Other elements of the whole-school approach include encouraging peer disapproval of bullying, encouraging bystanders to help victims, and encouraging victims and bystanders to report bullying to teachers. Similar programs have been recommended by Jones (1991) and Mellor (1991), who proposed that teachers, parents, and children should be involved in formulating antibullying policies and codifying what was acceptable or unacceptable behavior.

Undoubtedly, the most important evaluation of a whole-school approach was completed by Olweus (1990, 1991a). The Olweus program was theory-driven and aimed to increase awareness and knowledge of teachers, parents, and children about bullying and to dispel myths about it (see Olweus 1992a). In the autumn of 1983, a thirty-page booklet was distributed to all schools in Norway containing children aged eight to sixteen, describing what was known about bullying and recommending what steps schools and teachers could take to reduce it. Also, a twenty-five-minute video about bullying was made available to schools at a subsidized price. Simultaneously, the schools distributed to all parents a four-page folder containing information and advice about bullying. In addition, anonymous self-report questionnaires were completed by all children.

The program had additional elements in Bergen. Each of the forty-two participating schools received feedback information from the questionnaire about the prevalence of bullies and victims, in a specially arranged school conference day. Also, teachers were encouraged to develop explicit rules about bullying (e.g., do not bully, tell someone when bullying happens, bullying will not be tolerated, try to help victims, try to include children who are being left out) and to discuss bullying in class, using the video and role-playing exercises. Also, teachers were encouraged to improve monitoring and supervision of children, especially in the playground.

The success of the program was evaluated in the forty-two Bergen schools, using before-and-after measures of bullying and victimization of children at each age. For example, the prevalence of bullies and victims among thirteen-year-olds before the program was compared with the prevalence of bullies and victims among (different) thirteen-year-olds twenty months after the program. Generally, the prevalence of victims decreased by about half after the program, and the prevalence of bullies also decreased substantially (Olweus 1990, 1991a). Hence, the program seemed to be successful in reducing bullying in Bergen.

Roland (1989) then carried out a follow-up study three years later, in the autumn of 1986, to assess the lasting effects of the nationwide campaign. In Rogaland (a representative part of Norway), information about bullying was collected using anonymous questionnaires from nearly 7,000 children in thirty-seven schools that had participated in 1983. Using the criterion of "once a week or more often," the prevalence of male bullies and victims was greater in 1986 than in 1983. However, the prevalence of female victims was somewhat less, especially at the younger ages. The prevalence of female bullies had not changed, but this was very small (less than 2 percent at all ages). The use of the criterion of "sometimes or more often" would have permitted a more sensitive test of changes in bullying.

These results seemed rather disappointing. However, since Roland was not involved in the 1983 data collection, the comparability of the follow-up data with the original data is not clear. Roland also reported that schools that had been heavily involved in the antibullying campaign showed decreases in bullying, while schools which had been less involved showed increases. Unfortunately, he did not furnish the data on which these statements were based, and he had not had contact with the schools at the time of the campaign. It may be that the whole-school program requires the Bergen elements to be successful and that merely providing information about bullying to teachers and parents is not enough to have a lasting effect.

A somewhat similar program to that used in Norway was introduced in 1992 in twenty-three Sheffield schools by Peter Smith in a project funded by the United Kingdom Department for Education. The Smith program is based not only on the Olweus program but also on other bullying prevention approaches. It is planned to include elements that were not part of the Olweus program, such as bully courts, "quality circles" (having children produce ideas to improve schools that teachers act on), and the "Heartstone Odyssey" (a story that introduces experiences of racial harassment). The Smith program's intervention package is individually tailored to the needs of each school (Ahmad, Whitney, and Smith 1991; Sharp and Smith 1991). The anonymous questionnaires were completed in the autumn of 1990, and they were scheduled to be repeated in the autumn of 1992 to evaluate the success of the program. A national campaign against bullying in English schools was also launched in April 1992, and all 34,000 schools were sent a copy of the booklet by Tattum and Herbert (1990). The Olweus program is being tested in the United States (Perry et al. 1990) and in Canada (Pepler et al. 1993).

An interesting example of an environmentally focused program is provided by the antibullying program devised by McGurk and McDougall (1991) in an institution for young offenders in the North of England with a high proportion of dormitory accommodation. Using interviews, they found that bullying occurred mainly in the dormitories at night, when the young offenders were unsupervised. It occurred mainly on Tuesday and Friday nights; Tuesday was the new intake day, and bullying was often part of an initiation ceremony, while the dormitories were not inspected on Saturday mornings, so bullying on

Friday would be likely to go undetected. Generally, bullying was most likely to occur when there was least surveillance and a low probability of detection. The account of the techniques of bullying used in this institution makes horrific reading and shows the severity of the problem.

Despite the fact that fourteen of the twenty-three inmates interviewed said that they had personally witnessed bullying at least once in the previous week, bullying was rarely detected or punished. Only one of the previously recorded offenses against discipline involved bullying. McGurk and McDougall (1991) devised a number of environmental strategies to reduce bullying, which were adopted by the prison governor. Their aim was to increase staff surveillance, increase the risk of being apprehended, and increase the punishment received by detected bullies.

Every dormitory was visited at least once every night by a governor-grade officer. A switch operating the lights inside each dormitory was placed on the outside wall of the dormitory, so that the night patrol officer could turn the light on and see what was happening if he suspected that inmates were being bullied. Previously, an officer had to go through the time-consuming business of opening doors with keys, giving the inmates ample warning of his visit. Color television sets were located in each dormitory to combat boredom. Body checks were made on inmates each morning to detect injuries. Inmates with any previous history of violence or bullying were differentially allocated to cells rather than dormitories. Problem checklists were included in assessment techniques so that inmates could communicate problems without having to talk to officers. Officers were trained to increase vigilance by night patrols and to improve interrogation skills of those interviewing suspected bullies. Also, severe penalties were given to detected bullies.

McGurk and McDougall (1991) found that, according to inmate self-reports over a seven-month period, their program was successful in reducing bullying. The proportion of inmates who reported that they had witnessed bullying in the previous week declined from 61 percent before the program to only 13 percent afterward (although the numbers interviewed remained small). The method used in their program was somewhat similar to "crime analysis," which has been used widely in crime prevention research (e.g., Ekblom 1986; Burrows 1988). This environmentally focused approach could be used more often in the prevention of bullying.

## D. Designing and Evaluating Prevention Research

Methods of preventing bullying can be targeted on bullies, victims, or schools. These different targets, of course, imply different design and measurement strategies. In research targeted on individuals, the individual is the unit of analysis. For example, the effectiveness of social skills training targeted on bullies or victims should be evaluated by before-and-after measures of bullying by or victimization of these children. It is also important to have before and after measures of bullying by and victimization of comparison children. The best way to ensure equivalence of treated and control children is to allocate children at random to treatment and control conditions, as in the Tremblay et al. (1991) research. However, some type of matching method based on the before measures would also be appropriate, given the present state of knowledge about the prevention of bullying. It is arguable to what extent it is necessary to measure bullying by and victimization of children who are not in treatment or control conditions, except insofar as it is possible that, as some bullies and victims are "cured," other children may emerge to take the roles of bullies and victims. This could only happen if bullies and victims were in some way created by the social environment, which is not clear at present.

In research targeted on schools, the school is the unit of analysis. For example, the effectiveness of a whole-school approach to bullying should be evaluated by before and after measures of bullying by and victimization of all children in treated schools and in nontreated comparison schools. However, except in very large-scale research, the equivalence of treated and comparison schools could not be ensured by random allocation. Random allocation can only ensure equivalence of experimental units (within the limits of small statistical fluctuations) when the number of such units is large. If, say, 100 schools could be randomly allocated to treatment or comparison conditions, the random allocation would ensure equivalence. However, most school research will be based on a small number of schools, especially at the present state of knowledge, so the equivalence of treated and comparison schools will have to be achieved by matching on (or statistically adjusting for) the before measures of bullying and victimization. Hence, it is likely that research based on schools will have poorer control of extraneous variables than research based on individuals, but at the present state of knowledge about the prevention of bullying this is not too serious. In other words, the first priority is to carry out some prevention research that meets minimal methodological standards; further refinements can be achieved in due course, if the initial results are promising.

Some prevention research could be based on school classes, as in the Hawkins et al. (1991) program. For example, bully courts could be introduced in some classes of a school but not in others, and treated classes could be compared with nontreated classes on before-and-after measures of bullying. However, the effectiveness of bully courts is unclear. Olweus (1991b) argued that they were not and would not be effective because bullies were good at talking themselves out of situations, some bullies liked the notoriety of being labeled, victims were afraid of accusing bullies, the bully courts did not deal with the root causes of bullying but focused only on the most dramatic and severe cases and on punishment rather than prevention, and punishments were not very effective because they were long delayed after the bullying incidents.

The measurement strategies depend to some extent on the interventions. For example, if the intervention were to improve playground supervision, then it would be necessary to measure bullying and victimization in the playground separately from other places. This would establish whether improved supervision had its intended effect of decreasing playground bullying and whether this caused any displacement of bullying to other locations. Also, of course, it would be necessary to carry out a "process evaluation," in this case, to establish whether the playground supervision had improved as planned. It would be desirable to carry out some systematic observations in playgrounds to record bullying incidents and the behavior of supervisors (in monitoring the playground and in intervening to deal with bullying). However, it is not clear that the frequency and visibility of bullying incidents would be sufficient to justify the use of this method on a large scale.

The first step in any bullying prevention study in schools should be to establish the nature and extent of bullying. Questionnaires completed by children and teachers would be useful for this purpose and could also be used to furnish baseline measures of bullying. The questions asked should be chosen in the light of the intervention planned. For example, in a primarily environmental intervention (e.g., McGurk and McDougall 1991), it would be important to establish the times and places that bullying most often occurred. It is also desirable to investigate the methods currently used against bullying by schools in advance of any experimental intervention.

Ideally, the questionnaires should yield sensitive outcome measures of the prevalence and frequency of different types of bullying. The Olweus questionnaire inquires about bullying and victimization at school and on the way to school, being alone at school, the number of good friends a child has, age and sex of bullies, how often teachers intervene, how often victimization is reported to teachers and parents, and opinions of bullies. Other items about bullying that might be included in a questionnaire are whether the child is usually bullied by or usually bullies the same person or persons, the effects of being bullied (e.g., unhappiness, crying, illness, staying away from school, dislike of school), why the child thinks he or she bullies or is bullied, and more systematic information about the age, sex, and ethnicity of the child and his or her bullies and victims.

The questionnaire could also include items designed to throw more light on characteristics of bullies and victims, on such topics as impulsiveness, clumsiness, caution/daring, restlessness, poor concentration, angering easily, aggressiveness, strength, self-esteem, depression, anxiety, sensitivity, empathy, attractiveness, physical defects, leading or being easily led, popularity, intelligence, school attainment, truancy, and being cheeky to teachers. It would then be possible to specify which of these factors changed when bullying changed and, hence, to interpret the effects of any intervention more adequately. Given the link between bullying and other types of antisocial behavior such as violence, vandalism, stealing, and substance abuse, it would also be desirable to inquire about these other behaviors. It would then be possible to establish whether interventions targeted on bullying had wider benefits in reducing other types of antisocial behavior.

Of the possible types of interventions, the whole-school approach has evidence in favor of its effectiveness (Olweus 1991a) and can be implemented cheaply and on a large scale. Improving playground supervision by better training of existing supervisors, by paying teachers to supervise, or by extending a prefect system is also promising and can be implemented relatively cheaply. The effectiveness of bully courts is not clear, despite the promising results of Brier and Ahmad (1991). Social skills training, parent training, and other measures targeted on individuals may be effective, but they are likely to be relatively expensive. Hence, the priority at present should be to evaluate the effectiveness of the whole-school approach and of improvements in playground supervision.

The first step in implementing any program for the prevention of bullying in schools is to obtain cooperation from head teachers. My experience of discussing bullying with head teachers in London and Liverpool primary and secondary schools is that they are very willing to cooperate with research on the prevention of bullying because they see it as a problem for which their school should take responsibility. Also, other teachers see the point of this research and are willing to cooperate, as are local education departments. The influential Elton Report of the United Kingdom Department of Education and Science (1989) recommended that teachers should be alert to signs of bullying and should take firm action on it based on clear rules backed by appropriate sanctions.

The first step in evaluating an antibullying program is to have all children in each school complete the self-report questionnaire first, then implement the program, and then have all children complete the questionnaire again. The key test is whether the prevalence of bullies and victims and the frequency of bullying incidents decrease between the first and second administration of the questionnaire. It would be advisable, of course, to have before and after measurements of bullying in comparison schools that do not receive an antibullying program. If bullying decreases in this initial experiment, it would then be worthwhile to mount more complex, more extensive, and better designed replication experiments.

Specifically, the key elements of the antibullying program should be as follows:

1. Organize a school conference day about bullying for the teachers in which the questionnaire results are presented. Provide teachers with information booklets about bullying, show them a video about bullying, solicit their ideas about preventing bullying, and agree on a plan of action and commitment to reduce bullying.
2. Organize a parent-teacher meeting to inform parents about bullying and what is being done to prevent it. Provide parents with short information booklets about bullying, show them a video about bullying, and solicit their ideas about preventing bullying.
3. Improve playground supervision of children and the speed and certainty of intervention to stop bullying incidents, either by training supervisors, by paying teachers to supervise, or by extending a prefect system. If possible, make the playground better equipped, more attractive, and more diverting.
4. Teachers should discuss bullying with children in class (and use role-playing exercises and video) to develop a set of explicit rules

against bullying, for example: "Do not bully," "Tell someone when bullying happens," "Bullying will not be tolerated," "Try to help children who are being bullied," and "Try to include children who are being left out."

5. Teachers should talk to identified bullies and victims (and to their parents) about bullying. Where appropriate, sanctions should be applied against bullies. Teachers should try to find ways to help victims to increase their status with other children by being successful in class and receiving praise. Parents of bullies should be encouraged to monitor their behavior carefully and to praise their desirable acts and punish their undesirable ones. Parents of victims should be asked to help them develop potential talents and to facilitate their friendships with other children (especially popular ones).

This program is admittedly rather global, and some elements of it may be more effective than others. According to Olweus (1991b), the key element is the school showing its concern about bullying and setting the general tone that bullying will not be tolerated. If this program proved to be effective in reducing bullying in the initial experiment, further experiments could be carried out to investigate which were the more or less important ingredients. Since the success of this program in reducing bullying in England or the United States has not yet been proved, it is probably most appropriate to test the global program first and not to plan disentangling experiments unless and until the initial test showed a decrease in bullying.

## V. Future Research Needs

Future research on bullying should aim to study and disentangle the different types of bullying (e.g., teasing, intimidation, physical aggression) more carefully. While they may all be interrelated, some results may apply to one type of behavior rather than another. Researchers should furnish details about the definition of bullying, time periods inquired about, and so on. Information about ethnicity is needed in bullying research, so that it is possible to specify how the prevalence of bullying and victimization varies with ethnicity and whether some ethnic groups differentially bully others. Studies of bullying in other settings are also needed: between siblings, between spouses or cohabitees, and particularly in institutions for offenders.

Researchers on bullying should be more concerned with issues of measurement, reliability, and validity. For example, they should seek to validate self-reports concurrently and predictively against school records and teacher reports. Incidents reported by teachers and in school records should also be reported by children. Research should also be carried out on the feasibility of measuring bullying by systematic observation (e.g., in the playground).

There are many key issues to address. For example, research is needed to establish the concurrent overlap between bullies and victims according to different definitions of bullying, the extent to which victims at one age become bullies at a later age and vice versa, and the causal effect (if any) of victimization on later bullying. It has been suggested that shy and aggressive children might be simultaneously bullies and victims. Another important issue is to what extent a victim is always bullied by the same bully or bullies, to what extent a victim is bullied by children together in groups as opposed to several children consecutively, to what extent children in groups are victimized, and to what extent one child bullies several different victims consecutively. Following the criminal career paradigm, research is needed on when and why bullying and victimization careers begin, how long they persist, and when and why they end. Information about why bullying ends should be helpful in designing programs to reduce bullying. It is also important to investigate the onset, duration, and desistance of bully-victim pairs and bullying groups and the intertwining of bullying and victimization careers. This approach would encourage the developmental study of bullying and victimization, and explain why bullying by females seems to decline with age (from eight to sixteen) while bullying by males remains relatively constant.

Another important question to address is whether bullies are popular or unpopular with other children. It may be that they are popular among deviant groups but unpopular among more conventional children. Another issue concerns the effect on an observer of seeing a child victimized. This may depend on the degree of empathy felt by the observer toward the victim. Researchers on bullying have identified categories of anxious bullies and provocative victims, but the prevalences of these categories is unclear. It is also important to investigate why some schools have a higher prevalence of bullying than others, and the extent to which this reflects characteristics of children entering the schools or features of the schools themselves. To the extent that features of the schools are important, this might have implications for prevention measures focusing on the school environment.

Future research should investigate the developmental sequence through which bullying escalates into criminal violence and how and why bullying is related to other types of antisocial behavior. This leads naturally to the question of whether victims of bullying have a disproportionate probability of being victims of criminal violence and how and why bullying victimization is related to other types of internalizing or mental health problems. Another important issue is how and why there is intragenerational continuity and intergenerational transmission of bullying and victimization. In particular, it is important to establish to what extent the consistency lies in the personality of individuals and to what extent in the consistency of the environment. It would be useful to study children whose environments change markedly over time, and to compare them with children in stable environments.

It is desirable to try to develop and test theories of how bullying incidents arise from interactions between potential bullies and potential victims in environments that provide opportunities for bullying. By studying interactions between bullies and victims in detail, it may be possible to make recommendations about how potential victims might behave in order to minimize their probability of being bullied. Prevention methods should be based on explicitly formulated and empirically tested theories of bullying, and prevention strategies targeted on bullies or victims should be evaluated in controlled experiments. Environmentally focused prevention strategies based on a type of "crime analysis" could be implemented and evaluated more often, especially those focusing on improvements in playground supervision. The evaluation of the whole-school approach to bullying prevention should be designed so that the active ingredients of the program can be isolated.

A program of research on the prevention of bullying could lead not only to significant advances in knowledge but also to less distress and unhappiness suffered by children at school and to the fostering of prosocial behavior by potentially antisocial children, which might have long-term benefits in reducing their later offending. That would be in everyone's interests.

APPENDIX

Intragenerational and Intergenerational Continuity
in Bullying

The Cambridge Study in Delinquent Development is a prospective longitudinal survey of 411 males. When first contacted in 1961 to 1962, they were all living in a working-class area of London, England. The vast majority were chosen by taking all the boys who were then aged eight and on the registers of six state primary schools within a one-mile radius of a research office that had been established. The boys were overwhelmingly white, working-class, and of British origin. The major results have been reported in four books (West 1969, 1982; West and Farrington 1973, 1977) and in more than sixty papers listed by Farrington and West (1990).

The major aim was to measure as many factors as possible that were alleged to be causes or correlates of offending. The boys were interviewed and tested in their schools when they were aged about eight, ten, and fourteen by male or female psychologists. They were interviewed in the research office at about age sixteen, eighteen, and twenty-one and in their homes at about age twenty-five and thirty-two by young male social science graduates. The tests in schools included measures of intelligence, attainment, personality, and psychomotor impulsivity, while information was collected in the interviews about such topics as living circumstances, employment histories, relationships with females, leisure activities, and offending behavior. On all occasions except at ages twenty-one and twenty-five, the aim was to interview the whole sample, and it was always possible to trace and interview a high proportion. For example, 389 of the 410 males still alive at eighteen (94.9 percent) were interviewed, and 378 of the 403 still alive at age thirty-two (93.8 percent).

In addition to the interviews and tests with the boys, interviews with their parents were carried out by female social workers who visited their homes. These took place about once a year from when the boy was about age eight until he was aged fourteen to fifteen and was in his last year of compulsory education. The primary informant was the mother, although many fathers were also seen. The parents provided details about such matters as family income, family size, their employment histories, their child-rearing practices (including attitudes, discipline, and parental agreement), their degree of supervision of the boy, and his temporary or permanent separations from them.

The boys' teachers completed questionnaires when the boys were aged about eight, ten, twelve, and fourteen. These provided information about the boys' troublesome and aggressive school behavior, their attention deficit, their school attainments, and their truancy. Ratings were also obtained from the boys' peers when they were in their primary schools about such topics as their daring, dishonesty, troublesomeness, and popularity.

Searches were also carried out in the national Criminal Record Office in London to try and locate findings of guilt of the boys, of their parents, of their brothers and sisters, and (in recent years) of their wives and cohabitees. Convictions were only counted if they were for offenses normally recorded in this office, thereby excluding minor crimes such as common assault, traffic offenses, and drunkenness. The most frequent offenses included were thefts and burglaries. However, we did not rely only on official records for information about offending because we also obtained self-reports of offending from the boys themselves at every age from fourteen onward.

For these analyses, each variable was dichotomized, as far as possible, into the "worst" quarter (e.g., the quarter with lowest income or lowest intelligence) versus the remainder. This was done in order to compare the importance of different variables and also to permit a "risk-factor" approach. Because most variables were originally classified into a small number of categories and because fine distinctions between categories could not be made very accurately, this dichotomizing did not usually involve a great loss of information. The one-quarter/three-quarters split was chosen to match the prior expectation that about one-quarter of the sample would be convicted.

Summarizing, the Cambridge Study in Delinquent Development has a unique combination of features. Eight face-to-face interviews have been completed with the subjects over a period of twenty-four years, between ages eight and thirty-two. The attrition rate is unusually low for such a long-term survey. The main focus of interest is on crime and delinquency, but the survey also provides information about alcohol and drug abuse, educational problems, poverty and poor housing, unemployment, sexual behavior, aggression, and other social problems. The sample size of about 400 is large enough for many statistical analyses but small enough to permit detailed case histories of the males and their families. Information has been obtained from multiple sources, including the subjects themselves, their parents, teachers, peers, and official records. Generally, the information came from parents, teachers, peers, or tests completed by the males between ages eight and fourteen, but primarily from the males themselves between ages sixteen and thirty-two. Data have been collected about a wide variety of theoretical constructs at different ages, including biological (e.g., heart rate), psychological (e.g., intelligence), family (e.g., discipline), and social (e.g., socioeconomic status) factors.

## A. Measures of Bullying

Self-report measures of bullying, on four-point scales, were obtained at ages fourteen, eighteen, and thirty-two. The measure at fourteen was derived from a semantic differential test (West and Farrington 1973, pp. 174–77) in which the male essentially indicated whether he was "a bit of a bully" at one extreme or whether he "did not bully" at the other extreme. The measures at ages eighteen and thirty-two were derived from an attitude questionnaire (West and Farrington 1977, pp. 185–89) in which the male essentially indicated whether it was true or false that he was "sometimes a bit of a bully."

Nearly half of the males admitted bullying at age fourteen (49.3 percent of 406), in comparison with less than a quarter at age eighteen (21.3 percent of 389), and only about one in seven at age thirty-two (14.3 percent of 378). The three measures of bullying were significantly interrelated (see table A1), showing intragenerational continuity in bullying. For example, 32.5 percent of eighty bullies at age eighteen were also bullies at age thirty-two, in comparison with only 9.5 percent of 287 who were not bullies at age eighteen. In this essay, one-tailed statistical tests are used where there are clear directional predictions, and two-tailed tests in other cases.

An important question is how far bullying is merely one manifestation of aggression. The aggressive males at age fourteen were the 134 whose teachers (at ages twelve or fourteen) gave them most points for being disobedient, difficult to discipline, unduly rough during playtime, quarrelsome and aggressive, overcompetitive with other children, and unduly resentful of criticism or punishment. The aggressive males at age eighteen were the seventy-nine who

## TABLE A1

### Bullying, Aggression and Violence at Different Ages

| Variable 1 | Variable 2 | Percent on Variable 2 | | $\chi^2$ | $p$ | Odds Ratio |
|---|---|---|---|---|---|---|
| | | NB1 | B1 | | | |
| Bully 14δ | Bully 18 | 17.3 | 25.5 | 3.85 | .025 | 1.63 |
| Bully 14 | Bully 32 | 10.4 | 18.1 | 4.50 | .017 | 1.90 |
| Bully 18 | Bully 32 | 9.1 | 32.5 | 28.27 | .0001 | 4.83 |
| Bully 14 | Agg 14 | 22.8 | 43.0 | 18.77 | .0001 | 2.55 |
| Bully 18 | Agg 18 | 17.0 | 32.5 | 9.74 | .0009 | 2.36 |
| Bully 32 | Agg 32 | 33.1 | 61.1 | 15.52 | .0001 | 3.17 |
| Bully 32 | Violence | 10.5 | 20.4 | 4.31 | .019 | 2.18 |

NOTE.—Agg = aggressive; NB1 = not bully on variable 1; B1 = bully on variable 1. One-tailed significance tests were used in view of directional predictions.

most frequently admitted getting into fights, starting fights, and carrying and using weapons (in the previous three years). The aggressive males at age thirty-two were the 140 who admitted being involved in fights in the previous five years. Fights were defined as incidents in which blows were struck, and fights in the course of work (e.g., as a police officer, prison officer, or security guard) and men who were purely victims (e.g., of mugging) were not counted. In addition, fifty males were convicted of violent crimes up to age thirty-two (assaults, robberies, and threatening behavior). All these measures of aggression and violence were significantly interrelated (see Farrington 1991*b*).

Table A1 shows that bullying at each age was significantly related to aggression at the same age. For example, 43.0 percent of bullies at age fourteen were aggressive according to teachers at age fourteen, in comparison with 22.8 percent of nonbullies at age fourteen. Also, 20.4 percent of bullies at age thirty-two were convicted of violence, in comparison with 10.5 percent of nonbullies at age thirty-two. These results increase our confidence in the external validity of the self-reports of bullying.

### B. Is There Specific Intragenerational Continuity in Bullying?

This essay demonstrates that there is significant continuity in bullying from adolescence (age fourteen) to adulthood (age thirty-two). However, bullying is also significantly related to aggression in general, and there is significant continuity in aggression from adolescence to adulthood. This raises the question of whether the continuity in bullying is merely a consequence of the general continuity in aggression or whether there is some specific continuity in bullying over and above the general continuity in aggression.

These hypotheses were investigated using logistic regression analyses that essentially tested whether bullying at a first age predicted bullying at a second age independently of both aggression at the first age and aggression at the second age. Given the association between bullying and aggression, this is a

## TABLE A2

### Testing Specific Continuity in Bullying

#### A. Continuity

| | | | Percent Bully at Age 2 | | |
|-----|-----|-----|-----|-----|-----|
| Agg 1 | Agg 2 | Bully 1 | 14–18 | 14–32 | 18–32 |
| No | No | No | 15.6 | 5.3 | 4.9 |
| No | No | Yes | 23.1 | 14.9 | 27.3 |
| Yes | No | No | 18.8 | 8.7 | 4.5 |
| Yes | No | Yes | 15.7 | 7.0 | 25.0 |
| No | Yes | No | 17.6 | 15.9 | 15.3 |
| No | Yes | Yes | 44.4 | 35.1 | 42.9 |
| Yes | Yes | No | 33.3 | 23.8 | 21.4 |
| Yes | Yes | Yes | 37.5 | 21.1 | 35.7 |

#### B. Logistic Regression

| | LRCS | | |
|-----|-----|-----|-----|
| | 14–18 | 14–32 | 18–32 |
| Agg 1 | .6 | .0 | 2.3 |
| Agg 2 | 8.3* | 14.9** | 11.4** |
| Agg 1 × Agg 2 | .3 | .0 | .0 |
| Bully 1 | 2.6* | 4.9* | 21.6** |
| Agg 1 × Bully 1 | 1.5 | 3.6* | .8 |
| Agg 2 × Bully 1 | 1.0 | .0 | 1.2 |

NOTE.—Agg = Aggressive; LRCS = likelihood ratio $\chi^2$.
* $p < .05$.
** $p < .001$ (one-tailed).

very rigorous test. The results are shown in table A2, and can be explained most easily by comparing ages eighteen and thirty-two. If bullying at age eighteen predicts bullying at age thirty-two independently of aggression at both ages, then the percentage who are bullies at age thirty-two should be greater for those who are bullies at age eighteen irrespective of whether the males are aggressive at ages eighteen or thirty-two.

Comparing males who are nonaggressive at both ages eighteen and thirty-two, 27.3 percent of thirty-three bullies at age eighteen, as opposed to 4.9 percent of 164 nonbullies at age eighteen, were bullies at age thirty-two. Comparing males who are aggressive at age eighteen and nonaggressive at age thirty-two, 25.0 percent of twelve bullies at age eighteen, as opposed to 4.5 percent of twenty-two nonbullies at age eighteen, were bullies at age thirty-two. Comparing males who are nonaggressive at age eighteen and aggressive at age thirty-two, 42.9 percent of twenty-one bullies at age eighteen, as opposed to 15.3 percent of seventy-two nonbullies at age eighteen, were bullies at age thirty-two. Comparing males who are aggressive at both ages eighteen and thirty-two, 35.7 percent of fourteen bullies at age eighteen, as opposed to 21.4 percent of twenty-eight nonbullies at age eighteen, were bullies at age thirty-two.

Merely comparing the percentages in this case suggests that bullying at age eighteen predicts bullying at age thirty-two independently of aggression at ages eighteen and thirty-two. However, a logistic regression analysis, predicting bullying at age thirty-two, provided a more systematic test. Aggression at age eighteen was first entered into the equation, and it had a near-significant predictive effect (likelihood ratio $\chi^2$ [LRCS] = 2.3, $p$ = .066). Aggression at age thirty-two then significantly added predictive efficiency (LRCS = 11.4, $p$ = .0004). The interaction between the two aggression measures was not significant. However, the addition of bullying at age eighteen caused a highly significant increase in predictive efficiency (LRCS = 21.6, $p$ = .0001). No other interactions were significant.

Bullying at the first age also predicted bullying at the second age in comparing ages fourteen and thirty-two (LRCS = 4.9, $p$ = .014) and, marginally, in comparing ages fourteen and eighteen (LRCS = 2.6, $p$ = .054). Hence, it can be concluded that bullying at one age predicts bullying at another age independently of the tendency of aggression at one age to predict aggression at another age. Therefore, there is specific continuity in bullying superimposed on the general continuity in aggression.

## C. Predictors and Correlates of Bullying

The extensive range of variables measured in the Cambridge Study provide a unique opportunity to investigate the predictors and correlates of bullying at different ages. Table A3 summarizes the strength of relationships with bullying using odds ratios. For example, 31.5 percent of eighty-nine boys from low income families at age eight admitted bullying at age eighteen, compared with 18.3 percent of the remaining 300 known on low income and bullying. The odds of bullying were .46 (28/61) for low income boys and .22 (55/245) for the remainder, giving an odds ratio of 2.04 ([245 × 28]/[61 × 55]). Roughly speaking, an odds ratio of 2 signifies a doubling of the risk. The relationship between low income at age eight and bullying at age eighteen was statistically significant ($\chi^2$ = 7.05, 1 df, $p$ = .008, two-tailed; two-tailed tests are used in table A3 because the direction of the prediction is not always clear), as indicated by the asterisk. Nearly a quarter of the boys (22.6 percent) came from low-income families at age eight. Negative signs before odds ratios indicate negative relationships. The number of variables included in these analyses was thirty-four at ages eight to ten, twenty-four at ages twelve to fourteen, twenty-eight at age eighteen, and forty at age thirty-two.

The bullies at age fourteen tended to have convicted parents by their tenth birthday, tended to have low attainment at their junior school, and tended to be rated troublesome at ages eight to ten by their peers and teachers. In

# TABLE A3

## Predictors and Correlates of Bullying

| Variable | Percent Identified | Odds Ratios for Bullying 14 | 18 | 32 |
|---|---|---|---|---|
| **Age 8–10:** | | | | |
| Low family income | | | 2.04* | −1.02 |
| Poor housing | | | .83* | 1.17 |
| Large family size | | | 75* | 1.26 |
| Convicted parent | | | 42 | 1.15 |
| Poor parental supervision | | | 5* | 2.11* |
| Physical neglect | | | 4** | 2.47* |
| Low attainment | | | | −1.26 |
| Low school track | | | * | 1.58 |
| Attends church | | | | 1.34 |
| Few friends | | | 1.31 | 1.08 |
| Vulnerable | | 1.12 | 2.46* | 1.82 |
| Troublesome | 22 | 1.90* | 2.06* | 1.34 |
| Antisocial | 24 | 1.81* | 1.69 | 1.37 |
| **Age 12–14:** | | | | |
| Poor housing | 20 | −1.58 | 1.80* | 1.06 |
| Large family size | 21 | 1.71* | 2.09* | 1.35 |
| Father does not join in | 28 | −1.04 | 2.35* | 1.98* |
| Low nonverbal IQ | 29 | 1.76* | 1.05 | −1.13 |
| Low verbal IQ | 23 | 2.39** | 1.39 | 1.08 |
| Lacks concentration/restless | 26 | 1.31 | 1.69* | 1.10 |
| Daring | 13 | 3.32** | 2.13* | 1.17 |
| Frequently lies | 30 | 1.45 | 1.04 | 2.28* |
| High neuroticism | 25 | 1.71* | 2.01* | −1.10 |
| Unpopular | 17 | −1.99* | 1.57 | 1.68 |
| Had sex | 29 | 1.82* | −1.27 | 1.10 |
| Delinquent friends | 25 | 2.39** | 1.36 | 2.00* |
| Self-reported delinquent | 23 | 2.43** | −1.02 | 1.79 |
| Antisocial | 21 | 2.72** | 1.39 | 1.45 |
| **Age 18:** | | | | |
| Impulsive | 27 | 1.38 | 2.22* | 1.70 |
| Poor reader | 7 | −1.62 | 2.48* | 1.66 |
| Hangs about | 16 | 1.15 | 2.70** | −1.06 |
| Sexually promiscuous | 29 | 1.09 | −1.27 | 2.64* |
| Antisocial group member | 17 | 1.33 | 2.21* | 2.15* |
| Self-reported delinquent | 25 | 1.84* | 1.63 | 2.04* |
| Antisocial | 23 | 1.75* | 1.54 | 1.58 |
| **Age 32:** | | | | |
| Impulsive | 22 | 1.09 | 1.18 | 2.25* |
| Wears glasses | 31 | −1.07 | −1.09 | −2.46* |
| Heavy gambler | 29 | 1.90* | 1.31 | 1.29 |
| Heavy smoker | 32 | 1.64* | 1.10 | −1.36 |
| Alcoholism (Cage)[a] | 29 | −1.14 | 1.49 | 2.08* |
| Serious drug user | 10 | 1.07 | −2.39 | 2.60* |
| Antisocial | 24 | 1.10 | 1.32 | 1.53 |

[a] Cage Alcoholism Screening Test (see Mayfield, McLeod, and Hall 1974).
* $p < .05$.
** $p < .001$ (two-tailed).

addition, they were identified as antisocial in a variety of respects at age ten (see Farrington [1991*a*] for a description of the "antisocial" variables). They tended not to attend church at age eight and not to "have few or no friends" at age eight (according to their parents).

The bullies at age fourteen tended to come from large-sized families at age fourteen, to have low verbal and nonverbal IQ on tests, to be rated as daring by teachers, to have high neuroticism according to the New Junior Maudsley Inventory, and to be antisocial. The bullies were not unpopular. In addition, they tended to have had sexual intercourse by age fourteen, had many delinquent friends, and had committed many delinquent acts according to their own admissions. They were also high on self-reported delinquency and antisocial at age eighteen, and tended to be heavy gamblers and heavy smokers at age thirty-two.

The bullies at age eighteen tended to come from poor, large-sized families at ages eight to ten, living in poor housing. They tended to be poorly supervised and physically neglected by their parents at age eight. They were placed in low streams of schools and rated as troublesome at ages eight to ten. They also tended to be among the sixty-three most "vulnerable" boys at ages eight to ten, based on a combination of low family income, large family size, convicted parents, poor parental child-rearing behavior (harsh and erratic discipline), and low nonverbal IQ (see West and Farrington 1973, p. 131). The bullies at age eighteen also tended to be living in poor housing and large families at age fourteen, and their fathers rarely participated in their leisure activities at age twelve. They were rated by teachers as lacking in concentration or restless in class and as daring, and they tended to have high neuroticism at age fourteen. At age eighteen, they tended to be impulsive according to questionnaire items such as, "I generally do and say things quickly without stopping to think," were poor readers, spent a lot of time hanging about on the streets, and were involved in antisocial groups.

The bullies at age thirty-two also tended to have been poorly supervised and physically neglected by their parents at age eight, and to have fathers who did not join in their leisure activities at age twelve. They were rated as frequent liars by teachers at ages twelve to fourteen and reported that they had many delinquent friends at age fourteen. At age eighteen, they tended to be sexually promiscuous, in having intercourse with two or more girls in the previous six months, and were also antisocial group members and self-reported delinquents. At age thirty-two, concurrently with their bullying, they tended to be impulsive, to show symptoms of alcoholism, and to report that they had used prohibited drugs other than marijuana in the previous five years. However, they tended not to wear glasses or contact lenses.

In some cases, the absence of significant relationships was surprising. For example, the bullies did not significantly tend to be truants at ages twelve to fourteen, and they were not significantly likely to leave school at the earliest possible age or to have taken no examinations. There was nearly a significant tendency for the bullies at age thirty-two to hit their wives or cohabitees (23.8 percent of 42 bullies, as opposed to 13.0 percent of 247 nonbullies).

## TABLE A4

### Regression Analyses for Bullying

|  | OLS Regression | | Logistic Regression | |
| --- | --- | --- | --- | --- |
| Characteristics at Age: | F Change | p | LRCS Change | p |
| Bullying 14: | | | | |
| Few friends 8 (−) | 8.56 | .002 | 6.15 | .007 |
| Low attainment 11 | 4.74 | .015 | 3.30 | .04 |
| Attends church 8 (−) | 3.56 | .03 | 4.94 | .013 |
| Convicted parent 10 | 2.21 | .07 | 7.86 | .003 |
| Bullying 18: | | | | |
| Physical neglect 8 | 9.02 | .002 | . . . | . . . |
| Father does not join in 12 | 5.08 | .013 | 8.27 | .002 |
| High neuroticism 14 | 3.45 | .03 | . . . | . . . |
| Poor parental supervision 8 | . . . | . . . | 3.57 | .03 |
| Bullying 32: | | | | |
| Physical neglect 8 | 4.41 | .018 | . . . | . . . |
| Father does not join in 12 | 2.20 | .07 | 3.05 | .04 |

NOTE.—OLS = ordinary least squares; LRCS = likelihood ratio $\chi^2$; $p$ values are one-tailed; "(−)" indicates a negative relationship.

### D. Independent Predictors of Bullying

In attempting to explain the development of bullying, an important first step is to establish which factors are independent predictors of bullying. In view of the likelihood that bullying is one symptom of an antisocial personality, it is essential in these analyses to exclude any other factors that might also be symptoms of an antisocial personality (such as troublesomeness, delinquency, lying, and sexual promiscuity), so that all predictive factors are possibly causal. Two methods of investigating independent predictors were used, namely ordinary least squares (OLS) regression, and logistic regression. In practice, the two methods tend to produce similar results with dichotomous data (Cleary and Angel 1984). The main differences follow from the fact that missing cases can be deleted variable by variable in OLS regression (thereby using as much of the data as possible), whereas in logistic regression a case that is missing on any one variable has to be deleted from the whole analysis (sometimes causing a serious loss of data). The most reliable predictors are those identified by both regression methods.

So that the analysis would be truly predictive, only variables measured up to age twelve were studied as predictors of bullying at age fourteen, only variables measured up to age fourteen were studied as predictors of bullying at age eighteen, and only variables measured up to age eighteen were studied as predictors of bullying at age thirty-two. Table A4 shows that the best independent predictors of bullying at age fourteen were not "having few or no friends" at age eight, low junior attainment at age eleven, not attending church

## TABLE A5

### Age, Gender, and Child Bullying and Victimization

| Gender and Age | N | Percent Bullies | Percent Victims |
|---|---|---|---|
| Male: | | | |
| 3–6 | 90 | 6.7 | 11.1 |
| 7–10 | 53 | 9.4 | 32.1 |
| 11–15 | 26 | 19.2 | 15.4 |
| Female: | | | |
| 3–6 | 76 | 7.9 | 9.2 |
| 7–10 | 53 | 1.9 | 20.8 |
| 11–15 | 25 | .0 | 12.0 |

at age eight, and having a convicted parent up to the tenth birthday. The only independent predictor of bullying at ages eighteen and thirty-two identified by both regression methods was having a father who rarely joined in the boy's leisure activities at age twelve. However, physical neglect at age eight was important in both OLS regressions. Also, high neuroticism at age fourteen and poor parental supervision at age eight were identified as independent predictors of bullying at age eighteen by one regression method.

### E. Measures of Child Bullying and Victimization

When the males were aged thirty-two, they were asked whether they had any children. Of 378 males interviewed, 119 reported no children; 66, one; 119, two; 52, three; 12, four; 8, five; and 2, six; giving a total of 560 children. For each child living with them aged between three and fifteen, they were then asked about sixteen specified difficulties that children might have: lying, stealing at home, stealing outside home, running away from home, truancy, disobedience, fighting, temper tantrums, bullying, destroying things, restlessness, bedwetting, sleep disturbance, fears, nervous habits, and being bullied. These questions were answered by 178 study males for 323 eligible children; most of the other children were excluded because they were age inappropriate (123, mostly under age three) or living elsewhere (101).

Of these 323 children, 23 (7.1 percent) were reported to be bullies, and 52 (16.1 percent), victims of bullying. Table A5 shows how bullying and victimization varied with the age and gender of the child. Bullying was most prevalent among boys aged eleven to fifteen (19.2 percent) and virtually absent among girls aged seven or over (only one bully out of seventy-eight). The low rate of bullying by older girls is in agreement with research cited earlier (e.g., Olweus 1991a; Whitney and Smith 1991). Victimization was most prevalent among boys and girls aged seven to ten (32.1 percent of boys and 20.8 percent of girls).

From this point, the analyses are based on the study males, not on their children. Because bullying was virtually absent among girls aged seven or over, study males were considered at risk of having a child bully only if they had a

## TABLE A6

### Number of Children versus Child Bullying and Victimization

|  | Bullies | | Victims | |
| --- | --- | --- | --- | --- |
| Number of Children | Percent | N | Percent | N |
| 1 | 8.3 | 84 | 22.2 | 63 |
| 2 | 13.4 | 67 | 21.3 | 89 |
| 3–4 | 22.2 | 9 | 34.6 | 26 |
| Total males | 11.3 | 160 | 23.6 | 178 |

NOTE.—This is based on study males, not their children.

girl aged three to six or a boy aged three to fifteen. Hence, 160 study males were at risk of having a child bully, while 178 males were at risk of having a child victim.

Table A6 shows how the likelihood of having a child bully or a child victim varied with the number of children at risk. Overall, 11.3 percent of the study males had a child bully and 23.6 percent had a child victim of bullying. The percentage with child bullies and child victims was greater for the small number of study males with three or four children at risk than for those with only one or two children, as might have been expected. However, since the numbers were small and the differences were not startling, no attempt was made to adjust future results for the number of children at risk.

In about two-thirds of the cases (123 out of 178), the study male's wife or cohabitee was in the home when he was interviewed, and the interviewers often reported that he would ask her to help him to answer the questions about children. However, the prevalence of reported child bullying and victimization was not significantly greater when the wife or cohabitee was present than when she was absent.

There was some tendency for study males who had child bullies also to have child victims. Of eighteen males with child bullies, seven ( 38.8 percent) also had child victims, in comparison with 19.7 percent of 142 males with child nonbullies who had child victims. This was partly because children who were bullies tended also to be victims and partly because study males who had one child who was a bully tended to have another child who was a victim. About a quarter of child bullies (26.9 percent) were also victimized, compared with 18.1 percent of child nonbullies. Also, in about a quarter (26.9 percent) of child-child pairs in the same families where one child was a bully, the other child was victimized (as opposed to 12.7 percent of child-child pairs where one child was not a bully).

### F. Intergenerational Continuity of Bullying

Table A7 shows that there was a significant tendency for study males who were bullies to have children who were bullies. For example, 16.1 percent of eighty-seven study males who were bullies at age fourteen had child bullies at

## TABLE A7
### Aggression, Bullying, and Child Bullying

| Aggression Measure | Percent Child Bully 32 | | $\chi^2$ | $p$ | Odds Ratio |
| --- | --- | --- | --- | --- | --- |
| | NA | A | | | |
| Bully 14 | 5.5 | 16.1 | 4.48 | .017 | 3.31 |
| Bully 18 | 8.7 | 19.0 | 3.25 | .04 | 2.47 |
| Bully 32 | 9.4 | 22.7 | 3.37 | .03 | 2.83 |
| Aggressive 14 | 13.7 | 6.9 | 1.73 | N.S. | −2.15 |
| Aggressive 18 | 10.7 | 13.3 | .22 | N.S. | 1.28 |
| Aggressive 32 | 8.4 | 17.0 | 2.61 | .05 | 2.23 |
| Violence | 7.9 | 35.0 | 12.91 | .0002 | 6.31 |

NOTE.—NA = Not aggressive/bully; A = Aggressive/bully. One-tailed significance tests were used in view of directional predictions. N.S. = not significant.

age thirty-two, compared with only 5.5 percent of seventy-three study males who were not bullies at age fourteen. Because less than half of the study males (160) had children at risk of bullying at age thirty-two, these analyses are based on small numbers, and relationships have to be very strong to reach conventional levels of statistical significance.

There was less tendency for study males who were aggressive to have children who are bullies. However, the relationship between aggression at age thirty-two (fighting in the previous five years) and having child bullies was on the borderline of statistical significance. More strikingly, there was a strong tendency for study males convicted of violent crimes to have children who were bullies: seven (35.0 percent) out of twenty convicted violent men had child bullies, compared with only 7.9 percent of the remaining 140 study males.

### G. Is There Specific Intergenerational Continuity in Bullying?
The fact that bullying by the study males predicts bullying by their children may follow merely because general antisocial behavior by the study males predicts general antisocial behavior by their children. It is important to investigate how far there is specific intergenerational continuity in bullying as opposed to general intergenerational continuity in antisocial behavior. The best measures of general antisocial behavior of the study males are the "antisocial personality" measures at ages ten, fourteen, eighteen, and thirty-two. However, it was necessary to develop a measure of antisocial behavior of their children.

Table A8 shows the prevalence of the fourteen child problems inquired about (other than child bullying and victimization), for male and female children of different ages. As might perhaps have been expected, truancy was not reported for any child aged three to six, and bedwetting was reported for only one child aged eleven to fifteen. Truancy and stealing outside home were more

## TABLE A8
### Child Problems, Child Bullying, and Child Victimization

| | Percent of Males | | | Percent of Females | | | Odds Ratio (Significance) vs. | |
|---|---|---|---|---|---|---|---|---|
| | 3–6 | 7–10 | 11–15 | 3–6 | 7–10 | 11–15 | Child Bully | Child Victim |
| N | 90 | 53 | 26 | 76 | 53 | 25 | | |
| Lying | 43.3 | 62.3 | 65.4 | 47.4 | 58.5 | 80.0 | 3.55(.02) | 1.65(N.S.) |
| Stealing at home | 1.1 | 7.5 | 3.8 | .0 | 5.7 | 8.0 | −1.01(N.S.) | 3.54(.02) |
| Stealing outside home | 2.2 | 3.8 | 15.4 | 1.3 | 3.8 | 4.0 | 8.72(.0001) | 1.94(N.S.) |
| Running away from home | .0 | 3.8 | .0 | 1.3 | .0 | .0 | * | * |
| Truancy | .0 | 1.9 | 3.8 | .0 | 1.9 | 12.0 | * | * |
| Disobedience | 50.0 | 50.9 | 50.0 | 48.7 | 41.5 | 48.0 | 1.74(N.S.) | 1.12(N.S.) |
| Fighting | 63.3 | 73.6 | 65.4 | 50.0 | 64.2 | 48.0 | 2.71(.04) | −1.34(N.S.) |
| Temper tantrums | 45.6 | 35.8 | 53.8 | 59.2 | 52.8 | 40.0 | 1.64(N.S.) | 1.38(N.S.) |
| Destroys things | 13.3 | 7.5 | 7.7 | 6.6 | 3.8 | 8.0 | 2.61(.06) | 1.18(N.S.) |
| Restlessness | 22.2 | 18.9 | 11.5 | 11.8 | 11.3 | 12.0 | 3.90(.003) | 1.93(.05) |
| Bedwetting | 21.1 | 9.4 | .0 | 9.2 | 9.8 | 4.3 | 1.64(N.S.) | 1.42(N.S.) |
| Sleep disturbance | 21.1 | 9.4 | 3.8 | 21.1 | 7.5 | 4.0 | 1.42(N.S.) | 1.02(N.S.) |
| Fears | 25.6 | 22.6 | 1.5 | 28.9 | 18.9 | 16.0 | 2.69(.04) | 1.68(N.S.) |
| Nervous habits | 11.1 | 17.0 | 15.4 | 11.8 | 11.3 | 32.0 | 1.50(N.S.) | −1.31(N.S.) |

NOTE.—Percent of males and females are based on children of study males. Odds ratios are based on study males. Significance levels (one-tailed) are in parentheses. N.S. = not significant.
* Numbers insufficient to calculate.

common among older children, while bedwetting, sleep disturbance, and fears were more common among younger children. The most commonly reported problems were lying, disobedience, fighting, and temper tantrums.

Each study male was scored according to whether he had at least one child showing each problem, and each child problem was then related to child bullying and victimization. For example, 83.3 percent of eighteen study males with child bullies also had children who lied, compared with 58.5 percent of the remaining 142 study males with child nonbullies, a significant difference ($\chi^2 = 4.17$, $p = .02$, one-tailed, odds ratio = 3.55). Table A8 shows that child bullying was significantly associated with stealing outside home, restlessness, lying, fighting, and fears, while child victimization was significantly related only to stealing at home and restlessness.

Each of the fourteen child problems was intercorrelated with each other problem, although some of these comparisons were hindered by the small numbers involved (e.g., only three study males with runaway children and only six with truants; at least ten study males had a child with a problem in all other cases). Stealing at home, stealing outside the home, running away, and truancy were clearly associated, as were lying and fighting, disobedience and destructiveness, sleep disturbance, and fears and bedwetting. Nervous habits were not clearly related to any other problem, while restlessness was associated with most other problems (the "externalizing" stealing, disobedience, and destructiveness, as well as the "internalizing" fears and sleep disturbance).

An externalizing child problems scale (excluding child bullying) was developed on the basis of lying, stealing at home, stealing outside home, running away, disobedience, fighting, destructiveness, and restlessness. Truancy was not included in this scale because the younger children were not at risk. Each study male was scored according to the number of these eight problems that his child showed, and the main comparison was between sixty-one study males with a child with three or more problems and 117 with a child with two or less. From now on, "child problems" will refer to the children with three or more problems. Child bullying was significantly related to this measure of child problems since 72.2 percent of eighteen study males with child bullies also had three or more child problems (compared with 30.3 percent of 142 study males with child nonbullies; $\chi^2 = 12.35$, $p = .0001$, odds ratio = 5.99). However, child victimization was not significantly related to child problems (42.9 percent of forty-two study males with child victims also had three or more child problems, compared with 31.6 percent of the 136 with child nonvictims; $\chi^2 = 1.80$, not significant, odds ratio = 1.62).

Table A9 shows that the relationships between the study male's bullying and his child having problems were much weaker than those between the study male's bullying and his child bullying (table A7). Also, the relationships between the study male's antisociality at different ages and his child having problems were rather weak; only antisociality at age eighteen was on the borderline of statistical significance in predicting child problems. Also, the study males convicted of violent offenses were not significantly more likely to report child problems.

All these results suggest that the continuity between the study male bullying

## TABLE A9

### Antisocial Personality and Child Problems

| Aggression/Antisocial Measure | Percent Child Problem | | $\chi^2$ | $p$ | Odds Ratio |
|---|---|---|---|---|---|
| | NA | A | | | |
| Bully 14 | 31.3 | 36.7 | .59 | N.S. | 1.28 |
| Bully 18 | 34.4 | 34.8 | .00 | N.S. | 1.02 |
| Bully 32 | 32.0 | 48.0 | 2.43 | .06 | 1.96 |
| Antisocial 14 | 33.6 | 36.2 | .10 | N.S. | 1.12 |
| Antisocial 18 | 30.6 | 43.4 | 2.68 | .05 | 1.74 |
| Antisocial 32 | 31.3 | 43.2 | 2.06 | N.S. | 1.66 |
| Violence | 32.5 | 45.8 | 1.65 | N.S. | 1.76 |

NOTE.—NA = Not aggressive/antisocial; A = Aggressive/antisocial. One-tailed significance tests were used in view of directional predictions. N.S. = not significant.

and his child bullying is not likely to be merely a consequence of continuity between the study male being generally antisocial and his child being generally antisocial. Also, the weak relationship between the study male's antisociality and child problems suggests that the relationship between the study male's bullying and child bullying is not primarily caused by any tendency of the male to project his own traits onto his child.

Table A10 presents a more systematic test of how far the relationship between the study male's bullying and child bullying holds independently of any relationship between the study male's antisociality and child problems. Its rationale is similar to that of table A2. For example, comparing males who were not antisocial at age fourteen and did not have child problems at age thirty-two, 10.8 percent of thirty-seven bullies at age fourteen, as opposed to 2.4 percent of forty-two nonbullies at age fourteen, had child bullies at age thirty-two. None of the males who were antisocial at age fourteen, but who did not have child problems at age thirty-two, had child bullies at age thirty-two. However, comparing males who were not antisocial at age fourteen and who had child problems at age thirty-two, 30.4 of twenty-three bullies at age fourteen, as opposed to 11.8 percent of seventeen nonbullies at age fourteen, had child bullies at age thirty-two. Comparing males who were antisocial at age fourteen and who had child problems at age thirty-two, 30.0 percent of ten bullies at age fourteen, as opposed to 16.7 percent of six nonbullies at age fourteen, had child bullies at age thirty-two.

Merely comparing the percentages suggests that the study males' bullying at age fourteen predicted child bullying at age thirty-two independently of his antisociality at age fourteen and his child problems at age thirty-two. However, a logistic regression analysis, predicting child bullying at age thirty-two, provided a more systematic test. Antisociality at age fourteen was entered first in the equation, but it had no significant predictive effect (LRCS = 0.1, not significant). Child problems at age thirty-two were then added, and had a

## TABLE A10

Testing Specific Intergenerational Continuity in Bullying

### A. Continuity

| | Child | | Percent Child Bully at 32 | | |
|---|---|---|---|---|---|
| Ant | Problem | Bully | 14 | 18 | 32 |
| No | No | No | 2.4 | 5.0 | 6.6 |
| No | No | Yes | 10.8 | 10.5 | .0 |
| Yes | No | No | .0 | .0 | .0 |
| Yes | No | Yes | .0 | .0 | .0 |
| No | Yes | No | 11.8 | 16.0 | 16.1 |
| No | Yes | Yes | 30.4 | 44.4 | 44.4 |
| Yes | Yes | No | 16.7 | 18.8 | 23.1 |
| Yes | Yes | Yes | 30.0 | 40.0 | 33.3 |

### B. Logistic Regression

| | LRCS | | |
|---|---|---|---|
| | 14 | 18 | 32 |
| Ant | .1 | .0 | .0 |
| Child Problem | 11.9** | 12.2** | 11.9** |
| Ant × Child Problem | 2.6 | 2.2 | 2.0 |
| Bully | 4.7* | 4.1* | 1.3 |
| Ant × Bully | .2 | .0 | .0 |
| Child Problem × Bully | .1 | .2 | 2.9* |

NOTE.—Ant = Antisocial; LRCS = likelihood ratio $\chi^2$.
* $p < .05$.
** $p < .001$ (one-tailed).

significant effect (LRCS = 11.9, $p$ = .0003). The interaction between antisociality at age fourteen and child problems at age thirty-two was nearly significant (LRCS = 2.6, $p$ = .055), reflecting the tendency for antisociality at age fourteen to be negatively associated with child bullying in the absence of child problems and positively associated in the presence of child problems. Controlling for antisociality at age fourteen and child problems at age thirty-two, bullying at age fourteen significantly predicted child bullying at age thirty-two (LRCS = 4.7, $p$ = .015). No other interactions were significant.

Bullying at age eighteen also predicted child bullying at age thirty-two independently of antisociality at age eighteen and child problems at age thirty-two (LRCS = 4.1, $p$ = .02). However, bullying at age thirty-two did not significantly predict child bullying at age thirty-two independently of antisociality at age thirty-two and child problems at age thirty-two (LRCS = 1.3, not significant). This was probably an artifactual result caused by small numbers. The percentages show a clear effect of bullying at age thirty-two, but only in the presence of child problems at age thirty-two, and this is seen in the significant interaction between bullying at age thirty-two and child problems at age thirty-two (LRCS = 2.9, $p$ = .045). Overall, it can be concluded that the intergenerational continuity in bullying is specific and holds independently of any general continuity in antisocial behavior.

### H. Predictors and Correlates of Child Bullying

Table A11 summarizes the strength of relationships using odds ratios. Because of the small numbers involved in the child bullying analyses (160 study males with children at risk and only eighteen with child bullies), relationships had to be very strong to reach statistical significance at $p$ = .05 (two-tailed). For example, 20.0 percent of thirty-five study males who were separated from a parent up to their tenth birthdays for reasons other than death or hospitalization had child bullies, compared with 8.8 percent of the 125 nonseparated males who were at risk. Despite the high odds ratio of 2.59, this relationship was not quite significant ($\chi^2$ = 3.44, $p$ = .06, two-tailed). Similarly, 18.2 percent of forty-four study males with low verbal IQs at ages eight to ten had child bullies, compared with 7.9 percent of the remaining 114 at risk ($\chi^2$ = 3.50, $p$ = .06, odds ratio = 2.59).

The most significant predictors of child bullying were authoritarian parents (on a questionnaire) at age twelve, unpopularity at ages twelve to fourteen (according to teachers), poor reading ability at age eighteen, heavy gambling at age eighteen, and spending time hanging about the streets at age eighteen. Separation from parents and low verbal intelligence were the best predictors at ages eight to ten. In addition, going out frequently (four or more evenings per week), high debts, and not wearing glasses or contact lenses at age thirty-two were significant correlates of child bullying. There was some tendency for men who had struck their wives or cohabitees and for those who used physical punishment on their children to have child bullies, but these relationships were not statistically significant.

As before, OLS and logistic regression analyses were carried out to investigate the independent predictors of child bullying. Table A12 shows that being a poor reader at age eighteen, a heavy gambler at age eighteen, being unpopular at ages twelve to fourteen, and bullying at age fourteen were the best independent predictors of child bullying, while authoritarian parents at age twelve and hanging about at age eighteen also had some independent importance.

It is instructive to investigate the extent to which child bullying at age thirty-two could be predicted by the variables measured up to age eighteen. In the logistic regression analysis, eighteen males had a probability greater than .2 of having a child bully, and eight of them (44.4 percent) actually had a child bully. In contrast, 139 males had a probability less than .2 of having a child bully, and only ten of them (7.2 percent) actually had a child bully. When the prediction criterion was reduced to .18, eleven of twenty-nine predicted males (37.9 percent) had a child bully, compared with seven out of 128 nonpredicted males (5.5 percent). These results suggest that half or more of the males who had child bullies at age thirty-two might have been predicted at age eighteen.

### I. Predictors and Correlates of Child Victimization

The best predictors at ages eight to ten of child victimization at age thirty-two were having few or no friends at age eight (according to parents), being physically neglected by parents, being unpopular, being relatively lightweight, having parents with poor child-rearing behavior (providing harsh or erratic discipline), and going to a high-delinquency-rate school. For example, 50 percent of sixteen study males who had few or no friends at age eight had child victims at age thirty-two, compared with 19.6 percent of the remaining 153 at risk.

The best predictors at ages twelve to fourteen of child victimization at age thirty-two were nervousness (as rated by parents) and regular smoking, while unpopularity (as rated by teachers) was nearly significant. However, high neuroticism on the New Junior Maudsley Inventory was not a significant predictor. At age eighteen, the best predictor was an antiestablishment attitude, and poor reading ability was nearly significant. At age thirty-two, the most significant correlates were problems with accommodation (e.g., dampness, heating or structural problems, overcrowding) and problems with the area (e.g., noise, violence, dirt, difficult neighbors). In addition, high indebtedness was nearly significant.

Table A12 also shows the results of the regression analyses carried out to investigate the independent predictors of child victimization at age thirty-two. The most important predictors were unpopularity at ages eight to ten, having few or no friends at age eight, regular smoking at age fourteen, poor parental child-rearing behavior at age eight, and nervousness at age fourteen.

Once again, the extent to which variables measured up to age eighteen could predict child victimization was investigated. In the logistic regression analysis, twenty-six males had a probability greater than .4 of having a child victim, and fifteen of them (57.7 percent) actually had a child victim. In contrast, 130 males had a probability less than .4 of having a child victim, and only twenty of them (15.4 percent) actually had a child victim. When the prediction criterion was reduced to .35, twenty-one out of forty predicted males (52.5 percent) had a child victim, compared with fourteen out of 116 nonpredicted males (12.1 percent). These results suggest that half or more of the males who had child victims at age thirty-two might have been predicted at age eighteen.

### J. Measuring Probable Victimization of Study Males

The study males were never asked directly whether they were bullied. However, the literature suggests that boys who have few or no friends and those who are nervous and unpopular are most at risk of being bullied. Consequently, a measure of probable victimization of the study males was derived by counting males who had few or no friends at age eight, or who were both nervous and unpopular at ages eight to ten, or who were both nervous and

# TABLE A11

## Predictors and Correlates of Child Bullying and Victimization

| Variable | Percent Identified | Odds Ratio Child Bully 32 | Child Victim 32 | Probable Victim 8–14 |
|---|---|---|---|---|
| **Age 8–10:** | | | | |
| Low family income | 23 | 1.28 | 1.39 | 1.95* |
| Poor housing | 37 | 1.19 | −1.07 | 1.67* |
| Large family size | 24 | 1.97 | 1.20 | 1.98* |
| Working mother | 23 | −1.12 | 1.05 | −2.26* |
| Poor child rearing | 24 | 1.42 | 2.40* | 2.13* |
| Physical neglect | 12 | 1.44 | 2.98* | 1.75 |
| Separated | 22 | 2.59 | −1.31 | 2.03* |
| Low verbal IQ | 25 | 2.59 | 2.08* | 1.58 |
| Low attainment | 23 | 1.67 | 1.60 | 1.89* |
| Low school track | 79 | 1.72 | 1.98 | 2.48** |
| Delinquent school | 21 | 1.23 | 2.40* | 2.08* |
| Few friends | 12 | 1.50 | 4.10* | . . . |
| Unpopular | 32 | 1.85 | 2.95* | . . . |
| Daring | 30 | −1.50 | −1.80 | −2.00* |
| High clumsiness | 25 | 1.28 | 1.34 | 1.84* |
| Light | 18 | −1.63 | 2.60* | 1.47 |
| Vulnerable | 15 | 1.72 | 1.39 | 2.18* |
| **Age 12–14:** | | | | |
| Large family size | 21 | 1.84 | 1.77 | 1.90* |
| Authoritarian parents | 24 | 3.65* | 1.14 | 1.01 |
| Poor child rearing | 29 | 1.34 | 1.16 | 2.26* |
| Nervous | 28 | −1.03 | 2.82* | . . . |
| Unpopular | 17 | 4.23* | 2.38 | . . . |
| Daring | 13 | −1.71 | −1.51 | −2.72* |
| Frequent truant | 18 | −1.51 | 1.43 | 1.77* |
| Tall | 25 | −2.72 | 1.10 | 1.81* |
| Regular smoker | 17 | 1.06 | 2.48* | 1.27 |
| Had sex | 29 | 1.67 | −1.32 | −2.40* |
| **Age 18:** | | | | |
| Poor relationship with parents | 22 | −4.68 | 1.58 | 2.06* |
| No girlfriend | 42 | 1.85 | −1.08 | 1.84* |
| Poor reader | 7 | 5.56* | 2.68 | 2.64* |
| Tall | 22 | −1.44 | 1.05 | 1.99* |
| Hangs about | 16 | 3.21* | 1.58 | 1.22 |
| No sex | 26 | 1.75 | 1.28 | 3.10** |
| Heavy gambler | 22 | 3.96* | −1.42 | −1.62 |
| Heavy drinker | 25 | −1.75 | −1.01 | −2.14* |
| Antiestablishment | 25 | 2.22 | 2.11 | 1.22 |

## TABLE A11 (*Continued*)

| | | Odds Ratio | | |
| Variable | Percent Identified | Child Bully 32 | Child Victim 32 | Probable Victim 8–14 |
|---|---|---|---|---|
| Age 32: | | | | |
| Accommodation problems | 15 | 1.09 | 3.23* | −1.05 |
| Area problems | 19 | −1.12 | 2.60* | 1.88* |
| Low class job | 25 | −1.23 | −1.01 | 1.96* |
| Unstable job record | 25 | −4.55 | −1.61 | −2.13* |
| Wears glasses | 31 | −7.63* | 1.39 | 1.16 |
| Frequently out | 17 | 5.48* | −1.25 | 1.03 |
| No wife or girlfriend | 15 | . . . | . . . | 3.74** |
| High debts | 26 | 2.72* | 1.95 | −1.22 |
| Heavy smoking | 32 | −1.37 | −1.28 | −2.06* |
| Heavy drinking | 21 | 1.47 | 1.20 | −1.98* |

NOTE.—The variables "few friends" and "unpopular" are not shown as correlates of probable victims because they were included in the definition of this variable. The variable "no wife or girlfriend" is not shown as a correlate of child bullying or child victimization because males with no wife or girlfriend generally did not have children living with them.

\* $p < .05$.

\*\* $p < .001$ (two-tailed).

unpopular at age fourteen. Both nervousness and unpopularity were required in case unpopularity alone tended to identify bullies rather than victims. All the interrelationships among these five factors were statistically significant, except for three of those concerning unpopularity (as rated by peers) at ages eight to ten (with nervousness at ages ten and fourteen and unpopularity as rated by teachers at age fourteen). These criteria identified eighty-three presumed victims, of whom forty-six had few or no friends at age eight.

Interestingly, probable victims at ages eight to fourteen significantly tended at age thirty-two to have children who were victims. Nearly half of probable victims (44.8 percent of twenty-nine) had child victims, in comparison with 18.4 percent of the remaining 147 study males at risk. This is evidence in favor of the intergenerational transmission of victimization. Probable victims at ages eight to fourteen were significantly unlikely to be bullies at age fourteen; 35.8 percent of eighty-one probable victims were also bullies, compared with 53.1 percent of the remaining 320. Probable victimization at ages eight to fourteen was not significantly related to bullying at ages eighteen or thirty-two or to child bullying.

### K. Correlates of Probable Victimization

The most important correlates at ages eight to ten of probable victimization were low family income, poor housing, large family size, poor parental child-rearing behavior, separation from parents, low junior school attainment, low

TABLE A12

Regression Analyses for Child Bullying and Victimization

| | OLS Regression | | Logistic Regression | |
|---|---|---|---|---|
| | F Change | p | LRCS Change | p |
| Child Bully 32: | | | | |
| Poor reader 18 | 6.85 | .005 | 6.45 | .006 |
| Heavy gambler 18 | 5.33 | .011 | 4.55 | .017 |
| Unpopular 12–14 | 5.23 | .012 | 4.84 | .014 |
| Bully 14 | 5.40 | .011 | 5.49 | .01 |
| Authoritarian parents 12 | 3.68 | .03 | . . . | . . . |
| Hangs about 18 | . . . | . . . | 2.25 | .07 |
| Child Victim 32: | | | | |
| Unpopular 8–10 | 9.02 | .002 | 7.50 | .003 |
| Few friends 8 | 6.87 | .005 | 3.60 | .03 |
| Regular smoker 14 | 5.52 | .01 | 3.08 | .04 |
| Poor child rearing 8 | 4.11 | .02 | 4.97 | .013 |
| Nervous 14 | 2.80 | .05 | 8.68 | .002 |
| Antiestablishment 18 | 3.00 | .05 | . . . | . . . |
| Light 8–10 | 2.37 | .06 | . . . | . . . |
| Probable Victim 8–14: | | | | |
| Low school track 11 | 12.76 | .0002 | 9.88 | .0009 |
| Poor child rearing 8 | 6.60 | .005 | 5.43 | .01 |
| Working mother 8 (−) | 4.02 | .03 | 4.30 | .02 |
| Separated 10 | 5.07 | .013 | 3.14 | .04 |

NOTE.—OLS = ordinary least squares; LRCS = likelihood ratio $\chi^2$; p values are one-tailed; "(−)" indicates = negative relationship.

school tracking, going to a high-delinquency-rate school, high psychomotor clumsiness, and coming from the vulnerable group. In contrast, working mothers and daring were negatively related to probable victimization. Having a nervous father or a nervous mother was not related to probable victimization. Of the measures at ages twelve to fourteen, large family size, poor parental child-rearing behavior, and tallness were related to probable victimization, while probable victims were unlikely to be rated as daring or to report having sexual intercourse by age fourteen. Just on the borderline of statistical significance, probable victims tended to be frequent truants according to their teachers (Farrington 1980). However, they did not significantly tend to be lacking in concentration or restless.

At age eighteen, probable victims tended to have a poor relationship with their parents, to have no girlfriend, to be poor readers, to be relatively tall, and to report that they had not had sexual intercourse. However, they were unlikely to be heavy drinkers. At age thirty-two, probable victims tended to have no wife or girlfriend, reported problems with their area of residence, and tended to have low social class jobs. However, they did not have unstable job records and were not heavy smokers or heavy drinkers. There was no significant tendency for probable victims to score highly on the General Health Questionnaire at age thirty-two, reflecting psychiatric disturbance.

Only factors measured at ages eight to ten were studied as possible "predictors" of probable victims. Table A12 shows that the most important independent predictors were a low school track, poor parental child-rearing behavior, nonworking mothers, and separation from parents.

The probable victims are quite similar to the unconvicted males from vulnerable backgrounds studied by Farrington et al. (1988a, 1988b). Of the sixty-three vulnerable males, forty-six were convicted up to age thirty-two. The best predictors of avoiding conviction included having few or no friends at age eight, low daring, low family income and nonworking mothers. The unconvicted vulnerable males at age thirty-two were unlikely to commit offenses, to take drugs, or to go out in the evenings. However, they were likely to have never married, to have no wife or cohabitee, to be in conflict with their parents, living in dirty home conditions and having low-class, low-paid jobs. Farrington et al. (1988a) concluded that there was continuity from social isolation at age eight to social isolation at age thirty-two. It seems likely that the social isolates tend to be bullied and that, if they do have children, their children also tend to be bullied. The majority of the unconvicted vulnerable males (nine out of sixteen measured) were probable victims.

*L. Conclusions from the Analyses*

These analyses of data collected in the Cambridge Study indicate for the first time the intragenerational and intergenerational continuity of bullying: adolescent bullies tend to grow up to be adult bullies and tend to have children who are bullies. A particularly worrying result is that men convicted of violence tend to have children who are bullies. Furthermore, there seems to be continuity from childhood to adulthood in social isolation, with adolescent victims tending, when they grow up, to have children who are victims. Generally, adolescent victims tended not to be adolescent bullies.

While these results are very interesting, it is important not to lose sight of measurement problems. Bullying was measured by self-report and, while there was significant continuity, it could be that the nature and quality of bullying was rather different at age thirty-two than at age fourteen. Child bullying and victimization were measured by parental reports. In future research, it would be desirable to have at least two independent measures of bullying and child bullying, for purposes of validation, and it would be desirable to obtain more detailed information about the nature and quality of bullying.

The investigation of the predictors and correlates of bullying replicated some prior results. For example, the best predictor of bullying at ages eighteen and thirty-two was the father rarely joining in the boy's leisure activities at age twelve, and Olweus (1978) also found that this was an important factor. However, one of the best predictors of bullying at age fourteen was not "having few or no friends" at age eight, and other results also showed that bullies at age fourteen were likely to be popular rather than unpopular. Future researchers should propose and test theories about the development and continuity of bullying in more detail than was possible in this analysis.

REFERENCES

Achenbach, Thomas M., C. Keith Conners, Herbert C. Quay, Frank C. Verhulst, and C. T. Howell. 1989. "Replication of Empirically Derived Syndromes as a Basis for Taxonomy of Child/Adolescent Psychopathology." *Journal of Abnormal Child Psychology* 17:299–323.

Achenbach, Thomas M., and Craig S. Edelbrock. 1981. "Behavioral Problems and Competencies Reported by Parents of Normal and Disturbed Children Aged 4 through 16." *Monographs of the Society for Research in Child Development*, serial no. 188, vol. 46.

———. 1983. *Manual for the Child Behavior Checklist and Revised Child Behavior Profile.* Burlington: University of Vermont, Department of Psychiatry.

———. 1984. "Psychopathology of Childhood." *Annual Review of Psychology* 35:227–56.

Ahmad, Yvette S., and Peter K. Smith. 1990. "Behavioral Measures Review: I. Bullying in Schools." *Newsletter of the Association for Child Psychology and Psychiatry* 12:26–27.

Ahmad, Yvette S., Irene Whitney, and Peter K. Smith. 1991. "A Survey Service for Schools on Bully/Victim Problems." In *Practical Approaches to Bullying*, edited by Peter K. Smith and David Thompson. London: David Fulton.

American Psychiatric Association. 1987. *Diagnostic and Statistical Manual of Mental Disorders*, 3d ed., revised. Washington, D.C.: American Psychiatric Association.

Arora, Tina. 1991. "The Use of Victim Support Groups." In *Practical Approaches to Bullying*, edited by Peter K. Smith and David Thompson. London: David Fulton.

Arora, Tina, and David A. Thompson. 1987. "Defining Bullying for a Secondary School." *Education and Child Psychology* 4:110–20.

Bastian, Lisa D., and Bruce M. Taylor. 1991. *School Crime.* Washington, D.C.: U.S. Department of Justice, Bureau of Justice Statistics.

Beck, Mitchell. 1985. "Understanding and Managing the Acting-out Child." *Pointer* 29(2):27–29.

Besag, Valerie E. 1989a. *Bullies and Victims in Schools.* Milton Keynes: Open University Press.

———. 1989b. "Management Strategies with Vulnerable Children." In *Bullying: An International Perspective*, edited by Erling Roland and Elaine Munthe. London: David Fulton.

———. 1991. "The Playground." In *Bullying: A Practical Guide to Coping for Schools*, edited by Michele Elliott. Harlow: Longman.

Bjorkvist, Kaj, Kerstin Ekman, and Kirsti Lagerspetz. 1982. "Bullies and Victims: Their Ego Picture, Ideal Ego Picture and Normative Ego Picture." *Scandinavian Journal of Psychology* 23:307–13.

Blackburn, Ronald. 1988. "On Moral Judgments and Personality Disorders: The Myth of Psychopathic Personality Revisited." *British Journal of Psychiatry* 153:505–12.

Borg, Mark G., and Joseph M. Falzon. 1989. "Primary School Teachers' Perception of Pupils' Undesirable Behaviors." *Educational Studies* 15:251–60.

Brier, Joan, and Yvette Ahmad. 1991. "Developing a School Court as a Means of Addressing Bullying in Schools." In *Practical Approaches to Bullying*, edited by Peter K. Smith and David Thompson. London: David Fulton.

Brown, Jennifer M., and R. Armstrong. 1982. "The Structure of Pupils' Worries during Transition from Junior to Secondary School." *British Educational Research Journal* 8:123–31.

Bureau of Justice Statistics. 1991. *Criminal Victimization in the United States, 1989*. Washington, D.C.: U.S. Department of Justice, Bureau of Justice Statistics.

Burrows, John. 1988. *Retail Crime: Prevention through Crime Analysis*. London: Home Office.

Chazan, Maurice. 1989. "Bullying in the Infant School." In *Bullying in Schools*, edited by Delwyn P. Tattum and David A. Lane. Stoke-on-Trent: Trentham.

Cleary, P. D., and R. Angel. 1984. "The Analysis of Relationships Involving Dichotomous Dependent Variables." *Journal of Health and Social Behavior* 25:334–48.

Cohn, Tessa. 1987. "Sticks and Stones May Break My Bones but Names Will Never Hurt Me." *Multicultural Teaching* 5(3):8–11.

Coie, John D. 1990. "Toward a Theory of Peer Rejection." In *Peer Rejection in Childhood*, edited by Stephen R. Asher and John D. Coie. Cambridge: Cambridge University Press.

Coie, John D., and Kenneth A. Dodge. 1983. "Continuities and Changes in Children's Social Status: A Five-Year Longitudinal Study." *Merrill-Palmer Quarterly* 29:261–82.

Coie, John D., Kenneth A. Dodge, Robert Terry, and Virginia Wright. 1991. "The Role of Aggression in Peer Relations: An Analysis of Aggression Episodes in Boys' Play Groups." *Child Development* 62:812–26.

Coie, John D., Marion Underwood, and John E. Lochman. 1991. "Programmatic Intervention with Aggressive Children in the School Setting." In *The Development and Treatment of Childhood Aggression*, edited by Debra J. Pepler and Kenneth H. Rubin. Hillsdale, N.J.: Erlbaum.

Croft, I. John, and Tadeusz G. Grygier. 1956. "Social Relationships of Truants and Juvenile Delinquents." *Human Relations* 9:439–66.

Dale, Ronald R. 1991. "Mixed versus Single-Sex Schools: The Social Aspect of Bullying." In *Bullying: A Practical Guide to Coping for Schools*, edited by Michele Elliott. Harlow: Longman.

Dodge, Kenneth A., John D. Coie, Gregory S. Pettit, and Joseph M. Price. 1990. "Peer Status and Aggression in Boys' Groups: Developmental and Contextual Analyses." *Child Development* 61:1289–1309.

Dumas, Jean E. 1989. "Treating Antisocial Behavior in Children: Child and Family Approaches." *Clinical Psychology Review* 9:197–222.

Duyme, Michel. 1990. "Antisocial Behavior and Postnatal Environment: A French Adoption Study." *Journal of Child Psychology and Psychiatry* 31: 699–710.

Edelbrock, Craig S., and Anthony J. Costello. 1988. "Convergence between Statistically Derived Behavior Problem Syndromes and Child Psychiatric Diagnoses." *Journal of Abnormal Child Psychology* 16:219–31.

Ekblom, Paul. 1986. *The Prevention of Shop Theft: An Approach through Crime Analysis.* London: Home Office.

Elliott, Michele, ed. 1991a. *Bullying: A Practical Guide to Coping for Schools.* Harlow: Longman.

———. 1991b. "A Whole-School Approach to Bullying." In *Bullying: A Practical Guide to Coping for Schools,* edited by Michele Elliott. Harlow: Longman.

———. 1991c. "Bully 'Courts.'" In *Bullying: A Practical Guide to Coping for Schools,* edited by Michele Elliott. Harlow: Longman.

Eron, Leonard D., L. Rowell Huesmann, Eric Dubow, Richard Romanoff, and Patty W. Yarmel. 1987. "Aggression and Its Correlates over 22 Years." In *Childhood Aggression and Violence,* edited by David H. Crowell, Ian M. Evans, and Clifford R. O'Donnell. New York: Plenum.

Farrington, David P. 1972. "Delinquency Begins at Home." *New Society* 21:495–97.

———. 1978. "The Effectiveness of Sentences." *Justice of the Peace* 142:68–71.

———. 1980. "Truancy, Delinquency, the Home and the School." In *Out of School,* edited by Lionel Hersov and Ian Berg. Chichester: Wiley.

———. 1991a. "Antisocial Personality from Childhood to Adulthood." *Psychologist* 4:389–94.

———. 1991b. "Childhood Aggression and Adult Violence: Early Precursors and Later Life Outcomes." In *The Development and Treatment of Childhood Aggression,* edited by Debra J. Pepler and Kenneth H. Rubin. Hillsdale, N.J.: Erlbaum.

———. 1992. "Criminal Career Research: Lessons for Crime Prevention." In *Studies on Crime and Crime Prevention,* vol. 1, edited by Artur Solarz and Viveka Engwall. Oslo: Scandinavian University Press.

Farrington, David P., Bernard Gallagher, Lynda Morley, Raymond J. St. Ledger, and Donald J. West. 1988a. "A 24-Year Follow-up of Men from Vulnerable Backgrounds." In *The Abandonment of Delinquent Behavior: Promoting the Turnaround,* edited by Richard L. Jenkins and Waln K. Brown. New York: Praeger.

———. 1988b. "Are There Any Successful Men from Criminogenic Backgrounds?" *Psychiatry* 51:116–30.

Farrington, David P., and Donald J. West. 1990. "The Cambridge Study in Delinquent Development: A Long-Term Follow-up of 411 London Males." In *Criminality: Personality, Behavior and Life History,* edited by Hans-Jurgen Kerner and Gunter Kaiser. Berlin: Springer-Verlag.

Foster, Pat, Tina Arora, and David Thompson. 1990. "A Whole-School Approach to Bullying." *Pastoral Care in Education* 8(3):13–17.

Foster, Pat, and David Thompson. 1991. "Bullying: Towards a Non-violent Sanctions Policy." In *Practical Approaches to Bullying,* edited by Peter K. Smith and David Thompson. London: David Fulton.

Frost, Linda. 1991. "A Primary School Approach: What Can Be Done about the Bully?" In *Bullying: A Practical Guide to Coping for Schools*, edited by Michele Elliott. Harlow: Longman.

Goddard, Sarah, and Jenny Cross. 1987. "A Social Skills Training Approach to Dealing with Disruptive Behavior in a Primary School." *Maladjustment and Therapeutic Education* 5:24–29.

Gottfredson, Gary D., and Denise C. Gottfredson. 1985. *Victimization in Schools*. New York: Plenum.

Graham, Philip, and Michael Rutter. 1985. "Adolescent Disorders." In *Child and Adolescent Psychiatry*, edited by Michael Rutter and Lionel Hersov. Oxford: Blackwell.

Greenbaum, Stuart, Brenda Turner, and Ronald D. Stephens. 1989. *Set Straight on Bullies*. Malibu, Calif.: National School Safety Center.

Hawkins, J. David, Elizabeth Von Cleve, and Richard F. Catalano. 1991. "Reducing Early Childhood Aggression: Results of a Primary Prevention Program." *Journal of the American Academy of Child and Adolescent Psychiatry* 30:208–17.

Herbert, Graham. 1989. "A Whole-Curriculum Approach to Bullying." In *Bullying in Schools*, edited by Delwyn Tattum and David Lane. Stoke-on-Trent: Trentham.

Hindelang, Michael J., Travis Hirschi, and Joseph G. Weis. 1981. *Measuring Delinquency*. Beverly Hills, Calif.: Sage.

Hoover, John H., and Richard J. Hazler. 1991. "Bullies and Victims." *Elementary School Guidance and Counselling* 25:212–19.

Hough, Michael, and Patricia Mayhew. 1983. *The British Crime Survey*. London: H.M. Stationery Office.

Huizinga, David, and Delbert S. Elliott. 1986. "Reassessing the Reliability and Validity of Self-Report Delinquency Measures." *Journal of Quantitative Criminology* 2:293–327.

Jones, Eric. 1991. "Practical Considerations in Dealing with Bullying in Secondary School." In *Bullying: A Practical Guide to Coping for Schools*, edited by Michele Elliott. Harlow: Longman.

Junger, Marianne. 1990. "Intergroup Bullying and Racial Harassment in the Netherlands." *Sociology and Social Research* 74:65–72.

Kagan, Jerome, J. Steven Reznick, and Nancy Snidman. 1988. "Biological Bases of Childhood Shyness." *Science* 240:167–71.

Kazdin, Alan E. 1987. "Treatment of Antisocial Behavior in Children: Current Status and Future Directions." *Psychological Bulletin* 102:187–203.

Kellam, Sheppard G. 1990. "Developmental Epidemiological Framework for Family Research on Depression and Aggression." In *Depression and Aggression in Family Interaction*, edited by Gerald R. Patterson. Hillsdale, N.J.: Erlbaum.

Kellam, Sheppard G., C. Hendricks Brown, Barnett R. Rubin, and Margaret E. Ensminger. 1983. "Paths Leading to Teenage Psychiatric Symptoms and Substance Use: Developmental Epidemiological Studies in Woodlawn." In *Childhood Psychopathology and Development*, edited by Samuel B. Guze, Felton J. Earls, and James E. Barrett. New York: Raven Press.

Kikkawa, Masao. 1987. "Teachers' Opinions and Treatments for Bully/Victim

Problems among Students in Junior and Senior High Schools: Results of a Fact-finding Survey." *Human Development* 23:25–30.

Kulik, James A., Kenneth B. Stein, and Theodore R. Sarbin. 1968. "Disclosure of Delinquent Behavior under Conditions of Anonymity and Nonanonymity." *Journal of Consulting and Clinical Psychology* 32:506–9.

La Fontaine, Jean. 1991. *Bullying: The Child's View.* London: Gulbenkian Foundation.

Lagerspetz, Kirsti M. J., Kaj Bjorkvist, Marianne Berts, and Elizabeth King. 1982. "Group Aggression among School Children in Three Schools." *Scandinavian Journal of Psychology* 23:45–52.

Lane, David. 1989. "Violent Histories: Bullying and Criminality." In *Bullying in Schools*, edited by Delwyn Tattum and David Lane. Stoke-on-Trent: Trentham.

Laslett, Robert. 1980. "Bullies: A Children's Court in a Day School for Maladjusted Children." *British Columbia Journal of Special Education* 4:391–97.

———. 1982. "A Children's Court for Bullies." *Special Education* 9(1):9–11.

Lefkowitz, Monroe M., Leonard D. Eron, Leopold O. Walder, and L. Rowell Huesmann. 1977. *Growing Up to Be Violent.* New York: Pergamon.

Loeber, Rolf, Magda Stouthamer-Loeber, Welmoet B. Van Kammen, and David P. Farrington. 1989. "Development of a New Measure of Self-reported Antisocial Behavior for Young Children: Prevalence and Reliability." In *Cross-national Research in Self-reported Crime and Delinquency*, edited by Malcolm W. Klein. Dordrecht: Kluwer.

Lowenstein, Ludwig F. 1978*a*. "The Bullied and Non-bullied Child." *Bulletin of the British Psychological Society* 31:316–18.

———. 1978*b*. "Who Is the Bully?" *Bulletin of the British Psychological Society* 31:147–49.

———. 1991. "The Study, Diagnosis and Treatment of Bullying in a Therapeutic Community." In *Bullying: A Practical Guide to Coping for Schools*, edited by Michele Elliott. Harlow: Longman.

Lyons, J., L. A. Serbin, and K. Marchessault. 1988. "The Social Behavior of Peer-identified Aggressive, Withdrawn, and Aggressive/Withdrawn Children." *Journal of Abnormal Child Psychology* 16:539–52.

McGurk, Barry J., and Cynthia McDougall. 1991. "The Prevention of Bullying among Incarcerated Delinquents." In *Practical Approaches to Bullying*, edited by Peter K. Smith and David Thompson. London: David Fulton.

Magnusson, David. 1988. *Individual Development from an Interactional Perspective.* Hillsdale, N.J.: Erlbaum.

Manning, M., J. Heron, and T. Marshall. 1978. "Styles of Hostility and Social Interactions at Nursery, at School, and at Home: An Extended Study of Children." In *Aggression and Antisocial Behavior in Childhood and Adolescence*, edited by Lionel A. Hersov, Michael Berger, and David Shaffer. Oxford: Pergamon.

Mathai, John, and Bill Taylor. 1985. "Staff Perceptions of Adolescent Behavior Problems." *Journal of Adolescence* 8:243–54.

Mayfield, Demmie, Gail McLeod, and Patricia Hall. 1974. "The Cage Ques tionnaire: Validation of a New Alcoholism Screening Instrument." *American Journal of Psychiatry* 131:1121–23.

Mayhew, Patricia, David Elliott, and Lizanne Dowds. 1989. *The 1988 British Crime Survey*. London: H.M. Stationery Office.

Mellor, Andrew. 1990. *Bullying in Scottish Secondary Schools*. Edinburgh: Scottish Council for Research in Education.

———. 1991. "Helping Victims." In *Bullying: A Practical Guide to Coping for Schools*, edited by Michele Elliott. Harlow: Longman.

Michelson, Larry. 1987. "Cognitive-behavioral Strategies in the Prevention and Treatment of Antisocial Disorders in Children and Adolescents." In *Prevention of Delinquent Behavior*, edited by John D. Burchard and Sara N. Burchard. Beverly Hills, Calif.: Sage.

Mooney, Ann, Rosemary Creeser, and Peter Blatchford. 1991. "Children's Views on Teasing and Fighting in Junior Schools." *Educational Research* 33:103 -12.

Munthe, Elaine. 1989. "Bullying in Scandinavia." In *Bullying: An International Perspective*, edited by Erling Roland and Elaine Munthe. London: David Fulton.

Newson, John, and Elizabeth Newson. 1984. "Parent's Perspectives on Children's Behavior at School." In *Disruptive Behavior in Schools*, edited by Neil Frude and Hugh Gault. Chichester: Wiley.

Olweus, Dan. 1973. *Hackkycklinger och oversittare*. Stockholm: Almqvist & Wiksell.

———. 1978. *Aggression in the Schools*. Washington, D.C.: Hemisphere.

———. 1979. "Stability of Aggressive Reaction Patterns in Males: A Review." *Psychological Bulletin* 86:852–75.

———. 1981. "Continuity in Aggressive and Withdrawn, Inhibited Behavior Patterns." *Psychiatry and Social Science* 1:141–59.

———. 1984. "Development of Stable Aggressive Reaction Patterns in Males." In *Advances in the Study of Aggression*, vol.1, edited by Robert J. Blanchard and Diana C. Blanchard. Orlando, Fla.: Academic Press.

———. 1987. "Bully/Victim Problems among Schoolchildren." In *Psykologprofesjonen mot ar 2000*, edited by J. P. Myklebust and R. Ommundsen. Oslo: Universitetsforlaget.

———. 1990. "Bullying among Schoolchildren." In *Health Hazards in Adolescence*, edited by Klaus Hurrelmann and Friedrich Losel. Berlin: De Gruyter.

———. 1991*a*. "Bully/Victim Problems among Schoolchildren: Basic Facts and Effects of a School Based Intervention Programme." In *The Development and Treatment of Childhood Aggression*, edited by Debra J. Pepler and Kenneth H. Rubin. Hillsdale, N.J.: Erlbaum.

———. 1991*b*. Personal communication with author, March 13.

———. 1992*a*. Bullying at School: What We Know and What We Can Do. Unpublished manuscript, in possession of the author.

———. 1992*b*. "Victimization by Peers: Antecedents and Long-Term Outcomes." In *Social Withdrawal, Inhibition, and Shyness in Childhood*, edited by K. H. Rubin and J. B. Asendorf. Hillsdale, N.J.: Erlbaum.

O'Moore, A. Mona. 1988. "Report on Course/Seminar on 'Bullying in Schools' (Stavanger, Norway)." Strasbourg: Council of Europe.

O'Moore, A. Mona, and Brendan Hillery. 1989. "Bullying in Dublin Schools." *Irish Journal of Psychology* 10:426–41.

———. 1991. "What Do Teachers Need to Know?" In *Bullying: A Practical Guide to Coping for Schools*, edited by Michele Elliott. Harlow: Longman.

Parker, Jeffrey G., and Steven R. Asher. 1987. "Peer Relations and Later Personal Adjustment: Are Low-accepted Children at Risk?" *Psychological Bulletin* 102:357–89.

Parker, Robert N., William R. Smith, D. Randall Smith, and Jackson Toby. 1991. "Trends in Victimization in Schools and Elsewhere, 1974–1981." *Journal of Quantitative Criminology* 7:3–17.

Patterson, Gerald R. 1982. *Coercive Family Process*. Eugene, Oreg.: Castalia.

Pearce, John. 1991. "What Can Be Done about the Bully?" In *Bullying: A Practical Guide to Coping for Schools*, edited by Michele Elliott. Harlow: Longman.

Pepler, Debra J., Wendy Craig, Suzanne Ziegler, and Alice Charach. 1993. "A School-based Antibullying Intervention." In *Understanding and Managing Bullying*, edited by Delwyn Tattum. London: Heinemann.

Pepler, Debra J., Gillian King, and William Byrd. 1991. "A Social-cognitively Based Social Skills Training Programme for Aggressive Children." In *The Development and Treatment of Childhood Aggression*, edited by Debra J. Pepler and Kenneth H. Rubin. Hillsdale, N.J.: Erlbaum.

Pepler, Debra J., and Kenneth H. Rubin, eds. 1991. *The Development and Treatment of Childhood Aggression*. Hillsdale, N.J.: Erlbaum.

Perry, David G., Sara J. Kusel, and Louise C. Perry. 1988. "Victims of Peer Aggression." *Developmental Psychology* 24:807–14.

Perry, David G., J. G. Willard, and Louise C. Perry. 1990. "Peers' Perceptions of the Consequences That Victimized Children Provide Aggressors." *Child Development* 61:1310–25.

Priest, Simon. 1989. "Some Practical Approaches to Bullying." In *Bullying: An International Perspective*, edited by Erling Roland and Elaine Munthe. London: David Fulton.

Pulkkinen, Lea. 1987. "Offensive and Defensive Aggression in Humans: A Longitudinal Perspective." *Aggressive Behavior* 13:197–212.

Reid, Ken. 1989. "Bullying and Persistent School Absenteeism." In *Bullying in Schools*, edited by Delwyn Tattum and David Lane. Stoke-on-Trent: Trentham.

Rigby, Ken, and Phillip T. Slee. 1991. "Bullying among Australian School-children: Reported Behavior and Attitudes toward Victims." *Journal of Social Psychology* 131:615–27.

Roland, Erling. 1989. "Bullying: The Scandinavian Research Tradition." In *Bullying in Schools*, edited by Delwyn Tattum and David Lane. Stoke-on-Trent: Trentham.

Ross, Robert R., and Bambi D. Ross. 1988. "Delinquency Prevention through Cognitive Training." *New Education* 10:70–75.

Rutter, Michael. 1967. "A Children's Behavior Questionnaire for Completion by Teachers: Preliminary Findings." *Journal of Child Psychology and Psychiatry* 8:1–11.

Rutter, Michael, Barbara Maughan, Peter Mortimore, and Janet Ouston. 1979. *Fifteen Thousand Hours.* London: Open Books.

Sharp, Sonia, and Peter K. Smith. 1991. "Bullying in UK Schools: The DES Sheffield Bullying Project." *Early Child Development and Care* 77:47–55.

Shields, Ian W., and David J. Simourd. 1991. "Predicting Predatory Behavior in a Population of Incarcerated Young Offenders." *Criminal Justice and Behavior* 18:180–94.

Skinner, Alison. 1992. *Bullying: An Annotated Bibliography of Literature and Resources.* Leicester: Youth Work Press.

Smith, Peter K. 1991. "The Silent Nightmare: Bullying and Victimization in School Peer Groups." *Psychologist* 4:243–48.

———. 1992. Personal communication with author, February 8.

Smith, Peter K., and David Thompson, eds. 1991a. *Practical Approaches to Bullying.* London: David Fulton.

———. 1991b. "Dealing with Bully/Victim Problems in the UK." In *Practical Approaches to Bullying*, edited by Peter K. Smith and David Thompson. London: David Fulton.

Stattin, Hakan, and David Magnusson. 1989. "The Role of Early Aggressive Behavior in the Frequency, Seriousness and Types of Later Crime." *Journal of Consulting and Clinical Psychology* 57:710–18.

Stephenson, Pete, and Dave Smith. 1989. "Bullying in the Junior School." In *Bullying in Schools*, edited by Delwyn Tattum & David Lane. Stoke-on-Trent: Trentham.

———. 1991. "Why Some Schools Don't Have Bullies." In *Bullying: A Practical Guide to Coping for Schools*, edited by Michele Elliott. Harlow: Longman.

Tattum, Delwyn. 1989. "Violence and Aggression in Schools." In *Bullying in Schools*, edited by Delwyn Tattum and David Lane. Stoke-on-Trent: Trentham.

Tattum, Delwyn, and Graham Herbert. 1990. *Bullying: A Positive Response.* Cardiff: Cardiff Institute of Higher Education.

Tattum, Delwyn, and David Lane, eds. 1989. *Bullying in Schools.* Stoke-on-Trent: Trentham.

Tattum, Delwyn, and Eva Tattum. 1992. *Social Education and Personal Development.* London: David Fulton.

Thompson, David, and Peter K. Smith. 1991. "Effective Action against Bullying: The Key Problems." In *Practical Approaches to Bullying*, edited by Peter K. Smith and David Thompson. London: David Fulton.

Toby, Jackson. 1983. "Violence in School." In *Crime and Justice: An Annual Review of Research*, vol. 4, edited by Michael Tonry and Norval Morris. Chicago: University of Chicago Press.

Townsend-Wise, Kristyn, and Hereward Harrison. 1991. "A Child's View: How Childline Helps." In *Bullying: A Practical Guide to Coping for Schools*, edited by Michele Elliott. Harlow: Longman.

Tremblay, Richard E. 1991. Personal communication with author, January 16, Montreal, Quebec.

Tremblay, Richard E., Joan McCord, Helene Boileau, Pierre Charlebois, Claude Gagnon, Marc LeBlanc, and Serge Larivee. 1991. "Can Disruptive Boys Be Helped to Become Competent?" *Psychiatry* 54:148–61.

Tremblay, Richard E., Frank Vitaro, Lucie Bertrand, Marc LeBlanc, Helene Beauchesne, Helene Boileau, and Lucille David. 1992. "Parent and Child Training to Prevent Early Onset of Delinquency: The Montreal Longitudinal-Experimental Study." In *Preventing Antisocial Behavior*, edited by Joan McCord and Richard E. Tremblay. New York: Guilford.

United Kingdom Department of Education and Science. 1989. *Discipline in Schools (Elton Report)*. London: H.M. Stationery Office.

Verhulst, Frank C., and Monika Althaus. 1988. "Persistence and Change in Behavioral/Emotional Problems Reported by Parents of Children Aged 4–14: An Epidemiological Study." *Acta Psychiatrica Scandinavica*, vol. 77, suppl. no. 339.

Verhulst, Frank C., and Jan Van der Ende. 1991. "Four-Year Follow-up of Teacher-reported Problem Behaviors." *Psychological Medicine* 21:965–77.

Vieira da Fonseca, Maria M., Isabel Fernandez Garcia, and Gumersindo Quevedo Perez. 1989. "Violence, Bullying and Counselling in the Iberian Peninsula." In *Bullying: An International Perspective*, edited by Erling Roland and Elaine Munthe. London: David Fulton.

West, Donald J. 1969. *Present Conduct and Future Delinquency*. London: Heinemann.

———. 1982. *Delinquency: Its Roots, Careers and Prospects*. London: Heinemann.

West, Donald J., and David P. Farrington. 1973. *Who Becomes Delinquent?* London: Heinemann.

———. 1977. *The Delinquent Way of Life*. London: Heinemann.

White, Jennifer L., Terrie E. Moffitt, Felton Earls, Lee Robins, and Phil A. Silva. 1990. "How Early Can We Tell? Predictors of Childhood Conduct Disorder and Adolescent Delinquency." *Criminology* 28:507–33.

Whitney, Irene, and Peter K. Smith. 1991. "A Survey of the Nature and Extent of Bullying in Junior/Middle and Secondary Schools." Final report to the Gulbenkian Foundation. Sheffield: University of Sheffield, Department of Psychology.

Widom, Cathy S. 1989. "The Cycle of Violence." *Science* 244:160–66.

Yates, Colin, and Peter K. Smith. 1989. "Bullying in Two English Comprehensive Schools." In *Bullying: An International Perspective*, edited by Erling Roland and Elaine Munthe. London: David Fulton.

Ziegler, Suzanne, and Merle Rosenstein-Manner. 1991. *Bullying in School*. Toronto: Board of Education.

*Robert F. Meier and Terance D. Miethe*

# Understanding Theories of Criminal Victimization

ABSTRACT

Current theories of victimization have generated a sizable body of
empirical research, mostly within the last two decades. The two most
widely known perspectives, lifestyle-exposure and routine activities
theories, have been the object of much current thinking and empirical
testing, but their maturation has been hampered by many of the same
problems impeding theories of criminality. These include inadequate
attention to variation by type of crime, compartmentalized thinking, poor
links between theory and data, inadequate measures of key concepts, and
failure to specify clearly functional relationships between sets of variables.
Many of these problems can be addressed by closer examination of the
interrelationships among victims, offenders, and criminal situations.
Victimization theories should be incorporated into comprehensive
integrated theories of crime.

Victimization theories are now a common feature of criminological
work, but it has not always been so. In spite of their obvious appeal,
perspectives on victim behavior have only recently gained sufficient
scholarly respectability to join forces with the mainstay of the criminological arsenal, theories of offender behavior. Work that has incorporated victim perspectives, such as Wolfgang's (1958) research on homicide and especially Amir's (1971) related work on rape, encountered
political difficulty because it appeared that the victim bore some responsibility for the crime. This was an idea that smacked of "blaming
the victim," a cornerstone of liberal crime control ideology and some-

Robert F. Meier is professor and chair of sociology at Iowa State University. Terance
D. Miethe is associate professor of criminal justice at the University of Nevada at Las-
Vegas

thing to be avoided at all scholarly cost, even truth. But the impediments to a defensible notion of victim involvement in crime were more long-standing than this, and even relatively unenlightened criminologists must surely have known that no picture of predatory crime can ever be complete without information about the victim of these offenses. Only in the last two decades have victimization theories generated empirical, as well as anecdotal, support, most notably in the form of lifestyle-exposure (Hindelang, Gottfredson, and Garofalo 1978) and routine activities theories (Cohen and Felson 1979). This long road to respectability is hard to explain, but the high (or low) points can at least be identified.

In this essay, we argue that the current popularity of and support for victimization surveys is well deserved but that investigators must also consider the major limitations of the theoretical and empirical work that has been done on victimization. Although it is beyond the scope of this essay to provide a complete critique of victimization studies, we do note that much previous research has suffered from a number of problems, including the use of inadequate measures of key concepts, few statistical controls, and the absence of multilevel models and contextual effects that could provide alternative explanations for the results of victimization research. We also note that, while some versions of victimization theories suggest that victims and offenders are tied together in a broader social ecology of crime, these theories do not provide testable propositions about the conditions of offending and victimization to permit adequate predictions of crime. In spite of these problems, we are encouraged about the current status of victimization surveys.

We begin our analysis by examining the historical context of victimization theories in Section I. We also identify major sources of information concerning these theories, predominantly victimization surveys. Section II identifies major current theories of victimization with particular attention to lifestyle theories and routine activities theories. Alternative models of victimization are identified in Section III, and major concepts used in victimization theories are examined in Section IV with an eye toward improving conceptual clarity. Section V discusses what we consider to be major problems with victimization theories. The context of crime plays an important role in modeling victimization, and its effects are discussed in Section VI. We discuss the prospects of integrating theories of victimization with theories of criminality in Section VII. Conclusions are offered in Section VIII.

## I. Historical Foundations for Current Victimization Theories

The use of such expressions as "the victim-offender problem" (Mac-Donald 1939), "the duet frame of crime" (Von Hentig 1948), "the penal couple" (Ellenberger 1955), and, more generally, "the victim-offender relationship" (Von Hentig 1940; Schafer 1968; Schultz 1968) clearly indicates the significance of crime victims to the understanding of crime. Garofalo (1914) was one of the first to note that a victim may provoke another into attack, whereas Mendelsohn (1956) developed a victim typology that distinguishes victims who are more culpable than their offenders from those who are considered totally guiltless. Von Hentig (1948) described general classes of crime victims (e.g., the young, females, the old, the mentally defective, the depressed, the acquisitive, the lonesome and heartbroken) and some of the characteristics associated with these personal attributes that increase their vulnerability to crime.

Such a list of phrases is not a history, and it would be incorrect to claim that modern victim theories are merely the latest variants in a long lineage of earlier victim theories. These early writers did not propose theories, and even some of the concepts they used were primitive. Furthermore, it is speculative at best to attempt to sketch a victim theory ancestry since there seem to be few connections among these early works. Although it is difficult to trace the origins of any particular theoretical perspective, two fairly recent research traditions appear to be the antecedents to current theories of victimization. These include research on victim precipitation and the development of victimization surveys.

### A. Victim Precipitation

The first systematic study of victim involvement in crime was conducted in the late 1950s by Marvin Wolfgang. The term he introduced, "victim precipitation," became a popular descriptor for all direct-contact predatory crime (e.g., murder, assault, forcible rape, robbery). When applied to homicide, victim precipitation is restricted to those cases in which "the victim is the first in the homicide drama to resort to physical force against the subsequent slayer" (Wolfgang 1958, p. 252; see also Wolfgang 1957). A similar definition is used in the case of aggravated assault except that insinuating language or gestures might also be considered provoking actions (Curtis 1974; Miethe 1985). Victim-precipitated robbery involves cases in which the victim has acted without reasonable self-protection in the handling of money, jewelry, or other valuables (Normandeau 1968; Curtis 1974), whereas this concept in forcible rape applies to "an episode ending in forced sexual intercourse in which the victim first agreed to sexual relations, or clearly invited them verbally or through gestures, but then retracted before the act" (Amir 1967; Curtis 1974). Under each of these definitions, there is an explicit time ordering of events in which victims initiate some type of action that results in their subsequent victimization.

Previous studies using police reports suggest some level of victim involvement in a large proportion of violent crimes. The extent of victim precipitation, however, varies widely by type of offense. Estimates of victim precipitation range from 22 to 38 percent for homicide, 14 percent for aggravated assault, between 4 and 19 percent for rape cases, and about 11 percent of armed robberies are characterized by carelessness on the part of the victim (see, for review, Curtis 1974). These figures are best considered low estimates of the rate of victim involvement because of the fairly restrictive definition of victim precipitation for some crimes (i.e., murder, assault) and the large number of cases with incomplete information. The national survey of aggravated assaults reported by Curtis (1974), for example, had insufficient data for determining the presence of victim precipitation in 51 percent of the cases. Nonetheless, the importance of the notion of victim precipitation is clearly revealed in many cases of homicide where who becomes labeled the victim and who the offender (Wolfgang 1957) is a matter of chance or circumstance.

There are several reasons why previous research on victim-precipitated crime was influential in the emergence of current theories of victimization. First, the prevalence of victim precipitation signified the importance of victims' actions in explaining violent crime but also brought attention to the less direct ways by which citizens contribute to their victimization. These less direct forms of victim involvement would include such acts as getting involved in risky or vulnerable situations, not exercising good judgment when in public places, leaving property unprotected, and interacting on a regular basis with potential offenders.

Second, the notion of victim precipitation, by definition, attributes some responsibility for crime to the actions of its victims. That victim-precipitation researchers had to deal directly with such an unpopular public and political stance may have made it easier for subsequent scholars to examine victim culpability and how the routine activities and lifestyles of citizens provide opportunities for crime. Thus, current theories of victimization may have benefited greatly from the prior work on victim precipitation.

The implication of blame in victim-precipitation analyses has inhibited full development of the concept. When Wolfgang's student Menachim Amir (1971) adopted the concept in a study of forcible rape that parallels Wolfgang's research on homicide, it caused a major political controversy. Amir, like Wolfgang, used official police reports in the city of Philadelphia; he also used the subculture of violence as a unifying theoretical notion to explain this crime. But Amir was not sufficiently sensitive to the differences between murder and rape in using the idea of victim precipitation. While it is neither counterintuitive nor politically contentious to acknowledge that murder victims sometimes strike the first blow or otherwise provoke a violent response, it was politically aberrant to suggest that rape victims were provocative, at least in the same sense. In suggesting the nature of victim precipitation in rape, Amir reported that 20 percent of the victims had a prior record for some sort of sexual misconduct (usually prostitution or juvenile intercourse) and another 20 percent had "bad reputations." Wolfgang's research offered a promising idea to further explore the relationship between offender and victim, but Amir's study blunted the promise by not developing the idea beyond Wolfgang's pioneering work.

Actually, Amir was either too far ahead, or too far behind, his times. The 1970s were politically charged in criminology as well as in society at large with much concern about victim blaming and women's rights. Research on rape would shortly be done correctly only by women. The idea that men had anything reasonably objective to say about rape was not given much credence. Surely this overstates the matter, but there is no mistaking the fact that there were very few male authors on rape, and Amir himself took an academic assignment in Israel never really to publish on rape again. The concept of victim precipitation remained comatose under the feminist assault never to resurface, even for homicide.

In fairness, the concept of victim precipitation was never really defined very well, and Amir's application of the concept to include "bad reputation" was a serious mistake scientifically. Such an indicator clearly smacked of subjectivity, and no validity checks were made of the Philadelphia Police Department records in which this phrase appeared.

## B. Victimization Surveys

The second major contributor to the emergence of current victimization theories is the development of large-scale victimization surveys. Prior to the advent of victimization surveys in the late 1960s and early 1970s, official reports on crimes known to the police and self-reports of offending were the only systematically available data on criminal activities. However, neither of these sources give any systematic information about the actions and characteristics of crime victims. Although it is possible to understand crime without directly surveying its victims (e.g., by interviewing offenders about their choice of crime sites, doing observation studies of areas with high rates of crime), victim surveys provide information about aspects of the criminal event that is not routinely collected from other sources.

There were three early studies: one by Reiss of business victimization; Biderman's study in Washington, D.C.; and Ennis's survey through the National Opinion Research Center (NORC) (President's Commission on Law Enforcement and Administration of Justice 1967, pp. 38–43). These surveys, thoroughly reviewed by Sparks (1982), paved the way for more systematic studies. Of these initial efforts, one deserves more than passing comment.

The first national project was sponsored by the President's (Lyndon Johnson) Commission on Law Enforcement and Administration of Justice. The report was published in the commission proceedings the following year, and the findings were startling even to criminologists, let alone citizens (Ennis 1967). This first systematic survey of victims used a probability sample of nearly ten thousand households. The major conclusions included the findings that forcible rape was three and a half times more frequent than the reported rate, burglaries were three times the reported rate, and robbery was 50 percent higher than the reported rate. Thus, not only were most crimes underreported to a significant degree, the extent of underreporting varied from crime to crime. This meant that official estimates of crimes were not only "off" by some factor but that the degree to which they were off was variable and could not be estimated without separate surveys for each crime category.

The largest current victimization survey, the National Crime Victimization Survey (NCS), involves yearly reports based on surveys of from between 59,000 and 72,000 U.S. households in which questions are asked to identify personal attributes of crime victims and characteristics of the offense. The interviews are conducted by Bureau of the Census personnel, and the results are coordinated by the Department of Justice. Actually, the NCS is a series of surveys rather than a survey at a single point in time. The NCS series involves probability samples of households that are interviewed a maximum of seven times at six-month intervals. Started in 1973, the NCS series involves interviews with persons over twelve years of age. Persons who move out of a household are not followed to their new address, but, if a new family or person moves into a sampled housing unit between waves, they are interviewed as part of the series. Skogan (1990) outlines the major changes in the implementation of the NCS series.

Even at their earlier stages of development, victimization surveys addressed fundamental questions about crime. Victim surveys represent an alternative barometer of the extent and distribution of crime. They also identify factors associated with reporting crime to the authorities, and they yield detailed information about the consequences of crime for the victim. For present purposes, however, the major contribution of victimization surveys is that they provide detailed information about the ecology of crime (e.g., where it occurred, type of injury, victim-offender relationship) and about the demographic characteristics of victims. It is the distribution of crime and the characteristics of victims identified in victimization surveys that are the social facts to be explained by current theories of victimization.

## II. Current Major Theories of Victimization
Like theories of the behavior of criminals, theories of the behavior of crime victims are many and variable. Some, like the notion of victim precipitation, are little more than an idea, let alone a scientific concept. Others either are little more than victim typologies (Von Hentig 1948; Mendelsohn 1956) or highlight the distribution and characteristics of individuals who have repeat or multiple victimization experiences (Nelson 1980; Gottfredson 1981; Sparks 1981; Skogan 1990). Two major theories considered here are more sophisticated and have been the object of substantial empirical testing. The two most advanced theories are the lifestyle-exposure perspective and the routine activities theory.

There are points of conceptual and explanatory overlap between them, but they each offer a distinctive view of the role of victims in the crime process.

## A. Lifestyle-Exposure Theories of Victimization

One of the first systematic theories of criminal victimization was the lifestyle-exposure approach developed by Hindelang, Gottfredson, and Garofalo (1978) less than twenty years ago. This theory was originally proposed to account for differences in the risks of violent victimization across social groups, but it has been extended to include property crime, and it forms the basis for more elaborate theories of target-selection processes.

The basic premise underlying the lifestyle-exposure theory is that demographic differences in the likelihood of victimization are attributed to differences in the personal lifestyles of victims. Variations in lifestyles are important because they are related to the differential exposure to dangerous places, times, and others—that is, situations in which there are high risks of victimization. A graphic representation of this theoretical perspective is presented in figure 1.

From this perspective, an individual's lifestyle is the critical factor that determines risks of criminal victimization. Lifestyle is defined in this context as "routine daily activities, both vocational activities (work, school, keeping house, etc.) and leisure activities" (Hindelang, Gottfredson, and Garofalo 1978, p. 241). People's daily activities may naturally bring them into contact with crime, or they merely increase the risk of crime that victims experience. Time spent in one's home generally decreases victim risk, while time spent in public settings increases risk.

Differences in lifestyles are socially determined by individuals' collective responses or adaptations to various role expectations and structural constraints (see fig. 1). Both ascribed and achieved status characteristics (e.g., age, gender, race, income, marital status, education, occupation) are important correlates of predatory crime because these status attributes carry with them shared expectations about appropriate behavior and structural obstacles that both enable and constrain one's behavioral choices. Adherence to these cultural and structural expectations leads to the establishment of routine activities patterns and associations with others similarly situated. These lifestyles and associations, in turn, are expected to enhance one's exposure to risky or vulnerable situations that increase individuals' chances of victimization. Several

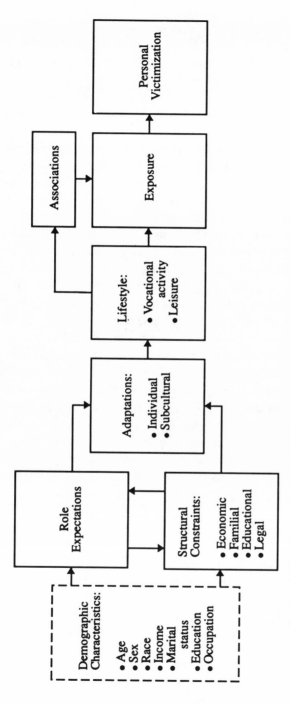

FIG. 1.—A lifestyle-exposure model of victimization. Source: adapted from Hindelang, Gottfredson, and Garofalo (1978)

examples should clarify the basic logic underlying this lifestyle-exposure model.

1. *Gender.* Despite major efforts to promote gender equality in American society, there remain fundamental differences in role expectations and structural opportunities for men and women. Gender stereotyping results in gender differences in such basic activities as where and with whom time is spent, the degree of supervision in daily activities, the likelihood of having contact with strangers, and exposure to risky and dangerous public places. For example, females spend a greater proportion of their time inside the home because as adolescents they are more closely supervised than males, and as adults they are more likely to assume housekeeping and child-rearing responsibilities (Hindelang, Gottfredson, and Garofalo 1978). Greater familial responsibilities and the systematic denial of educational and economic opportunities may severely impede women's participation in public life. Furthermore, even when engaged in public activity, women's routine activities are more likely to take place in the presence of friends and intimate others than in isolation. These role expectations and structural impediments are assumed to increase private domestic activities among women, increase supervision of their public behavior, decrease their exposure to high-risk persons and places, and subsequently decrease their relative risks of criminal victimization. Males, by contrast, are traditionally socialized to be active in the public domain, assertive and aggressive in social situations, have fewer restrictions on their daily lives, and spend more time away from a protective home environment. Accordingly, gender differences in traditional lifestyles are said partly to explain the higher victimization risks of men.

2. *Income.* Another strong determinant of lifestyle and exposure to crime is economic resources, such as income. As a fundamental aspect of stratification, income determines whether structural conditions either enable or constrain various aspects of social life. Low income severely restricts one's choices in regard to housing, transportation, associations with others, and leisure activities. Individuals' abilities to move out of crime-prone environments, live in apartments or homes with elaborate security measures (e.g., security guards, video surveillance, burglar alarms), avoid contact with potential offenders, and undertake leisure activities in safer areas are limited when living under conditions of economic deprivation. As family income increases, there is greater flexibility to adjust one's lifestyle to select the area in which to live, the mode of transportation for daily activities, the amount of

time spent in private versus public places, and the type of leisure activities (Hindelang, Gottfredson, and Garofalo 1978). The greater choices afforded persons with higher economic resources allow them to more easily avoid risky and vulnerable situations. Thus, by patterning the nature of social life, income is a lifestyle characteristic that is expected to lead to differential risks of victimization.

3. *Empirical Predictions.* From a lifestyle-exposure perspective, differences in risks of violent victimization by gender, high-income, and other status characteristics are attributed to differences in lifestyles that increase individuals' exposure to risky and vulnerable situations. Given that victimization risks are not uniformly distributed across time and space, lifestyles are assumed to affect the probability of victimization because different lifestyles are associated with differential risks of being in particular places, at particular times, under particular circumstances, and interacting with particular kinds of persons. Accordingly, persons who are younger, male, not married, low income, and black should have higher risks of violent victimization than their counterparts because each group is said to engage in more public activity (especially at night), spend less time with family members, or associate more frequently with persons who have offender characteristics. Under this theoretical model, individuals' risks of property victimization should also be higher among those social groups (e.g., young, male, single persons) who spend more time engaged in public activity because such persons would be less able to protect their dwelling from crime.

If a lifestyle-exposure theory is an adequate explanation for differential risks of predatory victimization, several outcomes would be expected. First, if demographic differences in victimization risks are due to differences in lifestyles and routine activities, the impact of each demographic variable (e.g., age, gender, race, social class) should decrease in importance once separate measures of lifestyles and routine activities are included as control variables. Second, persons with the configuration of status characteristics commonly recognized as having the most vulnerable lifestyles (i.e., young, single, low-income, black males) should have a greater risk of victimization than any other configuration, and their exact opposites (i.e., older, married, high-income, white females) should have the lowest relative risks. Third, given increases in efforts to promote gender and racial equality in all institutional domains over the last two decades, differences in victimization risks by these factors should decrease over time. In other words, smaller differences in victimization risks by gender and race would be expected over time if there were fewer group-specific role expectations and fewer structural obstacles that impede the life chances of persons within each of these groups.

While these hypotheses from lifestyle-exposure theories are relatively straightforward, they have not been adequately examined. In fact, only the first hypothesis has been examined empirically. The results of previous research (Miethe, Stafford, and Long 1987; Kennedy and Forde 1990) indicate that some demographic differences in victim risks (e.g., gender and age differences) can be attributed to differences in individuals' routine activities and lifestyles. Differences in victimization risks by configuration of status characteristics or changes over time in demographic predictors of victimization risks have not been investigated.

### B. Routine Activity Theory

The routine activity perspective developed by Cohen and Felson (1979) has many similarities with the lifestyle-exposure theory. Both emphasize how patterns of routine activities or lifestyles in conventional society provide an opportunity structure for crime. Each theory also downplays the importance of offender motivation and other aspects of criminality in understanding individuals' risks of victimization and the social ecology of crime. These theories are also representative of a wider "criminal opportunity" perspective because they stress how the availability of criminal opportunities is determined, in large part, by the routine activity patterns of everyday life (Cohen 1981; Cohen and Land 1987). The fundamental differences between these theories are in terminology and in the fact that routine activity theory was originally developed to account for changes in crime rates over time whereas lifestyle-exposure theory was proposed to account for differences in victimization risks across social groups. Over the past decade, however, each theory has been applied across units of analysis and in both cross-sectional and longitudinal designs.

According to Cohen and Felson (1979, p. 589), structural changes in routine activity patterns influence crime rates by affecting the convergence in time and space of three elements of direct-contact predatory crimes: motivated offenders, suitable targets, and the absence of capable guardians against a violation. As necessary elements, the lack of any of these conditions is sufficient to prevent criminal activity. Furthermore, Cohen and Felson (1979) note that increases in crime rates could occur without any increase in the structural conditions that motivate offenders to engage in crime as long as there has been an increase in the supply of attractive and unguarded targets for victimization. Their argument about how crime rates can increase even if offender motivation remains constant is important because it allows them to account for the apparent contradiction underlying most theories of criminality that crime rates continued to rise throughout the 1960s and 1970s in the United States even though conditions that foster criminality (e.g., unemployment, racial segregation, economic inequality) were decreasing.

From this perspective, routine activities are defined as "any recurrent and prevalent activities that provide for basic population and individual needs" (Cohen and Felson 1979, p. 593). Similar to the notion of lifestyle, these routine activities include formalized work, leisure, and the ways by which humans acquire food, shelter, and other basic needs or desires (e.g., companionship, sexual expression). Drawing from work in human ecology (e.g., Hawley 1950), Cohen and Felson (1979) argue that humans are located in ecological niches with a particular tempo, pace, and rhythm in which predatory crime is a way of securing these basic needs or desires at the expense of others. Potential victims in this environment are likely to alter their daily habits and take evasive actions that may persuade offenders to seek alternative targets. It is under such predatory conditions that the routine activities of potential victims are said both to enhance and to restrict the opportunities for crime.

1. *Social Change and Routine Activities.*   The basic premise underlying routine activity theory is that various social changes in conventional society increase criminal opportunities. For example, given the assorted costs for stealing items with great weight (e.g., their theft requires more physical energy, they are harder to conceal), it is not surprising that burglars are most attracted to items that are easily portable and have high resale value (e.g., cash, jewelry, electronic equipment). Accordingly, any changes in manufacturing or production activities that decrease the size or increase the demand for expensive durable goods (e.g., televisions, tape decks, VCRs, home computers, compact disk players) are expected to increase the attractiveness of these goods for victimization. Similarly, increases over time in the level of safety precautions taken by the public would apparently decrease crime rates by reducing the accessibility of potential crime targets to would-be offenders. Such changes, of course, might also result in alternative outcomes such as no net reduction in crime rates because crime

is being displaced to other objects, victims, or times depending on the structural conditions.

Of the various social changes in routine activities that have occurred over the last four decades, Lawrence Cohen, Marcus Felson, and their colleagues have placed primary importance on changes in sustenance and leisure activities away from domestic life and family-based living arrangements. A basic proposition underlying this theory is that any decrease in the concentration of activities within family-based households will increase crime rates (Cohen and Land 1987). There are several ways by which such social changes are assumed to increase criminal opportunities. First, a rise in single-person households or households consisting of unrelated persons requires a greater supply of durable consumer goods and other merchandise that are considered attractive property to steal. Such a duplication of consumer goods is unnecessary in family-like living arrangements. Second, increases in nonfamilial activities and households decrease the level of personal guardianship over others. The mere presence of a spouse, child, or other relative in a household provides greater protection for individuals and their property than is true of persons who live alone, and living with other relatives also increases the likelihood that public activities will be undertaken in groups. Third, increases in nonfamily households alter the location of routine activities from a private domain to a public domain, thereby also increasing one's exposure to risky and vulnerable situations. Thus, changes in domestic activities and living arrangements may increase the supply of attractive crime targets, decrease the level of guardianship, and consequently increase criminal opportunities.

Although applicable to various social science disciplines, there are several reasons why routine activity theory is especially attractive to sociologists. First, this theoretical approach clearly highlights the symbiotic relationship between conventional and illegal activity patterns. Illegal activities are presumed to "feed on" the routine activities of everyday life (Felson and Cohen 1980; Messner and Blau 1987). Second, this theory identifies a fundamental irony between constructive social change and crime rates. Specifically, many social changes that have improved both the quality and equality of social life in the United States (e.g., increased labor force participation and educational attainment among women, increases in out-of-home leisure activities) are the same factors predicted to increase rates of predatory crime. Third, both routine activity and lifestyle-exposure theory attempt to explain crime, not in the actions or numbers of motivated offenders, but in the activities and lifestyles of potential victims. Accordingly, these approaches have more relevance to a wider range of sociologists than most theories because they ignore the sources of criminal motivation and other major topics in traditional criminology (i.e., you do not have to be a criminologist to understand these theories) and direct attention to how the habits, lifestyles, and behavioral patterns of ordinary citizens in their daily lives create an environment for predatory crime.

   2. *Applying Routine Activities.*   Over the last decade, routine activity theory has been used to explain aggregate rates and individuals' risks of victimization, changes in crime rates over time, and the social ecology of crime. Each of these applications focuses on how the nature of nonhousehold activity influences one's exposure to crime. For example, Cohen and Felson (1979) examine the relationship between crime rates and the "household activity ratio" (i.e., the sum of the number of married female labor force participants and the number of nonhusband/nonwife households divided by the total number of households). Felson and Cohen (1980) investigate the impact of increases in the rate of primary households on increasing burglary rates over time. Arguing that high rates of unemployment lead to decreases in nonhousehold activity, Cohen, Felson, and Land (1980) also apply this approach to study how unemployment rates and the household activity ratio influence temporal changes in rates of robbery, burglary, and automobile theft. Messner and Blau (1987) examine the relationship between crime rates for standard metropolitan statistical areas (SMSAs) in the United States and measures of the volume of household activity (i.e., size of television viewing audience) and nonhousehold activity (i.e., the supply of sport and entertainment establishments). Miethe, Hughes, and McDowall (1991) use this perspective to examine how measures of guardianship, nonhousehold activity, and target attractiveness influence offense-specific crime rates and changes in crime rates in 584 U.S. cities for the three decades from 1960 to 1980. Finally, Messner and Tardiff (1985) apply routine activity theory to examine the social ecology of urban homicide.

   Most previous studies using the individual or household as the unit of analysis can be interpreted as tests of both routine activity and lifestyle-exposure theories. Cohen and Cantor (1980), for example, examine how characteristics of individuals and their lifestyles (e.g., income, age, race, major daily activity, household size) influence risks of residential burglary and personal larceny. Cohen, Kluegel, and Land

(1981) evaluate whether measures of exposure, guardianship, proximity to motivated offenders, and target attractiveness mediate the impact of income, race, and age on individuals' risks of predatory victimization. The impact of measures of nonhousehold activity, target suitability, and guardianship on individuals' risks of victimization has also been examined in other studies (e.g., Clarke et al. 1985; Lynch 1987; Maxfield 1987; Miethe, Stafford, and Long 1987; Sampson and Wooldredge 1987; Massey, Krohn, and Bonati 1989; Kennedy and Forde 1990). In the only study that uses longitudinal data on individuals, Miethe, Stafford, and Sloane (1990) explore the interrelationships between changes in the level of nonhousehold activity, guardianship patterns, and temporal changes in individuals' risks of personal and property victimization. The utility of this theoretical formulation for predicting multiple victimizations was also suggested by other researchers (Gottfredson 1981; Sparks 1981).

3. *Empirical Predictions.*   Although studies vary widely in terms of their units of analysis and measurement of key concepts, the predictive validity of routine activity theory rests ultimately on the empirical observation of three outcomes. First, routine activity patterns that indicate greater levels of nonhousehold activity should increase individuals' risks and aggregate rates of predatory crime by increasing potential victims' visibility and accessibility as crime targets. Second, routine activity patterns that indicate higher levels of self-protection or guardianship should decrease individuals' risks and aggregate rates of predatory crime. Third, persons and property with higher subjective or material value to offenders should have higher risks of victimization than less attractive crime targets. Taken together, a routine activity approach predicts the greatest risks for predatory crime when potential victims have high target suitability (i.e., high visibility, accessibility, and attractiveness) and low levels of guardianship.

## III. Alternative Theoretical Models

Lifestyle-exposure and routine activity theories have been the most widely applied perspectives to account for individuals' risks and aggregate rates of criminal victimization. However, other work has attempted to integrate these perspectives more directly, derive a clearer conceptual framework for explaining the process of target selection, and examine the context-specific effects of routine activities and lifestyles on risks of criminal victimization.

## A. A *Structural-Choice Model of Victimization*

Miethe and Meier (1990) examined the feasibility of integrating routine activity and lifestyle-exposure theories into what is called a "structural-choice" theory of victimization. Consistent with other work (Cohen, Kluegel, and Land 1981), we argued that current theories of victimization highlight the importance of physical proximity to motivated offenders, exposure to high-risk environments, target attractiveness, and the absence of guardianship as necessary conditions for predatory crime.

Two central propositions were derived from routine activity and lifestyle-exposure theories. First, routine activity patterns and lifestyles each contribute to the creation of a criminal opportunity structure by enhancing the contact between potential offenders and victims. Second, the subjective value of a person or object and its level of guardianship determine the choice of the particular crime target. In combination, these propositions imply that "routine activities may predispose some persons and their property to greater risks, but the selection of a particular crime victim within a sociospatial context is determined by the expected utility of one target over another" (Miethe and Meier 1990, p. 245). Under this revised theoretical model, proximity and exposure are considered "structural" features (because they pattern the nature of social interaction and predispose individuals to riskier situations), whereas attractiveness and guardianship represent the "choice" component (because they determine the selection of the particular crime target within a sociospatial context).

There are several reasons why this "structural-choice" model may be a useful integration of current victimization theories. First, the revised model emphasizes both macrodynamic forces that contribute to a criminal opportunity structure (as identified by routine activity theory) and microlevel processes that determine the selection of particular crime victims (as implied by lifestyle-exposure theory).

Second, the structural-choice model retains the view that exposure, proximity, attractiveness, and guardianship are necessary conditions for victimization, meaning that the absence of any of these factors is sufficient to eliminate predatory crime.

Third, the structural-choice model follows closely the distinction between "predisposing" and "precipitating" factors. Specifically, both characterizations assume that living in particular environments increases one's exposure and proximity to dangerous situations, but whether a person becomes a crime victim depends on their presumed subjective utility over alternative targets.

Fourth, the structural-choice perspective emphasizes the context-specific effects of routine activities and lifestyles on risks of predatory crime. For example, target attractiveness and guardianship may have little impact on victimization risks for residents of areas with a low criminal opportunity structure because, by definition, such environments are not conducive to predatory crime in the first place. Alternatively, geographical areas with a high concentration of offenders may have such a high criminal opportunity structure that all residents, regardless of their perceived attractiveness or level of guardianship, are equally susceptible to criminal victimization.

## B. Conceptualizing Target-Selection Processes

Both routine activity and lifestyle-exposure theories are designed to explain crime rates and why particular groups of individuals have higher risks of victimization than others. Differences in victimization risks for different demographic groups (e.g., males, young persons, nonwhites, the low income) are attributed to differences in lifestyles and routine activities that enhance persons' exposure to risky times, places, and potential offenders. However, neither of these approaches develops an adequate microlevel theory to account for the selection of particular crime targets within a particular sociospatial context. This is the case because both theories pay little attention to factors associated with criminality and offender motivation. Offender motivation is either assumed to be constant or there is no explicit reference to what motivates people to commit crime (Cohen and Land 1987).

A closer examination of these theories, however, reveals two specific images of criminality. First, an implicit assumption underlying these criminal opportunity theories is that offender motivation is at least partially caused by the lack of external physical restraints. Criminal intentions are translated into actions when there is a suitable person or object for victimization and "an absence of ordinary physical restraints such as the presence of other people or objects that inhibit, or are perceived to inhibit, the successful completion of direct contact predatory crime" (Cohen and Land 1987, p. 51). In this image, offenders are in some sense constantly motivated to commit crimes, and crime is explained only in mechanisms of restraint (Hirschi 1969). Second, offenders are assumed to make choices, no matter how rudimentary, in the selection of targets for victimization. It is this rational conception of criminal behavior underlying current victimization theories that, in our opinion, offers the most promise in explaining target-selection processes.

From the perspective of a "reasoning criminal" (Cornish and Clarke 1986), offenders seek to benefit themselves by their criminal behavior and select victims who offer a high payoff with little effort or risk of detection. The decision to get involved in crime and the subsequent choice of particular crime victims are influenced by the constraints of time, ability, energy, limited information, and the availability of alternatives, both conventional and unconventional. Nonetheless, it is hardly outrageous to assume that most offenders engage in some level of planning and foresight and adapt their behavior to take into account situational contingencies (Cornish and Clarke 1986). Through the selective filtering and processing of information, the rational offender is said to select from a pool of potential victims those targets that are thought to offer the greatest net rewards.

Interviews with convicted offenders reveal that many personal and situational factors are considered in the selection of crime targets. Burglars, for example, report that the risks of detection (i.e., the likelihood of getting caught), the potential yield or reward, and the relative ease with which the home can be entered are the critical factors in selecting targets for victimization (Bennett and Wright 1985). Similar aspects of the physical environment and victim characteristics are considered by other offenders (e.g., robbers, muggers) when selecting crime targets (Cornish and Clarke 1986).

Hough (1987) has developed a conceptual framework for explaining target selection that clarifies the importance of routine activities and lifestyles in this process. According to Hough (1987, p. 359), this revised conceptual scheme takes it as axiomatic that, if members of one group are selected as crime targets more frequently than another, they must meet at least one of three conditions: they must be exposed more frequently to motivated offenders (proximity), be more attractive as targets in that they afford a better "yield" to the offender (reward), or be more attractive in that they are more accessible or less defended against victimization (absence of capable guardians). This theoretical approach is diagrammed in figure 2. The virtue of this perspective for understanding criminal victimization is that it clearly states that differences in proximity, attractiveness, or guardianship can account for differences in individuals' risks of victimization and that persons who possess each of these characteristics are especially vulnerable to crime.

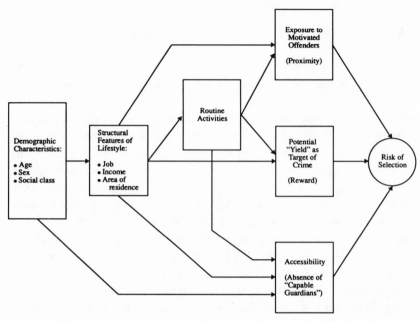

FIG. 2.—A target-selection model. Source: adapted from Hough (1987)

Consistent with both routine activity and lifestyle-exposure theory, these differences in target-selection factors are determined by individuals' routine activities and lifestyles.

Although a model that incorporates both structural and choice elements clarifies the role of routine activities and lifestyles in target-selection processes, the model is still limited in several respects. First, while it is reasonable to predict that criminal victimization is most likely under conditions of proximity, reward, and no guardianship, the model does not specify which factor is most important. Second, while interviews with convicted offenders suggest that target-selection factors may vary widely for different types of predatory crime (Bennett and Wright 1985; Carroll and Weaver 1986; Cornish and Clarke 1986; Feeney 1986; Walsh 1986), the model does not capture these crime-specific differences. Third, even within particular types of crime (e.g., among muggers), there appear to be major differences in factors associated with target selection, such as those found between novice and seasoned offenders (Cornish and Clarke 1986). These within-crime differences are also not directly incorporated in the revised model. Nonetheless, the conceptual framework outlined by Hough (1987) is a major improvement over the original formulations of routine activity and lifestyle theories.

## IV. Major Concepts in Victimization Theories

Although the terminology differs across studies, the central concepts underlying theories of victimization are essentially the same: proximity to crime, exposure, target attractiveness, and guardianship. Indeed, the major difference among victimization theories is the extent to which these concepts are interrelated.

### A. *Proximity to Crime*

Physical proximity to high-crime areas is a major factor that increases victim risk. Proximity is best represented as the physical distance between areas where potential targets of crime reside and areas where relatively large populations of potential offenders are found (Cohen, Kluegel, and Land 1981, p. 507). Living in a high-crime area increases the likelihood of frequent contact with offenders and thus increases one's risks of victimization. That persons spend a majority of their time around the home and that offenders tend to select victims in close proximity to their residences (Hindelang, Gottfredson, and Garofalo 1978) further increase the adverse consequences of living in a high-crime area.

Both theories of criminality and research in the spatial ecology of crime identify characteristics of high-crime areas. Macrosociological theories of criminality (e.g., social disorganization, anomie, differential social organization) suggest that high-crime geographical areas have high levels of population turnover, ethnic heterogeneity, and low socioeconomic status. However, the work on deviant places and "hot spots" (Stark 1987; Sherman, Gartin, and Buerger 1989) indicates that even within a large geographical area with a high crime rate (e.g., neighborhood, subdivision, a side of town) there is variation in the amount of crime. From this perspective, some places (e.g., bars, convenience stores, adult bookstores, apartment complexes) are more dangerous than others because they attract people for whom crime is more likely, provide more targets for victimization, and have a diminished capacity for social control. Living near major transportation arteries, fast-food restaurants, bus stops, schools, and other places that attract larger numbers of strangers would also increase one's vulnerability to crime for similar reasons.

Common measures of physical proximity used in previous research include place of residence (e.g., rural or urban resident), socioeconomic characteristics of the area (e.g., income level, unemployment rate, racial composition), and the perceived safety of the immediate neighborhood (Cohen, Kluegel, and Land 1981; Hough 1987; Lynch 1987; Sampson and Wooldredge 1987). The average rate of offending in an individual's immediate neighborhood is probably the best single indicator of proximity, but self-report or official measures of offending are rarely available at the neighborhood level of observation. Studies using the British Crime Survey (Sampson and Wooldredge 1987; Miethe and Meier 1990) are notable exceptions. As discussed shortly, the absence of multilevel research designs in a variety of settings has been a major limitation in previous research and has limited the development of measures of offending rates in models of victimization risks.

There is substantial empirical support for the relationship between proximity and increased risks of victimization. For example, we found in our study of British residents (Miethe and Meier 1990) that persons who lived in inner-city areas perceived their neighborhoods to be unsafe at night and that persons who lived in areas with higher levels of offending had higher risks of burglary, personal theft, and assault victimization. Using a seven-category variable based on the income of neighborhoods and urban-rural residence, Cohen, Kluegel, and Land (1981) found that persons who lived in central cities and low-income areas had higher risks of assault, burglary, and personal larceny than persons who live in other types of areas. Given high levels of residential segregation in the United States based on status characteristics, the observed association between particular demographic factors (e.g., low income, being single, being nonwhite, high residential mobility) and individuals' risks of victimization may also be attributed to the proximity of these social groups to pools of motivated offenders (Hindelang, Gottfredson, and Garofalo 1978; Smith and Jarjoura 1989). However, as discussed below, it is important to note that such findings are also consistent with other major components of victimization theories.

## B. Exposure to Crime

While proximity reflects the physical distance between large numbers of offenders and victims, "exposure to crime" is indicative of one's vulnerability to crime (Cohen, Kluegel, and Land 1981). A building or dwelling has higher exposure to burglary if it is detached from other units, has multiple points of entry, and is located on a corner lot. Persons are exposed to higher risks of personal theft and assault when placed in risky or vulnerable situations at particular times, under particular circumstances, and with particular kinds of persons. Usually, such exposure can result from the routine activities and lifestyles of persons. For example, risks of personal victimization are assumed to be directly related to the amount of time spend in public places (e.g., streets, parks) and, especially, public places at night (Hindelang, Gottfredson, and Garofalo 1978, p. 251). Furthermore, frequent contact with drinking establishments, bus depots, public transit, convenience stores, shopping malls, and other dangerous public places also increases one's exposure to crime (Sherman, Gartin, and Buerger 1989).

Exposure has usually been measured in terms of the level and nature of nonhousehold activity. One such common measure is the individual's primary daily activity (e.g. Cohen and Cantor 1980, 1981; Cohen, Kluegel, and Land 1981). Persons who are employed or are in school have greater exposure to crime because they spend more time away from home and they are more often in public places. More detailed indicators of this concept include the average number of evenings per week spent outside the home for leisure activities and the average number of hours per week the dwelling is unoccupied during the day or night (Sampson and Wooldredge 1987; Massey, Krohn, and Bonati 1989). When applied to the study of crime rates, measures of exposure have included the household activity ratio (Cohen and Felson 1979) and aggregate rates of television viewing, the supply of entertainment establishments (e.g., commercial cinemas, profit-making sport activities, opera and symphony orchestra companies), public transportation, female labor force participation, and retail sales from eating and drinking establishments.

Increases in nonhousehold activity are associated with higher crime rates in some studies (e.g., Cohen and Felson 1979; Felson and Cohen 1980; Cohen, Kluegel, and Land 1981) but not in others (Miethe, Hughes, and McDowall 1991). Increases in individuals' level of daytime and nighttime activity outside the home over time do not necessarily lead to increased risks of violent or property victimization, although cross-sectional analyses generally reveal that victimization risks are higher for persons who have higher levels of activity outside the home (Hough 1987; Sampson and Wooldredge 1987; Massey, Krohn, and Bonati 1989; Kennedy and Forde 1991).

Studies of the physical characteristics of burgled households and interviews with known offenders also suggest that the visibility and accessibility of attractive targets influence risks of victimization (Reppetto 1974; Waller and Okihiro 1978; Bennett and Wright 1985; Walsh 1986; Hough 1987). Unfortunately, little research has examined how active participation in particular types of routine activities (e.g., bar visits, visiting places where teenagers "hang out") influences risks of violent victimization.

### C. Target Attractiveness

A central assumption underlying current victimization theories is that particular targets are selected because they have symbolic or economic value to the offender. However, crime targets are also attractive to offenders when they are smaller in size (i.e., more portable) and there is less physical resistance against attack or illegal removal (Cohen, Kluegel, and Land 1981). Under a structural-choice model of victimization, it is the differential value or subjective utility associated with crime targets that determines the source of victimization within a social context (Miethe and Meier 1990, p. 250).

A variety of indicators of target attractiveness have been employed. In the original work on routine activity theory, Cohen and Felson (1979) compared the theft rate for portable and movable durables (e.g., electronic components, television sets, radios, automobiles and their accessories) with their overall circulation rate. The decreased size of these durable goods from the early 1960s through the mid-1970s also corresponds with increases in official crime rates in the United States. However, the supply of many of these portable durable goods (e.g., televisions, radios, car tape players, phonograph cartridges) may not be a good indicator of target attractiveness for studies of crime rates over time when one considers that the reduced costs and increased availability of many of these items may lead to their devaluation as "attractive" crime targets. As a general proxy for purchasing power and the supply of expensive goods, median family income and the gross national product are aggregate measures of target attractiveness that are not susceptible to such a devaluation over time.

The major measures of target attractiveness at the individual level of analysis have been the ownership of expensive and portable consumer goods (e.g., videocassette recorders, color television sets, bicycles, motorcycles), carrying cash and jewelry in public, family income, and social class (Sampson and Wooldredge 1987; Miethe and Meier 1990). As a measure of economic attractiveness, family income is commonly recognized as a proxy of this concept because it can be immediately recognized by offenders in most cases (e.g., through the geographical location of a dwelling within a city, its exterior condition, or the general appearance of the individual). In the case of expressive acts of interpersonal violence, it has been difficult to think of an unambiguous measure of target attractiveness.

Similar to the findings of research on exposure, findings on the effects of target attractiveness have not been consistent. Higher risks of victimization for persons with higher income are observed in some studies but not in others (Cohen and Cantor 1980, 1981; Cohen, Kluegel, and Land 1981; Hough 1987; Miethe and Meier 1990; Miethe, Stafford, and Sloane 1990). Persons who carry larger sums of money while in public places have a greater net risk of assault victimization, but ownership of a videocassette recorder was found either to decrease or to have no significant impact on individuals' risks of burglary (Sampson and Wooldredge 1987; Miethe and Meier 1990). Studies of crime rates for geographic areas also yield inconsistent results about the relationship between economic conditions and crime rates (Cohen, Felson, and Land 1980; Cohen 1981; Stahura and Sloan 1988; Miethe, Hughes, and McDowall 1991). Clearly, the effects vary according to the indicator chosen, suggesting that more conceptual attention must be devoted both to exposure and target attractiveness.

*D. Capable Guardianship*

The final major component of current victimization theories involves the ability of persons or objects to prevent the occurrence of crime. Guardianship has both social (interpersonal) and physical dimensions. Social guardianship includes the number of household members, the density of friendship networks in the neighborhood, and having neighbors watch property or a dwelling when the home is unoccupied. The availability of others (e.g., friends, neighbors, pedestrians, law enforcement officers) may prevent crime by their presence alone or through offering physical assistance in warding off an attack. Physical guardianship involves target-hardening activities (e.g., door/window locks, window bars, burglar alarms, guard dogs, ownership of firearms), other physical impediments to household theft (e.g., street lighting, guarded public entrances), and participation in collective activities (e.g., neighborhood watch programs, home security surveys). Regardless of its particular form, the availability of capable guardianship is deemed important because it indicates increased "costs" to would-be offenders (e.g., greater effort, greater risk of detection and apprehension) and thus should decrease the opportunity for victimization.

A review of previous research on guardianship activities reveals several general trends. First, target-hardening efforts are widespread in the United States and may be regarded as the most widespread and common forms of crime prevention. The majority of people in urban and suburban areas take routine precautions against crime such as locking doors and windows, using exterior lighting, and having neighbors watch their property (Dubow 1979; Skogan and Maxfield 1981; Miethe 1991). Collective crime prevention activities (e.g., property-marking projects, Neighborhood Watch) have also been organized throughout the country (Rosenbaum 1987, 1990).

Second, the success of guardianship activities has been mixed. Physical and social guardianship is associated with lower rates of victimization in several studies but not in others (Scarr 1973; Reppetto 1974; Lavrakas et al. 1981; Skogan and Maxfield 1981; Winchester and Jackson 1982; Yin 1986; Rosenbaum 1987, 1990; Miethe and Meier 1990). However, several authors (e.g., Mayhew 1984) argue that the use of cross-sectional designs has contributed to these inconsistent results because of what is called the "victimization effect." The victimization effect is the tendency for persons to take precautions as a consequence of being victimized. Because cross-sectional designs cannot determine the temporal ordering of victimization experiences and heightened awareness of crime prevention, an observed positive relationship may mask the deterrent effect of precautions on victimization risks.

Third, few studies of guardianship have exercised sufficient controls for other factors influencing victimization risks. Under such conditions, it is impossible to ascertain unambiguously whether differences between protected and unprotected residents are due to the deterrent effect of protective actions or to other factors (e.g., lifestyles, target attractiveness, proximity to high-crime areas) that also alter the likelihood of victimization.

## V. Problems with Previous Evaluations of Victimization Theories

Although theories of victimization have been the object of much research, there are several recurring problems that preclude complete confidence in the results of this research. These involve inadequate measures of key concepts, the lack of sufficient statistical controls, and the failure to examine multilevel and context-specific models of victimization.

### A. Inadequate Measures of Key Concepts

The development of clear empirical indicators of key theoretical concepts has been a major problem in the development of victimization theory. This is a problem in many theoretical areas in criminology, but the popularity of criminal opportunity theories of victimization makes this problem somehow more pressing than in areas where there is little research activity. We refer to this problem as one of *theoretical indeterminacy*, or the ability of the same indicator to serve more than one theoretical master. Consider the following alternative interpretations of the indicators of key concepts in victimization theories.

*Proximity* to motivated offenders is generally considered the physical distance between pools of offenders and victims, but this concept has usually been measured by the degree of population concentration (e.g., living in an urban versus rural area) and the socioeconomic characteristics of the geographical area. From this perspective, living in a large urban area and a low socioeconomic neighborhood are widely used as proxy measures of proximity (Cohen, Kluegel, and Land 1981; Hough 1987). However, it is easy to see that these variables may not only measure proximity but also a breakdown in social control, population heterogeneity, diminished economic opportunity, and other factors underlying traditional theories of criminality that attempt to explain the motivation of offenders. Using such indicators, higher victimization risks for persons who live in urban areas or low-income neighborhoods would not empirically distinguish theories of victimization from theories of criminality. Without greater conceptual refinement, it is hard to know what is being tested.

We have already mentioned that *exposure* to crime is usually indicated by the level of nonhousehold activity. Accordingly, persons who are employed outside the home or are going to school are assumed to be more exposed to crime than persons whose daily activities are more likely to take place around the home (e.g., unemployed, homemakers, retired, disabled). Yet such nonhousehold activities may actually be associated with "low exposure" because both work and school take place in a confined environment with a relatively high level of guardianship and supervision. However, only in the case of the Victim-Risk Supplement of the NCS and the British Crime Survey (BCS) are activities in particular public places (e.g., going to bars/taverns, taking public transit) included as variables that may be used to develop better measures of exposure to risky and vulnerable situations. Furthermore, without controlling for other factors, measuring exposure in this manner is consistent with some theories of criminality (e.g., differential association) that predict a relationship between nonhousehold activity and crime because of the acquisition of criminal norms, not because of greater risk of victimization.

When examining crime rates and social trends, Cohen and Felson (1979) used the "household activity ratio" as a measure of exposure. As defined earlier, this ratio is a composite index of the number of married women in the labor force and the number of nonhusband/nonwife households. Cohen and Felson (1979) assume that this ratio measures both the dispersion of the population away from households and the supply of durable goods susceptible to theft, but it is equally indicative of the prevalence of nontraditional families and reductions in social integration, ideas that are consistent with several theories of criminality as well as Cohen and Felson's theory of routine activities. In this sense, the positive association between crime rates and non-household activity could be due as much to social disorganization processes (e.g., problems of norm transmission and community control) or a breakdown of bonds to mainstream society (i.e., lower attachment, commitment, involvement and belief in conventional activity) as to increases in the supply of criminal opportunities from greater exposure and lower guardianship. If findings fit both sets of theories equally, then opportunity-based theories, while plausible, do not tell us anything unique about the social ecology of crime (Miethe, Hughes, and McDowall 1991, p. 168).

"Target attractiveness" is defined in terms of both its material and symbolic value to offenders (Cohen, Kluegel, and Land 1981). However, measures of individual ownership and the circulation of small but expensive durable goods (e.g., jewelry, audiovisual equipment) are not routinely available in the NCS yearly data or census reports. Thus, target attractiveness is usually measured by general economic conditions (e.g., family income, unemployment rate) even though such indicators may equally serve as surrogates for lower criminal motivation (because higher income and lower unemployment indicate greater legitimate economic opportunities) and greater exposure to crime (because higher income affords greater leisure activity outside the home).

The only available measure of guardianship in the NCS series and census data is the number of members in the household. Neither source provides measures of safety precautions and other types of guardianship on a routine basis. In the case of property crimes against the dwelling (e.g., burglary, vandalism, theft of property around the home), larger households should have lower victimization risks because the dwelling would be less likely to be unoccupied. As a measure of guardianship for violent crime, it must be assumed that the greater the household size, the less likely a person will be alone in a public place.

However, household size may also have a crime-enhancing effect as a result of the impact of household size on household crowding and, in turn, the possible adverse consequences of crowding on criminal motivation.

## B. The Use of Secondary Data

What these examples also show is that the reliance on secondary data has contributed to the use of inadequate measures of proximity, exposure, attractiveness, and guardianship. The proxy measures typically do not tap each dimension of the underlying concepts and have ambiguous meanings. Substantive inferences about the predictive utility of victimization theories are questionable under such conditions.

Indeed, we would argue that reliance on secondary data sources is one of the basic causes of measurement problems in studies of victimization. Given that victimization is such a rare event (only about 25 percent of U.S. households are "touched" by any crime each year and most of that is relatively minor), it is not surprising that the enormous costs of getting a large sample of particular types of crime victims and nonvictims prohibit many researchers from collecting their own data. However, the largest data source on individuals' victimization experiences, the yearly National Crime Victimization Survey series, was designed primarily to provide alternative estimates of the rate of crime rather than to test theories of victimization. The victim-risk supplement of the NCS data and the current NCS redesign are the only national data in this series that have potential for such theoretical analyses (Skogan 1990). Similarly, census data are the primary data source for studies of crime rates in geographical areas. Unfortunately, census data are collected primarily for political and administrative reasons. Thus, although both NCS data and census reports for various aggregate units are widely available, neither of these sources provides complete and unequivocal measures of the key concepts underlying victimization theories.

## C. The Use of Statistical Controls

Statistical control for other variables is virtually a requirement for causal inference in nonexperimental designs. Statistical control allows for an assessment of the net impact of one variable on another once adjustments are made for the variation shared between the primary independent variable and other predictor variables. Empirical studies of victimization processes, however, have rarely included measures of each major concept and component underlying victimization theories even though proximity, exposure, attractiveness, and lack of guardianship are considered *necessary* conditions for predatory crime. The failure to include adequate statistical controls for all relevant variables may seriously distort inferences about the substantive impact of each of these factors on victimization risks.

When measures of a particular concept have multiple meanings, statistical control is one way of disentangling and isolating the unique effects of each theoretical component. Given the pervasiveness of ambiguous measures of key concepts underlying theories of victimization, statistical control is especially important. Most measures of theoretical concepts used in studies of victimization have ambiguous meanings (Miethe, Hughes, and McDowall 1991). The following are examples. *Female labor-force participation* may represent either wider exposure, decreased guardianship, increased target attractiveness, or reduced criminal motivations resulting from rising economic resources. *Income* may represent target attractiveness, higher exposure from nonhousehold activity, or reduced criminal motivation. *Unemployment* may indicate criminogenic conditions, reduced circulation of money, and reduced levels of nonhousehold leisure activities. And *household size* may represent higher guardianship or increases in criminogenic conditions due to the adverse impact of household crowding. It is not possible to assess the adequacy of theoretical concepts when their presumed empirical indicators have multiple meanings. Previous evaluations of criminal opportunity theories have not included sufficient measures of key concepts or exercised sufficient statistical controls to isolate the unique impact of each theoretical component.

## D. Level of Analysis and Model Specification

Previous evaluations of theories of criminality and victimization have relied on what is called a "main effects" or "additive model." Under such a specification, the impact of a variable is assumed to be identical across levels of another variable. When applied to theories of victimization, the additive specification assumes that the impact of target attractiveness, for example, is the same for persons who vary in their exposure to crime and have different levels of guardianship. The impact of guardianship is likewise presumed to be the same across various social contexts. Regardless of where individuals live and their particular routine activities and lifestyles, increases in household size or the number of safety precautions are assumed to decrease risks of predatory crime.

However, the failure to examine whether variables have different effects across different contexts is a type of model misspecification that may dramatically alter substantive conclusions about the predictive validity of current theories.

There are various ways in which contextual effects can occur in models of victimization. What is required are data that permit multilevel observation and sensitivity to alternative social contexts. Data that do not permit the examination of multilevel relationships or the estimation of separate models of victimization across different social contexts are severely limited. Most aggregate data sources are restricted to one level of analysis (e.g., individual, census tract, city, SMSA) and do not contain measures of contextual variables. The opportunity to perform contextual analyses is important because it may more clearly specify the conditions under which proximity, exposure, target attractiveness, and guardianship alter individuals' risks and aggregate rates of predatory crime. The results of the few studies using this approach also suggest its utility as a research tool for testing theories of victimization (Sampson and Wooldredge 1987; Smith and Jarjoura 1989; Miethe and McDowall 1993).

## VI. Contextual Effects in Models of Victimization
The context of crime is a particularly important dimension, and the further development of victimization or opportunity-based theories of crime may require greater sensitivity to contextual information. A fundamental aspect of predatory crime is that it occurs in a social context in which there is a convergence of victims and offenders in time and space. It is surprising that little research has incorporated aspects of the social context directly into theories of victimization. To their credit, routine activity and lifestyle-exposure theories acknowledge the importance of exposure and proximity to risky or vulnerable situations as necessary conditions for predatory crime. However, what is absent is a clear specification of how aspects of the wider social context influence risks of victimization. There are several ways in which the social context can both facilitate and constrain the occurrence of crime.

A major contribution of macrosociological theories of criminality is that they identify the structural conditions associated with crime. For example, population heterogeneity and density, residential mobility, and low economic opportunity are identified as criminogenic forces because they either increase cultural conflict, decrease economic resources, or hamper the development of effective mechanisms of social control (Kornhauser 1978; Bursik 1988; Sampson and Groves 1989). One primary way in which these social forces generate a facilitating context for crime is by increasing the pool of potential offenders. The greater an individual's proximity to these criminogenic areas, the greater one's risks of victimization.

According to current theories of victimization, an alternative way in which the social context influences predatory crime is by increasing the supply of criminal opportunities. Because routine activities of everyday life are said to create criminal opportunities, geographical areas with high levels of public activity, expensive and portable consumer goods, and lower levels of physical guardianship are presumed to have higher rates of crime. Some persons, regardless of their own routine activities and lifestyles, may be more vulnerable than others to crime simply by living in these "crime-attractive" areas. The composition and structure of a neighborhood may influence individuals' victimization risks because both give off cues to would-be offenders about the potential yield and costs for engaging in crime in that geographical area.

Research on the crime-reduction benefits of safety precautions is an example of how elements of the wider social context influence individuals' risks of victimization. As a form of guardianship, it is widely assumed that taking safety precautions (e.g., locking doors, installing alarms, owning dogs) reduces risks of predatory crime. However, what is less clear is how a person's chances of victimization are influenced by the safety precautions taken by others in their immediate neighborhood. The safety precautions of others may either enhance or reduce an individual's risks of victimization. According to the arguments about *crime displacement* (Gabor 1981, 1990; Cornish and Clarke 1987; Miethe 1991), persons are negatively affected by the protective actions of others in their neighborhood because these actions are assumed to deflect crime to less protected others. Alternatively, a "free-rider" effect suggests that persons benefit from the social control activities of their immediate neighbors because these actions convey to would-be offenders an image that this area, in general, is a risky place to commit crime. Regardless of whether these safety precautions of others inhibit or enhance victimization risks, the major point is that the community context of crime control in both cases is said to alter individuals' risks of victimization substantially.

The assumption underlying contextual analyses is that victimization risks and its predictors vary by characteristics of the wider social context. These contextual effects can take various forms. First, living near "hot spots" for crime (Sherman, Gartin, and Buerger 1989) may be especially harmful because of proximity to areas with high concentration of offenders. Second, routine activities and lifestyles may have context-specific effects on victimization risks. For example, the crime-enhancing effects of exposure and proximity to motivated offenders may be important only in neighborhoods with low levels of informal and formal social control. When there are high levels of social integration and safety precautions in an area, these social control mechanisms may be of sufficient strength to deter crime and overwhelm the adverse effects of exposure and proximity to crime. Alternatively, the supply of expensive consumer goods in the immediate environment may influence the risks of property victimization even for residents who lack these possessions. As indicated by the conflicting predictions about displacement and free-rider effects, it may be unclear in other cases whether the same contextual factor impedes or enhances an individuals' risks of victimization. However, regardless of the particular type of contextual effect, what is important about multilevel models and contextual analysis is that victimization risks are seen as a function of both the routine activities of residents and the composition and structure of the wider geographical area.

It is difficult to overemphasize the potential import of including both measures of individuals' lifestyles and contextual variables in studies of victimization. First, a major premise of sociological theory is that social conditions enable and constrain human activity. Although not denying that individuals' lifestyles influence their vulnerability to crime, most sociological theories assume that the community context has a direct impact on victimization risks independent of individual characteristics. Second, it is possible that many of the presumed individual-level effects are actually reflective of community dynamics. For example, the strong impact of being young or unmarried on victimization risks is commonly attributed to the lifestyles of such persons. Yet the influence of these factors may simply reflect the tendency for both single persons and young adults to live in transitional neighborhoods with more potential offenders, lower internal social control, and high rates of public activity (see also Smith and Jarjoura 1989). Under these conditions, too much importance would be placed on these individual-level causes of victimization risks.

The importance of contextual factors has been empirically documented in several recent studies. For example, Miethe and McDowall

(1993) found that contextual factors had significant main and interactive effects on risks of both violent and property victimization. The impact of individuals' routine activities and lifestyles depends on the particular composition of the wider neighborhood. Sampson and Wooldredge (1987) found that personal risks of burglary were influenced by the level of family disruption, single-person households, and density of ownership of portable consumer goods (i.e., VCRs) in the wider community. Smith and Jarjoura (1989) found that risks of burglary were influenced by several neighborhood factors (e.g., racial heterogeneity, population instability, median income). Aspects of community composition and structure have been included in several additional studies of individuals' risks of victimization (e.g., Cohen, Kluegel, and Land 1981; Simcha-Fagan and Schwartz 1986; Sampson and Lauritsen 1990).

## VII. Prospects for Integrating Theories of Victimization and Theories of Offending

The development of theories of victimization requires the development of theories of offending. The objectives of theories of crime can only be attained with an understanding of the processes by which victims come to experience risk of crime and offenders come to be motivated to commit crime and of the social contexts that unite these parallel sets of processes. For these reasons, the theoretical objective in criminology should be identified as the development of defensible theories of crime, not just theories of victimization or just theories of offending.

The development of testable propositions about crime requires information about both victims and offenders. This information may involve data pertaining to group differences in offending and victimization (sometimes referred to as "structural" information) or to social psychological processes in offending and victimization (sometimes called "processual" information). These levels of observation and analysis have served criminologists well in the development of theoretical perspectives on both offending and victimization, but there has been no systematic attempt to formulate integrated theories of offending *and* victimization.

The prospects for such an integration are bright, but it must be admitted that previous efforts at theoretical integration in criminology have not been terribly successful. Several notable attempts in recent years have been made to integrate different theoretical traditions (Elliott, Ageton, and Cantor 1979; Pearson and Weiner 1985; Thornberry

1987), and there have been discussions about the issue of methods and desirability of theoretical integration in general (Hirschi 1979; Short 1979, 1985; Elliott 1985; Messner, Krohn, and Liska 1989). So far, the idea of theoretical integration has been applied only to theories of criminality, and theories of victimization have been relatively neglected.

The disadvantages of integrative efforts are initially conceptual and theoretical. That is, some perspectives do not lend themselves to integration because they make contradictory assumptions that cannot be reconciled. Cultural deviance and control theories, for example, have been said to contain irreconcilable differences in domain assumptions (Kornhauser 1978), which, if correct, would make any meaningful integration impossible. Several studies have attempted to unite variables from different theoretical traditions and have reported results as though they represented a unified perspective (Johnson 1979; Pearson and Weiner 1985). Such efforts are perhaps harmless (and perhaps even positive) unless they give the impression that the result of such efforts is a "new" rather than a logically recombined theory.

The problems of theoretical integration are significant (see also Meier 1989), but they may not be insurmountable. For one thing, there is no reason to believe that *any* theory of criminality and *any* theory of victimization make incompatible assumptions about the nature of crime or social reality. Furthermore, no theory of criminality makes explicit assumptions about victim processes that preclude integrative efforts; likewise, no theory of victimization makes any restrictive assumptions about offenders.

As a way of overcoming compartmentalized thinking, the integration of theories of criminality and victimization should improve substantially our understanding of crime. From their inception, theories of criminality (e.g., strain, social disorganization, differential association, social bond) have emphasized the structural and social psychological factors associated with criminal motivation, but they have ignored how the actions of potential crime targets condition the physical opportunities for victimization. The primary goal of these theories has been to explain the decision to engage in crime. In contrast, theories of victimization emphasize the causal role of personal characteristics that enhance the accessibility and attractiveness of crime victims, but these theories largely neglect sources of criminal motivation. By addressing both crime-commission and target-selection decisions, it is easier to see the value of an integrated perspective.

From an integrated perspective, crime is not simply what offenders do and what victims do. Rather, understanding crime from an integrated perspective requires an understanding of the social structure that surrounds both criminals and victims. It is that structure, or context, that creates both offender motivation and victim risk-taking. Integrated theories are theories sensitive to the nature and impact of that structure. Such theories are informed about offenders, victims, and structural facilitators that link them. Furthermore, such theories, if they are to be truly useful, will be testable and judged on their predictive validity. Traditional "isolationist" approaches that focus only on one component of the larger picture are necessarily limited and should be tolerated only insofar as they contribute to larger theoretical structures. Both more sophisticated offender and victim theories can make such a contribution.

## VIII. Conclusions

Current theories of victimization highlight the symbiotic relationship between conventional and illegal activities. Regardless of their particular terminology, routine activities and lifestyle-exposure theories emphasize how criminal opportunities develop out of the routine activities of everyday life. Routine activity patterns that increase proximity to motivated offenders, increase exposure to risky and dangerous situations, enhance the expected utility or attractiveness of potential crime targets, and reduce the level of guardianship are assumed to increase aggregate rates and individuals' risks of predatory crime. These criminal opportunity theories have been used to account for changes in crime rates in the United States over time, the level of crime in aggregate units (e.g., cities, SMSAs), differences in victimization risks for different social groups (e.g., males, single persons, younger people), and individuals' risks of victimization.

The results of previous studies give some indication of the explanatory power of these criminal opportunity theories. There is some evidence to support each of the major components underlying these theories (i.e., proximity, exposure, attractiveness, and guardianship). However, this supporting evidence is less impressive when the major limitations of previous work are acknowledged. That previous research has generally used inadequate proxy measures of key concepts, includes few statistical controls, and has not examined rigorously multilevel models and contextual effects casts doubt on the substantive conclusions from these studies.

While current theories of victimization suggest that victims and offenders are inextricably linked in an ecology of crime, they do not provide sufficient information about the conditions of offending to permit adequate predictions of crime. This is, of course, also a failing of theories of criminality that concentrate only on accounting for the pool of motivated offenders; the victim side of the equation is neglected. More adequate theories should be sought in the exploration of combinations of victim and offender theories and a sensitivity to the social contexts in which crimes are committed.

### REFERENCES

Amir, Menachem. 1967. "Victim-precipitated Forcible Rape." *Journal of Criminal Law, Criminology, and Police Science* 58:493–502.
———. 1971. *Patterns of Forcible Rape*. Chicago: University of Chicago Press.
Bennett, Trevor, and Richard Wright. 1985. *Burglars on Burglary: Prevention and the Offender*. Hampshire, England: Bower.
Bursik, Robert J., Jr. 1988. "Social Disorganization and Theories of Crime and Delinquency: Problems and Prospects." *Criminology* 26:529–51.
Carroll, John, and Frances Weaver. 1986. "Shoplifters' Perceptions of Crime Opportunities: A Process-tracking Study." In *The Reasoning Criminal: Rational Choice Perspectives on Offending*, edited by Derek B. Cornish and Ronald V. Clarke. New York: Springer-Verlag.
Clarke, Ronald, Paul Ekblom, Mike Hough, and Pat Mayhew. 1985. "Elderly Victims of Crime and Exposure to Risk." *Howard Journal of Criminal Justice* 24:1–9.
Cohen, Lawrence E. 1981. "Modeling Crime Trends: A Criminal Opportunity Perspective." *Journal of Research in Crime and Delinquency* 18:138–64.
Cohen, Lawrence E., and David Cantor. 1980. "The Determinants of Larceny: An Empirical and Theoretical Study." *Journal of Research in Crime and Delinquency* 17:140–59.
Cohen, Lawrence E., and David Cantor. 1981. "Residential Burglary in the United States: Lifestyle and Demographic Factors Associated with the Probability of Victimization." *Journal of Research in Crime and Delinquency* 18:113–27.
Cohen, Lawrence E., and Marcus Felson. 1979. "Social Change and Crime Rate Trends: A Routine Activity Approach." *American Sociological Review* 44:588–608.
Cohen, Lawrence E., Marcus Felson, and Kenneth C. Land. 1980. "Property Crime Rates in the United States: A Macrodynamic Analysis 1947–77 with Ex Ante Forecasts for the Mid-1980s." *American Journal of Sociology* 86:90–118.

Cohen, Lawrence E., James R. Kluegel, and Kenneth C. Land. 1981. "Social Inequality and Predatory Criminal Victimization: An Exposition and Test of a Formal Theory." *American Sociology Review* 46:505–24.

Cohen, Lawrence E., and Kenneth C. Land. 1987. "Sociological Positivism and the Explanation of Criminality." In *Positive Criminology*, edited by Michael Gottfredson and Travis Hirschi. Beverly Hills, Calif.: Sage.

Cornish, Derek B., and Ronald V. Clarke. 1986. *The Reasoning Criminal: Rational Choice Perspectives on Offending*. New York: Springer-Verlag.

———. 1987. "Understanding Crime Displacement." *Criminology* 25:933–43.

Curtis, Lynn. 1974. "Victim-Precipitation and Violent Crimes." *Social Problems* 21:594–605.

Dubow, Fred. 1979. *Reactions to Crime: A Critical Review of the Literature*. Washington, D.C.: U.S. Government Printing Office.

Ellenberger, T. 1955. "Psychological Relationships between the Criminal and His Victim." *Archives of Criminal Psychology* 2:257–90.

Elliott, Delbert. 1985. "The Assumption That Theories Can Be Combined with Increased Explanatory Power." In *Theoretical Methods in Criminology*, edited by Robert F. Meier. Beverly Hills, Calif.: Sage.

Elliott, Delbert, Suzanne Ageton, and R. J. Cantor. 1979. "An Integrated Theoretical Perspective on Delinquent Behavior." *Journal of Research in Crime and Delinquency* 16:3–27.

Ennis, Philip H. 1967. *Criminal Victimization in the U.S.* Field Survey 2. Report on a National Survey by the President's Commission on Law Enforcement and Administration of Justice. Washington, D.C.: U.S. Government Printing Office.

Feeney, Floyd. 1986. "Robbers as Decision-Makers." In *The Reasoning Criminal: Rational Choice Perspectives on Offending*, edited by Derek B. Cornish and Ronald V. Clarke. New York: Springer-Verlag.

Felson, Marcus, and Lawrence Cohen. 1980. "Human Ecology and Crime: A Routine Activity Approach." *Human Ecology* 8:389–406.

Gabor, Thomas. 1981. "The Crime Displacement Hypothesis: An Empirical Examination." *Crime and Delinquency* 26:390–404.

———. 1990. "Crime Displacement and Situational Prevention: Toward the Development of Some Principles." *Canadian Journal of Criminology* 32:41–73.

Garofalo, R. 1914. *Criminology*. Boston: Little, Brown.

Gottfredson, Michael. 1981. "On the Etiology of Criminal Victimization." *Journal of Law and Criminology* 72:714–26.

Hawley, Amos. 1950. *Human Ecology: A Theory of Community Structure*. New York: Ronald Press.

Hindelang, Michael S., Michael Gottfredson, and James Garofalo. 1978. *Victims of Personal Crime*. Cambridge, Mass.: Ballinger.

Hirschi, Travis. 1969. *The Causes of Delinquency*. Berkeley: University of California Press.

———. 1979. "Separate and Unequal Is Better." *Journal of Research on Crime and Delinquency* 16:34–38.

Hough, Michael. 1987. "Offenders' Choice of Targets: Findings from Victim Surveys." *Journal of Quantitative Criminology* 3:355–69.

Johnson, Richard E. 1979. *Juvenile Delinquency and Its Origins*. Cambridge: Cambridge University Press.

Kennedy, Leslie, and David Forde. 1990. "Routine Activity and Crime: An Analysis of Victimization in Canada." *Criminology* 28:137–51.

Kornhauser, Ruth. 1978. *Social Sources of Delinquency*. Chicago: University of Chicago Press.

Lavrakas, P. J., J. Normoyle, W. G. Skogan, E. J. Herz, G. Salem, and D. A. Lewis. 1981. *Factors Related to Citizen Involvement in Personal, Household, and Neighborhood Anti-Crime Measures*. Washington, D.C.: U.S. Government Printing Office.

Lynch, James P. 1987. "Routine Activity and Victimization at Work." *Journal of Quantitative Criminology* 3:283–300.

MacDonald, Robert. 1939. *Crime Is a Business*. Palo Alto, Calif.: Stanford University Press.

Massey, James L., Marvin D. Krohn, and Lisa M. Bonati. 1989. "Property Crime and the Routine Activities of Individuals." *Journal of Research in Crime and Delinquency* 26:378–400.

Maxfield, Michael G. 1987. "Household Composition, Routine Activity, and Victimization: A Comparative Analysis." *Journal of Quantitative Criminology* 3:301–20.

Mayhew, Pat. 1984. "Target-Hardening: How Much of an Answer?" In *Coping with Burglary*, edited by Ronald V. Clarke and Tim Hope. Boston: Kluwer-Nijhoff.

Meier, Robert F. 1989. "Deviance and Differentiation." In *Theoretical Integration in the Study of Deviance and Crime: Problems and Prospects*, edited by Steven F. Messner, Marvin D. Krohn, and Allen E. Liska. Albany, N.Y.: SUNY Press.

Mendelsohn, B. 1956. "The Victimology" (in French). *Etudes Internationales de Psycho-Sociologie Criminelle* 1956(3):25–26.

Messner, Steven F., and Judith R. Blau. 1987. "Routine Leisure Activities and Rates of Crime: A Macro-Level Analysis." *Social Forces* 65:1035–52.

Messner, Steven F., Marvin D. Krohn, and Allen E. Liska, eds. 1989. *Theoretical Integration in the Study of Deviance and Crime: Problems and Prospects*. Albany, N.Y.: SUNY Press.

Messner, Steven F., and Kenneth Tardiff. 1985. "The Social Ecology of Urban Homicide: An Application of the 'Routine Activities' Approach." *Criminology* 23:241–67.

Miethe, Terance D. 1985. "The Myth or Reality of Victim Involvement in Crime: A Review and Comment on Victim-Precipitation Research." *Sociological Focus* 18:209–220.

————. 1991. "Citizen-based Crime Control Activity and Victimization Risks: Examination of Displacement and Free-Rider Effects." *Criminology* 29:419–39.

Miethe, Terance D., Michael Hughes, and David McDowall. 1991. "Social Change and Crime Rates: An Evaluation of Alternative Theoretical Approaches." *Social Forces* 70:165–85.

Miethe, Terance D., and David McDowall. 1993. "Contextual Effects in Models of Criminal Victimization." *Social Forces* (forthcoming).

Miethe, Terance D., and Robert F. Meier. 1990. "Criminal Opportunity and Victimization Rates: A Structural-Choice Theory of Criminal Victimization." *Journal of Research in Crime and Delinquency* 27:243–66.

Miethe, Terance D., Mark C. Stafford, and J. Scott Long. 1987. "Social Differentiation in Criminal Victimization: A Test of Routine Activities/Lifestyle Theory." *American Sociological Review* 52:184–94.

Miethe, Terance D., Mark Stafford, and Douglas Sloane. 1990. "Lifestyle Changes and Risks of Criminal Victimization." *Journal of Quantitative Criminology* 6:357–76.

Nelson, James. 1980. "Multiple Victimization in American Cities: A Statistical Analysis of Rare Events." *American Journal of Sociology* 85:870–91.

Normandeau, Andre. 1968. "Trends and Patterns in Crimes of Robbery." Doctoral dissertation. University of Pennsylvania, Philadelphia.

Pearson, Frank S., and Neil Alan Weiner. 1985. "Toward an Integration of Criminological Theories." *Journal of Criminal Law and Criminology* 76:116–50.

President's Commission on Law Enforcement and Administration of Justice. 1967. *The Challenge of Crime in a Free Society*. Washington, D.C.: U.S. Government Printing Office.

Reppetto, Thomas A. 1974. *Residential Crime*. Cambridge, Mass.: Ballinger.

Rosenbaum, Dennis P. 1987. "The Theory and Research behind Neighborhood Watch: Is It a Sound Fear and Crime Reduction Strategy?" *Crime and Delinquency* 33:103–34.

———. 1990. "Community Crime Prevention: A Review and Synthesis of the Literature." *Justice Quarterly* 5:323–95.

Sampson, Robert J., and W. Bryon Groves. 1989. "Community Structure and Crime: Testing Social-Disorganization Theory." *American Journal of Sociology* 94:774–802.

Sampson, Robert J., and Janet L. Lauritsen. 1990. "Deviant Lifestyles, Proximity to Crime, and the Offender-Victim Link in Personal Violence." *Journal of Research in Crime and Delinquency* 27:110–39.

Sampson, Robert J., and John D. Wooldredge. 1987. "Linking the Micro- and Macro-Level Dimensions of Lifestyle-Routine Activity and Opportunity Models of Predatory Victimization." *Journal of Quantitative Criminology* 3:371–93.

Scarr, Harry A. 1973. *Patterns of Burglary*. Washington, D.C.: U.S. Government Printing Office.

Schafer, Stephen. 1968. *The Victim and His Criminal: A Study in Functional Responsibility*. New York: Random House.

Schultz, Lawrence. 1968. "The Victim-Offender Relationship." *Crime and Delinquency* 14:135–41.

Sherman, Lawrence W., P. R. Gartin, and M. E. Buerger. 1989. "Hot Spots of Predatory Crime: Routine Activities and the Criminology of Place." *Criminology* 27:24–55.

Short, James F., Jr. 1979. "On the Etiology of Delinquent Behavior." *Journal of Research on Crime and Delinquency* 16:28–33.

Short, James F., Jr. 1985. "The Level of Explanation Problem in Criminology." In *Theoretical Methods in Criminology*, edited by Robert F. Meier. Beverly Hills, Calif.: Sage.

Simcha-Fagan, Ora, and Joseph E. Schwartz. 1986. "Neighborhood and Delinquency: An Assessment of Contextual Effects." *Criminology* 24:667–99.

Skogan, Wesley G. 1990. "The Polls—a Review of the National Crime Survey Redesign." *Public Opinion Quarterly* 54:256–72.

Skogan, Wesley G., and Michael G. Maxfield. 1981. *Coping with Crime: Individual and Neighborhood Reactions*. Beverly Hills, Calif.: Sage.

Smith, Douglas A., and G. Roger Jarjoura. 1989. "Household Characteristics, Neighborhood Composition, and Victimization Risk." *Social Forces* 68:621–40.

Sparks, Richard F. 1981. "Multiple Victimization: Evidence, Theory, and Future Research." *Journal of Criminal Law and Criminology* 72:762–78.

———. 1982. *Research on Victims of Crime: Accomplishments, Issues, and New Directions*. Washington, D.C.: U.S. Government Printing Office.

Stahura, John, and John Sloan III. 1988. "Urban Satisfaction of Places, Routine Activities, and Suburban Crime Rates." *Social Forces* 66:1102–18.

Stark, Rodney. 1987. "Deviant Places." *Criminology* 25:893–908.

Thornberry, Terence P. 1987. "Toward an Interactional Theory of Delinquency." *Criminology* 25:863–92.

Von Hentig, Hans. 1940. "Remarks on the Interaction of Perpetrator and Victim." *Journal of Criminal Law, Criminology, and Police Science* 31:303–9.

Von Hentig, Hans. 1948. *The Criminal and His Victim*. New Haven, Conn.: Yale University Press.

Waller, Irvin, and Norman Okihiro. 1978. *Burglary: The Victim and the Public*. Toronto: University of Toronto Press.

Walsh, Dermot. 1986. "Victim Selection Procedures among Economic Criminals: The Rational Choice Perspective." In *The Reasoning Criminal: Rational Choice Perspectives on Offending*, edited by Derek Cornish and Ronald V. Clarke. New York: Springer-Verlag.

Winchester, S., and H. Jackson. 1982. *Residential Burglary: The Limits of Prevention*. Home Office Research Study no. 74. London: H.M. Stationery Office.

Wolfgang, Marvin. 1957. "Victim-precipitated Criminal Homicide." *Journal of Criminal Law, Criminology, and Police Science* 48:1–11.

Wolfgang, Marvin. 1958. *Patterns of Criminal Homicide*. Philadelphia: University of Pennsylvania Press.

Yin, Robert K. 1986. "Community Crime Prevention: A Synthesis of Eleven Evaluations." In *Community Crime Prevention: Does It Work?* edited by Dennis Rosenbaum. Criminal Justice System Annuals. Beverly Hills, Calif.: Sage.